Software Management

SEVENTH EDITION

Software Management

SEVENTH EDITION

Edited by

Donald J. Reifer

IEEE computer society
60TH anniversary

WILEY-INTERSCIENCE

A JOHN WILEY & SONS, INC., PUBLICATION

Published by John Wiley & Sons, Inc., Hoboken, New Jersey.
Published simultaneously in Canada.

For general information on our other products and services or for technical support, please contact our Customer Care Department within the United States at (800) 762-2974, outside the United States at (317) 572-3993 or fax (317) 572-4002.

Wiley also publishes its books in a variety of electronic formats. Some content that appears in print may not be available in electronic format. For information about Wiley products, visit our web site at www.wiley.com.

Library of Congress Cataloging-in-Publication Data is available.

ISBN-13 978-0-471-77562-1
ISBN-10 0-471-77562-2

Printed in the United States of America.

10 9 8 7 6 5 4 3 2 1

Contents

Foreword

In 1969, I received the following perspective on software management from an Air Force general trying to manage the development of a complex command-and-control system:

> You software guys are like the weavers in the story about the Emperor and his new clothes. Every time I come by to see how things are going, the weavers tell me that they 're fantastically busy weaving this magic cloth, and that I'll look great when I wear it in the big parade. But there's nothing I can see and no way that I can tell whether I'm going to be out in front of this big parade with nothing on.

In those days, this software invisibility was a significant concern, but only for a few people, because there weren't that many complex software systems around. And at the time, we were able to develop tightly integrated looms [the waterfall model with its sequential progression and traceability through requirements, design, code, and test; the unit development folder (UDF) with its similar micro milestones at the unit-of-code level; and software maturity models that focused on repeatability and allocation of prespecified requirements] that provided a framework of visibility and control for weaving the software.

But the times they have been a-changin. Software is now part of almost everything, and its defects increasingly affect our safety and quality of life. The tightly integrated looms of the waterfall, the UDF, and requirements-driven maturity models worked well while the requirements were relatively easy to specify and stayed relatively stable. But with the increasing pace of information technology change, the tightly integrated looms are increasingly likely to weave obsolete software.

Instead of simple stand-alone systems, the Web and the Internet connect everything with everything else. And with mobile platforms running out of power and running into tunnels, you don't know if they will be there or not. Autonomous agents that make deals for you in cyberspace create many opportunities for chaos. Systems of systems, networks of networks, and agents of agents create huge intellectual control and software management problems. The resulting complex adaptable systems spawn adaptive, emergent behavior, making it unrealistic to specify requirements in advance.

Further, the economics of software systems leave software developers with no choice but to incorporate large commercial off-the-shelf (COTS) components into their applications. Unfortunately, developers have no way of knowing what is inside these COTS components, and they have no control over the direction of their evolution. And with the market pressures of Internet time, software managers and architects have to make rapid decisions, with virtually no time to recover from decisions that turn out to be mistakes.

Into this software development tornado come new software management and development approaches. Risk-oriented maturity models and associated spiral model extensions integrate software and systems engineering and emphasize concurrent engineering with integrated multi-stakeholder teams. Open-source development turns the loom into more like a meritocratic quilting bee. Agile methods promise to instantly refactor the loom's structure and content to adapt to change.

All of this leaves today's software managers in a serious quandary about which of the traditional software management wisdoms is still applicable to their situation, and which of the new methods are a good fit for their projects. Fortunately, Don Reifer has been involved in many of these trends: running the Defense Department's Software Reuse Initiative, consulting for large aerospace companies and agile commercial companies, and developing new models and approaches for Web-based development, government software acquisition, computer security, COTS management, business case analysis, and software/system process improvement. This experience has enabled him to select and attract key new papers in his classic *Software Management* tutorial volume that illuminate the new issues and ways of dealing with them.

A good many still-valuable papers remain from the previous edition. There are also new papers and sections providing valuable insights on critical success factors, agile and extreme development methods, distributed development, integrated product teams, and resulting changes in such areas as configuration management, quality management, risk management, software cost estimation, software metrics, and software business case analysis. The business case that would encourage you to invest in buying and reading the book is an easy one to make. I hope it will prove to be a wise investment for you.

BARRY W. BOEHM
Director
Center for Systems and Software Engineering
University of Southern California

Preface to the Seventh Edition

Purpose and Scope

This new edition contains 62 articles of which five revise original materials prepared for the sixth edition, 25 are new, and 32 are reprints that have been carried over. The primary goal of this tutorial is to provide software project managers with the information they need to be successful. This includes providing managers with pointers on how to cope with current issues, challenges, and experiences that shape their jobs. By design, the tutorial is broad in scope. It must be in order to address the advances being made in such dissimilar fields as management theory, collaboration, knowledge management, motivation theory, process improvement, organization dynamics, and technology transfer. It must also speak to different levels of software managers and their viewpoints. For example, it must provide software executives and corporate officers with the knowledge they need to develop their software engineering management strategies for the future. At the same time, it must arm software project managers with insights into the tools and techniques that they can use to improve their ability to deliver high-quality software products to their users on time and within budgetary obligations now.

Intended Audience

This tutorial is intended for the following target audiences:

- **New Software Managers**—Provides new software managers with the information they need to plan, organize, staff, direct and control a software development project and deliver acceptable products on schedule and within budgetary constraints.
- **Experienced Software Managers**—Supplies experienced managers with the information they need to address current issues and use the latest state-of-the-art tools and techniques in their software management practice.
- **Nonsoftware Managers and Executives**—Provides managers from other disciplines with insight into how to succeed when managing software-intensive applications. The primary message communicated is that traditional project management techniques work for software. The trick is adapting management theory so that it can be used effectively for software.
- **Software Technologists and Change Agents**—Gives those focusing on change management the insights they need to take new technology and transition it into practice on existing projects without increasing risk.
- **Software Engineers, Programmers, and other Software Professionals**—Supplies software professionals with a general understanding of what software engineering project management is all about and why it should be of interest to newcomers to the profession.
- **University Teachers and Students**—Provides them with the needed instructional material to serve as the primary text for a course in either software or software management.

Overview of Contents

Every attempt was made to include the best available papers in this seventh edition. This was a difficult task due to the diversity of the target audience and the breadth of material that needed to be covered. In response to these challenges, I have included a wide range of papers within each chapter to fill the needs of various constituencies. My goal was to achieve a balance between theory and practice, with an emphasis on what works. I move from the basics to more advanced subjects as each chapter unfolds. I try to cover the full range of topics that I believe a software manager needs to know. When acceptable papers did not exist in the literature, I asked leaders in the field of software engineering and management to write original materials to fill the void. This is a departure from past editions for which I tried to handle the shortfalls myself.

This tutorial systematically addresses the skills, knowledge, and abilities that software managers, at any level of experience, need to have to practice their profession effectively. The key to being a successful software manager is to understand what I call the "3P's" and their conflicting relationships: process, products, and people. In simple terms, my success formula revolves around knowing what has to be built, establishing the building codes needed to build it, having the skilled and motivated staff who want to build it, and being in the position to deliver what you have promised on time and within budget.

The approaches advocated and the tools, techniques, and practices recommended for managing software within this volume are not unique. They tend to include what good managers use independent of their specialties. The trick to their effective use is to understand what works for software, and when and how to apply available management tools and techniques under a variety of situations. To support such tailoring, I have included a number of experience reports and case studies that stress what tools and techniques work in practice. These have been included to help you to figure out what makes sense under what circumstances.

Papers in this tutorial are organized into four groupings and 14 chapters in a top-down manner. This structure was used to assemble materials in groupings based upon the typical functions software managers perform.

- **Group 1—General Background Information (Chapters 1–3)**

  This group of papers provides background information needed to practice software engineering project management. Chapter 1 introduces you to the current concerns and challenges of software management and provides you with general background information. Chapter 2 introduces the reader to modern software life cycles and related extreme methodologies. Chapter 3 looks at the progress we have made in the area of software process improvement. All three chapters contain case studies that report experiences with the concepts summarized and lessons learned from the field.

- **Group 2—Seven Basic Functions of Management (Chapters 4–10)**

  The next group of papers focuses on the six basic functions of management as applied to software projects: planning, estimating, organizing, staffing, directing, and controlling. Chapter 4 introduces the reader to the discipline of software project management and provides insight into its theories and practices. Its articles set the stage for the rest of the papers in this group. Chapter 5 discusses the planning function and provides insight into the tools used to support the hierarchy of planning documents prepared to support software organizations. Chapter 6 provides a detailed look at the methods and models available to prepare estimates and perform economic analysis. Chapter 7 discusses organizational concepts and focuses on the use of core competencies to decide on the structure used for software within the firm. Chapter 8 looks at staffing and discusses how to acquire, coach and grow the staff resources needed to get the job done. Chapter 9 explains how to lead and direct these staff resources to achieve aggressive goals. Chapter 10 provides an overview of control tools and techniques, and includes papers on the related topics of configuration management, quality management, and inspections. Again, I have included case studies and experience reports whenever possible to show how the concepts work in practice.

- **Group 3—Advanced Software Management Topics (Chapters 11–14)**

  The third group of papers addresses advanced software management concepts. This is where we get into the more sophisticated subject matter. Four subjects are discussed, each as a separate chapter. Chapter 11 discusses risk management concepts and their application on large and complex projects. Chapter 12 focuses on the topic of metrics and measurement. Several case studies are included to demonstrate the value of the data collected after metrics programs are established. Chapter 13 contains a number of articles on the topic of acquisition management. Its focus is to help you put in place a process that allows you to improve how you manage your subcontractors and suppliers. Chapter 14 introduces a number of emerging management techniques developed to exploit emerging software technologies like the distributive project management concepts, product lines, and architecture-based reuse and change agent fundamentals.

- **Group 4—Support Materials for Readers and University Teachers (Appendices)**

  The fourth collection of papers primarily consists of support materials. A glossary of software project management terms, an annotated bibliography of recommended references, pointers to Web resources, and biographies for my guest authors are included as Appendices.

Unique Features of the Seventh Edition

This tutorial contains original articles as well as a collection of reprints. About sixty percent of the papers were taken from the previous edition. The primary reason for this update is to provide current and more topical materials. For example, excellent papers on the topics of distributed development, personnel motivation, and risk management have been added to this edition. As another example, new process-improvement case studies have been added because they seem more important today. Such papers have been included because they provide you with up-to-date tools that you can use to bring in and control new technologies.

When I think about it, I am amazed that this tutorial has maintained its popularity for over 27 years. In the early years, the volume's popularity was not surprising. There were just a few books on the topic of software management available for educators and practitioners to draw from. However, today there are many volumes available (see the Bibliography for what I consider the best of these). When I ask colleagues why they still use this tutorial, they often remark that they use it just for that reason. There are too many books and the tutorial helps them by providing pointers to the best information that is available on the topic today.

I hope this tutorial provides you with the information you need to both do your job and propel the practice of software and software engineering project management ahead during the current decade. The challenges we face and opportunities for advancement are many. I continue to be excited by the prospects. However, I understand that it is through your efforts that we continue to improve the practice. Your experiences are valuable, as are the lessons you will learn by trying new things. I encourage you to publish your work. It is through trial and error that we learn the most. My hope is that we can quickly overcome the trials and move on with the job of producing high-quality software on schedule and within budget.

DONALD J. REIFER

Chapter 1

Introduction

Under any social order from now to Utopia a management is indispensable and all enduring . . . the question is not "Will there be a management elite?" but "What sort of elite will it be?"

—Sidney Webb

Overview

The five papers selected for this introductory chapter provide insights into the concerns and challenges associated with software management and the framework composed to study ways to deal with them. Although each paper makes its own unique point, the majority of the papers were selected because they examine the root causes of what many of us in the industry have called "the software crisis." All too often, managers tend to treat the symptoms and not the root causes of their problems. They then use "gut feel" instead of "hard" data to develop a "quick fix" to the dilemma. For example, managers might try to tie task progress to an impossible schedule when they are falling behind instead of trying to convince their bosses that rescheduling based upon more realistic goals is a better option. They may not realize that rescheduling does not mean the end date has to change. In addition to permitting them to dedicate more time and effort to the tasks that are causing the delays, rescheduling allows them to refocus their resources and take advantage of opportunities to perform other tasks that are not on the critical path in parallel.

The papers included in this chapter were selected to provide you with help in figuring out the root causes of your problems. In the example in the previous paragraph, should progress be considered to be falling behind schedule because the people are not productive enough, the task is tougher to perform than expected, or the original schedule is overly optimistic? These are difficult questions. To develop answers, I have selected papers that establish frameworks to help you understand how different software process, product and people considerations relate to each other and the many life cycle management options that are available for use today. These frameworks are important because they establish a foundation that we will build upon and reference in later chapters in this tutorial.

Article Summaries

Software Management's Seven Deadly Sins, by Donald Reifer. This article is a reprint of an editorial I wrote for *IEEE Software* magazine about my reflections on the state of software and software management worldwide. The paper summarizes the results of a straw poll of experts from 20 organizations who identified what they believed were the major problems relative to managing software. What is surprising about the results is that they reflect problems that have been haunting software managers for the past three decades. The seven sins include: volatile requirements, poor planning, unrealistic schedules and budgets, inadequate controls, undercapitalization, the "we're different" syndrome, and lack of focus on quality. Read on if you are interested in reflections on what we have learned about these problems during the past 30 years.

Principles of Software Engineering Project Management, by Donald Reifer. I originally wrote this article to serve as an introduction to this tutorial. The article reinforces my message that software can be managed using classical project-management approaches. The article ties chapters together and provides you with a road map through this tutorial. The paper has been updated for this volume to reflect the state of the practice of software management and the current content of this volume. The paper's findings, conclusions, and recommendations are presented as principles that you can use to guide your management actions. It is important to note that these principles have not changed during the past decade. They provide you with basic truths or rules for managing software people, projects, and organizations.

The "3P's" of Software Management, by Donald Reifer. This paper communicates principles devised to improve how we address what I call the "3P's" of software management (i.e., the processes we use, the products we generate, and the people who perform the work on our software projects). The paper has been updated to show more clearly how these three important factors are related to one another and the methods, tools, and techniques that we use for software project management. My hypothesis in the paper is that you can increase your chances of success on a software project by reducing the conflicts that arise between the "3P's." Such conflicts arise as the factors take on different levels of importance as the project unfolds.

Why Big Software Projects Fail: The 12 Key Questions, by Watts Humphrey. Answers to the twelve questions asked within this article reveal that managers of large software projects can improve their ability to succeed by looking at past failures and learning from them. The answers to the questions posed provide the reader with insights provided by one of the old hands in software management. This piece is truly thought provoking and stimulating, especially for those professionals who are embarking on the task of managing software projects, both large and small. I recommend that you ponder its message and use the results accordingly.

Critical Success Factor in Software Projects, by John Reel. This excellent article looks at the things you can do on a software project to increase its chances of success. It suggests that you start off on the right foot by setting realistic objectives and expectations for those working on the project. Then, it recommends that you focus on building the team by carefully selecting the members and furnishing them with what they need to get the job done. To maintain your momentum, the paper recommends that you focus on tracking progress, keeping attrition low, and gathering the "hard" data to make smart decisions. The paper concludes by suggesting that you put a postmortem process in place, allowing you to learn from your mistakes.

Key Terms

For those worried about terminology, I have included an updated and expanded glossary at the end of this tutorial volume. To communicate the meanings of the words, 1 have sometimes taken liberties with standard definitions to make them more understandable. Common acronyms used in this chapter follow in a paragraph that follows right after the definitions.

The fourteen terms, which are defined as follows, are important to understanding the articles provided in this introduction:

1. **Activity.** A major unit of work to be completed in achieving the goals of a software project. An activity has precise starting and ending dates, has a set of tasks that need to be done, consumes resources, and results in work products. An activity may contain other activities arranged in a hierarchical order.
2. **Budget.** In management, a statement of expected results expressed in numerical terms.
3. **Case study.** An example employed to communicate lessons learned from trial use of a concept or idea.
4. **Critical success factors.** Those characteristics, conditions, or variables that have a direct influence on your customer's satisfaction with the products and services that you offer.
5. **Lessons learned.** The knowledge or experience gained by actually completing the project.
6. **Milestone.** A scheduled event for which some person is held accountable and that is used to demonstrate progress.
7. **Project.** An organized undertaking that uses human and physical resources, done once, to accomplish a specific goal.
8. **Project management.** The system of management established to focus resources on achieving project goals. Project management has been defined as the art of creating the illusion that any outcome is the result of a series of predetermined, deliberate acts when. in fact, it is not.
9. **Practice.** In management, a preferred course of action for getting the job done.
10. **Resources.** In management, the time, staff, capital, and money made available to a project to perform a service or build a project.
11. **Schedule.** The actual calendar time budgeted for accomplishing the goals established for activities or tasks at hand.
12. **Slack.** In networks, the term used to refer to marginal time available to complete a task or activity.
13. **Task.** In management, the smallest unit of work subject to management accountability.
14. **Tracking.** In management, the process of identifying cost and schedule variances by comparing actual expenditures to projects.

Common Acronyms

The following acronyms are used within the articles in this chapter:

3P's	Process, Product and People
CMM	Capability Maturity Model

CMMI	Capability Maturity Model Integration
GUI	Graphical User Interface
IEEE	Institute of Electrical and Electronics Engineers
IS	Information Systems
PC	Personal Computer
PBS	Product Breakdown Structure
PERT	Program Evaluation and Review Technique
PMBOK™	Project Management Body of Knowledge
SEI	Software Engineering Institute
WBS	Work Breakdown Structure

For Your Bookshelf

Although there are many books and articles on management theory, few of them apply this theory within the context of software projects. In addition, few of these publications provide software project managers with help in identifying issues, bounding solutions, and resolving their day-to-day problems. The texts that I have listed in the Annotated Bibliography appearing at the back of this tutorial volume bridge the gap and provide practical guidance aimed at helping to get the software management job done. They do this by providing readers with examples that they can relate to.

Many of the books on this list are relatively new. I have deliberately tried to make sure that these additions cover the latest concepts. I have eliminated most of the more technically oriented texts and referred readers instead to more management-oriented books like McConnel's *Software Project Survival Guide,* Wiegers's classic *Creating a Software Engineering Culture,* and my book, *Making the Software Business Case: Improvement by the Numbers.* I have also kept several classics on the list of recommended readings, as they are easy to read and contain important messages. For example, I believe that everyone in the field should read the *The Mythical Man-Month* by Fred Brooks. His messages are as relevant today as they were when he first published the book almost 40 years ago.

In addition, the *Project Management Body of Knowledge* (PMBOK™), prepared by the Project Management Institute, provides an excellent framework for putting the lessons learned and discussed into action on your project. I highly recommend that you become familiar with this work.

I will point out books you should consider for your bookshelf in my introduction to each chapter of this volume. I will also provide you with pointers to additional information that is available to assist you in these sections.

Finally, I will put updates to this volume and errata on my Web site (go to www. reifer. corn). Use of the site will allow me to keep you posted on developments in the software management field.

Software Management's Seven Deadly Sins

Donald J. Reifer

D uring the past month, I have participated in an online discussion to look at the state of software and software management worldwide. What a revelation! Apparently, at least for the past several years, I have been living a sheltered existence.

That's because most of my consulting clients have had their acts together when it 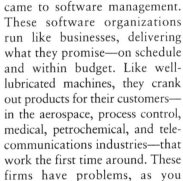 came to software management. These software organizations run like businesses, delivering what they promise—on schedule and within budget. Like well-lubricated machines, they crank out products for their customers— in the aerospace, process control, medical, petrochemical, and telecommunications industries—that work the first time around. These firms have problems, as you might expect, but not overwhelming ones. Most track progress, use metrics, and employ risk management techniques to solve their problems early.

Others in the discussion group contended that I haven't been living in the real world. They argued that software organizations still have a tainted reputation because most software groups fail to deliver what they promise when they promise it. In many firms, senior managers still view software with disdain. To them, it represents the tall pole in the tent: with hardware now typically purchased off the shelf, software consumes most of their engineering resources and represents most of the risk their firms face. As evidence, my interlocutors pointed

to statistics recently published by the Software Engineering Institute (SEI), which indicate that most firms recently rated using the Software Capability Maturity Model are still at Level 1.[1] Group members also pointed to the horror stories appearing far too often in the professional literature, documenting what many call death-march projects and software mismanagement.

I decided to poll my industry friends to determine who was right. I drafted questions and conducted fact-finding using email. In all, senior managers from 20 organizations responded to my questions. To my surprise, most of them indicated that we still have major problems when it comes to managing software (see Table 1). Even more surprisingly, this table could have been built 20 years ago. Have we made *no* progress?

While these findings are not statistically significant, they are revealing. Most of these senior managers view software as a drain on their organizations rather than a contributor. Many think software people are unmanageable prima donnas. Many perceive software organizations as unable to deliver what they promise when they promise it. Interestingly enough, when I called several of these managers and asked them to characterize their firms' software groups, three themes echoed through their answers: software groups never seem to have the time to do the job right, their cost and schedule expectations are unrealistic, and I'm scared of them (because these managers do not understand software).

As one of the field's old-timers, I remember how things were the 1970s and early 1980s. Then, as companies increasingly

Reprinted from *IEEE Software,* March/April, 20001.

bought their hardware off the shelf, they discovered that their products were becoming software-intense. Observers likened software development to hardware engineering, and the "software crisis" was on everyone's lips. Of course, the public did not have a clue about software. The PC was new and general use of the Internet was far in the future. To cope with this so-called software crisis, leading firms pursued software initiatives. Most embraced the following three-pronged attack:

- Standardize the process.
- Standardize the product.
- Professionalize the workforce.

The leaders among them also educated their senior members to set expectations. In the late 1980s, the SEI software maturity model came out.[2] This model formed the framework that enabled many firms to adopt the practices, methods, and tools needed to pursue process improvement. In the mid-1990s, architecture technology became the rage.[3] These same firms then could use their processes to develop standard products using product-line management techniques.[4] Because the technology used to develop software continued to change throughout this period, focus shifted to developing the workforce's skills. However, entire new industries emerged and software development

moved away from the world of the large monoliths to the Web.

Sally Lee

As Table 1 illustrates, some of us are apparently reliving this history. If so, perhaps we can reorient the solutions that worked in the past to help now. Let's turn our attention to what I call the seven sins of software management[5] and see how solutions that worked in the past might again be our salvation.

Sin 1: Volatile requirements

In the old days, requirements were where the action was. The software industry developed better specification techniques to reduce volatility and get the user involved in the process early. We adopted object-oriented techniques to provide better

mapping from problem to solution domains. We learned that we couldn't stabilize the software architecture and design if we let our customers alter requirements at will.

Today's quick-to-market projects seem to be teaching us this lesson anew. Although managers of such projects might use enlightened techniques such as prototyping and modern paradigms such as Mbase[6] and the Rational Unified Process,[7] they succeed only marginally when their organizations let requirements change whenever marketing staffs or customers and users suggest new features and functions. Clearly, better requirements-management processes are fundamental to making improvements.

Sin 2: Poor planning

Years ago, project teams would forsake requirements development and planning because management wanted them to get on with the coding. To cope with this foolishness, we likened software to hardware to illustrate the need for improvement. Firms developed planning templates only after they developed or bought into a life-cycle methodology. Then they brought in classical project-planning tools and techniques such as work breakdown structures and milestone schedules that worked for other disciplines. The software development community learned that we had to plan our future work in detail so we

Table 1

Software Management Straw Poll Findings

Question	Yes (%)	No (%)
Are your software organizations perceived as well managed?	18	82
Do these software organizations deliver what they promise when they promise it?	34	66
Do your customers and users view the products you deliver as high quality?	25	75
Do you employ classical management tools and techniques to manage software deliveries?	55	45
Does your senior management view software organizations as contributing to the bottom line?	30	70
Are software people treated as professionals within your firm?	85	15
Is your firm actively pursuing some form of software improvement strategy?	68	32

could control it and report its status. We invented terms such as *inch pebbles* to describe the depths to which our plans had to go so management would understand what we wanted.

Today, many firms have placed increased attention on planning, because they are trying to shorten the time-to-market interval by scheduling tasks in parallel using iterative and spiral techniques instead of sequential development approaches. They do so because there isn't enough time to plan all the options. To cope with such contingencies, we have learned that we can do planning in a just-in-time manner. We have also learned that plans should be living documents, iterating and evolving over time.

Sin 3: Unrealistic schedules and budgets

In the past, senior managers often set software budgets and schedules because they did not believe our estimates. We had little data to justify our contention that we just couldn't do what they expected with the resources allocated. In addition, many software managers had no idea what it would take to deliver a quality product. Consequently, these managers often said, "We will try our best," instead of "No! Based on our experience, it will take more resources to do this job." The tables have turned as modern cost-estimating methods and models have emerged.[8]

Today, software managers can say with conviction whether they can do the job with the budget authorized. But they still need better requirements and detailed plans to estimate more precisely. Models need to be calibrated to experience so they can achieve the desired accuracy. Improved management processes are not enough—that's what we need to learn here. To go the next yard, firms must bring in specialized management tools and calibrate them to their experience.

Sin 4: Inadequate controls

A decade ago, software managers rarely understood where they stood relative to their budgets and how long and how much it would take to complete their projects. As I've mentioned, their planning was poor and their schedules and budgets unrealistic. In addition, the tracking and measurement techniques software managers used were in their infancy. Few progress metrics and indicators were reported. Modern inspection techniques and statistical controls were still to come.

Today, only the most forward-looking firms seem to use such techniques. We can't properly control what we haven't properly planned. The easiest way to proceed according to schedule is to lie to ourselves. Again, adopting improved planning and tracking processes will go a long way toward slaying this dragon. But we have also learned that putting modern metrics and measures in place to supplement enhanced controls will improve our capabilities and create an atmosphere of trust with senior management.[9]

Sin 5: Undercapitalization

In the late 1980s, the Japanese startled the software world by introducing the software factory concept. They designed such factories as strategic resources that capitalized on the physical plant employed for software development.[10] In other words, they designed and built their software facilities with software development in mind. Trying to leapfrog the com-

> **The software development community has learned that we need to put effort today into developing the infrastructure needed to generate products tomorrow.**

petition, Japanese software developers wired, equipped, and tooled their buildings to optimize software productivity. In making much-needed capital improvements (buying workstations, improving the environment, and so forth), they released money that Corporate America held tightly. In addition, they increased budgets for software tools, especially in firms that had adopted new methods and were embracing process improvement technology.

Today, most firms are heavily undercapitalized regarding software. The reason is simple. These firms just haven't put the effort into assessing and justifying such investments to their management. Instead, they focus on getting their products out using whatever resources are available. The software development community has learned that we need to put effort today into developing the infrastructure needed to generate products tomorrow.

Sin 6: "We're different" syndrome

In the 1970s and 1980s, software developers tried to get management off their backs by hiding behind their product's intangibility. Too often, when senior managers asked questions, the developers would raise the "snow" level to shorten their "do list" and alleviate pressure to increase progress reporting. Clearly, exploiting our mystique this way was a mistake. Senior managers felt better when we told them that we could use what many considered to be best-management practices to report the status of our projects and track their progress. Senior managers also started promoting software people to positions of power when they felt that software managers could deliver what they promised on schedule.

Today, it seems that we have reverted to hiding behind the "we're different" syndrome, again to get management off our backs, especially when schedules are aggressive. Experience shows that it's better to focus on explaining why software is no different than other technical disciplines.

Sin 7: Lack of focus on quality

During the 1970s and 1980s, we had problems with software quality. Many software product releases were buggy. Even worse, consumers often didn't trust software to perform as advertised. Today's software products appear to be no better. Just look at industry-leading browsers and operating systems. Heavy use of commercial off-the-shelf packages, generators, and user application programs complicate the mix even further. In the early 1990s, when Total Quality Management was king, we learned that nobody prospers when defective products are released. As more systems come to depend on software, perhaps we should pay more attention to this lesson. Our customers and users demand that we do a better job when it comes to quality.

I hope that you can use these lessons learned to avoid making one or more of these seven deadly software management sins. When you think about it, most of these lessons convey nothing more than common sense. When I echoed these sentiments to several members of the discussion group, the few who responded agreed with me somewhat. I would be interested in receiving your opinions as well. ⬛

References

1. M.C. Paulk, D. Goldenson, and D.M. White, *The 1999 Survey of High Maturity Organizations*, Special Report CMU/SEI-2000-SR-002, Software Eng. Inst., Carnegie Mellon Univ., Pittsburgh, 2000.
2. W.S. Humphrey, *Managing the Software Process*, Addison-Wesley, Reading, Mass., 1989.
3. L. Bass, P. Clements, and R. Kazman, *Software Architecture in Practice*, Addison-Wesley, Reading, Mass., 1998.
4. D.J. Reifer, *Practical Software Reuse*, John Wiley & Sons, New York, 1997.
5. D.J. Reifer, "The Seven Sins of Software Management," *Software Summit Proc.*, Defense Information Systems Agency, Washington, D.C., 1993.
6. B.W. Boehm, *Guidelines for Life Cycle Objectives (LCO) and the Life Cycle Architecture (LCA) Deliverables for Model-Based (System) Architecting and Software Engineering*, Univ. Southern California, Los Angeles, 2000.
7. P. Kruchten, *The Rational Unified Process*, Addison-Wesley, Reading, Mass., 1998.
8. B.W. Boehm et al., *Software Cost Estimation with COCOMO II*, Prentice-Hall, Upper Saddle River, N.J., 2000.
9. Software Productivity Consortium, *The Software Measurement Guidebook*, Int'l Thomson Computer Press, Stamford, Conn., 1995.
10. M.A. Cusumano, *Japan's Software Factories*, Oxford Univ. Press, New York, 1991.

Donald J. Reifer is a teacher, change agent, consultant, contributor to the fields of software engineering and management, and author of *Tutorial on Software Management, Fifth Edition.* He is president of Reifer Consultants and serves as a visiting associate at the Center for Software Engineering at the University of Southern California. He is also a member of the *IEEE Software* Editorial Board and editor of its Manager column. Contact him at d.reifer@ieee.org.

Principles of Software Engineering Project Management

Donald J. Reifer

This paper communicates 14 principles of software engineering project management that are based upon the experience of seasoned software managers. To make these principles useful, each is related to the primary functions software managers perform. These principles are based on the fundamental premise that good engineering and classical project management methods, tools, and techniques can be applied in a cost-effective manner to cope with the challenges associated with delivering high-quality software products on schedule and within budget.

Introduction

This article introduces you to 14 principles of software management that revolve around the five primary functions software project managers perform to get their job done effectively: planning, organizing, staffing, directing, and controlling. Software managers must develop skills, knowledge, and abilities in each of these functions to successfully deliver an acceptable product on schedule and within budget. They start by planning their projects thoroughly and creating the road map that they will use to create baselines and expectations. Then they create organizations, staff them with the right mix of talent and capability, develop teams and teamwork, and motivate and direct their human resources toward achieving project-related goals. They have to integrate the work of many participants to pull the pieces of this puzzle together in such a manner that they can achieve aggressive budgets and schedules. They put into place controls and use them to track status and determine whether or not their teams are making suitable progress. They manage risk and deal with the day-to-day issues that can, if left unchecked, impede progress. They replan, refocus, and reenergize their teams as they take detours to overcome the obstacles that get in the way of achieving their goals. Software project managers are focused on delivering acceptable products on schedule and within budget. They intentionally avoid doing things that would distract them from accomplishing this goal.

Tutorial Organization

This article discusses the organization of this seventh edition of the tutorial and provides you with an overview of its contents. The volume is organized in 14 chapters and three appendices. As illustrated in Figure 1, the first three chapters in this volume provide you with necessary background for this tutorial and acquaint you with the topics of software life cycle models and process improvement. The next chapter introduces you to the discipline of software project management and its tools of the trade. The five chapters that follow discuss the five primary functions of software engineering project management: planning, organizing, staffing, direction, and visibility and control. Three additional chapters have been added over the years as extensions to the original material for the following topics: software estimating, risk management, and metrics and measurement. The final two tutorial chapters discuss areas of special interest to software managers: acquisition management and emerging management topics. Three appendices round out the volume. The glossary defines management terms used throughout the tutorial, and the annotated bibliography provides you with recommended readings to amplify the key points addressed within this volume. The final appendix provides biographies of the twelve authors who contributed original works to this edition of the tutorial.

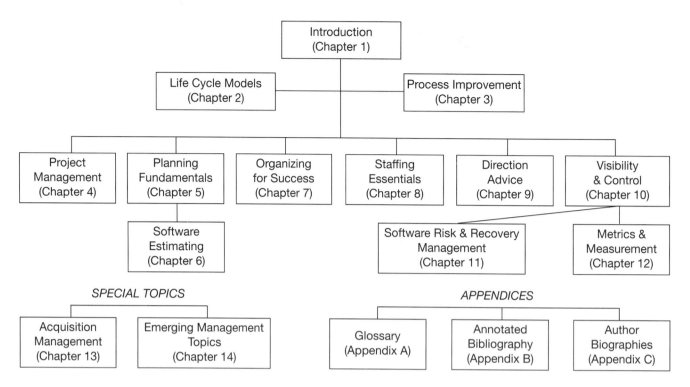

Figure 1. Software Management Tutorial Organization

Planning

Planning is defined as deciding in advance what has to be done, when and how to do it, and who should do it. It encompasses many related disciplines, such as estimating, budgeting, and scheduling. Software managers get involved in many types of planning exercises. For example, they plan projects, capital acquisitions, and/or training/skill development. As discussed in Chapter 5 of this tutorial, plans form the basis against which schedule and budgetary performance are assessed and project control is implemented. Plans create the foundations that project managers use to gain visibility into and control over progress. Based upon the experience of seasoned managers and the software project management body of knowledge,[1] the following three principles establish the basis for project planning:

- **Principle 1—Planning Takes Precedence.** Planning logically takes precedence over all other management functions. While often difficult and time-consuming to perform, plans form the basis for all future work. Managers are encouraged to devote the time needed to figure out what needs to be done, when to do it, who should do it, and how to address the contingencies. Budgets are financial plans, whereas schedules create a viable project time line.
- **Principle 2—Effective Plans Tap the Infrastructure.** Plans are most effective when they are consistent with policies and take full advantage of the organization's existing management infrastructure. This is especially true for those organizations that have initiated a software process improvement program aimed at institutionalizing a "preferred process" and "best practices" across groups.
- **Principle 3—Plans Should Be Living Documents.** Plans should be maintained as living documents or they will quickly become outdated and lose their value as control tools. Plans need to be periodically updated to add detail and reflect the current situation.

Because of their short timetable, most project plans tend to be tactical (near-term) instead of strategic (long-term). When capital and research budgets are impacted, this is a mistake because implementation of project plans may become dependent on others for their realization. The most basic elements of a project plan are its budgets (financial plans) and schedules (delivery timetables). The parts of these documents with the highest leverage are the risk management and contingency plans. It is not uncommon for a manager to spend as much as fifty percent of his/her time early in the project on planning. The better the plans, the more visibility and control you have over task progress. In addition, the higher in management you move, the more strategic your plans become. For example, product line or line-of-business managers generate product plans whose horizons may be 10 to 20 years long. Independent of the level of planning, each plan you develop represents a guide to some future course of action.

To establish a budget, you will have to prepare a resource estimate (time, staff, budget, etc.) based upon your understanding of what the work is that must be done and the resources you have available to handle the job. The ability to estimate resources accurately is a skill every software manager must possess. As discussed in Chapter 6, poor resource estimates can lead to problems that no amount of dedication, perseverance and hard work can correct. The more accurate the estimate, the higher your chances of success will be.

Organizing

Managers create organizations to achieve their goals and get the work they are responsible for done as efficiently as possible. Such organizations provide a structure that lets managers get work done by assigning responsibilities, delegating authority, and holding people accountable for results. Most managers work within an existing organizational structure. As discussed in Chapter 7, their function is to build teams, staff them, provide them with leadership, direct them, integrate their results, and manage communications up, down, and across the organization. Based upon extensive software engineering project management experience, these tasks lead to the following two organizational principles:

- **Principle 4—Assign Your Software Manager Early.** Recruit your software manager early in the project and empower this professional to perform all of the tasks for which he/she will be held responsible. Ensure that this person occupies a high enough position in the hierarchy to successfully compete for needed resources (staff, budget, etc.), talent, and management support.
- **Principle 5—Give Authority Commensurate with Responsibility.** Your software manager's responsibility should be commensurate with his/her authority. Because software managers are not always masters of their own destiny, they should not be held accountable for results when others' actions impede their performance. Such problems often occur when dealing with requirements. Software managers are not in charge of requirements, but rely on them to form the foundation of their architecture and design.

Many of the organizational factors that impact the performance of software managers fall outside their sphere of control. For example, marketing is often responsible for developing requirements (and their frequent change) and for customer liaison. Influence is the key for gaining control over this untenable situation. The software manager must be able to communicate effectively with others within, across, and up and down the existing organizational framework. As discussed in Chapter 7, working groups and use of integrated product teams are mechanisms that can be used specifically for this purpose.

Communications must flow up and down and across the organization to keep people informed. Staff members must keep abreast of current events or they will lose focus and their performance will be negatively impacted. Newsletters, colloquiums, brown-bag lunches, weekly team meetings and monthly "all hands" meetings, are proven mechanisms for improving communications. They should be exploited, along with software peer reviews and inspections.

Staffing

Staffing refers to recruiting, appraising, growing, and keeping the people you need to get the job done properly. Organizations are only as good as the people who populate them. As discussed in Chapter 8, software managers must be able to recognize talent, breed competence, and weed out deadwood. They must also be able to attract the right people to fill key slots within their organizations. Based upon a great deal of software engineering project management experience, the following two principles establish the basis for staffing:

Principle 6—Care about Your People. Software managers must be able to show their people that they truly care about them, their careers, and their goals. Because actions speak louder than words, managers must demonstrate their devotion by fighting for promotions, salary increases, and better working conditions for their people. They must also be able to coach poor achievers and be able to improve their job-related performance.

Principle 7—Provide Dual-Career Ladders. Promotion should be possible up either a technical or managerial career ladder. Technical people who do not want to move into management slots should be given the opportunity to follow other career paths. Chief software engineer positions that are equivalent to middle- and upper-level management slots should be made a visible part of the organizational chart.

In many organizations, dual-career paths act as powerful incentives for technical people who may or may not want to move into management. Knowing what is required to progress along dual lines provides software people with the growth and opportunity they desire. It acts as a motivator and stimulates high levels of achievement. It also makes career counseling easier, especially when people are not satisfied.

As in many other scientific disciplines, good technical performers are often promoted prematurely to management positions. This is frequently a mistake because the skills required for management differ from those required for engineering. Good software managers have to be developed. Training must be provided for those who have demonstrated management potential. Mentoring and other forms of coaching need to be available to help develop individual skills and abilities. In addition, new supervisors should be taught the fundamentals of management.

Directing

Managers get things done through the actions of others. They communicate their goals and lead and motivate their subordinates to achieve these goals typically under deadline pressures. Direction tends to be difficult because software people are highly creative and individualistic. As discussed in Chapter 9, leadership and direction are needed to eliminate mistrust and provide focus for work activities. Based upon lessons learned managing software projects, the following three direction principles create a foundation for our discussions on direction:

- **Principle 8—Provide Your People with an Opportunity to Excel.** Interesting work and the opportunity to excel will motivate your people to do the best that they can. Software managers need to understand how to channel behavior so that it is directed towards achieving work-related goals.
- **Principle 9—Lead by Satisfying Goals.** People will follow those individuals who lead by example and represent a means to satisfy their own personal goals. Success will come to those managers who can make satisfying personal and work-related goals possible on the job.
- **Principle 10—Keep Key People Focused.** Avoid giving your best people too much to do. Too many diversions causes a loss of efficiency that talent alone cannot correct. Learn to say "no" to distractions. To succeed, keep your people focused on the task at hand.

We would like to populate our organizations with talented, self-motivated professionals. Under such a system, tasks would be completed with little or no management interference. Unfortunately, such situations do not exist in most firms. Managers, like coaches, must build synergistic teams and motivate their players to perform at their fullest capability. Managers must be able to communicate, lead, and motivate the players so that they can survive the trials of combat. In addition, they must be able to focus the team, as necessary, to meet deadlines.

Controlling

Planning and control tend to be closely related activities. Managers control by tracking progress against plans and acting on observed deviations. They track actuals against targets and forecast trends. Controls should be diagnostic, therapeutic, accurate, timely, understandable, and, most important, economical. They should call attention to significant deviations from the norm and suggest ways of fixing the problems. They should be forward-looking and emphasize what you need to do in the future to make corrections relative to your plans.

Controls that should be imposed throughout the software development process are discussed in Chapter 10. To be in control, managers must manage risks (see Chapter 1 1) and use metrics to manage (see Chapter 12). Based upon extensive project management experience, this leads to the following three control principles:

- **Principle 11—Focus on the Significant Deviations.** Controls should be implemented to alert managers promptly to significant deviations from plans. The philosophy of "if it isn't broke, don't fix it" should be remembered. In other words, don't interfere if things are going well and the prognosis looks good for the future.

- **Principle 12—You Cannot Control What You Cannot Measure.** Effective control requires that we measure performance against standards. Normally, these standards are budgets and schedules established as targets within your project plan. However, other standards may exist, especially when metrics and other indicators are used to track status and measure progress. Independent of the system you use, you cannot determine where you are going if you do not know where you are or have been.
- **Principle 13—Make Risk Abatement Your Goal.** Risk management and abatement must be an integral part of any control system or else it will cease to work. Identifying obstacles and figuring out ways to avoid them in advance is an essential part of the control process.

Controls close the loop in the feedback system. They provide managers with the visibility and insight needed to make better and timely decisions. As noted in Chapters 10 to 12 of this tutorial, software managers rely on configuration management, metrics and measurement, quality assurance, software inspections, risk management, and verification and validation techniques to provide them with visibility into the project's status and control over its progress.

Instituting Technology Change

The software industry is in a constant state of change. Managers need to be aware of advances that are being made in order to harness them for their benefit. Although using new technology may lie risky, software managers must be able to figure out when and how to put it to work for their organization's benefit. Otherwise, the ability to get the job done may he hindered. Some of the emerging management concepts are discussed in Chapter 14. Experience with such new technology gives rise to the following final principle of software project management:

- **Principle 14—Match Technology Risk with Expected Benefits.** Technology should be used only when the risk associated with its use is acceptable. For projects on a tight schedule, the introduction of something new may be unacceptable. Yet, the same technology may be defensible on another project where adequate resources are available to insert it operationally.

I Firmly believe that technology transfer is the primary means we have to alleviate most of the software problems the industry is experiencing. We need to figure out how to tap the benefits of new technologies, like those explained in Chapter 14, without paying too high a price. We need to work smarter and harder, or we may not be able to handle the workload in the future.

Summary and Conclusions

I am indebted to many good managers with whom I have had the pleasure of working over the past thirty years. They have taught me a great deal. Their conduct has influenced my conduct. Their wisdom has made me wiser. Their experience has become a part of mine. They have provided me with role models, mentored and coached me, spurred me on when I needed motivation, and influenced my management style. My goal with this tutorial is to help you improve your management capabilities by communicating the lessons 1 have learned primarily from others in the form of the 14 principles of software management that I used to organize and shape this volume.

1 would like to thank the IEEE Computer Society for motivating me to keep this tutorial current. The field of software management has made great strides since the last edition of this tutorial. I hope the next few years will see us make even more progress.

Final Thoughts

It is interesting to reflect back 27 years when this tutorial was first published. At that time, I was teaching project management and could not find a suitable text. 1 wrote the first edition to fill that gap. Those universities and colleges that adopted this book as their text told me that they also could not find a suitable textbook. Now. when I ask my professor Friends why they are still using my text, they give a different reason. They say that there just are too many texts available. They use this tutorial because it distills the body of knowledge in software project management down to the point where it can be taught. It is nice to see such progress.

Reference

1. Project Management Institute, *A Guide to the Project Management Body of Knowledge,* 2000.

The "3 P's" Of Software Management

Donald J. Reifer

Abstract. This paper discusses the "3 P's" of software management, the principles devised to discipline the *processes,* standardize the *products,* and professionalize the *people* you use to generate software within your organization. This paper discusses each of the 3 P's and shows how each is related to the others and the methods, tools, and techniques you use to direct and control your software projects.

Introduction

Producing a large software system is fraught with the problems inherent in any highly labor-intensive activity. A large workforce must be assembled and organized into teams. The engineering and management processes must be defined and put into place before the work starts. A software engineering environment and associated tools must be acquired to support selected methods and to automate tedious tasks. Requirements must be specified and the customer's expectations must be known. Plans must be developed, tasks and related milestones must be defined, and budgets and schedules must be negotiated and agreed upon by the key players. A variety of controls must be put into place so that you can assess your progress, and metrics, reviews, reports, and risk management procedures must be provided. Staff must be brought on, trained and molded into teams to deliver quality products per the negotiated budgets and timetables. People must learn to collaborate, cooperate, communicate, and work together to achieve desired results.

As discussed in the previous paragraph, software project managers must address a wide range of issues when tasked with delivering a "high-quality" solution to the user's needs per an agreed-upon budget and schedule. Their job can be likened to putting a puzzle together while on the deck of a ship that is navigating through a storm. To deliver what is promised, software managers must put into place a management infrastructure that allows them to integrate the products of the many processes that their people use to get their work done. In conjunction with these activities, successful managers must address the variety of financial, social, psychological, political, and technical issues that arise and often impede their progress. To succeed, software managers must perform the following activities:

- Planning
- Organizing
- Staffing
- Directing
- Controlling
- Integrating

Based upon the nature of these activities, I do not believe that novices using recipes and cookbooks can practice software management. Success as a manager requires skill, knowledge, and the ability to get a tough job done under extreme deadline and budgetary pressures. Because managers must direct and coordinate the efforts of teams of highly creative people, their job can be simultaneously challenging and frustrating. By its very nature, the practice of software management requires a great deal of common sense, awareness, and sensitivity. Innovation is necessary at times to cope with the many challenges that arise. Persistence is needed to identify the true causes of their problems. Experience is needed to figure out what has to be done, by whom, and when. Openness to a continual stream of new ideas is a prerequisite for success.

In contrast to the articles written about "software failures," I would like to focus on "software successes." I believe many of us in the industry know how to manage a software project successfully. Unfortunately, because of the pressures to deliver, we do not always put this knowledge into practice when necessary. To help you correct this state of affairs, I have prepared both this book and this paper. The book's primary goal is to pull together the ingredients for success in software project management into one place so readers can use it. It provides the body of knowledge that every software manager should know in order to get their job done. I have prepared this paper to introduce you to the concept of the "3 P's of software management." This concept is important because it influenced the selection of papers for this volume. I have also prepared a follow-on paper entitled "Principles of Software Engineering Project Management" (see page 9) to introduce you to the structure and contents of the book.

Setting the Stage

People have often asked me, "Why have you succeeded as a software project manager when others have failed?" That's not an easy question to answer. After considerable thought, the idea of the "3 P's of software management" struck me. While simple, the idea is profound. I immediately tested the idea against the projects that I had managed, both successful and not. I became convinced that the concept had merit because it let me explain to others the attributes of success. What are the 3 P's? Simply stated, they are the *processes, products,* and *people* that populate today's software-intensive projects. To be successful, managers must control the 3 P's concurrently and constantly reconcile conflicts that occur among them.

Think about this concept for a minute. The idea suggests that just concentrating on any one of the 3 P's alone will not be enough to guarantee project success. For example, those who have focused on a process have learned that they need to motivate their people to use it. Just having a good process is not enough. Engineers must be convinced that the process makes their job easier and improves product quality. Otherwise, they will resist using it. However, a process is only one of the contributors to project success. In many organizations, people problems dominate process issues. For example, the pressures associated with deadlines might force key people to quit midway through testing. Social and psychological issues might cause a lack of teamwork just when you cannot afford it. In the product dimension, engineering decisions associated with poor performance might be the most important issue facing management. Using this concept of the "3 P's," you can glean principles that can be used to reconcile the conflicts between differing goals and provide criteria for action. Such principles by design are descriptive, not prescriptive.

Maturing the Process

Producing software involves more than just writing programs. Software should be thought of as a product that must be specified, designed, built, tested, and documented in a disciplined manner. It must be integrated with other products and with the hardware, and you must show your customers that it satisfies their requirements and works as expected in their operational environment. Software product development and maintenance progresses through a series of interrelated, time-phased activities called a life cycle model. Many different life cycle models exist that allow you to sequence activities and order your deliverables. In some, work is done in parallel whenever possible to speed developments and make impossible schedules possible. In others, work is done in spirals to address risk through rapid prototyping. Independent of the model you select, the process you employ must be fully defined, taught, and supported prior to being institutionalized for everyone in your organization to use.

The following three principles are provided to help you decide if the processes you have adopted for your organization are mature and robust enough to satisfy your needs:

- **Principle 1—Recognize that Good Processes Add Value.** Arm good people with processes that they understand and believe in and they will excel. As we have already stated, having either a good process or good people is not enough. You must have both to succeed when faced with the difficulties of generating complex products under budget and schedule pressures. Getting your people to use the process is the challenge. This can be handled most effectively by making your process the preferred way of doing business.

- **Principle 2—Use Your Processes to Share Your Lessons Learned.** Direct your process-definition efforts toward institutionalizing a preferred approach to doing business. This framework represents the scaffolding upon which you will build your management infrastructure (policies, practices, team mechanisms, etc.) and get work done. Such an infrastructure enables you to share your experiences and build on your lessons learned, both positive and negative.

- **Principle 3—Stress Continuous Process Improvement.** Aim your advanced efforts in process development toward using metrics, measurement data and quantitative methods that are directed toward continuously improving your processes. Make sure that the process you improve is the one that your people use. Be flexible and try to build on the past in a manner that lets you address the future. Try to take both people and products into account as you make your decisions based upon the data you collect as part of the normal way that you do business.

To emphasize the progress we have made in the area of process improvement, I have rewritten the chapter on this topic in the current edition of the tutorial. This chapter highlights the experience in using the Capability Maturity Model (CMM) developed at the Software Engineering Institute (SEI) as a process improvement framework. The CMM builds on the five-level process maturity model popularized by the SEI in the late 1980s to characterize the maturity of the practices your people use to generate their software products. The CMM creates a structure that makes insertion of a preferred process into organizations easier to accomplish. This model can be used to rate and rank the "effectiveness" of your current software process and identify shortcomings. Using information from this evaluation, you can implement an improvement program aimed at reaching higher levels of process maturity.

I would suggest that you become familiar with the newer version of the CMM called the CMM Integration (CMMI).[2] This new and more powerful version of the CMM permits you to improve your collective set of engineering and manufacturing practices. The CMMI is beginning to have a profound impact throughout industry because it helps to provide better ways of getting the work done. In addition, models like the CMMI let you both benchmark your process and compare it against your competition. This helps you to identify what practices you should use to develop quality products more quickly and efficiently.

As my principles suggest, emphasis on improving your process is a necessary, but not entirely sufficient, condition for project success. The reason for this is simple. In order to make the process perform as expected within your operational environment, you need to consider both its product and people implications. For example, selection of a process that does not support the specific engineering practices needed for a product could lead to catastrophe. And the process is doomed to failure if the people who are tasked to use it do not believe in its capabilities. Instead of using the process, your people will devote their time and energy to either finding ways of going around the process or justifying why it cannot be used.

Focusing on Product Issues

Let us now look at the issues associated with product management. To be successful, you really need to understand what you are building, why you are building it, and the related building codes. Good processes help you structure how to build; they do not tell you what to build. They do not establish requirements for form, Fit, and function. To build a software product that satisfies your customer, you must put an engineering methodology into place and follow it and its associated building codes to bring high-quality products to market. You must understand both the customer and technical requirements and design a solution that satisfies them. You must establish a product vision and pursue the technology that enables you to realize it now and over time. You must focus on both solidifying your architecture and taking advantage of the opportunities for sharing of components across families of like systems. You must also be able to demonstrate that the product works as specified in an operational setting so that end users will applaud your accomplishments.

The following additional four principles are provided to help you put the different product and product line characteristics into action when you are building software for your systems:

- **Principle 4—Recognize that Performance Is Always the Issue.** Focus your efforts on performance because that is what makes or breaks your product from a customer's point of view. Normally, about twenty percent of the software consumes eighty percent of the computational resources (e.g., memory, speed, I/O capacity). Identify these parts and build them carefully. If you are replacing an existing system, establish a baseline for the current performance. This enables you to make quantitative comparisons and demonstrate in the future that you have achieved your performance goals.

- **Principle 5—Realize that Quality Makes the Difference.** When faced with a choice, your customers will always select quality when functionality and price are nearly equivalent. However, remember that the price/performance trade-off is only important when the product has the features that your customers want and when it works as expected.

- **Principle 6—Emphasize that the Customer is Always Right.** Be customer directed in your functional choices because the customers are ultimately the ones who buy and use your product. Involve them in your process at strategic milestones and do everything you can to tap their knowledge and experience as you build the product. Aim your quality assurance activities at customer satisfaction, not specification conformance.

- **Principle 7—Avoid Gold Plating and Feature Creep.** Avoid gold plating and feature creep at all costs; they will doom your software development project to failure. No matter how hard you try, you cannot deliver an acceptable product on time and for a negotiated price when your requirements are changing and needless additions are being made to the system.

As these principles suggest, marketing rather than engineering issues drive product development. 1 learned early in my career to pay as much attention to product packaging as I did to content. A feature-rich product will not sell if it is not easy to understand and use. And the principles of total quality management definitely hold true. Your goal should be to build the right product the first time. To achieve this aim, you must package the features, functionality, and performance that your customers want, need, and expect in an acceptable form. You must also embed quality into the product and make sure it is reliable, maintainable, and usable when it is released to the field. Finally, you must avoid rework and take advantage of opportunities for commonality and reuse to keep your costs down and remain competitive.

Most of my discussion so far has focused on the deliverable products. Yet. there are many nondeliverable engineering products that are generated during the process that deserve attention. Most software engineering efforts generate documentation of some form. All too often, we produce either too little or too much paperwork. Planning is needed to make sure the documents produced are actually used. This discussion leads us to our fifth and final product principle:

- **Principle 8—Eliminate Unnecessary Paperwork.** Do not produce paper for the sake of producing paper. Such folly results in wasted effort. Understand what documentation you need and devise a plan to develop it. Distinguish between deliverable and nondeliverable documents. Make sure that every document you generate serves a worthwhile purpose.

Realize that generating documentation takes time and effort. It also takes effort to review, distribute, manage, and control versions. I suggest that you generate only those documents that are truly needed to service your user, developer, maintainer, management, and customer communities. Realize that documents come in four varieties: specifications, plans, test documents, and manuals. In addition, the code itself should be self-documenting. After all, that is what the programmers really trust and read.

Within the last few years, the concepts of agile methods for software product lines, architectures, and reuse have become popular as has the move to software patterns and components. My chapter on emerging management topics and some of the case studies in other chapters treat these important techniques. For those interested, I have included several agile method papers throughout the text and updated my paper on the topic of product lines in order to summarize where the state of the technology is today and where it is heading. I have also included a similar survey paper in my chapters on technology transfer and metrics and measurement to round out this update to the tutorial volume.

Addressing the People-Oriented Needs

The final "P" revolves around people. They are your most precious resource because it is through their efforts that you as a manager are successful. Good software managers know how to recruit, grow, motivate, and retain the best people. They know how to use the system to recognize and reward their high performers and provide them with interesting work and the opportunity to excel on the job. When their people are enthusiastic, they are smart enough to get out of the way and watch them shine. When their people are unmotivated, they know how and when to step in and take charge of the situation. When good people are involved, the impossible becomes possible. In my opinion, highly motivated, talented people are the key to software success.

As a manager, you know how to get things done through the work of others. Your primary job is to stimulate your staff to do the best that they can commensurate with their abilities. To motivate staff, you must be sensitive to their needs, understand what drives them, trust them implicitly, and he able to lead them. To get your people to work together, you must build teams and facilitate teamwork. For team building, you must stress the importance of collaboration, cooperation and communication as part of the job. To achieve high levels of performance, you must provide your people with a good work environment and a variety of tangible and intangible rewards. You must realize that when your people shine, you will shine. Your outward sign of success will he the "results" your people achieve. You must be able to plan, direct, and integrate the work of others so things will happen in predictable ways.

Good managers can be likened to good coaches. They know how to recruit the right talent, build teams, and get people to perform. Positive results occur on the playing field when things go well. When problems arise, they know when to step in and what to do to develop a remedy.

Again, I have tried to revise this tutorial to include better and more up-to-date papers on the people-oriented software management disciplines of organizing, staffing, and direction. I have also tried to include some case studies to show how to direct behavior when deadlines get tough and people are overworked. I have also developed the following five people-oriented principles to guide your future personnel actions:

- **Principle 9—Reward Your Top Performers.** Know who your top performers are and do everything you can to keep them happy. Realize that as much as eighty percent of the work is done by twenty percent of your staff. Recognize and reward these high producers and make sure they are not stretched too thin.

- **Principle 10—Commit to Personal Growth.** Make an open and visible commitment to staff development and growth. Know your people and help them achieve their personal goals through work-related training, mentoring, and job assignments. If you help people be all they can be, they will follow you anywhere. More important, they will expend whatever effort is needed to get the job done right the first time.

- **Principle 11—Recognize what Motivates Performance.** People will try their best when they are given interesting work, growth opportunities, feedback, praise, recognition for a job well done, and the ability to excel. To motivate your people, you must recognize, respect, and respond to their needs. You must tap potential, deal with personalities, and get your people to try their hardest, especially when the chips are down and the situation seems desperate.

- **Principle 12—Build Bridges through Open Communication.** Most disputes that occur between staff members are prompted by either intolerance or poor communication. To address these problems, you must stimulate a free exchange of information and ideas. You must permit your interdisciplinary and integrated product teams to go across organizational boundaries when necessary. You must set up vertical and horizontal channels to keep pertinent information flowing up, down, and across the organization. Most important, you must stay engaged with your people even when your work load is intolerable.

- **Principle 13—The Equality Principle.** Reward competence and incompetence with equal vigor. Otherwise, you will foster ineptitude and complacency. Help your people set aggressive but realistic goals and then hold them accountable for results. Be fair but austere in your convictions. Coach your staff and show them how to do a good job. After you have exhausted every other avenue, do not be afraid to terminate an employee for poor performance.

As these principles suggest, software managers need to focus more of their attention on the needs of their people. Many of these needs revolve around your people's desire for structure, leadership, coaching, direction, and attention. When your staff knows what is expected, they will achieve their objectives. They want to do a good job. Your job is to make such performance possible. Managers must also arm their people with the processes, tools, and work environment necessary to complete their assignments. They must be able to focus the energy of their teams so that daily distractions do not interfere with completing the task at hand. They must establish a communications infrastructure and do everything possible to get people to use it. Communications problems lead to many of the people problems that I have been exposed to over the years in large software projects.

Software managers often have difficulty in dealing with people issues because they come from technical specialties like engineering, mathematics or the sciences. They must learn to handle the conflicts that arise between logic and emotion fairly and openly. They must also learn to tap the knowledge base of experience that others have developed to manage the work of others. This edition of the tutorial contains several new papers that address the human side of the management process.

Summary and Conclusions

I believe the concept of the "3 P's of software management" is very meaningful. It allows you to separate concerns and address the relationships between the things that make a difference in a software development effort. In essence, the "3 P's" (process, product, and people) act as the three independent variables that you must control in any software development effort. By addressing each of these variables consciously, I believe you can greatly bolster your overall ability to manage either a software development effort or an organization. This paper provides you with principles that allow you to take advantage of the lessons we have learned relative to the "3 P's." These principles are aimed at helping you succeed when you are tasked with delivering an acceptable software product under deadline pressures.

References

1. M. C. Paulk, C. V. Weber, B. Curtis, and M. B. Chrissis, *The Capability Maturity Model: Guidelines/or Improving the Software Process,* Addison-Wesley, 1995.
2. M. B. Chrisis, M. Konrad, and S. Shrum, *CMMI,* Addison-Wesley, 2003.

Why Big Software Projects Fail: The 12 Key Questions

Watts S. Humphrey
The Software Engineering Institute

In spite of the improvements in software project management over the last several years, software projects still fail distressingly often, and the largest projects fail most often. This article explores the reasons for these failures and reviews the questions to consider in improving your organization's performance with large-scale software projects. Not surprisingly, considering these same questions will help you improve almost any large or small project with substantial software content. The principal questions concern why large software projects are hard to manage, the kinds of management systems needed, and the actions required to implement such systems. In closing, the author cites the experiences of projects that have used the methods described and cites sources for further information on introducing the required practices.

Software project failures are common, and the biggest projects fail most often. There are always many excuses for these failures, but there are a few common symptoms. Some years ago, before the invention of the Capability Maturity Model® (CMM®) and CMM Integration℠ (CMMI®) the principal problem was the lack of plans [1, 2]. In the early years, I never saw a failed project that had a plan, and very few unplanned projects were successful.

The methods defined for CMM and CMMI Levels 2 and 3 helped to address this problem. As the Standish data in Figure 1 shows, the success rate for software organizations improved between 1994 and 2000, and much of this improvement was due to more widespread use of sound project management practices [3]. Still, with less than 30 percent of our projects successful, those of us who are software professionals have little to be proud of.

The definition of a successful project is one that completed within 10 percent or so of its committed cost and schedule and delivered all of its intended functions. Challenged projects are ones that were seriously late or over costs or had reduced functions. Failed projects never delivered anything. Figure 2 (see page 26) shows another cut of the Standish data by project size. When looked at this way, half of the smallest projects succeeded, while none of the largest projects did. Since large projects still do not succeed even with all of the project management improvements of the last several years, one begins to wonder if large-scale software projects are inherently unmanageable.

Question 1: Are All Large Software Projects Unmanageable?

There are some large, unprecedented projects that are so risky that they would likely be challenged under almost any management system. But some large projects have succeeded. Two examples are the Command Center Processing and Display System Replacement (CCPDS-R) project, described by Walker Royce, and the operating system (OS)/360 project in my former group at IBM [4, 5]. The CCPDS-R was a U.S. Air Force installation at Cheyenne Mountain in Colorado. It had about 100 developers at its peak. The OS/360 was the operating system to support the IBM 360 line of computers, and included the control program, data management, languages, and support utilities. Its development team consisted of about 3,000 software professionals.

Both of these projects placed heavy emphasis on planning, and both adopted an evolutionary development strategy with multiple releases and phased specifications. Both projects also took a somewhat unconventional approach to motivating team member performance. For CCPDS-R, management distributed 50 percent of the project award fee to the development team members. This built their loyalty and commitment to success, and maintained team motivation throughout the job. The CCPDS-R project was delivered on schedule and within contracted costs.

By the time I took over the OS/360 project some years ago, we had all learned that the proper strategy for building big software-intensive systems was to break the job into as many small incremental releases as practical. Since this strategy required organization-wide coordination, our very first action was to have all the development teams in all the involved laboratories produce their own plans and coordinate them through a central build-and-release group. Then, we based the company's commitments on the dates that the teams provided. In no case did IBM commit to any date that was not supported by a plan that had been developed by the team that was to do the work.

These plans extended through 19 releases over a period of 30 months. Most importantly, they provided the focus we all needed to coordinate the work of 15 laboratories in six countries and to promptly recognize and address the myriad problems that inevitably arose. The developers were personally committed to their schedules, and they delivered every one of these releases on or ahead of the committed schedules. So, at least based on this limited sample, some large software projects can be managed successfully. However, because the success rate is so low, large-scale software projects remain a major project management challenge.

Question 2: Why Are Large Software Projects Hard to Manage?

While large software projects are undoubtedly hard to manage, the key question is "Why?"

Historically, the first large-scale management systems were developed to manage armies. They were highly autocratic, with the leader giving orders and the

Figure 1: *Project Success History [3]*

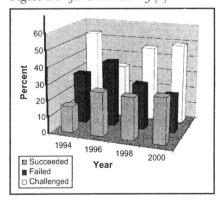

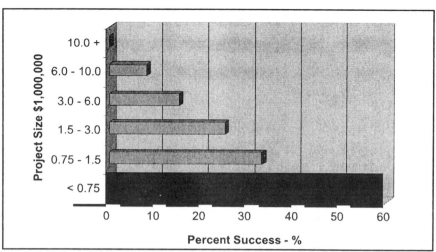

Figure 2: *Success Rate by Project Size [3]*

troops following. Over time, work groups were formed for major construction projects such as temples, palaces, fortifications, and roads. The laborers were mostly slaves, and again, the management system was highly autocratic. The workers did what they were told or they were punished.

This army-like structure was essentially the only management system for many years until the Greek city-states introduced democratic political systems. However, these democratic principles were primarily used for governing, not for project man-

The first large-scale management systems were developed for armies. Leaders gave orders and troops followed. With training and discipline, this approach could work even amid chaos and confusion.

Large-scale management systems were eventually applied to major construction projects. The system was highly autocratic; workers did what they were told or they were punished.

agement. Somewhat later, a totally different management system was used to build cathedrals. This work was largely done by volunteer artisans who managed themselves under the guidance of a master builder. Since building a cathedral often took 50 years or more, the cathedral-management system is not a good model for modern large-scale software projects. However, it did produce some beautiful results. This cathedral-building management system was not used for anything but cathedrals for many years, but it has recently had some success as the guiding principle for the open source software development community [6].

The next major management innovation was the factory. Factories started producing clothing and were soon used for making all kinds of goods. Again, however, the factory management system was autocratic, with management directing and workers doing. While the factory model improved productivity, it was not without its problems. The early work of Frederick Winslow Taylor about 100 years ago and the more recent work of W.E. Deming, J.M. Juran, and others has improved the effectiveness of this model by redefining the role of the worker. The modern view is that to do quality work for predictable costs and schedules, workers must be treated as thinking and feeling participants rather than merely as unfeeling drudges. However, to date, these methods have had limited application to software [7, 8, 9].

The factory/army system has persisted and now characterizes the modern corporate structure where senior management decides and everybody else follows. Many managers would contend that they listen to their people while making decisions. However, employees generally view corporate management as autocratic and few

feel that they could influence a senior manager's decisions. Some managers even argue that autocratic management is the only efficient style for running large projects and organizations. Democratic debates would take too long and decisions would not be made by the most important or knowledgeable people.

Regardless of the validity of this view, the hierarchical management style does not work well for managing large software projects. Unfortunately, except for the cathedral-building system, there is no other proven way to manage large-scale work. So, if we want to have successful large-scale software projects, we must develop a project management system that is designed for this purpose.

Question 3: Why Is Autocratic Management Ineffective for Software?

Before developing a new management system, we should first understand why the current one does not work. To answer this question, we must explore the nature of software work and how it differs from other, more manageable work. Software and software-like work have characteristics that are particularly difficult to manage. From a management perspective, the principal difference between managing traditional hardware projects and modern software work concerns management visibility.

With manufacturing, armies, and traditional hardware development, the managers can walk through the shop, battlefield, or lab and see what everybody is doing. If someone is doing something wrong or otherwise being unproductive, the manager can tell by watching for a few minutes. However, with a team of software developers, you cannot tell what they are doing by merely watching. You must ask them or carefully examine what they have produced. It takes a pretty alert and knowledgeable manager to tell what software developers are doing. If you tell them to do something else or to adopt a new practice, you have no easy way to tell if they are actually working the way you told them to work.

Some might argue that hardware work is not actually that different from software work and that, at least for some hardware tasks and most system engineering jobs, the work is equally opaque to management. This is certainly true, particularly when the hardware engineers are producing microcode, using hardware design languages, or working with simulation or layout tools. Today, as modern technical specialties increasingly overlap, many hard-

22

ware projects now share the same characteristics as large software projects. When hardware development and system-engineering work have the characteristics of software work, they should be managed like software. However, since these systems groups generally tend to be relatively small, they do not yet present the same project-manageability problems as large-scale software.

Question 4: Why Is Management Visibility a Problem for Software?

Since most software developers are dedicated and hard-working professionals, why is management visibility a problem?

The problem is that the manager cannot tell where the project stands. To manage modern large-scale technical work, you must know where the project stands, how rapidly the work is being done, and the quality of the products being produced. With earlier hardware-development projects, all of this information was more-or-less visible to the manager, while with modern software and systems projects it often is not.

This is a problem because large development projects, whether hardware or software, always run into problems, and every problem involves more work. While developers can invariably overcome small problems, every problem adds to the workload and delays the job. Each little slip is generally manageable by itself, but over time, problems add up, and sooner or later the project is in serious trouble.

The project manager's job is to identify these small daily slips and to take steps to counter them. As Fred Brooks said, "Projects slip a day at a time" [10]. With traditional hardware projects, the manager could usually see these one- and two-day slips and could do something about them. With modern, complex, software-intensive systems, the daily schedule slips are largely invisible. So, with large-scale software work, the managers generally do not see the schedule problem until it is so big that it is obvious. Then, however, it is usually too late to do much about it.

Question 5: Why Can't Managers Just Ask the Developers?

If the managers cannot see where the developers stand, why not just ask them?

Most developers would be glad to tell their managers where they stood on the job. The problem is that, with current software practices, the developers do not know where they stand any more than the

managers do. The developers know what they are doing, but they do not have personal plans, they do not measure their work, and they do not track their progress. Without these practices to guide them, software people do not know with any precision where they are in the job. They could tell the manager that they are pretty close to schedule or 90 percent done with coding, but the fact is that they do not really know. Again, as Brooks said, "...programmers generally think that they are 90 percent through with the coding for more than half of the project" [10].

Unless developers plan and track their personal work, that work will be unpredictable. Furthermore, if the cost and schedule of the developers' personal work is unpredictable, the cost and schedule of their teams' work will also be unpredictable. And, of course, when a project team's work is unpredictable, the entire project is unpredictable. In short, as long as individual developers do not plan and track their personal work, their projects will be uncontrollable and unmanageable.

Anyone who has managed software development will likely argue that this is an overstatement. Although you may not know precisely where each developer's work stands, you can usually get a general idea. Since about a third to a half of the small projects are successful when the developers do not plan and track their personal work, such projects can be managed. So why should the lack of sound personal software practices be a problem for large projects?

It is true that software projects are not totally unmanageable. As Figures 1 and 2 show, the worst problem is with the very large software projects. On small projects, some uncertainty about each team member's status is tolerable. However, as projects get bigger and communications lines extend, precise status information becomes more important. Without hard data on project status, people communicate opinions, and their opinions can be biased or even wrong. When filtered through just a few layers of management, imprecise project status reports become so garbled that they provide little or no useful information. Then these large-scale software projects end up being run with essentially no management visibility into their true status, issues, and problems.

Question 6: Why Do Planned Projects Fail?

Today, with CMM and CMMI, most large software projects are planned, and they use methods like Program and Evaluation

Work on cathedrals was done by volunteer artisans who managed themselves under the guidance of a master builder. This approach has had some success in open source software development.

and Review Technique (PERT) and earned value to track progress. Why is that not adequate?

The problem is with the imprecision and inaccuracy of most software project plans. Most projects have major milestones such as specifications complete, design complete, code complete, and the like. The problem is that on real software projects, few of these high-level tasks have crisp completion dates. The requirements work generally continues throughout design and even into implementation and test; coding usually starts well before design completion and continues through most of testing.

A few years ago, the management of a large software organization asked me to review their largest project. They told me that the code completion milestone had already been met on schedule. However, I found that very little code had actually been released to test. When I met with the development teams, they did not know how much code they had written or what remained to be done. It took a full week to get a preliminary count, and it was a month before we got accurate data. It was another 10 months before all of the coding was actually completed. It is not that developers lie, just that without objective data, they have no way to know precisely where they stand. When they are under heavy schedule pressure, people try to respond. Since we all know that the bearer of bad news tends to be blamed, no one dares to question the schedule and everyone gives the most optimistic story they can.

Question 7: Why Not Just Insist on Detailed Plans?

Why cannot management just insist on more detailed plans? Then they could have more precise measures of project status.

While this would seem reasonable, the issue is, "Whose plans are they?" Detailed plans define precisely how the work is to be done. When the managers make the plans, we have the modern-day equivalent of laborers building pyramids. The managers tell the workers what to do and how to do it, and the workers presumably do as they are told.

While this has been the traditional approach for managing labor, it has become progressively less effective for managing high-technology work, particularly software. The principal reason is that the managers do not know enough about the work to make detailed plans. That is why many of these software-intensive projects typically have very generalized plans. This provides the developers with the flexibility they need to do creative work in the way that they want to. The current system is therefore the modern equivalent of the cathedral-building system where the developers act like artisans. The unfortunate consequence is that, without Herculean effort, it often seems that the natural schedule for such projects could easily approach 50 years.

Question 8: Why Not Tell the Developers to Plan Their Work?

The obvious next step would be to tell the developers to make their own detailed plans. Why would this not work?

There are three problems. First, most developers do not want to make plans; they would rather write programs. They view planning as a management responsibility. Second, if you told them to make plans, they would not know how to do it. Few of them have the skill and experience to make accurate or complete plans. Finally, making accurate, complete, and detailed plans means that the developers must be empowered to define their own processes, methods, and schedules. Few managers today would be willing to cede these responsibilities to the software developers, at least not until they had evidence that the developers could produce acceptable results.

Question 9: How Can We Get Developers to Make Good Plans?

It seems that the problem of effectively managing large software projects boils down to two questions: How can we get the software developers and their teams to properly make and faithfully follow detailed plans, and how can we convince management to trust the developers to plan, track, and manage their own work?

To get the developers to make and follow sound personal plans, you must do three things: provide them with the skills to make accurate plans, convince them to make these plans, and support and guide them while they do it.

Providing the skills is just a question of training. However, once the developers have learned how to make accurate plans and to measure and track their work against these plans, they usually see the benefits of planning and are motivated to plan and track their own and their team's work. So, it is possible that developers *can* be taught to plan and, once they learn how, they are generally willing to make and follow plans [11].

Question 10: How Can Management Trust Developers to Make Plans?

This is the biggest risk of all: Can you trust developers to produce their own plans and to strive for schedules that will meet your objectives?

This question gets to the root of the problem with autocratic management methods: trust. If you trust and empower your software and other high-technology professionals to manage themselves, they will do extraordinary work. However, it cannot be blind trust. You must ensure that they know how to manage their own work, and you must monitor their work to ensure that they do it properly. The proper monitoring attitude is not to be distrustful, but instead, to show interest in their work. If you do not trust your people, you will not get their whole-hearted effort and you will not capitalize on the enormous creative potential of cohesive and motivated teamwork. It takes a leap of faith to trust your people, but the results are worth the risk.

Question 11: What Are the Risks of Changing?

Every change involves some risk. However, there is also a cost for doing nothing. If you are happy with how your large software projects are performing, there is no need to change. However, few managers or professionals are comfortable with the current state of software practice, particularly for large-scale projects. So, there are risks to changing and

risks to not changing. The management challenge is to balance these risks before deciding what to do.

There are two risks to changing to a new management system for large-scale software projects. First, it costs time and money to train the developers to plan and track their work and to train the managers to use a new management system. Then comes the risk of using these methods on a real project. While you will see some early benefits, you will not know for sure whether this new management system is truly effective for you until the first project is completed and you can analyze the results.

This brings up a related and even more difficult problem: On large multi-year projects, there is not time to run pilots. You must pick a management strategy and go with it. However, since almost all large software-intensive projects are now failing anyway, the biggest risk is *not changing*. Perhaps the biggest shock for most managers is realizing that they are part of the problem, and that they have to change their behavior to get the kind of large-system results they want.

These problems are common to all change efforts. The way to manage these problems is to examine the experiences of others and to minimize your exposure by carefully planning your change effort and getting help from people who have already used the methods you plan to introduce. Of course the alternative is to hope that things will get better without any changes. With this choice, however, your large-systems projects will almost certainly continue to perform much as they have in the past.

Question 12: What Has Been the Experience So Far?

The Software Engineering Institute (SEI[SM]) has developed a method called the Team Software Process[SM] (TSP[SM]) that follows the concepts described in this article [11]. With the TSP[1], if you properly train and support your development people and if you follow the SEI's TSP introduction strategy, your teams will be motivated to do the job properly. The team members' personal practices will be defined, measured, and managed; team performance will also be defined, measured, and managed; and the project's status and progress will be precisely reported every week. Although this will not guarantee a successful project, these practices have worked for the several dozen projects that have tried them so far.

Moreover, there is one caveat. These

practices have proven effective for teams of up to about 100 members, as well as for teams composed of multiple hardware, systems, and software professionals. They have even worked for distributed teams from multiple geographic locations and organizations. Although these methods should scale up to very large projects, the TSP has not yet been tried with projects of over 100 professionals. I know from personal experience, however, that these practices will address many of the problems faced by the managers of software organizations of several thousand developers.

The other articles in this issue describe the TSP experiences of several organizations. They describe how these practices have worked on various kinds of projects and how they could help your organization.◆

Acknowledgements

Many people have participated in the work that led to this article, so I cannot thank them all personally. However, without their willingness to try new methods and to take the risks that always accompany change, this work would not have been possible. So, to everyone who participated in the early CMM and CMMI work and to all of those who have learned and used the Personal Software Process^{SM} and TSP, you have my profound gratitude. I have also had the advice and support of several people in writing this article. My special thanks go to Dan Burton, Noopur Davis, Bill Peterson, Marsha Pomeroy-Huff, and Walker Royce.

References

1. Humphrey, Watts S. <u>Managing the Software Process</u>. Reading, MA: Addison-Wesley, 1989.
2. Chrissis, Mary Beth, Mike Konrad, and Sandy Shrum. <u>CMMI – Guidelines for Process Integration and Process Improvement</u>. Reading, MA: Addison Wesley, 2003.
3. The Standish Group International, Inc. <u>Extreme Chaos</u>. The Standish Group International, Inc., 2001.
4. Royce, Walker. <u>Software Project Management, A Unified Framework</u>. Reading, MA: Addison-Wesley, 1998.
5. Humphrey, Watts S. "Reflections on a Software Life." <u>In the Beginning, Recollections of Software Pioneers</u>. Robert L. Glass, Ed. Los Alamitos, CA: IEEE Computer Society Press, 1998.
6. Raymond, Eric S. <u>The Cathedral and the Bazaar</u>. Cambridge, MA: O'Reilly Publishers, 1999.
7. Deming, W. Edwards. <u>The New Economics for Industry, Government, Education</u>. 2nd ed. The MIT Press, Cambridge, MA, 2000.
8. Juran, J.M., and Frank M. Gryna. <u>Juran's Quality Control Handbook, Fourth Edition</u>. New York: McGraw-Hill Book Company, 1988.
9. Taylor, Frederick Winslow. <u>The Principles of Scientific Management</u>. New York: Harper and Row, Publishers, Inc., 1911.
10. Frederick P. Brooks. <u>The Mythical Man-Month</u>. Reading, MA: Addison Wesley, 1995.
11. Humphrey, Watts S. <u>Winning With Software: An Executive Strategy</u>. Reading, MA: Addison-Wesley, 2002.

Note

1. The Software Engineering Institute offers courses and transition services to help organizations introduce the TSP. Additional information is available at <tsp@sei.cmu.edu> or at <www.sei.cmu.edu/tsp>.

About the Author

Watts S. Humphrey joined the Software Engineering Institute (SEI^{SM}) of Carnegie Mellon University after his retirement from IBM in 1986. He established the SEI's Process Program and led development of the Software Capability Maturity Model®, the Personal Software Process^{SM}, and the Team Software Process^{SM}. During his 27 years with IBM, he managed all IBM's commercial software development and was vice president of Technical Development. He holds graduate degrees in physics and business administration. He is an SEI Fellow, an Association for Computing Machinery member, an Institute of Electrical and Electronics Engineers Fellow, and a past member of the Malcolm Baldrige National Quality Award Board of Examiners. He has published several books and articles and holds five patents.

Carnegie Mellon University
4500 Fifth AVE
Pittsburgh, PA 15213-2612
Phone: (941) 924-4169
Fax: (941) 925-1573
E-mail: watts@sei.cmu.edu

Software projects are still late, over budget, and unpredictable. Sometimes the entire project fails before ever delivering an application. This clear, commonsense review of fundamental project management techniques reminds us that we still have a long way to go.

Critical Success Factors In Software Projects

John S. Reel, Trident Data Systems

hroughout the fifty-odd years of software development, the industry has gone through at least four generations of programming languages and three major development paradigms. We have held countless seminars on how to develop software correctly, forced many courses into undergraduate degree programs, and introduced standards in our organizations that require specific technologies. Still, we have not improved our ability to successfully, consistently move from idea to product. In fact, recent studies document that, while the failure rate for software development efforts has improved in recent years, the number of projects experiencing severe problems has risen almost 50 percent.[1] There is no magic in managing software development successfully, but a number of issues related to software development make it unique.

Reprinted from *IEEE Software*, May/June 1999.

MANAGING COMPLEXITY

Several characteristics of software-based endeavors complicate management. First, software-based systems are exceptionally complex. In fact, many agree that "the basic problem of computing is the mastery of complexity."[2] Because software developers must deal with complex problems, they are generally very intelligent and complex individuals, which also complicates the management formula. Add the fact that developers are trying to hit a moving target—user requirements—and you get a volatile mixture of management issues.

These and many other influences contribute to a fantastically high failure rate among software development projects. The Chaos study, published by the Standish Group, found that 26 percent of all software projects fail (down from 40 percent in 1997), but 46 percent experience cost and schedule overruns or significantly reduced functionality (up from 33 percent in 1997).[1] The study also shows that the completion rate has improved because companies have trended towards smaller, more manageable projects—not because the management techniques have improved. Can you imagine a construction firm completing only 74 percent of its buildings and completing only 54 percent of the buildings within schedule and budget? To change this trend, we must place special emphasis on certain factors of the management process.

You may think the answers lie in elaborate analysis methodologies, highly advanced configuration management techniques, or the perfect development language. Those elements of the technology landscape are as important as highly scientific and analytical research in analysis and design methodologies, project management, and software quality. However, blueprints of the latest train technology didn't improve life in the Wild West until rail companies invested in the fundamental aspects of train transportation—tracks and depots. Likewise in software, more "advanced" technologies are far less critical to improving practice than embracing what I believe are the five essential factors to managing a successful software project:

1. Start on the right foot.
2. Maintain momentum.
3. Track progress.
4. Make smart decisions.
5. Institutionalize post-mortem analyses.

Granted, even a detailed review of these may leave you wondering what's new here. Not much—this is common-sense, basic management stuff. And yet these principles are not commonly employed. If they were, we would not see such high failure rates.

START ON THE RIGHT FOOT

It is difficult to call any of these factors most important, since they are all critical to the success of large development efforts. However, getting a project set up and started properly certainly leads this

> At least seven of 10 signs of IS project failures are determined before a design is developed or a line of code is written.

class of factors. Just as it is difficult to grow strong plants in weak soil, it is almost impossible to successfully lead a development effort that is set up improperly. Tom Field analyzed pitfalls in software development efforts and gave 10 signs of IS project failures—at least seven of which are fully determined before a design is developed or a line of code is written.[3] Therefore, 70 percent of the dooming acts occur before a build even starts.

Here are 10 signs of IS project failure:[3]

1. Project managers don't understand users' needs.
2. The project's scope is ill-defined.
3. Project changes are managed poorly.
4. The chosen technology changes.
5. Business needs change.
6. Deadlines are unrealistic.
7. Users are resistant.
8. Sponsorship is lost.
9. The project lacks people with appropriate skills.
10. Managers ignore best practices and lessons learned.

Given this information, what can we do to get projects off to a successful start?

Set realistic objectives and expectations—for everyone

The first objective in getting a project off to a good start is to get everyone on the same wavelength. Management, users, developers, and designers must all have realistic expectations. In case your customers haven't heard, remind them routinely that this system will not solve all of their problems and it will probably create new issues. The new system should cost-effectively solve more problems than it creates. The developers must also understand that the customers do not know exactly what they want, how they want it, or how it will help

By the time you figure out you have a quality problem, it is probably too late to fix it.

them. Often, they don't even know how much they can spend. Everyone has to come to the table with their eyes open, willing to cooperate and listen. To avoid later heartache, pay strict attention to the commitments made by both sides.

Build the right team

Next, you must put together the right team. First ensure that you have enough resources to get the job done. If you do not get commitments for resources up front, the effort is doomed. If management is not excited enough about the effort to give it enough resources, you may not have the support necessary for success. Remember, too, that you will likely need more resources than you think. We are all inherently optimistic, so guard your personnel projections and err on the high side from the start.

Building the right team means getting good people. This is hard because companies usually want to place personnel moving off other efforts. Sometimes these people are good resources, but not always. However, also recognize that you do not need, or want, all of the very best designers and developers. In my experience, staffing around 20 percent of the team with the best available works well. This figure is loosely supported in Fred Brooks' essay "The Surgical Team."[4] His team of about 10 people includes two who are real experts (the Chief Programmer and the Language Lawyer). Having too many stars creates ego issues and distractions, while not having enough can leave the team struggling with small problems.

The rest of the team should be good, solid developers with compatible personalities and work habits. The more advanced team members can step ahead into uncharted waters, develop the most critical algorithms and applications, and provide technical mentoring to the rest of the team.

The most critical element in selecting people is creating an environment in which they can excel, and that lets you focus more on technology than team dynamics. You don't want a team of clones, but you do want people who are compatible with one another and with the company and team environment you are striving to establish. For example, a married-with-kids, laid-back, nine-to-five developer might not work well on a team of young, single, forceful seven-to-eleven developers. This doesn't mean the former is any less qualified or productive. Actually, that laid-back developer may produce better code and be more productive than the rest of the group. If you think that first person brings a calming, focused influence without either "side" becoming overly frustrated, maybe it is a good fit after all. At any rate, you must take these factors into consideration when building your team.

Wherever possible, and it usually is possible, involve customers and users in the development. Not only does this help build higher levels of trust between developers and users, it also places domain experts within arm's reach of the developers throughout development. This increases the chance that you will develop a product that meets the user requirements.

Give the team what they think they need

Once you have built a strong team, you must next provide it with an environment that encourages productivity and minimizes distractions. First, do your best to arrange quiet, productive office spaces. This is often impossible given most corporate realities, but a comfortable office setting can yield dramatic results. Highly productive environments contain white boards, meeting areas (formal and informal), private office areas, and flexible, modern lab facilities. Add comfort elements such as stereos, light dimmers, coffee machines, and comfortable chairs; you will create an environment where people can focus on their work and forget the rest of the world.

Once you have a team with a productive office space, you need the proper equipment. Do not for any reason scrimp on equipment. The difference between state-of-the-art machines and adequate development systems is less than $1,000. You will probably spend at least $100,000 per year to keep a good developer, including salary, bonuses, benefits, training, and other related expenses. That extra $1,000 amortized over two years represents less

than 1/2 percent of the employee cost.

Finally, your team needs tools. Get good, proven tools from stable companies. Nothing will derail a project faster than using unsupported tools. The team also needs training on those tools; losing files and folders from ignorance and inexperience is painful and costly. The term tool does not just mean compiler. You also need analysis and design, configuration management, testing, back-up management, document production, graphics manipulation, and troubleshooting tools. This is, however, an area where going first-class does not necessarily mean spending the most money. Shop carefully, review a lot of options, and involve the entire team in the decision.

MAINTAIN THE MOMENTUM

By now, you have your development team energized with strong co-workers, a great working environment, and some high-end hardware. Congratulations, you have momentum. The next critical factor is maintaining and increasing this momentum. Building momentum initially is easy, but rebuilding it is dreadfully difficult. Momentum changes often during the course of a development effort. These changes add up quickly, so it is crucial to quickly offset the negative shifts with positive ones.

You should focus on three key items to maintain or rebuild team momentum:

♦ Attrition—keep it low.

♦ Quality—monitor it early on and establish an expectation of excellence.

♦ Management—manage the product more than the people.

Attrition

Attrition is a constant problem in the software industry. It can spell disaster for a mid-stream software project, because replacement personnel must quickly get up to speed on software that is not complete, not tested, and probably not well-documented yet. A tremendous amount of knowledge walks out the door with the person leaving, and those left behind have a scapegoat for every problem from then on. Also, in this tight labor market, the lag time between when a person quits and when a replacement is hired can wreak havoc with even the most pessimistic schedules.

Quality

You cannot go back and add quality. By the time you figure out you have a quality problem, it is probably too late to fix it. Establish procedures and expectations for high levels of quality before any other development begins and hire developers proven to develop high-quality code. Have the developers participate in regular peer-level code reviews and external reviews.

Invariably, when a project is cruising along, everybody is excited, the status reports look great, and the GUI is awesome, everything goes wrong. There may be a bad test report, a failed demo, or a small change request from the customer that becomes the pebble that starts an avalanche. You fix one bug, or make one change, and cause two more. Suddenly, the development team that was making fantastic progress is mired in repairing and modifying code that has been in the bank for months.

Management

Manage your product more than your personnel. After all, the product is what you are selling. So, if your corporate culture can handle it, don't worry about dress codes or fixed work hours. Relax and let people deliver things at the last minute. Then critique their

Project leaders often avoid confronting individuals and merely "fix" a problem by setting arbitrary team rules.

products. If the products are not acceptable, you can start working with the individuals to improve their products. The goal here is to not make individual issues team problems. Just because one or two people like to come in at 10:00 a.m. and work until 5:00 p.m., abusing the flexibility you give, doesn't mean you should dampen the environment for the whole team. Too often, project leads avoid confronting the individuals and merely "fix" the problem by setting arbitrary team rules. Soon, everyone is griping about deviant co-workers and the strict management. Those are the sounds of momentum slipping away. Roll a few of these decisions together, and the team is soon focused more on avoiding the rules or tattling on offenders than on producing a quality product.

When you do have a legitimate personnel problem, deal with it quickly. If you must let someone go, do it quickly and then meet with your team to explain what happened. As long as you are being fair, these experiences will contribute to the team's cohesiveness and allow them to rebuild momentum quickly.

TRACK PROGRESS

Consider the intangible nature of software compared to traditional brick-and-mortar construction. Construction results in a physical manifestation of a conceptual model—the blueprint becomes a building that people can touch and see. They can also touch and see all of the little pieces as they are

> If you don't take time to figure out what happened during a project, both the good and the bad, you're doomed to repeat it.

being nailed, welded, glued, or screwed to the framework during construction. Software development begins as a conceptual model and results in an application, so there is no physical manifestation of software that can be touched and measured, especially during construction.

A large problem in managing software development is figuring where you are in your schedule. How complete is a module? How long will it take to finish modules X, Y, and Z? These are hard questions to answer, but they must be addressed. If you don't know where you are in relation to the schedule, you cannot adjust and tweak to bring things back on track. Many methodologies exist for tracking progress; select one at the right level of detail for your effort, and use it religiously.

MAKE SMART DECISIONS

Making smart decisions often separates successful project leaders from failures. It shouldn't be hard to identify a bad decision before you make it. Choosing to rewrite a few of Microsoft's dynamically linked libraries to accommodate your design choices, for example, is a poor decision. Yet I have seen at least four major projects attempt such insanity. If your application needs to communicate across a serial connection, do you buy a commercial library of communications routines or develop your own from scratch? If you build it from scratch, you can then implement your own personally designed

protocol. Bad call. Always use commercial libraries when available, and never try to create a new communications protocol. At best, it will cost you a fortune. At worst, it will sink your project.

People also consistently make bad decisions in selecting technologies. For example, how many people chose to develop applications for the Next platform? Most never finished their applications before that platform went away. When you pick a fundamental technology, whether a database engine, operating system, or communications protocol, you must do a business and a technical analysis. If the technology isn't catching market share and if a healthy company doesn't support it, you are building your project on a sandy foundation.

Because your foresight is fallible, use your design to insulate yourself from the underlying technology. Encapsulate the interface to new or niche technologies as much as possible. Think about which technologies will be prone to change over your product's lifetime and design your application to insulate—to a practical level—your code from those changes.

You will have many opportunities to make good decisions as you negotiate the customer's requirements. Strive to move the requirements from the complicated, "never been done before" category to the "been there, done that" category. Often, users request things that are marginally valuable without understanding the complexity. Explain the ramifications of complicated requirements and requirements changes in terms of cost and schedule. Help them help you.

POST-MORTEM ANALYSIS

Few companies institutionalize a process for learning from their mistakes. If you do not take time to figure out what happened during a project, both the good and the bad, you are doomed to repeat it.

What can you learn from a post-mortem analysis? First, you learn why your schedule estimates were off. Compensating for those factors in the next project will dramatically improve your estimating techniques. A post-mortem will also help you develop a profile for how your team and company develop software systems. Most companies and teams have personalities that strongly impact the development cycle. As you go through post-mortem

analyses, these personalities emerge as patterns rather than as isolated incidents. Knowing the patterns allows you to circumvent or at least schedule for them on your next project.

In his book *Managing Software Development Projects*, Neal Whitten offers six steps for executing a post-mortem review of a project:[5]

♦ Declare the intent: Announce at the beginning of the project that you will hold the review. Also define what topics will be addressed, and set the procedures.

♦ Select the participants: Choose representatives from each major group associated with the project. To ensure an objective review, management should not participate directly.

♦ Prepare the review: After the project is complete, assign review participants to gather data. This should include metrics, staffing, inter- and intra-group communications, quality, and process.

♦ Conduct the review: The actual review should not require more than a few days of meetings. All participants should start by presenting their findings and experiences with the project. Next, the group prepares two lists: things that went right and things that went wrong. Participants can then begin to work on what went wrong to develop solutions.

♦ Present the results: The participants should present the results to the development team and executive leadership.

♦ Adopt the recommendations: The company must implement the recommendations on upcoming projects. Without this follow-through, the process yields a marginal benefit.

The premise and benefit of performing post-mortem analyses are validated by the process improvement movement inspired by W. Edwards Deming during the late 1980s and early 1990s. He suggests objectively measuring a given process and using those measurements to evaluate the influence of changes to the processes. Only by measuring a system and analyzing those incremental measurements can you truly improve the system.[6]

Guess what? Your company's software methods and habits for developing software constitute a system. It is far less defined than an assembly line, but it is still a system. The post-mortem analysis allows you to modify that system for the next "production run."

These five critical factors hold true regardless of the design and development methodology, the implementation language, or the application domain. However, this is not an exhaustive list—many other factors influence the successful management of a software development effort. But if you master these five, you greatly increase the odds of completing your project on time and within budget. Just as important, you increase your chances of actually delivering something your users want. ❖

REFERENCES

1. R. Whiting, "News Front: Development in Disarray," *Software Magazine*, Sept. 1998, p. 20.
2. J. Martin and C. McClure, *Structured Techniques for Computing*, Prentice Hall, Upper Saddle River, N.J., 1988.
3. T. Field, "When BAD Things Happen to GOOD Projects," *CIO*, 15 Oct. 1997, pp. 55-62.
4. F.P. Brooks, Jr., *The Mythical Man-Month: Essays on Software Engineering*, Addison Wesley Longman, Reading, Mass., 1995.
5. N. Whitten, *Managing Software Development Projects*, John Wiley & Sons, New York, 1995.
6. R. Aguayo, *Dr. Deming: The American Who Taught the Japanese About Quality*, Fireside Books, New York, 1990.

About the Author

John S. Reel is the chief technology officer of Trident Data Systems, an information protection and computer networking company. He is a co-inventor of patented COMSEC technology. He received a BS in computer science from the University of Texas at Tyler and a PhD in computer science from Century University. He also worked for the US Department of Defense in systems support, software development, and management.

He is a member of the IEEE, the IEEE Computer Society, Information Systems Security Association, and the Armed Forces Communications and Electronics Association.

Readers may contact Reel at 6615 Gin Road, Marion, Texas 78124; e-mail jreel@tds.com.

Chapter 2

Life Cycle Models

Discipline provides strength and comfort, while agility provides releases and invents.
—Barry Boehm and Rich Turner in *Balancing Agility and Discipline*

Overview

The three papers included in this chapter on life cycles were selected to make you think about the methods, processes, and approaches you should choose for developing software. In the old days, most professionals would develop software using an integrated collection of methods and tools according to the waterfall life cycle model. This conventional life cycle model was useful because it succeeded in focusing attention on the steps that we had to go through to get a software product out the door. Using this life cycle model, we would focus our early efforts on getting the requirements right before progressing with the design and code. In order to effectively prepare, long-lead activities like test planning were done in parallel with development activities. Feedback between activities was desirable as were milestone reviews to ensure that development products like requirements and designs were acceptable before venturing forth into the next task. Stability, flexibility, and feedback loops were the most desired attributes of the process because most of us wanted to avoid problems attributed to changing baselines. The common lore was that it was bad to start design without a firm set of requirements in hand.

The plan-driven or waterfall approach tends to be too rigid for today's quick-to-market software development projects. Most firms characterize this new software development model as agile and risk tolerant rather than rigid and risk averse. They place a premium on being low rather than high ceremony and focus their resources on generating software products rather than documentation. Parallelism and iteration tend to be the norm along with spirals, as is the notion that projects should move ahead if the potential gains are worth the pain. Yes, the life cycle still needs to be stable and provide measurable feedback on progress. Yes, it is OK to perform tasks in parallel when it makes sense. Yes, it is all right to take some shortcuts. But, you are warned to do so with your eyes wide open, and encouraged to build prototypes to firm the requirements and learn what the user truly wants.

The papers selected focus on what leaders in the industry are calling lightweight processes and Internet speed. The goal of these new life cycles is quickness to market. The context used to be small projects and Web applications. Recently, however, more and more firms seem to be using lightweight methods for larger projects. This is especially true for applications for which requirements are volatile and safety is not a concern. Instead of rigor and rigidity, the life cycles discussed emphasize agility and flexibility. The alternative life cycles models or paradigms that are introduced show you how to achieve speed and agility without sacrificing process discipline. But, as the papers emphasize, trade-offs need to be made to realize the balance needed to maintain visibility and control in an environment that places rewards on getting to the marketplace first with competitive and high-quality software products.

Article Summaries

A Spiral Model of Software Development and Enhancement, by Barry W. Boehm. The spiral model described in this paper is a risk-driven rather than a code-driven approach to the software development and enhancement process. Conventional software process models assume that projects can be done in a stepwise manner from requirements to designs, designs to code, and so on. They fail to recognize the need for prototyping and risk reduction at each stage of translation. This paper shows how the spiral model addresses these needs through the use of an evolutionary, iterative, risk-reduction process. The paper also introduces you to other process frameworks and serves as a useful introduction to the topic of life cycle models.

Bridging Agile and Traditional Development Methods: A Project Management Perspective, by Paul E. McMahon. This paper presents a case study that highlights the conflicts experienced when moving from traditional to extreme methodologies. Extreme methods focus on developing product quickly using an iterative, risk-driven, results-oriented, and collaborative approach. The author provides you recommendations that help you to navigate your way through the conflicts using lessons learned primarily from practice. The paper addresses they key questions many project managers have relative to the potential use of agile methods on their projects.

Coping with New Paradigms, by Walker Royce. This original paper builds on the previous two to present a critical commentary on modem software methods and life cycle models. The emphasis of the paper is to describe what works for the new business economy. The message is that old-school approaches just are not agile enough to cope with the demands of the Internet and the Web-based economy. Using real-world case studies and examples, the author builds a cogent and compelling case for changing the way modem firms attack software development. I think the paper is valuable because the arguments are insightful and make you think.

Key Terms

The ten terms, which are defined as follows, are important to understanding the articles provided in this chapter.

1. **Activity.** A major unit of work to be completed in achieving the goals of the software project. An activity has precise starting and ending dates, has a set of tasks that need to be done, consumes resources, and results in work products. An activity may contain other activities arranged in a hierarchical order.
2. **Agile method.** A software development process that evolves a product in a series of rapid iterations, most of which are scheduled to last weeks instead of months.
3. **Build.** An operational version of a software product that includes a specified subset of the capabilities provided by the final product.
4. **Infrastructure.** The underlying framework used by management for making decisions and allocating resources.
5. **Life cycle.** The period of time that starts when a software product is conceived and ends when that product is retired from service.
6. **Method.** The steps, notation, rules, and examples used to structure the approach used by a person or team for problem solving.
7. **Paradigm.** A modeling method for the software development process.
8. **Software development methodology.** The overall approach selected to develop software. Hopefully, an integrated set of methods supported by mature standards, practices, and tools will be used as part of the methodology.
9. **Software process.** A set of activities, methods, practices, and transformations people employ to develop and maintain software and associated products.
10. **Spiral development.** A software development process whose function is risk reduction; activities are performed iteratively until the software is completed and delivered.

Common Acronyms

The following acronyms are used within the articles in this chapter:

ASD	Adaptive Software Development
DBMS	Database Management System
EIA	Electronic Industries Association
IEEE	Institute of Electrical and Electronics Engineers
LAN	Local Area Network
RTT	Requirements Traceability Tool
RUP	Rational Unified Process
SDE	Software Development Environment
SEI	Software Engineering Institute
SW-CMM	Software Capability Maturity Model
UDF	Unit Development Folder
XP	Extreme Programming

For Your Bookshelf

As the topic of incremental and evolutionary life cycle processes became popular, several books on the topic appeared. The one that I like the best is highlighted in the bibliography. This book by Jacobson, Booch, and Rumbaugh entitled *The Rational Unified Development Process* was chosen to illustrate what I believe are the characteristics of a modem life cycle model.

For those interested in learning about the topic of lightweight or agile processes, I have included Kent Beck's popular book entitled *Extreme Programming Explained* in the bibliography. I selected it because it is one of the few books that provide a balanced discussion of when and when not to use this approach.

The best comparison of the virtues of plan-driven versus extreme methodologies in my opinion is the Boehm and Turner volume entitled *Balancing Agility and Discipline.* In addition to explaining the difference, it shows you how to use both approaches to realize benefits. I especially like the concept of anchoring the process because it provides you with gating criteria needed to determine whether you are making acceptable progress.

The *Project Management Book of Knowledge (PMBOK™),* published by the Project Management Institute, discusses the project phases and life cycle in Chapter 2. It characterizes representative project life cycles and discusses stakeholder roles, social–economic–environmental influences, and organizational impacts on their selection and use.

Finally, the IEEE has published the following three Life Cycle Standards and several other pertinent standards and guides:

- Software Life Cycle Processes, IEEE/EIA Std 12207.9-1996
- Software Life Cycle Processes—Life Cycle Data, IEEE/EIA Std 12207.1-1997
- Software Life Cycle Processes—Implementation Considerations, IEEE/EIA Std 12207.2-1997

You can order these standards directly from the IEEE Service Center in New Jersey via phone at 800-678-4333 or e-mail at customer.service@ieee.org.

A Spiral Model of Software Development and Enhancement

Barry W. Boehm, TRW Defense Systems Group

"Stop the life cycle—I want to get off!"
"Life-cycle Concept Considered Harmful."
"The waterfall model is dead."
"No, it isn't, but it should be."

These statements exemplify the current debate about software life-cycle process models. The topic has recently received a great deal of attention.

The Defense Science Board Task Force Report on Military Software[1] issued in 1987 highlighted the concern that traditional software process models were discouraging more effective approaches to software development such as prototyping and software reuse. The Computer Society has sponsored tutorials and workshops on software process models that have helped clarify many of the issues and stimulated advances in the field (see "Further reading").

The spiral model presented in this article is one candidate for improving the software process model situation. The major distinguishing feature of the spiral model is that it creates a *risk-driven* approach to the software process rather than a primarily *document-driven* or *code-driven* process. It incorporates many of the strengths of other models and resolves many of their difficulties.

This article opens with a short description of software process models and the issues they address. Subsequent sections outline the process steps involved in the

This evolving risk-driven approach provides a new framework for guiding the software process.

spiral model; illustrate the application of the spiral model to a software project, using the TRW Software Productivity Project as an example; summarize the primary advantages and implications involved in using the spiral model and the primary difficulties in using it at its current incomplete level of elaboration; and present resulting conclusions.

Background on software process models

The primary functions of a software process model are to determine the *order of the stages* involved in software development and evolution and to establish the *transition criteria* for progressing from one stage to the next. These include completion criteria for the current stage plus choice criteria and entrance criteria for the next stage. Thus, a process model addresses the following software project questions:

(1) What shall we do next?
(2) How long shall we continue to do it?

Consequently, a process model differs from a software method (often called a methodology) in that a method's primary focus is on how to navigate through each phase (determining data, control, or "uses" hierarchies; partitioning functions; allocating requirements) and how to represent phase products (structure charts; stimulus-response threads; state transition diagrams).

Why are software process models important? Primarily because they provide guidance on the order (phases, increments, prototypes, validation tasks, etc.) *in which a project should carry out its major tasks.* Many software projects, as the next section shows, have come to grief because they pursued their various development and evolution phases in the wrong order.

Evolution of process models. Before concentrating in depth on the spiral model, we should take a look at a number of others: the code-and-fix model, the stagewise model and the waterfall model, the evolutionary development model, and the transform model.

The code-and-fix model. The basic model used in the earliest days of software

Reprinted from *IEEE Computer,* May 1988.

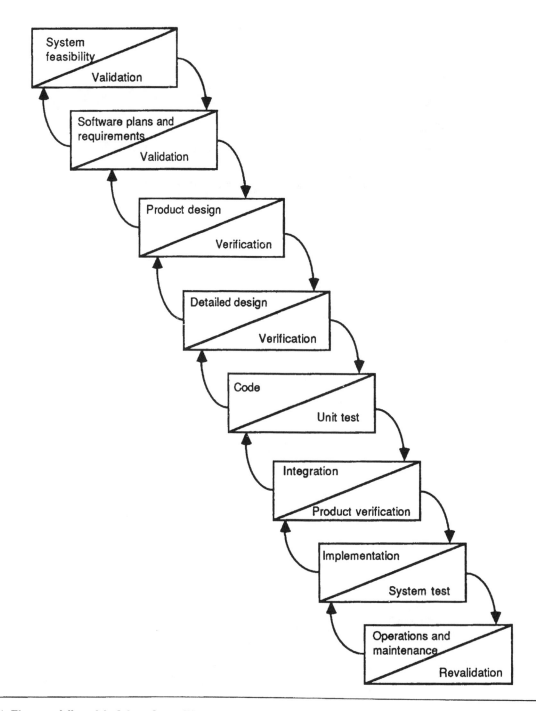

Figure 1. The waterfall model of the software life cycle.

development contained two steps:

(1) Write some code.

(2) Fix the problems in the code.

Thus, the order of the steps was to do some coding first and to think about the requirements, design, test, and maintenance later. This model has three primary difficulties:

(a) After a number of fixes, the code became so poorly structured that subsequent fixes were very expensive. This underscored the need for a design phase prior to coding.

(b) Frequently, even well-designed software was such a poor match to users' needs that it was either rejected outright or expensively redeveloped. This made the need for a requirements phase prior to design evident.

(c) Code was expensive to fix because of poor preparation for testing and modification. This made it clear that explicit recognition of these phases, as well as test-and-evolution planning and preparation tasks in the early phases, were needed.

The stagewise and waterfall models. As early as 1956, experience on large software systems such as the Semi-Automated Ground Environment (SAGE) had led to the recognition of these problems and to the development of a stagewise model[2] to address them. This model stipulated that software be developed in successive stages (operational plan, operational specifications, coding specifications, coding, parameter testing, assembly testing, shakedown, system evaluation).

The waterfall model,[3] illustrated in Figure 1, was a highly influential 1970 refinement of the stagewise model. It provided two primary enhancements to the stagewise model:

(1) Recognition of the feedback loops between stages, and a guideline to confine the feedback loops to successive stages to minimize the expensive rework involved in feedback across many stages.

(2) An initial incorporation of prototyping in the software life cycle, via a "build it twice" step running in parallel with requirements analysis and design.

The waterfall model's approach helped eliminate many difficulties previously encountered on software projects. The waterfall model has become the basis for most software acquisition standards in government and industry. Some of its initial difficulties have been addressed by adding extensions to cover incremental development, parallel developments, program families, accommodation of evolutionary changes, formal software development and verification, and stagewise validation and risk analysis.

However, even with extensive revisions and refinements, the waterfall model's basic scheme has encountered some more fundamental difficulties, and these have led to the formulation of alternative process models.

A primary source of difficulty with the waterfall model has been its emphasis on fully elaborated documents as completion criteria for early requirements and design phases. For some classes of software, such as compilers or secure operating systems, this is the most effective way to proceed. However, it does not work well for many classes of software, particularly interactive

---

The waterfall model has become the basis for most software acquisition standards.

---

end-user applications. Document-driven standards have pushed many projects to write elaborate specifications of poorly understood user interfaces and decision-support functions, followed by the design and development of large quantities of unusable code.

These projects are examples of how waterfall-model projects have come to grief by pursuing stages in the wrong order. Furthermore, in areas supported by fourth-generation languages (spreadsheet or small business applications), it is clearly unnecessary to write elaborate specifications for one's application before implementing it.

The evolutionary development model. The above concerns led to the formulation of the *evolutionary development* model,[4] whose stages consist of expanding increments of an operational software product, with the directions of evolution being determined by operational experience.

The evolutionary development model is ideally matched to a fourth-generation language application and well matched to situations in which users say, "I can't tell you what I want, but I'll know it when I see it." It gives users a rapid initial operational capability and provides a realistic operational basis for determining subsequent product improvements.

Nonetheless, evolutionary development also has its difficulties. It is generally difficult to distinguish it from the old code-and-fix model, whose spaghetti code and lack of planning were the initial motivation for the waterfall model. It is also based on the often-unrealistic assumption that the user's operational system will be flexible enough to accommodate unplanned evolution paths. This assumption is unjustified in three primary circumstances:

(1) Circumstances in which several independently evolved applications must subsequently be closely integrated.

(2) "Information-sclerosis" cases, in which temporary work-arounds for software deficiencies increasingly solidify into

---

unchangeable constraints on evolution. The following comment is a typical example: "It's nice that you could change those equipment codes to make them more intelligible for us, but the Codes Committee just met and established the current codes as company standards."

(3) Bridging situations, in which the new software is incrementally replacing a large existing system. If the existing system is poorly modularized, it is difficult to provide a good sequence of "bridges" between the old software and the expanding increments of new software.

Under such conditions, evolutionary development projects have come to grief by pursuing stages in the wrong order: evolving a lot of hard-to-change code before addressing long-range architectural and usage considerations.

The transform model. The "spaghetti code" difficulties of the evolutionary development and code-and-fix models can also become a difficulty in various classes of waterfall-model applications, in which code is optimized for performance and becomes increasingly hard to modify. The transform model[5] has been proposed as a solution to this dilemma.

The transform model assumes the existence of a capability to automatically convert a formal specification of a software product into a program satisfying the specification. The steps then prescribed by the transform model are

- a formal specification of the best initial understanding of the desired product;
- automatic transformation of the specification into code;
- an iterative loop, if necessary, to improve the performance of the resulting code by giving optimization guidance to the transformation system;
- exercise of the resulting product; and
- an outer iterative loop to adjust the specification based on the resulting operational experience, and to rederive, reoptimize, and exercise the adjusted software product.

The transform model thus bypasses the difficulty of having to modify code that has become poorly structured through repeated reoptimizations, since the modifications are made to the specification. It also avoids the extra time and expense involved in the intermediate design, code, and test activities.

Still, the transform model has various

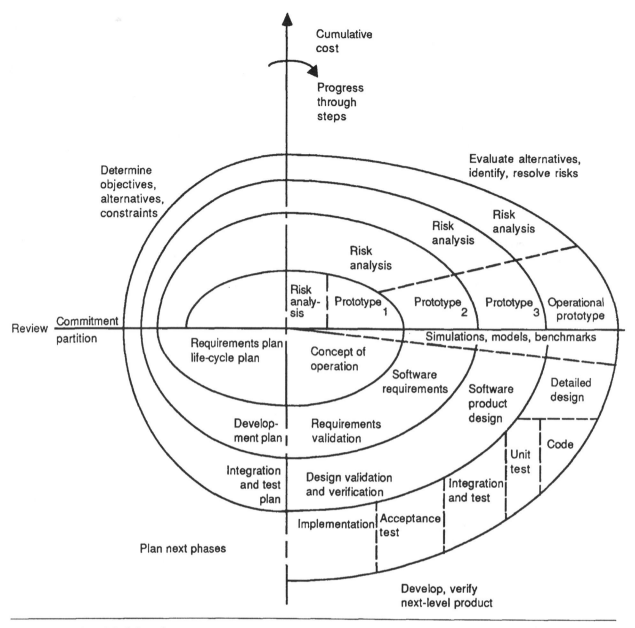

Figure 2. Spiral model of the software process.

difficulties. Automatic transformation capabilities are only available for small products in a few limited areas: spreadsheets, small fourth-generation language applications, and limited computer-science domains. The transform model also shares some of the difficulties of the evolutionary development model, such as the assumption that users' operational systems will always be flexible enough to support unplanned evolution paths.

Additionally, it would face a formidable knowledge-base-maintenance problem in dealing with the rapidly increasing and evolving supply of reusable software components and commercial software products. (Simply consider the problem of tracking the costs, performance, and features of all commercial database management systems, and automatically choosing the best one to implement each new or changed specification.)

The spiral model

The spiral model of the software process (see Figure 2) has been evolving for several years, based on experience with various refinements of the waterfall model as applied to large government software projects. As will be discussed, the spiral model can accommodate most previous models as special cases and further provides guidance as to which combination of previous models best fits a given software situation. Development of the TRW Software Productivity System (TRW-SPS), described in the next section, is its most complete application to date.

The radial dimension in Figure 2 represents the cumulative cost incurred in accomplishing the steps to date; the angular dimension represents the progress made in completing each cycle of the spiral. (The model reflects the underlying concept that each cycle involves a progression that addresses the same sequence of steps, for each portion of the product and for each of its levels of elaboration, from an overall concept of operation document down to the coding of each individual program.) Note that some artistic license has been taken with the increasing cumulative cost dimension to enhance legibility of the steps in Figure 2.

A typical cycle of the spiral. Each cycle of the spiral begins with the identification of

- the objectives of the portion of the product being elaborated (performance, functionality, ability to accommodate change, etc.);
- the alternative means of implementing this portion of the product (design A, design B, reuse, buy, etc.); and
- the constraints imposed on the application of the alternatives (cost, schedule, interface, etc.).

The next step is to evaluate the alternatives relative to the objectives and constraints. Frequently, this process will identify areas of uncertainty that are significant sources of project risk. If so, the next step should involve the formulation of a cost-effective strategy for resolving the sources of risk. This may involve prototyping, simulation, benchmarking, reference checking, administering user questionnaires, analytic modeling, or combinations of these and other risk-resolution techniques.

Once the risks are evaluated, the next step is determined by the relative remaining risks. If performance or user-interface risks strongly dominate program development or internal interface-control risks, the next step may be an evolutionary development one: a minimal effort to specify the overall nature of the product, a plan for the next level of prototyping, and the development of a more detailed prototype to continue to resolve the major risk issues.

If this prototype is operationally useful and robust enough to serve as a low-risk base for future product evolution, the subsequent risk-driven steps would be the evolving series of evolutionary prototypes going toward the right in Figure 2. In this case, the option of writing specifications would be addressed but not exercised. Thus, risk considerations can lead to a project implementing only a subset of all the potential steps in the model.

On the other hand, if previous prototyping efforts have already resolved all of the performance or user-interface risks, and program development or interface-control risks dominate, the next step follows the basic waterfall approach (concept of operation, software requirements, preliminary design, etc. in Figure 2), modified as appropriate to incorporate incremental development. Each level of software specification in the figure is then followed by a validation step and the preparation of plans for the succeeding cycle. In this case, the options to prototype, simulate, model, etc. are addressed but not exercised, leading to the use of a different subset of steps.

This risk-driven subsetting of the spiral model steps allows the model to accommodate any appropriate mixture of a specification-oriented, prototype-oriented, simulation-oriented, automatic transformation-oriented, or other approach to software development. In such cases, the appropriate mixed strategy is chosen by considering the relative magnitude of the program risks and the relative effectiveness of the various techniques in resolving the risks. In a similar way, risk-management considerations can determine the amount of time and effort that should be devoted to such other project activities as planning, configuration management, quality assurance, formal verification, and testing. In particular, risk-driven specifications (as discussed in the next section) can have varying degrees of completeness, formality, and granularity, depending on the relative risks of doing too little or too much specification.

An important feature of the spiral model, as with most other models, is that each cycle is completed by a review involving the primary people or organizations concerned with the product. This review covers all products developed during the previous cycle, including the plans for the next cycle and the resources required to carry them out. The review's major objective is to ensure that all concerned parties are mutually committed to the approach for the next phase.

The plans for succeeding phases may also include a partition of the product into increments for successive development or components to be developed by individual organizations or persons. For the latter case, visualize a series of parallel spiral cycles, one for each component, adding a third dimension to the concept presented in Figure 2. For example, separate spirals can be evolving for separate software components or increments. Thus, the review-and-commitment step may range from an individual walk-through of the design of a single programmer's component to a major requirements review involving developer, customer, user, and maintenance organizations.

Initiating and terminating the spiral. Four fundamental questions arise in considering this presentation of the spiral model:

(1) How does the spiral ever get started?
(2) How do you get off the spiral when it is appropriate to terminate a project early?
(3) Why does the spiral end so abruptly?
(4) What happens to software enhancement (or maintenance)?

The answer to these questions involves an observation that the spiral model applies equally well to development or enhancement efforts. In either case, the spiral gets started by a hypothesis that a particular operational mission (or set of missions) could be improved by a software effort. The spiral process then involves a test of this hypothesis: at any time, if the hypothesis fails the test (for example, if delays cause a software product to miss its market window, or if a superior commercial product becomes available), the spiral is terminated. Otherwise, it terminates with the installation of new or modified software, and the hypothesis is tested by observing the effect on the operational mission. Usually, experience with the operational mission leads to further hypotheses about software improvements, and a new maintenance spiral is initiated to test the hypothesis. Initiation, termination, and iteration of the tasks and products of previous cycles are thus implicitly defined in the spiral model (although they're not included in Figure 2 to simplify its presentation).

Using the spiral model

The various rounds and activities involved in the spiral model are best understood through use of an example. The spiral model was used in the definition and development of the TRW Software Productivity System (TRW-SPS), an integrated software engineering environment.[6] The initial mission opportunity coincided with a corporate initiative to improve productivity in all appropriate corporate operations and an initial hypothesis that software engineering was an attractive area to investigate. This led to a small, extra "Round 0" circuit of the spiral to determine the feasibility of increasing software productivity at a reasonable corporate cost. (Very large or complex software projects will frequently precede the "concept of operation" round of the spiral with one or more smaller rounds to establish feasibility and to reduce the range of alternative solutions quickly and inexpensively.)

Tables 1, 2, and 3 summarize the application of the spiral model to the first three rounds of defining the SPS. The major features of each round are subsequently discussed and are followed by some examples from later rounds, such as preliminary and detailed design.

Round 0: Feasibility study. This study involved five part-time participants over a two- to three-month period. As indicated in Table 1, the objectives and constraints were expressed at a very high level and in qualitative terms like "significantly increase," "at reasonable cost," etc.

Some of the alternatives considered, primarily those in the "technology" area, could lead to development of a software product, but the possible attractiveness of a number of non-software alternatives in the management, personnel, and facilities areas could have led to a conclusion not to embark on a software development activity.

The primary risk areas involved possible situations in which the company would invest a good deal only to find that

- resulting productivity gains were not significant, or
- potentially high-leverage improvements were not compatible with some aspects of the "TRW culture."

The risk-resolution activities undertaken in Round 0 were primarily surveys and analyses, including structured interviews of software developers and managers, an initial analysis of productivity leverage factors identified by the constructive cost model (Cocomo)[7]; and an analysis of previous projects at TRW exhibiting high levels of productivity.

The risk analysis results indicated that significant productivity gains could be achieved at a reasonable cost by pursuing an integrated set of initiatives in the four major areas. However, some candidate solutions, such as a software support environment based on a single, corporate, maxicomputer-based time-sharing system, were found to be in conflict with TRW constraints requiring support of different levels of security-classified projects. Thus, even at a very high level of generality of objectives and constraints, Round 0 was able to answer basic feasibility questions and eliminate significant classes of candidate solutions.

The plan for Round 1 involved commitment of 12 man-months compared to the two man-months invested in Round 0 (during these rounds, all participants were part-time). Round 1 here corresponded fairly well to the initial round of the spiral model shown in Figure 2, in that its intent was to produce a concept of operation and a basic life-cycle plan for implementing whatever preferred alternative emerged.

Round 1: Concept of operations. Table 2 summarizes Round 1 of the spiral along the lines given in Table 1 for Round 0. The features of Round 1 compare to those of Round 0 as follows:

- The level of investment was greater (12 versus 2 man-months).
- The objectives and constraints were more specific ("double software productivity in five years at a cost of $10,000 a person" versus "significantly increase productivity at a reasonable cost").
- Additional constraints surfaced, such as the preference for TRW products (particularly, a TRW-developed local area network (LAN) system).
- The alternatives were more detailed ("SREM, PSL/PSA or SADT, as requirements tools etc." versus "tools"; "private/shared" terminals, "smart/dumb" terminals versus "workstations").
- The risk areas identified were more specific ("TRW LAN price-performance

Table 1. Spiral model usage: TRW Software Productivity System, Round 0.

Objectives	Significantly increase software productivity
Constraints	At reasonable cost
	Within context of TRW culture
	• Government contracts, high tech., people oriented, security
Alternatives	Management: Project organization, policies, planning, control
	Personnel: Staffing, incentives, training
	Technology: Tools, workstations, methods, reuse
	Facilities: Offices, communications
Risks	May be no high-leverage improvements
	Improvements may violate constraints
Risk resolution	Internal surveys
	Analyze cost model
	Analyze exceptional projects
	Literature search
Risk resolution results	Some alternatives infeasible
	• Single time-sharing system: Security
	Mix of alternatives can produce significant gains
	• Factor of two in five years
	Need further study to determine best mix
Plan for next phase	Six-person task force for six months
	More extensive surveys and analysis
	• Internal, external, economic
	Develop concept of operation, economic rationale
Commitment	Fund next phase

42

within a "$10,000-per-person investment constraint" versus "improvements may violate reasonable-cost constraint").

• The risk-resolution activities were more extensive (including the benchmarking and analysis of a prototype TRW LAN being developed for another project).

• The result was a fairly specific operational concept document, involving private offices tailored to software work patterns and personal terminals connected to VAX superminis via the TRW LAN. Some choices were specifically deferred to the next round, such as the choice of operating system and specific tools.

• The life-cycle plan and the plan for the next phase involved a partitioning into separate activities to address management improvements, facilities development, and development of the first increment of a software development environment.

• The commitment step involved more than just an agreement with the plan. It committed to apply the environment to an upcoming 100-person testbed software project and to develop an environment focusing on the testbed project's needs. It also specified forming a representative steering group to ensure that the separate activities were well-coordinated and that the environment would not be overly optimized around the testbed project.

Although the plan recommended developing a prototype environment, it also recommended that the project employ requirements specifications and design specifications in a risk-driven way. Thus, the development of the environment followed the succeeding rounds of the spiral model.

Round 2: Top-level requirements specification. Table 3 shows the corresponding steps involved during Round 2 defining the software productivity system. Round 2 decisions and their rationale were covered in earlier work[6]; here, we will summarize the considerations dealing with risk management and the use of the spiral model:

• The initial risk-identification activities during Round 2 showed that several system requirements hinged on the decision between a host-target system or a fully portable tool set and the decision between VMS and Unix as the host operating system. These requirements included the functions needed to provide a user-friendly front-end, the operating system to be used by the workstations, and the functions necessary to support a host-target

operation. To keep these requirements in synchronization with the others, a special minispiral was initiated to address and resolve these issues. The resulting review led to a commitment to a host-target operation using Unix on the host system, at a point early enough to work the OS-dependent requirements in a timely fashion.

• Addressing the risks of mismatches to the user-project's needs and priorities resulted in substantial participation of the user-project personnel in the requirements definition activity. This led to several significant redirections of the requirements, particularly toward supporting the early phases of the software life-cycle into which the user project was embarking, such as an adaptation of the software requirements engineering methodology (SREM) tools

for requirements specification and analysis.

It is also interesting to note that the form of Tables 1, 2, and 3 was originally developed for presentation purposes, but subsequently became a standard "spiral model template" used on later projects. These templates are useful not only for organizing project activities, but also as a residual design-rationale record. Design rationale information is of paramount importance in assessing the potential reusability of software components on future projects. Another important point to note is that the use of the template was indeed uniform across the three cycles, showing that the spiral steps can be and were uniformly followed at successively detailed levels of product definition.

Table 2. Spiral model usage: TRW Software Productivity System, Round 1.

Objectives	Double software productivity in five years
Constraints	$10,000 per person investment Within context of TRW culture • Government contracts, high tech., people oriented, security Preference for TRW products
Alternatives	Office: Private/modular/. . . Communication: LAN/star/concentrators/. . . Terminals: Private/shared; smart/dumb Tools: SREM/PSL-PSA/. . .; PDL/SADT/. . . CPU: IBM/DEC/CDC/. . .
Risks	May miss high-leverage options TRW LAN price/performance Workstation cost
Risk resolution	Extensive external surveys, visits TRW LAN benchmarking Workstation price projections
Risk resolution results	Operations concept: Private offices, TRW LAN, personal terminals, VAX Begin with primarily dumb terminals; experiment with smart workstations Defer operating system, tools selection
Plan for next phase	Partition effort into software development environment (SDE), facilities, management Develop first-cut, prototype SDE • Design-to-cost: 15-person team for one year Plan for external usage
Commitment	Develop prototype SDE Commit an upcoming project to use SDE Commit the SDE to support the project Form representative steering group

Succeeding rounds. It will be useful to illustrate some examples of how the spiral model is used to handle situations arising in the preliminary design and detailed design of components of the SPS: the preliminary design specification for the requirements traceability tool (RTT), and a detailed design rework or go-back on the unit development folder (UDF) tool.

The RTT preliminary design specification. The RTT establishes the traceability between itemized software requirements specifications, design elements, code elements, and test cases. It also supports various associated query, analysis, and report generation capabilities. The preliminary design specification for the RTT (and most of the other SPS tools) looks different from the usual preliminary design specification, which tends to show a uniform level of elaboration of all components of the design. Instead, the level of detail of

the RTT specification is risk-driven.

In areas involving a high risk if the design turned out to be wrong, the design was carried down to the detailed design level, usually with the aid of rapid prototyping. These areas included working out the implications of "undo" options and dealing with the effects of control keys used to escape from various program levels.

In areas involving a moderate risk if the design was wrong, the design was carried down to a preliminary-design level. These areas included the basic command options for the tool and the schemata for the requirements traceability database. Here again, the ease of rapid prototyping with Unix shell scripts supported a good deal of user-interface prototyping.

In areas involving a low risk if the design was wrong, very little design elaboration was done. These areas included details of all the help message options and all the

report-generation options, once the nature of these options was established in some example instances.

A detailed design go-back. The UDF tool collects into an electronic "folder" all artifacts involved in the development of a single-programmer software unit (typically 500 to 1,000 instructions): unit requirements, design, code, test cases, test results, and documentation. It also includes a management template for tracking the programmer's scheduled and actual completion of each artifact.

An alternative considered during detailed design of the UDF tool was reuse of portions of the RTT to provide pointers to the requirements and preliminary design specifications of the unit being developed. This turned out to be an extremely attractive alternative, not only for avoiding duplicate software development but also for bringing to the surface several issues involving many-to-many mappings between requirements, design, and code that had not been considered in designing the UDF tool. These led to a rethinking of the UDF tool requirements and preliminary design, which avoided a great deal of code rework that would have been necessary if the detailed design of the UDF tool had proceeded in a purely deductive, top-down fashion from the original UDF requirements specification. The resulting go-back led to a significantly different, less costly, and more capable UDF tool, incorporating the RTT in its "uses-hierarchy."

Spiral model features. These two examples illustrate several features of the spiral approach.

• It fosters the development of specifications that are not necessarily uniform, exhaustive, or formal, in that they defer detailed elaboration of low-risk software elements and avoid unnecessary breakage in their design until the high-risk elements of the design are stabilized.

• It incorporates prototyping as a risk-reduction option at any stage of development. In fact, prototyping and reuse risk analyses were often used in the process of going from detailed design into code.

• It accommodates reworks or go-backs to earlier stages as more attractive alternatives are identified or as new risk issues need resolution.

Overall, risk-driven documents, particularly specifications and plans, are important features of the spiral model. Great amounts of detail are not necessary unless the absence of such detail jeopardizes the

Table 3. Spiral model usage: TRW Software Productivity System, Round 2.

Objectives	User-friendly system Integrated software, office-automation tools Support all project personnel Support all life-cycle phases
Constraints	Customer-deliverable SDE ⇒ Portability Stable, reliable service
Alternatives	OS: VMS/AT&T Unix/Berkeley Unix/ISC Host-target/fully portable tool set Workstations: Zenith/LSI-11/. . .
Risks	Mismatch to user-project needs, priorities User-unfriendly system • 12-language syndrome; experts-only Unix performance, support Workstation/mainframe compatibility
Risk resolution	User-project surveys, requirements participation Survey of Unix-using organizations Workstation study
Risk resolution results	Top-level requirements specification Host-target with Unix host Unix-based workstations Build user-friendly front end for Unix Initial focus on tools to support early phases
Plan for next phase	Overall development plan • for tools: SREM, RTT, PDL, office automation tools • for front end: Support tools • for LAN: Equipment, facilities
Commitment	Proceed with plans

project. In some cases, such as with a product whose functionality may be determined by a choice among commercial products, a set of weighted evaluation criteria for the products may be preferable to a detailed pre-statement of functional requirements.

Results. The Software Productivity System developed and supported using the spiral model avoided the identified risks and achieved most of the system's objectives. The SPS has grown to include over 300 tools and over 1,300,000 instructions; 93 percent of the instructions were reused from previous project-developed, TRW-developed, or external-software packages. Over 25 projects have used all or portions of the system. All of the projects fully using the system have increased their productivity at least 50 percent; indeed, most have doubled their productivity (when compared with cost-estimation model predictions of their productivity using traditional methods).

However, one risk area—that projects with non-Unix target systems would not accept a Unix-based host system—was underestimated. Some projects accepted the host-target approach, but for various reasons (such as customer constraints and zero-cost target machines) a good many did not. As a result, the system was less widely used on TRW projects than expected. This and other lessons learned have been incorporated into the spiral model approach to developing TRW's next-generation software development environment.

Evaluation

Advantages. The primary advantage of the spiral model is that its range of options accommodates the good features of existing software process models, while its risk-driven approach avoids many of their difficulties. In appropriate situations, the spiral model becomes equivalent to one of the existing process models. In other situations, it provides guidance on the best mix of existing approaches to a given project; for example, its application to the TRW-SPS provided a risk-driven mix of specifying, prototyping, and evolutionary development.

The primary conditions under which the spiral model becomes equivalent to other main process models are summarized as follows:

• If a project has a low risk in such areas

as getting the wrong user interface or not meeting stringent performance requirements, and if it has a high risk in budget and schedule predictability and control, then these risk considerations drive the spiral model into an equivalence to the waterfall model.

• If a software product's requirements are very stable (implying a low risk of expensive design and code breakage due to requirements changes during development), and if the presence of errors in the software product constitutes a high risk to the mission it serves, then these risk considerations drive the spiral model to resemble the two-leg model of precise specification and formal deductive program development.

• If a project has a low risk in such areas as losing budget and schedule predictability and control, encountering large-system integration problems, or coping with information sclerosis, and if it has a high risk in such areas as getting the wrong user interface or user decision support requirements, then these risk considerations drive the spiral model into an equivalence to the evolutionary development model.

• If automated software generation capabilities are available, then the spiral model accommodates them either as options for rapid prototyping or for application of the transform model, depending on the risk considerations involved.

• If the high-risk elements of a project involve a mix of the risk items listed above, then the spiral approach will reflect an appropriate mix of the process models above (as exemplified in the TRW-SPS application). In doing so, its risk-avoidance features will generally avoid the difficulties of the other models.

The spiral model has a number of additional advantages, summarized as follows:

It focuses early attention on options involving the reuse of existing software. The steps involving the identification and evaluation of alternatives encourage these options.

It accommodates preparation for life-cycle evolution, growth, and changes of the software product. The major sources of product change are included in the product's objectives, and information-hiding approaches are attractive architectural design alternatives in that they reduce the risk of not being able to accommodate the product-charge objectives.

It provides a mechanism for incorporating software quality objectives into software product development. This mechanism derives from the emphasis on identifying all types of objectives and constraints during each round of the spiral. For example, Table 3 shows user-friendliness, portability, and reliability as specific objectives and constraints to be addressed by the SPS. In Table 1, security constraints were identified as a key risk item for the SPS.

It focuses on eliminating errors and unattractive alternatives early. The risk-analysis, validation, and commitment steps cover these considerations.

For each of the sources of project activity and resource expenditure, it answers the key question, "How much is enough?" Stated another way, "How much of requirements analysis, planning, configuration management, quality assurance, testing, formal verification, etc. should a project do?" Using the risk-driven approach, one can see that the answer is not the same for all projects and that the appropriate level of effort is determined by the level of risk incurred by not doing enough.

It does not involve separate approaches for software development and software enhancement (or maintenance). This aspect helps avoid the "second-class citizen" status frequently associated with software maintenance. It also helps avoid many of the problems that currently ensue when high-risk enhancement efforts are approached in the same way as routine maintenance efforts.

It provides a viable framework for integrated hardware-software system development. The focus on risk-management and on eliminating unattractive alternatives early and inexpensively is equally applicable to hardware and software.

Difficulties. The full spiral model can be successfully applied in many situations, but some difficulties must be addressed before it can be called a mature, universally applicable model. The three primary challenges involve matching to contract software, relying on risk-assessment expertise, and the need for further elaboration of spiral model steps.

Matching to contract software. The spiral model currently works well on internal software developments like the TRW-SPS, but it needs further work to match it to the world of contract software acquisition.

Internal software developments have a great deal of flexibility and freedom to accommodate stage-by-stage commitments, to defer commitments to specific options, to establish minispirals to resolve critical-path items, to adjust levels of effort, or to accommodate such practices as prototyping, evolutionary development, or design-to-cost. The world of contract software acquisition has a harder time achieving these degrees of flexibility and freedom without losing accountability and control, and a harder time defining contracts whose deliverables are not well specified in advance.

Recently, a good deal of progress has been made in establishing more flexible contract mechanisms, such as the use of competitive front-end contracts for concept definition or prototype fly-offs, the use of level-of-effort and award-fee contracts for evolutionary development, and the use of design-to-cost contracts. Although these have been generally successful, the procedures for using them still need to be worked out to the point that acquisition managers feel fully comfortable using them.

Relying on risk-assessment expertise. The spiral model places a great deal of reliance on the ability of software developers to identify and manage sources of project risk.

A good example of this is the spiral model's risk-driven specification, which carries high-risk elements down to a great deal of detail and leaves low-risk elements to be elaborated in later stages; by this time, there is less risk of breakage.

However, a team of inexperienced or low-balling developers may also produce a specification with a different pattern of variation in levels of detail: a great elaboration of detail for the well-understood, low-risk elements, and little elaboration of the poorly understood, high-risk elements. Unless there is an insightful review of such a specification by experienced development or acquisition personnel, this type of project will give an illusion of progress during a period in which it is actually heading for disaster.

Another concern is that a risk-driven specification will also be people-dependent. For example, a design produced by an expert may be implemented by non-experts. In this case, the expert, who does not need a great deal of detailed documentation, must produce enough additional documentation to keep the non-experts from going astray. Reviewers of the specification must also be

Table 4. A prioritized top-ten list of software risk items.

Risk item	Risk management techniques
1. Personnel shortfalls	Staffing with top talent, job matching; teambuilding; morale building; cross-training; pre-scheduling key people
2. Unrealistic schedules and budgets	Detailed, multisource cost and schedule estimation; design to cost; incremental development; software reuse; requirements scrubbing
3. Developing the wrong software functions	Organization analysis; mission analysis; ops-concept formulation; user surveys; prototyping; early users' manuals
4. Developing the wrong user interface	Task analysis; prototyping; scenarios; user characterization (functionality, style, workload)
5. Gold plating	Requirements scrubbing; prototyping; cost-benefit analysis; design to cost
6. Continuing stream of requirement changes	High change threshold; information hiding; incremental development (defer changes to later increments)
7. Shortfalls in externally furnished components	Benchmarking; inspections; reference checking; compatibility analysis
8. Shortfalls in externally performed tasks	Reference checking; pre-award audits; award-fee contracts; competitive design or prototyping; teambuilding
9. Real-time performance shortfalls	Simulation; benchmarking; modeling; prototyping; instrumentation; tuning
10. Straining computer-science capabilities	Technical analysis; cost-benefit analysis; prototyping; reference checking

Table 5. Software Risk Management Plan.

1.	Identify the project's top 10 risk items.
2.	Present a plan for resolving each risk item.
3.	Update list of top risk items, plan, and results monthly.
4.	Highlight risk-item status in monthly project reviews. • Compare with previous month's rankings, status.
5.	Initiate appropriate corrective actions.

sensitive to these concerns.

With a conventional, document-driven approach, the requirement to carry all aspects of the specification to a uniform level of detail eliminates some potential problems and permits adequate review of some aspects by inexperienced reviewers. But it also creates a large drain on the time of the scarce experts, who must dig for the critical issues within a large mass of non-critical detail. Furthermore, if the high-risk elements have been glossed over by impressive-sounding references to poorly understood capabilities (such as a new synchronization concept or a commercial DBMS), there is an even greater risk that the conventional approach will give the illusion of progress in situations that are actually heading for disaster.

Need for further elaboration of spiral model steps. In general, the spiral model process steps need further elaboration to ensure that all software development participants are operating in a consistent context.

Some examples of this are the need for more detailed definitions of the nature of spiral model specifications and milestones, the nature and objectives of spiral model reviews, techniques for estimating and synchronizing schedules, and the nature of spiral model status indicators and cost-versus-progress tracking procedures. Another need is for guidelines and checklists to identify the most likely sources of project risk and the most effective risk-resolution techniques for each source of risk.

Highly experienced people can successfully use the spiral approach without these elaborations. However, for large-scale use in situations where people bring widely differing experience bases to the project, added levels of elaboration—such as have been accumulated over the years for document-driven approaches—are important in ensuring consistent interpretation and use of the spiral approach across the project.

Efforts to apply and refine the spiral model have focused on creating a discipline of software risk management, including techniques for risk identification, risk analysis, risk prioritization, risk-management planning, and risk-element tracking. The prioritized top-ten list of software risk items given in Table 4 is one result of this activity. Another example is the risk management plan discussed in the next section.

Implications: The Risk Management Plan. Even if an organization is not ready to adopt the entire spiral approach, one characteristic technique that can easily be adapted to any life-cycle model provides many of the benefits of the spiral approach. This is the Risk Management Plan summarized in Table 5. This plan basically ensures that each project makes an early identification of its top risk items (the number 10 is not an absolute requirement), develops a strategy for resolving the risk items, identifies and sets down an agenda to resolve new risk items as they surface, and highlights progress versus plans in monthly reviews.

The Risk Management Plan has been used successfully at TRW and other organizations. Its use has ensured appropriate focus on early prototyping, simulation, benchmarking, key-person staffing measures, and other early risk-resolution techniques that have helped avoid many potential project "show-stoppers." The recent US Department of Defense standard on software management, DoD-Std-2167, requires that developers produce and use risk management plans, as does its counterpart US Air Force regulation, AFR 800-14.

Overall, the Risk Management Plan and the maturing set of techniques for software risk management provide a foundation for tailoring spiral model concepts into the more established software acquisition and development procedures.

We can draw four conclusions from the data presented:

(1) The risk-driven nature of the spiral model is more adaptable to the full range of software project situations than are the primarily document-driven approaches such as the waterfall model or the primarily code-driven approaches such as evolutionary development. It is particularly applicable to very large, complex, ambitious software systems.

(2) The spiral model has been quite successful in its largest application to date: the development and enhancement of the TRW-SPS. Overall, it achieved a high level of software support environment capability in a very short time and provided the flexibility necessary to accommodate a high dynamic range of technical alternatives and user objectives.

(3) The spiral model is not yet as fully elaborated as the more established models. Therefore, the spiral model can be applied by experienced personnel, but it needs further elaboration in such areas as contract-

ing, specifications, milestones, reviews, scheduling, status monitoring, and risk-area identification to be fully usable in all situations.

(4) Partial implementations of the spiral model, such as the Risk Management Plan, are compatible with most current process models and are very helpful in overcoming major sources of project risk.☐

Acknowledgments

I would like to thank Frank Belz, Lolo Penedo, George Spadaro, Bob Williams, Bob Balzer, Gillian Frewin, Peter Hamer, Manny Lehman, Lee Osterweil, Dave Parnas, Bill Riddle, Steve Squires, and Dick Thayer, along with the *Computer* reviewers of this article, for their stimulating and insightful comments and discussions of earlier versions of the article, and Nancy Donato for producing its several versions.

References

1. F.P. Brooks et al., *Defense Science Board Task Force Report on Military Software*, Office of the Under Secretary of Defense for Acquisition, Washington, DC 20301, Sept. 1987.
2. H.D. Benington, "Production of Large Computer Programs," *Proc. ONR Symp. Advanced Programming Methods for Digital Computers*, June 1956, pp. 15-27. Also available in *Annals of the History of Computing*, Oct. 1983, pp. 350-361, and *Proc. Ninth Int'l Conf. Software Engineering*, Computer Society Press, 1987.
3. W.W. Royce, "Managing the Development of Large Software Systems: Concepts and Techniques," *Proc. Wescon*, Aug. 1970. Also available in *Proc. ICSE 9*, Computer Society Press, 1987.
4. D.D. McCracken and M.A. Jackson, "Life-Cycle Concept Considered Harmful," *ACM Software Engineering Notes*, Apr. 1982, pp. 29-32.
5. R. Balzer, T.E. Cheatham, and C. Green, "Software Technology in the 1990s: Using a New Paradigm," *Computer*, Nov. 1983, pp. 39-45.
6. B.W. Boehm et al., "A Software Development Environment for Improving Productivity," *Computer*, June 1984, pp. 30-44.
7. B.W. Boehm, *Software Engineering Economics*, Prentice-Hall, 1981, Chap. 33.

Further reading

The software process model field has an interesting history, and a great deal of stimulating work has been produced recently in this specialized area. Besides the references that appear at the end of the accompanying article, here are some additional good sources of insight:

Overall process model issues and results

Agresti's tutorial volume provides a good overview and set of key articles. The three recent *Software Process Workshop Proceedings* provide access to much of the recent work in the area.

Agresti, W.W., *New Paradigms for Software Development*, IEEE Catalog No. EH0245-1, 1986.

Dowson, M., ed., *Proc. Third Int'l Software Process Workshop*, IEEE Catalog No. TH0184-2, Nov. 1986.

Potts, C., ed., *Proc. Software Process Workshop*, IEEE Catalog No. 84CH2044-6, Feb. 1984.

Wileden, J.C., and M. Dowson, eds., Proc. Int'l Workshop Software Process and Software Environments, *ACM Software Engineering Notes*, Aug. 1986.

Alternative process models

More detailed information on waterfall-type approaches is given in:

Evans, M.W., P. Piazza, and J.P. Dolkas, *Principles of Productive Software Management*, John Wiley & Sons, 1983.

Hice, G.F., W.J. Turner, and L.F. Cashwell, *System Development Methodology*, North Holland, 1974 (2nd ed., 1981).

More detailed information on evolutionary development is provided in:

Gilb, T., *Principles of Software Engineering Management*, Addison Wesley, 1988 (currently in publication).

Some additional process model approaches with useful features and insights may be found in:

Lehman, M.M., and L.A. Belady, *Program Evolution: Processes of Software Change*, Academic Press, 1985.

Osterweil, L., "Software Processes are Software, Too," *Proc. ICSE 9*, IEEE Catalog No. 87CH2432-3, Mar. 1987, pp. 2-13.

Radice, R.A., et al., "A Programming Process Architecture," *IBM Systems J.*, Vol. 24, No.2, 1985, pp. 79-90.

Spiral and spiral-type models

Some further treatments of spiral model issues and practices are:

Belz, F.C., "Applying the Spiral Model: Observations on Developing System Software in Ada," *Proc. 1986 Annual Conf. on Ada Technology*, Atlanta, 1986, pp. 57-66.

Boehm, B.W., and F.C. Belz, "Applying Process Programming to the Spiral

Model," *Proc. Fourth Software Process Workshop*, IEEE, May 1988.

Iivari, J., "A Hierarchical Spiral Model for the Software Process," *ACM Software Engineering Notes*, Jan. 1987, pp. 35-37.

Some similar cyclic spiral-type process models from other fields are described in:

Carlsson, B., P. Keane, and J.B. Martin, "R&D Organizations as Learning Systems," *Sloan Management Review*, Spring 1976, pp. 1-15.

Fisher, R., and W. Ury, *Getting to Yes*, Houghton Mifflin, 1981; Penguin Books, 1983, pp. 68-71.

Kolb, D.A., "On Management and the Learning Process," MIT Sloan School Working Article 652-73, Cambridge, Mass., 1973.

Software risk management

The discipline of software risk management provides a bridge between spiral model concepts and currently established software acquisition and development procedures.

Boehm, B.W., "Software Risk Management Tutorial," Computer Society, Apr. 1988.

Risk Assessment Techniques, Defense Systems Management College, Ft. Belvoir, Va. 22060, July 1983.

Barry W. Boehm is the chief scientist of the TRW Defense Systems Group. Since 1973, he has been responsible for developing TRW's software technology base. His current primary responsibilities are in the areas of software environments, process models, management methods, Ada, and cost estimation. He is also an adjunct professor at UCLA.

Boehm received his BA degree in mathematics from Harvard in 1957 and his MA and PhD from UCLA in 1961 and 1964, respectively.

Readers may write to Boehm at TRW Defense Systems Group, One Space Park, R2/2086, Redondo Beach, CA 90278.

Bridging Agile and Traditional Development Methods: A Project Management Perspective

Paul E. McMahon
PEM Systems

Systems & Software Technology Conference
Monday, 19 April 2004
Track 4: 3:35 - 4:20
Ballroom D

Today, companies are reporting success in meeting rapidly changing customer needs through agile development methods. Many of these same companies are finding they must collaborate with organizations employing more traditional development processes, especially on large Department of Defense projects. While it has been argued that agile methods are compatible with traditional disciplined processes, actual project experience indicates conflicts can arise. This article identifies specific project management conflicts that companies face based on actual project experience, along with strategies employed to resolve these conflicts and reduce related risks. Rationale, insights, and related published references are provided along with lessons learned and recommendations. If you work for a company that is using or considering using agile development, or your company is collaborating with a company using an agile method, this article will help you understand the risks, issues, and strategies that can help your project and organization succeed.

This article was motivated by a case study where a small company using a well-known agile method – eXtreme Programming (XP) – requested help addressing specific conflicts that arose on the project where they were a subcontractor to a larger organization employing a traditional development method. The purpose of this article is not to compare agile and traditional methods, but to raise awareness of potential project management conflicts that can arise when a company employing an agile method collaborates with a company employing a traditional development methodology. It also identifies practical steps that can be taken to reduce related risks.

It is worth noting that the case study presented is not unique. Published references documenting similar conflicts are provided. Also notable is that the motivation for examining this project extends beyond the case study itself. Today there exist increasing opportunities for small companies to gain new work through software outsourcing from traditional development organizations.

Where Are We Going?

In this article, I first identify key case study facts along with relevant information and common misperceptions related to traditional and agile methods. Next, I identify four conflicts observed along with five recommendations and one lesson learned. The company named SubComp refers to the subcontractor employing an agile methodology. The company named PrimeComp refers to the prime contractor employing a traditional development methodology.

Case Study Key Facts

Shortly before I was asked to help SubComp, PrimeComp's customer had withheld a progress payment based on a perceived risk observed at a recent critical design review (CDR). Written comments provided to PrimeComp indicated that the customer wanted to see working software in order to *assess the proposed design and related risk*. The area of concern was SubComp's responsibility. Upon receiving the customer comments, PrimeComp requested that SubComp provide additional detailed design documentation.

It is important to note that PrimeComp required all correspondence between the customer and SubComp to go through them. It is also important to note that most of the contractually required documentation was not formally due until the end of the project, and, prior to the CDR, little had been communicated to SubComp with respect to documentation content and expectations. The project was planned using a traditional waterfall life cycle with a single CDR.

Early in the project, SubComp had identified multiple technical risks. However, it had decided in the early stages to focus its small agile team on a single technical risk that it had assessed to be of much greater significance than all other risks. At the recent CDR, SubComp had provided a demonstration with working software that addressed this risk to the customer's satisfaction.

The risk the customer was currently raising was one SubComp viewed as lower priority. To address this risk, the XP team was focusing on a second demonstration with working software to show to the customer at a follow-up CDR. In parallel, it was also driving to meet PrimeComp's request for additional detailed design documentation. This follow-up CDR had not originally been planned, and it was causing project tension because of the progress payment holdup.

Agile Development Methods

In the spring of 2001, 17 advocates of agile development methods gathered in Utah and agreed to a set of four values and 12 principles referred to as the Agile Manifesto [1]. The four values are expressed in the following:

We are uncovering better ways of developing software by doing it and helping others do it ... Through this work we have come to value:

- Individuals and interactions over processes and tools.
- Working software over comprehensive documentation.
- Customer collaboration over contract negotiation.
- Responding to change over following a plan.

That is, while there is value in the items on the right, we value the items on the left more. [1]

One misperception of agile methods is that they hold little or no value in documentation and plans. Note that the value statements express a relative value of documentation and plans with respect to working software and responding to change.

Traditional Development Methods

The traditional waterfall model is well known, but it is important to understand that it is not an incremental model. Today, Department of Defense policy 5000.1 and 5000.2 [2] strongly encourages using the spiral model for software development. Although the spiral model was first introduced by Barry Boehm in the mid-80s [3], the risk-driven essentials of the model frequently have been misunderstood. To help clarify, Boehm recently identified six spiral essentials [2]:

- Concurrent determination of key artifacts.
- Stakeholder review and commitment.
- Level of effort driven by risk.
- Degree of detail driven by risk.
- Use of anchor-point milestones.
- Emphasis on system and life-cycle artifacts (cost/performance goals, adaptability).

A Perspective on Waterfall, Spiral, and Agile Development

Historically, the waterfall life-cycle model has been closely associated with heavyweight documentation. The spiral model has also historically been misinterpreted as an incremental waterfall model, rather than as a risk-based model as clarified by Boehm. It is important to note the focus on people (individuals, stakeholders), products (working software, key artifacts), and change (responding to change, adaptability) common to both the Agile Manifesto and the spiral essentials.

Methods Compatibility or Conflict?

It would seem from this observation that a company using an agile methodology should be able to successfully collaborate with a company using a traditional development method, especially if the project contained risk. To further support this position, Mark Paulk, co-author of the Software Engineering Institute's Capability Maturity Model® (CMM®), which has been associated with rigorous traditional development methods, has stated, "XP is a disciplined process, and the XP process is clearly well defined. We can thus consider CMM and XP complementary" [4].

Despite this evidence of methods compatibility, a different situation appears to exist in the developmental trenches. This is clearly pointed out by Don Reifer in the following statement

made in reference to one of his own studies:

> Instead of trying to make XP work rationally with the firm's existing processes, each side is pointing fingers at the other. No one seems to be trying to apply XP within the SW-CMM context rationally and profitably as the sages have suggested ... XP adherents feel they don't have time for the formality … Process proponents argue … quality will suffer and customer satisfaction will be sacrificed. [5]

One proposal to address this conflict has been put forth by Scott Ambler in the form of a *blocker* who runs *interference* for

---

"Using an incremental life-cycle model is critical because many of the conflicts observed are rooted in the all up-front thinking that comes with the single-increment waterfall model. Incremental thinking is fundamental to agile methods and crucial to bridging the two methods."

---

the team by providing, in Ambler's words, "the documents that the bureaucrats request" [6]. The term blocker essentially means someone whose sole job is to keep non-agile project stakeholders from hindering the agile development team's progress.

In the following paragraphs we identify four conflicts observed on the PrimeComp case study project.

Conflict 1: Working Software vs. Early Design Documentation

Part of the difficulty faced by SubComp is the conflict between what they perceive the end-customer wants with respect to risk management, and what is being asked for by their immediate-customer, PrimeComp. The end-customer has asked

to *see working software*. It appears that the end-customer wants more than a *paper* design to assess the risk, yet PrimeComp is asking SubComp to provide more detailed design documentation.

Conflict 2: Single vs. Multiple-Increment Life Cycle

Assuming SubComp succeeds in addressing the immediate high visibility risk, what if yet another risk pops up at the follow-up CDR? Will there be a follow-up to the follow-up CDR with further delays of progress payments?

Agile teams often tackle tough issues first, as did SubComp. They focus on achieving customer satisfaction through frequent software deliveries based on clear priorities. Agile teams are also usually small and often do not have adequate resources to work multiple risks in parallel. The single iteration through the waterfall model with the planned single CDR milestone was a major project management conflict for the agile team. From a project management perspective, it was a critical conflict since a significant payment was withheld.

Conflict 3: Formal Deliverable Documentation Weight

Hearing that the documentation was not due until the end of the project led me to ask two questions:

- What exactly were the contractual documentation requirements?
- Did SubComp know PrimeComp's documentation expectations?

Companies that employ agile methods tend to provide *lightweight* documentation. This is, at least partially, because they value working software more than documentation. Although large documents are not a requirement of traditional development methods, cultural expectations often tend to the *heavyweight* side.

Waiting to deliver documentation until late in the project creates a potential conflict, especially if expectations have not been set through early communication. Because of the stress being placed on the agile team to complete the demo software and to provide additional detailed documentation, the possibility of using a blocker was considered.

Conflict 4: On-Site Customer Collaboration

Agile methods *embrace* [7] changing requirements, even late in development. During my discussions with SubComp personnel, I discovered that the contractual project requirements were, in the words of one team member, "high level and open to many interpretations." When contractor and customer work closely on an agile development project, embracing change is eased through close collaboration. When a prime contractor inserts itself in the middle, effective collaboration can be stifled, creating additional conflict and risk.

During my discussions with SubComp personnel, one member of the agile team said,

> What is difficult from my perspective is that the details they [PrimeComp] are asking for are the lowest risk and lowest value technically … spending time on what they feel they need puts our small team at risk for actually completing the product, which is what ultimately matters, I think.

This statement led me to stop and consider just what ultimately did matter. The agile team was addressing the technical risks in a planned manner, but a key ingredient to effective XP operation was missing. How could the agile team determine and act based on what ultimately mattered to the customer when the customer was not collaborating closely on-site?

Given these four observed conflicts, what strategies make sense and what can be done to bridge agile and traditional development?

Recommendation 1: Plan Collaboratively and Use an Incremental Life Cycle

Some believe those who use agile methods do not follow a plan. This is a misunderstanding. Planning is actually a core principle of agile methods [7]; however, agile teams tend to plan in smaller time increments and more frequently than those who use traditional methods. This distinction has been clarified by the characterization of XP as *planning driven* rather than *plan driven* [8]. Planning takes place with both methods, but with agile methods the focus is on the act of planning, rather than a document.

I recommend for similar projects that the initial planning be done collaboratively, with the prime contractor, subcontractor, and customer working closely. I also recommend that an incremental life-cycle model be employed to aid in aligning the agile subcontractor's work within the overall project schedule. Using an incremental life-cycle model is critical because many of the conflicts observed are rooted in the all up-front thinking that comes with the single-increment waterfall model. Incremen-

tal thinking is fundamental to agile methods and crucial to bridging the two methods.

In the case study, it was too late to re-plan the project with an incremental life cycle, but I did recommend that SubComp step back and re-evaluate their strategy to the upcoming follow-up CDR. The following questions needed to be answered:
- Were there other risks that the customer felt had to be addressed at this point for the project to move forward successfully?
- What else would it take to close the CDR?

We had to find out the customer's CDR completion criteria, but we had to do it within an agile mind-set. That is, quickly and with minimal resources given that the small agile team was already over-extended working to complete the demo and the prime contractor's request for additional documentation.

> "The frequent feedback from multiple spirals can help your risk mitigation visibility and ultimately your project's success."

Recommendation 2: Use the Spiral Model and Well-Defined Anchor-Point Milestones to Address Risk

If one of the risk-responsible collaborating team members is employing an agile method, a spiral model with well-defined anchor points [2, 9] can go a long way to reduce potential project conflict and risk. This model can help the traditional development prime contractor as well as the agile subcontractor.

Providing working software early to address high-risk areas makes sense, but it is not sufficient to meet all project management needs. If you are the prime contractor, you want to make sure all the risks are being addressed in a timely and prioritized fashion. The frequent feedback from multiple spirals can help your risk mitigation visibility and ultimately your project's success.

From the agile subcontractor's perspective, you want your team to be able to focus and solve the highest priority risks early, but you also want to know what the prime contractor's expectations are along the way. By agreeing to the anchor-point milestones during the early collaborative planning activity, expectations can be

made clear on both sides, allowing the project to operate more effectively. One of the reasons an incremental life-cycle model is recommended is because it often leads to earlier communication concerning priorities and risks. When a traditional waterfall life-cycle model is selected, early discussions concerning priorities are often missed.

Recommendation 3: Plan for Multiple Documentation Drops and Use a Bridge Person

One reason collaborative initial planning is recommended is to get discussions going early concerning product deliverables thereby reducing the likelihood of late surprises. In the case study, it was decided not to use a *blocker* to provide the contractual documentation. Discussions led the agile team to the conclusion that the blocker notion brought with it a negative view of documentation. The blocker was seen as someone outside the agile team whose job it was to develop the documentation without *bothering* the team. This was not consistent with SubComp's view of documentation, nor was it consistent with the values expressed in the Agile Manifesto.

Our solution was to use what we called a *bridge* person, rather than a blocker. The bridge person, unlike the blocker, was a member of the agile team who participated in team meetings providing a valuable service to the team by capturing key verbal points and whiteboard sketches thereby providing useful maintainable *lightweight* documentation that would ultimately help both contractors and the customer.

I recommended that multiple drops of documentation be provided to PrimeComp prior to the contractual delivery date to get early feedback and reduce late surprises. Waiting until late in the game to deliver documentation is risky, especially when expectations are uncertain.

Recommendation 4: Find a Way to Make Customer Collaboration Work for Effective Requirements Management

The reason establishing a close collaborative working relationship with the customer was not easy in our case study was because PrimeComp was sensitive to any contact between the end-customer and SubComp. This sensitivity was, at least partially, motivated by the desire to maintain control. It is also possible that uncertainty surrounding how the end-customer would perceive the use of an agile methodology fueled PrimeComp's desire to maintain a separation between

SubComp and the end-customer.

A recommendation I would make today to a prime contractor facing similar situations is to recognize that the key to maintaining real project control is the management of risks associated with the subcontractor's effort. One of the most common risks in similar situations is requirements creep, which often fails to get recognized until late in the project's test phase when the customer starts writing new discrepancies because the product does not meet what they now perceive the requirements to mean.

This situation frequently occurs because the end-customer and product developer (agile subcontractor) fail to collaborate sufficiently in the early stages reaching common agreements on potentially ambiguous requirements statements. In an agile development environment, this risk increases because requirements are often written as *story cards* [7], which have an implicit dependence on face-to-face communication to resolve potential differing requirements interpretations.

One common misperception of agile methods is that the requirements are not controlled since they are allowed to change late in the game. This is a legitimate concern that could also fuel why a prime contractor might want to keep an end-customer away from an agile subcontractor, but it also demonstrates a fundamental misunderstanding of agile methods.

As Craig Larman explains, "Iterative and agile methods embrace change, but not chaos" [10]. The following rule clarifies the distinction: "Once the requests for an iteration have been chosen and it is under way, no external stakeholders may change the work" [10].

If you are a prime contractor, I recommend that you check with your agile subcontractor to ensure they understand this crucial distinction between embracing change and living in chaos. I also recommend that a member of the prime contractor's team be placed on the agile team. Then encourage and support as much customer collaboration as you can between the agile team and the end-customer to help manage your own risk.

If you are an agile subcontractor, you want to demonstrate to the prime contractor that you are effectively managing your allocated requirements. Those employing agile methods often use *story point* [11] charts to depict work remaining and requirements creep. While story points and anchor points are different, they can be used together to help bridge the two methods.

Anchor points can be viewed as spiral model progress checkpoints [2, 9]. One weakness with traditional approaches has been the accuracy of the methods employed to measure progress. Story points provide an objective progress-measurement method based on stories verified through successfully completed tests [11].

At the start of each increment, I recommend that the agile subcontractor provide the prime contractor with a documented list of agreed-to stories to be completed in the upcoming increment. Story point charts can then be used to objectively back up anchor-point progress assessments, leading to improved team communication and trust.

Recommendation 5: Document and Communicate Your Process

I recommended to SubComp that they put together a presentation documenting their agile process from the project management perspective. This presentation

---

> "If you are an agile subcontractor, you want to demonstrate to the prime contractor that you are effectively managing your allocated requirements."

---

would include key terms, roles, and responsibilities. Terms unique to the agile method such as coach, tracker, and metaphor [7] would be mapped to traditional terms such as project manager and architecture.

Recommendations for incremental lifecycle model, contract deliverables, and reviews compatible with both agile and traditional development methods should be included. Key to the presentation is a description of how SubComp's agile method fits within a traditional project management framework using a spiral model focusing on risk management. I then recommended to SubComp that they take every opportunity to communicate the key points in the presentation to PrimeComp, the end-customer, and to other traditional development contractors who might hold potential new business opportunities through software outsourcing.

Lesson Learned

When on-site customer collaboration exists, conflicts associated with vague requirements can often be resolved quickly. However, when the customer is not easily accessible, an agile subcontractor with vague requirements can quickly be placed at great risk.

We have learned that today's multi-contractor collaborative projects often do not lend themselves well to full-time, on-site customer collaboration. However, this does not mean that these projects cannot benefit from agility.

In such cases, I recommend a hybrid agile method with a focus on a more traditional requirements development and management method. Successful hybrid agile methods are not new [8, 12]. Keep in mind that hybrid does not imply all requirements up-front, but it does imply that once an iteration is under way, requirements must remain fixed to avoid chaos.

Conclusion

Today, we know how to manage geographically distributed teams formed from companies with divergent cultures and experiences [13]. Bridging agile and traditional development is the next step for organizations looking to take advantage of increasing new business opportunities through collaboration.

If you are experiencing conflicts similar to what has been described in this article, first examine your lines of communication. Look at your terminology. Are you communicating effectively what it is you do and how you do it? If you heard recently that a customer review did not go well, consider that the cause could be as simple as your agile terminology not connecting to the ear of a listener familiar only with traditional methods.

Allowing late requirements changes can work when your customer is on-site working next to you. But if you do not have an on-site collaborative customer, consider a hybrid approach to avoid major trouble late in the project.

Consider bridging, rather than blocking to meet milestone deliverables. More importantly, consider communicating to your collaborative partners and customers through examples of your products to gain their buy-in early, including the weight of your proposed documentation. Let them know that being agile is not cheating, but is in the best interests of everyone.

While many of the solutions described in this article are similar to those employed on non-agile projects, these solutions should not be taken for granted for two reasons. First, too often on hybrid agile-traditional projects, we find emotion getting in the way of clear thinking, often leading to a fundamental breakdown of communication. Second, we are learning through agile methods more effective techniques to measure progress and communicate. As Robert Martin pointed out in referring to agile methods:

They're not a regression to the cave, nor are they anything terribly new: Plain and simple, the agile bottom line is the production of regular, reliable data – and that's a good thing. [11]

Don Reifer said, "No one seems to be trying to apply XP within the SW-CMM context rationally and profitably as the sages have suggested" [5]. In our case, studying the proactive steps taken based on the recommendations led to a successful follow-up CDR and to improved communication and early documentation agreements. Today, SubComp recognizes the value of XP, but they also recognize the value and need for fundamental project management, and they are looking to the CMM Integration℠ framework [14] to help guide related improvements.

Agility is not counter to effective project management, but agile methods do not provide all of the project management needs necessary for success. Wrap your agile development process in a lightweight project management framework, and watch your communication and collaboration improve and your project and company succeed.◆

References

1. Cockburn, Alistair. Agile Software Development. Addison-Wesley, 2002: 215-218.
2. Boehm, Barry. "Spiral Model as a Tool for Evolutionary Acquisition." CROSSTALK May, 2001 <www.stsc. hill.af.mil/crosstalk/2001/05/index. html>.
3. Boehm, Barry. A Spiral Model of Software Development and Enhancement. Proc. of An International Workshop on Software Process and Software Environments, Trabuco Canyon, CA., Mar. 1985.
4. Paulk, Mark. "Extreme Programming from a CMM Perspective." IEEE Software Nov./Dec. 2001: 19-26.
5. Reifer, Don. "XP and the CMM." IEEE Software May/June 2003: 14-15.
6. Ambler, Scott. "Running Interference." Software Development July, 2003: 50-51.
7. Beck, Kent. Extreme Programming Explained: Embrace Change.
   Addison-Wesley, 2000.
8. Boehm, Barry, and Richard Turner. Balancing Agility and Discipline: A Guide for the Perplexed Addison-Wesley, 2003: 33-34, 233.
9. Boehm, Barry, and Daniel Port. "Balancing Discipline and Flexibility With the Spiral Model and MBASE." CROSSTALK Dec. 2001 <www. stsc. hill.af.mil/crosstalk/2001/12/ boehm.html>.
10. Larman, Craig. Agile and Iterative Development: A Manager's Guide. Addison-Wesley 2003: 14.
11. Martin, Robert C. "The Bottom Line." Software Development Dec. 2003: 42-44.
12. McMahon, Paul E. "Integrating Systems and Software Engineering: What Can Large Organizations Learn From Small Start-Ups?" CROSS-TALK Oct. 2002: 22-25 <www.stsc. hill.af.mil/crosstalk/2002/10/ mcmahon. html>.
13. McMahon, Paul. E. Virtual Project Management: Software Solutions for Today and the Future. St. Lucie Press, 2001.
14. CMMI Product Team. Capability Maturity Model® Integration (CMMI®), Version 1.1. Pittsburgh, PA: Software Engineering Institute <www.sei. cmu.edu>.

About the Author

Paul E. McMahon, principal of PEM Systems, provides technical and management services to large and small engineering organizations. He has taught software engineering at Binghamton University; conducted workshops on engineering process and management; and published over 20 articles, including articles on agile development and distributed development in CROSSTALK, and a book on collaborative development, "Virtual Project Management: Software Solutions for Today and the Future." McMahon also presented at the 2003 Software Technology Conference on "Growing Effective Technical Managers."

PEM Systems
118 Matthews ST
Binghamton, NY 13905
Phone: (607) 798-7740
E-mail: pemcmahon@acm.org

Coping with the New Paradigms

Walker Royce

Getting More for Your Money

For more than 20 years, Rational Software has been working with the world's largest software development organizations across the entire spectrum of software domains. Today, the company employs more than 1,000 software engineering professionals who work on-site with organizations that depend on software. Rational Software has harvested and synthesized many lessons from this in-the-trenches experience. They have diagnosed the symptoms of many successful and unsuccessful projects, identified root causes of recurring problems, and packaged patterns of software project success into a set of best practices captured in the Rational Unified Process. Rational is also a large-scale software development organization, with more than 750 software developers. They use their own techniques, technologies, tools, and processes internally, with outstanding results, as evidenced by their own business performance and product leadership in the market.

One of Rational's primary goals is to apply what they have learned in order to enable software development organizations to make substantial improvements in their software project economics and organizational capabilities. The following section of this paper summarizes the key approaches that deliver these benefits.

Part I. Trends in Software Development

Over the past two decades, the software industry has moved unrelentingly toward new methods for managing the ever-increasing complexity of software projects. We have seen evolutions, revolutions, and recurring themes of success and failure. Although software technologies, processes, and methods have advanced rapidly, software engineering remains a people-intensive process. Consequently, techniques for managing people, technology, resources, and risks have profound leverage.

The early software approaches of the 1960s and 1970s can best be described as craftsmanship, with each project using a custom process and custom tools. In the 1980s and 1990s, the software industry matured and transitioned to more of an engineering discipline. However, most software projects in this era were still primarily research-intensive, dominated by human creativity and diseconomies of scale. The next generation of software processes is driving toward a more production-intensive approach dominated by automation and economies of scale. Next-generation software economics are already being achieved by some advanced software organizations.

A Simplified Model for Assessing Software Economics

There are many cost models in use today for software. The most popular, open, and well-documented model is the Constructive COst MOdel (COCOMO), which has been widely used by industry for 20 years. The latest version, COCOMO II, is the result of a collaborative effort led by the University of Southern California (USC) Center for Software Engineering, with the financial and technical support of numerous industry affiliates. The objectives of this team are threefold:

1. To develop a software cost and schedule model for the life-cycle practices of the post-2000 era
2. To develop a software project database and tool support for improvement of the cost model
3. To provide a quantitative analytic framework for evaluating software technologies and their economic impacts

The accuracy of COCOMO II allows its users to estimate cost within 30% of actuals, 74% of the time. This level of unpredictability in the outcome of a software development process should be truly frightening to any software project investor, especially in view of the fact that few projects ever miss their financial objectives by doing better than expected.

The COCOMO II cost model includes numerous parameters and techniques for estimating a wide variety of software development projects. For the purposes of this discussion, we will abstract COCOMO II into a function of four basic parameters:

1. **Complexity.** The complexity of the software solution is typically quantified in terms of the size of human-generated components (the number of source instructions or the number of function points) needed to develop the features in a usable product.
2. **Process.** This refers to the process used to produce the end product, and in particular its effectiveness in helping developers avoid non-value-added activities.
3. **Team.** This refers to the capabilities of the software engineering team, and particularly their experience with both the computer science issues and the application domain issues for the project at hand.
4. **Tools.** This refers to the software tools a team uses for development, that is, the extent of process automation.

The relationships among these parameters in modeling the estimated effort can be expressed as follows:

$$\text{Effort} = (\text{Team}) \cdot (\text{Tools}) \cdot (\text{Complexity}) \cdot (\text{Process})$$

Schedule estimates are computed directly from the effort estimate and process parameters. Reductions in effort generally result in reductions in schedule estimates. To simplify this discussion, we can assume that the "cost" includes both effort and time. The complete COCOMO II model includes several modes, numerous parameters, and several equations. This simplified model enables us to focus the discussion on the more discriminating dimensions of improvement.

What constitutes a good cost estimate is a very tough question. In our experience, a good estimate can be defined as one that has the following attributes:

- It is conceived and supported by the project manager, the architecture team, the development team, and the test team accountable for performing the work.
- It is accepted by all stakeholders as ambitious, but realizable.
- It is based on a well-defined software cost model with a credible basis and a database of relevant project experience that includes similar processes, similar technologies, similar environments, similar quality requirements, and similar people. •
- It is defined in enough detail for both developers and managers to objectively assess the probability of success and to understand key risk areas.

Although several parametric models have been developed to estimate software costs, they can all be generally abstracted into the form given above. One very important aspect of software economics (as represented within today's software cost models) is that the relationship between effort and size (see the equation above) exhibits a diseconomy of scale. The software development diseconomy of scale is a result of the "process" exponent in the equation being greater than 1.0. In contrast to the economics for most manufacturing processes, the more software you build, the greater the cost per unit item. It is desirable, therefore, to reduce the size and complexity of a project whenever possible.

Software Engineering: A 40 Year History

Software engineering is dominated by intellectual activities focused on solving problems with immense complexity and numerous unknowns in competing perspectives. We can characterize three generations of software development as follows:

1. **1960s and 1970s.** Virtually all custom tools, custom processes, and custom components used by conventional organizations were built in primitive languages. Project performance was highly predictable: cost, schedule, and quality objectives were almost never met.
2. **1980s and 1990s.** This period was dominated by software engineering. Organizations used more repeatable processes, off-the-shelf tools, and about 70% of their components were built in higher-level languages. About 30% of these components were available as commercial products, including the operating system, database management system, networking, and graphical user interface. During the 1980s, some organizations began achieving economies of scale, but with

the growth in applications complexity (primarily in the move to distributed systems), the existing languages, techniques, and technologies were just not enough.

3. **2000 and later.** We are now in the next generation. Modern practice is rooted in the use of managed and measured processes, integrated automation environments, and mostly (70%) off-the-shelf components. Typically, only about 30% of components need to be custom built.

Figure 1 illustrates the economics associated with these three generations of software development. The ordinate of the graph refers to software unit costs (per source line of code [SLOC], per function point, per component—take your pick) realized by an organization. The abscissa represents the life-cycle growth in the complexity of software applications developed by the organization.

Technologies for achieving reductions in complexity/size, process improvements, improvements in team proficiency, and tool automation are not independent of one another. In each new generation, the key is complementary growth in all technologies. For example, the process advances could not be used successfully without new component technologies and increased tool automation.

Keys to Improvement: A Balanced Approach

Improvements in the economics of software development have been not only difficult to achieve, but also difficult to measure and substantiate. In software textbooks, trade journals, and market literature, the topic of software economics is plagued by inconsistent jargon, inconsistent units of measure, disagreement among experts, and unending hyperbole. If we examine only

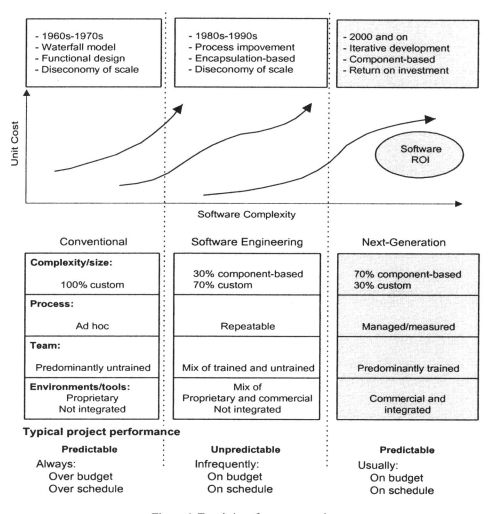

Figure 1. Trends in software economics.

one aspect of improving software economics, we are able to draw only narrow conclusions. Likewise, if an organization focuses on improving only one aspect of its software development process, it will not realize any significant economic improvement, even though it may make spectacular improvements in this single aspect of the process.

The key to substantial improvement in business performance is a balanced attack across the four basic parameters of the simplified software cost model: complexity, process, team, and tools. These parameters are in priority order for most software domains. In Rational's experience, the following discriminating approaches have made a difference in improving the economics of software development and integration:

1. Reduce the size or complexity of what needs to be developed.
   - Manage scope.
   - Reduce the amount of human-generated code through component-based technology.
   - Raise the level of abstraction, and use visual modeling to manage complexity.
2. Improve the development process.
   - Reduce scrap and rework by transitioning from a waterfall process to a modern, iterative development process.
   - Attack significant risks early through an architecture-first focus.
   - Use software best practices. 3. Create more proficient teams.
   - Improve individual skills.
   - Improve project teamwork.
   - Improve organizational capability.
4. Use integrated tools that exploit more automation.
   - Improve human productivity through advanced levels of automation.
   - Eliminate sources of human error.
   - Enable process improvements.

Most software experts would also stress the significant dependencies among these trends. For example, new tools enable complexity reduction and process improvements, size-reduction approaches lead to process changes, and process improvements drive tool advances.

In addition, IT executives need to consider other trends in software economics whose importance is increasing. These include the life-cycle effects of commercial components-based solutions and rapid development (often a source of maintenance headaches); the effects of user priorities and value propositions (often keys to business case analysis, and to the management of scope and expectations); and the effects of stakeholder/team collaboration and shared vision achievement (often keys to rapid adaptation to changes in the IT marketplace). Rational Software is accumulating and distilling experience and best practices in these areas, again in collaboration with the pioneering software economics research ongoing at USC.

In the next four sections, I will elaborate on the approaches listed above for achieving improvements in each of the four dimensions. These approaches represent patterns of success we have observed among Rational's most successful customers who have made quantum leaps in improving the economics of their software efforts.

Part II. Reducing Software Product Size or Complexity

The most significant way to improve economic results is usually to achieve a software solution with the minimum amount of human-generated source material. Our experience shows that managing scope, raising the level of abstraction through component-based technology, and using visual modeling notations are the highest leverage techniques that make a difference in reducing complexity.

Managing Scope

The scope of a software product is usually defined by a set of features, use cases, or requirements that specify what the product needs to do and how well it needs to do it. Managing scope requires an understanding of the economic trade-offs inherent in a set of features or requirements. At a minimum, you need to understand the relative value and cost of achieving each unit of scope. Typically, the development cost and user value associated with the required product features are fuzzy in the early phases of a project, but they evolve and become clearer with time.

Consider a trivial product with four features, as represented in Figure 2. This illustration abstracts the units of cost, value, and economic leverage to simplify a very complex and context-dependent discipline. In most applications, representations of cost, value, and economic leverage assessments do not need to be precise to manage scope. They could be as simple as "low, moderate, high," or they could be represented by an integer ranging from 1 to 10, as in the illustration. The main point is that all requirements are not created equal. To manage scope, the units of scope need to be objectively differentiated. Simple coarse-grained assessments are usually good enough to make most of the significant decisions. Obvious conclusions to be drawn from the Figure 2 trade-offs are that delivering a subset of the features faster may be a highly desirable option for the end product, or that a certain subset of features constitutes the best target for the first increment of capability demonstration.

Most products are not so trivial. A product might consist of tens, hundreds, or even thousands of requirements that are somewhat interrelated and cannot simply be added to or subtracted from the scope. Nevertheless, if you recognize the relative importance of different requirements and define some simple objective measures of cost and value for each unit of scope, you will succeed in managing scope and evolving a product toward a solution with more optimal economic leverage.

Reducing the Size of Human-Generated Code

Component-based technology is a general term for reducing the size and complexity of human-generated code necessary to achieve a software solution. Commercial components, domain-specific reuse, architectural patterns, and higher-order programming languages are all elements of component-based approaches focused on achieving a given system with fewer lines of human-specified source directives (statements). For example, to achieve a certain application with a fixed number of features, we could use any of the following potential solutions:

- Develop 1,000,000 lines of custom assembly language.
- Develop 400,000 lines of custom C++.
- Develop 100,000 lines of custom C++, integrate 200,000 lines of existing reusable components, and purchase a commercial middleware product.
- Develop 50,000 lines of custom Visual Basic and purchase and integrate several commercial components on a WinDNA platform.
- Develop 5,000 lines of custom Java, develop 10,000 lines of custom HTML, and purchase and integrate several commercial components on a J2EE platform.

Each of these solutions represents a step up in exploiting component-based technology, and a commensurate reduction in the total amount of human-developed code, which in turn reduces the time and the team size needed for development. Since the difference between large and small projects has a greater-than-linear impact on the life-cycle cost, the use of the highest-level language and appropriate commercial components has the highest potential cost impact. Furthermore, simpler is generally better. Reducing the size of custom-developed software usually increases understandability, reliability, and the ease of making changes.

Required Feature	Cost	Value
A	1	2
B	3	7
C	4	5
D	5	4

Product Option 1: Produce **All** Features A, B, C, and D
Development Cost = 13, User Value = 18
Development Time =14 months
Economic Leverage: 18/13 = 1.4

Product Option 2: Produce **Only** Features B and C
Development Cost = 7, User Value = 12
Development Time = 8 Months
Economic Leverage: 12/7 = 1.7

Figure 2. Trade-offs in managing scope.

Managing Complexity through Visual Modeling

Object-oriented technology and visual modeling achieved rapid acceptance during the 1990s. The fundamental impact of object-oriented technology has been in reducing the overall size and complexity of what needs to be developed through formalized notations for capturing and visualizing software abstractions. A model is a simplification of reality that provides a complete description of a system. We build models of complex systems because we cannot comprehend any such system in its entirety. Modeling is important because it helps the development team visualize, specify, construct, and communicate the structure and behavior of a system's architecture.

Using a standard modeling notation such as the Unified Modeling Language (UML), different members of the development team can communicate their decisions unambiguously to each other. Using visual modeling tools facilitates the management of these models, letting you hide or expose details as necessary. Visual modeling also helps maintain consistency among a system's artifacts: its requirements, designs, and implementations. In short, visual modeling helps improve a team's ability to manage software complexity.

Part III. Improving the Development Process

In order to achieve success, real-world software projects require an incredibly complex web of sequential and parallel steps. As the scale of the project increases, more overhead steps must be included just to manage the complexity of this web.

Project Processes

All project processes consist of productive activities and overhead activities:

- Productive activities result in tangible progress toward the end product. For software efforts, these activities include prototyping, modeling, coding, integration, debugging, and user documentation.
- Overhead activities have an intangible impact on the end product. They include plan preparation, requirements management, documentation, progress monitoring, risk assessment, financial assessment, configuration control, quality assessment, testing, late scrap and rework, management, personnel training, business administration, and other tasks. Although overhead activities include many value-added efforts, in general, when less effort is devoted to these activities, more effort can be expended on productive activities.

The main thrust of process improvement is to improve the results of productive activities and minimize the impact of overhead activities on personnel and schedule. Based on our observations, these are the three most discriminating approaches for achieving significant process improvements:

1. Transitioning to an iterative process.
2. Attacking the significant risks first through a component-based, architecture-first focus.
3. Using key software engineering best practices, from the outset, in requirements management, visual modeling, change management, and assessing quality throughout the life cycle.

Using an Iterative Process

The key discriminator in significant process improvement is making the transition from the conventional (waterfall) approach to a modern, iterative approach. The conventional software process was characterized by transitioning through sequential phases, from requirements to design to code to test, achieving 100% completion of each artifact at each life-cycle stage. All requirements, artifacts, components, and activities were treated as equals. The goal was to achieve high-fidelity traceability among all artifacts at each stage in the life cycle.

In practice, the conventional process resulted in:

- Protracted integration and late design breakage
- Late risk resolution

- Requirements-driven functional decomposition
- Adversarial stakeholder relationships
- Focus on documents and review meetings

These symptoms almost always led to a significant diseconomy of scale, especially for larger projects involving many developers. By contrast, a modern (iterative) development process framework is characterized by:

1. Continuous round-trip engineering from requirements to test, at evolving levels of abstraction.
2. Achieving high-fidelity understanding of the architecturally significant decisions as early as practical.
3. Evolving the artifacts in breadth and depth based on risk management priorities.
4. Postponing completeness and consistency analyses until later in the life cycle

A modern process framework attacks the primary sources of the diseconomy of scale inherent in the conventional software process. Figure 3 provides an objective perspective of the difference between the conventional waterfall process and a modern iterative process. It graphs development progress versus time, where progress is defined as percent coded, that is, demonstrable in its target form. At that point, the software is compilable and executable. It is not necessarily complete, compliant, or up to specifications.

In the waterfall project life cycle, software development typically progressed without issue until the integration phase. Requirements were first captured in complete detail in ad hoc text. Design documents were then fully elaborated in ad hoc notations. Coding and unit testing of individual components followed. Finally, the components were compiled and linked together into a complete system. This integration activity was the first time that significant inconsistencies among components (their interfaces and behavior) could be tangibly recognized. These inconsistencies, some of which were extremely difficult to uncover, resulted from using ambiguous formats for the early life-cycle artifacts. Getting the software to operate reliably enough to test its usefulness took much longer than planned. Budget and schedule pressure drove teams to shoehorn in the quickest fixes; redesign was usually out of the question. Then the testing of system threads, usefulness, requirements compliance, and quality was performed through a series of releases until the software was judged adequate for the user. About 90% of the time, the end result was a software system that was late, over budget, fragile, and expensive to maintain.

A review of numerous conventional projects that followed a waterfall model shows a recurring symptom: Although it was not usually planned this way, the resources expended in the major software development workflows resulted in an excessive al-

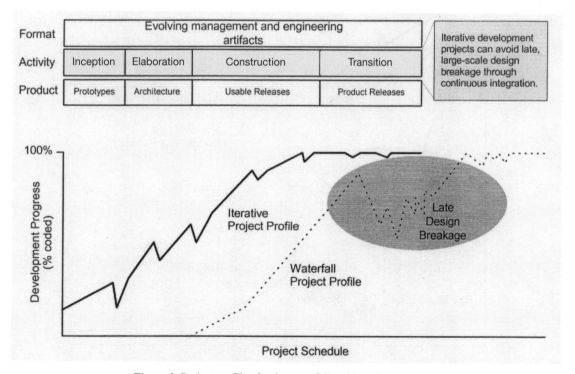

Figure 3. Project profiles for the waterfall and iterative processes.

location of resources (time or effort) to accomplish integration and test. Successfully completed projects consumed 40% of their effort in these activities; the percentage was even higher for unsuccessful projects. The overriding reason was that the effort associated with the late scrap and rework of design flaws was collected and implemented during the integration and test phases. Integration is a non-value-added activity, and most integration and test organizations spent 60% of their time integrating (that is, getting the software to work by resolving the design flaws and the frequently malignant scrap and rework associated with these resolutions). It is preferable for integration to take little time and little effort so the integration and test team can focus on demonstrating and testing the software, which are value-added efforts.

Attacking Significant Risks Early

Using an iterative development process, the software development team produces the architecture first, allowing integration to occur as the "verification" activity of the design phase and allowing design flaws to be detected and resolved earlier in the life cycle. This replaces the big-bang integration at the end of a project with continuous integration throughout the project. Getting the architecturally important things to be well understood and stable before worrying about the complete breadth and depth of the artifacts should result in scrap and rework rates that decrease or remain stable over the project life cycle.

The architecture-first approach forces integration into the design phase and demonstrations provide the forcing function for progress. The demonstrations do not eliminate the design breakage; they just make it happen in the design phase where it can be fixed correctly. In an iterative process, the system is "grown" from an immature prototype to a baseline architectural skeleton, to increments of useful capabilities to complete product releases. The downstream integration nightmare is avoided, and a more robust and maintainable design is produced.

Major milestones provide very tangible results. Designs are now guilty until proven innocent: The project does not move forward until the objectives of the demonstration have been achieved. Results of the demonstration and major milestones contribute to an understanding of the trade-offs among the requirements, design, plans, technology, and other factors. Based on this understanding, changes to stakeholder expectations can still be renegotiated.

The early phases of the iterative life cycle (inception and elaboration) focus on confronting and resolving the risks before making the big resource commitments required in later phases. Managers of conventional projects tend to do the easy stuff first, thereby demonstrating early progress. A modern process, like that in Figure 4, needs to attack the architecturally significant stuff first, the important 20% of the requirements: use cases, components, and risks.

The "80/20" lessons learned during the past 30 years of software management experience provide a useful perspective for identifying some of the key features of an iterative development philosophy:

- 80% of the engineering is consumed by 20% of the requirements. Do not strive prematurely for high fidelity and full

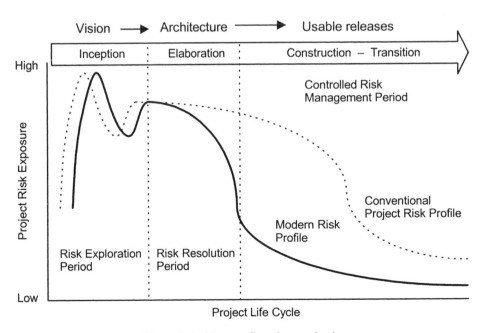

Figure 4. Architecture first, then production.

traceability of the complete requirements set. Instead, strive to understand the driving requirements completely before committing resources to full-scale development.

- 80% of the software cost is consumed by 20% of the components. Elaborate the cost-critical components first so that planning and control of cost drivers are well understood early in the life cycle.

- 80% of the errors are caused by 20% of the components. Elaborate the reliability-critical components first so that assessment activities have enough time to achieve the necessary level of maturity.

- 80% of software scrap and rework is caused by 20% of the changes. Elaborate the change-critical components first so that broad-impact changes occur when the project is nimble.

- 80% of the resource consumption (execution time, disk space, memory, etc.) is consumed by 20% of the components. Elaborate the performance-critical components first so that engineering trade-offs with reliability, changeability, and cost-effectiveness can be resolved as early in the life cycle as possible.

- 80% of the progress is made by 20% of the people. Make sure the initial team that plans the project and designs the architecture is of the highest quality. An adequate plan and adequate architecture can then succeed with an average construction team. An inadequate plan or inadequate architecture will probably not succeed, even with an expert construction team.

Using Software Best Practices

Best practices are a set of commercially proven approaches to software development that, when used together, strike at the root causes of software development problems. The Rational Unified Process integrates six industry best practices into one process framework:

1. Develop iteratively
2. Manage requirements
3. Use component architectures
4. Model visually
5. Continuously verify quality
6. Manage change

The techniques and technologies inherent in these best practices are discussed in detail in the Rational Unified Process. One way to view the impact of these best practices on the economics of software projects is through the differences in resource expenditure profiles between conventional projects and modern iterative projects.

Conventional principles drove software development activities to overexpend during implementation and integration activities. A healthy iterative process, an architecture-first focus, and incorporation of software best practices should result in less total scrap and rework through relatively more emphasis on the high-value activities of management planning, requirements analysis, and design. This results in a more balanced expenditure of resources across the core workflows of a modern process.

One critical lesson learned from successful iterative development projects is that they start out with a planning profile different from the standard profile of a conventional project. If you plan modern iterative projects with the old waterfall planning profile, the chance of success is significantly diminished. By planning a modern project with a more appropriate resource profile derived from successful iterative projects, there is much more flexibility in optimizing the project performance for improvements in productivity, quality, or cycle time, whichever is the business driver.

During the past decade, Rational Software has participated in the software process improvement efforts of numerous companies, including most of the leading software development organizations in the Fortune 500 companies. Typical goals are to achieve a $2X$, $3X$, or $10X$ increase in productivity, quality, time to market, or some combination of all three, where X corresponds to how well the organization does now. The funny thing is that most of these organizations have only a coarse grasp on what X is, in objective terms.

Table 1 characterizes the impact on project expenditure profiles associated with making about a $3X$ reduction in scrap and rework. This improvement is the primary goal of transitioning from the conventional waterfall software development process to a modern iterative software development process.

Standardizing on a common process is a courageous undertaking for a software organization, and there is a wide spectrum of implementations. I have seen organizations attempt to do less (too little standardization, or none) and more (too much standardization) with little success in improving software return on investment. Process standardization requires a very balanced approach.

Table 1. Resource expenditures

Life cycle activity	Conventional	Modern
Management	5%	10%
Requirements	5%	10%
Design	10%	15%
Implementation	30%	25%
Test and assessment	40%	25%
Deployment	5%	5%
Environment	5%	10%
	100%	100%

Part IV. Improving Team Proficiency

Getting more done with fewer people is the paramount underlying need for improving software economics. The demand for competent software professionals continues to outpace the supply of qualified individuals. In almost every successful software development project and software organization that Rational Software encounters, there is a strong commitment to configuring the smallest, most capable team.

However, most troubled projects are staffed with more people than they require. "Obese" projects usually occur because the project culture is more focused on following a process rather than achieving results. In the previous section covering process improvement, and in the Rational Unified Process, there is a continuous, life-cycle emphasis on achieving results. This is a subtle but paramount differentiator between successful, results-driven, iterative development projects and unsuccessful process-driven projects.

So, how can organizations use smaller, more capable teams? Rational Software has identified three different levels that need to be addressed: enhancing individual performance, improving project teamwork, and advancing organizational capability.

Enhancing Individual Performance

Organizations that analyze how to improve their employees' proficiency generally focus on only one dimension: training. Although training is an important mechanism for enhancing individual skills, team composition and experience are equally important dimensions that should be considered. Balance and coverage are two important characteristics of excellent teams.

Balance requires leaders and followers, visionaries and crank-turners, optimists and pessimists, conservatives and risk takers. Whenever a team is out of balance, it is vulnerable. Software development is a team sport. A team loaded with superstars, each striving to set individual records and be the team leader, can be embarrassed by a balanced team of solid players with a few leaders focused on the team result of winning the game. Managers must nurture a culture of teamwork and results rather than individual accomplishment. The other important characteristic—coverage—requires a complement of skill sets that span the breadth of the methods, tools, and technologies.

Two dimensions of experience necessary to achieve sustained process improvements are equally important: software development process maturity and domain knowledge. Unprecedented systems are much riskier endeavors than systems that have been built before. Experience in building similar systems is one of the paramount qualities needed by a team. This precedent experience is the foundation for differentiating the 20% of the stuff that is architecturally significant in a new system. A mature organization that builds real-time command-and-control systems will not be capable of exhibiting its usual mature performance if it takes on a new application domain such as e-business Web site development.

Improving Project Teamwork

Although it is difficult to make sweeping generalizations about project organizations, some recurring patterns in successful projects suggest that a core organization should include four distinct subteams: management, architecture, development, and assessment. The project management team is an active participant, responsible for producing as well as managing. Project management is not a spectator sport. The architecture team is responsible for design artifacts and for the integration of components. The development team owns the component construction and maintenance activities. The assessment team is kept separate from development, to foster an independent quality perspective as well as to focus on testability and product evaluation activities concurrent with ongoing development throughout the life cycle. There is no separate quality team because quality is everyone's job, integrated into all activities and checkpoints. However, each team takes responsibility for a different quality perspective.

Some proven practices for building good software architectures are equally valid for building good software organizations. The organization of any project represents the architecture of the team and needs to evolve in synch with the project plans. Defining an explicit architecture team with ownership of architectural issues and integration concerns can provide simpler and less error-prone communications among project teams. Figure 5 illustrates how project team staffing and the organizational center of gravity evolves over the life cycle of a software development project. There are four phases in this process:

1. **Inception.** A management team focus on planning, with enough support from other teams to ensure that the plans represent a consensus of all perspectives.
2. **Elaboration.** An architecture team focus, in which the driving forces of the project reside in the software architecture team and are supported by the software development and software assessment teams as necessary to achieve a stable architecture baseline.
3. **Construction.** A development team focus, in which most of the activity resides in the software development and software assessment teams.
4. **Transition.** A customer-focused organization, in which usage feedback drives the organization and activities.

Teamwork is much more important than the sum of individual skills and efforts. Project managers need to configure balanced teams with a foundation of solid talent and put highly skilled people in the high-leverage positions. These are some project team management maxims:

- A well-managed project can succeed with nominal engineering talent.
- An expert team of engineers will almost never succeed if a project is mismanaged.
- A well-architected system can be built by a nominally talented team of software builders.
- A poorly architected system will flounder even with an expert team of builders.

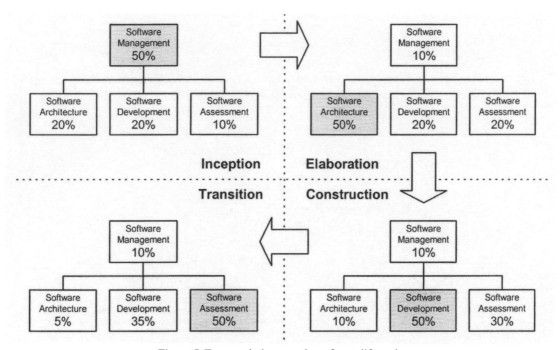

Figure 5. Team evolution over the software life cycle.

65

Advancing Organizational Capability

Organizational capability is best measured by trends in project performance rather than by key process area checklists, process audits, and so forth. Figure 6 provides some simple graphs of project performance over time to illustrate the expectation for four different levels of organizational capability:

1. **Random.** Immature organizations use ad hoc processes, methods, and tools on each new project. This results in random performance that is frequently unacceptable. Probably 60% of the industry's software organizations still operate with random, unpredictable performance.

2. **Repeatable.** Organizations that are more mature use foundation capabilities roughly traceable to industry best practices. They can achieve repeatable performance with some relatively constant return on investments in processes, methods, training, and tools. In our experience, about 30% of the industry's software development organizations have achieved repeatable project performance.

3. **Improving.** The industry's better software organizations achieve common process frameworks, methods, training, and tools across an organization within a common line of business. Consistent, objective metrics can be used across projects, which can result in an improving return on investment from project to project. This is the underlying goal of ISO 9000 or SEI CMM process improvement initiatives, although most such initiatives tend to take process- and activity-focused perspectives rather than project-result-focused perspectives. At most, 10% of the industry's software development organizations operate today at this level of capability.

4. **Market leading.** Organizations achieve excellent capability, which should align with market leadership, when they have executed multiple projects under a common framework with successively better performance, have achieved an objective experience base from which they can optimize business performance across multiple performance dimensions (trading off quality, time-to-market, and costs), and practice quantitative process management.

In any engineering venture in which intellectual property is the real product, the dominant productivity factors will be personnel skills, teamwork, and motivations. To the extent possible, a modern process encapsulates the requirements for high-leverage people in the early phases, when the team is relatively small. The later production phases, when teams are typically much larger, should then operate with far less dependency on scarce expertise.

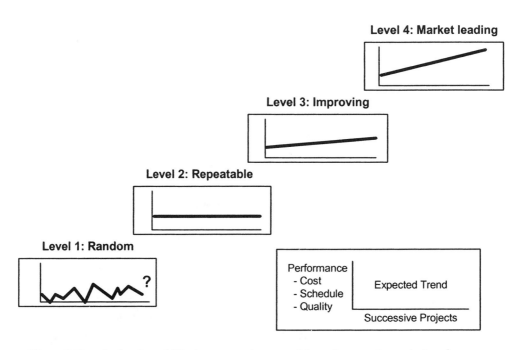

Figure 6. Organizational capability improvement measured through successive project performance.

66

Part V. Improving Automation through Integrated Tools

In Part III, I described process improvements associated with transitioning to iterative development. These improvements are focused on eliminating steps and minimizing the scrap and rework inherent in the conventional process. Another form of process improvement is to improve the efficiency of certain steps by improving automation through integrated tools.

Today's software development environments, combined with rigorous engineering languages like UML, enable many tasks that were previously manual to be automated. Activities such as design analysis, data translations, quality checks, and other tasks involving a deterministic production of artifacts can now be done with minimal human intervention. Environments should include tools for requirements management, visual modeling, document automation, host/target programming tools, automated regression testing, integrated change management, and feature/defect tracking.

Today, most software organizations are facing the need to integrate their own environment and infrastructure for software development. This typically results in the selection of more or less incompatible tools with different information repositories, from different vendors, on different platforms, using different jargon, and based on different process assumptions. Integrating and maintaining such an infrastructure has proved to be much more problematic than expected. An important emphasis of a modern approach is to define an integrated development and maintenance environment as a first-class artifact of the process. Commercial processes, methods, and tools have synthesized and packaged industry best practices into mature approaches applicable across the spectrum of software development domains. The return on investment in these commercial environments scales up significantly with the size of the software development organization, promotes useful levels of standardization, and minimizes the additional organizational burden of maintaining proprietary alternatives.

Improving Human Productivity

Planning tools, requirements management tools, visual modeling tools, compilers, editors, debuggers, quality assurance analysis tools, test tools, and user interfaces provide crucial automation support for evolving the intermediate products of a software engineering effort. Moreover, configuration management environments provide the foundation for executing and instrumenting the process. Viewed in isolation, tools and automation generally yield 20 to 40% improvements in effort. These same tools and environments, however, are also primary vehicles for reducing complexity and improving process automation, so their impact can be much greater.

Tool automation can help reduce the overall complexity in automated code generation from UML design models, for example. Designers working at a relatively high level of abstraction in UML may compose a model that includes graphical icons, relationships, and attributes in a few diagrams. Visual modeling tools can capture the diagrams in a persistent representation and automate the creation of a large number of source code statements in a desired programming language. Hundreds of lines of source code are typically generated from tens of human-generated visual modeling elements. This 10-to-1 reduction in the amount of human-generated stuff is one dimension of complexity reduction enabled by visual modeling notations and tools.

Eliminating Error Sources

Each phase of development produces a certain amount of precision in the product/system description called software artifacts. Life-cycle software artifacts are organized into five sets that are roughly partitioned by the underlying language of:

1. Requirements (organized text and UML models of the problem space)
2. Design (UML models of the solution space)
3. Implementation (human-readable programming language and associated source files)
4. Deployment (machine-processable languages and associated files)
5. Management (ad hoc textual formats such as plans, schedules, metrics, and spreadsheets)

At any point in the life cycle, the different artifact sets should be in balance, at compatible detail levels, and traceable to each other. As development proceeds, each part evolves in more detail. When the system is complete, all five sets are fully elaborated and consistent with each other. As the industry has moved into maintaining different information repositories for the engineering artifacts, we now need automation support to ensure efficient and error-free transition of data from one artifact to another. Round-trip engineering describes the environment support needed to change an artifact freely and have other artifacts automatically changed so that consistency is maintained among the entire set of requirements, design, implementation, and deployment artifacts.

Enabling Process Improvements

Real-world project experience has shown that a highly integrated environment is necessary both to facilitate and to enforce management control of the process. An environment that captures artifacts in rigorous engineering languages such as UML and programming languages can provide semantic integration (by which the environment understands the detailed meaning of the development artifacts) and significant process automation to improve productivity and software quality. An environment that supports incremental compilation, automated system builds, and integrated regression testing can provide rapid turnaround for iterative development, allow development teams to iterate more freely, and accelerate the adoption of modern techniques.

Objective measures are required for assessing the quality of a software product and the progress of the work, which provide different perspectives of a software effort. Architects are more concerned with quality indicators; managers are usually more concerned with progress indicators. The success of any software process whose metrics are collected manually will be limited. The most important software metrics are simple, objective measures of how various perspectives of the product/project are changing. Absolute measures are usually much less important than relative changes with respect to time. The incredibly dynamic nature of software projects requires that these measures be available at any time, tailorable to various subsets of the evolving product (subsystem, release, version, component, team), and maintained such that trends can be assessed (first and second derivatives). Such continuous availability has only been achieved in development/integration environments that maintain the metrics online, as an automated by-product.

Part VI. Accelerating Culture Change through Common Sense

In the software marketplace, the track record has been that three out of four projects do not succeed. Project managers and organizations tend to "play defense," which typically results in an overemphasis on risk management. In Rational's experience, the organizations that have truly achieved a quantum leap in improving their software economics are the ones that have demonstrated judicious risk management and savvy success management by playing offense, attacking each of the four dimensions—complexity, process, teams, and tools—in an aggressive, yet balanced fashion.

Profiles of Successful Organizations

Figure 7 illustrates the target project profiles that result when a software organization attacks all four dimensions of our simplified software economics framework. These organizations execute projects with a profile similar to that of the upper shaded

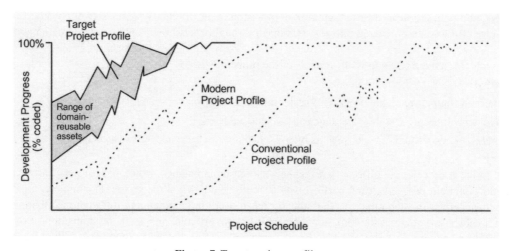

Figure 7. Target project profiles.

region, using a modern iterative process, capable teams supported by an integrated environment, and a component-based architecture that reduces the complexity of custom development through the use of an architectural pattern with a rich supply of existing components.

Today, roughly 60% of the industry still operates according to the conventional project profile. About 30% has transitioned to the modern project profile. Less than 10% is already achieving improved software economics and experiencing results similar to the target project profile. Organizations that have succeeded are deploying software products that are constructed largely out of existing components in 50% less time, with 50% less development resources, maintained by teams 50% the size of those required by legacy systems.

In making the transition to new techniques and technologies, there is always apprehension and concern about failing. Maintaining the status quo and relying on existing methods is usually considered the safest path. In the software industry, however, where most organizations succeed on only a small percentage of their software projects, maintaining the status quo is not always safe. When an organization does decide to make a transition, two pieces of conventional wisdom are usually offered both by internal champions and by external change agents: (1) Pioneer any new techniques on a small pilot program; (2) Be prepared to spend more resources (money and time) on your first project that makes the transition. In our experience, both recommendations are counterproductive. The organizations that succeed take the opposite approach: They implement the changes on a business-critical project, and they explicitly plan to demonstrate the business improvements (in resources or time required) on that first critical project.

Keys to Success

Why does the bold approach succeed? Our experience shows that meaningful organizational change depends on A-players and committed middle-level managers. A-players are typically assigned to the front lines, working on business-critical projects. These are the projects that will have the most impact on near-term business. Most organizations cannot afford to assign A-players to noncritical pilot projects.

Middle-level managers are important because they lay out resource plans and schedules. When they propose to improve a process by making a change, and then sell their proposal by giving the change initiative as the reason, it is a sure sign that these leaders (and their teams) believe that a new method, process, technique, or tool will make a difference. On the other hand, if a manager accountable for performance proposes that a project will take more time or need more people because of a new approach, this is usually a sign that the project is incorporating a change that the manager and team only half-heartedly support. The change may have been mandated, or it may have come about because of some line of reasoning the team has not completely bought into. The first team that believes that a certain change will achieve better results will usually do whatever it takes to make that claim come true. Ownership by the right people is the key to success. Look for it.

Successful software management is hard work. Technical breakthroughs, process breakthroughs, and new tools will make it easier, but management discipline will continue to be the crux of software project success. New technological advances will be accompanied by new opportunities for software applications, new dimensions of complexity, new avenues of automation, and new customers with different priorities. Accommodating these changes will perturb many of our ingrained software management values and priorities. However, striking a balance among requirements, designs, and plans will remain the underlying objective of future software management endeavors, just as it is today.

Improving software economics is not revolutionary; numerous projects have been practicing some of these techniques for years. However, many of the disciplines suggested here will require nontrivial paradigm shifts. It is important to be prepared for these shifts in order to avoid as many sources of friction as possible. Some of these changes will be resisted by certain stakeholders or by certain contingencies within a project or organization. This resistance must be overcome to transition successfully to a modern software management process and supporting methods and tools. In some cases, distinguishing objective opposition from stubborn resistance will be a challenge.

The following paragraphs discuss some rough indicators of a successful transition to a modern culture focused on improved software business performance. These are things to look for in order to differentiate projects and organizations that have made a genuine cultural transition from those that have only put up a facade.

Lower and Middle Level Managers Are the Key Performers

Hands-on management skills vary, but competent first-line managers typically spend much of their time performing, especially focused on understanding the status of the project first-hand and developing plans and estimates. Above all, the person managing an effort ought to plan it. This does not mean approving the plan; it means participating in its development.

In independent project assessments we have performed, a good indicator of trouble ahead is a manager who did not author the plan or take ownership in it. The stakeholders affected by this transition are software project managers and team leaders.

Requirements, Designs, and Plans Are Fluid and Tangible

The conventional software development process focused too much on producing documents that attempted to describe the software products and too little on producing tangible increments of the products themselves. Major milestones were defined solely in terms of specific documents. Development organizations were driven to produce tons of paper to meet milestones rather than expend their energy on tasks that would reduce risk and produce quality software. An iterative process requires actual construction of a sequence of progressively more complete systems that demonstrate the architecture, enable objective requirements negotiations, validate the technical approach, and address resolution of key risks. Ideally, all stakeholders will focus on these real milestones, with incremental deliveries of useful functionality and commensurate increases in objective understanding of the trade-offs among requirements, designs, and plans rather than speculative paper descriptions of the end-item vision. The transition to a less document-driven environment will be embraced by the engineering teams; it will probably be resisted by traditional product and project monitors.

Ambitious Demonstrations Are Encouraged

The purpose of early life-cycle demonstrations is to expose design flaws, not to put up a facade. Stakeholders should not overreact to early mistakes, digressions, or immature designs. Evaluation criteria in early release plans are coarse goals, not requirements. If early engineering obstacles are overemphasized, development organizations will set up future iterations to be less ambitious. On the other hand, stakeholders should not tolerate lack of follow-through in resolving issues. If negative trends are not addressed with vigor, they can cause serious perturbations later on. Open and attentive follow-through is necessary to resolve issues. The management team is most likely to resist these demonstrations (especially if the project was oversold) because they will expose any engineering or process issues that were easy to hide using the conventional process. Customers, users, and the engineering team will embrace them for exactly the same reason.

Good and Bad Project Performance Is Much More Obvious Earlier in the Life Cycle

In an iterative development, success breeds success; early failures are extremely difficult to turn around. Real-world project experience has shown time and again that it is the early phases that make or break a project. It is therefore of paramount importance to have absolutely the right start-up team for the early planning and architecture activities. If these early phases are done right with good teams, projects can be completed successfully with nominal teams evolving the applications into the final product. If the planning and architecture phases are not performed adequately, all the expert programmers and testers in the world will probably not make the project successful. No one should resist early staffing with the right team. Most organizations, however, have scarce resources for early life-cycle roles and are hesitant to make the necessary staff allocations.

Early Iterations Will Be Immature

External stakeholders, including customers and users, cannot expect initial deliveries to perform up to specification, to be complete, to be fully reliable, or to have end-target levels of quality or performance. On the other hand, development organizations must be held accountable for, and demonstrate, tangible improvements and positive trends in successive increments. These trends usually indicate convergence toward specifications. Objectively quantifying changes, fixes, and upgrades will help all stakeholders evaluate the quality of the process and environment for future activities. Objective insight into performance issues occurs early in the life cycle in almost every successful project. This is a sign of an immature design but a mature design process. All stakeholders will initially be concerned with early performance issues. Development engineers will embrace the emphasis on early demonstrations and the ability to assess and evaluate performance trade-offs in subsequent releases. Although customers and users may have difficulty accepting the flaws of early releases, they should be impressed by later increments. The development team will accept immaturity as a natural part of the process.

Detailed and Complete Artifacts Are Less Important Early, More Important Later

It is a waste of time to worry about the details (traceability, thoroughness, and completeness) of the artifact sets until a baseline is achieved that is useful enough and stable enough to warrant time-consuming analyses of these quality factors. Project leaders should avoid squandering early engineering cycles and precious resources on adding content and quality precision to artifacts that may quickly become obsolete. Although the development team will embrace the transition to this approach wholeheartedly, traditional contract monitors will resist the early deemphasis on completeness.

Real Issues Surface and Get Resolved Systematically

Successful projects recognize that requirements and designs evolve together through a process of continuous negotiation, trade-off, and bartering toward best value; they do not blindly adhere to some ambiguous contract clause or requirements statement. On a healthy project that is making progress, it should be easy to differentiate between real and apparent issues.

Quality Assurance Is Everyone's Job, Not a Separate Discipline

Many organizations have a separate group called Quality Assurance. We are generally against the concept of separate quality assurance activities, teams, or artifacts. Quality assurance should be woven into every role, every activity, and every artifact. True quality assurance is measured by tangible progress and objective data, not by checklists, meetings, and inspections. The software project manager or delegate should assume the role of ensuring that quality assurance is properly woven into the process. The traditional policing by a separate team of inspectors should be replaced by the self-policing teamwork of an organization with a mature process, common objectives, and common incentives. Traditional managers and quality assurance personnel will resist this transition, but engineering teams will embrace it.

Investments in Automation Are Viewed as Necessary

Because iterative development projects require extensive automation, it is important not to underinvest in the capital environment. It is also important for stakeholders to acquire an integrated environment that permits efficient participation in an iterative development. Without this, interactions with the development organization will degenerate to paper exchanges and many of the issues of the traditional process. These investments may be opposed either by managers who are overly focused on near-term financial results or project personnel who favor a narrow project focus over a global solution that serves both the project and the organization's goals.

Recommendation: Select the Right Project, the Right People, and the Right Goals

In our experience, the most successful organizational paradigm shifts resulted from similar sets of circumstances. Organizations took their most critical project and highest caliber personnel, gave them adequate resources, and demanded better results. If an organization expects a new method, tool, or technology to have an adverse impact on the results of the trailblazing project, that expectation is almost certain to come true. Why? Because no organization manager would knowingly cause an adverse impact on the most important projects in an organization, to which the best people are assigned. Therefore, the trailblazing project will be a noncritical project, staffed with noncritical personnel of whom less is expected. The expectation of an adverse impact ends up being a self-fulfilling prophecy.

The best way to transition to improved software economics is to take the following approach:

- **Ready.** Understand modern processes, approaches, and technologies. Define (or improve, or optimize) your process to support iterative development in the context of your business priorities. Support the process with mature environments, tools, architectural patterns, and components.

- **Aim.** Select a project critical to the organization's business. Staff it with the right team of complementary resources.
- **Fire.** Execute the organizational and project-level plans with vigor and follow through.

In this paper, I have presented key lessons about improving software economics that Rational's field organization has learned through 20 years of working in the trenches with thousands of customers. When all the buzzwords and cosmetics are stripped away, most of our advice boils down to simple (un)common sense.

Chapter 3

Process Improvement

Order is not pressure which is imposed on society from without, but an equilibrium which is set up from within.

—Jose Ortega y Gasset, *Mirabeau and Politics*

Overview

The Software Engineering Institute's (SEI) publication of its process maturity framework in the mid-1980s ranks as one of the major developments in the software management field during the past two decades. This framework provided organizations with a structure that they could use to assess where they stood relative to an industry norm. Using this information, software organizations could plan and sell process improvement programs whose cost could be justified based on competitive factors.

Since the early 1990s, the U.S. Department of Defense (DoD) has strongly promoted the use of the process maturity model as a means to select contractors who have the capability and capacity to perform on large weapon systems acquisitions. Based upon the results of these early efforts, many commercial and overseas organizations have embraced the SEI model and used it to structure their process improvement activities.

In the mid-1990s, the SEI published its Capability Maturity Model (CMM). This natural refinement of the original five-level maturity model was built based upon suggestions from the communities who were using it as the foundation of their process assessment and improvement activities. The CMM more precisely defined clusters of activities and practices upon which the capabilities at a given maturity level were based in its model architecture. These were called the Key Process Areas (KPAs). Transition to the CMM began even before the revision was finalized when several of the numerous organizations, who were involved in its development, committed to its use. The CMM was widely embraced by the international community, and many firms in Europe, India, and the People' Republic of China (PRC) adopting it as a means to booster their off-shore businesses.

During the past five years, a new version of the CMM has been published as part of a concentrated effort to address process improvement in engineering (and sometimes manufacturing) organizations. To broaden the scope of the maturity model beyond just software, a joint government/industry team developed a new version of the model called the CMMI (Capability Maturity Model Integration). This new version of the model integrates previously developed systems and software engineering frameworks into a composite model that organizations can use to structure their process improvement efforts. The harmonization activities conducted were primarily directed toward eliminating overlap and developing a common architecture that could be used to tailor the provisions of the CMMI using process areas arranged in either a discrete or continuous manner. Experience reported to date with the CMMI has been positive, and organizations have started to adopt it widely, along with its revamped assessment methodology.

In the decade since the process maturity model's emergence, considerable evidence has been gathered that justifies the framework's utility, cost-effectiveness, and continued enhancement. Although there are still many perceived issues associated with the use of the CMM and the CMMI, even its harshest critics agree that it provides value to its users. In response, I have revamped this chapter to reflect the changes that have been made to the CMM and more current experience with its use in both the aerospace and commercial worlds. I have selected the following four papers to be in this edition to summarize the challenges, issues, and experiences associated with the application of the CMM and CMMI within their engineering organizations.

Article Summaries

Successful Process Implementation, by Anna Borjesson and Lars Mathiassen. This paper details Ericsson's experience with its software process improvement efforts. It discusses what techniques worked and what did not as the firm tried to move to higher levels of maturity on the SEI's CMM process maturity scale. Besides giving you valuable insight into what it takes to pull such an effort off in practice, the paper provides valuable evidence that the investments made in process improvement were justified in terms of productivity and quality gains made over time. The investments made, and the returns, are detailed in the text.

The Definitive Paper: Quantifying the Benefits of Software Process Improvement, by Donald Reifer, Doug Walters, and Al Chatmon. This new paper provides insight into how Northrop Grumman computed their return-on-investment for their software process improvement program within their Electronics Systems' operations. Although focused on quantifying the gains made due to their process initiatives, Northrop's push for improvement took a different tack than Ericsson's did, as outlined in the previous paper. The paper shows how they built their business case to sustain their focus and propel their organization toward making large gains in productivity and product line engineering.

Process Improvement for Small Organizations, by Declan P. Kelly and Bill Culleton. Because they believe it may be overkill, small organizations often resist investing in process improvement initiatives. The authors debunk this myth as they discuss their experience that provides evidence to the contrary. The paper discusses what they did to bring process into their firm, how they sold it, their training and rollout approach, and, most importantly, their experience on pilot projects. Although little hard data is presented, the authors make the case for process improvement in small firms through their subjective evaluation of their results.

The Clash of Two Cultures: Project Management versus Process Management, by Rob Thomsett. This final paper highlights the conflicts that exist today between the process and project management camps. One camp is product oriented, whereas the other focuses on improving the processes used in production. This conflict has existed for thirty years as the two separate cultures have coexisted and thrived. I have included this article to help you understand and address the conflict as part of your process improvement efforts, especially when considering agile approaches (they put a premium on product, not process). To succeed, compromises must be made so both camps can flourish.

Key Terms

Seven terms, defined as follows, are important for understanding the topics of process maturity and improvement:

1. **Capability Maturity Model (Software).** A description of the stages through which organizations evolve as they define, implement, measure, control, and improve their software processes. This model provides a guide for selecting process improvement strategies.

2. **Institutionalization.** The building of infrastructure and culture to support making whatever is changed a part of the ongoing way a firm does business.

3. **Key Process Area (KPA).** A cluster of related activities that, when performed collectively, achieve a set of goals considered to be important for establishing process capability.

4. **Process.** In management, the sequence of steps, actions, or activities taken to bring about a desired result or achieve a goal.

5. **Process maturity.** A relative assessment of an organization's ability to achieve its goals through the technical and managerial processes it uses to develop its products and services.

6. **Productivity.** In economics, productivity is defined as the ratio of output to input so that the efficiency and effectiveness with which resources (people, equipment, facilities, etc.) are used to produce output of value can be calculated.

7. **Return on investment.** The amount of savings gained (via increased productivity, cost savings, etc.) divided by the investments made to obtain them.

Common Acronyms

The following acronyms are used within the articles in this chapter:

CM	Configuration Management
CMM	Capability Maturity Model
CMMI	Capability Maturity Model Integration
COTS	Commercial-off-the-Shelf
DoD	Department of Defense
EIA	Electronics Industries Alliance
IEEE	Institute of Electrical and Electronics Engineers

KPA	Key Process Area
MA	Measurement and Analysis
NDIA	National Defense Industrial Association
PPQA	Process and Product Quality Assurance
PSP	Personal Software Process
RES	Raytheon Electronic Systems
ROI	Return on Investment
SCAMPI	Standard CMMI Appraisal Method for Process improvement
SEI	Software Engineering Institute
SEPG	Software Engineering Process Group
SPI	Software Process Improvement
SPIN	Software Process Improvement Networks
SW-CMM	Software Capability Maturity Model
TQM	Total Quality Management
TSP	Team Software Process

For Your Bookshelf

The two texts that I recommend for understanding process maturity models and concepts are Humphrey's *Managing the Software Process* and Chrisis's *CMMI*. The first book provides insight into the CMM model and how it was derived, whereas the second details the processes and practices upon which the CMMI is currently based. For those interested in a more top-level book on Capability Maturity Model Integration (CMMI), the book that I would recommend is Ahern's *CMMI Distilled: A Practical Introduction to Integrated Process Improvement* (2nd Edition).

The Software Engineering Institute (SEI) publishes a great deal of material on process maturity on its web site (http://www.sei.cmu). Besides the most up-to-date frameworks, it publishes a Process Maturity Profile of the Software Community, the SPIN Directory, a listing of local groups interested in process improvement, and a list of SEI Qualified Appraisers. It holds an annual conference and offers a variety of seminars on CMM topics including the CMMI and its associated appraisal methods. It also has published a number of experience reports on the topic. Contact SEI customer relations in Pittsburgh, PA, directly via phone at 412-268-5000 or e-mail at customer-relations@sei.cmu.edu to get more information on the products and services they offer.

Finally, the IEEE has published a *Standard for Developing Life Cycle Processes,* IEEE Std 1074-1997 and several other pertinent standards and guides. Unfortunately, the IEEE Standard is not fully compatible with those in the SEI Software CMM or CMMI. If you are SEI compliant, mappings will have to be made to address this problem. You can order the standard directly from the IEEE Service Center in New Jersey via phone at 800-678-4333 or e-mail at customer.service@ieee.org.

Successful Process Implementation

Anna Börjesson, *Ericsson*

Lars Mathiassen, *Georgia State University*

How do you measure success in software process improvement? The answer is perhaps not as straightforward as it seems. Success is traditionally measured as the difference in quality and productivity between the old and new engineering practices.[1] However, this measure requires systematic benchmarking and data collection over long periods of time, and few software organizations can meet this demand. So, how can we more realistically measure SPI and

practically guide our SPI efforts toward success?

We propose measuring SPI success through *implementation success*—the extent to which initiatives lead to actual changes in software engineering practice. First, without implementation success, SPI success is impossible. Second, only when implementation succeeds can we see how SPI initiatives affect software practices. Third, implementation success is easy to assess. Finally, focusing on implementation success is a pragmatic way to steer SPI initiatives toward success.

We studied the approach and outcome of 18 different SPI initiatives conducted over a five-year period at the telecom company Ericsson AB, based in Gothenburg, Sweden. Doing so gave us insight into how SPI initiatives can best

- Ensure stakeholder commitment

- Support organizational learning
- Distribute resources over different activities
- Manage customer relations

The Ericsson experience

Ericsson has provided packet-data solutions for the international market for more than 20 years and is among the world leaders in this area. Between 1995 and 2001, the company grew from 150 to 900 employees. During this period, SPI played a key role in improving software productivity and quality, and the company conducted many SPI initiatives with varying degrees of success. The initiatives were executed in the same organizational context and, in most cases, involved the same SPI people. The initiatives also followed the same IDEAL approach[2] to SPI (see "The IDEAL Model" sidebar): After *initiation*, the initiatives went through one or more cycles of *diagnosing* problems, *establishing* focused improvements, *acting* to improve, and *learning* from results.

However, the SPI initiatives had important differences (see Table 1). They focused on different improvement areas, had different vol-

> Traditional approaches to measuring software process improvement are typically lengthy, data intensive, and cost prohibitive. A simple indicator, the extent to which engineering practices change, can provide enough information to guide initiatives toward success.

Reprinted from *IEEE Software,* July/August 2004.

The IDEAL Model

The IDEAL (Initiating, Diagnosing, Establishing, Acting, and Learning) approach,[1] developed in 1996 by the Carnegie Mellon University Software Engineering Institute (www.sei.cmu.edu/ideal), presents a five-phase, cyclic approach to software process improvement.

The initiating phase (see Figure A) is where you establish the initial improvement infrastructure, define the initial roles and responsibilities for the infrastructure, and assign initial resources. You create an SPI plan to guide the organization through the completion of the initiating, diagnosing, and establishing phases. Also, you obtain approval for the SPI initiative along with a commitment of future resources for the tasks ahead.

The diagnosing phase lays the groundwork for the later phases. The SPI action plan is initiated in accordance with the organization's vision, strategic business plan, lessons learned from past improvement efforts, key business issues the organization faces, and long-range goals. You perform appraisal activities to establish a baseline of the organization's current software operation. You reconcile the results and recommendations from the appraisals with existing and planned improvement efforts for inclusion into the SPI action plan.

During the establishing phase, you prioritize the issues that the organization has decided to address with its improvement activities and develop strategies for pursuing the solutions. You detail and complete the SPI action plan on the basis of the adopted strategy and the decisions made. You design focused projects to address each prioritized improvement area.

In the acting phase, you create, pilot,

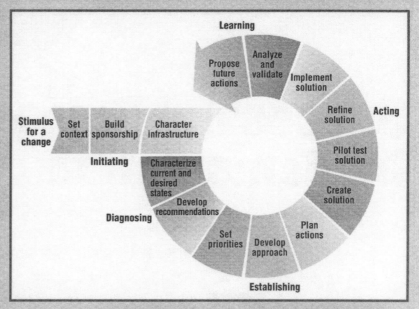

Figure A. The IDEAL model presents a five-phase approach to software process improvement. (Special permission to reproduce "Ideal Model Graphic," © 2003 by Carnegie Mellon University, is granted by the Software Engineering Institute.)

and deploy throughout the organization solutions to address the areas for improvement discovered during the diagnosing phase. You develop plans to execute pilots to test and evaluate the new or improved processes. After piloting these processes and determining their readiness for organization-wide adoption, deployment, and institutionalization, you develop and execute plans to accomplish the rollout.

The learning phase (called the "leveraging" phase when IDEAL debuted) aims to make the next pass through the IDEAL model more effective. By this time, you've developed solutions, learned lessons, and collected metrics on performance and goal achievement. These artifacts are added to the process database as a source of information for personnel involved in the next pass through the model. Also, on the basis of this information, you can evaluate the strategy, methods, and infrastructure used in the SPI program. By doing this, you can correct or adjust the strategy, methods, or infrastructure prior to executing the IDEAL model's next cycle.

Depending on the resources organizations commit to their SPI program, they can pursue IDEAL activities in parallel, and some parts of the organization can pursue activities in one phase of the model while others pursue activities in a different phase.

---

ume, and targeted different parts of the organization. In addition, the initiatives adopted assorted improvement tactics and went through a varying number of IDEAL model cycles. Also, while commitment is generally recognized as a key factor in SPI success,[1,2] different social forces drove each initiative.[3] The *process push* depends on the competence, commitment, and active participation of *process engineers* in developing and implementing new engineering practices. The *practice pull* instead depends on

the competence, commitment, and active participation of *software practitioners* in developing and adopting new practices. These differences in improvement tactics (that is, the number of iterations, degree of process push, and degree of practice pull) resulted in varying levels of implementation success.

SPI participants collected data both during and after the initiatives using time-reporting systems, project specifications, final reports, and interviews with process engineers and

Table I

Process implementation data on Ericsson's software process improvement projects

SPI initiative	Improvement area	Volume	Target	Ideal iterations	Process push
1	Configuration management	10 weeks 300 person-hours 4 participants	Several units	1 full cycle	Weak. Process engineers focused on designing a generic process, with no commitment to or plan for actually deploying the process.
2	Design information	21 weeks 400 person-hours 6 participants	Several units	1 full cycle; stopped during establishing in the second cycle	Weak. Process engineers focused on designing a generic process, with no commitment to or plan for actually deploying the process.
3	Estimation and planning	14 weeks 600 person-hours 11 participants	Several units	1 full cycle; stopped during establishing in the second cycle	Weak. Process engineers focused on designing a generic process. Time for mentoring and process deployment was limited.
4	Historical data	16 weeks 200 person-hours 4 participants	Several units	1 full cycle	Weak. Process engineers focused on identifying historical data, little of which had been recorded. SPI participants planned very few activities to communicate the results.
5	Introductory training	14 weeks 620 person-hours 11 participants	Several units	1 full cycle	Weak. Process engineers were dedicated to defining and describing the process. No plans for how to deploy the process and support its actual use.
6	Module tests	12 weeks 400 person-hours 10 participants	Several units	1 full cycle; stopped during establishing in the second cycle	Weak. Process engineers focused on designing a generic process. Too little time was planned to help the project actually use the result.
7	Project tracking	9 weeks 300 person-hours 7 participants	Several units	1 full cycle; stopped during establishing in the second cycle	Weak. Process engineers were given time only to define a process, not to implement it in projects.
8	Resource handling	4 weeks 250 person-hours 8 participants	Several units	1 full cycle	Weak. Process engineers focused on solving the problem through a well-defined process.
9	Requirements management	10 weeks 200 person-hours 5 participants	Several units	1 full cycle	Weak. Participants spent most of the time defining requirements management; they planned little time to help implement the results.
10	Requirements management implementation	12 weeks 330 person-hours 7 participants	Project	1 full cycle; stopped during establishing in the second cycle	Strong. Management made time for the process engineers to help implement the project results.
11	Subcontract management	18 weeks 650 person-hours 9 participants	Several units	1 full cycle	Weak. Process engineers were strongly committed to solving the problems, but the resulting process wasn't grounded in current practices. No time was planned for activities to make change happen.
12	Requirements management	30 weeks 1,200 person-hours 3 participants	Project	4 full cycles; stopped during diagnosing in the fifth cycle	Strong. Management made time for process engineers to mentor and support the project in action. The SPI initiative was dedicated to solving the problems for one project.
13	Analysis and design	30 weeks 1,000 person-hours 4 participants	Unit	5 full cycles; stopped during establishing in the sixth cycle	Strong. Process engineers planned the deployment activities and made time available for mentoring and support.
14	Implementation	30 weeks 1,000 person-hours 4 participants	Project	4 full cycles	Strong. Management gave process engineers time to participate in the project to support implementing the results.
15	Test	30 weeks 1,300 person-hours 2 participants	Unit	4 full cycles	Strong. Process engineers participated in software tests and came to understand the tester's specific needs.
16	Configuration management	30 weeks 1,650 person-hours 6 participants	Unit	4 full cycles; stopped during diagnosing in the fifth cycle	Strong. Management dedicated sufficient resources to daily mentoring and support to make the change happen.
17	Project management	10 weeks 150 person-hours 2 participants	Unit	3 full cycles	Strong. Some process engineers were also customers who would be using the results. The SPI commitment to the initiative was very high.
18	Process development map	30 weeks 200 person-hours 2 participants	Unit	4 full cycles	Strong. Process engineers saw the need for a well-defined process development map to help communicate and deploy all SPI work.

Practice pull	Implementation success
Weak. Projects focused mainly on making generic process descriptions. Practitioners were eager to solve problems on a general level but had little commitment to using the results.	Low. Potential users considered results hard to use. SPI participants used part of the result indirectly, when they applied the knowledge gained to other projects.
Weak. Projects focused mainly on making generic process descriptions. Practitioners were eager to solve problems on a general level but had little commitment to using the results.	Medium/low. The intention was to provide a design framework. The results were mainly implemented in one project that one process engineer worked on.
Medium. Projects were dedicated to solving generic process problems, but only one project manager was interested in actually testing the results.	Low. The results were tested in one project, but the project ran into difficulties. Support was weak, and no one helped the project; resources from the SPI initiative were no longer available to make necessary changes.
Weak. Managers were eager to find out about historical data. When they found very little, their commitment to change dropped dramatically.	Low. The purpose was to build a database of old data and take action from there. Participants found no interesting data and thus made no changes.
Strong. The result was focused on supporting managers who were asking for help and interested in applying the results.	Medium. An estimated 50 percent of managers used the process. Some didn't know about it and weren't given the opportunity to learn about it. The SPI initiative gave managers supporting guidelines. More assistance was sometimes needed.
Weak. Many practitioners believed in performing systematic module tests, but no one was committed or given the time to implement the results.	Medium/low. The process was used only when process engineers were members of a project or when section managers strongly believed in systematic module tests.
Weak. Most project managers believed good follow-up on a project was necessary, but only one was committed and willing to try out the results in practice. Everyone else waited to see if someone else benefited from the process.	Medium/low. Only one project, which was supported by the SPI initiative's driver, used the process. That project team was content with the outcome.
Medium. The managers believed in supporting resource handling, and most of them were willing to use the result.	Medium. An estimated 75 percent of managers used the new process. Those not using the results either didn't get the help they needed or didn't believe in the approach.
Weak. Everyone knew that managing requirements was important, but no one was committed to acting on the results in his own project.	Low. The results were hard to use. They were used mainly as a framework by the members of the SPI initiative.
Weak. The targeted project was interested but not committed to spending the time required to make the change happen.	Medium. Initiative 9's low impact spurred this initiative. This initiative focused on one project, and all results were designed to suit its needs.
Weak. Managers were strongly committed to creating better routines for subcontract management, but no time was planned for the projects to actually implement the new process.	Low. The results needed further adaptation to be useful for different projects, but no one tried to tailor them. Project engineers used some results indirectly in other projects.
Strong. A few highly respected practitioners were strongly committed to the initiative. They helped ensure the results would actually be used.	High. The process was adapted to a specific project but needed further adaptation to be useful. Process engineers and practitioners solved these problems jointly and made the change happen.
Strong. A few well-respected practitioners were convinced (after a few difficult weeks) of the need for improved practices and committed to making them happen.	Medium/high. This is a complex area and required several iterations of experimenting with processes before the result was satisfactory.
Strong. The practitioners were receptive to adopting a stronger focus on implementation, and they participated actively in the change process.	High. Two slightly different adaptations were made to fit the needs of different products developed on different sites. Collaboration between process engineers and software practitioners made the change happen.
Strong. The practitioners came to understand that the SPI initiative was responsive to their specific needs, and they became committed to using the results.	High. The result was adapted to the specific needs of a specific project. Process engineers and software practitioners solved difficulties together.
Strong. The configuration managers were highly involved in both defining and deploying the results.	High. Each specific situation has hundreds of possible solutions. Choosing one and focusing on making that happen required extra attention. The software practitioners' dedication played a key role.
Strong. The project managers wanted to implement their own ideas and took the time to do it.	High. The results were actually used, and the project managers' dedication to SPI work within project management continued.
Strong. All software practitioners needed a process description that would provide templates, guidelines, and other relevant information.	High. The development-process map's use is measured in both "hits" to a site on the process web and subjective opinions of need. All measurements are very positive.

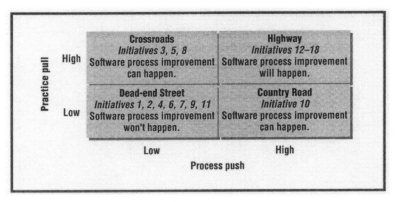

Figure 1. Four roads to process implementation.

software practitioners. One of us was directly involved in and responsible for all of these initiatives; the other had conducted SPI research in many other organizations. Analyzing the data revealed how important it is to actively manage commitment, learning, resource distribution, and customer relations if SPI efforts are to succeed.

Managing commitment

Categorizing Ericsson's SPI initiatives on the basis of the degree of process push and practice pull, we arrive at four different roads to process implementation (see Figure 1).

The Dead-end Street initiatives focused on the process itself—specifically, on process definition and specification. The initiatives targeted several Ericsson units, but the new process was often hard to apply because process engineers had to make many compromises to meet everyone's needs. The process push toward implementation was low because the process engineers focused on defining a generally applicable process. Few resources and incentives existed for the process engineers to become engaged in the involved units' different engineering cultures. The practice pull was also low because it was difficult to engage software practitioners from different units in one common initiative. Needs and backgrounds differed across the units, and they had no tradition for communication and collaboration across units. The Dead-end Street initiatives never amounted to much. No one was seriously committed to implement the processes, so the organization saw little overall benefit.

The Country Road initiative targeted a specific project's engineering practices. The process engineers worked in the project and had time to help implement the results. The

process engineers, therefore, understood the particular culture and practices in the project, and they were strongly committed to support and change practices. They focused on requirement issues and created a process that fit the project's particular needs. However, the practitioner commitment was weak. The software practitioners weren't motivated to change requirements practices. They didn't understand why they had to be involved and didn't allocate time to work with process implementation. The process push was high, but the practice pull was low. A typical Country Road initiative can happen, but it's slow going and likely to fall short of changing engineering practices.

The Crossroads initiatives targeted several company-level units with similar requirements. Practices and needs across the units had little variation, so process compromises were unnecessary. The practice pull was high: Software practitioners understood the need for new processes and were committed to using them. But the process engineers failed to allocate sufficient time and resources to implement the process, so the process push was low. A typical Crossroads initiative can happen, and at Ericsson, the initiatives might succeed. However, the software practitioners might yet face barriers to effective implementation,[4] and process engineers are no longer available to guide them and facilitate the change process.

The Highway initiatives targeted practices in a single unit or project. The main focus was on solving specific problems identified by software practitioners, and they required few compromises. Both process push and practice pull were high. The process engineers were committed and allocated time to process implementation, and the software practitioners understood why they needed the new approaches and appreciated the SPI initiative. The process engineers and the software practitioners worked closely together and communicated intensively about needs, problems, and progress. A typical Highway initiative will happen, and engineers will implement and use the results. Organizations directly benefit from such initiatives.

Managing learning

Successfully changing software practices requires learning, and helping organizations learn is by no means easy.[5,6] Iterations support learning by letting you correct failures and modify processes based on practical experience. Although CMM founder Watts Humphrey doesn't use the word *iteration*, he does discuss the importance of performing SPI work in steps and repeatable sequences.[1] Several SPI approaches emphasize iterative development, including the IDEAL model[2] and methods that implement plan-do-act-check cycles.[7]

We examined how Ericsson's SPI initiatives used iterations and feedback from practice to support learning. Figure 2 illustrates the relation between the initiatives' implementation success and the number of iterations they executed. As the figure shows, the number of iterations significantly affected SPI implementation success: As the number of iterations increased, so too did implementation success.

However, because factors apart from iterations affect implementation success, this pattern has exceptions. Initiatives 5 and 8, for example, executed a single iteration but still achieved moderate implementation success. One possible explanation is that both initiatives had high practice pull. Also, Initiative 13 executed two iterations in the last phase alone and still failed to achieve high implementation success, while Initiative 17 executed only three iterations total and was highly successful. Compared to the other initiatives, however, Initiative 13 was by far the most complex and difficult and consumed the most time and expertise. In contrast, Initiative 17 had an experienced project manager who exercised considerable practice pull. So, projects can succeed with few iterations. In general, however, more iterations support more learning and better facilitate change.

To further illustrate the importance of iterations, we mapped each initiative to Gerald Weinberg's four phases of successful change (see Figure 3).[8] As the figure shows, initial attempts to introduce a new process lead to chaos. The process then becomes integrated as engineers attempt to practice it, eventually giving rise to a new and stable status quo of engineering practices. However, each phase has barriers that make implementation difficult, and these barriers can cause the process to regress to previous phases.

As Figure 3 illustrates, an initiative typically took one full iteration to pass one phase in Weinberg's change model. Most SPI initiatives must pass the chaos phase and enter the

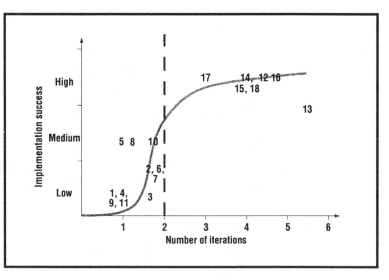

Figure 2. Implementation success and number of iterations (1 through 18). More iterations meant more implementation success.

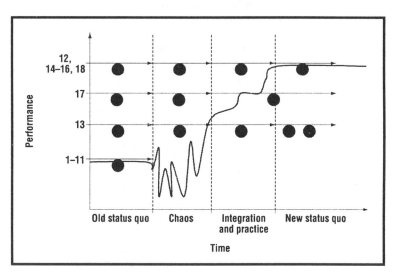

Figure 3. Performance and distribution of iterations (numbered 1 through 18). The jagged line illustrates Weinberg's optimum learning curve. The circles denote the number and distribution of iterations over phases.

integration and practice phase to successfully implement a new or modified process. SPI initiatives that execute only a single iteration will therefore seldom enter the phase of using the new process as an integral part of engineering practices. Thus, the process simply won't be adopted as intended.

Managing resources

As Humphrey says, "SPI requires investment—it takes planning, dedicated people, management time, and capital investment," and, for an organization to improve, "someone must work on it."[1] To drive SPI work toward success, organizations must commit and manage their resources accordingly, and they

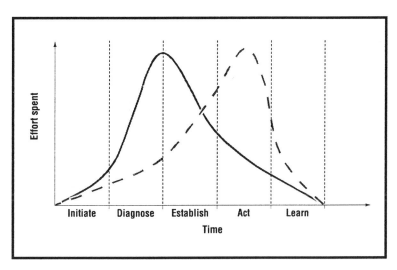

Figure 4. Effort spent over IDEAL phases. Initiatives that overinvested in early phases, represented by Initiative 1 (the red curve), had low implementation success. Initiatives that invested most resources in later phases, represented by Initiative 12 (the green curve), had high implementation success.

must constantly motivate people to participate and contribute. Any significant change can create substantial fear and uncertainty throughout the organization. It's essential that process engineers possess change-management skills.[8] Skillful change agents can work closely with software practitioners to solve potential difficulties that arise regarding both the new process and the change process itself.

Ericsson's process engineers managed resources quite differently in the SPI initiatives. Figure 4 shows how the process engineers distributed their time over the IDEAL model's phases[2] in two ways. Initiative 1 is representative of the pattern in initiatives 1 through 11. It had low implementation success, and engineers invested most of their effort into the model's early phases (the red curve). Initiative 12 is representative of initiatives 12 through 18. It had high implementation success, and the process engineers invested most of their effort in the model's later phases (the green curve). As this comparison indicates, spending considerable effort in the model's later phases might be more successful than putting most effort into early phases. Most of Initiative 1's process-engineering resources were used to analyze, design, and describe the new process. This meant few resources were available during the difficult implementation phases, in which software practitioners can experience

significant fear and uncertainty. Because Initiative 12 invested considerable resources in these later phases, the process engineers could better manage and address change issues as they emerged.

Managing customer relations

To achieve SPI success, process engineers must have a positive, collaborative relationship with their customers, the software practitioners.[9] Positive customer relations will help process engineers better understand engineering practices and problems and thus develop more useful processes. A good relationship also helps software practitioners overcome their resistance to change: When the status quo is challenged, they often become defensive and alienated.[8]

For managing customer relations, a dedicated SPI approach seems more likely to succeed. As Table 1 shows, Initiatives 1 through 11 generally supported several units and thus used a relatively generic SPI approach that achieved moderate success at best. Initiatives 12 through 18 supported only one project or unit and used a more dedicated approach with greater overall success. Of course, other factors influence SPI outcome, and rules always have exceptions. Nonetheless, generic approaches make it difficult for process engineers to build and maintain good customer relations—there are too many different relationships, needs, and requirements. In dedicated approaches, process engineers and software practitioners can work closely together and focus on the project's specific challenges. Also, in generic approaches, it's difficult to handle the many personalities and requirements when relationships with the software practitioners become fragile. In such situations, it's much easier for process engineers to simply focus on the process design and description and forget about troublesome implementation issues.

Lessons learned

Our experiences with the Ericsson initiatives offered several lessons about how organizations can more successfully manage SPI.

Focus on implementation

When it comes to software, we already know that test-and-repair strategies fail to deliver quality. To achieve quality, software projects must consider it and plan for it from the start. Similarly, in an SPI initiative, you should consider implementation issues early on. Such considerations should include[10]

- Critically evaluating the new process from an easy-to-adopt standpoint
- Examining the roles that stakeholders must play during implementation
- Choosing an implementation strategy that suits the initiative
- Assessing and resolving implementation risks
- Outlining an initial plan for implementation

Such early focus on implementation can help you design processes that software practitioners are more likely to adopt and thereby reduce the risk of failure.

Take the Highway

To succeed with SPI, you need a serious commitment from key stakeholders.[1,7] To develop this commitment, you must ensure that process engineers have sufficient change-management skills and resources to create high process push. This in turn facilitates the active involvement of software practitioners to create high practice pull. Also, it's important to focus on the cultural environment of the change process.[11] Are the involved actors motivated? Are senior and middle managers involved? Are the recognition and reward systems appropriate? And, is communication between the involved actors supportive? The Highway is the best route to SPI implementation success. The Country Road and Crossroads are risky and require additional attention and resources to create complementary pull and push, respectively. As its name implies, the Dead-End Street leads nowhere.

Iterate, iterate, iterate

SPI initiatives that execute only a single iteration never enter the phase in which the new process is exposed to practice. In such initiatives, the process engineers get no feedback on whether the process is useful, and the process won't likely be used. SPI initiatives that execute several iterations are more likely to enter and pass through the phase in which practitioners resist change; when the defined process meets actual practice, process engineers can learn and react. The result is a process that practitioners will likely use. If you plan for several itera-

tions, you're more likely to overcome resistance to change and facilitate learning.

Expect chaos

At Ericsson, process engineers initially perceived some initiatives, such as Initiative 1, as successful because the operations went smoothly. They viewed other initiatives, such as 12, as problematic because they caused debate, anxiety, and active resistance among software practitioners. Paradoxically, Initiative 1's implementation ultimately met with low success, while Initiative 12 was highly successful. The explanation is simple: If you emphasize process analysis and design, you won't experience the tension that arises between your design and current engineering practices. If, on the contrary, you engage in process implementation activities, you'll be confronted with misfits and psychological reactions. You should therefore expect a certain level of chaos in SPI initiatives. Chaos is often a sign that the implementation process is on its way and that you're about to receive valuable information that will help you succeed.

Focus on action

Achieving SPI success is difficult if process engineers aren't involved in the action phase of the IDEAL model, in which practitioners experience considerable fear and uncertainty.[2] During implementation, process engineers with change artistry[8] should work closely with software practitioners to resolve difficulties with both the new process and the process of change. You should, therefore, distribute available resources to ensure that process engineers and software practitioners are actively involved throughout the initiative, until the process has been successfully implemented.

Organize dedicated initiatives

SPI initiatives that target several units and projects often lack the resources and motivation needed to address the extremely complex change issues involved. Process engineers also sometimes prefer the early IDEAL model phases, in which they analyze and design the process, rather than the later phases, in which their challenge is to handle resistance and other barriers to change.[2] SPI initiatives supporting a single project or unit are less time consuming, require no compromises, and make it easier to create an open, collaborative relation-

> **Chaos is often a sign that the implementation process is on its way and that you're about to receive valuable information that will help you succeed.**

About the Authors

Anna Börjesson is a software process improvement manager at Ericsson AB in Gothenburg, Sweden, and an industrial PhD student at the IT University in Gothenburg. Her software engineering skills cover such areas as CMM, Rational Unified Process, Rational Tool Suite, SW metrics, SW quality assurance, change management, SW diffusion and implementation theories, and SW process adaptation work. She received her M.Sc. in informatics from Gothenburg University. She's a member of the IEEE and ACM. Contact her at Ericsson AB, Lindholmspiren 11, 417 56 Gothenburg, Sweden; anna.borjesson@ericsson.com.

Lars Mathiassen is a professor of computer information systems at Georgia State University. His research interests include information systems and software engineering, with a particular focus on business process innovation. He received his Dr. Techn. in software engineering from Aalborg University. He's a member of the IEEE, ACM, and AIS and coauthor of *Computers in Context* (Blackwell, 1993), *Object Oriented Analysis & Design* (Marko Publishing, 2000), and *Improving Software Organizations* (Addison-Wesley, 2002). Contact him at the Center for Process Innovation, J. Mack Robinson College of Business, Georgia State Univ., PO Box 5029, Atlanta, GA 30302-5029; lmathiassen@gsu.edu; www.mathiassen.eci.gsu.edu.

O ur experiences at Ericsson focus on improvement tactics that affect SPI implementation success. You should, however, be cautious when you transfer the lessons to other software organizations. Factors such as process complexity, volume of initiative, organizational culture, and individual skills also affect SPI outcome. And, of course, there are always exceptional situations and those in which other approaches to process implementation are feasible. Ultimately, these are guidelines, not absolute truths. Our advice is to stay pragmatic but actively use these lessons to guide your SPI initiatives toward success. ∿

ship between process engineers and software practitioners. You should, therefore, opt for dedicated SPI initiatives over generic ones whenever possible.

References

1. W.S. Humphrey, *Managing the Software Process*, Addison-Wesley, 1989.
2. B. McFeeley, *IDEAL: A User's Guide for Software Process Improvement*, tech. report CMU/SEI-96-HB-001, Software Eng. Inst., Carnegie Mellon Univ., 1996; www.sei.cmu.edu/pub/documents/96.reports/pdf/hb001.96.pdf.
3. R.W. Zmud, "An Examination of 'Push-Pull' Theory Applied to Process Innovation in Knowledge Work," *Management Science*, vol. 30, no. 6, 1984, pp. 727–738.
4. R.G. Fichman and C.F. Kemerer, "The Assimilation of Software Process Innovations: An Organizational Learning Perspective," *Management Science*, vol. 43, no. 10, 1997, pp. 1345–1363.
5. C. Argyris and D. Schön, *Organizational Learning*, Addison-Wesley, 1978.
6. J.S. Brown and P. Duguid, "Organization Learning and Communities-of-Practice: Toward a Unified View of Working, Learning and Innovation," *Organization Science*, vol. 2, no. 1, 1991, pp. 40–57.
7. R.B. Grady, *Successful Software Process Improvement*, Prentice Hall, 1997.
8. G.M. Weinberg, *Quality Software Management, Volume IV: Anticipating Change*, Dorset House, 1997.
9. L. Mathiassen, P.A. Nielsen, and J. Pries-Heje, "Learning SPI in Practice," *Improving Software Organizations: From Principles to Practice*, L. Mathiassen, J. Pries-Heje, and O. Ngwenyama, eds., Addison-Wesley, 2002, pp. 3–21.
10. S. Tryde, A.-D. Nielsen, and J. Pries-Heje, "A Framework for Organizational Implementation of Software Process Improvement in Practice," *Improving Software Organizations: From Principles to Practice*, L. Mathiassen, J. Pries-Heje, and O. Ngwenyama, eds., Addison-Wesley, 2002, pp. 257–271.
11. P. Fowler and M. Patrick, *Transition Packages for Expediting Technology Adoption: The Prototype Requirements Management Transition Package*, tech. report CMU/SEI-98-TR-004, Software Eng. Inst., Carnegie Mellon Univ., 1998.

The Definitive Paper: Quantifying the Benefits of Software Process Improvement

Don Reifer, Al Chatmon, and C. Doug Walters

This paper summarizes the tangible and intangible benefits that Northrop Grumman Electronics Systems has reaped from its process improvement program. It puts facts and figures in the public domain to help others make the business case for process improvement. This is an actual case study that shows that investing in process improvement pays off.

1. Introduction

Northrop Grumman Electronics Systems (ES) initiated its process improvement program in the late 1980s. They were forced to do it because it was a customer requirement (i.e., these were not forced but were instead recognized as an implied requirement). At the time, there was lots of resistance to change. ES was rated a level 2 in 1987 and level 3 in 1989 by an in-house team with observers from the Software Engineering Institute present during the assessment. As an early adopter, ES went through all the trials and tribulations that you normally read about in the case studies that have appeared since that time.

ES stayed at level 3 for almost a decade. Investment in process improvement was refocused onto ISO compliance and management viewed the business requirement as having been met. ES was winning contracts and performing well. However, in 1996 the General Manager resurrected process improvement when a customer survey identified software as an area needing improvement. In response, an aggressive program to be recertified a level 3 and reach level 4 was mounted.

2. Environment

Northrop Grumman ES builds some of the best sensors in the world. Their radars fly in the F 16 and F22 fighters. They build air traffic control systems and outfit eyes in the sky like the Defense Meteorological Support Program. They have a professional workforce of more than 600 software engineers working on hundreds of embedded system projects that provide the intelligence for such systems. Their programs are large and small, new and old. The software ES produces is complex, life-critical, and runs in real time.

Engineering management has run hot and cold over the years when it comes to process improvement. However, ES has had solid support from its executive staff since 1996. Like most in the industry, ES has formed a process group and used it to write processes and put them into practice. Unlike most, ES has staffed its process group with 30 year veterans, senior management, and technical personnel, some of whom came back from retirement, to lead projects through the transition. Use of people who are known and are respected by those in the organization is deemed one of ES's critical success factors.

Costs for the software process improvement program have averaged about $2 million annually. This budget covers the process group, training, and the transition activities. ES's philosophy has been and remains one of partnership with projects. They let their projects tailor the process to the specifics of the application. The process group budget provides charge numbers for key people to participate in working groups, process authorship, and reviews. Projects fund the remainder of the activities, including training, deployment, and tailoring.

3. Process Improvement Strategy

The goal of ES's process improvement program was to put processes in place that made a difference. They were not concerned with process for the purpose of process. Instead, they wanted to generate products quicker, better, and cheaper than their competition. They succeeded because they tied process improvement to business goals. Their strategy, initiated in 1996, revolved around achieving these goals. The two primary objectives were:

1. **Accelerate productivity gains.** Investment strategy for productivity was reoriented to process in order to accelerate gains made through improvement in management practices.
2. **Move to the use of product lines, architecture, and systematic reuse.** ES was convinced that developing avionics product lines that permitted systematic reuse of software from project to project based upon a reference architecture was the way to go.

Prior to 1996, ES had pursued these two strategies piecemeal. In 1996, they developed a process improvement plan that focused attention and investment dollars on making these four things happen in a planned and systematic manner. This plan has yielded both tangible benefits that justify the investment and justify process improvement based upon its returns.

4. Tangible Benefits

Most of the information we have seen in the literature about process improvement has harped on the benefits without putting numbers around them. Although useful, such discussions do not help the community make a strong business case for process improvement. Because we have developed such numbers to convince our internal critics that process improvement pays dividends, we want to share them with the community. However, we must do so in such a way that we do not let our competition know our actual costs.

4.1. Accelerating Productivity Gains through Process

The average gain in productivity that ES experienced during the past 5 years as it moved from Level 3 to 4 was approximately 20% annually. During their static years, the nominal gain was 10% annually. We can thereby conclude that gain accelerated by 10% a year based upon a strategy that was heavily software-process-improvement based. Such acceleration results in a cost avoidance averaging $25 million annually over a 5 year investment time span based upon the analysis in Table 1. It should be noted that we assume no gain during the first year of the investment strategy. We also assume a static workforce. Both of these assumptions simplify the analysis and make the results very conservative.

The nondiscounted ROI due to productivity improvements alone is calculated as follows:

$$ROI = (\$125.1M - \$10M)/\$10M = 1251, \text{ or } 250 \text{ annually}$$

Of course, this is not a true number. However, it does illustrate the benefits that have accrued, which are more than the numbers provided in this paper suggest.

Table 1. Dollar savings attributed to accelerating productivity from 10 to 20% annually

	Year 1	Year 2	Year 3	Year 4	Year 5
Current productivity (SLOC/staff-month) (10 nominal gain)	105	116	127	140	154
Accelerated gain (20%)	—	126	151	181	218
Additional number of SLOCs that can be generated via acceleration, assuming 600 engineers	—	72,000	172,800	295,200	460,800
Cost avoidance ($125/SLOC)	$9.0 million	$21.6 million	$36.9 million	$57.6 million	
Cumulative cost avoidance	—	$9.0 million	—	—	—

Note: For competitive reasons, we have used a base productivity of 105 SLOC/staff-month as the basis of our analysis. This is not current productivity. The cost of $125/SLOC assumed is also not actual cost/SLOC. These numbers are industry averages taken from a productivity report that represents the cost for the military airborne domain. These numbers are conservative and used to illustrate the benefits.

4.2. Movement to Product Lines, Architecture, and Systematic Reuse

The hardest part of the strategy to implement was moving to architecture-based avionics software product lines. The reason behind this is that the SW-CMM and CMMI offer little structure for initiatives in this area. For the most part, ES was on its own to develop processes in this area. Because they are a defense contractor, they also have many restrictions that make it difficult to share software developed for one project with another. Sharing is not something that customers encourage or provide financial incentives for. But ES wanted to leverage its previous work to be more competitive. Therefore, they took the risk and moved ahead, paving the way for others to follow.

Northrop Grumman ES has been pursuing systematic reuse for over a decade on internal research and development and technology research projects. They completed a domain analysis and developed a radar system architecture, both hardware and software, that facilitates reuse at the system level in the mid-1990s. Their goal was to deploy this architecture using product line management concepts by making it part of the processes their engineers used to do their work. In response, the engineers incorporated reuse provisions into processes as they were developed or updated for Level 4.

The benefits attributed to systematic reuse are many and substantial. Reuse saves money and time by making big jobs smaller. Table 2 illustrates this savings by using an example. It shows how exploiting an existing architecture that is maintained using product line management concepts can reduce the effective size in SLOCs of a typical job by half. Although these numbers are hypothetical, they are in the ballpark for a real system that has many more modes.

The benefits of cutting the size in half can be quantified using a simple cost model like COCOMO II. Using the model with its nominal settings for cost drivers for the example summarized in Table 2 results in the effort and duration estimates in Table 3. Both nominal and shortest development time options are estimated. The only cost driver varied was Process Maturity (PMAT). It was set to reflect a Level 4 organization.

The example in Table 3 illustrates the benefits associated with reuse. It suggests that about half the cost (e.g., about $5 million) and as much as a year can be saved through systematic reuse for this basic radar.

In reality, ES's radar systems are much bigger and more complex than what is shown in Table 3. ES estimated that their cost saving exceeded $5 million on each new radar using the reference architecture developed and the infrastructure introduced. Multiply this savings across the four product lines that were developed and we estimate savings of at least $20 million annually. However, there are increased costs associated with maintaining architecture and designing assets for reuse. The cost/benefits that result as a product of this fourth prong of the initiative are summarized in Table 4 across all product lines.

The ROI associated with this part of our strategy alone is therefore computed as follows:

ROI = $19.2M/$800K = 240, or 48 a year across the 5 year planning horizon

Table 2. Size of application with/without reuse

Application	Without reuse	With Reuse
Executive	10,000	500
Radar Scheduler	30,000	0
Radar Mode 1—Search	50,000	10,000
Radar Mode 2—Precision Track	50,000	25,000
BIT/FIT (hardware specific)	60,000	60,000
Total	200,000	95,500

Table 3. Effort and duration estimates with and without reuse

	Without reuse	With reuse
Nominal development time (months)	30	23.4
Nominal effort (staff-months)	845.3	383.7
Shortest development time (months)	22.5	17.6
Shortest development time effort (staff-months)	1208.7	548.7

Table 4. Cost/benefits associated with product lines, architectures, and systematic Reuse

Nonrecurring costs		Tangible benefits	
• Domain engineering	Completed on IR&D	• Cost avoidance	$20 million
• Infrastructure	Done by process development group		
		Intangible benefits	
Recurring costs		• Deliver 12 months earlier than the norm	
• Architecture maintenance	$200K	• 10 times reduction in errors upon delivery	
• Asset maintenance	$500K	• Architecture stable, proven, and can be be demonstrated	
• Process updates	$100K	• Scheduling algorithms for the radar can be optimized and improved each time a new radar is built	
Total costs = S800K		Total benefits = $20 million	

Note: This analysis assumes that the nonrecurring costs are treated as sunk costs.

Again, this is not the true number. EH has in reality been able to realize larger gains through reuse than were first anticipated.

In summary, ES's successes in process improvement and architectural reuse strategies exceeded their initial expectations, even considering that process improvement cannot take credit for all of the productivity gains (i.e., the move toward the use of COTS products, improved tool sets, and increased training also contribute directly to the bottom line). The business case is clear and is being extended to encompass all enterprise disciplines, systems engineering, hardware design, program management, and business operations.

5. Conclusion

Based on the tangible benefits accrued, Northrop Grumman ES has become a true believer in process improvement. Either accelerated productivity or move to product lines alone would have justified our investments. However, the real scorecard is presented monthly at their internal financial reviews. Before the process initiative, ES used to spend hours explaining why many of their software projects had problems delivering acceptable products on schedule and within budget. Today, life is easier. The software organization is run like a business. Few projects are in trouble. Yes, there are still challenges that must be addressed. But ES is not scolded any longer for being the problem on the project. Other organizations are now taking their place in the hot seat.

Although While the numbers we presented are fictitious, the facts are not. Because they have the improvement data, ES can justify its investments. That is why their initiatives have been funded and they are well on the path to achieving level 5, hopefully in a year.

Process Improvement for Small Organizations

To introduce and sustain a software process improvement initiative, a smaller organization must minimize the limitations of its size and maximize the benefits inherent in its culture. The authors describe how this was done at Silicon & Software Systems.

Declan P.
Kelly
Bill Culleton
Silicon &
Software Systems

Software process improvement (SPI) has been a hot topic within the software industry for a number of years. Its high profile has been due in part to the introduction and industry acceptance of standard improvement models, most notably the Capability Maturity Model (CMM)[1] developed by the Software Engineering Institute at Carnegie Mellon University. Large organizations, such as Motorola's Government Electronics Division with 1,500 software engineers, have successfully implemented SPI initiatives and reaped significant benefits.[2] For smaller organizations, these benefits are no less significant, but smaller organizations often operate under different constraints.

For a small organization to introduce and sustain a process improvement initiative, it must minimize the limitations of its smaller size and maximize the benefits inherent in its culture. In this article, we describe an approach to SPI that has been used successfully in an organization of approximately 150 software engineers. Our approach involved as many software engineers as possible while avoiding disruption to ongoing projects.

SMALL-COMPANY ISSUES

The ratio of the effort required to implement a CMM-based SPI initiative in a company of 1,500 software engineers and a company of 150 software engineers will not be 10:1. In fact, for the core activities, excluding training and support, the effort required will not be significantly different. Clearly, the investment that a larger company can afford will usually be significantly greater than the investment that a smaller company can justify. Therefore, smaller organizations have an even more acute need to use SPI resources efficiently; if they don't, the cost of SPI can become prohibitively expensive.

Significant cultural differences exist between small organizations and larger ones. In smaller organizations, employees expect to be involved in all aspects of the software engineering process. Often, this practice is a result of the company's history. When a software company starts off with a handful of people, by necessity, everyone is involved in all aspects of software development. As these start-up companies grow, they often retain this culture of involvement. On the other hand, large organizations can leverage significant efficiency improvements by, for example, having a dedicated group choose computer-aided software engineering (CASE) tools or standards. Therefore, in a large organization, it is not unusual for decisions about the software process to be made outside the software engineering groups. In contrast, software engineers in smaller organizations expect to influence decisions that affect the way they work.

The culture of smaller organizations can often be characterized as creative, dynamic, and innovative. The success of these organizations is often due in no small part to the creativity and innovation of their employees. SPI is frequently viewed as the antithesis of these qualities, leading to bureaucracy that restricts the freedom of individuals. This aspect of small-company culture affects the SPI initiative in two ways. First, the SPI initiative should use the creativity of individuals within the organization to provide innovative solutions to SPI problems. Second, the result of the SPI initiative should not stifle creativity; it should focus creativity on project-specific problems, not standard process issues.

S3'S SPI PROJECT

Silicon & Software Systems (S3) has been providing design services in silicon, software, and hardware design since it was established in 1986. Within the software division, application areas include telecommunications, consumer electronics, Internet, and digital broadcasting.

Reprinted from *Computer,* October 1999.

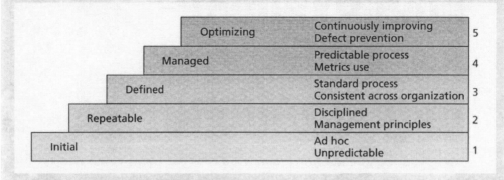
The customer base is diverse and includes many major multinational companies. Because software projects in S3 cover a range of application areas and involve working with many different customers, the SPI process must be flexible enough to accommodate S3's diverse and constantly evolving projects. It would certainly be simpler to mandate a common programming language, design methodology, and set of CASE tools for all projects, but such an approach clearly is not an option for a company like S3. The diversity of S3's projects at first seems a complicating factor, but in practice it results in simplified procedures. This may seem surprising. However, applying quality procedures to such a diverse range of projects forces the procedures to focus on the essential details. The result is that the quality procedures mandate requirements essential to the quality of all projects, but they do not bound the freedom of projects by including arbitrary restrictions.

The starting point for our SPI initiative was an existing quality system—a set of quality procedures and tools to support their use. Throughout its history, S3 has used quality procedures, in many cases based on IEEE software engineering standards. The existing quality system had been certified ISO 9001-compliant.

Goals

The business objectives of our process improvement initiative were to reduce project lead time and improve the quality of the results, which in turn would increase customer satisfaction to the point that customers would keep using S3 as a preferred supplier. We had four main goals.

Maximize involvement, minimize disruption. In pursuing our SPI program, we wanted to involve as many of the software engineering staff as possible. There were two reasons for this. First, it would not be practical to have a dedicated group assigned full-time for the entire project. Second, given the organizational culture, it would not be acceptable to have solutions imposed by a small group.

All the people we wanted to involve were active on projects, which we did not want to disrupt. To deal with this, we broke the SPI work into small tasks, and we defined exactly what was required and how much effort it would take for each task. This approach allowed people to evaluate their project commitments and then commit to the SPI work only if it would not conflict with other project requirements. A single full-time coordinator was assigned to manage the project and coordinate the work of part-time participants.

We made sure that we involved people with varying degrees of experience from all sections of the software group. In particular, we tried to involve people who were skeptical about the need for a defined quality system and for a CMM-based SPI program. The skeptics generally think they know better and so object to what they perceive as restrictions on how they work. In practice, they often do have good ideas about ways of working; the trick is to channel their skepticism into improving the quality system. Involving them can often dissolve their skepticism. As they become immersed in the SPI initiative, they begin to see that it is not an attempt to impose restrictions but rather a way to improve the efficiency and effectiveness of the complete software group. Skeptics can also be some of the most influential individuals within the organization. Consequently, a benefit of converting them to SPI is that they influence others to become involved.

Stress quality, not CMM compliance. Although we were basing our initiative on the CMM, we did not focus exclusively on moving up the levels (see the "Why the Capability Maturity Model?" sidebar). Level 1 has no defined key process areas (KPAs) because it is the starting point; there *is* no defined process. In CMM terms, we were at Level 1 (although we had partially addressed all Level 2 KPAs), and we wanted to be formally assessed for Level 2. First and

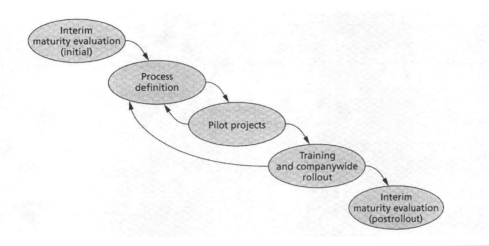

Figure 1. S3's software process improvement initiative. Improvement efforts began in September 1997 with an interim maturity evaluation to determine how S3 assessed relative to the CMM and its key process areas. The next step was to define a proposal for improving the weaker areas. Pilot projects helped validate the proposals. In June 1998, the team was ready to expand the process companywide and establish training. Shortly thereafter, we performed another interim maturity evaluation to gauge progress in addressing the key process areas.

foremost, however, we wanted an efficient and flexible quality system that would promote continuous process improvement.

Although achieving a particular CMM level will no doubt improve software quality,[1,3] there is always the danger of introducing a CMM-compliant process that does not fit your organization or that involves too much overhead. Thus, you have short-term process improvement, but it will be hard to sustain. If, however, the emphasis is on an efficient, flexible, quality system, the process improvement team is likely to keep working on the process definition until that efficiency and flexibility are achieved—even after a CMM-compliant process has been defined.

Also, CMM compliance should never be used to justify a process change. It is always tempting to counter objections to process changes by stating that the changes are a CMM requirement. It is more difficult, but ultimately more rewarding, to explain where the requirement comes from and then discuss the objections with a view to finding an acceptable solution.

Emphasize the advisory role. Most people view a quality system as a set of requirements to be enforced. We wanted the engineers to view it as both defining mandatory requirements and providing helpful advice. Our motto was, "Quality standards should seek to help the user do the job well, rather than just prevent the user from doing it badly."

To follow this motto, we structured the quality procedures in two layers. On the bottom is a set of mandatory requirements (which all projects follow). On the top is a set of optional guidelines, or best practices, which are based on the requirements. We deliberately put best practices in the guidelines layer because not all practices apply to all projects. The choice of which best practice to use is left to the project leader and the project team under the guidance of an independent quality assurance group. This is important because the final responsibility for a project's quality rests with that project's leader and team.

Promote efficiency. To make the quality system efficient, we wanted to be sure that the quality procedures were well written and clearly structured. People should be able to find the information they need without searching through multiple documents or following a chain of cross-references. We also wanted adequate tool support to make the quality system easy to use.

Interim maturity evaluation

Figure 1 shows the steps in our SPI initiative. The first step was a maturity evaluation. Before embarking on the SPI project, we wanted to evaluate our existing process against CMM KPAs. This would give us a baseline against which to measure our improvement. We based our evaluation on an Interim Maturity Evaluation Questionnaire—a set of questions, derived from the KPAs, about the way the organization worked. The evaluation consisted of a discussion based on the questionnaire and guided by an external consultant. The participants first individually scored each question and then as a group discussed questions they disagreed on. The discussion continued until participants agreed on the appropriate score for the organization for each question. We calculated an estimate of compliance for each KPA by averaging the scores for individual questions. In addition to providing us with an objective measure of our current status, the evaluation helped raise awareness of the issues we needed to address to achieve compliance at the next CMM level.

Where we were. In terms of CMM levels, S3 was a Level 1, but the typical description of a Level 1 organization as "unpredictable" (see Figure A) didn't apply. In our opinion, at that time, S3 most closely resembled the CMM Level 3 description: "standard process, consistent across organization." This situation is probably found in many Level 1 organizations: The company has not fully addressed all the Level 2

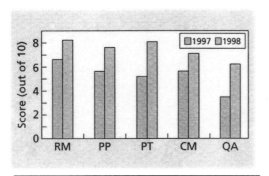

Figure 2. S3's compliance rating in the CMM Level 2 key process areas in September 1997, when the initiative began, and in June 1998, when the initiative was ready to go companywide. The Level 2 KPAs are requirements management (RM), software project planning (PP), software project tracking and oversight (PT), software configuration management (CM), and software quality assurance (QA). The software subcontract management KPA, also in Level 2, is not shown because S3 does not use subcontractors.

KPAs and so remains at Level 1, but it has partially addressed Level 2 and higher KPAs.

Figure 2 shows our compliance rating in Level 2 KPAs when we started our initiative. As the figure indicates, the existing quality system partially addressed all of these issues. It also covered some Level 3 KPAs, such as peer reviews. Many organizations starting a CMM-based SPI initiative will have some level of documented process. Starting an SPI initiative in a pure Level 1 company would be much more difficult.

Where we wanted to go. To achieve CMM Level 2, we needed to address requirements management, software project planning, software project tracking and oversight, software quality assurance, and software configuration management.

In addition to these CMM KPAs, we defined two non-CMM KPAs: completed work analysis and software metrics. CMM purists would object to including these with the CMM Level 2 KPAs because each represents a topic covered by a KPA at a higher CMM level. The CMM philosophy is that the KPAs at each level form a foundation for the process improvement at higher levels. Therefore, it isn't effective to implement higher level KPAs before the required foundation is in place. Although this may be true for a pure Level 1 organization, we started with a quality system that partially addressed all the relevant Level 2 KPAs and some Level 3 KPAs. We thus took a pragmatic approach and defined KPAs for issues we believed could offer significant benefits.

The completed work analysis KPA was a central part of our continuous process improvement plan. Its goal was to define a procedure for analyzing the work done

on projects and for feeding back the experience so that it could be used in future projects. The scope was thus wider than process issues, encompassing tool use and communication and coordination on individual projects. We wanted to use the procedure from the completed work analysis to ensure that we learned not just from our mistakes but also from our successes. By analyzing the experience on all projects, we hoped to ensure that the lessons learned from individual projects were also learned by the complete organization. A group of 150 software engineers gains 150 person-years of experience every year. This represents a significant source of knowledge for the organization if it can be tapped.

The Level 2 software project tracking and oversight KPA covers some metrics, but we added a non-CMM KPA to define additional metrics. The goal was to define data to be collected by projects that would identify weaknesses in our existing process. Knowing the weaknesses would allow us to focus our process improvement effort on them. For example, we collected metrics on the defects introduced per project phase. This let us focus our improvements on the phases where the most serious defects are introduced. When defining the metrics to collect, we wanted to be clear about why we were collecting them, so for each metric, we also defined what we planned to conclude from the data.

Process definition

For the KPAs we defined ourselves (complete work analysis and software metrics), we had a clear understanding of what we wanted to achieve and the requirements. For the Level 2 KPAs, we chose to buy expertise so that we could get the project moving as quickly as possible.

KPA definition workshop. We organized a workshop and chose participants from across the software group so that all types of projects were represented. We did not assume that the participants had any knowledge of CMM, so the workshop started with a CMM introduction. The rest of the workshop focused on the Level 2 KPAs that were relevant for S3. The workshop's goal was to produce proposals for implementing these KPAs in the S3 environment. The consultant first described the requirements of two KPAs and gave some ideas about how to implement them. The participants then broke into two groups and worked out an implementation proposal. This approach was very effective. The groups were able to consider various options in the context of how people work in S3, and the consultant was there to answer any questions about CMM.

Once the two groups had agreed on a proposal, each group presented its proposal to the other, and the proposals were discussed further. At the end of the workshop, the participants had produced concrete proposals

Table 1. How the task force tailored an activity from the CMM Level 2 key process area (software project planning) to meet S3's needs.

Key process area	Description
Activity	The software engineering group participates on the project proposal team.
S3 context	The participants in the proposal are the sales team and software development team in conjunction with management. The sales department and senior management deal with the commercial and financial aspects.
Interpretation	Experienced software engineers prepare the technical aspects of the project proposal. These engineers normally form the core of the project team that will perform the work. At this stage, this team prepares an initial plan that documents the main aspects of the project.
	Once the customer and S3 senior management make a commitment in the form of a signed contract or letter of intent, the plan is further developed. Any further development or modifications at later stages must always involve the project team as well as any organizations outside the project that are affected by it.

for implementing two CMM KPAs. The success of the workshop was due in large extent to the consultant, who not only understood the CMM theory but also had experience with its practical application. This was a great help to us as we designed an implementation of the KPAs to suit our working environment.

One striking outcome of the workshop was that all the participants, without exception, were enthusiastic about the SPI project and were highly motivated to contribute further. They all agreed to meet again the following week to work on the remaining KPAs. This follow-on workshop also resulted in implementation proposals.

Task forces. To involve as many people as possible in the SPI project, we used task forces. In each task force, one person was responsible for implementing the changes, and approximately five people reviewed and guided the implementation. Each CMM Level 2 and internally defined KPA was assigned to a task force. This ensured that a large proportion of the organization was directly involved in the SPI project. Indeed, after this step in the initiative, approximately 45 percent of the software group had been directly involved.

Each task force followed a standard approach to KPA implementation. First, they wrote a proposal describing how the KPA would be implemented. For CMM KPAs, they produced a detailed proposal document that was based on the workshop results. For the non-CMM KPAs, they wrote a proposal document. In each case, the task force reviewed and discussed the KPA proposal and agreed on how to implement the KPA. The next step was to implement the agreed-on changes. This involved updating existing quality procedures, writing new procedures, and, in some cases, providing tool support. The task force also reviewed any new or updated quality procedures. Table 1 shows how the task force proposed to implement an activity from the software project planning KPA.

Pilot projects

Once the task force approved the changes for a KPA, we were ready to introduce them on real projects. For KPAs that had significant changes, we chose to test the changes on a pilot project. This allowed us to monitor the effects of the changes very closely and take corrective action if problems arose with the KPA requirements.

We tested our changes to the software project planning KPA on an Internet application project that had a short life cycle. The project let us not only verify the completeness of the process, but also test the downward scalability of the KPA definition to a small project. The project team implemented all the improvements and tracked their effects. From the customer and the S3 management point of view, the documented project plan provided excellent visibility and greatly aided tracking. The project team was more confident in their plan and, because they spent less time replanning, as had been typical of previous projects, they had more time to concentrate on technical issues and product quality. Also, increasing the level of detail (relative to previous plans) produced a more complete schedule, thus reducing the number of tasks that might otherwise have been forgotten.

In general, the pilot project test of the project planning KPA definition went very smoothly, and the KPA definition did not change significantly.

In contrast, the pilot project to test the quality assurance KPA definition did encounter problems. After less than a month, it became apparent that the KPA definition was not practical, although it had been set and reviewed by many people and seemed to be a reasonable approach. The amount of overhead to both the project and supporting infrastructure was not acceptable, and the return on invested time was questionable. When we analyzed the KPA definition, we found that we had spent too little time tailoring the KPA to S3's environment, and we had not sufficiently defined the supporting infrastructure. The project immediately stopped using this KPA definition, and the original task force, in conjunction with the pilot project team, redesigned it. We put the new version and an improved infrastructure in place only after the project was completed. The updated KPA definition has since been tested and is proving effective.

Training and rollout

Before introducing the updated quality system throughout the software group, we arranged training on the new system for all software engineers and relevant managers. To stimulate discussion, the training was conducted in groups of 12. The training course for each group lasted a full day. During the course, we tried to get as much feedback as possible from the software engineers who would use the updated quality system. Also, we tried to instill an understanding of the context and purpose of the changes so that the engineers would not only understand what was required of them but also why. The training courses included a walk-through of some of the updated quality procedures, which generated much useful discussion and many suggestions for improvements.

The training course initiated the rollout of the new processes to all projects. Process mentors were assigned to each project to support the introduction of the new processes. For existing projects, the process mentor and project leaders decided case by case which parts of the new processes to adopt and at what point to introduce the changes.

Infrastructure. To make the updated quality system easy to use, we developed a supporting infrastructure and used the companywide intranet to support it. We provided an easy-to-use Web interface to the quality documents and tools to support specific changes that resulted from KPA implementation. Among these was a lessons-learned database that provided easy access to suggestions arising from the completed work analysis performed on projects. A software process group also reviews these lessons and looks for ways to provide feedback into the quality system.

Version control. Our goal to start a continuous improvement process conflicted with the need for stability within the quality system. If the quality procedures are constantly changing, the multitude of versions will cause confusion. To avoid this, we released modified documents only when we released a new quality system version, which was at most every three months. With each quality system version release, we provided a full description of all changes. This gave projects visibility into any changes that had been introduced. When a project starts, it uses the latest version of the quality system. A project might later adopt a newer version of the quality system, depending on how significantly it has changed. Typically, projects will change versions only at the start of a major new phase.

RESULTS

In evaluating an SPI project, you cannot consider only objective measurements because the software process is ultimately about helping people do their jobs. Trying to measure process improvement while ignoring the people involved provides a very one-sided view. If the people who use the quality system do not feel that the SPI is improving things, there is a problem.

Measurements

At the start of our SPI project, we conducted an interim maturity evaluation to assess our status with respect to CMM KPAs. After we introduced the new quality procedures and tool support, we again performed an interim maturity evaluation. Figure 2 shows the results of this evaluation.

When we started our SPI initiative, we were reasonably strong in all areas except quality assurance. The strength in the other KPAs was due to our ISO 9001-compliant quality system, which in our opinion was already a very strong foundation. Figure 2 shows real improvements in all KPAs. The most striking improvement is in quality assurance—understandable because this was our weakest area initially and hence where we could gain the most. The large improvement is due to CMM's emphasis on a supportive role, for example, support at the planning stage, in contrast to ISO 9001's audit-based approach. The figure also shows that we can benefit even more, especially in quality assurance. We decided that before seeking a formal CMM assessment, we should score at least nine for each KPA in the interim maturity evaluation. Moreover, given that our primary goal was to achieve real improvements, with CMM certification as a secondary goal, we also decided to look at further improvement benefits before seeking the assessment.

Since the first rollout in June 1998, all projects have moved to the new process definitions, with the help of the training course and mentoring by process experts. The feedback from customers has been very positive. Before the project, most of our customers required that we use their process; now, after one and a half years, most customers are happy to see projects use the S3 process. An excellent example is S3's recent recognition as a qualified software supplier to a CMM Level 4 company. The positive feedback from customers proves that the SPI program is contributing to S3's business goals.

Subjective evaluation

The subjective evaluation of our SPI project is also very positive. Software engineers feel greater ownership of the quality system and are more inclined to suggest improvements through a structured change proposal mechanism, as evidenced by the increased number of change proposals. They also greatly appreciated our addition of a strong support infrastructure. Managers feel that the SPI initiative has given them greater visibility, though not yet complete, into projects and their progress.

The effort expended to date, excluding the project leader, is 180 person-days on process redefinition, 70 person-days on training, and 20 person-days on evaluations. Two new procedures were introduced, one on requirements management and the other on risk management (as part of project planning). We have revised six existing procedures, one of which is the project planning documentation procedure.

O ur approach to process improvement has proved very effective. There has been a noticeable shift in attitudes toward the quality system. Where once it was seen as something static to be tolerated, it is now seen as a living thing that is constantly evolving. Thus, although not everyone agrees with all aspects of the quality system, people are far more willing than in the past to make constructive suggestions.

The SPI approach described in this article was targeted for S3's software division. A process improvement initiative that follows a similar approach is now being introduced across S3. ❖

Acknowledgments

We thank Dave Murrells of Silicon & Software Systems for reviewing an earlier version of this article and providing valuable comments.

References

1. K.M. Dymond, *A Guide to the CMM: Understanding the Capability Maturity Model for Software*, Process Transition Int'l, Annapolis, Md., 1995.

2. M. Diaz and J. Sligo, "How Software Process Improvement Helped Motorola," *IEEE Software*, Sept./Oct. 1997, pp. 75-81.

3. J. Herbsleb et al., "Software Quality and the Capability Maturity Model," *Comm. ACM*, June 1997, pp. 30-40.

Declan P. Kelly is a research scientist at Philips Research Laboratories in Eindhoven, The Netherlands. Before joining Philips Research, he worked in the software division at Silicon & Software Systems as software process improvement coordinator, among other roles. His research interests include digital video processing, storage applications, software engineering, formal methods, and software process improvement. He received an MSc in computer science from Trinity College, Dublin, and a joint honors BSc in mathematics and computer science from University College, Dublin. He is a member of the IEEE Computer Society and the ACM.

Bill Culleton is process and quality manager at Silicon & Software Systems, Dublin, where his responsibilities include managing a CMM-based process improvement project in the software division as well as project management mentoring and training. He also supports process improvement in S3's other divisions. He received an MSc in microelectronics design and a BA BAI in telecommunications engineering from Trinity College, Dublin. He is a member of the Institute of Engineers of Ireland. Contact Culleton at bill_c@ s3group.com.

The Clash of Two Cultures: Project Management Versus Process Management

by Rob Thomsett

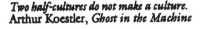

Two half-cultures do not make a culture.
Arthur Koestler, *Ghost in the Machine*

The current focus in organizations on reengineering, downsizing, strategic value analysis, total quality management (TQM), and self-managing teams is an attempt to meet the challenges that have evolved from the "excesses of the '80s" and the global recession of the early 1990s. However, as Charles Handy [10], Tom Peters [20], John Huey [11], John Byrne [4] and many others discuss, rather than being isolated remedial actions, these concepts signal the emergence of a new paradigm of organizational structure and behavior. Terms such as the "virtual organization," the "network organization," and the "unglued organization" are used to propose radical solutions for the senior executives of organizations facing a chaotic environment of social, legislative, and technological change.

In computing, a similar paradigm change is beginning to emerge. Concepts such as object-oriented development, client-server architectures, information resource management, rapid application development, networks,

Reprinted from *American Programmer,* Vol. 7, No. 6, June 1994, pp. 18–28. Reprinted with permission.

I-CASE, and groupware are seen as the solution to the productivity, service, and quality pressures that clients are bringing to bear on computing groups [14, 15, 34]. Furthermore, the move from technically oriented service to business-oriented service has forced many computing groups to reevaluate their well-established processes of strategic and project management [28].

Yet the benefits of improved organizational structures and information technology (IT) infrastructures will be diminished unless organizations and their IT service groups address and resolve a much more fundamental issue: the existence of two conflicting cultures within their organizations.

PROJECT AND PROCESS CULTURES: A HIDDEN CONFLICT

The process culture in organizations has existed since at least the Industrial Revolution. Formalizing the factory culture that had emerged in the 1800s, Frederick Taylor [24] and Max Weber [31] laid the theoretical framework in the early 1900s for the bureaucratic model of organizations, which is still the prevailing organizational paradigm.

However, from the formalization of project management as a discrete technical discipline during the Polaris Program in the 1950s, the growth of an alternative project culture has been accelerated in most organizations through the impact of information technology. By the 1960s, such analysts as Paul Gaddis [8], C.J. Middleton [16], and Gerald Weinberg [33] had begun to draw attention to the special nature of projects, project people, and, in the case of Weinberg's seminal book, project teams.

But as those who had begun to experiment with teams and project cultures in the 1970s discovered, the predominant process culture negated many of the advantages of the emerging project culture [26]. For example, in a project culture, the whole team must be rewarded for a good job. In a process culture, the boss is rewarded for the team's good work.

The clash between process and project cultures has been ignored for many years, forcing the project culture to coexist within the process culture like some alien immigrant. In the emerging organizational paradigm, the project culture will become the dominant culture. The impact of this shift will have a broader and more far-reaching impact than the latest management fad or technological fix.

The differences between the two cultures can be seen by examining three elements: organizational structure, the control and authority structure, and job design. There are clearly many

other aspects of organizational culture, such as behavioral norms, socialization processes, and professional attitudes; however, these tend to be dominated by the three elements listed above.

A BLAST FROM THE PAST: THE PROCESS CULTURE

The process culture is based on routinized work undertaken in a stable environment by people and technologies that are interchangeable and "plug-compatible." The primary (if covert) concern is that when machines or people break down, they must be quickly replaced so productivity is not impacted and business as usual can resume. Process culture tasks and procedures are engineered through scientific analysis and time-and-motion studies, and a system is designed to optimize the efficiency of the work. This factory mentality applies to all forms of process cultures, whether they are car manufacturers, banks, insurance companies, or hospitals.

Organizational Structure

The organizational structure of the process culture is hierarchical and rigid. To quote Weber, "The organization of offices follows the principle of hierarchy; that is, each lower office is under the control and supervision of a higher one" [31]. In addition, the organization is divided into subhierarchies that are designed with specialized technical competencies. For example, in a bank there might be a retail division, a corporate division, and an overseas division.

The key to this structure is the concept of legitimized ownership of the knowledge, data, practices, and standards of an organizational unit. As many have observed, this ownership often results in dysfunctional behavior, such as protecting one's territory at all costs. Stafford Beer has noted that the more threatened the bureaucracy, the more its efforts are diverted from serving its clients to ensuring its own survival [1]. These preservation efforts go beyond people and procedures. Many a naive information resource manager has experienced senior managers' strong sense of data ownership when attempting to introduce data-naming standards.

Weber conceived of a technically competent hierarchy in which a position was separate from the person occupying it. According to Weber, "The office is filled by a free contractual relationship. Thus, in principle, there is free selection based on a sphere of competence" [31]. However, as many of us have experienced, this concept has been distorted over time by the personalization of a position by an occupant who seeks to build and protect his or her turf to justify higher remuneration, organizational status, and power. The psychological needs for social acceptance, esteem, and reward accentuate the inherent concept of higher and lower positions in hierarchies. Richard Pascale [18] provides a detailed description of the "turf" wars between the various functional divisions in Ford Motor Company in the early 1980s. He quotes a senior executive: "It was civil war at the top. The question was never, 'Are we winning against the Japanese?'

but rather, 'Are we winning against each other?' "

For the past 30 years, computing has had to exist within the process culture, and as a result, many major systems reflect the hierarchical divisions of the larger organization. A bank's information resource managers are, for example, well aware of the retail banking system's inability to share data with the personal loan system. Similarly, many project managers have been caught in turf wars between their various clients as they attempt to balance conflicting system requirements. In part, the move to new, more organic organizational structures — virtual networks, for example — is a long overdue reaction to the failing of hierarchical structures.

Control and Authority

It is in the areas of control and authority that the process culture is most evident. Structure and control are closely linked, and the higher the position in the structure, the more control and authority the occupant of the position has formally vested in him or her.

The rules many organizations have regarding finance and human resources are good examples of the link between organizational structure and control. In many bureaucracies, senior management will attempt to increase its control by restricting spending authority. A typical rule might be that all expenditures over $50,000 must be approved by the CEO. It is also common for organizations to require executive-level approval for new recruitment and the hiring of

contract workers — another attempt to retain control over expenses and to maintain the status quo. The inevitable outcome of these restrictions is that the organization becomes controlled by the finance and accounting experts [18]. Pascale quotes a senior Ford executive, who explained, "Finance occupied the critical spot at the top of the pyramid."

In a process culture, technical elites also engage in turf battles using their expertise as a basis for control and authority. Engineers and computing people use their expertise to determine strategic technical decisions, the technical feasibility of new products and projects, and the choice of technical infrastructures. For example, an internal computing group might dictate a rigid IBM PC environment, excluding Unix and Macintoshes. While the technical control is explained by the need for a service ethic and for consistency and standards, in many cases the inflexible control of technical infrastructure is nothing more than an exercise in bureaucratic control and authority by technocrats [28].

Many attempts to restructure hierarchical organizations over the past 15 years have failed to realize that the shifting of people and positions in an organization chart does not alter the basic control and authority structures, nor does it address the existence of informal networks, which eventually undermine the expected outcomes of the restructuring. The phrase "rearranging deck chairs on the Titanic" has become associated with endless organizational restructuring that fails to address the control and

authority that people have accumulated over many years.

Job Design

If organizational structure and the associated control and authority form the architectural framework of the process culture, the design of jobs is the day-to-day manifestation of that culture. The key to process job design, as noted by Taylor in 1910, is that "the initiative of workmen is obtained practically with absolute regularity" [24].

Jobs in a process culture are characterized by the following attributes:

Repeating tasks. The typical process job will be repeated many times a day. In a bank, a teller will service a customer in two minutes or less. In some factories, scientific analysis (as Taylor proposed some 80 years ago) has reduced the individual task to one minute or less.

Routinization and standardization. It is key to process work that the same job be performed according to a routine and standards independent of the person performing it. As a result, a bank teller may move from branch to branch without being retrained. Standard operating procedures are developed and used as a guide for training, evaluation, and enforcement of standardization.

Reduced variation. In process work, any variation in performance is seen as a "defect." This covert value has become institutionalized in the TQM movement. W. Edwards Deming [30] and Joseph Juran [13], who are credited with founding TQM, both see special cases (i.e., a person acting in a nonstandard manner) as a major cause of poor quality in process work.

Clear performance measures.
Process work is easily measured and there are clearly established performance standards that must be met each period. Most process organizations have highly developed performance measurement systems that monitor the rate of task completion. For example, the bank manager knows the number of clients that a teller should serve on an average day. Performance in a process culture is based on the speed, accuracy, and consistency of task completion.

Precise scope. As a result of the years of scientific analysis and bureaucratic territory protection, process culture jobs have a clearly defined scope. A teller handles general inquiries, and a housing loan expert handles loans. This demarcation is even more evident in union environments, where each trade has precisely defined boundaries and skills.

Operates within status quo. The most significant attribute of process work is that it constitutes business as usual for the organization. In other words, at the end of a normal day, the bank branch, its people, and its tasks are unchanged. The next day will be the same as the day before, and any change is framed as a once-only project and is undertaken by experts.

Process work and tasks are the lifeblood of a process culture. The very nature of the work provides consistency and predictability that is also manifest in the organization's structure and control. People know where they fit and what they have to do.

Taylor and Weber were seeking to obtain consistency without sacrificing workmanship, but the process culture let consistency and standards become ends in themselves. To quote Taylor, "The principles of scientific management . . . must in all cases produce far larger and better results . . . than can be obtained under the management of initiative and incentive in which those on the management's side deliberately give a large incentive to their workmen, and in return, the workmen respond by working at the very best of their ability."

AND NOW FOR SOMETHING COMPLETELY DIFFERENT: THE PROJECT CULTURE

The project culture is the exact opposite of the process culture. While the concept of projects probably predated the process culture (the construction of buildings, the conduct of wars, and the mounting of major explorations can all be considered projects), the formalization of the project culture did not begin until the 1950s. Although elements of the project culture (e.g., project plans) were developed by Henry Gantt and others in World War I, a formalized body of knowledge and a specific organizational model first emerged in the post–World War II U.S. Defense Department. The Atlas Missile Program and

the Polaris Program under Admiral John Raborn were early examples of what is now recognized as the project culture [17].

Organizational Structure

Organizational structures in the project culture are still evolving. However, whereas the process culture is based on hierarchies, the project culture is based on project teams. So, in many ways, the organizational structure of the project culture reflects the micro-organizational structure of project teams; the primary design is one of dynamic networks rather than rigid hierarchies.

At first, the project culture adopted the more dominant process model of organizational structure, and as a result, project teams were themselves mini-hierarchies. The traditional project team consisted of a project manager, who had project leaders reporting to him or her, and technical specialists (analysts, designers, etc.), who reported to the project leaders [27]. But as early as the 1970s, computing experts were challenging the effectiveness of the hierarchical structure and its ability to deal with the dynamic and participatory nature of decision making in teams [6, 27].

Advocates of the sociotechnical system model were asking similar questions about the effectiveness of hierarchical team structures in other industries. In the 1960s, the work of Fred Emery and Eric Trist [7] and others in coal mines, car factories, and steelworks laid the theoretical foundation for the self-directed team model that is now central to the project culture. In 1961,

Emery and Trist predicted that the inflexibility of the process culture in responding to environmental changes could lead to its failure. They write, "The very survival of an enterprise may be threatened by its inability to face up to such demands, as for instance, switching the main effort from production of processed goods to marketing."

The project culture's emerging organizational model is one of flexible team structures based on leadership as a series of roles rather than a position. Weinberg's egoless teams, Larry Constantine's structured open teams, and Rob Thomsett's X-team are all based on the concept of leadership moving between team members based on their specific skills, personality, and roles.

In summary, there is not one preferred organizational structure; rather, the organizational structure of the project culture is dynamic and depends on the organization's mission, team members, and the specific project. Two early models of the project culture's organizational structure can be seen in Handy's Shamrock structure [10] and Charles Savage's network design [22]. Both models share the concept of a small strategic and policy cell (which may be hierarchical) and a flexible network of project teams.

Control and Authority

Whereas control and authority in the process culture are based on position in the hierarchy and formal delegation of authority, control and authority in the project culture are more complex.

The fact that a manager in a process culture can review his or her subordinates' performance and make other major decisions regarding their careers gives control and authority to the manager. In the project culture, control and authority are won through performance rather than given through position. The complex communications, negotiations, and decision making required in a project culture are beyond most individuals, and there is a need for full participation by project team members and project stakeholders (providers of service to the project team) [29]. As I discuss later, the predominance of teamwork in the project culture challenges many concepts — such as leadership, rewards, recognition, and performance measurement — that are well established in the process culture.

In contemporary team models, leadership within a team or organization moves from person to person depending on the specific competencies of the person and the specific issue facing the team. For example, when planning a project that requires many service providers to cooperate, the person with the best negotiation and communication skills may be the dominant team member. Once the project is under way, a team member with superior technical skills may move into the leadership role. The move to self-directed or autonomous teams in manufacturing [32] indicates that the majority of organizations that are adopting the project and team culture use the rotating team leaders model.

However, there is a variety of team structures, ranging from highly structured teams based on specific expertise and roles to open team structures with no specific structure [6]. The key is that the team structure is project specific and team member specific.

Job Design

The design of jobs in the project culture provides the clearest indication of the differences between the process and project culture. In fact, the attributes of jobs in the project culture are the exact opposite of those in the process culture.

Jobs in a project culture can be characterized by the following attributes:

Nonrepeating tasks. The typical project task will vary between projects, reflecting the unique nature of the project. Furthermore, project tasks can last for a considerable time. For example, the tasks undertaken by a systems analyst in a project may last many months.

Unique and entrepreneurial. While project work may follow some established processes, such as requirements analysis, design, development, and implementation, the specific outcomes of the work are project specific. As a result, the focus in project work moves from standardizing the output to standardizing (where possible) the techniques and technology. Many companies have developed standard systems analysis techniques, such as data or process modeling, but the outcome of the product analysis depends on the specific system or product involved and upon the expertise of the person performing the analysis.

Amplified variation. Project work requires flexibility and creativity. As a result, the success of a project often depends on people breaking the rules and questioning the status quo. Variation between individuals and teams is expected and encouraged. Studies by Capers Jones [12], Lawrence Putnam and Ware Myers [21], and many others have revealed individual and team performance variations of 10:1 and greater in information systems work. This has profound implications for the process culture, as I discuss later.

Vague performance measures. Project work is extremely difficult to measure and evaluate. While the use of formal planning techniques (e.g., work breakdown structures) can provide a basis for dividing project work into shorter activities, the assessment of process in project work tends to be subjective. True assessment of progress requires completion and quality review of task outputs. Given that many projects involve hundreds of tasks that are interrelated, it is often impossible to measure whether a project is progressing successfully until it is completed.

Dynamic scope. The scope of a project is flexible and reflects the dynamic nature of organizational systems. While project management seeks to control variations in project scope, it cannot stop the variation; it is inevitable for project scope and objectives to change during the project development cycle [12, 29]. These changes are driven by external requirements changes and by the iterative and progressively more detailed processes of analysis and design.

Changes status quo. The most significant attribute of project work is that it is designed to change the status quo. The development of a new product or service, the implementation of a new human resources program, and the installation of reengineered work practices are typical projects that have an impact beyond the project manager and team.

In other words, the project culture is designed for continuous change, and the basic organizational structure and job design pattern are dynamic and innovative. When a project has implemented the initial product or system, a continuous process of enhancement and refinement is typical. The innovative nature of the project culture also relies on the creativity of people who are working at "the very best of their ability."

TWO CULTURES IN CONFLICT

For the past 30 years, these two cultures have coexisted, with the project culture being mainly found in the remote and technically oriented areas of organizations, such as computing and engineering. But with the focus of senior management moving to radical organization changes, the project culture has begun to emerge in all areas. For example, two major Australian organizations have reported that they have over 200 projects under way at any one time.

Given the vast differences between the cultures, it is easy to identify the conflicts between them and the resulting confusion that many people are now experiencing. Examples can be found in the issues of project stakeholders, financial processes, reward systems, and career paths.

Stakeholder Versus Line Reporting

A project stakeholder is a person who has to provide services to the project manager or who is expecting service from the project. In the development of a new insurance product, for example, typical stakeholders would be agency, administration, marketing, advertising, actuarial, audit, and computer specialists, together with the product clients.

The project manager must negotiate with the various stakeholders, as most of them will "belong" to other organizational areas within the traditional hierarchy. In turn, each stakeholder must get the approval of his or her line manager before providing services to the project. When a stakeholder is unable to fulfill his or her obligations to the project manager, the project manager is caught between the two cultures.

To resolve the conflict, the project manager must first inform his or her line manager and the project sponsor (who may be from a different organizational area). Then the sponsor and/or line manager must raise the conflict with the stakeholder's line manager, who must then raise the issue with the stakeholder in question. In all, at least 5 people are involved, as the line management concerns must be balanced with the project concerns. With 10 stakeholders, the project manager must negotiate with up to 20 people to resolve disputes and ensure that the process culture's concerns with turf and boundaries are addressed. This complexity is one of the major causes of project failure [29].

Project Finance Versus Process Budgeting

Financial management in the process culture is based on clearly defined cycles and accountable items. Calendar year, financial year, account receivables, balance sheets, inventories, fixed assets, and zero-base budgeting are the lifeblood of traditional accounting. However, the need for process culture accountants to balance the books yearly is in clear conflict with the flexible budgeting required in the project culture.

Return on investment (ROI) is the focus of the project culture finance model, and for many projects, the "balance sheet" cannot be done yearly, quarterly, or on any other fixed cycle. The balancing of the books begins with the implementation of the project's deliverable and ends when the ROI time frame is ended. For example, in Company A the ROI cycle is two years and in Company B the ROI cycle is seven years. In Company B, the accounts for the project cannot be balanced until Year 7.

In other words, process culture budgets are broken into spe-

cific account items, which are allocated to an organizational unit for a year. In a project culture, the budget is allocated to a project (which will cross organizational areas) and for the period of the project life cycle (however long that is). Of course, the use of project management tracking techniques can provide "interim" results.

Individual Versus Team Rewards

In the process culture, the individual is rewarded based on performance and position. Managers get rewarded for the performance of their subordinates, and, as reported by John Byrne [5], it is typical for managers to be rewarded disproportionally. (Byrne reports that the average gap between CEOs' pay and that of their technical experts has grown from 19:1 in the 1960s to 65:1 in the 1990s.)

As discussed by Thomsett, Weinberg, Constantine, and many others, in a project environment each team member's unique skills are part of a synergistic process in which the whole is greater than the sum of the parts. If a project is successful, all team members should share equally in (or at least participate in determining the allocation of) the rewards, since all were vital to the success.

Specialist/Horizontal Career Paths Versus Vertical Career Paths

The conflict involving technical career paths in the process culture has been well documented in all specialist project areas;

among them, engineering, computing, and research. Promotion and career paths in a process culture involve explicit expansion of the number of people a person manages. For example, as a person is promoted from Technical Expert Grade 3 to Senior Technical Expert (STE) Grade 1, he or she is expected to supervise more technical experts. The Peter Principle reported by Laurence Peter and Raymond Hull [19] is invoked, as the person spends more time managing subordinates than applying his or her technical expertise. Rapid changes in techniques and technology eventually render STE Grade 1's technical skills obsolete, and with all the management demands, he or she has no time to attend training programs to update them.

In a project culture, the career of technical and project management experts becomes horizontal [10]. By moving from project to project, workers in a project culture are rewarded by new skills, challenges, and knowledge rather than position. In the project culture, a career focuses on the building of specific portfolios of knowledge, skills, and experience rather than organizational empires.

Other conflicts between the two cultures can be seen in competency development (the orientation of human resources development toward supervision, management, and bureaucratic processes rather than project-oriented competencies), physical building construction (where office layouts suitable for process work are inadequate for project and team work), human resources allocation (the line manager decides whom he or she can spare rather than the project manager selecting the appropriate people), and organizational reporting systems (where executive information systems are process rather than project oriented).

CAN THESE CULTURES PEACEFULLY COEXIST?

During the transition from process cultures to project cultures, the two must learn to coexist. This coexistence will require some creativity, and as a result, hybrid organizational structures and approaches have begun to emerge.

One common model is the streaming of technical experts into management or administrative and technical careers. This goes some way toward avoiding the "Peter Principle," as it allows technical experts whose preference is for a technical career to move to senior technical positions (labeled "Consultant" or "Technical") that offer management-level salaries but do not require supervising subordinates. In many projects, it is possible for the project manager to earn less than the technical consultants who report — in a project sense — to the project manager. Clearly, this can lead to conflict, as the organizational status of the process culture can become confused with the authority vested in the project manager by the project culture.

Program budgeting and activity-based costing [3] represent two attempts to break the time-based cycle of process culture accounting. With program budgeting, a "trust" account is set up for the project, which en-

ables flexibility in the allocation of the funds and the reporting cycle. Activity-based costing attempts to prevent the use of generic project on-costing guidelines, such as salary plus 155 percent on-costs [29]. For example, the equipment costs and other nonsalary costs are identified project by project, enabling tailored on-costing calculation. Unfortunately, both of these approaches are consistently compromised by the long-established accounting systems and reporting structures built around the process culture accounting models.

The establishment of separate organizational units (often called "skunkworks," independent business units, SWAT teams, etc.) is another common attempt to build hybrid structures. However, as IBM's PC group and other isolated project cultures have discovered, the "reentry" of their product into the process culture is hindered by the very fact that the product was developed by an organizationally remote group. This reentry problem is also experienced by people seconded into project teams as project managers, business analysts, and client representatives. The longer these people work in the project culture, the less likely it is that their process culture colleagues will accept them and the harder it is for them to readjust to the process culture.

Other hybrid approaches, such as the matrix structure [23] and expert resource pools, attempt to provide the flexibility of skills required during the project development cycle with the hierarchical structures of the process culture. These are generally ineffective, however, as people are

caught between the two cultures. The matrix structure is constantly dealing with conflicts of interest between the technical specialists and their culture and the project manager and the process culture.

In computing, the concept of software engineering exhibits many of the features of the hybrid approach. Implicit in the concept of engineering is the Taylorist view of predictability and conformity. In other words, the goal of software engineering is minimizing the variability of individuals and maximizing the use of repeatable, engineered processes. Yet detailed studies have shown that computing work is highly creative and individualistic [12, 21].

Even organizations that have structured and standardized their project development technology and techniques have found that data modeling techniques cannot eliminate the 10:1 productivity variance between developers. Coupling the software engineering model with the process culture, which is unable to reward and develop exceptional performance, simply leads to a "leveling down" of expertise and performance as the best performers leave.

In summary, hybrid cultures are at best a temporary fix, and at worst, they result in confusion and conflict to both cultures' disadvantage.

WHERE TO NOW?

The emergence of the project culture and its associated dynamic structures, reward systems, and leadership models is inevitable as the rate of change and competition increases for the remainder of the 1990s.

The shift from process to project culture must be seen as an integrated and long-term process rather than a series of isolated initiatives, such as business reengineering and self-directed teams. While these and other popular management concepts are part of a suite of enabling techniques, the culture shift will impact all existing components of the process culture, including the service/business processes (the focus of reengineering), the accounting/finance procedures, the human resources/appraisal/reward practices, organization and team structures, physical office design, and so on.

Senior managers must steer the culture shift and provide everyone in the process culture with extensive education in the areas of project management, team building, business analysis, and other competencies well established in project cultures. In addition, they must integrate the implementation of strategic value analysis and planning, business process reengineering, activity-based accounting, competency-based human resources development, flexible reward systems, flexible IT infrastructures, TQM, project management, and performance appraisal systems.

While this integrated approach is expensive, the cost of the culture shift is far outweighed by the expensive failures of the current process culture, as giant organizations such as IBM, GM, and other icons are outmaneuvered by smaller project culture organizations such as Microsoft and Intel.

At last, the project culture identified in the 1960s by pioneers Emery, Trist, and Beer and popularized later by Alvin Toffler [25] (and more recently by Peters [20] and others) is slowly becoming the dominant paradigm. Whereas Emery, Trist, and Beer based their arguments on a value system oriented toward enriching people's working lives, the current focus [29] is oriented toward a more urgent value — survival! But while organizations and their clients will clearly reap substantial benefits, the real winners will still be people in organizations who will join teams in dynamic and challenging projects and experience "working at the very best of their ability."

REFERENCES

1 Beer, Stafford. *Platform for Change*. New York: John Wiley & Sons, 1975.

2 Belbin, R. Meredith. *Management Teams: Why They Succeed or Fail*. London: Heinemann, 1981.

3 Brimson, James A. *Activity Accounting*. New York: John Wiley & Sons, 1990.

4 Byrne, John A. "The Virtual Corporation." *International Business Week* (February 8, 1993).

5 Byrne, John A. "Executive Pay Ain't Over Yet." *International Business Week* (April 26, 1993).

6 Constantine, Larry L. "Teamwork Paradigms and the Structured Open Team." In *Proceedings of the Embedded System Conference*. San Francisco: Miller Freeman, 1989.

7 Emery, Frederick E., and Eric A. Trist. "Socio-technical Systems." In Fred Emery, ed., *Systems Thinking*. London: Penguin Books, 1969.

8 Gaddis, Paul O. "The Project Manager." *Harvard Business Review* (March–April 1959), pp. 89–119.

9 Galbraith, John Kenneth. *The Anatomy of Power*. Boston: Houghton Mifflin, 1983.

10 Handy, Charles B. *The Age of Unreason*. Boston: Harvard Business School Press, 1989.

11 Huey, John. "Managing in the Midst of Chaos." *Fortune International*, Vol. 7 (April 5, 1993), pp. 30–36.

12 Jones, Capers. *Applied Software Measurement*. New York: McGraw-Hill, 1991.

13 Juran, Joseph M. *Juran on Leadership for Quality*. New York: Free Press, 1989.

14 Keen, Peter G.W. *Shaping the Future*. Boston: Harvard Business School Press, 1991.

15 Martin, James. *Rapid Application Development*. New York: Macmillan, 1991.

16 Middleton, C.J. "How to Set Up a Project Organization." *Harvard Business Review* (March–April 1967), pp. 76–91.

17 Morris, Peter W.G., and George H. Hough. *The Anatomy of Major Projects*.

New York: John Wiley & Sons, 1987.

18 Pascale, Richard T. *Managing on the Edge*. New York: Simon & Schuster, 1990.

19 Peter, Laurence J., and Raymond Hull. *The Peter Principle*. New York: William Morrow, 1969.

20 Peters, Thomas J. *Liberation Management*. New York: Knopf, 1992.

21 Putnam, Lawrence H., and Ware Myers. *Measures for Excellence*. Englewood Cliffs, NJ: Prentice Hall, 1992.

22 Savage, Charles M. *Fifth Generation Management*. Bedford, MA: Digital Press, 1990.

23 Struckenbruck, Linn C. *The Implementation of Project Management*. Reading, MA: Addison-Wesley, 1989.

24 Taylor, Frederick W. "Scientific Management." In Derek S. Pugh, ed., *Organization Theory*. London: Penguin Books, 1971.

25 Toffler, Alvin. *The Third Wave*. New York: Morrow, 1980.

26 Thomsett, Rob. *People and Project Management*. Englewood Cliffs, NJ: Prentice Hall, 1980.

27 Thomsett, Rob. "The X-team: An Innovative Team Structure for Systems Development." *American Pro-grammer*, Vol. 5, no. 1. (January 1992), pp. 23–33.

28 Thomsett, Rob. "Computer and Business Professionals: An Evolutionary Perspective." *Professional Computing*, Australian Computer Society (July 1992), pp. 8–10.

29 Thomsett, Rob. *Third Wave Project Management*. Englewood Cliffs, NJ: Prentice Hall, 1992.

30 Walton, Mary. *The Deming Management Method*. New York: Dodd, Mead & Company, 1986.

31 Weber, Max. "Legitimate Authority and Bureaucracy." In Derek S. Pugh, ed., *Organization Theory*. London: Penguin Books, 1971.

32 Wellins, Richard S., William C. Byham, and Jeanne M. Wilson. *Empowered Teams*. San Francisco: Jossey-Bass, 1991.

33 Weinberg, Gerald M. *The Psychology of Computer Programming*. New York: Van Nostrand Reinhold, 1971.

34 Yourdon, Edward N. *Decline and Fall of the American Programmer*. Englewood Cliffs, NJ: Prentice Hall, 1992.

Rob Thomsett is a director of Rob Thomsett & Associates. He is the author of People and Project Management *(Yourdon Press–Prentice Hall, 1980) and* Third Wave Project Management *(Yourdon Press–Prentice Hall, 1992). He has worked with Ed Yourdon, Larry Constantine, Gerald Weinberg, and Meilir Page-Jones. During his 23 years in computing, Mr. Thomsett has continued to explore the relationship between project and team management and the broader issues of the impact of computing on organizational culture. He is currently implementing new approaches to both project and team management in leading Australian and Asian organizations. He is also developing the accreditation course in project management for the Australian Computer Society and is writing a new book on advanced project management approaches. He can be reached at Rob Thomsett & Associates, 2 Buntine Crescent, Isaacs, ACT, Australia 2607 (fax +61-6-290-1517; CompuServe: 100250,1157).* ★

Chapter 4

Project Management

Project management is the art of creating the illusion that any outcome is the result of a series of predetermined, deliberate acts when, in fact, it was dumb tuck.

—Kerzner, in *Project Management*

Overview

This chapter contains four papers on the topic of project management. Each article was selected to describe how to apply related management tools and techniques to software projects. For the uninitiated, project management directs resources (people, investments, etc.) toward the delivery of acceptable products per agreed-upon specifications and approved plans, budgets, and schedules. To achieve its goals, project management requires trade-offs to be made between desired functionality, quality, cost, and schedules. To make things happen in a responsive manner, it may require the efforts of diverse groups, often geographically separated, to be integrated and evaluated. Its disciplined practice takes guts, patience, smarts, skills, understanding, and perseverance. Teamwork is required and conflicts between people and organizations must be minimized. As you will see in the articles that follow, there are many tools and techniques available to help you deal with deadline and customer pressures. The real trick to project management is using the proper technique at the right time to cope with the problems that spring up as you do the job.

Projects are living organisms. Like people, they are born, grow up, age, and die. Each project can be portrayed simply by using the following recognizable characteristics:

- There is a well-defined objective and some tangible product to be delivered.
- The requirements for the product have been defined and approved by the user.
- There is a plan to generate the product that identifies the tasks that need to be performed and their relationships.
- There is an agreed-upon schedule for completing the tasks, with start and stop dates identified.
- Budgets for the resources that are needed to realize these schedules have been defined and approved by the customer.
- There will be roadblocks that occur while conducting the project that will block management from achieving their goals.
- Management is successful when they deliver a quality product on schedule and within budget.

Project management provides you with the tools and techniques you need to plan and control a project. The primary tool used to relate the process, products, and people involved is the Work Breakdown Structure (WBS). Relationships between tasks that need to be performed to keep you on track are identified using schedule networks devised for that purpose. Performance relative to schedules and budgets is determined using metrics and schemes that measure successful milestone completions. Schedule networks clearly show when and where teams can be put to work in parallel to generate pieces of the product that will be integrated together at a later time. Tracking actuals to plan lets you to assess your progress and measure how well you are performing per your plan.

Article Summaries

The Mythical Man-Month After 20 Years, by Frederick P. Brooks, Jr. This book review highlights why Professor Brooks feels his book *The Mythical Man-Month* just keeps selling and selling. It highlights why the author's experiences managing the OS/360 project 40 years ago still seem relevant today. The book emphasizes the managerial aspects of software engineering, not the technical issues. It suggests that people are the most important ingredient for success and then goes on to discuss how to tap their potential. I have included this update because I am sure that you will find it stimulating and exciting. I also strongly recommend reading the original book.

Traditional Software Management Approaches, by Donald Reifer. This updated article summarizes the tools and techniques that project managers use to get the job done. After introducing you to a variety of classical yet available options, the paper assesses their use in information system projects. This paper provides you with a good overview of tools and techniques that are available to help you do your job. You will find that reading this paper will help you to better understand how to use the tools of project management.

In-House Software Development: What Project Management Practices Lead to Success? by June M. Verner and William M. Evanco. This paper reports the results of a survey conducted by the authors to determine the factors that lead to success in in-house software development. Although most of those managers who responded dedicated the resources needed for planning, few used their plans during development to proactively manage risk. Surprisingly, unclear requirements were identified as a pacing function as was the need to conduct retrospectives. The article highlights other practices that I am sure will interest you.

The Nine Deadly Sins of Project Planning, by Steve McConnell. This short article discusses the nine deadliest sins that the author found in project planning. None should be a surprise to experienced software managers. Most stem from either under- or overplanning. Some stem from making unreasonable assumptions, whereas others evolve from the lack of follow-through. All are truly sins that you should make an effort to avoid in your organization.

Key Terms

The ten terms that are important to understanding the topic of project management are defined as follows:

1. **Earned value.** In project management, a technique used to assess progress and budgetary performance using milestone completions. Actuals and projections are compared to earned value in order to compute trends and variances.
2. **Project.** An organized undertaking that uses human and physical resources, done once, to accomplish a specific goal.
3. **Product breakdown structure (PBS).** A family tree that organizes, defines, and graphically illustrates the structure of the product (i.e., its bill of materials).
4. **Project management.** The system of management established to focus resources on achieving project goals.
5. Project manager. A person who is held responsible for planning, controlling, and directing project activities. Many times, these responsibilities involve coordinating and integrating activities and products across functional units or organizations.
6. **Project organization.** The form of organization in which all of the people working on the project report to the project manager.
7. **Work breakdown structure (WBS).** A family tree that organizes, defines, and graphically illustrates the products, services, or tasks necessary to achieve project objectives.

In addition, the following three popular laws are widely quoted and referenced in articles included within this chapter:

1. **Murphy's Law:** Whatever can go wrong, will.
2. **Parkinson's Law:** Work expands to fill (and often exceed) the time allocated.
3. **Reifer's Law:** The easiest way to proceed according to schedule is to lie to yourself about your current state of progress.

Common Acronyms

The following acronyms are used within the articles in this chapter:

CCB	Change Control Board
CPI	Cost Performance Index
EVS	Earned Value System
IEEE	Institute of Electrical and Electronics Engineers
OBS	Organizational Breakdown Structure
PBS	Product Breakdown Structure
PERT	Program Evaluation and Review Technique
PMBOK	Project Management Book of Knowledge

| **SOW** | Statement of Work |
| **WBS** | Work Breakdown Structure |

For Your Bookshelf

There are many good books on the topic of project management. In my opinion, Devauz's book entitled *Total Project Control: A Project Manager's Guide to Integrated Project Planning, Measuring and Tracking* does the best job in communicating the theory of project management. Walker Royce's book, *Software Project Management: A Unified Framework,* on the other hand, focuses on putting the theory into practice in software projects that use the spiral life cycle paradigm. However, of the many books I have read on the topic of project management, probably the most readable was a nonsoftware text authored by H. Kerzner entitled *A Systems Approach to Planning, Scheduling and Controlling.* It has both the depth and breadth needed to communicate the rudiments of project management to just about anyone interested in the topic, independent of their application discipline. Though lacking software examples, it still provides the best overview.

The Project Management Book of Knowledge (PMBOK™*)* contains a storehouse of information relative to project management. Its first three chapters introduce you to project management and establish the context in which its recommended processes and knowledge operate. It is highly informative and chock-full of practical advice on how to put project management principles into action with your stakeholders, within the context of your life cycle.

For those interested in an outline for a project plan, let me refer you to the Standard for *Software Project Management Plans,* ANSI/IEEE Std 1058-1998, available through the IEEE Computer Society. This standard provides an outline for what many in the industry believe represents a good project plan. You can order the standard directly from the IEEE Service Center via phone at 800-678-4333 or e-mail at customer.service@ieee.org.

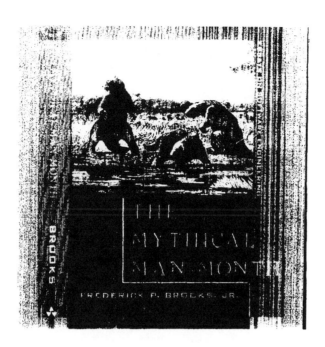

The Mythical Man-Month

AFTER 20 YEARS

Frederick P. Brooks, Jr.

WHY IS THERE A TWENTIETH ANNIVERSARY EDITION?

The plane droned through the night toward LaGuardia. Clouds and darkness veiled all interesting sights. The document I was studying was pedestrian. I was not, however, bored. The stranger sitting next to me was reading *The Mythical Man-Month*, and I was waiting to see if by word or sign he would react. Finally as we taxied toward the gate, I could wait no longer:

"How is that book? Do you recommend it?"

"Hmph! Nothing in it I didn't know already."

I decided not to introduce myself.

Why has *The Mythical Man-Month* persisted? Why is it still seen to be relevant to software practice today? Why does it have a readership outside the software engineering community, generating reviews, citations, and correspondence from lawyers, doctors, psychologists, sociologists, as well as from software people? How can a book written 20 years ago about a software-building experience 30 years ago still be relevant, much less useful?

One explanation sometimes heard is that the software development discipline has not advanced normally or properly. This view is often supported by contrasting computer software development productivity with computer hardware manufacturing productivity, which has multiplied at least a thousandfold over the two decades. As Chapter 16 explains, the anomaly is not that software has been so slow in its progress but rather that computer technology has exploded in a fashion unmatched in human history. By and large this comes from the gradual transition of computer man-

Reprinted from *IEEE Software,* September 1995.

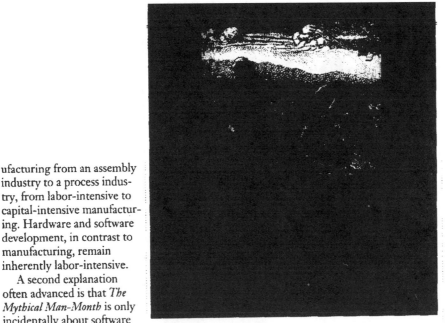

ufacturing from an assembly industry to a process industry, from labor-intensive to capital-intensive manufacturing. Hardware and software development, in contrast to manufacturing, remain inherently labor-intensive.

A second explanation often advanced is that *The Mythical Man-Month* is only incidentally about software but primarily about how people in teams make things. There is surely some truth in this; in the preface to the 1975 edition I said that managing a software project is more like other management than most programmers initially believe. I still believe that to be true. Human history is a drama in which the stories stay the same, the scripts of those stories change slowly with evolving cultures, and the stage settings change all the time. So it is that we see our twentieth-century selves mirrored in Shakespeare, Homer, and the Bible. So to the extent that *The MM-M* is about people and teams, obsolescence should be slow.

Whatever the reason, readers continue to buy the book, and they continue to send me much-appreciated comments. Nowadays I am often asked, "What do you think was wrong when written? What is now obsolete? What is really new in the software engineering world?" These quite distinct questions are all fair, and I shall address them as best I can. Not in that order, however, but in clusters of topics.

PARNAS WAS RIGHT AND I WAS WRONG ABOUT INFORMATION HIDING

In Chapter 7 I contrast two approaches to the question of how much each team member should be allowed or encouraged to know about the designs and code of other team members. In the Operating System/360 project, we decided that *all* programmers should see *all* material, i.e., each programmer having a copy of the project workbook, which came to number over 10,000 pages. Harlan Mills has argued persuasively that "programming should be a public process," that exposing all the work to everybody's gaze helps quality control both by peer pressure to do things well and by peers actually spotting flaws and bugs.

This view contrasts sharply with David Parnas's teaching that modules of code should be encapsulated with well-defined interfaces, and that the interior of such a module should be the private property of its programmer, not discernible from outside. Programmers are most effective if shielded from, not exposed to, the innards of modules not their own.

I dismissed Parnas's concept as a "recipe for disaster" in Chapter 7. Parnas was right, and I was wrong. I am now convinced that information hiding, today often embodied in object-oriented programming, is the only way of raising the level of software design.

One can indeed get disasters with either technique. Mills' technique ensures that programmers can know the detailed semantics of the interfaces they work to by knowing what is on the other side. Hiding those semantics leads to system bugs. On the other hand, Parnas's technique is robust under change and is more appropriate in a design-for-change philosophy. Chapter 16 argues the following:

♦ Most past progress in software productivity has come from eliminating non-inherent difficulties such as awkward machine languages and slow batch turnaround.

♦ There are not a lot more of these easy pickings.

♦ Radical progress is going to have to come from attacking the essential difficulties of fashioning complex conceptual constructs.

The most obvious way to do this recognizes that programs are made up of conceptual chunks much larger than the individual high-level language statement — subroutines, or modules, or classes. If we can limit design and building so that we only do the putting together and parameterization of such chunks from prebuilt collections, we have radically raised the conceptual level, and eliminated the vast amounts of work and the copious opportunities for error that dwell at the individual statement level.

Parnas's information-hiding definition of modules is the first published step in that crucially important research program, and it is an intellectual ancestor of object-oriented programming. He defined a module as a software entity with its own data model and its own set of operations. Its data can only be accessed via one of its proper operations. The second step was a contribution of several thinkers: the upgrading of the Parnas module into an *abstract data type*, from which many objects could be derived. The abstract data type provides a uniform way of thinking about and specifying module interfaces, and an access discipline that is easy to enforce.

The third step, object-oriented programming, introduces the powerful concept of *inheritance*, whereby classes (data types) take as defaults specified attributes from their ancestors in the class hierarchy. Most of what we hope to gain from object-oriented programming derives in fact from the first step, module encapsulation, plus the idea of prebuilt libraries of modules or classes *that are designed and tested for reuse.* Many people have chosen to ignore the fact that such modules are not just programs, but instead are program products in the sense discussed in Chapter 1. Some people are vainly hoping for significant module reuse without paying the initial cost of building product-quality modules — generalized, robust, tested, and documented. Object-oriented programming and reuse are discussed in Chapters 16 and 17.

PEOPLE ARE EVERYTHING (WELL, ALMOST EVERYTHING)

Some readers have found it curious that *The MM-M* devotes most of the essays to the managerial aspects of software engineering, rather than the many technical issues. This bias was due in part to the nature of my role on the IBM Operating System/360 (now MVS/370). More fundamentally, it sprang from a conviction that the quality of the people on a project, and their organization and management, are much more important

factors in success than are the tools they use or the technical approaches they take.

Subsequent researches have supported that conviction. Boehm's COCOMO model finds that the quality of the team is by far the largest factor in its success, indeed four times more potent than the next largest factor. Most academic research on software engineering has concentrated on tool. I admire and covet sharp tools. Nevertheless, it is encouraging to see ongoing research efforts on the care, growing, and feeding of people, and on the dynamics of software management.

Peopleware. A major contribution during recent years has been DeMarco and Lister's 1987 book, *Peopleware: Productive Projects and Teams.* Its underlying thesis is that "The major problems of our work are not so much *technological* as *sociological* in nature." It abounds with gems such as, "The manager's function is not to make people work, it is to make it possible for people to work." It deals with such mundane topics as space, furniture, team meals together. DeMarco and Lister provide real data from their Coding War Games that show stunning correlation between performances of programmers from the same organization, and between workplace characteristics and both productivity and defect levels.
The top performers' space is quieter, more private, better protected against interruption,

and there is more of it.... Does it really matter to you ... whether quiet, space, and privacy help your current people to do better work or [alternatively] help you to attract and keep better people?

I heartily recommend the book to all my readers.

Moving projects. DeMarco and Lister give considerable attention to team *fusion,* an intangible but vital property. I think it is management's overlooking fusion that accounts for the readiness I have observed in multilocation companies to move a project from one laboratory to another.
My experience and observation are limited to perhaps a half-dozen moves. I have never seen a successful one. One can move *missions* successfully. But in every case of attempts to move projects, the new team in fact started over, in spite of having good documentation, some well-advanced designs, and some of the people from the sending team. I think it is the breaking of fusion of the old team that aborts the embryonic product, and brings about restart.

THE POWER OF GIVING UP POWER

If one believes, as I have argued at many places in this book, that creativity comes from individuals and not

from structures or processes, then a central question facing the software manager is how to design structure and process so as to enhance, rather than inhibit, creativity and initiative. Fortunately, this problem is not peculiar to software organizations, and great thinkers have worked on it. E.F. Schumacher, in his classic, *Small is Beautiful: Economics as if People Mattered,* proposes a theory of organizing enterprises to maximize the creativity and joy of the workers. For his first principle he chooses the "Principle of Subsidiary Function" from the Encyclical *Quadragesimo Anno* of Pope Leo XIII:

It is an injustice and at the same time a grave evil and disturbance of right order to assign to a greater and higher association what lesser and subordinate organizations can do. For every social activity ought of its very nature to furnish help to the members of the body social and never destroy and absorb them.... Those in command should be sure that the more perfectly a graduated order is preserved among the various associations, in observing the principle of subsidiary function, the stronger will be the social authority and effectiveness and the happier and more prosperous the condition of the State.

Schumacher goes on to interpret:

The Principle of Subsidiary Function teaches us that the centre will gain in authority and effectiveness if the freedom

and responsibility of the lower formations are carefully preserved, with the result that the organization as a whole will be "happier and more prosperous."

How can such a structure be achieved? ... The large organization will consist of many semi-autonomous units, which we may call quasi-firms. Each of them will have a large amount of freedom, to give the greatest possible chance to creativity and entrepreneurship.... Each quasi-firm must have both a profit and loss account, and a balance sheet.

Among the most exciting developments in software engineering are the early stages of putting such organizational ideas into practice. First, the microcomputer revolution created a new software industry of hundreds of start-ups. These firms, all of them starting small, and marked by enthusiasm, freedom, and creativity. The industry is changing now, as many small companies continue to be acquired by larger ones. It remains to be seen if the larger acquirers will understand the importance of preserving the creativity of smallness.

More remarkably, high management in some large firms have undertaken to delegate power down to individual software project teams, making them approach Schumacher's quasi-firms in structure and responsibility. They are surprised and delighted at the results.

Jim McCarthy of Microsoft described to me his experience at emancipating

his teams:

Each feature team (30-40 people) owns its feature set, its schedule, and even its process of how to define, build, ship. The team is made up for four or five specialties, including building, testing, and writing. The team settles squabbles; the bosses don't. I can't emphasize enough the importance of empowerment, of the team being accountable to itself for its success.

Earl Wheeler, retired head of IBM's software business, told me his experience in undertaking the downward delegation of power long centralized in IBM's division managements:

The key thrust [of recent years] was delegating power down. It was like magic! Improved quality, productivity, morale. W° have small teams, with no central control. The teams own the process, but they have to have one. They have many different processes. They own the schedule, but they feel the pressure of the market. This pressure causes them to reach for tools on their own.

Conversations with individual team members, of course, show both an appreciation of the power and freedom that is delegated, and a somewhat more conservative estimate of how much control really is relinquished. Nevertheless, the delegation achieved is clearly a step in the right direction. It yields exactly the benefits Leo XIII predicted: the center gains in real authority by delegating power, and the organization as a whole is happier and more prosperous. ◆

Traditional Software Management Approaches

Donald J. Reifer

This paper reviews the traditional management approaches professionals use independent of discipline to manage the on-time delivery of products within allocated budgets. It highlights the tools and techniques that are normally used and serves as an introduction to many of the other papers within this tutorial.

Introduction

In the earlier chapters, I took you through the organizational framework that I used for this edition of the tutorial. This framework embraced the 3 P's of software management[1] and the functions that a software manager performs.[2] The message of these papers was that software management was not unique. To succeed, good software managers must perform the same functions that other managers tackle, independent of discipline. However, such words are easy to say, but often difficult to implement. You are probably wondering why. The following three reasons immediately come to mind:

1. Software management is, to many, an oxymoron. There is confusion over best practices and a perception that software development is unmanageable.
2. The term "management" is confusing because people use it to mean project management, general management, and product line management.
3. Project management of software projects is difficult because the product generated is intangible and hard to make visible.

Of course, there are many other reasons why software managers have difficulty succeeding. When tasked with delivering a product, managers may rely on intuition instead of planning. As we explained in earlier papers in this tutorial, managers must take product complexity, personnel skills and motivation, risk, and many other factors into account as they push their project ahead.

How do you distinguish one form of management from another? That is not difficult to do when you think about it. Project and application area management operates within an established context that tries to take full advantage of generally accepted principles of management practice. Like this book, most textbooks on general management focus on the five conventional functions of management that are conducted to run any business:

1. **Planning.** Those management activities conducted to establish a future course of action at all levels of the organization. At the executive levels, plans tend to be strategic. At lower levels, plans tend to be more tactical. At all levels, plans establish the baselines against which progress is measured and project level decisions are made.
2. **Organizing.** Those management activities conducted to structure efforts that involve collaboration and communication so that work can be effectively performed.
3. **Staffing.** The management activities conducted to acquire, develop, and retain staff resources within an organization with the prerequisite skills, knowledge, and abilities to get the work done.
4. **Directing.** Those management activities conducted to energize, motivate, and guide staff to achieve organizational and project goals.
5. **Controlling.** Those management activities conducted to determine whether or not progress is being made according to plan. Control involves measuring, monitoring, and acting on information to correct deviations, focus resources, and mitigate risk.

Each of these functions is so important that we have devoted entire chapters to them elsewhere in this tutorial. However, many of the papers that I included in these chapters focus more heavily on traditional management concepts rather than those most would associate exclusively with software. That is because I believe that software management must be placed in context with those more traditional practices used by others in the organization to run the business. As an example, project plans generated for software should employ organizational planning practices that permit senior managers to determine if they satisfy organizational goals, identify external inputs and interfaces, and, most importantly, extract commitments that the organization must make in order for the plan to succeed. Such commitments include personnel, investments in capital equipment and facilities, and intellectual property. These commitments to the project must be then factored into other plans that go across many organizations (capital, hiring, R&D, etc.) and must be balanced against the needs of the enterprise as a whole.

Classical Project Management Approaches

As we stated in the introduction to this chapter, projects are living organisms. They are born, grow up, age and die. Each project can be portrayed simply by using the following recognizable characteristics:

- There is a well-defined objective and some tangible product to be delivered.
- The requirements for the product have been defined and approved by the user.
- There is a plan to generate the product that identifies the tasks that need to be performed and their relationships.
- There is an agreed-upon schedule for completing the tasks, with start and stop dates identified.
- Budgets for the resources that are needed to realize these schedules have been defined and approved by the customer.
- There will be roadblocks that spring up during the conduct of the project that will block management from achieving their goals.
- Management is judged to be successful when they deliver a quality product on schedule and within budget.

Project management provides organizations and people with the tools and techniques they need to plan, organize, staff, direct and control a project. The primary tool used to relate the process, products and people involved is the work breakdown structure (WBS). Relationships between tasks that need to be performed to keep you on track are identified using schedule networks devised for that purpose. Performance relative to schedules and budgets is determined using metrics and schemes like earned value that organizations use to assess progress based on successful milestone completions. Networks clearly show when and where teams can be put to work in parallel to generate pieces of the product that will be integrated together at a later time. For the most part, these management techniques are amplified by the papers selected for this and other chapters within the tutorial.

Project Management Knowledge Areas

To address all of the knowledge needed to practice project management, the Project Management Institute has published the Project Management Body of Knowledge[3] (PMBOK™). The PMBOK™ organizes the knowledge a project manager needs to learn using the taxonomy shown in Figure 1. The PMBOK™ highlights the high-level processes associated with each knowledge area along with the typical inputs, outputs, and tools and techniques you can use to perform the subsidiary tasks.

Traditional Management Functions

To succeed, good project managers know that they must use their organization's system of management to perform the tasks at hand. Even when the system is broken, using it is easier than trying to fix it in most organizations. Such systems of management complement those inserted for project management. They provide project managers with specialists who can help them address issues that arise in the following areas aligned with their projects:

- **Contracting.** Their help is especially needed when structuring relationships with subcontractors and suppliers.
- **Finance and accounting.** Receiving timely reports telling you what you spent on which tasks is essential, as is a workable charter of account that accurately reports your charges.

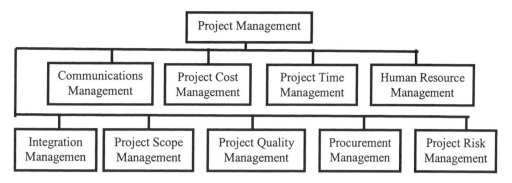

Figure 1. PMBOK™ knowledge areas.

- **Human resources.** Getting their assistance in hiring, firing, and promoting key staff members makes your job so much easier.
- **Legal.** When dealing with contractors, suppliers, and licenses for software packages, you may need your legal department's help in getting favorable terms and discounts.
- **Marketing.** Marketing can help you get accurate information about potential clients and establish relationships. They can also maintain these relationships on a day-to-day basis as you manage the delivery of products and services.
- **Purchasing.** Their help is useful when trying to purchase people's time, material, and equipment. They can coordinate the purchase order and expedite its accomplishment.
- **Research and development.** Getting your research and development departments to perform work that you can apply to your project is useful, especially if you do not have the talent to address the long-term technical issues.

As indicated, project managers cannot do everything in a vacuum. They must rely on other people and parts of the organization for help in areas in which their expertise may be lacking. They must maintain focus on their primary job, which is managing the delivery of acceptable products per the agreed-upon budget and schedule.

Tools and Techniques of the Trade

There are eight classical project management tools that software managers use to manage the delivery of products on budget and schedule. Each of these tools is discussed in turn as follows.

1. **Planning Framework.** The project normally relates the work it plans to perform to generate the product to the organization using the following three breakdown structures as illustrated in Figure 2: work breakdown structure (WBS), a product breakdown structure (PBS), and organizational breakdown structure (OBS). The WBS illustrates the work tasks needed to build the product, the OBS the parts of the organizations who will perform these tasks, and the PBS the products that will result once the work is completed. Typically, the work in the WBS is decomposed layer by layer to the lowest level of the WBS possible, the work package level. As such, a work package defines at least the following:

- The work associated with completing the task
- Work product(s) to be generated by the task
- The staffing needs, including the name of the responsible individual(s)
- The resources to be used and the expected schedule
- The reviews to be held and any scheduled work product inspections
- The acceptance criteria to be used for the work products
- Any special considerations for and/or constraints on the work

2. **Estimates.** Based on the work structure, project managers estimate the staff and schedule time it will take to perform each task. Estimates are used to predict the resources that will be needed to complete tasks per the agreed-upon requirements.

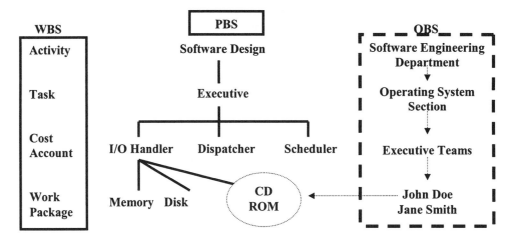

Figure 2. Work structuring concepts. *Note:* This structure arranges the work to be performed in developing a piece of executive software using a family tree so that it can be assigned to people, progress can be tracked, and those responsible can be held accountable for results.

Estimates can be developed top-down or bottom-up using any of the methods and models summarized in Table 1. It is important to remember that estimates normally exceed the budgets authorized once the project is approved. The difference is due in part to reserves that project managers retain to deal with unknowns later in the project (often about 10 to 20% of the budget). It is also important to note that many budgets are overrun because they may be arbitrary and low to begin with and, once obliged, their scope is allowed to expand out of control.

To develop their estimates, many software project managers use a cost model. As noted in the Boehm and Chulani article in this volume,[4] these models use statistical techniques like regression to accurately estimate the effort and duration associated with a software job, at least at the project level. They also allow their users to assess the many "what-if questions that arise as the estimate is being formulated. Popular cost models discussed include COCOMO-II,[5] Checkpoint,[6] PRICE S,[7] SEER,[8] and SLIM.[9]

3. **Schedules.** Schedules represent the actual calendar time budgeted for accomplishing the goals established for activities or the tasks at hand. On most projects, the customer sets final delivery dates in stone. As a consequence, project managers must try to fit the work they have estimated into a top-level milestone schedule. They do this by pursuing many tasks in parallel. They develop a network to identify previous relationships between tasks and the critical path through the schedule. Based on these relationships, they can assess how changing one task will impact another. They adjust the schedule and staff estimates at the task level to account for speeding up or slowing down the work. Based on Brook's Law,[10] they recognize that there are limits on the impact of adding manpower to preserve the schedule. They then develop schedules for WBS tasks from the top-

Table 1. Estimating methods and models

Estimating methods	Estimating models
Algorithms. Use mathematical formulas based on rules of thumb or experience (i.e., it takes fo many staff hours to generate a work package based on past experience) to estimate the resources needed for the job.	**Models.** Develop an estimate using statistical formulas that are adjusted to reflect a number of factors that resource forecasts have been found to be sensitive to (experience of people, complexity of the application, etc.
Analogy. Use past experience on similar jobs to develop an estimate using similarities and differences for a part of or the entire promect.	**Parkinson.** Develop an estimate that equates the cost estimate to the resources available (people, time, etc.) to complete the project.
Bottom up. Estimate each work package and/or component and sum them up for the entire work breakdown structure to develop an estimate for the total project.	**Price to win.** Develop an estimate of what you believe your customer is willing to pay in terms of money, staff, or schedule time to get the project done.
Delphi. Have one or more experts develop, circulate, and reach consensus on an estimate for a part of or the entire project.	**Top down.** Estimate using job's global properties and then split the total among the various components of the project.

down and bottom-up in parallel, achieving balance and overcoming inconsistencies by meeting in the middle (i.e., typically at the cost account level). Finally, as shown in Figure 3, they plot out the schedule for each tier of the WBS using milestone or Gantt charts as their primary form of representation. These tiered schedules are then used as inputs to the budgeting process.

4. **Budgets.** A budget is a statement of expected results expressed in numerical terms. Management uses budgets as benchmarks to track progress and manage the effort at the work package level. Budgets are formulated at the task level for staff and other expenditures (travel, purchases, subcontracts, etc.). As we discussed above, trade-offs between budget and time are made as the schedule is developed to address fixed delivery dates. The results of these trade-offs are an adjusted forecast of the number and type of people needed to perform each task that appears on the work breakdown structure (along with any other associated expenditures). However, synergy between tasks that occurs as a function of teamwork and intergroup coordination is often not factored into the estimate. Neither are the reserves that project managers take off the top to handle the unknowns as they occur later in the project. As a consequence, budgets allocated are most likely slimmer than estimates. However, reconciliation of the differences between estimates and budgets may not be as difficult as you think. There may be cost accounts that you can tap into in order to offset some of the cost differential. For example, you could purchase workstations as capital equipment instead of handling them as a project charge. In their last budget preparation iteration, project managers again adjust schedules and budgets to level out the number of people assigned to perform individual work breakdown structure tasks and their transition onto the project (i.e., staff-loading considerations). An example of a staff-loading diagram is shown in Figure 4 to illustrate typical staffing curves at the task level and tracking mechanisms (e.g., used to determine whether you are staffing the task at the planned rate).

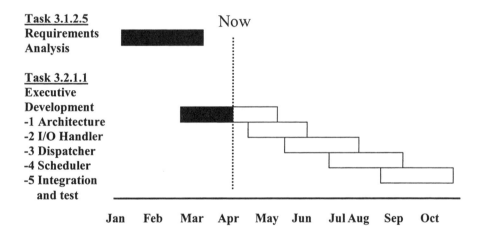

Figure 3. Typical milestone schedule. *Note:* The darkened part of the box indicates the percentage of the task that has been completed computed using rate-of-progress charts.

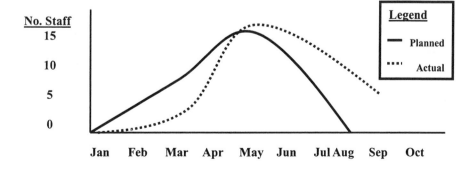

Figure 4. Staff-loading diagram for a typical task.

123

5. **Networks.** As shown in Figure 5, networks refer to diagrams that show the logical relationships that exist between schedule activities and their precedence relationships. Networks can either be drawn as a function of activities or milestones. Networks are very useful when adjusting schedules because they show you the impact of your actions based on the relationships that exist between tasks. Networks also provide you with the following management information:

- **Slack paths.** Refers to tasks that you can delay starting because they are not on the critical path through the network.
- **Critical chains.** Refers to the chain of critical tasks on a project.
- **The critical path.** The longest path from start to finish in the network or the path that does not have any slack; thus, the path corresponding to the shortest time in which the project can be completed.
- **Schedule buffers.** The extra time or reserve that project managers have in their schedules that can be allocated to handle contingencies that arise as the project unfolds.

6. **Organizational Processes.** The main reason that I and many other project managers like the Software Capability Maturity Model (CMM)[11] is that it simplifies the job. Instead of having to worry about developing processes, the project manager only has to tailor them in his/her project plan. Most of the important processes are covered. However, there are known holes (e.g., risk and supplier management). Some of these have been addressed by the new CMM Integration (CMMI).[12] Other things that you need to be concerned about for which there are no current fixes include COTS and product line management.

7. **Metrics and Management Indicators.** The next variety of tools and techniques that we will discuss are metrics and management indicators. Metrics are quantitative measures that rate the degree to which a system, process, or component possesses a given attribute. In contrast, indicators use metrics to characterize the prescribed state of affairs relative to performance. As an example, error density can be used to characterize the reliability of a piece of software. If the error density is high, the reliability tends to be low. Error density can also provide management with indicators relative to whether or not the software has been thoroughly tested. For this example, the actual error density as a function in time would be compared to some benchmark that management would use to make the decision relative to whether the software has been adequately tested. As I explained in my paper on the topic,[13] managers use metrics to help answer questions that they have about the process, product, and people that populate their projects. For example, they use the rework rate to determine whether the processes that they are using on the project are effective. If a lot of rework occurred, they would question their use. As a second example, they would measure the complexity of their products. They would try to keep them as simple as possible because this effort would make the products easier to understand and test. They would instruct their staffs to measure and report complexity using one of the commonly used metrics like cyclomatic number.[14] They would plot complexity trends by component to focus on achieving their simplicity goal and periodically track status.

8. **Reviews.** Project managers should conduct frequent technical, managerial and customer reviews to gain insight into what is happening on their project. Because managers are often removed from the daily action, they need to delve deeply to

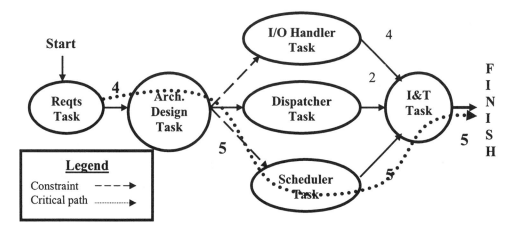

Figure 5. Schedule network and critical path. *Note:* The critical path will take 19 weeks because the scheduler task paces the way through the network (i.e., it doesn't matter that the dispatcher and I/O handler can be done more quickly). This means that the dispatcher task can be started later than originally scheduled because it will take three weeks less to get through the network.

leam what the project status is and where the problems lie. Technical reviews are held to determine whether the product is technically sound, the process is working, and the people possess the skills that are needed to get the job done. Such reviews, which most often materialize as software inspections, are held throughout the life cycle. They are used to build teams, get several sets of eyes involved in reviewing products, and pinpoint problems before they have a chance to propagate. In contrast, management reviews are held to determine project status and progress and manage risk. Such reviews typically assess budgetary, schedule, and technical performance using metrics and management indicators. When variances from plans arise at these meetings, the issues raised are addressed until satisfactorily handled. Customer reviews are the final type of reviews held on a project. They are conducted to provide the customer with assurance that the product they will receive functions and performs as specified and expected. Such meetings can be more than handholding sessions. The customer representative can work closely with the developers to communicate their view of what the requirements mean and how their usability/support concerns can be adequately addressed.

9. **Reports.** As expected, a large number of reports are also generated as a by-product of reviews and the systems and procedures utilized for managing a project. Project managers are interested in gaining insight, not generating paperwork. They gather data from a variety of sources to assess their performance, determine rates of progress, confirm variances, identify the issues, and pinpoint the problems. The bigger the project, the more difficult it is to get a true picture of status. In response, project management uses all of the information at its disposal to try to paint an accurate picture. That is why the information provided to them must be current, accurate, and indicative of what is really going on in the project.

Focusing on Results

The nine tools we described provide project managers with the infrastructure they need to manage a project. The planning framework structures the work and relates it to the products being generated and organizations involved. Estimates are the first step in establishing budgets and schedules. Networks permit managers to make trade-offs between time and effort and to determine what tasks are on the critical path. Organizational processes, once tailored, provide the project manager with the detailed work-related practices that he/she needs to get the job done once the project is initiated. As scoped, project management's initial goal is to develop a workable plan that has a high probability of being successful.

Once the plan is approved, project managers focus on building teams, providing direction, determining status, tracking progress, resolving risks, and, most importantly, controlling the effort. In essence, project management's main task is facilitating getting the job done by getting the right people involved at the right times. In addition to tracking progress and controlling cost, schedule, and technical performance on the project, the project manager's major responsibilities include working problems, resolving issues, mitigating risks, getting experts in needed specialties involved (engineering as well as contracts, legal, etc.), empowering teams, energizing and motivating subordinates, and holding the customer's hand. Many projects fail during execution because the project manager tracks instead of manages the effort.

The key to managing the effort is taking action. All of the tools we discussed provide managers with an infrastructure by which to manage. Good managers use this infrastructure to collect the information they need to determine where they are, where they are heading, and whether they can deliver an acceptable product on schedule and within budget. If the pointers indicate they will not meet these goals, management needs to figure out how to recoup, turn the project around, and meet their commitments. This often forces everyone into a replanning exercise.

Project managers can recover from disaster. They can do this because they have the power to:

- Provide subordinates with interesting and challenging work assignments.
- Recommend subordinates for promotion and advancement.
- Approve the opening of cost accounts.
- Authorize approved work to either start or stop.
- Approve budgets and schedules.
- Establish work priorities for individuals and teams.
- Authorize the use of resources and reserves.
- Delegate actions to subordinates via action items.

By using these powers, project managers can realign work priorities so that issues they feel are important are addressed as the first order of business. They can allocate buffers (i.e., the extra time in the schedule allocated to handling contingencies that arise) and reserves (i.e., the budget or schedule that has been held in reserve to mitigate cost and/or schedule risk and

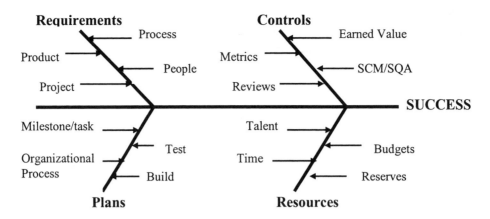

Figure 6. Software management fishbone diagram.

growth) to cope with problems as they arise. They can off-load the team of conflicting responsibilities and provide them with the additional support and encouragement to resolve the issue. They can bring in outside experts and get the customer involved when help is needed in developing and selling the solution. It has been my experience that problems do not happen all at once. They occur over time because management fails to read the trouble signs. It has also been my experience that easy solutions typically do not work for hard problems.

Summary, Conclusion, and Recommendations

Figure 6 summarizes many of the points made in this article. It uses a fishbone diagram to identify what I believe are the key successful attributes for software projects. The four branches specify the key attributes: requirements, plans, controls, and resources. The extensions identify the critical attributes. For example, to succeed you need the following four critical resources: talent, budget, time, and reserves. Each of these attributes is of equal importance as evidenced during retrospectives[15] held on past projects, both successful and failures.

In conclusion, there is no mystery when it comes to being a successful software project manager. The classical techniques (structuring the work via a WBS and relating it to the product and those doing the work, using networks to identify the critical path, controlling progress using metrics and management indicators, etc.) that others use to foster delivery of acceptable products on time and within budget work for software as well. The trick to making these techniques work is to tailor them to the specifics of the project. For those who want to learn more about these techniques, see the following references and those in the many articles that appear in this edition of the tutorial.

References

1. Donald J. Reifer, "The "3 P's" of Software Management," page 15, this volume.
2. Donald J. Reifer, "Principles of Software Engineering Project Management," page 9, this volume.
3. Project Management Institute, *A Guide to the Project Management Body of Knowledge (PMBOK™)*, 2000.
4. Barry W. Boehm and Sunita Chulani, "Software Engineering Economics," page xxxxxxxxxxxxxxxxx, this volume.
5. Barry W. Boehm, Chris Abts, A. Winsor Brown, Sunita Chulani, Bradford K. dark, Ellis Horowitz, Ray Madachy, Donald Reifer, and Bert Steece, *Software Cost Estimation with COCOMO II*, Prentice-Hall, 2000.
6. T. Capers Jones, *Applied Software Measurement*, McGraw-Hill, 1997.
7. Robert Park, "The Central Equations of the PRICE Software Cost Model," in *Proceedings of the 4th COCOMO User's Group Meeting*, November 1988.
8. Galorath Inc., *SEER-SEM User's Manual*, 2000.
9. Lawrence Putnam, Sr. and Ware Myers, *Measures of Excellence*, Prentice-Hall, 1992.
10. Frederick P. Brooks, Jr., *The Mythical Man-Month* (Anniversary Edition), Addison-Wesley, 1995.
11. M. Paulk., C. V. Weber, B. Curtis, and M. B. Chrises, *The Capability Maturity Model: Guidelines for Improving the Software Process*, Addison-Wesley, 1995.

12. Dennis M. Ahem, Aaron Clouse, and Richard Turner, *CMMI Distilled,* Addison-Wesley, 2001.

13. Donald J. Reifer, "Metrics and Management," page xxxxxxxxxxx, this volume.

14. Dick B. Simmons, Newton C. Ellis, Hiroko Fujihara, and Way Kuo, *Software Measurement: A Visualization Toolkit,* Prentice-Hall, 1997.

15. Norman L. Kerth, *Project Retrospectives,* Dorset House Publishing Co., 2001.

In-House Software Development:
What Project Management Practices Lead to Success?

June M. Verner, *National Information and Communications Technology Australia*

William M. Evanco, *Drexel University*

Project management is an important part of software development, both for organizations that rely on third-party software development and for those whose software is developed primarily in-house. However, most software engineering research emphasizes "technical matters above behavioral matters."[1] Moreover, quantitative survey-based research regarding software development's early, nontechnical aspects is lacking. Additionally, in-house software development failures are unlikely

to receive the same attention as third-party software development failures with their attendant litigation and negative media coverage.

To help provide a project management perspective for managers responsible for in-house software development, we conducted a survey in an attempt to determine the factors that lead to successful projects. We chose a survey because of its simplicity and because we hoped to find relationships among variables. Also, a survey let us cover more projects at a lower cost than would an equivalent number of in-

terviews or a series of case studies. Our results provide general guidance for business and project managers to help ensure that their projects succeed.

Our questionnaire

We conducted wide-ranging, structured discussions with 21 senior software practitioners at a large financial organization to document their views regarding software project success or failure and the practices they consider important. We developed our questionnaire on the basis of these discussions, which focused on the practitioners' recent projects.

This practitioner group responded to our questionnaire twice—for a project they considered successful and for one they considered a failure (42 projects total). Later, we distributed our questionnaire to practitioners who developed in-house software for a variety of

A survey of in-house software development practices investigated why projects succeed or fail. A clear vision of the final product, good requirements, active risk management, and postmortem reviews can all help increase the odds of success.

Reprinted from *IEEE Software,* January/February 2005.

commercial US organizations such as financial institutions, banks, pharmaceutical companies, and insurance companies. This set of questionnaires included descriptions of 80 unique projects. In total, we surveyed 101 respondents about 122 projects. Our sample wasn't random, but rather a convenience sample of practitioners we know.

We organized the questionnaire into seven sections, three of which we discuss in this article: project management, requirements elicitation and management, and cost and effort estimation and scheduling. We also asked respondents if they considered the referenced project successful (according to their own definitions of success). We discuss the questionnaire's remaining four sections elsewhere.[2]

Results and analysis

Our sample size (standard error 0.002) was reasonably large for empirical software engineering research. Of all the projects in the survey, the respondents regarded 62 percent as successful and 38 percent as unsuccessful. Eighty-seven percent were development projects (55 percent successful), and 13 percent were large (in terms of effort) maintenance or enhancement projects (60 percent successful). Overall, 64 percent of our projects had nine or fewer full-time employees, 27 percent had between 10 and 19, and the rest had 20 or more, with a median of eight.

Nineteen percent of the projects had no prescribed development methodology. Fifty-seven percent used a waterfall methodology, five percent a modified waterfall, five percent prototyping, two percent incremental delivery, two percent a spiral model, and 10 percent an in-house proprietary methodology.

Table 1 shows the percentage of yes responses to the survey questions. It also shows significant correlations with project success (<0.05) as well as some associations between responses to selected questions. The table shows five aspects of project management: the project manager (prefixed with M in column one), requirements analysis (R), cost and effort estimation and scheduling (C), risk assessment (A), and postmortem (P).

Project management

Because we assume that project management and the project manager (PM) are pivotal to a project's outcome, we begin by analyzing PM participation in the development process. Although you'd expect software development projects to have PMs, five percent of our sample projects didn't. Most of these projects were small, with fewer than seven full-time personnel equivalents. However, one failed project with 100 internal practitioners and 25 contractors had no PM. In 16 percent of the projects, the PM changed at least once. This volatility, practitioners reported, was very disruptive. The largest project in our survey had 80 internal practitioners and 100 contractors, and the PM was changed; the practitioners viewed it as a failure. For all projects, changing the PM was significantly negatively correlated with project success.

The PMs' software development experience ranged from under six months to 22 years, with a median of five years. Fifty-one percent of PMs had a software development background, 35 percent had a business background, and the rest had other backgrounds, such as engineering. Neither a PM with a software development background (M14) nor one experienced in the application area (M2) was significantly associated with project success. This result agrees with observations that a broad background is more useful than expertise in any particular technical area. According to Jaak Jurison, "[s]uccessful project managers are generalists, not technical specialists." Although some technical competence is helpful, managerial and interpersonal skills are more important.[3] Our results support this perspective; we found that the abilities to communicate (M5) and relate well with staff (M6) were significantly associated and positively correlated with success (this type of relationship is referred to as "positively associated" from here on).

An above-average PM (M1) was also positively associated with project success. This isn't surprising, because "poor management can increase software costs more rapidly than any other factor."[4] Table 1 also shows that an above-average PM (M1) is involved with good schedule estimates (C4) made with appropriate requirements information (C2). A PM with a clear vision of the project (M4) was also positively associated with success. Lack of a clear vision leads to poorly defined goals and specifications, poor requirements, insufficient project-planning time, lack of a project plan, and unrealistic deadlines and budgets.[3]

For all projects, changing the project manager was significantly negatively correlated with project success.

Table 1

Survey results

ID	Question	Yes answers (%)			Direction of success relationship	χ^2 association with project success	Association with other questions*†
		Successful projects	Failures	All projects			
M0	Did the project have a project manager (PM)?	97	95	96	**	**	**
M1	Was the PM above average?	76	34	55	+	0.000	M2, M3, M4, M5, M7, M8, R1, R2, R4, R5, R7, R8, C2, C3, C4, C5(–), C6, C7, P1
M2	Was the PM experienced in the application area?	68	73	62	**	**	M3, M5
M3	Did the PM understand the customer's problems?	79	49	67	+	0.001	M7, R1, R4, R5, R7, R9, R10(–), C4, C6
M4	Did the PM have a clear vision of the project?	86	44	71	+	0.000	M4, M7, R2, R4, R5, R7, C2, C4
M5	Did the PM communicate well with the staff?	68	32	54	+	0.000	M3, M4, M5, M7, R1, R2, R4, R5, R7, R8, C2, C4, C5(–), C6, C7
M6	Did the PM relate well with the development staff?	70	35	57	+	0.001	**
M7	Did the PM delegate authority?	94	83	90	**	**	R4, R9, C2, C7
M8	Did the PM pitch in and help when necessary?	56	61	58	**	**	M2, M3, M5, R2(–), C1(–), C5, C6(–))
M9	Did the PM control the project?	74	56	68	+	0.042	M1, C5(–), C6
M10	Did the PM treat the staff equally?	78	56	70	+	0.020	M1, M2, M3, M4, M9, R2, R4, R5, R7, R8, C2, C3, C5(–)
M11	Did the PM let the staff know he/she appreciated their working long hours?	74	51	65	+	0.008	M1, M3, M4, M5, M10, R7, C2, C3, C4, C5(–), C7(–)
M12	Did the PM ensure the staff was rewarded for working long hours?	48	21	37	+	0.003	M1, M3, M4, M5, M9, M10, M11, R1, R2, R5, C2, C3, C4
M13	Was the PM changed during the project?	11	24	16	–	0.05	M4(–), M8(–), R2(–), A2(–)
M14	Did the PM have a software development background?	49	54	51	**	**	**
R1	Were requirements gathered using a specific method?	50	49	50	**	**	R2, R8
R2	Were requirements complete and accurate at the project's start?	45	19	52	+	0.004	R1, R6
R3	If not complete at start, were the requirements completed later?	76	26	53	+	0.000	**

* All associations are reciprocal but are only shown once.
** There is no relationship or the relationship is shown as its reciprocal.
† A negative symbol in parentheses means variables are significantly associated with a negative correlation.

Our data supports the view that management support of the development team is essential to motivate the team to work effectively toward organizational goals.[5] Appreciating and rewarding staff who worked long hours (M11, M12) were positively associated with success.

Using logistic regression (we required in our logistic regressions that the explanatory variable have at least a five percent level of significance), we found that the best PM predic-

Table 1

Survey results (cont.)

ID	Question	Yes answers (%)			Direction of success relationship	χ^2 association with project success	Association with other questions*†
		Successful projects	Failures	All projects			
R4	Overall, were the requirements good?	86	39	68	+	0.000	R2
R5	Did the project have a well-defined scope?	79	40	64	+	0.000	R2, R4
R6	Did the scope increase during the project?	61	74	66	**	**	R2(−), R9(−), R10
R7	Did users make adequate time available for requirements gathering?	83	40	66	+	0.000	R1, R2, R4, R6(−), R8
R8	Was there a central repository for requirements?	73	42	61	+	0.003	R4, R5
R9	Did the requirements result in well-defined deliverables?	76	35	60	+	0.000	R1, R2, R4, R5, R8
R10	Did the project's size have an impact on the requirements?	23	54	35	−	0.000	R4(−), R5(−), R7(−)
C1	Was the PM involved in making initial cost and effort estimates?	35	27	32	**	**	R4(-)
C2	Was the delivery decision made with appropriate requirements information?	73	17	51	+	0.000	R2, R4, R5, R7, R8, R10(−), C1
C3	Did the project have a schedule?	83	79	81	**	**	R2, R5
C4	If yes, were the effort and schedule estimates good?	49	12	33	+	0.000	R1, R2, R4, R5, R7, R8, R10(−), C2, C5(−), C6, C7(−)
C5	At some stage, were the developers involved in making estimates?	20	44	29	−	0.007	R2(−), R4(−), R7(−), R8(−), C2(−)
C6	Did the project have adequate staff to meet the schedule?	82	44	67	+	0.000	R1, R2, R4, R5, R7, R8, R10(−), C2, C5(−)
C7	Were staff added late to meet an aggressive schedule?	19	54	32	−	0.000	R4(−), R7(−), R10, C2(−), C6(−)
A1	Were potential risks identified at the project's start?	72	49	62	+	0.029	M1, M3, M5, M10, M12, R1, R2, R4, R5, R7, R8, C2, C4, C5(−), C6, C7(−), A2, A3
A2	Were risks incorporated into the project plan?	63	40	53	**	**	M1, M5, M10, M11, M12, R7, R8, C1, C2, C4, C6, C7(−)
A3	Were the risks managed throughout the project?	60	20	43	+	0.000	M1, M3, M4, M5, M9, M10, M12, R2, R4, R5, R7, R8, C2, C4, C5(−), C6, C7(−), A1, P1
P1	Was a postmortem review held?	35	21	29	NA	NA	R4, A1, A2, A3, P2
P2	If there was a postmortem review, were its results made available to other groups?	43	14	32	NA	NA	A1

tor of project success was M4 (Did the PM have a clear vision of the project?). This variable predicted 86 percent of successes, 56 percent of failures, and 75 percent correctly overall.

Requirements elicitation and management

Good project management necessitates complete, consistent requirements.[6] Although gathering requirements with a specific methodology (R1) was significantly associated with

We found that if requirements were initially incomplete, completing them during the project was positively associated with success.

requirements being complete and accurate at the project's start (R2), it wasn't significantly associated with project success. However, in 54 percent of our projects, respondents didn't know what requirements methodology their project's systems analysts used. Again, this didn't surprise us, because most respondents had no interaction with the systems analysts.

Requirements-gathering methods. Among the 46 percent of respondents who knew about requirements gathering, four projects used prototyping and nine used JAD (joint application design) sessions with prototyping. Eleven of these 13 projects were successful. Interviews and focus groups were the remaining projects' main requirements-gathering methods. Eight projects used UML to document requirements, but only three of these were successful. Practitioners commented that there were "too many new things without a pilot" and "unfamiliar methods." However, the failed UML projects had other problems such as poor estimates and no risk management, so their failures weren't necessarily due to using UML.

Managing changing requirements. Nearly half the projects began with incomplete requirements (R2); predictably, the scope changed for many of these projects during development (R6). A χ^2 test of R2 with R6 was significant. The scope was more likely to change for larger projects. Given that an organization needs control over the requirements function to advance from the lowest CMMI (Capability Maturity Model Integration, see www.sei.cmu.edu/cmmi) level, it's obvious that many of our sample's organizations are still at that level. These results agree with a survey Colin J. Neill and Philip A. Laplante conducted in 2002,[7] whose respondents thought that their companies didn't do enough requirements engineering. The number of projects that began with poor requirements suggests that these organizations should develop their projects using methodologies designed to deal with unclear requirements. However, this isn't the case.

The importance of requirements management. Our results, shown in Table 1, demonstrate that requirements continue to be an enormous problem for IS development and one of the most common causes of runaway projects.[8] Consistent with Robert Glass's observations,[9]

we found that good requirements (R4) that were complete and accurate at the project's start (R2) with a well-defined project scope (R5), resulting in well-defined software deliverables (R9), were positively associated with project success. The importance of user involvement in requirements gathering (R7) supports observations by Glass[9] and Carl Clavedetschers.[10]

Although Barry Boehm includes a "continuing stream of requirements changes" in his top 10 risk items,[11] we didn't find an association between changing the scope during the project (R6) and project success. Instead, we found that if requirements were initially incomplete, completing them during the project (R3) was positively associated with success, as was being able to manage requirements and any changes to them through a central repository (R8). Only 60 percent of our projects used a central repository, supporting Clavedetscher's suggestion that software developers "fail to use requirements management to surface (early) errors or problems."[12]

When a project's size impacted requirements gathering (R10), project success was negatively influenced. This result agrees with another of Glass's observations,[9] suggesting that large projects hamper requirements gathering and lead to unclear, incomplete, and potentially unstable requirements.

Using logistic regression, we found that the best risk management predictor of project success was R4 (the requirements were good), which predicted 89 percent of successes, 58 percent of failures, and 78 percent correctly overall.

Cost and effort estimation and scheduling

Good cost and schedule estimates (C4) affect project success.[5] As early as 1975, Frederick Brooks stated that more projects have gone awry for lack of calendar time than from all other causes combined.[12] Optimistic estimation is still one of the two most common causes for runaway projects,[8] with cost and schedule failures exceeding any other kind of software failures in practice.[13] Boehm includes unrealistic schedules and budgets in his top 10 risk items.[11] However, having a schedule (C3) wasn't associated with project success; not having a schedule means you don't have to meet one.

Who's making the estimates? We initially assumed that the PM would be involved in deciding the delivery date because he or she would likely know the project's technology, participants, and development practices better than anyone else. This assumption was mainly incorrect. Higher-level management, marketing, or the customer or user generally made initial estimates. The PM was involved in making initial cost and effort estimates for only 33 percent of the projects (C1), but responses to this question weren't associated with project success. PMs were able to negotiate the schedule in just under half (48 percent) of the projects where they weren't included in the initial delivery date or budget decisions.

In these organizations, the wrong people are making the estimates. This observation agrees with Glass.[9] When the PM had no say in project estimates, our respondents indicated that only 31 percent of those estimates were good. Given the lack of PM participation in estimation, it's understandable that only about half of the projects' delivery dates were made with appropriate requirements information (C2). Our result agrees with Glass[8] that most software estimates are performed at the beginning of the life cycle before the requirements phase and thus before the problem is understood. It's noteworthy that 76 percent of the estimates considered to be above average had some kind of PM input.

Estimate accuracy. Seventy-four percent of the projects were underestimated, 36 percent were accurately estimated, and no projects were overestimated. Overall, respondents thought that 38 percent of the estimates were either poor or very poor (33 percent of these projects were successful), 27 percent were average (66 percent successful), and 35 percent were either good or very good (86 percent successful). Many estimates initially thought to be of average quality were underestimates. Developers were more likely to contribute to project estimates when the requirements were incomplete, and developer involvement in making the estimates (C5) was negatively associated with project success. Furthermore, developers might not have a global perspective of the project, which could handicap them in producing projectwide estimates.

Project size was significantly related to whether a project had a schedule. Larger projects were more likely to have a schedule but were also more likely to have inadequate staffing levels, staff added late, and estimates that didn't take staff leave into account. Finally, adding staff late to meet an aggressive schedule (C7) was negatively related to project success, in agreement with Brooks's findings in *The Mythical Man Month*.[12]

Using logistic regression, we found that C2 (making delivery decisions with the appropriate requirements information) was the best C predictor of project outcomes, predicting 73 percent of successes, 83 percent of failures, and 77 percent correctly overall.

Risk assessment and postmortem reviews

Unfortunately, most developers and PMs perceive risk management processes and activities as creating extra work and expense, and risk management is the least-practiced project management discipline.[14] Respondents indicated that 33 percent of the projects had no risks, even though 62 percent of these projects failed. As Tom DeMarco and Timothy Lister noted, "if a project has no risks, don't do it."[5] Large projects were significantly less likely to have risks incorporated into their project plans. Active risk management characterizes software project management quality,[6] and managing risks throughout the project (A3) was significantly associated with project success.[5] The association between responses to questions A1, A2, and A3 and the PM being above average (M1) supports this observation.

Using logistic regression, we found that A3 (risks were managed throughout the project) predicted project success the best, predicting 60 percent of successes, 80 percent of failures, and 69 percent correctly overall.

Postmortem reviews are important for process improvement,[8] but companies seldom perform them. As a result, they tend to repeat the same mistakes project after project.[1,15] Few organizations conducted project postmortems, and those that conducted them didn't do so consistently (for our first 42 projects from the same organization, only 33 percent had postmortem reviews). Holding postmortem reviews (P1) was significantly associated with good requirements (R4) and managing risks throughout the process (A1, A2, and A3).

Discussion and recommendations

Our respondents' organizations rely heavily on software for many business functions. While we wouldn't assume our results are typ-

> **Postmortem reviews are important for process improvement, but companies seldom perform them. As a result, they tend to repeat the same mistakes.**

134

ical of all organizations, we believe they're reasonably typical of organizations that develop software in house. Surveys are based on self-reported data, which reflects what people say happened, not what they actually did or experienced. Because we surveyed software developers, our results are limited to their knowledge, attitudes, and beliefs regarding the projects and PMs with which they were involved. However, because most of the projects were fairly small, we believe that our respondents had a reasonable knowledge of most project events. The overall preponderance of small projects might, however, bias our results.

The best predictors of successful project outcomes, using logistic regression, were M4 (Did the project manager have a clear vision of the project?) with R4 (Overall, were the requirements good?) and C2 (Was the delivery decision made with adequate requirements information?). Combining these factors, 90 percent of successes, 70 percent of failures, and 82 percent of projects overall were predicted correctly.

We were surprised that so many projects started (and continued) with unclear requirements. Why are PMs prepared to go ahead with projects that don't have appropriate requirements, or without at least using a life-cycle methodology that can deal with unclear requirements? It's common wisdom that good requirements lead to software development success, so why are PMs prepared to jeopardize project success in this fashion? Poor requirements negatively affect the estimation process, leading to schedule and cost underestimates and inadequate staffing; staffing itself then becomes a major risk factor.

Business management seems to lack an appreciation of the steps necessary to successfully execute a project. Not only were PMs excluded from initial discussions, they subsequently weren't permitted to negotiate what the business managers had decided. Consequently, PMs are frequently short-circuited in managing their projects; they should be proactive in ensuring their participation in the estimation process rather than leaving it to someone else. Senior management needs better education regarding the importance of adequate requirements, systematic effort and schedule estimates, and the need to consult the PM for projects with fixed budgets. At the other end of the spectrum, developer input to the estimates improved neither the chances of

success nor the estimates, probably because developers appeared to be asked for estimates only if the requirements were unclear.

A mismatch also exists between risk identification and control. Although most PMs identified risks at the project's start, fewer than half followed through during development. No respondent addressed risk assessment and management or the lack of it during our early discussions. Again, this underscores that risk management isn't routinely part of development.[5]

We found that managers viewed each project as a standalone entity and therefore didn't perceive postmortem reviews as important. Neither business managers nor project managers appeared to understand the specific causes of failed projects; consequently, they're unlikely to improve their performance on subsequent projects. Do these organizations have a culture of not admitting to mistakes? Managers ought to view finding out what went wrong with a project as a good thing, not something to hide. If PMs can't admit to or investigate failure, their projects will likely continue to fail.

nalysis of our survey suggests that a number of questions require further research. For example, what kinds of pressures lead PMs to not only start projects with poor requirements but also complete them without really knowing what the requirements are? How can PMs arrange to be part of estimation and scheduling, and how can they ensure that estimates are done with adequate requirements information? Why are risk planning and management so frequently ignored? And finally, why do so few organizations conduct postmortem reviews, and why don't they perform them consistently?

Table 1 shows that current practices are fair at best. The opportunity for greatest improvement is at a project's start, in the requirements and risk identification and control areas. We must face these issues if we wish to increase software project management quality and success. ⦿

References
1. R. Glass, "Project Retrospectives, and Why They Never Happen," *IEEE Software*, vol. 19, no. 5, 2002, pp. 112, 111.
2. J.M. Verner and W.M. Evanco, "An Investigation into Software Process Knowledge," *Managing Software En-*

gineering Knowledge, A. Aurum et al., eds., Springer-Verlag, 2003, pp. 29-47.

3. J. Jurison, "Software Project Management: The Manager's View," *Comm. Assoc. for Information Systems*, vol. 2, article 17, 1999; http://cais.isworld.org/articles/2-17/default.asp?View=html&x=33&y=6.

4. B.W. Boehm, *Software Engineering Economics*, Prentice Hall, 1981.

5. T. DeMarco and T. Lister, *Waltzing with Bears*, Dorset House, 2003.

6. J.S. Osmundson et al., "Quality Management Metrics for Software Development," *Information and Management*, vol. 40, no. 8, 2003, pp. 799–812.

7. C.J. Neill and P.A. Laplante, "Requirements Engineering: State of the Practice," *IEEE Software*, vol. 20, no. 6, 2003, pp. 40–45.

8. R. Glass, "Frequently Forgotten Fundamental Facts about Software Engineering," *IEEE Software*, vol. 18, no. 3, pp. 112, 110–111.

9. R. Glass, "How Not to Prepare for A Consulting Assignment and Other Ugly Consultancy Truths," *Comm. ACM*, vol. 41, no. 12, 1998, pp. 11–13.

10. C. Clavedetscher, "User Involvement Key to Success," *IEEE Software*, vol. 15, no. 2, 1998, pp. 30, 32.

11. B.W. Boehm, "Software Risk Management Principles and Practice," *IEEE Software*, vol. 8, no. 1, 1991, pp. 32–41.

12. F.P. Brooks Jr., *The Mythical Man Month: Essays on Software Engineering*, Addison-Wesley, 1975.

13. R. Glass, "Error-Free Software Remains Extremely Elusive," *IEEE Software*, vol. 20, no. 1, 2003, pp. 104, 103.

14. Y.H. Kwak and C.W. Ibbs, "Calculating Project Management's Return on Investment," *Project Management J.*, vol. 31, no. 2, 2000, pp. 38–47.

15. B. Collier, T. DeMarco, and P. Fearey, "A Defined Process for Project Postmortem Review," *IEEE Software*, vol. 13, no. 4, 1996, pp. 65–72.

About the Authors

June M. Verner is a senior principal research scientist in the Empirical Software Engineering group at National Information and Communications Technology Ltd. Australia. Her research interests include software project management, risk management, and software process and product measurement. She received her PhD in software engineering from Massey University. She's a member of the IEEE Computer Society and the British Computer Society. Contact her at National ICT Australia, Australian Technology Park, Alexandria, Sydney, Australia; june.verner@nicta.com.au.

William M. Evanco is an associate professor in Drexel University's College of Information Science and Technology. His research interests include software product and process measurement and software performance analysis. He's also worked at Mitretek and MITRE in software development and intelligent transportation systems. He received his PhD in theoretical physics from Cornell University. Contact him at the College of Information Science and Technology, Drexel Univ., 3141 Chestnut St., Philadelphia, PA 19104; william.evanco@cis.drexel.edu.

The Nine Deadly Sins of Project Planning

Steve McConnell

At a time when some software organizations have achieved close to perfect on-time delivery records,[1] others continue to suffer mediocre results. Surveys generally indicate that poor project planning is one of the top sources of problems.

How can you recognize a badly planned software project? Here are nine of the deadliest sins I've found in project planning.

1. Not planning at all

By far the most common planning problem is simply not planning at all, and this sin is easily avoided. A person need not be an expert planner to plan effectively. I've seen numerous instances of projects planned by rank amateurs that have run well simply because the people in charge had carefully considered their project's specific needs. Forced to choose between an expert project planner who doesn't carefully think through his plan or an amateur who has thoroughly evaluated his project needs, I'll bet on the amateur every time.

2. Failing to account for all project activities

If Deadly Sin #1 is not planning at all, Deadly Sin #2 is not planning *enough*. Some project plans are created using the assumption that no one on the software team will get sick, attend training, go on vacation, or quit. Core activities are often underestimated to a great degree. Plans created using unrealistic assumptions like these set up a project for disaster.

There are numerous variations on this theme. Some projects neglect to account for ancillary activities such as the effort needed to create setup programs, convert data from previous versions, perform cutover to new systems, perform compatibility testing, and other pesky kinds of work that take up more time than we would like to admit.

Some late projects propose to catch up by reducing their originally planned testing cycle; they reason that there probably won't be very many defects to detect or correct. (I leave as an exercise for the reader to determine why—if this is really the case—they didn't plan for a shorter testing cycle in the first place.)

3. Failure to plan for risk

In *Design Paradigms*,[2] Henry Petroski argues that the most spectacular failures in bridge design were generally preceded by periods of success that led to complacency in the creation of new designs. Designers of failed bridges were lulled into copying the attributes of successful bridges and didn't pay enough attention to each new bridge's potential failure modes.

For software projects, actively avoiding failure is as important as emulating success. In many business contexts, the word "risk" isn't mentioned unless a project is already in deep trouble. In software, a project planner who isn't using the word "risk" every day and incorporating risk management into his plans probably isn't doing his job. As Tom Gilb says, "If you do not actively attack the risks on your project, they will actively attack you."[3]

4. Using the same plan for every project

Some organizations grow familiar with a particular approach to running software projects, which is known as "the way we do things around here." When an organization uses this approach, it tends to do well as long as the new projects look like the old projects. When new

Reprinted from *IEEE Software,* September/October 2001.

projects look different, however, reusing old plans can cause more harm than good.

Good plans address specific conditions of the project for which they are created. Many elements can be reused, but project planners should think carefully about the extent to which each element of a previous plan still applies to the new project context.

5. Applying prepackaged plans indiscriminately

A close cousin to Deadly Sin #3 is reusing a generic plan someone else created without applying your own critical thinking or considering your project's unique needs. "Someone else's plan" usually arrives in the form of a book or methodology that a project planner applies out of the box. Current examples include the *Rational Unified Process*,[4] *Extreme Programming*,[5] and to some extent (despite my best intentions to the contrary) my own *Software Project Survival Guide*[6] and my company's Cx-One. These prepackaged plans can help avoid Deadly Sins #1 and #2, but they are not a substitute for thinking about and optimizing your plans to the unique demands of your project.

No outside expert can possibly understand a project's specific needs as well as the people directly involved. Project planners should always tailor the "expert's" plan to their specific circumstances. Fortunately, I've found that project planners who are aware enough of planning issues to read software engineering books usually also have enough common sense to be selective about the parts of the prepackaged plans that are likely to work for them.

6. Allowing a plan to diverge from project reality

One common approach to planning is to create a plan early in the project, then put it on the shelf and let it gather dust for the remainder of the project. As project conditions change, the plan becomes increasingly irrelevant, so by mid-project the project runs free-form, with no real relationship between the unchanging plan and project reality.

This Deadly Sin is exacerbated by Deadly Sin #5—project planners who embrace prepackaged methodologies whole-hog are sometimes reluctant to change them midstream when they're not working. They think the problem is with their application of the plan when, in fact, the problem is with the plan. Good project planning should occur and recur incrementally throughout a project.

7. Planning in too much detail too soon

Some well-intentioned project planners try to map out a whole project's worth of activities early on. But a software project consists of a constantly unfolding set of decisions, and each project phase creates dependencies for future decisions. Since planners do not have crystal balls, attempting to plan distant activities in too much detail is an exercise in bureaucracy that is almost as bad as not planning at all.

The more work that goes into creating prematurely detailed plans, the higher the likelihood the plan will become shelfware (Deadly Sin #6). No one likes to throw away previous work, and project planners sometimes try to force-fit the project's reality into their earlier plans rather than laboriously revising their prematurely detailed plans.

I think of good project planning like driving at night with my car's headlights on. I might have a road map that tells me how to get from City A to City B, but the distance I can see in detail in my headlights is limited. On a medium-size or large project, macro-level project plans should be mapped out end-to-end early in the project. Detailed, micro-level planning should generally be conducted only a few weeks at a time and "just in time."

8. Planning to catch up later

For projects that get behind schedule, one common mistake is planning to make up lost time later. The typical rationalization is that, "The team was climbing a learning curve early in the project. We learned a lot of lessons the hard way. But now we understand what we're doing and should be able to finish the project quickly." Wrong answer! A 1991 survey of more than 300 projects found that projects hardly ever make up lost time—they tend to get further behind.[7] The flaw in the rationalization is that software teams make their highest-leverage decisions earliest in the project—the time during which new technology, new business areas, and new methodologies are the least well understood. As the team works its way into the later phases of the project, it won't speed up; it will slow down as it encounters the consequences of mistakes it made earlier and invests time correcting those mistakes.

9. Not learning from past planning sins

The deadliest sin of all might be not learning from earlier deadly sins. Software projects can take a long time, and people's memories can be clouded by ego and the passage of time. By the end of a long project, it can be difficult to remember all the early decisions that affected the project's conclusion.

One easy way to counter these tendencies and prevent future deadly sins is to conduct a structured project postmortem review.[8] A postmortem review might not erase the sins of projects past, but it can certainly help prevent sins on future projects. 🕮

References

1. S. Ahuja, "Laying the Groundwork for Success," *IEEE Software*, vol. 16, no. 6, Nov.–Dec. 1999, pp. 72–75.

2. H. Petroski, *Design Paradigms*, Cambridge Univ. Press, Cambridge, U.K., 1994.

3. T. Gilb, *Principles of Software Engineering Management*, Addison-Wesley, Reading, Mass., 1988.

4. P. Kruchten, *The Rational Unified Process: An Introduction*, 2nd ed., Addison-Wesley, Reading, Mass., 2000.

5. K. Beck, *Extreme Programming: Embrace Change*, Addison-Wesley, Reading, Mass., 2000.

6. S. McConnell, *Software Project Survival Guide*, Microsoft Press, Redmond, Wash., 1997.

7. M. van Genuchten, "Why Is Software Late? An Empirical Study of Reasons for Delay in Software Development," *IEEE Trans. Software Eng.*, vol. 17, no. 6, June 1991, pp. 582–590.

8. B. Collier, T. Demarco, and P. Fearey, "A Defined Process for Project Postmortem Review," *IEEE Software*, vol. 13, no. 4, July–Aug. 1996, pp. 65–72.

Chapter 5

Planning Fundamentals

But since the affairs of men rest still uncertain, let us reason with the worst that may befall.
—Shakespeare, in *Julius Caesar*

Overview

Planning is the most basic function of management. It involves deciding in advance what needs to done, by whom, and when, why, and how it will be done. Those involved in planning set objectives for some future course of action, scope the work that needs to be done, break the work down into tasks, define completion milestones for these tasks and their deliverables, figure out who can best perform the work, agree upon acceptable schedules and budgets, determine how progress will be measured, and establish the means to manage risk and handle contingencies as the project unfolds. Because planning revolves around requirements, both of these important topics are discussed in this chapter. I have also included a paper on agile development to provide you with an alternate point of view.

Everyone in an organization develops plans. At the upper levels, executives address such things as research and development (R&D) needs, facilities and capital equipment, and acquisitions and mergers in their planning activities. Such plans, by their very nature, are aligned with the long-term vision and strategies they have set for the organization. In contrast, project managers develop plans of action and appropriate milestones aimed at satisfying customer requirements per agreed-upon schedules that go across shorter planning horizons (e.g., three to five years). Functional managers have even nearer-term goals as they typically determine what staffing levels are needed on an annual basis to handle the workload. They also set in motion short-term plans to develop the skills, knowledge, and abilities of the workforce and to decide what technology the organization needs to perform its work tasks. Supervisor's plans are aimed at integrating the products of each of the members of their teams into a work product over a time span of weeks as opposed to months. They, by design, are aligned with the plans of both the project and functional managers. Individual plans are more closely directed to figuring out how to meet weekly commitments. In addition, all plans need to be tied to organizational goals. As you can see, everyone needs to develop planning skills.

The five papers that follow focus attention on requirements and project plans because they are important and related topics. Requirements form the foundations of plans. When they are volatile, so are the plans developed to mechanize them. The first paper was written to kick off this section. It spells out the secrets to planning success. The next two papers focus on the topic of requirements and the practices that you can use to get them under control. The fourth paper discusses project planning and highlights the tools and techniques available to balance scope, cost, time, and quality with stakeholder expectations. The next paper considers how to tailor classical techniques for use on small projects, and the final paper provides an agile perspective. All of the papers selected amplify this chapter's underlying theme that classical planning tools and techniques can be used effectively by software managers at any level of the organizational hierarchy to develop responsive plans.

Article Summaries

21 Project Management Success Tips, by Karl Wiegers. This paper provides 21 tips for project success that were generated based upon experience. Most of these tips focus on establishing goal-related plans and estimates early in the project's life cycle. Others emphasize the need to create a solid management infrastructure. All revolve around the concept of root-level management, in which the software job is first broken into its elementary tasks and then planned, estimated, budgeted, scheduled, tracked, and controlled using inch-pebbles or root-level milestones. The tips provide project managers with a planning checklist of things to do.

Requirements Management: The Search for Nirvana, by Donald Reifer. Poor requirements have for years often been a source of frustration within the software community. Everyone agrees that we need to write better requirements specifications because they serve as the foundation for software development activities. Although software managers can manage using such specifications, often their development is outside of their control. This paper discusses the problems in generating requirements and how to cope using clear objectives, teamwork, discipline, and knowledge of both the application and operational environment.

Requirements Engineering as a Success Factor in Software Projects, by Hubert F. Hofmann and Franz Lehner. Based on their study of 15 requirements engineering teams, the authors identify requirements engineering practices that contribute to project success, particularly in terms of project performance. The article first discusses the process of requirements engineering as well as what stakeholders want and what they offer. The paper then examines three critical factors that contribute to project success and their impact on project performance. Finally, best practices are shared as the paper concludes by emphasizing that the requirements engineering activity should be perceived of as a learning process.

The Secrets of Planning Success, by Michael Deutsch. This paper starts by setting the context for software project management. Within this perspective, the paper emphasizes four planning best practices that should underlie the management philosophy of every project. These principles are: protect a core capability, have an antideception measure, make two parts for every plan, and get involved early if you want an achievable schedule. A laziness metaphor is halfheartedly used to underscore the payoff of key planning decisions that are made early in the project. The paper concludes by discussing how planning decisions can give a project the ability to gracefully degrade and remain viable when trouble arrives.

The Slacker's Guide to Project Tracking, by James Davison, Tim Mackinnon, and Michael Royle. This article explains how to use plans as tracking tools within the context of agile development. It identifies the steps involved in planning and how to develop the plan iteratively. It then discusses how to use the results to track progress and focus attention on risks. It provides some insights into release planning and the role of the iteration or build manager. Be warned that this is an article for those interested in the more agile approaches to project management, like extreme programming. Its premise is that little rather than big plans should be developed as the project progresses.

Key Terms

Nine terms, defined as follows, are important to understanding the topic of planning as used within this chapter:

1. **Budget.** In management, a statement of expected results expressed in numerical terms.
2. **Critical path.** In a network diagram that shows how tasks in your work plan are related, the longest path from start to finish or the path that does not have any slack; thus, the path corresponding to the shortest time in which the project can be completed.
3. **Customer.** The individual or organization that specifies and accepts the project deliverables. The customer may be internal or external to the parent organization and may or may not be the end user of the software. A financial transaction between the customer and developer is not implied by this definition.
4. **Management reserve.** In project management, resources set aside for contingency purposes.
5. **Milestone.** A scheduled event for which some person is held accountable and that is used to demonstrate progress.
6. **Network.** A diagrammatic display showing the logical relationships that exist between schedule activities and their previous relationships.
7. **Planning.** Those management activities conducted to establish a future course of action at all levels of the organization. At the top, plans tend to be strategic. At lower levels, plans tend to be more tactical. At all levels, plans set the baselines against which progress is measured.
8. **Resource management.** In management, the identification, estimation, allocation, and monitoring of the resources used to develop a product or perform a service.
9. **Work breakdown structure (WBS) .** A family tree that organizes, defines, and graphically illustrates the products, services, or tasks necessary to achieve project objectives.

Common Acronyms

The following acronyms are used within the articles in this chapter:

COTS   Commercial off the shelf
CPM   Critical path method

RE	Requirements engineering
R&D	Research and development
TPI	Technical Performance Indicator
WBS	Work breakdown structure

For Your Bookshelf

There are several books that I would recommend on planning. For middle managers, the recently released Devauz text entitled *Total Project Control: A Manager's Guide to Integrated Project Planning, Measuring and Tracking* provides excellent guidance on the process and usable examples of planning and control products. Of course. Pressman's *Manager's Guide to Software Engineering* and Humphrey's *Managing the Software Process* both provide useful information on planning processes and practices. However, my favorite book is a nonsoftware classic that I have found myself referring to time and time again. Because of its age and generality, I have not included this old friend in the Bibliography, but you might search out a copy of Rosenau's *Successful Project Management* (Lifetime Learning Publications, Belmont, CA, 1981) if you have time and take a look at its simple step-by-step recipe for generating project plans.

21 Project Management Success Tips

Karl E. Wiegers

Managing software projects is difficult under the best circumstances. The project manager must balance competing stakeholder interests against the constraints of limited resources and time, ever-changing technologies, and unachievable demands from unreasonable people. Project management is people management, technology management, business management, risk management, and expectation management. It's a juggling act, with too many balls in the air at once.

Unfortunately, many new project managers receive little training in how to do the job. Anyone can learn to draw a Gantt chart, but effective project managers also rely on the savvy that comes from painful experience. Coaching and survival tips from people who have already done their tour of duty in the project management trenches can save you from learning such lessons the hard way. Here are 21 such tips for success, which I have learned from both well-managed and challenged projects. The tips are organized into five categories:

1. Laying the groundwork for success
2. Planning the project
3. Estimating the work
4. Tracking your progress
5. Learning for the future

Together, the practices in these five categories define a project-management control system that can help your project deliver on expectations. Keep these suggestions in mind on your next project, recognizing that none of them is a silver bullet for your project management problems.

Laying the Groundwork

Tip #1: Define Project Success Criteria

At the beginning of the project, make sure the stakeholders share a common understanding of how they will determine whether this project is successful. Too often, meeting a predetermined schedule is the only apparent success factor, but there are certainly others. Begin by identifying your stakeholders and their interests and expectations. Next, define some clear and measurable business goals. Some examples are:

- Increasing market share by a certain amount by a specified date
- Reaching a specified sales volume or revenue
- Achieving certain customer satisfaction measures
- Saving money by retiring a high-maintenance legacy system
- Achieving a particular transaction processing volume and correctness

These business goals should imply specific project success criteria, which should again be measurable and trackable. They could include achieving schedule and budget targets, delivering committed functionality in a form that satisfies customer acceptance tests, complying with industry standards or government regulations, or achieving specific technological milestones.

Also, keep your eye on team-member job satisfaction, sometimes indicated by staff turnover rate and the willingness of

---

A condensed version of this paper was published in *Software Development* magazine, November 1999.

team members to do what it takes to make the project succeed. The business objectives define the overarching goal, though. It does not matter if you deliver to the specification on schedule and budget if those factors do not clearly align with business success.

Remember that not all of these defined success criteria can be your top priority. You will have to make some thoughtful trade-off decisions to ensure that you satisfy your most important priorities. If you do not define clear priorities for success, team members can wind up working at cross-purposes, leading to frustration, stress, and reduced teamwork effectiveness.

Tip #2: Identify Project Drivers, Constraints, and Degrees of Freedom

Every project must balance its functionality, staffing, cost, schedule, and quality objectives [Wiegers, 1996]. Define each of these five project dimensions as either a *constraint* within which you must operate, a *driver* strongly aligned with project success, or a *degree of freedom* you can adjust within some stated bounds. There is bad news: not all factors can be constraints and not all can be drivers. The project manager must have some flexibility to react to schedule slips, demands for increased functionality, staff turnover, and other realities.

A "flexibility diagram" such as that shown in Figure 1 visually depicts your constraints, drivers, and degrees of freedom. A constraint gives the project manager no flexibility in that dimension, so it is plotted at the zero value on its axis. A driver yields a small amount of flexibility, so its point is plotted a bit higher than zero. Degrees of freedom provide varying degrees of latitude. They represent parameters the project manager can adjust to achieve the project's success drivers within the limits imposed by its constraints. Connecting the five plotted points creates an irregular pentagon. The smaller the area inside the pentagon, the more constrained the project is.

I once heard a senior manager ask a project leader how long it would take to deliver a planned new large software system. The project leader replied, "Two years." The senior manager said, "No, that's too long. I need it in six months." The project leader's response was simply, "Okay," despite the fact that nothing had changed in the few seconds of that conversation to make the six-month target achievable. A better response would have been to negotiate a realistic outcome through a series of questions such as the following:

- How critical is the six-month target? Does something drastic happen if we do not deliver in six months (schedule is a constraint), or is that just a desirable target date (schedule is a driver)?
- If the six months is a firm limit, what subset of the requested functionality do you absolutely need delivered by then?
- Can I get more people to work on it? (Staff is a degree of freedom.)
- Do you care how well it works? (Quality is a degree of freedom.)

Tip #3: Define Product Release Criteria

Early in the project, decide what criteria will indicate whether the product is ready for release. Possible release criteria might include the following:

- There are no open high-priority defects.
- The number of open defects has decreased for X weeks and the estimated number of residual defects is acceptable.
- Performance goals are achieved on all target platforms.
- Specific required functionality is fully operational.
- Quantitative reliability goals are satisfied.
- X of system tests have been passed.
- Specified legal, contractual, or regulatory goals are met.
- The optimum marketplace time to release has arrived.
- Customer acceptance criteria are satisfied.

Whatever criteria you choose should be realistic, objectively measurable, documented, and aligned with what "quality" means to your customers. Decide early on how you will tell when you are done, track progress toward your goals, and stick to your guns when confronted with pressure to ship before the product is ready for "prime time."

Carefully consider your target market segments when deciding on release criteria [Rothman, 1999]. The early adopters and

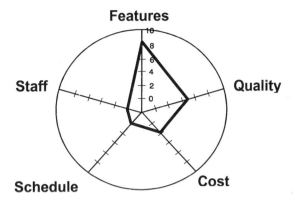

Figure 1. A flexibility diagram for a project that is staff constrained and schedule constrained, with cost being a driver and quality and features being decrees of freedom.

enthusiasts have a higher tolerance for defects than do the pragmatic early majority of customers or the conservative late majority, m contrast, time to market and innovative features or technology usage are most important to the early adopters.

Tip #4: Negotiate Achievable Commitments

Despite pressure to promise the impossible, never make a commitment you know you cannot keep. Engage in good-faith negotiations with customers, managers, and team members about goals that are realistically achievable. Negotiation is required whenever there is a gap between the schedule or functionality the key project stakeholders demand and your best prediction of the future as embodied in project estimates. Principled negotiation involves four precepts [Fisher, 1991]:

- Separate the people from the problem.
- Focus on interests, not positions.
- Invent options for mutual gain.
- Insist on using objective criteria.

Any data you have from previous projects will help you make persuasive arguments, although there is no real defense against truly unreasonable people.

I once met with an aggressive and intimidating senior manager to discuss our department's software process improvement plans. Jack was eager to see our department achieve CMM Level 2 by July of 1996. My process improvement group had carefully studied the problem and estimated that the end of 1997 was the earliest date that was even remotely feasible. After some debate. Jack grudgingly agreed to the end of 1996, but I regarded even that goal as pure fantasy. After additional discussion, I finally said, "Jack, I'm not going to commit to the end of 1996." I do not think anyone had ever told Jack he would not make a commitment that Jack demanded. He wasn't sure what to say next. Jack eventually agreed to the target date to which I was willing to commit.

Plan to renegotiate commitments when project realities (such as staff, budget, or deadlines) change, unanticipated problems arise, risks materialize, or new requirements are added. No one likes to have to modify his commitments. However, if the reality is that the initial commitments will not be achieved, do not pretend that they will up until the moment of unfortunate truth.

Planning the Project

Tip #5: Write a Plan

Some people believe the time spent writing a plan could be better spent writing code, but I do not agree. The hard part is not writing the plan. The hard part is actually doing the planning—thinking, negotiating, balancing, asking, listening, and thinking some more. Actually writing the plan is mostly transcription at that point. The time you spend analyzing what it will take to solve the problem will reduce the number of surprises you have to cope with later in the project. Today's multisite and cross-cultural development projects demand even more careful planning and tracking than do traditional projects undertaken by a co-located team.

A useful plan is much more than a schedule or work breakdown structure of tasks to perform. It also includes:

- Staff, budget, and other resource estimates and plans
- Team roles and responsibilities
- How you will acquire and train the necessary staff
- Assumptions, dependencies, and risks
- Descriptions of, and target dates for, major deliverables
- Identification of the software development life cycle that you will follow
- How you will track and monitor the project
- Metrics that you will collect
- How you will manage any subcontractor relationships

Your organization should adopt a standard software project plan template, which can be tailored for various kinds of projects. An excellent starting point is IEEE Std 1058-1998, the "IEEE Standard for Software Project Management Plans" [IEEE, 1998]. This standard describes a comprehensive template, sufficient for the largest projects. Study this template to see what sections would make sense for the types and sizes of projects that you work on.

If you commonly tackle different kinds of projects, such as major new product development as well as small enhancements, adopt a separate project plan template for each. Avoid overburdening small projects with excessive documentation that adds little value. The project plan should be no any longer nor more elaborate than necessary to make sure you can successfully execute the project. But always write a plan.

Tip #6: Decompose Tasks to Inch-Pebble Granularity

Inch-pebbles are miniature milestones (get it?). Breaking large tasks into multiple small tasks helps you estimate them more accurately, reveals work activities you might not have thought of otherwise, and permits more accurate, fine-grained status tracking. Select inch-pebbles of a size that you feel you can estimate accurately. I feel most comfortable with inch-pebbles that represent tasks of about 5 to 15 labor-hours, or about one to three days in duration. Overlooked tasks are a common contributor to schedule slips, so breaking large problems into small bits reveals more details about the work that must be done and improves your ability to make accurate estimates.

You can track progress based on the number of inch-pebbles that have been completed at any given time, compared to those you planned to complete by that time. Defining the project's work in terms of inch-pebbles is an aid to tracking status through earned value analysis [Lewis, 2000]. The earned value technique compares the investment of effort or dollars that you have made to date with progress as measured by completed inch-pebbles.

Tip #7: Develop Planning Worksheets for Common Large Tasks

If your team frequently undertakes certain common tasks, such as implementing a new object class, executing a system test cycle, or performing a product build, develop activity checklists and planning worksheets for these tasks. Each checklist should include all of the steps the large task might require. These checklists and worksheets will help each team member identify and estimate the effort associated with each instance of the large task he or she must tackle. People work in different ways and no single person will think of all the necessary tasks, so engage multiple team members in developing the worksheets. Using standard worksheets will help the team members adopt common processes that they can tune up as they gain experience. Tailor the worksheets to meet the specific needs of individual projects.

Tip #8: Plan to do Rework after a Quality Control Activity

I have seen project task lists in which the author assumed that every testing experience will be a success that lets you move into the next development activity. However, almost all quality control activities, such as testing and peer reviews, find defects or other improvement opportunities. Your project schedule or work breakdown structure should include rework as a discrete task after every quality control activity. Base your estimates of rework time on previous experience. For example, you might have historical inspection data indicating that, on average, your developers find 25 defects per thousand lines of code by inspection and that it takes an average of 40 minutes to fully repair each code defect. You can crunch these kinds of numbers to come up with average expected rework effort for various types of work products. If you do not actually have to do any rework after a test, great; you are ahead of schedule on that task. Do not count on it, though.

Tip #9: Manage Project Risks

If you do not identify and control project risks, they will control you. A risk is a potential problem that could affect the success of your project, a problem that has not happened yet—and you want to keep it that way [Wiegers, 1998]. Risk management has been identified as one of the most significant best practices for software development [Brown, 1996]. Simply identifying the possible risk factors is not enough. You also have to evaluate the relative threat each one poses so you can focus your risk management energy where it will do the most good.

Risk exposure is a combination of the probability that a specific risk could materialize into a problem and the negative consequences for the project if it does. To manage each risk, select mitigation actions to reduce either the probability or the impact. You might also identify contingency plans that will kick in if your risk control activities are not effective. Suppose you are concerned that your top developer might move to Australia to be with her new boyfriend. Consider the following actions:

- Pay her more money, offer to hire the boyfriend, or give her more vacation time to fly to Australia periodically (reduces probability).
- Keep her on as a telecommuting employee or contractor, have her document her work, or have her impart her specialized knowledge to other employees (reduces impact).
- Line up a consultant or contract specialist to replace her if she leaves anyway (contingency plan).

A risk list does not replace a plan for how you will identify, prioritize, control, and track risks. Incorporate risk tracking into your routine project status tracking. Record which risks materialized and which mitigation actions were effective for reference on future projects.

Tip #10: Allow Time for Process Improvement

Your team members are already swamped with their current project assignments, but if you want the group to rise to a higher plane of software engineering capability, you will have to invest some time in process improvement [Wiegers, 1999]. Set aside some time from your project schedule, because software project activities should include making process changes that will help your next project be even more successful. Do not allocate 100 percent of your team members' available time to project tasks and then wonder why they do not make any progress on the improvement initiatives. Some process changes can begin to pay off immediately, whereas you will not reap the full return on your investment in other improvements until the next project. View process improvement as a strategic investment in the sustained effectiveness of your development organization. I liken process improvement to highway construction: it slows everyone down a little bit for a time, but after the work is done, the road is a lot smoother and the throughput greater.

Tip #11: Respect the Learning Curve

The time and money you spend on training, reading and self-study, consultants, and developing improved processes are part of the investment your organization makes in project success. Recognize that you will pay a price in terms of a short-term productivity loss when you first try to apply new processes, tools, or technologies. Do not expect to get fabulous benefits from new software engineering approaches on the first try, no matter what the tool vendor's literature or the methodology consultant's brochure claims. Instead, build extra time into the schedule to account for the inevitable learning curve. Make sure your managers and customers understand the learning curve and accept it as an inescapable consequence of working in a rapidly changing high-technology field.

Estimating the Work

Tip #12: Estimate Based on Effort, Not Calendar Time

People generally provide estimates in units of calendar time. I prefer to estimate the effort (in labor-hours) associated with a task, then translate the effort into a calendar-time estimate. A 20-hour task might take 2.5 calendar days of nominal full-time effort, or two exhausting days. However, it could also take a week if you have to wait for critical information from a customer or stay home with a sick child for two days. The translation of effort into calendar time is based on estimates of how many effective hours I can spend on project tasks per day, any interruptions or emergency bug fix requests I might get, meetings, and all the other places into which time disappears. If you keep track of how you actually spend your time at work, you will know how many effective weekly project hours you have available on average [Wiegers, 1996]. Typically, this is only about 50 to 60% of the nominal time people spend at work, far less than the assumed 100% effective time on which so many project schedules are planned.

Tip #13: Do Not Schedule Multitasking People for More than 80% of Their Time

The task-switching overhead associated with the many activities we are all asked to do reduces our effectiveness significantly. Excessive multitasking introduces communication and thought process inefficiencies that reduce individual productivity. I once heard a manager say that someone on his team had spent an average of eight hours per week on a particular activity, so she could do five of them at once. m reality, she will be lucky if she can handle three such tasks. Some people multitask more efficiently than others. If some of your team members thrash when working on too many tasks at once, set clear priorities and help them succeed by focusing on just one or two objectives at a time.

Tip #14: Build Training Time into the Schedule

Estimate how much time your team members spend on training activities annually, and subtract that from the time available for them to work on project tasks. You probably already subtract out average values for vacation time, sick time, and other assignments; treat training time the same way. Recognize that the high-tech field of software development demands that all practitioners devote time to ongoing education, both on their own time and on the company's time. Arrange just-in-time training when you can schedule it, as the half-life of new technical knowledge is short unless the knowledge is put to use promptly. Attending a training seminar can be a team-building experience, as project team members and other stakeholders hear the same story about how to apply improved practices to their common challenges.

Tip #15: Record Estimates and How You Derived Them

When you prepare estimates for your work, write down those estimates and document how you arrived at each of them. Understanding the assumptions and approaches used to create an estimate will make them easier to defend and adjust when necessary. It will also help you improve your estimation process. Train the team in estimation methods, rather than assuming that every software developer and project leader is instinctively skilled at predicting the future. Develop estimation procedures and checklists that people throughout your organization can use.

An effective group estimation technique is the Wideband Delphi method [Wiegers, 2000]. Wideband Delphi builds on the principle that multiple heads are better than one. The Delphi estimation method asks a small team of experts to anonymously generate individual estimates from a problem description and reach consensus on a final set of estimates through iteration. Figure 2 illustrates the Wideband Delphi process flow. The outputs from the process include a complete list of project and

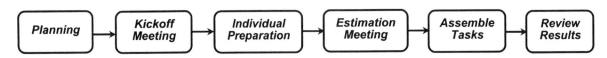

Figure 2. The Wideband Delphi process flow.

quality-related tasks and an estimate for each task, in whatever units the team chose (such as dollars, weeks, or labor-hours). Participation by multiple estimators and the use of anonymous estimates to prevent one participant from biasing another make the Delphi method more reliable than simply asking a single individual for his best guess.

Tip #16: Use Estimation Tools

Many commercial tools are available to help you estimate entire projects. Based on large databases of actual project experience, these tools can give you a spectrum of possible schedule and staff allocation options. They will also help you avoid the "impossible region," combinations of product size, effort, and schedule where no known project has been successful. The tools incorporate a number of "cost drivers" you can adjust to make the tool more accurately model your project, based on the technologies used, the team's experience, and other factors. Over time, you can calibrate the tool with your own project data to make it an even more reliable predictor of the future. A good tool to try is Estimate Pro from the Software Productivity Center (www.spc.ca). Others include KnowledgePlan (www.spr.com), SLIM (www.qsm.com), and Cost Xpert (www.costxpert.com). You can compare the estimates from the tools with the bottom-up estimates generated from a work breakdown structure. Reconcile any major disconnects so you can generate the most realistic overall estimate.

Tip #17: Plan Contingency Buffers

Projects never go precisely as planed. The prudent project manager incorporates budget and schedule contingency buffers (also known as management reserve) at the end of major phases to accommodate the unforeseen. Use your project risk analysis to estimate the possible schedule impact if several of the risks materialize and build that projected risk exposure into your schedule as a contingency buffer. Even more sophisticated is the use of critical chain analysis, a technique that pools the uncertainties in estimates and risks into a rational overall contingency buffer [Zultner, 1999].

Your manager or customer might view these contingency buffers as padding, rather than as the sensible acknowledgement of reality that they are. To help persuade skeptics, point to unpleasant surprises on previous projects as a rationale for your foresight. If a manager elects to discard contingency buffers, he has tacitly absorbed all the risks that fed into the buffer and assumed that all estimates are perfect, no scope growth will occur, and no unexpected events will take place. The reality on most projects is quite different. I would rather see us deal with reality, however unattractive, than to live in Fantasyland, which leads to chronic disappointments.

Tracking Your Progress

Tip #18: Record Actuals and Estimates

Someone once asked me where to get historical data to improve her ability to estimate future work. My answer was, "If you write down what actually happened today, that becomes historical data tomorrow." Unless you record the actual effort or time spent on each task and compare them to your estimates, you will never improve your estimating approach. Your estimates will forever remain guesses. Each individual can begin recording estimates and actuals, and the project manager should track these important data items on a project task or milestone basis. In addition to effort and schedule, you could estimate and track the size of the product, in units of lines of code, function points, classes and methods, GUI screens, or other units that make sense for your project.

Tip #19: Count Tasks as Complete Only When They are 100% Complete

We give ourselves a lot of partial credit for tasks we have begun but not fully completed: "I thought about the algorithm for that module in the shower this morning, and the algorithm is the hard part, so I'm probably about 60% done." It is difficult to accurately assess what fraction of a sizable task has actually been done at a given moment. One benefit of using inch-pebbles for task planning is that you can break a large activity into a number of small tasks and classify each small task as either done or not done—nothing in between. Your project status tracking is then based on the fraction of the tasks that are completed, not the percent completion of each task. If someone asks you whether a specific task is complete and your reply is, "It's all done except . . . ," it's not done! Do not let people "round up" their task completion status; use explicit criteria to tell whether a step truly is completed.

Tip #20: Track Project Status Openly and Honestly

An old riddle asks, "How does a software project become six months late?" The answer is, "One day at a time." The painful problems arise when you do not know just how far behind (or, occasionally, ahead) of plan the project really is. Create a climate in which team members feel it is safe for them to report project status accurately. Strive to run the project from a foundation of accurate, data-based facts, rather than from the misleading optimism that sometimes arises from the fear of reporting bad news. Use project status information and metrics data to take corrective actions when necessary and to celebrate when you can. You can only manage a project effectively when you really know what is done and what is not, what tasks are falling behind their estimates and why, and what problems and issues remain to be tackled. The five major areas of software measurement are size, effort, time, quality, and status. Remember the cardinal rule of software metrics: metrics data must never be used to punish or reward individuals for their performance.

Learning for the Future

Tip #21: Conduct Project Retrospectives

Retrospectives (also called postmortems or postproject reviews) provide an opportunity for the team to reflect on how the last project or the previous phase went and to capture lessons learned that will help enhance your future performance [Kerth, 2001]. During such a review, identify the things that went well, so you can create an environment that enables you to repeat those success contributors. Also look for things that didn't go so well, so you can change your approaches and prevent those problems in the future, hi addition, think of events that surprised you. These might be risk factors for which you should be alert on the next project.

Conduct retrospectives in a constructive, honest atmosphere. Do not make them an opportunity to assign blame for previous problems. Capture the lessons learned from each review and share them with the entire team and organization, so all can benefit from your painfully gained experience. I like to write lessons learned in a neutral way, such that it is not obvious whether we learned the lesson because we did something right or because we made a mistake.

These 21 project management tips will not guarantee success, but they will help you get a solid handle on your project and ensure that you are doing all you can to make it succeed in an unpredictable world.

Bibliography

Brown, Norm. "Industrial-Strength Management Strategies," *IEEE Software,* vol. 13, no. 4 (July 1996), pp. 94–103.

Fisher, Roger, William Ury, and Bruce Patton. *Getting to Yes: Negotiating Agreement Without Givingin,* 2nd Edition. New York: Penguin Books, 1991.

IEEE. "IEEE Standard for Software Project Management Plans, Std 1058-1998." *IEEE Standards Software Engineering, 1999 Edition.* Volume 2: Process Standards. New York: The Institute of Electrical and Electronics Engineers, Inc., 1999.

Kerth, Norman L. *Project Retrospectives: A Handbook for Team Reviews.* New York: Dorset House Publishing, 2001.

Lewis, James P. *The Project Manager's Desk Reference,* 2nd Edition. Boston, Mass.: McGraw-Hill, 2000.

Rothman, Johanna. "Determining Your Project's Quality Priorities," *Software Development,* vol. 7, no. 2 (February 1999), pp. 22–25.

Wiegers, Karl E. *Creating a Software Engineering Culture.* New York: Dorset House Publishing, 1996.

Wiegers, Karl. "Know Your Enemy: Software Risk Management," *Software Development,* vol. 6, no. 10 (October 1998), pp. 38–42.

Wiegers, Karl. "Process Improvement that Works," *Software Development,* vol. 7, no. 10 (October 1999), pp. 24–30.

Wiegers, Karl. "Stop Promising Miracles," *Software Development,* vol. 8, no. 2 (February 2000), pp. 49–54.

Zultner, Richard. "Project Estimation with Critical Chain: Third-Generation Risk Management," *Cutter IT Journal,* vol. 12, no. 7 (July 1999), pp. 4–12.

Requirements Management: The Search for Nirvana

Donald J. Reifer

Software engineers have been trying for years to manage requirements better. The reasons are simple. A slight change to requirements can profoundly affect cost and schedule because their definition underlies all design and implementation. We have been taught to spell out the requirements at the beginning of a project and not to change them. Experience has shown that these lessons are impractical and impossible to achieve.

The Search for Nirvana

For years, I have watched software engineers strive to create requirements specifications. They have tried to scope the functional, performance, and interface requirements using a variety of specification techniques and notations. Often, they developed specifications long before starting their projects because that's what the experts taught. The experts advised us to define what we wanted before we figured out how to develop our software. Involving the user or customer was considered a key to success. Firming up the requirements before starting was the industry best practice because specifications formed the foundation of our design and coding activities. We were taught to negotiate each modification with the user because of the cost and schedule impacts. After all, nobody in his or her right mind would expect something for nothing.

The only thing wrong with these techniques is that they don't work in today's environment. As most start-ups have figured out, rapid prototyping and application methods have supplanted the waterfall life-cycle model on which these techniques were based. Architecture-driven methods have eliminated the need for these document-driven development approaches. What's most important is that we finally have the guts to admit to ourselves that we don't know precisely what the system should do when we start the project. *We have discovered that requirements development is a learning, rather than a gathering, process.* We know we need to work with users or customers to understand their expectations and win conditions for success. We also know that we might need to build prototypes to explore options, including those that exploit legacy and commercial off-the-shelf (COTS) solutions.

I have seen development of the requirements specifications take longer than development of the software. This lengthy development is especially common in government software acquisitions when the specifications form the basis for competitive procurements. Most often, the specifications are trashed right after the contract is awarded because they are out of date and out of tune with the user's real needs. Commercial firms face the same dilemma when developing Web applications. By the time they are finished writing a decent specification, they have completed the development.

After the contract is awarded, I have seen the winning teams spend countless hours checking each version of the requirements specification for consistency, completeness, and traceability. They seem to be looking for

Reprinted from *IEEE Software*, May/June 2000.

the perfect specification—that is, one that completely, consistently, and clearly specifies what the customer wants. Some teams bog down in methods. They lose sight of the task at hand—figuring out what functions the software should perform—and instead generate pictures and argue over the object diagram's form. Although these tasks are sometimes valuable, they often waste time and effort.

In contrast, in the quick-to-market commercial environment, software engineers iteratively formulate requirements, using a spiral model. Each cycle provides the engineers with more detail about the product's architecture and necessary functions. Users, customers, and other stakeholders impacted by the requirements are drawn in as members of the team who develop the specification. Prototyping is a natural way of quickly firming up designs that are mechanize requirements with tools such as use cases and operational scenarios.

As we have moved to rapid-development paradigms, the way we develop software has changed. Let's look at other concepts we must change as we migrate to more iterative software development life-cycle approaches.

Software Engineers Don't Control Requirements

Software engineers are not masters of their own destiny. For instance, they are not in charge of requirements and never have been. You are probably asking, "If you can't control the definition and evolution of requirements, how can you manage them?" and "Who specifies requirements?" More often than not, a team comprising marketing and system-engineering people defines the features and functions that form the product's crux. These people work with the customer or user to set expectations and then communicate these prospects to the software engineers, using a variety of means and notations. They identify what the customer wants, the performance expectations, and the interfaces that must be maintained with other systems or the platform. Luckily, this

team specifies the functions the software should perform, not how it will be built. This provides the software team with some latitude during implementation. Often, software people are part of the requirements definition teams. However, when changes occur, the software engineer's job is to figure out how to implement the new requirements, not argue that implementation is either impossible or too costly because of retrofit.

As the development progresses and people and situations change, so do requirements. That's natural. As the spiral model unfolds, the customer and the requirements definition team learn more about what the product should do through continuous exploration and refinement. It is therefore naïve to believe that we can specify in detail what the customer wants at the beginning of the job. The best that we can do is control the continuing definition of the requirements as they change throughout the life cycle. Yes, we can and should manage a requirements baseline and track its changes. We can also trace requirements to their source and show their evolution. But managing traceability is quite different from managing requirements changes. We can only anticipate and respond to requests for change. We cannot dictate either the frequency or desirability of changes. That's a task for those in charge of the job. And, based on past experience, we can expect requests for change to come at the worst possible moment and greatly impede our ability to finish the job with the available resources.

Volatile Requirements Make Success Hard to Achieve

Software managers will argue that they will have a hard time meeting

Software engineers are not masters of their own destiny.

their budgets and schedule targets if they can't control the requirements. "How can you deliver an acceptable product on time and within budget when the requirements change all the time?" they will ask. Cynics such as I will counter by suggesting that these managers can deliver what they promise by maintaining and allocating budget and schedule reserves scoped to address these changes. Those of us who have tried this approach know that software engineers are often asked to implement such changes throughout a project. After all, the primary reason we implement functions in software is that it is easy to change. When the hardware doesn't work as advertised, don't we patch the software to fix it? When the customer realizes that the product and business processes that it implements are at odds, don't we change the software to preserve past operational procedures? I would argue that although you can't control requirements evolution and volatility, you can plan for and control the chaos that ensues throughout the process.

Requirements Today

Requirements are not worthless, however. They need to be specified and managed. But pulling this off requires a clear objective, teamwork, discipline, and knowledge. Let's look at each element of our success formula and see what we can do about it:

- *Clear objectives*: "Why are you writing the requirements? And for whom?" should be the first questions asked. If the specification will form the basis of a competitive procurement or will address safety concerns in a critical system, then by all means write one. But don't waste much time defining requirements if you are building a rapid prototype to drive out requirements. Wait until the requirements become clearer before spending a lot of time and effort on them.
- *Teamwork*: Software engineers can and should influence requirements and the changes made to them by participating on the team that de-

fines the requirements. Of course, the marketing and systems people who head these teams should invite you to participate. More important, you need to earn these people's respect so that your recommendations might be implemented. To get their ideas accepted, software engineers need to change their image from that of specialists to that of generalists whose ideas complement those of other team members.

- *Discipline*: Yes, you do need a process, methods, and tools to define requirements and track their changes. The process should be flexible enough to accommodate the problem domain and the many different viewpoints in it. I like use cases; they let me define what differ-

ent parties expect the system to do, using a common lexicon. I also like to use a well-founded process such as the Rational Unified Process. Although vendor specific, it is well supported by modern methods and tools.

- *Knowledge*: Finally, you need knowledge of the application and the environment or domain in which it will operate. When nonsoftware people generate requirements with no input from software engineers about the consequences of their specification decisions, the results are often disastrous. Nonsoftware people typically haven't the foggiest idea of what we software people need in the specification to scope the job and build a responsive solution. We need to edu-

cate them, letting them know the software concerns and implications. As my wife taught me, we need to convince them that it was their idea to put what we want into the specification.

Hopefully, you've gotten two messages from this column: We don't always need to spell out completely requirements before development, and, regarding requirements, we are not always masters of our own destiny. I hope you will rethink how you specify requirements. And I hope you will manage the changes that others make that negatively impact your ability to get the job done. ⓜ

Requirements Engineering as a Success Factor in Software Projects

Hubert F. Hofmann, *General Motors*

Franz Lehner, *University of Regensburg*

Deficient requirements are the single biggest cause of software project failure. From studying several hundred organizations, Capers Jones discovered that RE is deficient in more than 75 percent of all enterprises.[1] In other words, getting requirements right might be the single most important and difficult part of a software project. Despite its importance, we know surprisingly little about the actual process of specifying software. "The RE Process" sidebar provides a basic description.

> **Based on their field study of 15 requirements engineering teams, the authors identify the RE practices that clearly contribute to project success, particularly in terms of team knowledge, resource allocation, and process.**

Most RE research is conceptual and concentrates on methods or techniques, primarily supporting a single activity. Moreover, the rare field studies we actually have do not establish a link between RE practices and performance. We therefore conducted this study to identify the RE practices that clearly contribute to software project success.

Stakeholders and teams

Stakeholders are individuals and organizations that are actively involved in a software project or whose interests the project affects. Stakeholders of any computer system can include customers, users, project managers, analysts, developers, senior management, and quality assurance staff. Table 1 illustrates the wide range of expertise and motivations that stakeholders typically exhibit.[2]

A typical software project team consists of a project manager, analysts, developers, and quality assurance personnel. Often it includes users or their representatives. In the case of commercial off-the-shelf (COTS) software, marketers such as sales representatives and account managers tend to substitute for users and customers.

Field study

Seven field studies have reported on RE in practice.[3-9] Unfortunately, these rare studies have not established a clear link to performance and tend to focus on a narrow set of variables. Our study provides a more integrated view of RE by investigating team knowledge, allocated resources, and deployed RE processes (see Figure 1) and their contribution to project success. In addition, we incorporate the observations of previous field studies.

Fifteen RE teams, including six COTS and nine customized application develop-

Reprinted from *IEEE Software,* July/August 2001.

The RE Process

Requirements engineering denotes both the process of specifying requirements by studying stakeholder needs and the process of systematically analyzing and refining those specifications.[1] A *specification*, the primary result of RE, is a concise statement of the requirements that the software must satisfy—that is, of the conditions or capabilities that a user must achieve an objective or that a system possesses to satisfy a contract or standard.[2] Ideally, a specification enables stakeholders to quickly learn about the software and developers to understand exactly what the stakeholders want.

Despite heterogeneous terminology throughout the literature, RE must include four separate but related activities: elicitation, modeling, validation, and verification. In practice, they will most likely vary in timing and intensity for different projects.

Typically, we first elicit requirements from whatever sources are available (experts, repositories, or the current software) and then model them to specify a solution. Eliciting and modeling requirements are interrelated. Modeling describes a perceived solution in the context of an application domain using informal, semiformal, or formal notations. The gradual normalization of such models in terms of the requirements leads to a satisfactory candidate specification, which then must be validated and verified. This gives stakeholders feedback on the interpretation of their requirements so they can correct misunderstandings as early as possible.

Elicitation

Elicitation is often treated as a simple matter of interviewing users or analyzing documents, but several other elicitation methods are available. Some emphasize group sessions in the form of focus groups or workshops; others are employed primarily to elicit requirements for specific types of systems. For example, developers frequently use repertory grids, sorts, and laddering methods in specifying knowledge-based systems.

Elicitation also includes those activities that explore how software can meet organizational goals, what alternatives might exist, and how they affect various stakeholders.

Modeling

Experts have proposed many modeling methods and specification languages to make requirements precise and consistent. Traditionally these methods have separated the data, functional, and behavioral aspects of requirements and specified software by creating one or more distinct models. Prototypes, for instance, attempt to create an operational model that stakeholders can directly experience.

Paul Ward and Stephen Mellor, followed by many others, proposed extensions to basic models. Most of these extensions focus on modeling real-time systems. Developments in OO programming and design have introduced a more integrated approach to modeling requirements. In addition, advanced modeling methods attempt to establish a closer link between models and "the customer's voice," stakeholders' viewpoints, and business goals.

Validation and verification

The purpose of validating requirements is to certify that they meet the stakeholders' intentions: Am I specifying the right software? In other words, validation examines a work product (for example, a specification) to determine conformity with stakeholder needs. Verification, on the other hand, determines whether a work product conforms to the allocated requirements: Am I specifying the software correctly? That is, it checks a specification for internal consistency through mathematical proofs or inspection techniques.

An important point in validating and verifying requirements is prioritizing them. By addressing high-priority requirements before considering low-priority ones, you can significantly reduce project costs and duration. Moreover, throughout RE you should revisit the priorities assigned, for example, during elicitation to ensure that they continue to adequately reflect the stakeholders' needs. This highlights the recurrent nature of requirements validation and verification.

Methods for validating and verifying requirements are relatively scarce. Peer reviews, inspections, walk-throughs, and scenarios figure most prominently. Moreover, the recording of decisions and their rationales is quite useful.

References

1. H.F. Hofmann, *Requirements Engineering: A Situated Discovery Process*, Gabler, Wiesbaden, Germany, 2000.
2. *IEEE Guide to Software Requirements Specification*, IEEE Std. 830-1998, IEEE Press, Piscataway, N.J., 1998.

Table I

What Stakeholders Want and What They Offer

Stakeholder	Motivation	Expertise areas
Customer	Introduce change with maximum benefit	Business and information system strategies, industry trends
User	Introduce change with minimum disruption	Business process, operating procedures
Project manager	Successfully complete the project with the given resources	Project management, software development and delivery process
Analyst	Specify requirements on time and within budget	RE methods and tools
Developer	Produce technically excellent system, use latest technologies	Latest technologies, design methods, programming environments and languages
Quality assurance	Ensure compliance to process and product standards	Software process, methods, and standards

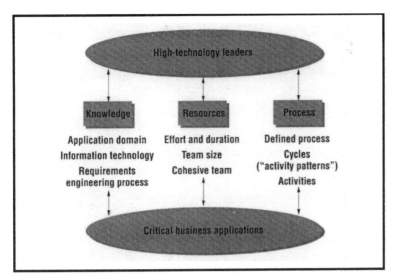

Figure 1. We studied three factors that contribute to project success: team knowledge, allocated resources, and exhibited RE processes.

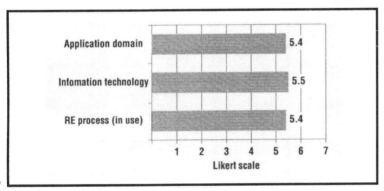

Figure 2. Research results regarding knowledge of application domain, information technology, and the RE process being used.

accuracy of statements (such as "the project has a well-documented process for specifying requirements") by assigning a value from 1 (very inaccurate) to 7 (very accurate). The Likert scale let us calculate a total numerical value from the responses.

Our research approach

We decided to study knowledge because, as Bill Curtis, Herb Krasner, and Neil Iscoe have emphasized, deep application-specific knowledge is required to successfully build most large, complex systems.[4] We investigated team knowledge with regard to application domain, the technology needed to implement the proposed solution, and the RE process used. To gather the participants' perceptions of team knowledge, we employed a 7-point Likert scale for each focus area.

Allocated resources included team size, expended effort in person-months, and duration (in months) of RE. With regard to team size, the project managers provided data on full- and part-time members of the RE and project teams. We also gathered perceptions about the teams' coordination and interaction capabilities during RE. In the questionnaire, we used the construct of "cohesiveness," measured on the Likert scale, to address this aspect of RE. During follow-up interviews, we further investigated communication breakdowns, quality of interaction, and conflict resolution.

We gathered the stakeholders' perceptions of the defined RE process by considering the extent of standardization (for example, is it well-documented? is it tailored from an organizational standard?) and the configuration of work products and their changes, as well as by obtaining independent reviews of RE activities and deliverables. We measured these constructs on the Likert scale.

To enable the participants to characterize the practiced RE process, we gave them a list of typical elicitation, modeling, verification, and validation activities, some of which we identified by surveying the RE literature. We also applied the construct of *RE cycles* to distinguish activity patterns over time. An RE cycle is a set of activities that contain at least one each of elicitation, modeling, validation, and verification activities. Generally, a specific deliverable (for example, a prototype or data model) also characterizes a completed RE cycle.

ment projects in nine software companies and development organizations in the telecommunications and banking industries, participated in our study. There were 76 stakeholders: 15 project managers, 34 team members, and 27 other stakeholders such as customers, management, and quality assurance personnel. The development projects we targeted were recently released critical business applications. On average, the participating projects finished in 16.5 months with an expended effort of approximately 120 person-months.

Through questionnaires and interviews, we collected data directly from each project's stakeholders to avoid an eventual bias and to obtain a more complete understanding of the RE process. We assessed the participants' confidence in their responses by using a 1–7 Likert scale in the questionnaires. That is, individuals rated their own perceived degree of

We gathered stakeholders' perceptions of RE performance in terms of process control, the quality of RE service, and the quality of RE products. Process control addresses the team's capability to execute according to plan; thus, we gathered data to compare planned and actual cost, duration, and effort. We evaluated the quality of RE service in terms of the stakeholders' satisfaction with the RE process and the perceived "organizational fit" of the proposed solution. The stakeholders rated the quality of RE products using these quality attributes: correct, unambiguous, complete, consistent, prioritized, verifiable, modifiable, and traceable.[10] Requirements *coverage*, the functional and nonfunctional requirements addressed by a project's RE products, also influences quality. We assessed functional requirements from the perspective of functions, data, and behavior, and nonfunctional requirements by gathering perceived coverage of product, process, and external requirements.[11]

Findings

We focused on three factors that contribute to project success—knowledge, resources, and process—and analyzed their contribution to a project's success (performance).

Knowledge

Group research emphasizes the impact of experience and expertise on team effectiveness. For instance, in the study by Curtis, Krasner, and Iscoe, project managers and division vice presidents consistently commented on how differences in individual talents and skills affected project performance.[4] The authors identified the thin spread of application domain knowledge as one of the most salient problems in software projects.

In this study, stakeholders perceived the team's domain knowledge as relatively good. It reached 5.4 on a 7-point Likert scale, where 7 indicates an RE team with a high degree of knowledge (see Figure 2). Several teams repeatedly referred to their "good use of domain experts." (The quotes here and throughout this article indicate a direct quote from a participant in our study.) They also included "end users and customers from the very beginning" and "tried to get as much feedback as possible from team members when defining requirements." Some teams, however, worked with marketing personnel rather than the actual customer, assuming

that marketing knew what was best for the customer. This produces, in some instances, "unrealistic" requirements due to the fact that the marketing staff's understanding often differs from the application-specific information about the software use that is needed for design.[4]

On half of the participating projects, senior management, project managers, and system analysts defined at least the initial requirements. Only a few software teams involved technically knowledgeable stakeholders such as software developers, quality assurance, test, and configuration management personnel early in the project. In the rare case that they were involved in RE, they were selected because they had greater application domain knowledge than their colleagues.

Involving stakeholders early also resulted in an increased understanding of the RE process being used. On the other hand, a lack of training and "weak project management" led to teams that were less familiar with the RE process. For instance, some organizations assign project managers based on their availability rather than their capabilities.[5] In those cases, both project managers and team members must learn the basics as they work. Participants in this study confirmed that this can result in severe budget overruns, frequent schedule adjustments, and canceled projects.[3]

Resources

Traditionally, RE receives a relatively small percentage of project resources throughout the software life cycle. For example, in 1981 Barry Boehm found that 6 percent of a project's cost and 9 to 12 percent of project duration are allocated to specifying requirements.[12] Over the last 20 years, the resources allocated to RE activities have increased. In this study, perhaps due to the projects' high-tech leaders, the resource allocation to RE was significantly higher. Project teams expended on average 15.7 percent of project effort on RE activities. The average amount of RE time equaled 38.6 percent of total project duration.

Patricia Guinan gives an average RE team size of 5.6 members in the 66 projects she studied.[7] For the 15 projects in our study, we calculated an average RE team headcount of 6.2 (see Figure 3). The varied

> **Some teams worked with marketing personnel rather than the actual customer, assuming that marketing knew what was best for the customer.**

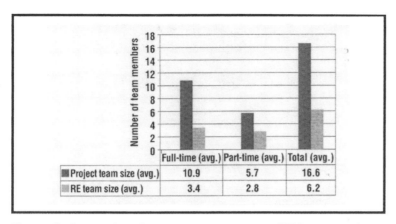

Figure 3. Comparing the resources spent on RE by team size and part-time versus full-time allocation of people.

uses of full- and part-time resources during RE were interesting: Some projects allocated only dedicated resources ("product teams") to RE, whereas others relied on RE "experts" whom various projects "shared."

We also investigated participants' perceptions of team cohesiveness. The teams rated themselves as relatively cohesive—5.5 on a 7-point Likert scale. Overall, stakeholders gave higher scores to RE teams that frequently communicated with customers and other teams involved in the development project. In other words, such teams executed more "boundary management activities."[7] While some teams leveraged "a lot of confidence and trust between customers and developers," others struggled to achieve "buy-in from all stakeholders" or to secure "the necessary participation of other teams to stay on track and complete the specification."

Several RE teams used specification templates to facilitate communication among stakeholders. They also included "comprehensive examples" to improve specification readability. The most common tool used during RE was an internal Web site, accessible to all stakeholders, where the project team posted and maintained the requirements. Some RE teams experimented with commercially available RE tools. In all but one case, these tools interfered with rather than supported RE activities. We believe that either a lack of well-defined RE processes or the RE team members' lack of training in the selected tools caused this undesired effect.

Process

Only some projects defined their RE process explicitly or tailored an organizational ("standard") RE process (see Figure 4) to their needs. A tailored RE process uses

sets" such as methods, templates, and tools to better fit a specific project's characteristics. Although several RE teams executed a documented RE process, with quality assurance providing insight into the compliance of a team's actions to their plan, most stakeholders perceived RE as an ad hoc process.

Most projects specify software in a dynamic environment and therefore struggle with the classic problem of rapidly fluctuating requirements.[4] This requires "flexible requirements" that "can be clarified and changed as the product progresses." In other words, the RE process has to account for stakeholders' learning curves and for requirements negotiation throughout the development project. Early on, some projects lamented the lack of "a detailed enough system architecture to adequately specify requirements," while others "froze the specification early" only to face customers that "kept changing requirements late in the cycle." The average ratings of configured RE work products (for example, prototypes and object-oriented models) and configured requirement changes reflect the stakeholders' struggle to balance the "drivers for change and the desire for stability." The most successful projects, however, recognized elusive requirements early in the process (with such statements as "the specification is a living document"). They managed requirements change explicitly rather than "freezing the whole specification."

Most of the RE teams performed multiple RE cycles. This is consistent with Pradromas Chatzoglou's research finding that more than half of the 107 projects he studied exhibited three or more RE cycles.[3] In our study, RE teams focused significantly more on eliciting and modeling requirements than on validating and verifying them (6.4 and 6.2 percent compared to 3.1 percent of project effort).

All teams performed some level of document analysis. Some, for instance, analyzed business plans and market studies while others derived requirements from contracts and requests for proposals. Most of the projects also used unstructured interviews, brainstorming, and focus groups. Only two projects held workshops to elicit requirements.

Most RE teams did not use "textbook" modeling methods,[8] but they did adopt abstraction and partitioning. The majority of projects developed prototypes ranging from simple mock-ups to operational prototypes. A third of the RE teams developed OO models.

Most projects verified and validated requirements with multiple stakeholders. More than half the projects performed peer reviews or walk-throughs to verify or validate requirements. Repeatedly, participants emphasized the importance of including customers and users in peer reviews. Moreover, several teams created scenarios to validate requirements. Only five of the 15 RE teams explicitly tracked requirements throughout their projects' life cycles.

Performance

We considered three dimensions of performance: quality of RE service, quality of RE products, and process control. Using existing preference measures,[5] we calculated the product of weighted performance dimensions to obtain a total performance indicator (TPI). That is, quality of RE service is most important (with a weight of 1.438), followed by the quality of RE products (1.126) and process control (0.438).

Stakeholders rated the quality of service at 76 percent on average. Several stakeholders mentioned their early and frequent involvement in RE activities and the "good interaction between all groups" as important aspects that influenced their rating. They were more satisfied with the fit of the recommended solution than with RE, however. Frequently, this was due to difficulties in project planning (for example, "planning for high-priority items slipped" or "maintaining requirements in later development phases not planned").

The quality of RE products considers both requirements coverage and specification quality. Stakeholders gave it an average rating of 66 percent; the customers' perception of requirements coverage was relatively low, particularly with regard to nonfunctional requirements. Management seemed satisfied with data requirements, whereas the team and project managers focused on functions. Stakeholders emphasized, however, that concentrating on functions and data resulted in a "lack of total system requirements attention" and in "incomplete performance, capacity, and external interface requirements."

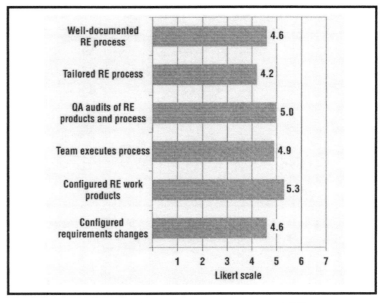

Figure 4. Evaluation of the participating teams' RE processes, based on a 7-point Likert scale.

The stakeholders also scored specification quality. Overall, they were most satisfied with the specification's consistency and the ability to modify it as necessary, but they emphasized that the lack of traceability hurt their project. Prioritization of requirements, however, caused the most difficulty for RE teams. The average stakeholder rating for this quality attribute was significantly lower than any other attribute. RE teams struggled with adequately involving customers to identify high-priority requirements, management's inattention to resolving "unknowns," and nonfunctional requirements that were not managed "in the same process or as tightly." Several teams also mentioned the inability to consistently execute RE according to stakeholders' priorities rather than their own interpretation of "what's important," and some reported difficulties in keeping everybody on the project informed of changing priorities.

Process control, the third dimension of RE performance, was rated at 59 percent on average. The less variance between actual and planned cost, duration, and effort, the better the process control of a particular project. On average, project teams contained cost overruns within less than 2 percent and effort overruns within less than 6 percent. In addition, their cost and effort performance was predictable, with a standard deviation of less than 25 percent. Project duration, however, showed an average overrun of 20 percent, with a standard deviation of 47 percent. Managers frequently focused on cost to

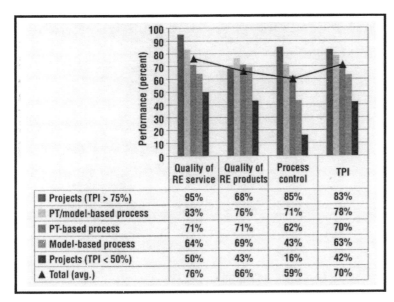

	Quality of RE service	Quality of RE products	Process control	TPI
■ Projects (TPI > 75%)	95%	68%	85%	83%
▨ PT/model-based process	83%	76%	71%	78%
■ PT-based process	71%	71%	62%	70%
▨ Model-based process	64%	69%	43%	63%
■ Projects (TPI < 50%)	50%	43%	16%	42%
▲ Total (avg.)	76%	66%	59%	70%

Figure 5. Comparing the deployed processes and their total performance indicator (TPI), the quality of RE service, the quality of RE products, and process control.

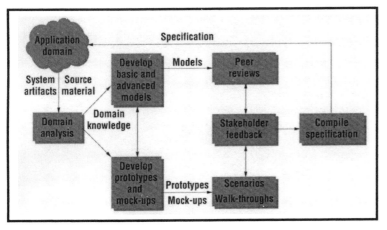

Figure 6. A successful RE process.

throughout the project's duration, while lower-rated RE teams (TPI < 50 percent) were primarily involved during the "front end" of the project. For both types of projects, about four full-time team members participated in the RE team. On the most successful projects, however, several part-time members also supported the team.

For projects with a higher TPI, stakeholders reported that RE teams were more knowledgeable about the application domain, IT, and the RE process. Whereas Mitchell Lubars suggests that a "better atmosphere" contributes to project success,[8] Guinan concludes that an environment where team members share positive and friendly feelings is unrelated to team performance.[7] In our study, we found low cohesiveness only on projects with a TPI of less than 50 percent. This suggests that cohesiveness is a "trouble" indicator rather than a performance predictor. In other words, an increase in cohesiveness reduces the risk of failure but does not guarantee success.

Successful teams performed on average three iterations of the RE process (see Figure 6). They identified major stakeholders and domain boundaries, examined system artifacts and source material from current and previous systems, and frequently obtained stakeholder feedback and expert guidance on how to proceed. This resulted in much more explicit "win conditions" for stakeholders.

The successful RE teams used advanced modeling methods such as OO models, knowledge models, and quality function deployment matrices that translated "the voice of the customer" into quantitative technical requirements. However, they did not abandon basic models (for example, the entity-relationship model or state transition diagrams). They simply tried "to create a more complete model of the system." Moreover, the teams developed (basic and advanced) models and prototypes together to clarify "known" requirements and to guide the discovery of new ones. A combination of models and prototypes helped the stakeholders, especially customers and users, envision the proposed solution.

During peer reviews, the RE team, technical and domain experts, and customers and users examine the models. The resulting feedback enables the RE team to create acceptable models that accurately specify the

control the RE process, leading to undesired changes of expended effort and predicted duration. Moreover, some project managers perceived "pressure" to underestimate effort and duration to meet cost targets determined outside their control.

The "top" performers in this study (TPI > 75 percent) dynamically balance knowledge, resources, and process. For example, as Figure 5 shows, RE teams that used either prototypes or models exclusively faired better on average than projects with a TPI below 50 percent. A combined prototyping and model-based (PT/M) process resulted in higher ratings in all performance dimensions. The most successful projects also expended twice the effort to specify requirements. They performed RE activities

Table 2

Best Practices

Focus area	Best practice	Cost of introduction	Cost of application	Key benefit
Knowledge	Involve customers and users throughout RE	Low	Moderate	Better understanding of "real needs"
Knowledge	Identify and consult all likely sources of requirements	Low to moderate	Moderate	Improved requirements coverage
Knowledge	Assign skilled project managers and team members to RE activities	Moderate to high	Moderate	More predictable performance
Resources	Allocate 15 to 30 percent of total project effort to RE activities	Low	Moderate to high	Maintain high-quality specification throughout the project
Resources	Provide specification templates and examples	Low to moderate	Low	Improved quality of specification
Resources	Maintain good relationships among stakeholders	Low	Low	Better satisfy customer needs
Process	Prioritize requirements	Low	Low to moderate	Focus attention on the most important customer needs
Process	Develop complementary models together with prototypes	Low to moderate	Moderate	Eliminate specification ambiguities and inconsistencies
Process	Maintain a traceability matrix	Moderate	Moderate	Explicit link between requirements and work products
Process	Use peer reviews, scenarios, and walk-throughs to validate and verify requirements	Low	Moderate	More accurate specification and higher customer satisfaction

requirements. Scenarios and walk-throughs further guide the discovery of requirements. The breakdowns experienced while using prototypes and mock-ups lead to an evolutionary improvement of the specification.

Best practices

Successful RE teams have in-depth knowledge of the application domain, IT, and the RE process. In other words, successful projects have the "right combination" of knowledge, resources, and process. Table 2 summarizes the best practices exhibited by the most successful RE teams.

Stakeholder feedback plays a decisive role from the beginning to the end of successful RE projects. The most successful teams always involve customers and users in the RE process and maintain a good relationship with stakeholders. They have an ongoing collaboration with stakeholders to make sure that requirements are interpreted properly, to deal with fluctuating requirements, and to avoid communication breakdowns. Research supports this best practice: according to one study, user participation is one of the most important factors contributing to RE success.[5]

Successful RE teams identify the boundaries of the application domain and of the major stakeholders. To validate their understanding of the application domain, they identify and consult all likely requirements sources. They examine, for example, system artifacts and source material from current and previous systems.

As other research points out,[4] some individuals perform "10 times better than others." Thus, managers of successful RE teams should

- carefully select team members skilled in the application domain, IT, and the RE process;
- always assign experienced, capable project managers to RE; and
- consult domain experts and stakeholders early on to augment and validate the team's knowledge base.

Successful projects allocate a significantly higher amount of resources to RE (28 percent) than the average project in this or previous field studies, and they expend these resources according to a well-defined process. Successful teams also maintain a balance between RE activities. That is, they allocate on average 11 percent of project effort to elicitation, 10 percent to modeling, and 7 percent to validation and verification. To streamline RE activities, successful teams frequently leverage specification templates and examples from previous projects.

Requirements prioritized by stakeholders drive successful RE teams. This allows the

RE team to decide which requirements to investigate when and to what degree of detail. To specify prioritized requirements, the RE team develops various models together with prototypes. Moreover, they maintain a requirements traceability matrix to track a requirement from its origin through its specification to its implementation. This lets the team show how its work products contribute to satisfying the requirements. In addition, successful teams repeatedly validate and verify requirements with multiple stakeholders. They use peer reviews, scenarios, and walk-throughs to improve the specification throughout the software's life cycle.

Teams often struggle with fluctuating requirements, communication breakdowns, and difficulties in prioritizing requirements. RE goes through recurrent cycles of exploring the perceived problem, proposing improved specifications, and validating and verifying those specifications. It is a learning, communication, and negotiation process; to succeed, you must integrate your technical, cognitive, social, and organizational processes to suit your project's particular needs and characteristics. In other words, you must progressively discover your project requirements to specify software successfully. 🔟

Acknowledgments

We thank the participating companies and the outstanding executives managing their software development and procurement processes for making this study possible. We also thank Steve McConnell and the reviewers, especially Karl E. Wiegers, for their helpful comments and suggestions. Further thanks go to Theresa Hofmann and John Overmars.

References

1. C. Jones, *Applied Software Measurement: Assuring Productivity and Quality*, McGraw-Hill, New York, 1996.
2. L.A. Macaulay, *Requirements Engineering*, Springer, London, 1996.
3. P.D. Chatzoglou, "Factors Affecting Completion of the Requirements Capture Stage of Projects with Different Characteristics," *Information and Software Technology*, vol. 39, no. 9, Sept. 1997, pp. 627–640.
4. B. Curtis, H. Krasner, and N. Iscoe, "A Field Study of the Software Design Process for Large Systems," *Comm. ACM*, vol. 31, no. 11, Nov. 1988, pp. 1268–1287.
5. K.E. Emam and N.H. Madhavji, "A Field Study of Requirements Engineering Practices in Information Systems Development," *Second Int'l Symp. Requirements Eng.*, IEEE CS Press, Los Alamitos, Calif., 1995, pp. 68–80.
6. N.F. Doherty and M. King, "The Consideration of Organizational Issues during the System Development Process: An Empirical Analysis," *Behavior & Information Technology*, vol. 17, no. 1, Jan. 1998, pp. 41–51.
7. P.J. Guinan, J.G. Cooprider, and S. Faraj, "Enabling Software Development Team Performance During Requirements Definition: A Behavioral Versus Technical Approach," *Information Systems Research*, vol. 9, no. 2, 1998, pp. 101–125.
8. M. Lubars, C. Potts, and C. Richter, "A Review of the State of the Practice in Requirements Modeling," *First Int'l Symp. Requirements Eng.*, IEEE CS Press, Los Alamitos, Calif., 1993, pp. 2–14.
9. S.R. Nidumolu, "A Comparison of the Structural Contingency and Risk-Based Perspectives on Coordination in Software-Development Projects," *J. Management Information Systems*, vol. 13, no. 2, 1995, pp. 77–113.
10. *IEEE Guide to Software Requirements Specification*, IEEE Std. 830-1998, IEEE Press, Piscataway, N.J., 1998.
11. H.F. Hofmann, *Requirements Engineering: A Situated Discovery Process*, Gabler, Wiesbaden, Germany, 2000.
12. B.W. Boehm, *Software Engineering Economics*, Prentice Hall, Englewood Cliffs, N.J., 1981.

About the Authors

Hubert F. Hofmann is manager of information systems and services for General Motors. His professional interests include strategic planning, enterprise-wide program management, software development, and system delivery processes. He received a PhD in business informatics from the University of Regensburg and an MBA from the University of Linz and the University of Zurich. He is a member of the IEEE Computer Society. Contact him at 7000 Chicago Rd., Warren, MI 48090; hubert.hofmann@gm.com.

Franz Lehner is a professor of management and information systems at the University of Regensburg, Germany, and head of the Department of Business Informatics. His fields of interest are software engineering and reengineering, knowledge management, and distance education. Contact him at the University of Regensburg, Business Informatics, D-93040 Regensburg, Germany; franz.lehner@wiwi.uni-regensburg.de.

For further information on this or any other computing topic, please visit our Digital Library at http://computer.org/publications/dlib.

The Secrets of Planning Success

Michael S. Deutsch
Texas A&M University
Department of Information and Operations Management
College Station, Texas
mdeutsch@cgsb.tamu.edu

Success Through Laziness

This is a story about software project planning. In this connection, the world's oldest profession is not what we have been told but is that of the storyteller. Here is a fable that should be weighed as you see fit:

It was a relatively large project, so the Project Manager developed a very detailed plan. Tasks and dependencies were defined at a minute level, and people were allocated to each task. Team interfaces were elaborated and followed. The Manager thought that he could gauge status and foresee problems by relying on this plan. On the morning of the project review with upper management, the status metrics in fact told him the project was behind. He showed the trend charts to the big boss and proclaimed: "Yes, we have slipped schedule. We can recover because all the major problems are behind us." This prediction was accepted. The Project Manager next called a team meeting exhorting the participants to work hard with diligence. He drew a line in the sand: "No more slips!" The team responded. Indeed the slippage was made up, and a good product was delivered to the customer on time. Success happened because of a motivated team with a good plan.

Really? In some instances myth can be more powerful than fact. This could be true possibly in organized crime fighting: *"After you testify your safety is guaranteed by the witness protection program."* or perhaps in athletics: *"We play better coming from behind."* However, our little story does not bear the slightest resemblance to the real world. The actuality is when a sizeable project falls behind schedule, it usually gets worse! If you believe the story, it may well be that your purpose in life is to serve as a bad example to others, and there is considerable value to that. In my project experiences over thirty years, you need more than a detailed plan and hard work to avoid failure.

Hard work may pay off over time. Conceivably, but laziness always pays off now. Here are a few "planning secrets" derived from my failures, and occasional successes, in project management. These emanate from the easygoing way of life describing how to succeed without unnecessary hard work.

KEY PLANNING PRINCIPLES:
1. Protect a core capability.
2. Have an anti-deception measure.
3. Make two parts to every plan.
4. Achievable plan? Get involved early.

Each of these "lazy planning principles" is explained in turn. A further personal thought on leisure: After years in industry I do not presently lhave a real job, yet they are paying me. Is this a great country, or what?

Finally, it is common knowledge that a plan must address certain fundamental factors: What needs to be done? When? By whom? Where? How much will it cost? Others have expertly articulated how to represent these in software project plans. This paper seeks to concentrate on how planning helps project management make better decisions. Isn't decision making the real value that is added by management? From a decision support perspective, these are the typical questions that confront the project manager and his superiors: What is the status of the project? What are its problems? and Why?

Principle #1: Protect a Core Capability

The project is sliding out of control in part because the original schedule was unrealistic. The project manager asserts that the slippage can be recovered. Hence, today's question is: What should be done?

QUIZ - When a large project gets behind:
❑ Accept manager's prediction that the schedule will be met.
❑ Fire the project manager repeating as necessary.
❑ Bring in the "Review Committee."
❑ Add more staff.
❑ Do not make it worse.

Any or all of these may be warranted under specific circumstances. We can briefly reflect on the choices. The veracity of the project manager's prediction that the schedule can be recovered becomes less likely beyond about the first third of the duration; more on this in Principle #2. Dumping the project manager is cosmetically pleasing and may be justified. A number of factors comes into play including whether the project manager can pass this quiz. The Review Committee says "We're from headquarters, and we are here to help." Maybe they can if they are unobtrusive. On the matter of adding staff, it is impossible not to recall Frederick Brooks' illustrious advice [1]:

> *"Adding manpower to a late software project makes it later."*

All the choices so far may arguably further decay the situation depending on specifics. Perhaps the smart course is to muster some courage against upper management pressure then resist the first four options. You can, however, protect the project, and your job, by re-prioritizing tasks to assure that a minimum core capability of the most important functionality is delivered to customers on the originally appointed date. The customer and your management undoubtedly will be displeased. Nonetheless, the extent of their displeasure will be far less than if their only option is to wait. It may even be possible to salvage a reputation for rational project management under adverse circumstances.

A superior approach is to *include the prioritized core capability in the original plan*. Not only do you avoid making things worse, but you also accrue a built-in graceful degradation to schedule slippages. Very little has to be done after initial planning to gain these advantages. Here is how the prioritization strategy looks in concept:

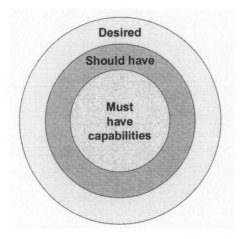

The requirements are stratified into multiple priority categories. At the core of the "onion" are the critical capabilities that constitute the core capability to be preserved within the original schedule. The implementation schedule proceeds incrementally from the core of the onion outward. The requirements objects that can be used to actualize this priority scheme are:

- Operational scenarios
- Use cases
- Features
- Services

Naturally it would be better to obtain the concurrence of your customer, internal or external, and other stakeholders when formulating the core capability. Regrettably, this does require some real effort.

I am reminded of a related anecdote from my project management career. The project entailed development of an Air Traffic Control system. An interdisciplinary team of system engineers and users was chartered to define the system's operational scenarios. Unfortunately, the team over achieved by delineating eight hundred scenarios. This was clearly unbalanced with cost and schedule resources. As good project managers we applied Win-Win principles [2] to the situation: The users were amenable to the business limitations. In return, they were given the primary authority for prioritizing the scenarios into a core capability structure. In the end only a subset of scenarios was delivered on schedule, but the users received the highest valued capabilities within the schedule limitation.

Perhaps everyone reading this paper will always manage flawlessly with on-time performance. For our less gifted colleagues, here is what I like about the core capability planning principle: 1) when the schedule slips you are no longer "mediocre" but instead are "agile;" and 2) this agility, i.e., avoidance of painful repercussions, is bought with a minimum of exertion.

Principle #2: Have an Anti-Deception Measure

All of us in management are victims and perpetrators of deception; let's be generous and say that almost invariably the deception is unwitting. Of paramount concern is self-deception. Even experienced project managers incline toward optimism and unconscious denial as things go off-course little by little. Degradation is seldom seen as a single major calamity. I rely again on wisdom from Brooks' to lucidly characterize this phenomenon [1]: *"How does a project get to be a year late?....One day at a time."* One pay back for a strong project planning and tracking infrastructure is that you can head off denial before it happens.

Another reason to confront self-denial is to help recognize the need to make decisions before it is too late. The best general manager I ever worked for had a test he applied whenever a project manager asserted that the project would finish on schedule. He referred to this as the anti-deception measure. He actually called the measure something else that cannot be written in a publication of any repute.

The essence of this measure involves comparison of two rates of task efficiency. The first is rate of work accomplished over the schedule duration cumulative-to-date:

$$\overline{T}_{Cum} = \frac{WorkUnits_{Cum}}{Duration_{Cum}}$$

The rate chart below from a phase of a real project plots planned rate of work unit accomplishment along with actual accomplishment to-date. About 110 work units have been completed over a 12 week duration; therefore $\overline{T}_{Cum}$ is 9.2.

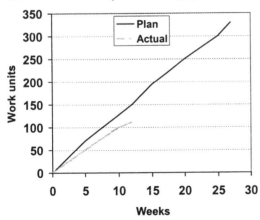

The second calculation is rate of work accomplishment required over the remaining schedule duration to complete on time:

$$\overline{T}_{ToGo} = \frac{WorkUnits_{ToGo}}{Duration_{ToGo}}$$

The number of work units yet to be accomplished is 220 (330-110) while the remaining duration is 15 weeks (27-12); therefore $\overline{T}_{ToGo}$ is 14.7.

My old boss was fond of noting that a study of over 700 projects (unfortunately I am unable to retrieve a specific reference) showed that when a project has advanced beyond 30-35% of its schedule, the task efficiency never increased and even decreased in many cases. Hence, when a project manager (or sub-project manager) alleges that he/she can make up a schedule slippage, these two comparative task efficiencies are a good anti-deception test. The above example takes a snapshot at 12 weeks into a 27 week total duration, well surpassing the 30-35% threshold. The proposition that task efficiency can improve from 9.2 to 14.7 is clearly not credible based upon this model. This suggests that corrective actions are only likely to be influential during that early 30-35% of the timeline. To recount, the person who most often needs a shock to see the situation impartially is you, the project manager; this furnishes the opportunity to make corrective action decisions early when they can make a difference. Further, these task efficiency metrics are only possible if the plan includes frequent completion milestones.

When a project is well into its schedule, this anti-deception measure fortifies the notion that the best course of action may be to do nothing. This option is also attractive if you are lazy especially when extra activity is likely to be harmful. Superb project managers are rare. For the rest of us who perform at a lesser level we need to do so impressively, and upper management probably will not notice the difference anyway.

Principle #3: Make Two Parts to Every Plan

The core concept on this one is fairly simple. On any project there are two important dimensions of knowledge: 1) what you do know about the problem; and 2) what you do not know. The unknowns are preponderant during the project's early stages. The project plan should reflect both aspects.

Traditional planning processes are based upon the fallacy that all major tasks can be delineated in a Work Breakdown Structure at project inception then transferred into a plan. Each project has open issues that prevent this. These open issues, if forthrightly addressed, require a healthy dose of resources to resolve. It is counter-cultural in some organizations to acknowledge that these uncertainties exist. Perish the thought of conceding that the problem is not fully understood! Some unprincipled project managers explicitly suppress these uncertainties, move on to another assignment unscathed before anything has to be delivered, and leave it to their successors to deal with the unpleasant impacts when the unresolved problems emerge.

It can safely be asserted then that there are two categories of things to be done and planned. The first are those generic tasks that can be anticipated during early planning. On the partial plan shown below from the requirements phase of a real project these include the first three task lines. The second category is the open issues and uncertainties that constitute the residue from the basic tasks with some becoming evident only after initial work is done. Examples such as capacity studies, exception scenarios, and other tradeoffs are shown in the example.

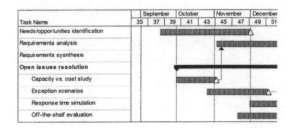

The basic principle here is that open issues are a certainty. It is only the specifics of the open items that may not become clear until later. Therefore, there should be a general open issue sub-task for each major WBS category. When they become evident the specific task items are entered into the plan, are scheduled, and are assigned resources. It has been my observation that good project managers during the requirements phase of a project reserve about 15-20% of the phase budget for open issue resolution. Open issue control is more or less an operationalization of risk management. As many companies have a predisposition against the "risk" word, characterizing uncertainty as open issues can help you remain popular with your management and customers.

Open issue management is entirely cosmetic without resources to fight the battle. The budget part is probably the easiest. What about the more perplexing matter of personnel? You do not exactly have good people sitting on the bench waiting to come into the game whenever an open issue shows up. The real answer is to not overload your best people at the very beginning of a project explicitly limiting them to a forty-hour week. The open issue reserve becomes this available overtime bandwidth. It will be utilized soon enough.

Lastly, dealing with open issues resembles intense work. It is difficult to dispatch this hard reality with levity or flippancy. We can only rationalize that treating the open questions now within an evolving plan averts harder work with painful consequences later.

Principle #4: Want an Achievable Schedule? Get Involved Early

Have you ever observed a situation like the following especially in commercial product organizations? I have in my consulting practice. The schedule is unattainable, and everybody knows it. The product organization or equivalent internal customer has unilaterally determined the feature content and delivery schedule based upon market needs. Engineering passively accepts the delivery date with token protest or none at all. There is essentially an unspoken conspiracy. When the product is delivered late, the product manager blames engineering for the slip; engineering disclaims the original schedule saying they had no voice in its formulation. Everyone has a built-in defense valve, and there is no real final accountability. This situation is certainly not helpful to the company's business interests.

The real losers in the above scenario are the software engineers who are forced to participate in death-march schedules. This culture eventually precipitates a human resources disaster. DeMarco and Lister furnish a scathing commentary [3] on such corporate policies. While software engineers do not expect flawless decision making from their leaders, they are entitled to protection from wish-based plans.

The ultimate responsibility for an unrealistic schedule lies with the software Project Manager. He or she should have the estimation, negotiation, and interpersonal skills to participate early with the marketing and product organizations to influence determination of the schedule. A good project manager will find a way to participate even if initially uninvited. The fundamentals of this process are outlined below:

Estimating Principals

- Iterative process to bring effort, schedule, and technical scope into balance through tradeoffs.
- Work with, not against, your customer through mutual exploration of options, alternatives.
- Avoid impossible schedules by being a good ethical negotiator when the project is being conceived.

A reasonable schedule results from interaction not confrontation. A typical starting conversation might be:

> **Product Manager:** "We need to deliver in 12 months."
>
> **Project Manager:** "What? This job cannot be done in less than 16 months."

A deadlock? This is not necessarily the case. A market window likely drives the requested twelve-month schedule. A good start would be for the Project Manager to recognize this. The Project Manager's challenge is to identify the resource needs, decisions, and tradeoffs that could enable a twelve-month delivery. Some of the exploration parameters are:

Schedule compression options

- Parallelize some tasks
- Schedule vs. effort tradeoffs
- Reconsider feature content
- Resolve conflicts to make key personnel available
- Incremental deliveries

Within these dimensions lies a probable path of decisions that can help converge a give and take solution that satisfies most of the business goals. It is incumbent upon the project manager to propose options jumpstarting the negotiation while avoiding the aforementioned impasse. An estimation system including parametric models such as COCOMO II [4] (for custom development) and COCOTS [5] (for COTS intensive systems) can assist a convergence toward a shared vision.

Using calibrated estimation models helps, but something needs to be said about reverse estimation. This entails starting with management's answer then manipulating and rationalizing model parameters to produce the expected numbers. As one acquires experience in this practice, the results can be quite convincing. Unscrupulous? Yes! Lamentably, some have advanced their careers doing this and have been skillful enough to be someplace else before the project gets into trouble.

Returning to the laziness theme, there are two choices: You can be lazy now or lazy later. I would favor the latter. Why traverse the agony of long hours to meet an impossible schedule? The only way of realizing this is to engage early during the project's conception and negotiate a reasonable schedule. This does have the side effect of making you accountable.

Alternately, you can be lazy now avoiding this intense early interaction. This option likely involves the hectic death march to a difficult or unachievable deadline. For everybody, these circumstances make going to the office somewhat like visiting Hell with fluorescent lighting. The human resource ramifications are indeed acute.

Final Thoughts

Planning artifacts such as the Work Breakdown Structure, Gantt charts, network diagrams, and resource tables are blueprints for the internal execution of the project. These documents also reply to upper management's continual concerns of "How much?" and "How long?" The documentation is only the culmination of a stream of strategy decisions. These decisions should supply the project with the agility, gracefulness, and ability to remain afloat when trouble arrives in River City. I convey in this paper what I think are the key flagship principles that shape those planning decisions designed to keep a project viable through the inevitable bog of problems and obstacles. While these guidelines have served me well, it is more significant to note that I adapted them from the two or three most talented project managers with whom I worked during my industrial career.

These "planning secrets" are hardly arcane; they denote a set of planning best practices that should underlie the management philosophy of every project. They are not difficult and can be readily tailored to most situations. The "laziness" metaphor has been employed halfheartedly to emphasize that conservation of energy pays dividends. Finally, notwithstanding a few diehards, who really does want to live at the office? It is very disconcerting when your dog no longer recognizes you.

References

1. Brooks, Frederick P., *The Mythical Man-Month: Essays on Software Engineering,* Addison-Wesley, Reading, MA, 1975.
2. Boehm, B. and R. Ross, "Theory W Software Project Management: Principles and Examples," *IEEE Transactions on Software Engineering,* July 1989, pp. 902-916.
3. DeMarco, T. and T. Lister, *Peopleware: Productive Projects and Teams,* 2nd ed., Dorset House, New York, 1999.
4. Boehm, B., C. Abts, A. Brown, S. Chulani, B. Clark, E. Horowitz, R. Madachy, D. Reifer, and B. Steece, *Software Cost Estimation with COCOMO II,* Prentice Hall PTR, Upper Saddle River NJ, 2000.
5. Abts, C., *Constructive COTS,* http://sunset.usc.edu/research/COCOTS/index.html, University of Southern California Center for Software Engineering, 2001.

The Slacker's Guide to Project Tracking

or spending time on more important things...

James Davison, Tim Mackinnon, Michael Royle

ThoughtWorks UK
Berkshire House, 168-173 High Holborn
London WC1V 7AA

{jdavison, tmackinn, mlroyle} @thoughtworks.com

Abstract

As a Project Manager, your time is far too important to be wasted on mundane tasks like detailed tracking of the day-to-day activities of each of your developers. Wouldn't it be nice if you spent your time negotiating project scope and identifying and removing team impediments? Our experience has shown that consistency in card sizes and estimates allows you to perform full project planning with little effort. Additionally, it results in diagrams that accurately reflect your project's status. With this, release planning sessions take hours not days, freeing up valuable time for both you and your developers.

1. Introduction

While it's easy to convince Project Managers that some form of project tracking is important, what is difficult is to get the right degree of tracking that adequately helps them make informed decisions. This paper is based on our work with a large organisation that had a very formal process for project selection, definition and execution. However, one of their software delivery departments was open to suggestions about how to make their process more agile and better able to deliver working solutions on time and on budget. By working with several of their development teams, all of whom had little agile experience, we began to discover basic techniques for making project tracking both simple and extremely effective. In turn, these teams have developed a great track record for delivery that our tracking techniques have both facilitated and made more visible within the organisation.

We found it made sense to break down the tracking process into three areas: iteration planning, progress tracking, and release planning. Each of these areas presents specific information that helps organize and understand project status by tracking at different levels of granularity. For instance, release planning deals with the entire release at a high level by considering a unit of measure of weeks. Thus after a release planning session we can't say that we will be finished at precisely 12 p.m. on July 15, but we can say that the current scope seems to be a reasonable fit for 3 months of work. This is then supplemented by other tracking techniques which look at a finer level of detail and help confirm or contradict the initial release plan. It is important to remember that this is not a science because this process is based on estimates. Estimates are inherently inaccurate but with continued tracking and attention these risks can be mitigated, as we will show in this article.

2. Why Track Progress?

When we began looking at what tracking would be necessary for a team, we started with first principles and examined who the audiences were for the results of our tracking data. This enabled us to tailor the tracking process to meet these needs without doing unnecessary work.

In a large organisation, such as the one we were working with, one of the main stakeholders for any project is business management. For this group, development of software is an investment, and they contribute time and money to make projects happen. This also means that their reputations are on the line for delivering the value from the software, and like any investor, they want to know how that investment is proceeding. Most of the time these stakeholders will not have in-depth knowledge of how the software development process works, so they want information presented to them in such a way that they can easily digest it and can decide if there are any actions they need to take to help ensure the delivery of the solution.

Along with business management, the users are another important group that have significant interest in the progress of the project. In larger organisations, a nominated person or smaller group of people represents the entire user group on the team. This person (or smaller group) is not always technical and so they need an easy way of understanding progress in such a way that they can simply and accurately communicate it back to their peers.

Alongside management and the users, the Project Manager is accountable for the delivery of the project. Having accurate information that can be used to quickly and easily discuss progress with all of these groups is extremely important. Furthermore the Project Manager

Reprinted from *Proceedings of the Agile Development Conference (ADC'04).*

needs to be able to interpret this information so that any corrective adjustments can be made to ensure the success of the project. For example, if progress is slow, it might be possible to hire more developers or remove barriers that are impeding progress. If there are indications of creeping scope, there needs to be a discussion with the stakeholders as early as possible to show how this will impact delivery.

Finally the development team itself needs to have an understanding of how well they are doing both for pacing and morale purposes. This can be vital to the success of a project. If the project is behind schedule then the team can adjust its approach or make any necessary changes that will help mitigate the risk of the project not delivering.

3. Iteration Planning

One of the first teams we encountered in the organisation was a collocated team of about 13 people. They had been waiting for final project approval to proceed with the execute phase of the project. They had been spending time spiking [2] different user interface libraries and persistence mechanisms in Microsoft .Net [1].

The time spent, while useful, was rather unstructured and wasn't being measured in a way that could be used for predicative purposes. Borrowing from the practices of eXtreme Programming (XP) [2], we immediately held a "Planning Game" and planned for "Short Iterations" of 1 week. We also began implementing and tightening up the other XP practices, however that work is outside the scope of this paper.

3.1 First Steps

As there was already a proposed project plan in place due to the organisation's gated acceptance process, we chose to concentrate on getting repeatable development iterations working. We also concentrated on measuring a development velocity [3], which would give an indication of how much work the team could achieve in a new development technology (.Net).

We held a planning game based on a velocity from a different team and selected some initial stories that dealt with persistence and reference data administration.

3rd Party Setups (#5.1)	1.00	100%
Sort on product (#53.16)	1.00	0%
Group by Country (#93.1)	0.25	100%
Transfer Simple Product (#62.5)	0.25	100%
Transfer Complex Product (#66.2)	2.00	100%
Totalling (#53.20)	0.25	100%
Country Product Setup (#16.2)	0.25	100%
Velocity Total	4.00	

Figure 1 – Iteration 3 results

Our planning process was similar to that described in [2], whereby cards were estimated in ideal days, and we tracked the total of how many cards were completed in an iteration. We also adopted the velocity simplification described in [3] and used a fixed iteration length that avoided using slightly more complicated "load factor" arithmetic. As an example, by the end of the third iteration, the measured results looked like Figure 1. The developers had finished 6 story cards, giving a velocity total of 4.

In Figure 1, notice how the team didn't finish card #53.16 which is why the completed total adds up to 4 and not 5. Therefore in the next iteration, using the concept of "yesterday's weather" [2], the team signed up for another 4 units of work. The potential stories for the next iteration were laid out on a table and the team collectively discussed new estimates based on their previous experience. Note, we differed slightly from the technique presented in [2], and used team estimates. These were much simpler than having individual developers track personal velocities and also helped with motivation by avoiding any blame culture related to not finishing cards. By using this set-up, planning games were quite simple although they did require someone in the role of Iteration Manager (IM), which will be discussed later in more detail, to facilitate team discussions to keep them focused. We found that in these meetings, the best strategy for the IM was to periodically ask the team "Do you have enough information to put an estimate on that?" This reinforces the message that not all decisions have to be made collectively with the team, just that enough common strategy needs to be agreed and recorded on task cards for a later pair to pick up and work with.

Once the estimates were in place, the users were then able to select from the estimated stories up to a total of 4 as shown in Figure 2. Notice card #53.16 was given highest priority since it had "hungover" from the previous iteration.

Sort on product (#53.16)	1.00
Product Setup (#62.2)	0.25
Transfer New Product (#66.3)	0.50
Database Qualifiers	0.50
Transfer Multiples (#62.3.5)	0.50
Stock Counts (#62.4)	0.50
Warehouse Isle Setup (#62.1)	0.50
Display Type of Trade (#89.1)	0.25
Total	4.00

Figure 2 - Iteration 4

3.2 Steady Iterations

As we continued planning 1-week iterations with the team, we found that they were very effective at giving quick feedback on story progress. More importantly, were much faster to plan due to their small size. This is an important point as many developers dislike planning meetings, and so the smaller duration makes them much more acceptable. We found that the users, who were also initially sceptical, also began to like them because any cards that were deferred due to velocity constraints were available for reconsideration in a short space of time.

Once an iteration had been created, the development team were encouraged by the Iteration Manager to take any cards larger than half a day and split them into meaningful development tasks to ensure that measurable progress could be made. We also noticed that stories that were larger than 2 days tended to run into difficulty and so we typically suggested that these stories be split into smaller but still useful chunks that could be more easily completed and tracked. While we didn't strictly enforce this, we found that the users noticed this trend as well, and so they started getting better at writing smaller stories of their own accord.

As the development iterations occurred every week, we also found that physically moving the cards to a meeting room was laborious. To overcome this, we used some simple story card wallets[1] which we created by duct taping CD protective wallets together and hanging them on a white board using bull clips (Figure 3). To ensure that we had smooth running planning games we also stuck helpful tips on the back of the wallets to indicate placeholders for Story Card format (title, text, author etc.), Acceptance tests (Action, Result), Pair History and Tasks 1 to 5.

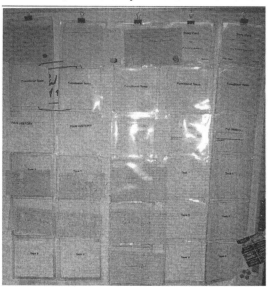

Figure 3 - Iteration Planning Wallets

In addition to the logistical advantages, it also enabled visibility of the process. Often when cards are just placed on a board by themselves, it is difficult to work out the relationships between them. The card wallets allowed us to group relevant cards and communicate their relationship in an easy and effective manor. We have even noticed that another team using the wallets has decided to put an "End"

marker after that last task so that they can see if there are any missing cards.

As we continued to complete iterations we found that our users felt a bit divorced from the development process. They often noticed that cards were being considered complete when in fact they had known problems. In an attempt to increase the visibility of the card status, we instituted a coloured sticker scheme[2] to indicate the status of cards as shown in Figure 4.

Originally we only had 3 states for the cards: Not Started (Red), Developer Complete (Yellow), and User Accepted (Green). We gave the green stickers to the users and the red and yellow stickers to the Iteration Manager. However we found that sometimes, even though a card was a place holder for a conversation, that conversation was not always happening. To overcome this, we added an extra state, Story Discussed with User (Blue) that must always happen before a story is Developer Complete.

A nice side effect of the colored stickers was that they had the effect of showing iteration status in a quick glance. As more stories were accepted, the iteration board would slowly turn green. In our experience, without this it was often difficult to determine the state of each card played in an iteration. Usually, this was because this information resided entirely within the Project Manager's head, or worse, spread out amongst the team members.

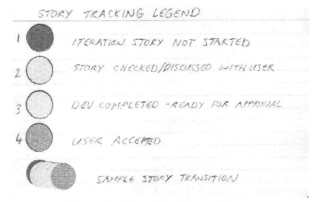

Figure 4 - Story Card Transitions

3.3 Later Refinements

Once the team was used to working on weekly iterations we noticed that we didn't always have as many pairs working as we thought. This was typically because some project members were required to help other teams or were on a short holiday. To easily account for this without getting too detailed, we decided to simply count the number of pairs available at the stand-up meeting and use the weekly average for the following iteration. This simple solution worked very well and also emphasised everyone's commitment to the project. At the beginning of each

---

[1] The original wallet idea came from Connextra

[2] An idea we also saw used at Connextra

planning meeting we reviewed our previous velocity and then discussed the number of pairs available to determine our velocity for the next iteration as shown in Figure 5. Although the table shows 2 decimal points, the Iteration Manager would normally round to the nearest quarter day.

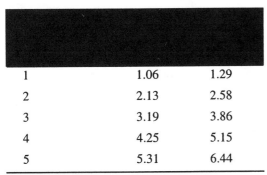

1	1.06	1.29
2	2.13	2.58
3	3.19	3.86
4	4.25	5.15
5	5.31	6.44

Figure 5 - Velocity Matrix

Another issue that we encountered when measuring a pure velocity was referred to as the "Friday Afternoon" syndrome. On the last day of the iteration, if there was only 1 large card left to work on that was obviously not possible to complete it in the time available, one developer came to the conclusion that he might as well do nothing and "go to the pub". This was especially the case if the work was not going to count in some way towards the velocity (admittedly this developer had a tendency to look for excuses to "go to the pub").

As the team felt strongly about this, we decided that partially completed work should be visible when measuring velocity. Rather than losing the benefits of "yesterday's weather", we introduced a second "optimistic" velocity that also counted a percentage of ideal time that had been measured on incomplete stories. In reality these percentages were very coarse grained and were normally one of 25%, 50%, 90% and 99%. At the end of each iteration the IM queried developers for the percentage on any incomplete stories, and this was added to the normal "pessimistic" velocity to form a range on the velocity matrix as shown in Figure 5. This was not meant to be used as an excuse to not finish whole cards, but it did mean that in a planning game the team could guarantee to finish the pessimistic velocity but could stretch to finish the optimistic target. This range of velocities enabled the IM to use their judgement on how much work should be attempted. Sometimes there was evidence that the optimistic target was uncharacteristic and so the team reverted to just using the pessimistic velocity. At other times the team was unlucky and they wanted to stretch to try and achieve a more optimistic figure. This helps address the complaint that strict adherence to "yesterday's weather" removed any judgement from the planning process. The IM (as well the team and customers) all have the necessary information needed to make an

informed decision, and set the correct expectations in an easy to maintain manner.

This technique does come with a health warning. Teams that consistently have a wide divergence between pessimistic and optimistic velocities are exhibiting a project smell of not properly completing cards. However, if used sensitively, a range helps gain team support for using an appropriately measured velocity. We also found that our users were very supportive of this technique as they could see that attempts were being made to actively make improvements.

4. Progress Tracking

While significant progress was being made on each iteration, and we had a functionally running application to demonstrate, our steering group continuously asked about project progress. As we were using XP as a development methodology, we were able to easily tell them the number of stories finished, the number of stories remaining, the number of bugs fixed as well as other typical metrics like man days used. In practice, they could never really grasp how this related to the success of the project. These numbers were alien to them and so the Project Manager decided that we needed something that would capture their interest as well as convey an accurate picture of the project.

4.1 The PM's Time Constraints

While it's easy to promise timely information on project status, the reality was that consolidating and massaging this data into a presentable form could easily use up half a day. Our Project Manager was keen to take an agile and pragmatic approach to this, partly because he had a lot of other work to do.

In fact it's very easy to lose sight of the full extent of the Project Manager's job and become too focused on simply collecting project metrics. In the case of this particular team, spending time with both customers and project sponsors was an important aspect of the job. As with any relationship, open communication needs to be nurtured, especially as previous projects for this particular user group had failed. To make things even more challenging, the customer base was geographically diverse and so couldn't be meet all at once.

As well as meetings, fiscal reporting was also another important activity that took a significant amount of time. This tracking is detailed and must be accurate as it can affect departmental performance; therefore, it required adequate time to get right.

We also noticed that "other" activities were not unique to this particular team. When we examined the results from retrospectives [4] held by four other similar teams at the end of their release deliveries (roughly every 2 months), the Project Manager's were all faced with other common items that "didn't go so well" and needed to be addressed:

- Team communication
- Getting customer feedback
- Lack of appropriate documentation
- Difficulty of achieving adequate testing

We were concerned that we didn't want a new way of reporting to divert the Project Manager from these other more important responsibilities.

4.2 First Steps

The original template for project reports (Figure 6) detailed project performance by reporting Costs, Man Days and Milestone Targets with columns for planned, actual, forecast and variance. While complete, this data seemed complicated and not in keeping with the agile approach being used for development.

Man Days				
Resource Type	Planned days	Actual days	Forecast to End	% Variance
Project Manager	88	21	67	0%
Technical Architect	88	22	66	0%
Business Analysts	141	19	105	(12.1%)
Lead Developer	88	22	66	0%
TOTAL	405	84	304	(4.2%)

Figure 6 - Original reporting format

In designing a new report, the first obvious question to answer was "what data would be easy to obtain but still show progress". As data from several XP iterations was available, the Project Manager tried to show something graphical that gave a sense of progress (Figure 7.). These graphs were intended to show what percentage of stories had been completed and how much time remained. Graphs are particularly useful because they can convey a lot of information that would be difficult to follow in textual form, however we found this first attempt was still difficult to interpret.

What we really wanted the stakeholders to understand was the trend towards an on-time completion. Therefore after some brainstorming, we decided to try a stacked bar graph approach as shown in Figure 8.

The lower segment of each bar indicates the number of stories completed, while the top portion represents the total number of story cards remaining (split into those defined, and those estimated to be defined).

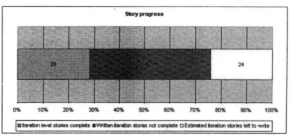

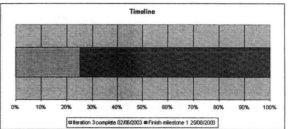

Figure 7 - First reporting attempt

As you can see this is a powerful yet simple technique for presenting this information. The format is similar in concept to a "Profit Graph", where increasing profits and decreasing expenses are viewed as a good indication of success. In our case, the reader's eye will fill in the trend line of completed stories, which is what the Project Manager wanted readers to notice. Additionally, it also shows other information about possible scope creep and other issues that may impact the delivery. Our graphs are opposite to the "Burn Down Charts" [5] used in Scrum, which show a decrease in remaining hours. We felt that showing an increase in completed work was psychologically more pleasing.

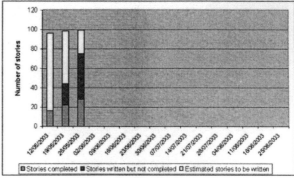

Figure 8 - The first report

In Figure 8, the first iteration bar in this graph shows only "stories completed" and "estimated stories to be written". This reflected that the users had not yet been able to translate their high level requirements into concrete user stories. Based on progress in the first iteration, the Project Manager took the high level functional areas of the system and estimated that these would translate into approximately 90 user stories which he indicated on the graph. With this graph in place it was clearer how much work there was for the users to finish writing the story cards. In fact, as the users were now seeing progress they became better at writing more stories.

As the project progressed, the next monthly report (Figure 9) continued to show development progress as well as the completion of all of the story cards (show in iteration 7, the last bar on the graph). This indication of story completion removed a large amount of risk from the project.

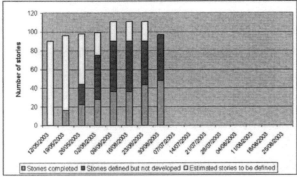
Figure 9 - The second report

At the end of the first project release (Figure 10), you can see that development progressed at a relatively constant pace (shown on the graph as the bottom segment of each bar). However, we can also see that the Project Manager had to manage scope creep very carefully. These scope changes were partially due to:

- The lack of completely defined stories at the beginning of the project
- The inexperience of users, new to writing story cards
- Some stories that were intended for the next release being "accidentally" moved earlier

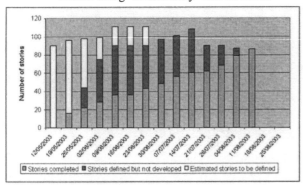
Figure 10 - The final report for release one

For the next release (Figure 11), the situation was quite different as all of the stories were defined up front. In fact in this release it was even possible to add more features than were initially specified. Again it's interesting to notice that the development progress of stories completed increased at a steady rate just as in the previous release.

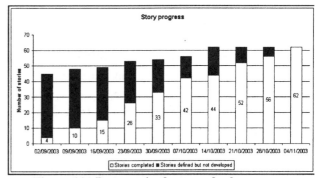
Figure 11 - Progress in the second release

4.3 More Detailed Tracking

As good as this tracking was, the Iteration Manager was worried about the inaccuracy of this method of reporting progress. The problem was that not every story was of equal size, and he feared that by treating them as if they were, the reported progress would be skewed. Instead, his idea was to plot the number of completed ideal days as a function of the iteration. Figure 12 shows an example of this graph. Again this shows a similar overall trend of increasing development as well as how many ideal days of work were left (the line).

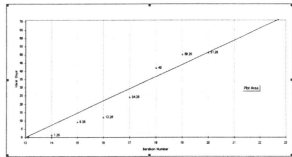
Figure 12 - A more detailed measure of story progress

Unfortunately, as we progressed through several iterations, this graph became more problematic. The difficulty was in dealing with story cards that spanned multiple iterations. For example, if card #x was initially started in iteration 3 with an estimate of 1 ideal day, it required additional effort to track the history of the card if it wasn't completed. If the card was finished in the next iteration, we had to take the original estimate and add any additional estimated time and put this on the graph. While not terribly difficult, the additional tracking overhead began to add extra time to creating the graph. We also noticed that this method of tracking didn't easily lend itself to showing scope creep.

About halfway through the release, we decided to compare results from the two graphing techniques to see if either of them was better able to predict an end date for the project. We were initially surprised to find that both methods predicted the same end date. At the same time we were quite relieved as the story count method of tracking was much easier to maintain and so we decided to abandon the second tracking technique.

After considering the results of our experiment, the explanation we came up with was two-fold. The first centred on our philosophy for estimation consistency over accuracy. Estimates by definition are fuzzy and not particularly accurate. Therefore, how do we use them to accurately predict how long it will take to develop an application? There are two schools of thought on this. The first and most often used is to keep track of the actual time taken to finish something and then use this actual as the basis for the next set of estimates. For instance, let's say we wrote a personal contact screen and the estimate was one day but it actually took two days. When the card for a screen for business contacts is being estimated it would be given an estimate of 2 days as it is similar in size to the personal contacts screen. The biggest advantage of this method is that it incorporates past experience when producing new estimates. This means that over time the difference between the estimated and actual time will tend towards zero. However, it also means that you need to accurately keep track of the actual time taken for each card and present that information in such a way that the team can quickly recall the amount of time taken for any one card.

Because of the extra effort involved in the first approach, we chose to use the second method, which is to keep estimates consistent. To use the example from above, rather than giving the business contacts screen a two day estimate we would give it a one day estimate. The reason this works is because if the estimates are consistent then we should have a nearly constant load factor [2] which can then be used for any estimates to determine relatively accurately how long they will take. This simplifies the tracking process because we don't need to record the actual time taken for each card. Additionally, we found that we didn't even need to record the original estimate because we used a simple guideline for estimation. For any estimate, we asked that it should be based on the amount of time the developers thought it would take to "Hack" the solution. Therefore, we didn't include testing, refactoring [6], or non-development time in estimates and simply tracked all of these within our development velocity. Thus the time taken to "spike" a possible solution can be used as an ideal estimate, as re-implementing a production worthy version incorporates refactoring and proper unit testing in the measured velocity.

The second factor in the success of the simple tracking model was our tendency to keep cards to a manageable size. Our goal for every card was to keep it between 0.25 and 2 ideal days. As we estimated cards, if we found cards larger than 2 ideal days we generally broke them down into meaningful pieces that could be easily completed. As previously mentioned, while this wasn't strongly enforced we found that users began to notice that smaller cards were

much easier for them to test and accept as finished. Thus they also began to write cards of this size.

The combination of these two simple factors: estimation consistency and small card size, created an environment where simply counting cards was enough to track progress.

4.4 Exciting Observations

After the introduction of the new graphs, we began to notice that at steering group meetings, the attendees would immediately turn to the page with the graph on it to see what progress had been made. Although they were used to a common format for project reports, it was clear that the new graph was conveying to them more than what they had seen in previous reports. Furthermore, because a lot of information was captured in one picture it became a good catalyst for some of the best project discussions.

The last refinement we made to the graph was adding a predictive aspect to it. This was just a simple average weighted by the anticipated number of pairs available. Figure 13 shows a graph with these projections added. You can see that from the seventh iteration onwards, the bars are a different colour. This is the predictive section of the graph. It shows the predicted number of cards completed based on a weighted average and the anticipated total number of cards. In this example, the predicted total number of cards remains constant. We tried to be more accurate by predicting how many cards would be added and split-up. However, at that point we decided that the extra information would only confuse the matter and make the results more ambiguous.

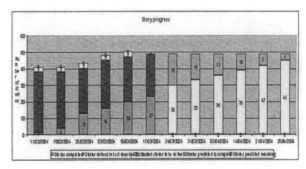

Figure 13 - Progress tracking with predictions

One downside of the predictions is that it adds a level of precision that in reality isn't there. For instance, at one steering group meeting about halfway though a release we had to fend off questions about why it was predicting that there would be two cards remaining that couldn't be finished. As with most things, people will believe numbers even if they know they are just a guess or estimate. Therefore, you should try to judge your audience and their propensity for believing numbers before showing them a simplistic predictive model.

In retrospect, there is a lot to be said for not even using a predicative model and simply showing current progress.

With a single end bar that shows the expected number of completed stories, you would then rely on the reader to imagine the trend curve themselves. When you have only completed 2 or 3 iterations, the line they imagine will be (in their minds) fairly inaccurate as they understand that they don't have enough data points. As you get more iterations, the visualisation of a trend line becomes much easier and it becomes much more obvious if you are on track or not. We haven't tried reverting to this model but it would definitely be in line with our tendency to question the appearance of too much accuracy and look for simplifications wherever possible.

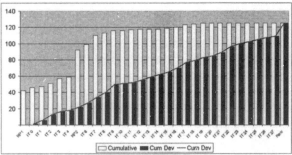

Figure 14 - Another progress tracking example

Finally, after seeing the success of our progress tracking, other teams within our department have begun using similar methods. Figure 14 is a diagram used by another team where the bars represent the same information but they have added a trend line to aid visualisation.

An interesting point about this graph is that it is obvious when the scope changed. In iteration 5, the users asked the team to deliver more functionality. This information could be presented to a steering group to show why the team may not make the deadline. In this case, they were able to get additional time and budget to cover the new scope.

5. Release Planning

The organization we were working for had insisted that no project would be approved unless it had a "defined" project plan. Thus for our project, there was already a high level plan that had been created by the Project Manager and the Technical Architect. While this plan was mainly methodology neutral, it was a more traditional plan with pieces of work shown in a Gant chart. As development was progressing in an agile, needs driven basis, we saw that the reality of the emerging iterative solution was diverging from the original plan. Therefore, we couldn't continue to rely upon it to adequately predict if any changes would endanger the team hitting the required schedule.

5.1 Reluctance

The lack of a clear plan that truly reflected the stories of work that needed to be completed made us feel rather uncomfortable. Although we didn't like moving forward with development without an adequate release plan, our fears were tempered by the desire of the team to start

writing code. The thought of taking several days to wade through cards and get high level estimates was met with a large amount of resistance from the entire team. As previously mentioned, we felt that it was in the best interest of the team to actually get some real experience delivering some software. At the same time, we kept looking for opportunities to fill in a release plan.

5.2 A Simple Strategy

The breakthrough for simplified release planning occurred almost half way into the first milestone of the project (after about 6 iterations). During an iteration planning meeting, the planning had gone quickly but we were still a bit uneasy about the breadth of the project that was unfolding (a smell that a release plan was missing). As we had a little more time available in the meeting room, we suggested that our customers read out some of the higher level stories that remained. We felt that this would give us an idea about what they intended to get done for the first official release of the product.

As an experiment, one of the authors began to write on a card, "gut feel" estimates for the amount of time required to finish those high level items. After a few minutes he realised that this was a useful technique for everyone to try and so he gave all the developers a card and asked them to try the following:

- On a card write down a high level estimate for each story card

- Keep your estimate to yourself

- Try and keep conversation to a minimum, limiting it to clarification of story details or technical questions

We then proceeded to record an estimate for each requirement that was described. Sometimes we needed a bit more detail from the user, like "how many reports would need to be produced" or "what kind of response time was required". Occasionally someone would ask a technical question like "does the current database technology provide support for offline replication". Often some of the questions that were asked caused people to go back and scribble out an estimate and increase it, or sometimes even decrease it. In cases where conversation was dwelling on a decision about a particular implementations we just asked everyone to make their estimate reflect their uncertainty. After about an hour we had covered all of the stories. The results looked similar to the cards shown in Figure 15, although these cards are a later example of the technique where we asked developers to give high and low estimates.

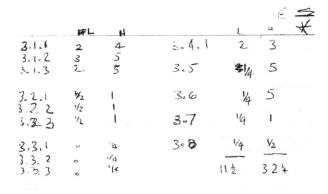

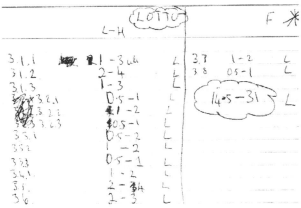

Figure 15 - Release Planning Estimates

Once we had completed estimates for each of the stories, we then went around the room and asked each developer to read out their estimate for each high level story, which we recorded on a flip chart. This proved to be quite entertaining as we quickly saw who was optimistic in the team and who had more knowledge of a particular area. We then simply averaged the estimates to get a total for the estimated time remaining.

This grand total was then divided by the development velocity (that we had been measuring in our iterations) to get an indication of how many weeks would be required to complete the first release. We also did the division with our "optimistic" velocity to get a best and worst case scenario. The good news was that our expected completion date fell roughly between our best and worst case estimates and so we felt that at least the first release was attainable.

When we left the planning room, there was a sense of relief from the entire team, as the project now felt like it was achievable. Furthermore, the feeling that release planning was going to be a monster, had now been dispelled.

5.3 Refinements

We have now repeated this process of release planning on several releases and with several teams, and have been happy with the outcome.

Time and time again we have to remind ourselves that planning is not an exact science – we are making judgements based on people's estimates, and while estimates can be fairly accurate, when you add them together they do not give you an exact answer. However, we have been pleased to find that overall our results have been accurate enough to properly meet our deadlines.

We have also noticed that in these release planning sessions, developers can get concerned about details that ultimately don't appear to affect the outcome of their estimates. For this reason we introduced high-low estimate boundaries more as a way to help make estimation more efficient so that they could express "either/or" decisions. For example in Figure 15, you can see ranges of 3 to 5 weeks in some cases.

Finally, we have also used this technique further up the project chain in the organisation. During the "Select" or "Define" phases we can quickly give high level estimates for different project options that can be used when making business cases for potential projects. Not only does this help the strategy teams put meaningful estimates on the projects for governance board selection, it also allows the development teams to feel more involved in the potential projects that might come through the pipeline for eventual development.

6. The Role of an Iteration Manager

Since the premise of this paper is enabling Project Managers to spend more time on the more important aspects of their job, a brief description of the Iteration Manager role is useful.

The Iteration Manager is a role to which the Project Manager can delegate most of the inward facing team responsibilities. You can think of these roles as two sides of the same coin, one facing outward (Project Manager) and one facing inward (Iteration Manager). This means that the Iteration Manager becomes the team tracker [2], communication enabler, and potentially overall team leader.

Therefore, the Iteration Manager should have many of the same skills you would look for in a Project Manager, such as leadership, understanding of team dynamics and motivation, as well as the ability to make the tough decisions. However, Iteration Managers can also add additional value to the team rather than just being an additional Project Manager. For instance, the Iteration Managers on our project have been from developer backgrounds, and in fact, they spent most of their time as developers on the project in addition to their responsibilities of Iteration Management. This was beneficial for several reasons: it freed up the Project Manager for more important duties, being an active member of the team gave them the understanding of the technical and business aspects necessary to perform the job, and it didn't add any additional levels of pure management that can often slow down a project.

7. Conclusion

We all know that Project Managers often need to divert their attention from the more important aspects of their work to focus on the useful but more mundane tracking tasks. We've presented a strategy for allowing managers to once again spend the necessary time on building and maintaining customer and business management relationships that ensure project success. The main idea is to keep tracking simple by figuring out exactly what information is necessary for all interested parties and only focusing on these items. Additionally, splitting out the inward facing responsibilities to another team member can free up more time.

If we had it to do over again, we would create the high level release plan even if there were some unknowns. This is especially true since we know they are not time consuming to perform, therefore any changes can be accommodated quickly. What is important is to establish a pattern of successful iterations, which show progress towards completion. As the project progresses, it is also important to be conscious of the team's velocity, keeping in mind the realities of "yesterday's weather" and the pit-falls of optimistically selecting an expected velocity. Lastly, progress tracking should give a simple overview without being too precise with its predictions. Simple graphs that show story completion are very effective.

8. Acknowledgements

We would like to thank the reviewers and the following colleagues for their contributions to this paper: members of the My Supply team (in particular Brent Cryder), Rebecca Parsons, Andy Pols, Laura Waite, The Bishop of Norwich and finally the Golden-T.

9. References

[1] Microsoft online at http://www.microsoft.com/net/basics/, last visited June 2004

[2]Beck, K. Extreme programming explained: embrace change. Reading Mass. Addison-Wesley, 1999

[3] Various authors online at http://www.c2.com/cgi/wiki?VelocityVsLoadFactor, last visited June 2004

[4] Kerth N. Project Retrospectives: A Handbook for Team Reviews, Dorset-House, 2001

[5] Control Chaos online at http://www.controlchaos.com/burndown.htm

[6] Fowler M, Refactoring: Improving the Design of Existing Code, Reading Mass. Addison-Wesley, 1999

Chapter 6

Software Estimating

If you can look into the seeds of time and say which grain will grow and which will not, speak then to me.

—Shakespeare, in *Macbeth*

Overview

Management has been mounting initiatives to improve the predictability and control of software costs and schedules ever since I entered the software field in the 1960s. Management wants to accurately forecast what resources are needed to deliver software products that satisfy specified requirements at any given time during the software life cycle. They also want to be able to control cost and schedule growth so they can deliver an acceptable product on schedule and within budget.

The field of software estimating has made a great deal of progress during the past decades. Today, we have put the processes and tools into place for generating accurate estimates. In addition, professional societies have been formed to address the issues that occur at conferences and in professional journals on the topic. Most of these responses have been prompted by a desire of the project management community to get a better handle on what it really costs to develop, field and maintain software products. Although certain issues remain in estimating, as the papers that follow indicate, current research is addressing them. Most of these issues revolve around the new technology (the Web, multimedia, etc.) and how to estimate its impact as we develop plans for future projects.

I have selected the four papers that follow to reflect advances being made in the field of software estimating. As the making, marketing, and manufacturing technology associated with software development changes, so must support technologies like software estimation. For example, what good do models and techniques that rely on source lines of code (SLOC) as their basis do when you are developing software using commercial off-the-shelf (COTS) components and visual languages for the Web using code generators and a host of other modem tools to streamline the effort? I asked Dr. Richard Stutzke to kick off this chapter with a survey article that addresses innovations made in the field. Because he has just published a definitive work in this area, I felt that it would be appropriate for him to provide a current survey of works in the field.

Article Summaries

Software Estimating: An Overview, by Richard Stutzke. This updated article provides a useful survey of past work done in the field of software cost and size estimating. The author summarizes the progress made over the last two decades and points out an important past work that has had a great deal of influence on the field (function points, Raleigh models, etc.). Based upon the survey and a look at future community needs, the author recommends how you can improve your ability to estimate software costs and schedules consistently and accurately now and in the future. His suggestions are aimed at helping you to take advantage of best industry practices in a manner compatible with SEI measurement and process maturity concepts.

Software Engineering Economics, by Barry W. Boehm and Sunita Chulani. This updated paper introduces you to the topic of software engineering economics and the COCOMO II cost estimation model. Being able to estimate resource needs is a skill that managers at every level in the organization should possess. This paper surveys the available tools and techniques of software economics. It focuses on the topic of estimating and rates their relative strengths and weaknesses of approaches devised to help you in this area. Details are then provided for the popular new version of the COCOMO software model, along with its cost drivers and scale factors. The paper concludes by providing guidance for calibrating, using and exploiting the model as you utilize it to conduct cost–benefit, cost estimating, and risk analysis.

Web Development: Estimating Quick-to-Market Software, by Donald J. Reifer. As we move to the Web, new challenges pop up that impact the methods and models we use to develop resource estimates. For example, current size metrics must be extended to address multimedia and other unique aspects of Internet applications. As another example, existing mathematics for estimating duration does not seem to accurately predict the time needed for developing Web applications. This paper advocates the use of a new size metric, Web Objects, and a new version of the COCOMO II mathematical model, WebMo, to address these and other challenges.

Software Size Estimation of Object-Oriented Systems, by Luiz A. Laranjeira. Most cost models use some measure of size as their primary input. To estimate cost, you must also estimate size as accurately as possible early in the development cycle of your product. This article helps you accomplish this by providing you with an excellent introduction to the techniques available for software size estimation. It goes further by proposing a method for capturing and representing knowledge about the architecture, which provides the basis for size estimates. It provides a good overview of the practice along with exciting concepts to advance the theory of size estimation.

Key Terms

Eight terms, defined as follows, are important to understanding the topic of software estimating:

1. **Costing.** In management, the process of developing a cost estimate for an item, task, or activity. Costing and pricing are separate but related activities typically done by different people and at different times during the software life cycle.
2. **Duration.** The number of time periods, excluding holidays and other scheduled periods of nonactivity, required to satisfactorily complete either a work task or activity.
3. **Effort.** The number of labor units required to satisfactorily complete either a work task or activity.
4. **Estimate.** A calculated prediction, typically of the resources required to complete a project.
5. **Forecasting.** In management, the prediction of future events. Forecasts differ from estimates in terms of the means used to derive them and their accuracy. For example, an estimate of the area of a curve is quite different from a market forecast.
6. **Metric.** A quantitative measure of the degree to which a system, process, or component possesses a given attribute. For example, generation of source lines of code per staff-month is an indicator of software productivity.
7. **Pricing.** In management, the process of determining how much to charge a customer or user for products or services. Costing and pricing are separate activities. Organizations can price services for less than their cost and still make a profit based upon economies of scale.
8. **Productivity.** In economics, productivity is defined as the ratio of output to input so that the efficiency and effectiveness with which resources (people, equipment, facilities, etc.) are used to produce output of value can be calculated.

Common Acronyms

The following acronyms are used within the articles in this chapter:

COCOMO	Constructive Cost Model
ESLOC	Equivalent (new) source lines of code
FP	Function points
IEEE	Institute of Electrical and Electronic Engineers
IFPUG	International Function Point User's Group
ISPA	International Society of Parametric Analysts
SEI	Software Engineering Institute
SEMA	Software engineering measurement analysis
SLOC	Source line of code
SM	Staff month (of effort)
WEBMO	Web Model

For Your Bookshelf

The classic text on software estimating is Barry Boehm's 1981 book entitled *Software Engineering Economics.* Although somewhat dated, this primer reviews techniques available for estimating and provides valuable guidelines for doing cost-effective decision and risk analysis using a variety of models. Another text, also authored by Barry Boehm and his team, is entitled

Software Cost Estimation with COCOMO II. It provides a current description of the COCOMO model (and a copy of the software) and explains how to use it to develop cost estimates and perform risk management. COCOMO is viewed by many as the most popular software estimating tool because of its simplicity and the fact that the mathematics it uses is public domain.

The new book by Richard Stutzke entitled *Estimating Software-Intensive Systems* surveys the field of software estimating and provides you with in-depth coverage of most of its topical areas. The book is comprehensive and full of factual appraisals of what works and what does not. In addition, it offers excellent guidance on what to do and when to do it. Finally, the book provides useful resources in the Appendices to help perform recommended tasks (spreadsheets, tables, etc.).

My book entitled *Making the Software Business Case: Improvement by the Numbers* is a more advanced text whose aim is to help software managers prepare business cases. The book shows you how to develop and use the numbers generated by cost models and other means to prepare credible justifications for just about any kind of improvement investment (software process improvement, replacement equipment and tools, infrastructure enhancement, etc.).

The *Project Management Book of Knowledge (PMBOK™)* devotes an entire chapter to the topic of project cost management. It also provides guidance and outlines the tools and techniques for resource planning, cost estimating, cost budgeting, and cost control.

The IEEE Computer Society has published a *Standard for Software Productivity Metrics,* IEEE Std 1045-1992. This standard provides useful conventions for comparing estimation results and claims.

The Software Engineering Institute (SEI) has also published counting convention recommendations and a set of core management measures that provide useful standards for estimating as part of their Software Engineering Measurement and Analysis (SEMA) project. Copies of the pertinent reports and guidebooks on this topic can be downloaded from the SEI Web site at http://www.sei.cmu.edu.

For those interested, the International Society of Parametric Analysts (ISPA) is a professional society dedicated to advancing the field of parameters. Its membership includes model builders, users, and decision makers who are interested in parametric analysis and estimation. The society publishes a newsletter and holds an annual conference.

Software Project Estimation: An Overview

Richard D. Stutzke

Introduction

Our world increasingly relies on software. There is a seemingly insatiable demand for more functionality, interfaces that are easier to use, faster response, and higher dependability. Developers must strive to achieve these objectives while simultaneously reducing development costs and cycle time. Above all, senior management wants software delivered on schedule and within cost, a rarity in past software development projects. Software Process Improvement (SPI), as advocated by the Software Engineering Institute (SEI), helps to achieve these objectives. Project planning and tracking are identified as two process areas in the Software Engineering Institute's (SEI) Integrated Capability Maturity Model (CMMI®).

Software cost and schedule estimation supports the planning and tracking of software projects. The formal study of software estimating technology did not begin until the 1960s, although Peter Norden did some earlier work on models of research and development [1]. Estimation received renewed attention during the 1990s decade to cope with new ways of building software and to provide more accurate estimates of project costs and schedules.

This article discusses the problems encountered in software estimation, surveys previous work in the field, and describes current work.

Description of the Problem

The estimator must estimate the effort (in person-hours) and duration (in calendar days) for the project to enable managers to assess important quantities such as product costs, return on investment, time to market, and quality. The estimation process is difficult for several reasons:

- Conflicting project goals
- Lack of a detailed product description
- Wide variations in developer productivity
- Difficulty of modifying existing code
- Emergence of new development processes, methods, and tools

First, projects often must satisfy conflicting goals. Projects to develop (or maintain) software must provide specified functionality according to specified performance criteria, within a specified cost and/or schedule, and with some desired level of quality (typically defined as the absence of defects). Software engineering processes can be chosen to meet any one of these project goals. Usually, however, more than one goal must be satisfied by a particular project. These multiple constraints complicate the estimating process.

Second, estimates are required before the product is well defined. Software functionality is very difficult to define, especially in the early stages of a project. This makes it difficult to estimate the amount of software to be produced (the product size). The basis for the first good cost estimate is not usually available for totally new systems until the top-level design has been defined. (This design is an instance of the product's "software architecture.") This level of design is only defined at the Preliminary Design Review (PDR) in United States Department of Defense (DoD) contracts. (More modem terms are the

---

This paper originally appeared in the May 1996 issue of the journal *CrossTalk*. An updated version appeared in the 6th edition of this book. This article updates the previous version. It contains additional information and references. All URLs cited are correct as of August 5, 2005.

Product Design Review and the Life Cycle Architecture review.) This milestone is reached after approximately 20 of the total effort and 40 of the total duration have been expended by the project staff At this point in a project, typical accuracies for the estimated effort and duration are within 25 of the final project actuals. In general, the accuracy of estimates increases as a project proceeds since more information becomes available, for example, product structure, product size, and team productivity. Figure 1 illustrates this and is adapted from Boehm [2]. (Commercial software projects behave similarly.) To reduce costs (as well as to improve quality and reduce development times), some projects use predefined "domain-specific software architectures" (DSSAs). The development costs for such projects can be estimated more accurately than for projects that build a totally new product since more information about the product is available earlier. (The Advanced Research Projects Agency and the SEI, among others, are sponsoring work on DSSAs.) In most cases, however, the estimator must apply considerable skill to estimate product size, project cost, and project schedule early in a project.

For modifications of existing code, more data are available earlier so more accurate estimates of product size are potentially possible than for totally new products. (But many factors affect the effort needed to modify existing code. See below.) This is important since approximately half of all software maintenance work is really a response to changes in the original requirements and/or in the system's external environment (e.g., mission or business objectives, or interfaces to external systems) and involves modification of existing code. (The choice of the software architecture significantly influences modifiability and, hence, maintainability. Architecture-based reuse is another motivation for the work on DSSAs.)

The third reason is that estimates of effort, cost, and schedule depend on programmer productivity. Software development is knowledge intensive. The main contributor to project cost is the labor expended by the development team. To the first order, the development effort is proportional to the amount of software to be developed (the product size), divided by the average productivity of the team. The productivity of different individuals can vary by a factor of 10 or more. As software-intensive

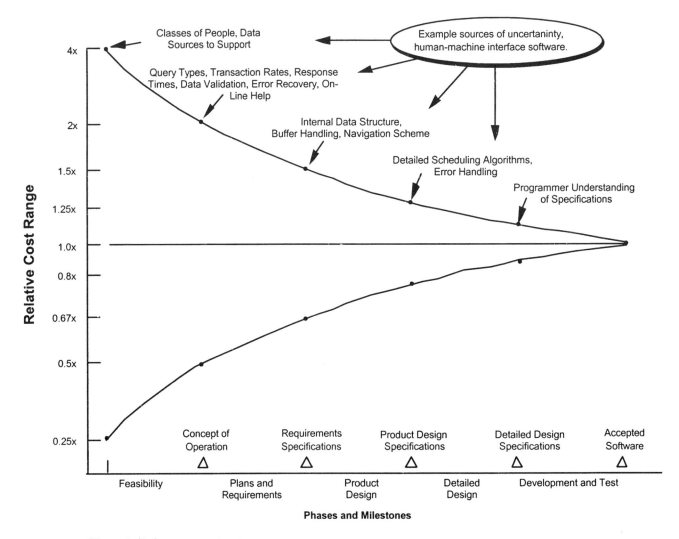

Figure 1. Software cost estimation accuracy versus phase. (Reproduced with permission from reference [1].)

190

systems become larger and more complex, teams of individuals must work together to design and build them. The productivity of a team depends not only on the knowledge and skills of its members, but also on how the members communicate and interact. Productivity is difficult to predict for newly formed teams, or for existing teams facing new application domains, product architectures, methods, or tools.[1]

The fourth reason that software cost estimating is difficult arises from the need to modify existing code. It is hard to identify and quantify the factors affecting the effort needed to incorporate existing code in a product. The code must be located, understood, modified, integrated, and tested. The associated effort depends on how the code is structured, the programmer's knowledge of the code, the amount of modification needed, and the amount of testing needed. Even if code is specifically designed for reuse, the same factors affect the associated effort. In addition, there may be costs for licenses and royalties.

Various cost-estimation models have been developed to quantify the economic costs of building and reusing software components. For example, Richard Selby [3] analyzed costs at NASA's Software Engineering Laboratory and found that there is a large increase in programmer effort as soon as a programmer has to "look inside" the component. The amount of effort continues to increase as the amount of existing code modified increases. The exact amount of effort depends on the suitability of the software component for the intended application, its structure, and other factors. Figure 2 illustrates this, and is based on a model that I developed using data from Richard Selby [3], Rainer Gerlich and Ulrich Denskat [4], and Barry Boehm et al. [5]. (For details, see [6].) The figure shows the modification effort measured relative to the effort to develop totally new code, plotted versus the fraction of code modified. The two curves shown correspond to the best and worst cases for reuse based on the factors mentioned above. There are three noteworthy features of these curves. First, the effort is never zero, even if no code is modified. Second, the effort increases faster than linearly at first. Such nonlinear behavior is not handled in most existing software-cost-estimation models. (COCOMO II, described later, does handle this.) Third, the effort needed to modify all of the existing code is more than the effort to develop the same amount of code from scratch. (Effort is wasted in understanding, and then discarding the existing code before the new code is written. This effort is never expended if the decision is made to develop totally new code from the start.) As shown in the figure, for the worst case, the economic break-even point occurs when only 23% of the code is modified; reuse is not cost-effective above the break-even point. For the highest-quality code, break-even occurs when 68 of the code must be modified.

The fifth reason that estimation is difficult is that the way software is being built is changing. New development processes endeavor to meet one or more of the following objectives: higher-quality software (i.e., fewer defects), more modular and maintainable software, faster delivery to end users, and lower development costs. To meet such objectives, developers are using combinations of prebuilt code components, labor-saving tools, and nontraditional development methods. For example, much programming is being put into the hands of the users themselves by providing macro definition capabilities in many products. These capabilities allow users to define sequences of frequently used commands.[2] A slightly more sophisticated approach is to allow domain experts to construct applications using special tools such as fourth-generation languages (4GLs) and application composition tools. Larger systems intended for specialized (one of a kind) applications are often built using commercial off-the-shelf (COTS) products to provide functionality in areas that are understood well enough to be standardized. Examples are graphical user interfaces (GUI) and relational database management systems. Object-oriented languages support component-based development by making it easier to identify and develop "plug compatible" components. Developing software for future reuse costs more, but reduces costs incurred to reuse the software to build software-intensive systems. New ways are needed to estimate the costs and schedules for these new processes.

During the 1990s, several authors described "agile methods" that produce software using a series of rapid iterations. Each iteration starts by identifying the features to be added to the evolving product. The iterations last from one to eight weeks. (Martin Fowler provides a good summary in [7].) The developers are also expected to evolve the method itself *during* the project. Planning and estimating projects that use such development processes and methods prior to the start of the project is impossible. Controlling them will also be difficult. This continues to be an active area of research.

What is an Estimate?

At a minimum, the estimator must compute the effort (cost) and duration (schedule) for the project's process activities; identify associated costs such as equipment, travel, and staff training; and state the rationale behind the calculations (including the input values used and any assumptions). Estimation is closely tied to the details of the product's requirements and design (pri-

---

[1]Accurately communicating domain knowledge between individuals is a major problem. Experts use special terminology to convey information about a domain accurately and concisely. People unfamiliar with the domain do not know this terminology. In addition, experts and nonexperts may assign different meanings to the same word, often without realizing it.

[2]There is an analogy here to the situation shortly after telephones were introduced in the United States. Someone predicted that soon the majority of the United States' population would have to be employed as telephone operators in order to handle the workload of connecting calls. Instead, technology changed and now everyone serves as their own operator, using direct dialing to connect nearly all calls.

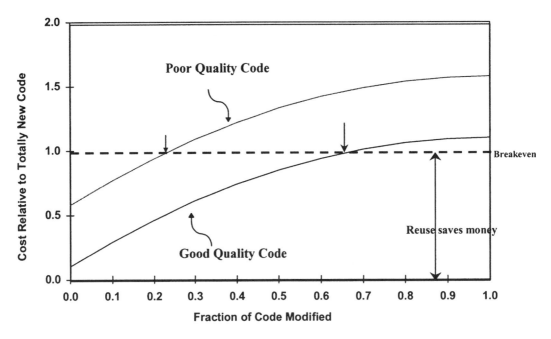

Figure 2. Reusing software is not always cost-effective. (Adapted from reference [6].)

marily the software architecture), the activities of the chosen development process, and the necessary resources (people, tools, and facilities). The requirements, architecture, and reuse of existing code all affect the product size. The process activities and the project resources affect the productivity. Estimators must understand all of these factors in order to produce accurate estimates for project planning (i.e., these factors also affect estimates of product performance and quality).

It is also highly desirable for the estimator to indicate the confidence in the reported values via ranges or standard deviations. The estimator should also try to state the assumptions and risks to highlight any areas of limited understanding relating to the requirements, product design, or development process.

All estimates have errors, so how accurately must you estimate? The short answer is "accurately enough so that you can control the production processes." The necessary accuracy depends on project goals, financial or business risk, the time needed to make decisions (or to convey information between the developers and the buyer, end user, or product manager), and other factors.

Steve McConnell notes that the purpose of a project estimate is not to make a perfect prediction of a project's cost and schedule. Due to the inevitable changes, you seldom end up with the same project that you originally estimated anyway. He states that a project estimate should be "sufficiently accurate" to allow the project manager to control the project to meet its business objectives. The required estimation accuracy depends on who well your feedback control systems work and on the needs of the project. Typically, ±20% is adequate for project cost and schedule. Accuracy goals typically tighten as the end of a project approaches because there is less time to correct problems.

Estimation determines feasible intended targets so that the project's feedback control system can guide the project to the desired targets. (The "targets" can be project, product, or process characteristics. They are the project's technical, cost, and schedule baselines.) The estimates of various quantities are moving targets, so you must update them during a project. In addition, the project manager must ensure that none of the assumptions and constraints underlying the estimate are violated during a project.

Estimation Techniques

Estimation techniques use a mixture of three elements: analytic models, historical data, and expert judgment. These techniques differ based on the emphasis they place on each element, and the rules they use to combine the three elements. The paper that follows this one in this tutorial volume, "Software Engineering Economics" by Barry Boehm and Sunita Chulani, describes six categories of estimation techniques.

The next section gives a chronological summary of work in the field over the past five decades, with emphasis on analytic models (also called "parametric models"). The paper by Boehm and Chulani contains detailed descriptions of several popular software estimation models. Their paper also explains the important role that estimation plays in decisions involving limited resources.

Survey of Past Work

From simple beginnings in the 1960s, software estimation technology has expanded due to the work of many individuals.

The 1960s

In the 1960s, while at RCA, Frank Freiman developed the concept of parametric estimating, and this lead to the development of the PRICE model for hardware. This was the first generally available computerized estimating tool. It was extended to handle software in the 1970s.

The 1970s

The decade of the 1970s was a very active period. During this decade, the need to accurately predict the costs and schedules for software development became increasingly important and so began to receive more attention. Larger and larger systems were being built and many past projects had been financial disasters. Frederick Brooks, while at IBM, described many of these problems in his book *The Mythical Man-Month* [8]. His book provides an entertaining but realistic account of the problems as perceived at that time.

During the 1970s, high-order languages, such as FORTRAN, ALGOL, JOVIAL and Pascal, were coming into increasingly wider use but did not support reuse. Also, programming tools (other than compilers for the languages and simple text editors) were in very limited use. For these two reasons, systems were essentially built by hand from scratch. The cost models of this period thus emphasized new development.

During this period, many authors analyzed project data using statistical techniques in an attempt to identify the major factors contributing to software development costs. Significant factors were identified using correlation techniques and were then incorporated in models using regression techniques. [Regression is a statistical method for predicting values of one or more dependent variables from a collection of independent (predictor) variables. Basically, the model's coefficients are chosen to produce the "best possible" fit to actual, validated project data.] Unfortunately, in practice there neither is enough data to define a model completely, nor are there any accepted "laws of software physics" that could constrain the form of the model's basic equations. As noted by Conte [9], researchers must thus resort to so-called "composite models" created using a combination of analytic equations, statistical data fitting, and expert judgment. Experts differ on which independent variables are significant and on the form of estimating equations, giving rise to diverse models. The coefficients of a particular model are determined using actual project data and regression techniques. Most estimating models are in fact composite models. Such models are one form of cost estimating relation (CER).

The prototypical composite model is the Constructive Cost Model (COCOMO) developed by Barry W. Boehm in the late 1970s and described in his classic book *Software Engineering Economics* [2]. Various implementations of COCOMO continue to be widely used throughout the world. COCOMO provides formulas for estimating the total development effort and time. The "nominal" effort depends on the amount of software to be produced, measured in delivered source instructions (essentially physical source lines of code without comments). The nominal effort is adjusted to account for the effects of 15 cost drivers, which describe attributes of the product, computer, personnel, and project. (The project attributes include the effects of modem methods and tools.) Estimators use five- or six-point Likert scales to rate each cost driver attribute [10]. These ratings are converted into quantitative values using tables. The quantitative values are multiplied to give the total effort adjustment factor (EAF). (The range of effort adjustment, based on the ratio of the highest possible to lowest possible values of EAF, is 817.) The adjusted effort is then used to compute the development schedule. Finally, additional tables are used to allocate the effort and development time by phase and by activity.[3]

---

[3]The names of the phases and activities are, unfortunately, nearly identical: analysis, design, code, test, and so on. The phases refer to the time when activities are performed. The problem is that activities span phases. For example, most of the effort for the requirements analysis activity is expended during the analysis phase, but some effort is also expended later to revise the requirements to reflect new knowledge obtained during the subsequent design and coding phases. This close correspondence of the phases and activities reflects the "waterfall" development of the 1970s. Other estimating tools do this also. Unfortunately, the close similarity of the names can sometimes cause users to misinterpret the numbers computed by such models.

COCOMO distinguishes three "development modes" that essentially correspond to the formality of the development process. For example, the "embedded" mode is used to estimate the development of large, complex systems such as those built to military specifications. Different coefficients are used in the effort and schedule equations for each mode. COCOMO also has three levels of detail. Basic COCOMO excludes the effects of the cost-driver attributes. Intermediate COCOMO uses the EAF as just described. Detailed COCOMO uses quantitative cost-driver values that are phase dependent. Intermediate CO-COMO is the version most commonly used. It predicts effort and schedule within ±20% of the final actual values approximately 70 of the time. COCOMO, like other composite models, also has ways to handle the reuse, modification, and maintenance of existing code.

The PRICE Software Cost Model (PRICE S), another software cost and schedule estimation model, was initially developed from 1975 through 1977 at RCA by Frank Freiman and Robert Park based on data from over 400 projects. Parametric models in the PRICE family were the first generally available computerized cost-estimation models. William Rapp programmed the models, among them PRICE S, to run on mainframe computers at RCA, making them available via a timesharing (dial-in) service.

The PRICE Software Cost Model (PRICE S) is described in [11] and [12]. The model operates as follows. The "central equation" computes the nominal effort to perform the tasks in an ideal world. The PRICE S central equation computes effort based on the "volume" of the software to be produced. Volume is computed based on the amount of code to be produced (measured in source lines of code (SLOC) or function points), the programming language used, and the complexity of the application. The nominal effort is then computed by raising the volume to a power that is a function of the organization's productivity factor (PROFAC).[4] PROFAC is determined based on language type, application complexity, and platform type (described below) using a table. (The value of PROFAC can also be determined by calibration using the organization's own historical data; this is preferable.) The nominal effort is then adjusted to account for the effects of the various cost drivers. There are approximately a dozen cost and schedule drivers used in the PRICE S model. These cost drivers adjust for nonnominal factors such as interface complexity, personnel skill, tools, utilization of available target computer resources, and so on. The platform-type cost driver describes the formality in which the development must take place. For example, software intended for internal use is developed less formally than software for manned space vehicles. The adjusted effort is then used to compute the nominal ("reference") schedule. Additional adjustments are made to obtain the final estimated schedule, as well as the final estimated effort (since compressing schedule and overlapping phases affect costs). The PRICE S calculations also handle the reuse/reengineering of code. Studies made in 1979, 1981, and 1984 found that PRICE S predicts costs within 8–15% of project actuals.

A shortcoming of these 1970s models is that the independent variables were often "result measures" such as the size in lines of code. Such values are readily measured, but only *after* the project has been completed. It is very difficult to predict the values of such variables before the start of the project.[5] This means that many of the models, although based on statistical analyses of actual result data, were hard to use in practice since the values of the independent variables were hard to determine before the project team had analyzed the requirements and had prepared a fairly detailed design. Another shortcoming of such models is that they assume that software will be developed using the same process as was used previously. This assumption is becoming increasingly unrealistic since new processes, methods, and tools continue to be developed.

At the end of the 1970s, Allan Albrecht and John Gaffhey of IBM developed function point analysis (FPA) for estimating the size and development effort for management information systems [13, 14]. Components of a system are classified into five types according to specific rules. These types are inputs, outputs, queries, logical internal files, and external interface files. Each type has an assigned weight based on characteristics of the component. These weights are proportional to the development effort needed to construct components of that type. The estimator counts the number of components of each type, multiplies these counts by the corresponding weight, sums these products, and multiplies the sum by a factor to account for global system characteristics. The result is the "size" of the system measured in "function points." The estimator then uses the team's productivity (in function points per person-month) to compute the development effort.

Later in the 1970s, two authors endeavored to define models based on theoretical grounds. Lawrence H. Putnam [15] based his Software Lifecycle Model (SLIM) on the Norden–Rayleigh curve plus empirical data from 50 U.S. Army projects. Putnam's data indicate that the development staffing rises smoothly and drops sharply during acceptance testing. The shape fits the first part of Norden–Rayleigh curve. Putnam uses this fact to relate the area under the curve (which corresponds to the development effort) to the curve's parameters. Putnam's other empirical results are expressed as two equations describing rela-

---

[4]Actually, effort is computed using separate equations for three phases: design, implementation (coding), and testing. The actual functions used to compute the volume, the exponent, and the adjustments for some of the cost drivers are proprietary and are not published.

[5]Some methods have been developed to help estimators estimate size. These methods rely on analogies to similar projects whose costs are recorded in a database, on averaging techniques to elicit the consensus of experts (Delphi, PERT) and combinations thereof. One such combination, developed by George Bozoki of Lockheed, uses sophisticated statistical techniques in conjunction with historical data. Bozoki's model is sold as the Software Sizing Model (SSM) by Galorath Associates.

tions between the development effort and the schedule. The first equation, called the "software equation," states that development effort is proportional to the cube of the size and inversely proportional to the fourth power of the development time. The second equation, the "manpower buildup equation," states that the effort is proportional to the cube of the development time. Solving these two coupled equations gives the basic predictive equations used in the commercial tool SLIM®. (SLIM is a registered trademark of Quantitative Software Management, Inc.) The solution represents the minimum development time (maximum development effort) for the project. The SLIM tool uses other management constraints (e.g., staffing caps and desired product reliability level) to define a bounded region of possible solutions representing minimum cost, minimum time, and so on.

Some authors, such as Conte [9], have criticized SLIM's modeling of the effort/schedule trade-off. Putnam's (and SLIM's) "software equation" implies that effort scales inversely as the fourth power of the development time, leading to severe cost increases for compressed schedules. Actually, Putnam's model limits the range of applicability of the fourth-power model relation using other constraints. Generally, development time computed by the Putnam model can range between some minimum development time and a time approximately 30 greater than this minimum time.

The second author attempting to define a model based on theoretical grounds was Maurice H. Halstead [16]. Halstead defined software size in terms of the number of operators and operands defined in the program and proposed relations to estimate the development time and effort. To obtain this size information before the start of a project is, of course, nearly impossible because a good understanding of the detailed design is not available until later. Subsequent work by S. D. Conte ([9], page 300) has shown that Halstead's relations are based on limited data, and Halstead's model is no longer used for estimation purposes. (Don Coleman, et al [17] have recently reported some success in using it to predict the "maintainability" of software.).

Comparison of the Major Composite Models

It is instructive to compare the basic equations of the 1970s era composite models. First, look at the development effort. SLIM has development effort proportional to the size raised to the 1.29 power. Both COCOMO ("embedded" mode) and Jensen's Software Estimation Model (SEM), described in the next section, have development effort proportional to the size raised to the 1.20 power. The PRICE S model is more complex, and the full equations have not been published. One complication is that PRICE S computes the effort for three phases and then sums these values. The other models, in contrast, compute a total core effort and then allocate it to the phases. We can say, however, that the effort estimated by PRICE S appears to increase approximately linearly with the volume (which is equivalent to the size used by the other models) for a given value of the productivity factor (PROFAC). The slope of the line decreases with increasing values of PROFAC.

Most of these models have the nominal development time ("schedule") proportional to the cube root of the estimated development effort (which includes all of the adjustments for non-nominal conditions). This is exactly true for the SLIM model and the Jensen model described in the next section. (For details, see Kitchenham, published as Chapter 9 of [18].) COCOMO's embedded mode uses an exponent ranging from 0.32 to 0.38. It is not so easy to make a clear statement for PRICE S since its schedule equations are complex, and not all details are published. PRICE S computes the nominal schedule as proportional to the volume raised to the 0.37 power. If we assume that the effort is proportional to the volume raised to a power of 1.1 or so, then the PRICE S model would have schedule proportional to effort raised to approximately the 0.34 power, and so PRICE S would appear to be consistent with the other models. [This is rather approximate, of course, since the PRICE S volume consists of size (in SLOC) multiplied by factors reflecting complexity and language. The other models use size directly.]

The COCOMO, SLIM, and SEM models all have effort proportional to the size raised to the 1.2 or 1.3 power, and development time proportional to the cube root of the effort. PRICE S has effort approximately proportional to the size raised to the 1.1 power, and development time is also approximately proportional to the cube root of the effort. The basic equations of these 1970s era composite models are thus similar even though the models were developed independently. These similarities suggest that there may be some common "laws of software estimating," at least for the case of new software development. Because of these similarities, these models have comparable accuracies, generally predicting effort within 10–20 of project actuals for some appreciable fraction of the projects analyzed.

The 1980s

During the 1980s, work continued to improve and consolidate the best models. As personal computers (PCs) started to come into general use, many models were programmed. Several firms began selling computerized estimating tools. Following the publication of the COCOMO equations in 1981, several tools that implemented COCOMO appeared during the latter half of the 1980s. (For proprietary models, the tool and the model are one and the same. The model exists only as implemented by the tool.)

The U.S. Department of Defense (DoD) introduced the Ada programming language in 1983 [American National Standards Institute (ANSI) and DOD-STD-1815A-1983] to reduce the costs of developing large systems. Certain features of Ada significantly impact development and maintenance costs and so Barry Boehm and Walker Royce defined a revised model called Ada COCOMO [19]. This model also addressed the fact that systems were being built incrementally in an effort to handle the inevitable changes in requirements.

Robert C. Tausworthe [20] extended the work of Boehm, Herd, Putnam, Walston and Felix, and Wolverton to develop a cost model for National Aeronautics and Space Administration (NASA) Jet Propulsion Laboratory. Tausworthe's model was further extended by Donald Reifer to produce the PC-based SOFTCOST-R model and a companion Ada estimating model called SOFTCOST-Ada. Both of these models are no longer sold commercially.

Randall W. Jensen [21] extended the work of Putnam by eliminating some of the undesirable behavior of Putnam's SLIM. Putnam's SLIM equation has development effort proportional to size (measured in source lines of code) cubed, divided by development time to the fourth power. Jensen asserted that development effort is proportional to the square of the size divided by the square of the development time. Both Jensen and Putnam apply the constraint that effort divided by the cube of the development time is less than some constant (which is chosen based on product and project parameters). Jensen's equations reduce to equations that are close to those of COCOMO's "embedded" mode but the effect of various cost drivers is handled quite differently. Daniel Galorath and coworkers continue to refine the Jensen model and market it as the Software Estimation Model (SEM), part of the System Evaluation and Estimation of Resources (SEER) tool set. (Jensen has recently proposed a new model that is described in the next section.)

In 1984, Albrecht [22] published a major revision to the FPA method. These revisions sharpened the rules for rating the complexity of the software. The original version of FPA had a single empirically derived weight for each type of component. The new method subdivided each type of component by complexity according to certain rules. Different weights are used for low-, medium-, and high-complexity components. This revised method is the basis for the current standard as defined by the International Function Point Users Group (IFPUG).

FPA was extended by Capers Jones [23] to include the effect of computationally complex algorithms on development costs. His "Feature Point Method" counts FPA's five types plus a sixth type called algorithms. His method eliminates the classification of the elements in terms of three levels of complexity; a single weight is used for each element type. Various PC-based tools implement these FPA-based methods, such as Function Point Workbench and Checkpoint from Software Productivity Research, and FPXpert and Estimacs from Computer Associates.

Charles Symons [24] proposed another revision of FPA to achieve the following major goals: reduce the subjectivity in dealing with files, make the size independent of whether the system was implemented as a single system or a set of related subsystems, and change the emphasis of function points away from gauging the value to users to predicting development effort. His method, called Mark II Function Points, bases the computation of size (functionality) on "logical transactions." Each processing activity done by the system is analyzed in terms of the number of data items input, referenced, and output. These are counted and weighted to compute the "size" in function points.

The 1990s

Because of the increasing diversity of software development processes, the 1990s saw renewed attention to developing improved cost models. In particular, Barry Boehm, now at the University of Southern California (USC), and his colleagues began to revise and extend the original COCOMO model in 1993. The new version of COCOMO, then called COCOMO 2.0, emerged in 1994 [5]. Since then, the model has been renamed COCOMO II and has matured [25]. The updated model explicitly handles the availability of additional information in later stages of a project, the nonlinear costs of reusing software components, and the effects of several factors on the diseconomies of scale. (Some of these are the turnover rate of the staff, the geographic dispersion of the team, and the "maturity" of the development process as defined by the SEI.) The updated COCOMO II model has three versions: the application point model for initial estimates, the prearchitecture model, and the postarchitecture model. (The application point model is described in the next paragraph.) The postarchitecture model has 17 cost drivers and five scale factors. The scale factors are used to compute the exponents in the equations for nominal effort and schedule. (This eliminates discontinuities in the 1981 model related to the three development modes.) Besides adding some cost drivers, the multiplier values for some of the cost drivers have been revised. The dynamic range for the postarchitecture model is 8800. (The five scale factors contribute a factor of 4.3 to this value.) The prearchitecture model is a simplified version of the postarchitecture model, obtained by combining cost drivers. It has seven cost drivers and the same five scale factors. Both of these modules measure size in logical statements ("LSLOC"), instead of using physical source lines of code like COCOMO 1981. Both models also accept size in unadjusted function points (UFPs), converting to size in LSLOC using language-specific "backfire values" defined by Capers Jones. (Many existing parametric models do this as well.) The model also revises the handling of maintenance and adaptation (code reuse). A group of industrial and academic affiliates reviewed the revised COCOMO equations and provided data to calibrate the postarchitecture model. The accuracy of COCOMO 11.2000 is ±30% of actuals 80% of the time for effort and for schedule. (For details, see Chapter 4 in [25].) Boehm and his coworkers expect to provide new calibrations biennially as more data is collected.

COCOMO II [25] defines an application point-estimation model for use in small projects that construct products by combining existing software components. This method is based on a procedure in Appendix B.3 of [26] and productivity data for 19 projects presented in [27]. The total size of the software is estimated in application points. Then a nominal productivity is determined based on two factors: developer experience and capability, and integrated computer-aided software engineering (ICASE) tool maturity and capability. Dividing the size by the productivity gives the estimated effort. Application points are based on the following three elements: screens, reports, and components (assumed to be written in a third-generation language). The "objects" to be produced are identified and each is assigned a complexity rating of low, medium, or difficult. These ratings depend on the number of screen views, report sections, and referenced data tables, as well as on the source of the data tables (client or server). Weights are assigned to each pairing of object type and complexity. Adding all of the weighted instances gives the total application point count. Multiplying by one minus the fraction of reuse expected or planned (i.e., 100% – reuse) decreases this count. This method combines simplified elements (similar to Gaffney's method described in the next paragraph) and complexity ratings of the elements (similar to FPA). The application point-estimation model, while considered to be part of the COCOMO II model, has not yet been calibrated. It will no doubt evolve in the future.

In 1996, John Gaffney [28] reported that using only a subset of the elements of a function point count provides estimates of development effort that are as accurate as those produced using classical function points. His analysis showed that the development effort was highly correlated with just the counts of the inputs and outputs. (Gaffney actually evaluated six linear models and five nonlinear models.) Gaffney's "simplified function point estimation method" does not use the three levels of complexity (i.e., low, medium, high) for the elements that are part of the official IFPUG FPA method. (Capers Jones' Feature Points method, as mentioned previously, also does not use the three levels of complexity.)

Scott Whitmire has proposed a way to extend FPA to handle scientific and real-time systems [29]. He acknowledges De-Marco's statement [30] that all software has three dimensions: data, function, and control. Whitmire asserts that classical FPA addresses only the data dimension of a software program. His three-dimensional (3D) function point method provides a way to quantify characteristics of the other two dimensions. The 3D function point index (i.e., the amount of functionality in the software) is computed in a way similar to that of classical FPA, with the addition of two new element types: transformations and transitions. The method is not yet rigorously validated. David Garmus has also described how to use function point counting in a real-time environment [31].

Randall Jensen has extended his original model [21] to explicitly handle the effects of management [32] on project costs and schedule. The new model, called SAGE (not an acronym), considers factors such as the working environment (multiple development sites), team experience, and the degree of resource dedication. (The COCOMO II model also considers similar factors.) The SAGE model was first formulated in 1995 and handles new development. A new version that handles software maintenance was released in 1997.

The 2000s

The technology used to build systems continues to evolve rapidly. This technology includes hardware platforms, operating systems, data formats, transmission protocols, programming languages, methods, tools, and commercial off-the-shelf (COTS) components. The half-life of software engineering knowledge is typically less than three years. Many project teams are using nontraditional development processes such as rapid application development (RAD), COTS integration, and agile methods to "grow" software systems. Such constant and rapid changes mean that little relevant historical data will be available to help us estimate future software projects and to develop new cost-estimation models. This may challenge SEI CMMI® criteria relating to estimating, planning, and tracking that require the use of historical data and assume a stable process. On the other hand, the CMMI model embraces change via its Level 5 Process Areas: Causal Analysis and Resolution, and Organization Innovation and Deployment. The challenge for the estimator is to balance the need for representative historical data with the need to evolve the baseline development process. Using data from many projects provides only aggregate, average behavior, making detailed, accurate estimates difficult to obtain. On the other hand, selecting only data from projects using very similar processes limits the sample size, and increases the uncertainty in the average values.

In an effort to keep up, researchers and model vendors are working to formulate, validate, and deploy new software estimation models. Much of this work is a continuation of work started in the 1990s. I cover it here because it is still in progress.

Allan Albrecht's function points, originally developed in the 1970s, are being extended to handle new software technologies and methods. Organizations such as the International Function Point Users Group (IFPUG) and the Netherlands Software

Metrics Users Association (NESMA) are working to modernize the rules for function point counting. (See www.ifpug.org and www.nesma.nl.) Lee Fischman has also proposed simplifying the counting rules for standard function points [33]. His paper has references to recent work in this area.

Alain Abran and his collaborators are working to update the measures of software size by extending function points to create what they call full function points. The two main organizations involved in this work are the Software Engineering Management Research Laboratory (Laboratoire de Recherche en Gestion des Logiciels) at the Universite du Quebec a Montreal (UQAM) and the Common Software Measurement International Consortium (COSMIC). Full function points are based on a solid theoretical foundation and will be validated using actual data from modem projects. See [34] and [35]. Full function points (FFP) are now referred to as COSMIC-FFP. For the latest information see: www.lr.gl.uqam.ca/cosmic-ffp or www.cosmicon.com.

Arlene Minkiewicz first proposed "predictive object points" (POPs) in 1997 [36]. The POP measure reflects three characteristics of object-oriented software. These are combined data and functions, object communication, and reuse via inheritance. The POP measure is a function of four metrics: the number of top level classes, the weighted methods per class, the average depth of the inheritance tree, and the average number of children per class. The function was validated using data from over 20 projects. For details see [37].

Some authors are attempting to link the products of analysis and design *directly* to the software size by tying the attributes of diagrams of the Unified Modeling Language (UML) to function points (or some variant thereof). This will make the counting of software size more objective. But this increased objectivity and precision comes at a price: we cannot count the size until after some analysis has been done. Some recent references are [35], [38], [39] and [40]. In particular, Fischman and McRitchie have proposed basing an 00 size measure on weighted methods per class [39]. Their "class-method points" has rules to identify and count only the "substantial" methods and classes. (Their paper also has references to 00 metrics defined by other authors.)

More desirable are techniques to estimate development costs before doing such detailed and expensive analyses. One avenue of attack is to use information contained in a system's operational concept. The operational concept describes the environment in which the system will operate, and explains how various types of users, external systems, and the system will function together to accomplish the "mission" of the organization or enterprise.[6] Many software products perform obvious, "easily understood" functions and so an operational concept is unnecessary. An operational concept is most useful for understanding large unprecedented systems (many classes of users, external stakeholders, functions, and modes of operation).

The operational concept is a key document for estimators because it assigns specific functions of the business process (i.e., the sociotechnical system) to the automated system, and other functions to human beings (or possibly other external systems). This assignment directly affects the sizes of the items that you must estimate. The product's requirements and design affect the software size, which in turn affects the development effort. The manual activities affect the effort to write user documentation and training materials.

The operational concept includes operational scenarios, which help estimators understand what users need to accomplish and how they will use the system to do it. Operational scenarios are called "use cases" in the newer software development methods. A use case captures the high-level interactions between an actor (the user or an external system) and the system being analyzed. The main elements of a use case are the purpose (business goal or action to be achieved), the actor(s) involved, the context, and the "scenario," which is a sequence of events. The use case records the main sequence needed to achieve the goal, and also includes alternate sequences to represent exceptional situations. Events may convey data, and so the use case identifies the information that is passed between the actor and the system. Use cases do not capture nonfunctional requirements, nor are they simply a functional decomposition of the system. Because they capture functions and data, however, they provide a possible way to size software during requirements analysis.

Some recent work has been done to estimate the effort for development projects using "user use case points" (UUCPs) [41]. UUCPs are counted similarly to function points. The counting procedure has the following steps. First, the estimator identifies actors and assigns a weight to each (simple, average, or complex), and then sums these to obtain the total unadjusted actor weights (UAW). Second, the estimator similarly identifies and weights use cases, summing the weights to obtain the unadjusted use case weights (UUCW). Third, the estimator rates nine technical and environmental factors. Each is rated from 0 (not applicable) to 5 (essential for the project). The contribution of each factor is computed by multiplying the rating (0 to 5) times the weight. (They use different weights for each of the nine factors.) Adding the resulting values gives the technical complexity factor (TCF). The size in adjusted use case points (AUCP) is computed as $UUCP \cdot (0.6 + 0.1 \cdot TEF)$. (This formula is similar to the function point calculation except the two coefficients are 0.6 and 0.1, compared to 0.65 and 0.35 used for

---

[6]The operational concept (Ops concept or OpsCon) is also called the concept of operations (ConOps). Both terms are used interchangeably. Note, however, that some manufacturers use the term concept of operations to denote the technical principles of operation of a system or device. (Other vendors call this document the "principles of operation.")

function point counting.) Using a productivity value determined from the organization's data, the estimator can compute the effort to implement the application. They tested this method using actual project data. The average error in the estimated effort was about 15%.

Geoffrey Sparks has adapted use case points as defined by Geri Schneider and Jason Winters [42]. The method only counts the use cases, assigning weights based on complexity (simple, medium, or complex). The method has separate factors for technical complexity (TCF) and environmental complexity (ECF). The adjusted use case points, denoted by UCP, equals UUCP · TCF · ECF. This multiplicative adjustment is similar to many other parametric models, and is unlike the adjustment used in function point counting. (Contrast this to the formula for AUCP in the preceding paragraph.). Sparx Systems in Castlemaine, Australia, has implemented the method in a tool. For details on project estimation using use case metrics, see their web site: www.sparxsystems.com.au.

Use case points have also been used to estimate testing effort [43]. Don Reifer has proposed "Web points" and a COCOMO-like model to estimate the effort and schedule for developing Web applications. (See the article entitled "Web Development: Estimating Quick-to-Market Software" in this chapter of this tutorial.)

Size is also difficult to define for prebuilt components. In many cases, the developer does not even have the source code, so measures such as source lines of code are not feasible. In addition, only the portion of the component's interfaces and functionality that is actually used needs to be understood, integrated, and tested by the developer. The size needs to reflect only this portion for the purpose of estimating the developer's effort.

During the 1990s, Boehm and his collaborators actually began to define a family of estimation models to estimate effort and schedule for different types of development processes. (They have also done some work on a model to estimate software defect densities and reliability.) The family presently includes:

COCOMO II	Constructive Cost Model Version II
COCOTS	Constructive COTS Model
CORADMO	Constructive Rapid Application Development Model
COPSEMO	Constructive Phased Schedule and Effort Model
COPROMO	Constructive Productivity Improvement Model
COQUALMO	Constructive Quality Model
COSYSMO	Constructive Systems Engineering Cost Model

This family of models continues to evolve. Additional models include Agile COCOMO and COCOSIMO, the constructive cost model for software-intensive systems of systems. The versions are identified by their year of release, for example, COCOMO 11.2000. For more information on these models see [25] and the COCOMO Web site (http://sunset.usc.edu/research/cocomosuite/index.html).

All model vendors periodically update their proprietary models to cope with many of these challenges. One trend is that the vendors are now packaging their estimation models with data-collection capabilities. This supports integrated planning and tracking, and also captures data needed to calibrate the estimation models to local development processes. (Many tools provide built-in calibration tools.) This enables organizations to use the basic tool set, yet adapt it to their changing development methods and processes.

Future Challenges

Technology and processes alone do not determine how businesses will develop software, license or sell their products, or calculate the return on investment. New business models may become possible. For example, instead of buying software products, users may instead rent them from service providers. (Costs would be based on actual usage.) Legal and security considerations may also affect the business models. Such influences will affect how software is built and sold. Estimating the trade-offs between development, operating, and maintenance costs will become more important and more difficult as new technologies and business models emerge. Estimators will require more knowledge of financial practices such as return on investment and discounted value. Barry Boehm covers such topics in Part III of his classic book [2].

Another factor that estimators must confront is the use of ephemeral teams. Projects need experts in multiple application and solution domains in order to build large, complex systems. No single person can understand all of these domains, so development teams will be more interdisciplinary. Because all of these experts are not needed continuously, project teams (and possibly entire companies) may consist of a core of permanent experts and groups of temporary workers hired just in time. The permanent staff would include managers, chief engineers, project controllers, and accountants. Temporary workers would include analysts, designers, engineers, testers, support staff, and various domain experts. It will be challenging to assemble and manage such diverse, dynamic teams. Advances in telecommunications, networking, and support software ("groupware") can help such teams function even though they are geographically and temporally dispersed. Such organizational structures affect estimators because they impact average productivity, which depends on parameters such as staff capability, experience, and turnover.

There will also be a growing need for estimates of quality (defects), reliability, and availability, as well as the usual cost and schedule estimates. Developers and customers will become more interested in ensuring the safety and reliability of complex software systems such as those used for financial and medical applications. Estimating such characteristics is especially challenging for systems built using COTS components. For other perspectives on emerging trends, see articles in [44], [45], [46], and [47]. Several articles discuss ways to improve the early estimation of software size, the main driver of software development costs. Other articles address estimates for developing Web applications and for large projects. Estimators today often have to estimate the performance of products and processes, as well as project cost and schedule. For a comprehensive look at the full scope of "software estimation" see [48].

Developers of software estimation models continue to face the obstacle that there are no universal laws of "software physics" that define quantitative relationships between the various independent variables characterizing the product and the project environment. Although some approximate equations can be found, software estimation will remain an experimental science for the foreseeable future. Estimators must rely on judgment and intuition to define heuristic rules and then validate these by analyzing actual project data. Once they have isolated the significant factors, they can define and calibrate simplified models for use by their organization.

Before you can prepare any project estimate, you must understand the six "precursors of estimation":

1. Customer's needs and operational environment
2. Products and services to be delivered
3. Production process to be used
4. Project goals and constraints
5. Estimate's purpose and constraints
6. Applicable estimating technique and tools

These precursors establish the context for the estimate: the data and assumptions that you must have to use the estimating techniques.[7] For further details, see Chapter 7 in [48].

References

[1] Peter V. Norden, "Curve Fitting for a Model of Applied Research and Development Scheduling," *IBM Journal of Research and Development,* Vol. 2, No. 3, July 1958.

[2] Barry W. Boehm, *Software Engineering Economics,* Prentice-Hall, 1981. Section 29.7 describes several models not discussed in this article, as well as the models developed by Herd, Putnam, Walston, and Wolverton.

[3] Richard Selby, "Empirically Analyzing Reuse in a Production Environment," in *Software Reuse: Emerging Technology,* W. Tracz, editor, IEEE Computer Society Press, 1988, pages 176-189.

[4] Rainer Gerlich and Ulrich Denskat, "A Cost Estimation Model for Maintenance and High Reuse," in *Proceedings of the European Software Cost Modeling Conference (ESCOM 1994),* Ivrea, Italy, May 1994.

[5] Barry W. Boehm, Bradford dark, Ellis Horowitz, Chris Westland, Ray Madachy, and Richard Selby, "Cost Models for Future Software Lifecycle Processes: COCOMO 2.0," *Annals of Software Engineering,* Volume 1, pp. 57–94, 1995. An earlier description was presented in the tutorial "COCOMO, Ada COCOMO and COCOMO 2.0" by Barry Boehm in the *Proceedings of the Ninth International COCOMO Estimation Meeting,* Los Angeles, CA, 6–7 October 1994.

[6] Richard D. Stutzke, "Deciding When It Is Cost Effective to Adapt Code," In *Proceedings of the 7th European Software Control and Measurement Conference,* Wilmslow, England, May 15–17, 1996.

[7] Martin Fowler, "The New Methodology," March 2001, available at: http://www.martinfowler.com/articles.html.

[8] Frederick P. Brooks, *The Mythical Man-Month,* Addison-Wesley, 1975. An updated and expanded edition was published in 1995.

[9] S. D. Conte, H. E. Dunsmore, and V. Y. Shen, *Software Engineering Metrics and Models,* Benjamin Cummings, 1986.

---

[7]Fred Heemstra provides essentially the same view, which he calls the "prerequisites for software cost estimation." He identifies characteristics of the product, process, production personnel, the production organization, and the user organization, plus the availability of estimation techniques and tools. For details, see [49].

[10] Rensis Likert, "A Technique for the Measurement of Attitudes," *Archives of Psychology,* Vol. 140, June 1932.

[11] Robert E. Park, *The Central Equations of the PRICE Software Cost Model,* PRICE Systems, 1988.

[12] Arlene Minkiewicz and Anthony DeMarco, *The PRICE Software Model,* Lockheed Martin PRICE Systems, 1995.

[13] Allan J. Albrecht, "Measuring Application Development Productivity," in *Proceedings of the Joint SHARE, GUIDE, and IBM Application Development Symposium,* October 14–17,1979.

[14] Allan J. Albrecht and John E. Gaffhey, "Software Function, Source Lines of Code and Development Effort Prediction: A Software Science Validation," *IEEE Transactions on Software Engineering,* Vol. 9, No. 2, November 1983.

[15] Lawrence H. Putnam, "A General Empirical Solution to the Macro Software Sizing and Estimating Problem," *IEEE Transactions on Software Engineering,* SE-4, July 1978, pages 345–361.

[16] Maurice H. Halstead, *Elements of Software Science,* Elsevier, New York, 1977.

[17] Don Coleman, Dan Ash, Bruce Lowther, and Paul Oman, "Using Metrics to Evaluate Software System Maintainability," *IEEE Computer,* Vol. 27, No. 8, August 1994, pages 44–49.

[18] Norman E. Fenton, *Software Metrics: A Rigorous Approach,* Chapman and Hall, 1995. A revised edition, co-authored with Shari Lawrence Pfleeger, appeared in 1998.

[19] Barry W. Boehm and Walker Royce, "Ada COCOMO and the Ada Process Model," in *Proceedings of the Third International COCOMO Users Meeting,* Software Engineering Institute, Pittsburgh, PA, November 1987, plus refinements presented at the Fourth International COCOMO Users Group Meeting held in November 1988.

[20] Robert C. Tausworthe, *Deep Space Network Estimation Model,* Jet Propulsion Report 81-7,1981.

[21] Randall W. Jensen, "A Comparison of the Jensen and COCOMO Estimation Models," in *Proceedings of the International Society of Parametric Analysts,* 1984, pages 96–106.

[22] Allan J. Albrecht, *AD/M Productivity Measurement and Estimate Validation,* IBM Corporate Information Systems, IBM Corp., Purchase, NY, May 1984.

[23] Capers Jones, *The SPR Feature Point Method,* Software Productivity Research, Inc., 1986.

[24] Charles Symons, *Software Sizing and Estimating: Mark II Function Points (Function Point Analysis),* Wiley, 1991.

[25] Barry W. Boehm, Chris Abts, A. Winsor Brown, Sunita Chulani, Bradford K. dark, Ellis Horowitz, Ray Madachy, Donald Reifer, and Bert Steece, *Software Cost Estimation with COCOMO II,* Prentice-Hall, 2000.

[26] R. Kauffman and R. Kumar, *Modeling Estimation Expertise in Object Based ICASE Environments,* Stem School of Business Report, New York University, January 1993.

[27] R. Banker, R. Kauffman and R. Kumar, "An Empirical Test of Object-Based Output Measurement Metrics on a Computer Aided Software Engineering (CASE) Environment," *Journal of Management Information Systems,* Winter 1991–92, Vol. 8, No.3, pages 127–150.

[28] John E. Gaffney, Jr., "Software Cost Estimation Using Simplified Function Points," in *Proceedings of the Eighth Annual Software Technology Conference,* Salt Lake City, May 1996.

[29] Scott A. Whitmire, *3D Function Points: Scientific and Real-Time Extensions to Function Points,* Boeing Airplane Company report BCS-G3252, dated 1992. It was published in the *Proceedings of the 1992 Pacific Northwest Quality Conference.* A more accessible reference by the same author is "An Introduction to 3D Function Points," *Software Development,* April 1995, page 43.

[30] Tom DeMarco, *Controlling Software Projects,* Yourdon Press, 1982.

[31] David Garmus, "Function Point Counting in a Real-Time Environment," *Cross Talk,* Vol. 9, No. 1, January, 1996, pages 11–14.

[32] Randall W. Jensen, "Management Impact on Software Cost and Schedule," *CrossTalk,* Vol. 9, No. 7, July 1996, pages 6–10.

[33] Lee Fischman, "Evolving Function Points," *CrossTalk,* Vol. 14, No. 2, February 2001, pages 24–27. CrossTalk is available at: http://stsc.hill.af.mil. Recent information available at: http://www.galorath.com.

[34] Alain Abran and P. N. Robillard, "Function Point Analysis: An Empirical Study of Its Measurement Processes," *IEEE Transactions on Software Engineering,* Vol. 22, No. 12, December 1996, pages 895–909.

[35] IWSM99, *Proceedings of the 9th International Workshop on Software Measurement,* Lac Supérieur, Québec, Canada, 8–10 September 1999. Stutzke, Labyad et al., and Bévo et al. presented three papers dealing with UML-based size measures.

[36] Arlene Minkiewicz, "Predictive Object Points—Measuring the Size of 00 Applications," in *Proceedings of the 9th Software Technology Conference,* Salt Lake City, 27 April–2 May 1997.

[37] Arlene Minkiewicz and John Staiger, "Estimating Object Oriented Software, An Automated Approach," in *Proceedings of the 22nd Annual ISPA Conference,* Noordwijk, The Netherlands, 8–10 May 2000.

[38] Richard D. Stutzke, "Possible UML-Based Size Measures," in *Proceedings of the 18th International Forum on COCOMO and Software Cost Modeling,* Los Angeles, CA, 6–8 October 1998.

[39] Lee Fischman and Karen McRitchie, "A Size Metric for UML," in *Proceedings of the ISPA/SCEA Joint International Conference,* San Antonio, 8–11 June 1999. Accessible at: users.erols.com/scea/Conference99_pdfs/Conf99_53.pdf. Related articles can be found at www.galorath.com/.

[40] Arlene Minkiewicz, *Measuring Object Oriented Software with Predictive Object Points,* PRICE Systems Technical Report, 2000. Available at www.pricesystems.com/downloads/pdf/pops.pdf.

[41] Rakesh Agarwal, Santanu Banerjee, and Bhaskar Gosh, "Estimating Internet Based Projects: A Case Study," in *Proceedings of the Quality Week 2001 Conference,* San Francisco, 29 May–1 June 2001, paper number 6W2. Accessible at www.soft.com/QualWeek/QW2001/papers/6W2.html.

[42] Geri Schneider and Jason Winters, *Applying Use Cases,* Addison-Wesley, 1998.

[43] Suresh Nageswaran, "Test Effort Estimation Using Use Case Points (UCP)," in *Proceedings of the Quality Week 2001 Conference,* San Francisco, 29 May–1 June 2001, paper number 4T2. Abstract accessible at www.soft.com/QualWeek/OW20Ql/papers/4T2.html.

[44] The April 2000 issue of *CrossTalk,* the Journal of Defense Software Engineering, has four articles addressing aspects of cost estimation. *CrossTalk,* Vol. 13, No. 4, April 2000, pages 4–12, 14–17, and 20–24. Page 30 lists several web sites dealing with cost estimation. This issue is accessible at: www.stsc.hill.af.mil/crosstalk/2000/04.

[45] The November/December 2000 issue of IEEE Software has several articles on software estimation. *IEEE Software,* Vol. 17, No. 6, November/December 2000, pages 22–43, 45–49, and 51–70.

[46] The June 2002 issue of *CrossTalk,* the Journal of Defense Software Engineering, has six articles addressing aspects of cost estimation. *CrossTalk,* Vol. 15, No. 6, June 2002. This issue is accessible at: www.stsc.hill.af.mil/crosstalk/2002/06.

[47] The April 2005 issue of *CrossTalk,* the Journal of Defense Software Engineering, has seven articles addressing aspects of cost estimation. *CrossTalk,* Vol. 18, No. 4, April 2005. This issue is accessible at: www.stsc.hill.af.mil/crosstalk/2005/04.

[48] Richard D. Stutzke, *Estimating Software-Intensive Systems: Projects, Products, and Processes,* Pearson Education, Inc., 2005.

[49] Fred Heemstra, "Software Cost Estimation," *Information and Software Technology,* Vol. 34, No. 10, 1992, pages 627–639.

Software Engineering Economics

Barry Boehm and Sunita Chulani

This paper summarizes the current state of the art and recent trends in software engineering economics. It provides an overview of economic analysis techniques and their applicability to software engineering and management. It surveys the field of software cost estimation, including the major estimation techniques available and the state of the art in algorithmic cost models.

1. Introduction

Definitions

The dictionary defines "economics" as "a social science concerned chiefly with description and analysis of the production, distribution, and consumption of goods and services." Here is another definition of economics that we think is more helpful in explaining how economics relates to software engineering: Economics is the study of how people make decisions in resource-limited situations. This definition of economics fits the major branches of classical economics very well.

Macroeconomics is the study of how people make decisions in resource-limited situations on a national or global scale. It deals with the effects of decisions that national leaders make on such issues as tax rates, interest rates, and foreign and trade policy.

Microeconomics is the study of how people make decisions in resource-limited situations on a more personal scale. It deals with the decisions that individuals and organizations make on such issues as how much insurance to buy, which word processor to buy, or what prices to charge for their products or services.

Economics and Software Engineering Management

If we look at the discipline of software engineering, we see that the microeconomics branch of economics deals more with the types of decisions we need to make as software engineers or managers.

Clearly, software engineers deal with limited resources. There is never enough time or money to cover all the good features you would like to put into your software products. If you have been in the software engineering field for any length of time, we are sure you can think of a number of decision situations in which you had to determine some key software product feature as a function of some limiting critical resource.

Throughout the software life cycle there are many decision situations involving limited resources in which software engineering economics techniques provide useful assistance.[1] To provide a feel for the nature of these economic decision issues, an example is given below for each of the major phases in the software life cycle:

- *Inception Phase.* How much should we invest in information system analyses (user questionnaires and interviews, current-system analysis, workload characterizations, simulations, scenarios, prototypes) so that we can converge on an appropriate definition and concept of operation for the system we plan to implement?

- *Elaboration Phase.* How rigorously should we specify requirements? How much should we invest in requirements and architecture validation activities (automated completeness, consistency, and traceability checks; analytic models; simulations; prototypes) before proceeding to design and develop a software system?

- Should we organize the software to make it possible to use a complex piece of existing software that generally but not completely meets our requirements?

---

[1] Economic principles underlie the overall structure of the software life cycle and its primary refinements of prototyping, incremental development, and advancemanship. The primary economic driver of the lifecycle structure is the significantly increasing cost of making a software change or fixing a software problem, as a function of the phase in which the change or fix is made. See [Boehm 1981, ch. 4].

- *Construction Phase.* Given a choice between three data storage and retrieval schemes that are primarily execution time efficient, storage efficient, and easy to modify, respectively, which of these should we choose to implement? How should we balance investments in code analysis tools, peer reviews, and testing?

- *Transition Phase.* How much operational testing and evaluation should we perform on a product before releasing it to users? How should we best sequence deployment to different sites?

- *Maintenance Phase.* Given an extensive list of suggested product improvements, which ones should we implement first?

- *Phaseout.* Given an aging, hard-to-modify software product, should we replace it with a new product, restructure it, or leave it alone?

Outline of This Paper

The economics field has evolved a number of techniques (cost–benefit analysis, present-value analysis, risk analysis, etc.) for dealing with decision issues such as the ones above. Section 2 of this paper provides an overview of these techniques and their applicability to software engineering.

One critical problem that underlies all applications of economic techniques to software engineering is the problem of estimating software costs. Section 3 describes the major software-cost-estimation techniques, including the available algorithmic models for software cost estimation.

Section 4 concludes by summarizing the major benefits of software engineering economics, and commenting on the major challenges awaiting the field.

2. Software Engineering Economics Analysis Techniques

Overview of Relevant Techniques

The microeconomics field provides a number of techniques for dealing with software life cycle decision issues such as the ones given in the previous section. Figure 1 presents an overall master key to these techniques and when to use them.[2]

As indicated in Figure 1, standard optimization techniques can be used when we can find a single quantity such as dollars (or pounds, yen, cruzeiros, etc.) to serve as a "universal solvent" into which all of our decision variables can be converted. Or, if the nondollar objectives can be expressed as constraints (system availability must be at least 98%, throughput must be at least 3000 transactions per second), then standard constrained optimization techniques can be used. And if cash flows occur at different times, then present-value techniques can be used to normalize them to a common point in time.

More frequently, some of the resulting benefits from the software system are not expressible in dollars. In such situations, one alternative solution will not necessarily dominate another solution. An example situation is shown in Figure 2, which compares the cost and benefits (here, in terms of throughput in transactions per second) of two alternative approaches to developing an operating system for a transaction processing system:

- *Option A.* Accept an available operating system. This will require only $65 OK in software costs, but will achieve a peak performance of 2400 transactions per second, using five parallel processors, because of a high multiprocessor overhead factor.

- *Option B.* Build a new operating system. This system would be more efficient and would support a higher peak throughput, but would require $1200K in software costs.

The cost-versus-performance curves for these two options are shown in Figure 2. Here, neither option dominates the other, and various cost–benefit decision-making techniques (maximum profit margin, cost–benefit ratio, return on investments, etc.) must be used to choose between Options A and B.

In general, software engineering decision problems are even more complex than those in Figure 2, as Options A and B will differ in several important criteria (e.g., robustness, ease of tuning, ease of change, functional capability). If these criteria are quantifiable, then some type of figure of merit can be defined to support a comparative analysis of the preference of one option over another. If some of the criteria are unquantifiable (user goodwill, programmer morale, etc.), then some techniques for comparing unquantifiable criteria need to be used. As indicated in Figure 1, techniques for each of these situations are available and are discussed in [Boehm 1981].

---

[2]The chapter numbers in Figure 1 refer to the chapters in [Boehm 1981], in which those techniques are discussed in further detail.

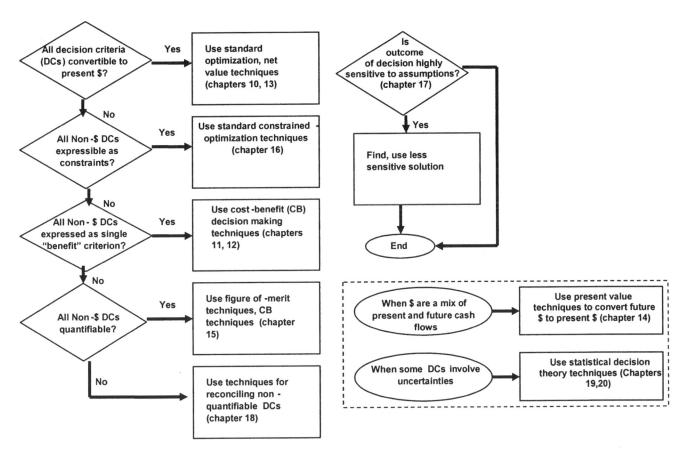

Figure 1. Master key to software engineering economics decision analysis techniques.

Analyzing Risk, Uncertainty, and the Value of Information

In software engineering, our decision issues are generally even more complex than those discussed above. This is because the outcome of many of our options cannot be determined in advance. For example, building an operating system with a significantly lower multiprocessor overhead may be achievable but, on the other hand, it may not. In such circumstances, we are faced with a problem of decision making under uncertainty, with a considerable risk of an undesired outcome.

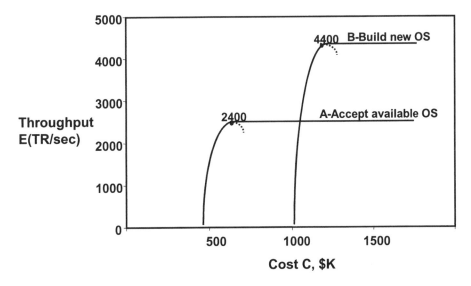

Figure 2. Cost-effectiveness comparison, transaction processing system options.

The main economic analysis techniques available to support us in resolving such problems are the following:

1. Techniques for decision making under complete uncertainty, such as the maximax rule, the maximin rule, and the Laplace rule [38]. These techniques are generally inadequate for practical software engineering decisions.

2. Expected-value techniques, in which we estimate the probabilities of occurrence of each outcome (successful or unsuccessful development of the new operating system) and complete the expected payoff of each option:

$$EV = Prob \text{ (success)} \cdot Payoff \text{ (successful OS)} + Prob \text{ (failure)} \cdot Payoff \text{ (unsuccessful OS)}$$

These techniques are better than decision making under complete uncertainty, but they still involve a great deal of risk if the Prob (failure) is considerably higher than our estimate of it.

3. Techniques in which we reduce uncertainty by buying information. For example, prototyping is a way of buying information to reduce our uncertainty about the likely success or failure of a multiprocessor operating system; by developing a rapid prototype of its high-risk elements, we can get a clearer picture of our likelihood of successfully developing the full operating system.

In general, prototyping and other options for buying information[3] are most valuable aids for software engineering decisions. However, they always raise the following question: "How much information-buying is enough?"

In principle, this question can be answered via statistical decision theory techniques involving the use of Bayes' law, which allows us to calculate the expected payoff from a software project as a function of our level of investment in a prototype or other information-buying option. (Some examples of the use of Bayes' law to estimate the appropriate level of investment in a prototype are given in [Boehm 1981, ch. 20].)

In practice, the use of Bayes' law involves the estimation of a number of conditional probabilities that are not easy to estimate accurately. However, the Bayes' law approach can be translated into a number of value-of-in formation guidelines, or conditions under which it makes good sense to decide on investing in more information before committing ourselves to a particular course of action:

Condition 1. There exist attractive alternatives -whose payoff varies greatly depending on some critical states of nature. If not, we can commit ourselves to one of the attractive alternatives with no risk of significant loss.

Condition 2. The critical states of nature have an appreciable probability of occurring. If not, we can again commit ourselves without major risk. For situations with extremely high variations in payoff, the appreciable probability level is lower than in situations with smaller variations in payoff.

Condition 3. The investigations have a high probability of accurately identifying the occurrence of the critical states of nature. If not, the investigations will not do much to reduce our risk of loss due to making the wrong decision.

Condition 4. The required cost and schedule of the investigations do not overly curtail their net value. It does us little good to obtain results that cost more than they can save us, or which arrive too late to help us make a decision.

Condition 5. There exist significant side benefits derived from performing the investigations. Again, we may be able to justify an investigation solely on the basis of its value in training, team building, customer relations, or design validation.

Some Pitfalls Avoided by Using the Value-of-Information Approach

The guideline conditions provided by the value-of-information approach provide us with a perspective that helps us avoid some serious software engineering pitfalls. The pitfalls below are expressed in terms of some frequently expressed but faulty pieces of software engineering advice.

Pitfall 1. Always use a simulation to investigate the feasibility of complex real-time software. Simulations are often extremely valuable in such situations. However, there have been a good many simulations developed that were largely an expensive waste of effort, frequently under conditions that would have been picked up by the guidelines above. Some have been relatively useless because, once they were built, nobody could tell whether a given set of inputs was realistic or not (picked up by Condition 3). Some have taken so long to develop that they produced their first results the week after the proposal was sent out, or after the key design review was completed (picked up by Condition 4).

---

[3]Other examples of options for buying information to support software engineering decisions include feasibility studies, user surveys, simulation, testing, and mathematical program verification techniques.

Pitfall 2. Always build the software twice. The guidelines indicate that the prototype (or build-it-twice) approach is often valuable, but not in all situations. Some prototypes have been built of software whose aspects were all straightforward and familiar, in which case nothing much was learned by building them (picked up by Conditions 1 and 2).

Pitfall 3. Build the software purely top-down. When interpreted too literally, the top-down approach does not concern itself with the design of low-level modules until the higher levels have been fully developed. If an adverse state of nature makes such a low-level module (automatically forecast sales volume, automatically discriminate one type of aircraft from another) impossible to develop, the subsequent redesign will generally require the expensive rework of much of the higher-level design and code. Conditions 1 and 2 warn us to temper our top-down approach with a thorough top-to-bottom software risk analysis during the requirements and product design phases.

Pitfall 4. Every piece of code should be proved correct. Correctness proving is still an expensive way to get information on the fault freedom of software, although it strongly satisfies Condition 3 by giving a very high assurance of a program's correctness. Conditions 1 and 2 recommend that proof techniques be used in situations in which the operational cost of a software fault is very large, that is, loss of life, compromised national security, or major financial losses. But if the operational cost of a software fault is small, the added information on fault freedom provided by the proof will not be worth the investment (Condition 4).

Pitfall 5. Nominal-case testing is sufficient. This pitfall is just the opposite of Pitfall 4. If the operational cost of potential software faults is large, it is highly imprudent not to perform off-nominal testing.

Summary: The Economic Value of Information

Let us step back a bit from these guidelines and pitfalls. Put simply, we are saying that, as software engineers, "It is often worth paying for information because it helps us make better decisions."

If we look at the statement in a broader context, we can see that it is the primary reason why the software engineering field exists. It is what practically all of our software customers say when they decide to acquire one of our products: that it is worth paying for a management information system, an online customer-relationship management system, a weather forecasting system, an air traffic control system, an inventory control system, and so on, because it helps them make better decisions.

Usually, software engineers are producers of management information to be consumed by other people, but during the software life cycle we must also be consumers of management information to support our own decisions. As we come to appreciate the factors that make it attractive for us to pay for processed information that helps *us* make better decisions as software engineers, we will get a better appreciation for what our customers and users are looking for in the information processing systems we develop for *them*.

3. Software Cost Estimation

Introduction

All of the software engineering economics decision analysis techniques discussed above are only as good as the input data we can provide for them. For software decisions, the most critical and difficult of these inputs to provide are estimates of the expected costs and expected benefits to be realized from a proposed software project. In this section, we will summarize the major software cost estimation techniques available and their relative strengths and difficulties, with detailed descriptions of some of the parametric models for software cost estimation.

Significant research on software cost modeling began with the extensive 1965 SDC study of the 104 attributes of 169 software projects [Nelson 1966]. This led to some useful partial models in the late 1960s and early 1970s.

The late 1970s produced a flowering of more robust models such as SLIM [Putnam and Myers 1992], Checkpoint [Jones 1997], PRICE-S [Park 1988], SEER [Jensen 1983], and COCOMO [Boehm 1981]. Although most of these researchers started working on developing models of cost estimation at about the same time, they all faced the same dilemma: as software grew in size and importance it also grew in complexity, making it very difficult to accurately predict the cost of software development. This dynamic field of software estimation sustained the interests of these researchers who succeeded in setting the stepping-stones of software engineering cost models.

Many software estimation models have evolved in the last two decades based on the pioneering efforts of the above-mentioned researchers. The most commonly used techniques for these models include classical multiple regression approaches. However, these classical model-building techniques are not necessarily the best when used on software engineering data, as illustrated in this paper.

Beyond regression, several papers [Briand et al. 1992; Khoshgoftaar et al. 1995] discuss the pros and cons of one software cost estimation technique versus another and present analysis results. In contrast, this section focuses on the classification of existing techniques into six major categories, as shown in Figure 3, providing an overview with examples of each category. The first category is discussed in more depth, comparing some of the more popular cost models that fall under model-based cost estimation techniques.

Model-Based Techniques

As discussed above, quite a few software estimation models have been developed in the last couple of decades. Many of them are proprietary models and, hence, cannot be compared and contrasted in terms of model structure. Theory or experimentation determines the functional form of these models. This section discusses six of the popular models, and Table 2 (presented at the end of this section) compares and contrasts these cost models based on the life-cycle activities covered and their input and output parameters.

All of the models discussed in this section use approximately the same form: software size as the main input adjusted for differences within projects in terms of project, process, product, and platform characteristics. COCOMO II, which is a completely published model, is discussed here in detail, followed by short descriptions of the other models.

COCOMO II

The COCOMO (Constructive Cost Model) cost and schedule estimation model was originally published in [Boehm 1981]. It became one of most popular parametric cost estimation models of the 1980s. But COCOMO '81 along with its 1987 Ada update experienced difficulties in estimating the costs of software developed to new life-cycle processes and capabilities. The COCOMO II research effort was started in 1994 at USC to address the issues on nonsequential and rapid-development process models, reengineering, reuse-driven approaches, object-oriented approaches, and so on.

COCOMO II was initially published in the *Annals of Software Engineering* in 1995 [Boehm et al. 1995] and is now fully published in [Boehm 2000]. The model has three submodels—Applications Composition, Early Design, and Post-Architecture—which can be combined in various ways to deal with the current and likely future software practices marketplace.

The Application Composition Model is used to estimate effort and schedule on projects that use integrated computer-aided software engineering tools for rapid application development. These projects are too diversified but sufficiently simple to be rapidly composed from interoperable components. Typical components include GUI builders, database or objects managers, middleware for distributed processing or transaction processing, and domain-specific components such as financial, medical, or industrial process-control packages. The Applications Composition Model is based on object points [Banker et al. 1994; Kauffman and Kumar 1993]. Object points are a count of the screens, reports, and 3 GL language modules developed in the application. Each count is weighted by a three-level—simple, medium, difficult—complexity factor. This estimating approach is commensurate with the level of information available during the planning stages of Application Composition projects.

The Early Design Model involves the exploration of alternative system architectures and concepts of operation. Typically, not enough is known to make a detailed fine-grained estimate. This model is based on function points (or lines of code when available) and a set of five scale factors and seven effort multipliers.

The Post-Architecture Model is used when the top-level design is complete, detailed information about the project is available, and, as the name suggests, the software architecture is well defined and established. It estimates for the entire development life cycle and is a detailed extension of the Early-Design Model. It uses source lines of code and/or function points for

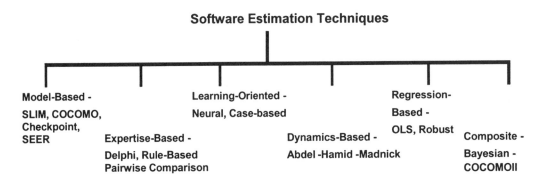

Figure 3. Software estimation techniques.

208

the sizing parameter, adjusted for reuse and breakage; a set of 17 effort multipliers; and a set of five scale factors, that determine the economies or diseconomies of scale of the software under development.

The Post-Architecture Model has been calibrated to a database of 161 projects collected from commercial, aerospace, government, and nonprofit organizations using the Bayesian approach [Chulani et al. 1998b]. This model is discussed further below and the Bayesian calibration approach is discussed later under the subsection Composite Techniques, in which where Table 3 presents the prediction accuracy of COCOMO II. The Early Design Model calibration is obtained by aggregating the calibrated effort multipliers of the Post-Architecture Model as described in [USC-CSE 1997]. The scale factor calibration is the same in both models. Unfortunately, due to lack of data, the Application Composition Model has not yet been calibrated beyond an initial calibration to the data presented in [Kauffman and Kumar 1993].

The Post-Architecture COCOMO II model has the following mathematical form:

$$Effort = A \cdot (size)^{B+0.01 \cdot \Sigma Sf_i} \cdot \prod EM$$

where A is the multiplicative constant, size is measured in terms of KSLOC (thousands of source lines of code) [Park92] or function points [IFPUG94] and programming language, B is the exponential constant, SF is the scale factor, and EM is the effort multiplier. The two constants, A and B, are calibrated constants and for the 2000 version of COCOMO II calibrated to 161 datapoints, $A = 2.94$ and $B = 0.91$. In the Post-Architecture Model, there are five scale factors and 17 effort multipliers. Table 1 summarizes them.

The following few paragraphs describe the use of the COCOMO II Post-Architecture Effort Estimation Model. Usually, software systems are comprised of multiple subsystems or components. The COCOMO II method for doing this does not use the sum of the estimates for each component as this would ignore effort due to integration of the components. The COCOMO II multiple module method has the following steps.

1. Sum the sizes for all of the components to yield an aggregate size:

$$Size_{Total} = \sum_{i=1}^{n} Size_{Component\,(i)}$$

2. Apply the project-level factors to the aggregated size to derive the nominal effort for the total project. Do not forget that the SCED effort multiplier is applied at the total project level:

$$PM_{Total\,Nominal} = A \times (Size_{Total})^{E} \times SCED$$

where

$$E = B + 0.01 \times \sum_{j=1}^{5} SF_j$$

where $B = 0.91$ (for COCOMO II.2000).

3. Apportion the total nominal effort to each component based on its contribution to the aggregate size:

$$PM_{Component\,(i)\,Nominal} = PM_{Total\,Nominal} \times \left(\frac{Size_{Component\,(i)}}{Size_{Total}} \right)$$

4. For each component, apply the component-level effort multipliers (excluding $SCED$) to the effort apportioned to that component:

$$PM_{Component\,(i)} = PM_{Component\,(i)\,Nominal} \times \sum_{j=1}^{16} EM_j$$

5. Sum the effort estimations from all of the components to derive the aggregate effort for the total project:

$$PM_{Total} = \sum_{i=1}^{n} PM_{Component\,(i)}$$

For description about schedule estimation, please refer to [Boehm 2001].

Table la. COCOMO II.2000 post-architecture effort multiplier descriptions

Cost Drivers	Very low	Low	Nominal	High	Very high	Extra high
RELY	Slight inconvenience	Low, easily recoverable losses	Moderate, easily recoverable losses	High financial loss	Risk to human life	
DATA		(DB bytes/Pgm SLOC) < 10	10 ≤ D/P < 100	100 ≤ D/P	D/P > 1000	
CPLX			See Table 1c			
RUSE		None	Across project	Across program	Across product line	Across multiple product lines
DOCU	Many life-cycle needs uncovered	Some life-cycle needs uncovered	Correct amount for life-cycle needs	Excessive for life-cycle needs	Very excessive for life-cycle needs	
TIME			≤ 50% use of available execution time	70% use	85% use	95% use
STOR			≤ 50% use of available storage	70% use	85% use	95% use
PVOL		Major change every 12 mo.; minor change every 1 mo.	Major: 6 mo.; minor: 2 wk.	Major: 2 mo.; minor: I wk.	Major: 2 wk.; minor: 2 days	
ACAP	15th percentile	35th percentile	55th percentile	75th percentile	90th percentile	
PCAP	15th percentile	35th percentile	55th percentile	75th percentile	90th percentile	
PCON	48/year	24/year	12/year	6/year	3/year	
APEX	≤ 2 months	6 months	1 year	3 years	6 years	
PLEX	≤ 2 months	6 months	1 year	3 years	6 years	
LTEX	≤ 2 months	6 months	1 year	3 years	6 years	
TOOL	Edit, code, debug	Simple, frontend, backend CASE, little integration	Basic life-cycle tools, moderately integrated	Strong, mature life-cycle tools, moderately integrated	Strong, mature, proactive life-cycle tools, well integrated with processes, methods, reuse	
SITE: Colocation	International	Multicity and multicompany	Multicity or multicompany	Same city or metro area	Same building or complex	Fully colocated
SITE: Communication	Some phone, mail	Individual phone, fax	Narrow-band e-mail	Wide-band electronic communication	Wide-band electronic communication, occasional video conference	Interactive multimedia
SCED	75% of nominal	85% of nominal	100% of nominal	130% of nominal	160% of nominal	

A primary attraction of the COCOMO II model is its fully available internal equations and parameter values. For up-to-date information please visit the COCOMO II website, http://sunset.usc.edu/COCOMOII/suite.html.

Putnam 's Software Life-Cycle Model (SLIM)

Larry Putnam of Quantitative Software Measurement developed the Software Life-Cycle Model (SLIM) in the late 1970s [Putnam and Myers 1992]. SLIM is based on Putnam's analysis of the life cycle in terms of a so-called Rayleigh distribution of project personnel level versus time (see Figure 4). It supports most of the popular size-estimating methods, including ball-park techniques, source instructions, function points, and so on. It makes use of a so-called Rayleigh curve to estimate project effort, schedule, and defect rate. A manpower buildup index (MBI) and a technology constant or productivity factor (PF) are

Table lb. COCOMO II.2000 scale driver descriptions

Scale Drivers	Very low	Low	Nominal	High	Very high	Extra high
PREC	Thoroughly unprecedented	Largely unprecedented	Somewhat unprecedented	Generally familiar	Largely familiar	Thoroughly familiar
FLEX*	Rigorous	Occasional relaxation	Some relaxation	General conformity	Some conformity	General goals
RESL†	Little (20%)	Some (40%)	Often (60%)	Generally (75%)	Mostly (90%)	Full (100%)
TEAM	Very difficult interactions	Some difficult interactions	Basically cooperative interactions	Largely cooperative	Highly cooperative	Seamless interactions
PMAT	SW-CMM Level 1 Lower	SW-CMM Level 1 Upper	SW-CMM Level 2	SW-CMM Level 3	SW-CMM Level 4	SW-CMM Level 5
			or the estimated Process Maturity Level			

*Degree of required adherence to stated system requirements.
†Percentage of module interfaces specified, subjectively averaged with the percentage of known significant risks mitigated.

used to influence the shape of the curve. SLIM can record and analyze data from previously completed projects, which are then used to calibrate the model; or if data are not available, then a set of questions can be answered to get values of MBI and PF from the existing database. For more details on the SLIM model please go to http://www.qsm.com.

Knowledge Plan

Knowledge Plan, as the name suggests, is a knowledge-based software project estimating tool from Software Productivity Research (SPR) developed from Capers Jones' studies [Jones 1997]. It has a proprietary database of about 8000 software projects and it focuses on four areas that need to be managed to improve software quality and productivity. It uses function points (or feature points) [Albrecht 1979; Symons 1991] as its primary input of size. SPR's Summary of Opportunities for

Table lc. CPLX, complexity and description

	Control operations	Computational operations	Device-dependent operations	Data management operations	User interface management operations
Very Low	Straight-line code with a few non-nested structured programming operators: DOs, CASES, IF-THEN-ELSEs. Simple module composition via procedure calls or simple scripts.	Evaluation of simple expressions: e.g., A=B+C*(D-E).	Simple read–write statements with simple formats.	Simple arrays in main memory, Simple COTS-DB queries, updates.	Simple input forms, report generators.
Low	Straightforward nesting of structured programming operators. Mostly simple predicates	Evaluation of moderate-level expressions: e.g., D= SQRT(B**2-4.*A*C).	No cognizance needed of particular processor or I/O device characteristics. I/O done at GET/PUT level.	Single file subsetting with no data structure changes, no edits, no intermediate files. Moderately complex COTS-DB queries, updates.	Use of simple graphic user interface (GUI) builders.
Nominal	Mostly simple nesting. Some intermodule control. Decision tables. Simple callbacks or message passing, including middleware-supported distributed processing.	Use of standard math and statistical routines. Basic matrix/vector operations.	I/O processing includes device selection, status checking and error processing.	Multifile input and single-file output. Simple structural changes, simple edits. Complex COTS-DB queries, updates.	Simple use of widget set.

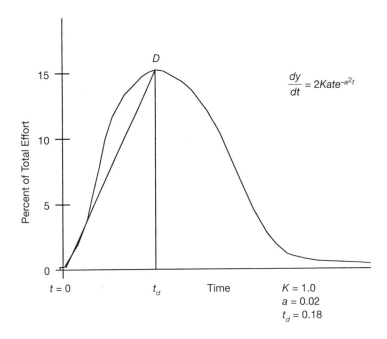

$$\frac{dy}{dt} = 2Kate^{-a^2t}$$

$t = 0$ t_d Time $K = 1.0$
$a = 0.02$
$t_d = 0.18$

Figure 4. The Rayleigh model.

software development is shown in Figure 5. For more information please refer to SPR's website, http://www.spr.com/ html/checkpoint.htm.

PRICE-S

The PRICE-S Model was originally developed at RCA for internal use on software projects such as some that were part of the Apollo moon program. It was then released in 1977 as a proprietary model and used for estimating several U.S. DoD, NASA, and other government software projects. The model equations were not released in the public domain, although a few of the model's central algorithms were published in [Park 1988]. The tool continued to become popular and is now marketed by PRICE Systems, which is a privately held company formerly affiliated with Lockheed Martin. As published on the PRICE

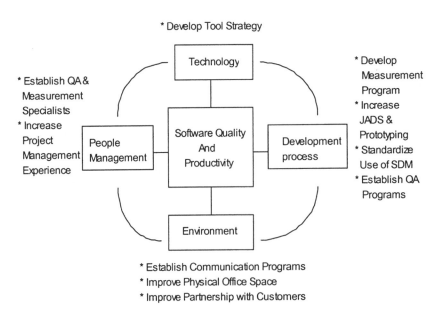

Figure 5. SPR's summary of opportunities. QA = quality assurance, JAD = joint application development, SDM = software development metrics.

Systems website (http://www.pricesvstems.com), the PRICE-S Model consists of three submodels that enable estimating costs and schedules for the development and support of computer systems. These three submodels and their functionalities are outlined below:

1. *The Acquisition Submodel.* This submodel forecasts software costs and schedules. The model covers all types of software development, including business systems, communications, command and control, avionics, and space systems. PRICE-S addresses current software issues such as reengineering, code generation, spiral development, rapid development, rapid prototyping, object-oriented development, and software productivity measurement.
2. *The Sizing Submodel.* This submodel facilitates estimating the size of the software to be developed. Sizing can be in SLOC, function points and/or predictive object points (POPs). POPs is a new way of sizing object-oriented development projects and was introduced in [Minkiewicz 1998] based on previous work in object-oriented (00) metrics done by Chidamber et al. and others [Chidamber and Kemerer 1994; Henderson-Sellers 1996].
3. *The Life-cycle Cost Submodel.* This submodel is used for rapid and early costing of the maintenance and support phase for the software. It is used in conjunction with the Acquisition Submodel, which provides the development costs and design parameters.

PRICE Systems continues to update their model to meet new challenges. Recently, they have added Foresight 2.0, the newest version of their software solution for forecasting time, effort, and costs for commercial and nonmilitary government software projects.

SEER-SEM

SEER-SEM is a product offered by Galorath, Inc. of El Segundo, California (http://www.gaseer.com). This model is based on the original Jensen model [Jensen 1983], and has been on the market some 15 years. During that time, it has evolved into a sophisticated tool supporting top-down and bottom-up estimation methodologies. Its modeling equations are proprietary, but they take a parametric approach to estimation. The scope of the model is wide. It covers all phases of the project life cycle, from early specification through design, development, delivery, and maintenance. It handles a variety of environmental and application configurations, such as client–server, stand-alone, and distributed, graphics. It models the most widely used development methods and languages. Development modes covered include object oriented, reuse, COTS, spiral, waterfall, prototype and incremental development. Languages covered are third- and fourth-generation languages (C++, FORTRAN, COBOL, Ada, etc.), as well as application generators. It allows staff capability, required design and process standards, and levels of acceptable development risk to be input as constraints.

Model specifications include these:

1. *Parameters:* size, personnel, complexity, environment, and constraints, each with many individual parameters; knowledge-base categories for platform and application, development and acquisition method, applicable standards; plus a user-customizable knowledge base.
2. *Predictions:* effort, schedule, staffing, defects, and cost estimates; estimates can be schedule or effort driven; constraints can be specified on schedule and staffing.
3. *Risk Analysis:* sensitivity analysis available on all least/likely/most values of output parameters; probability settings for individual WBS elements adjustable, allowing for sorting of estimates by degree of WBS element criticality.
4. *Sizing Methods:* function points, both IFPUG sanctioned plus an augmented set; lines of code, both new and existing.
5. *Outputs and Interfaces:* many capability metrics, plus hundreds of reports and charts; trade-off analyses with side-by-side comparison of alternatives; integration with other Windows applications plus user customizable interfaces.

Aside from SEER-SEM, Galorath, Inc. offers a suite of many tools addressing hardware as well as software concerns. One of particular interest to software estimators might be SEM [Bozoki 2001], a tool designed to perform sizing of software projects. For more information, please refer to http://www.gaseer.com

TASSC Estimator

TASSC Estimator [http://www.tassc-solutions.com] by TASSC is part of a suite of integrated products designed for components-based development modeling. The actual estimation technique is based upon ObjectMetrix developed by The Object Factory. TASSC Estimator works by measuring the size of a project by counting and classifying the software elements within a project. The project is defined in terms of business applications built out of classes and supporting a set of use cases, plus infrastructure consisting of reusable components that provide a set of services.

TASSC Estimator begins with a base metric of effort in person-days typically required to develop a given project element. This effort assumes that all the activities in a normal software development life cycle are performed, but assumes nothing about project characteristics or the technology involved that might qualify that estimate. Predefined activity profiles covering planning, analysis, design, programming, testing, integration, and review are applied according to type of project element, which splits that base metric effort into effort by activity. (These activity profiles are based upon project metric data.) The base effort is then adjusted by using "qualifiers" to add or subtract a percentage amount from each activity estimate. A "technology" factor addressing the impact of the given programming environment is then applied, this time adding or subtracting a percentage amount from the "qualified" estimate.

Summary of Model-Based Techniques

Table 2 summarizes the parameters used and activities covered by the models discussed. Overall, model-based techniques are good for budgeting, trade-off analysis, planning and control, and investment analysis. As they are calibrated to past experience, their primary difficulty is with unprecedented situations.

Expertise-Based Techniques

Expertise-based techniques are useful in the absence of quantified, empirical data. They capture the knowledge and experience of practitioners seasoned within a domain of interest, providing estimates based upon a synthesis of the known outcomes of all the past projects to which the expert is privy or in which he or she participated. The obvious drawback to this method is that an estimate is only as good as the expert's opinion, and there is usually no way to test that opinion until it is too late to correct the

Table 2. Activities covered and factors explicitly considered by various cost models*

Group	Factor	COCOMO II	SLIM	Checkpoint	PRICE-S	SEER-SEM	TASSC Estimator
Size attributes	Source instructions	YES	YES	YES	YES	YES	NO
	Function points	YES	YES	YES	YES	YES	NO
	OO-related metrics	YES	YES	YES	YES	YES	YES
Program attributes	Type/domain	NO	YES	YES	YES	YES	YES
	Complexity	YES	YES	YES	YES	YES	YES
	Language	YES	YES	YES	YES	YES	YES
	Reuse	YES	YES	YES	YES	YES	YES
	Required reliability	YES	?	?	YES	YES	NO
Computer attributes	Resource constraints	YES	YES	?	YES	YES	NO
	Platform volatility	YES	?	?	?	YES	NO
Personnel attributes	Personnel capability	YES	YES	YES	YES	YES	YES
	Personnel continuity	YES	?	?	?	?	NO
	Personnel experience	YES	YES	YES	YES	YES	NO
Project attributes	Tools and techniques	YES	YES	YES	YES	YES	YES
	Breakage	YES	YES	YES	YES	YES	YES
	Schedule constraints	YES	YES	YES	YES	YES	YES
	Process maturity	YES	YES	YES	?	YES	NO
	Team cohesion	YES	?	YES	YES	YES	YES
	Security issues	NO	?	?	?	YES	NO
	Multisite development	YES	?	YES	YES	YES	NO
Activities covered	Inception	YES	YES	YES	YES	YES	YES
	Elaboration	YES	YES	YES	YES	YES	YES
	Construction	YES	YES	YES	YES	YES	YES
	Transition and maintenance	YES	YES	YES	YES	YES	NO

*A question mark indicates that the authors were unable to determine from available literature whether or not a corresponding factor is considered ii model.

damage if that opinion proves wrong. Years of experience do not necessarily translate into high levels of competency. Moreover, even the most highly competent of individuals will sometimes simply guess wrong. Two techniques have been developed that capture expert judgment but that also take steps to mitigate the possibility that the judgment of any one expert will be off. These are the Delphi technique and the work breakdown structure.

Delphi Technique

The Delphi technique [Helmer 1966] was developed at The Rand Corporation in the late 1940s, originally as a way of making predictions about future events, thus its name, recalling the divinations of the Greek oracle of antiquity, located on the southern flank of Mt. Pamassos at Delphi. More recently, the technique has been used as a means of guiding a group of informed individuals to a consensus of opinion on some issue. Participants are asked to make some assessment regarding an issue, individually in a preliminary round, without consulting the other participants in the exercise. The first round results are then collected, tabulated, and then returned to each participant for a second round, during which the participants are again asked to make an assessment regarding the same issue, but this time with knowledge of what the other participants did in the first round. The second round usually results in a narrowing of the range in assessments by the group, pointing to some reasonable middle ground regarding the issue of concern. The original Delphi technique avoided group discussion; the Wideband Delphi technique [Boehm 1981] accommodated group discussion between assessment rounds.

This is a useful technique for coming to some conclusion regarding an issue when the only information available is based more on "expert opinion" than hard empirical data.

The authors have recently used the technique to estimate reasonable initial values for factors that appear in two new software estimation models they are currently developing. Soliciting the opinions of a group of experienced software development professionals, Abts and Boehm used the technique to estimate initial parameter values for effort adjustment factors (similar to factors shown in Table 1) appearing in the glue code effort-estimation component of the COCOTS (Constructive COTS) integration cost model [Abts 1997; Abts et al. 1998].

Chulani and Boehm used the technique to estimate software defect introduction and removal rates during various phases of the software development life cycle. These factors appear in COQUALMO (Constructuve Quality Model), which predicts the residual defect density in terms of number of defects/unit of size [Chulani 1997]. Chulani and Boehm also used the Delphi approach to specify the prior information required for the Bayesian calibration of COCOMO II [Chulani et. 1998b].

Work Breakdown Structure (WBS)

Long a standard of engineering practice in the development of both hardware and software, the WBS is a way of organizing project elements into a hierarchy that simplifies the tasks of budget estimation and control. WBS is usually the basis for bottom-up estimating, whereas model-based techniques are often used for top-down estimating. WBS helps determine just exactly what costs are being estimated. Moreover, if probabilities are assigned to the costs associated with each individual element of the hierarchy, an overall expected value can be determined from the bottom up for total project development cost [Baird 1989]. Expertise comes into play with this method in the determination of the most useful specification of the components within the structure and of those probabilities associated with each component.

Pairwise Comparison

Bozoki's Sizing Estimation Method (SEM) [Bozoki 2001] included in the SEER-SEM tool cited above is a good example of the use of pairwise comparison of known and upcoming projects as a way of estimating the upcoming project's size, cost, schedule, and so on. A good extension of these techniques has been developed by Miranda [Miranda, 2001].

Expertise-based methods are good for unprecedented projects and for participatory estimation, but encounter the expertise-calibration problems discussed above and scalability problems for extensive sensitivity analyses. WBS-based techniques are good for planning and control.

Aside from helping with estimation, the other major use of the WBS is cost accounting and reporting. Each element of the WBS can be assigned its own budget and cost-control number, allowing staff to report the amount of time they have spent working on any given project task or component, information that can then be summarized for management budget-control purposes.

Finally, if an organization consistently uses a standard WBS for all of its projects, over time it will accrue a very valuable database reflecting its software cost distributions. This data can be used to develop a software cost estimation model tailored to the organization's own experience and practices.

Learning-Oriented Techniques

Learning-oriented techniques include both some of the oldest as well as newest techniques applied to estimation activities. The former are represented by case studies, among the most traditional of "manual" techniques; the latter are represented by neural networks, which attempt to automate improvements in the estimation process by building models that "learn" from previous experience.

Case Studies

Case studies represent an inductive process, whereby estimators and planners try to learn useful general lessons and estimation heuristics by extrapolation from specific examples. They examine in detail elaborate studies describing the environmental conditions and constraints obtained during the development of previous software projects, the technical and managerial decisions that were made, and the final successes or failures that resulted. They try to root out from these cases the underlying links between cause and effect that can be applied in other contexts. Ideally, they look for cases describing projects similar to the project for which they will be attempting to develop estimates, applying the rule of analogy that says similar projects are likely to be subject to similar costs and schedules. The source of case studies can be either internal or external to the estimator's own organization. "Homegrown" cases are likely to be more useful for the purposes of estimation because they will reflect the specific engineering and business practices likely to be applied to an organization's projects in the future, but well-documented cases studies from other organizations doing similar kinds of work can also prove very useful.

Shepperd and Schofield did a study comparing the use of analogy with prediction models based upon stepwise regression analysis for nine datasets (a total of 275 projects), yielding higher accuracies for estimation by analogy. They developed a five-step process for estimation by analogy:

1. Identify the data or features to collect
2. Reconcile data definitions and collections mechanisms
3. Populate the case base
4. Tune the estimation method
5. Estimate the effort for a new project

For further details, the reader is urged to read [Shepperd and Schofield 1997].

Neural Networks

According to Gray and MacDonell [Gray and MacDonell 1996], the neural network is the most common software-estimation model-building technique used as an alternative to mean least squares regression. These are estimation models that can be "trained" using historical data to produce ever better results by automatically adjusting their algorithmic parameter values to reduce the delta between known actuals and model predictions. Gray and MacDonell go on to describe the most common form of a neural network used in the context of software estimation, a "backpropagation trained feed-forward" network (see Figure 6).

The development of such a neural model is begun by first developing an appropriate layout of neurons, or connections between network nodes. This includes defining the number of layers of neurons, the number of neurons within each layer, and the manner in which they are all linked. The weighted estimating functions between the nodes and the specific training algorithm to be used must also be determined. Once the network has been built, the model must be trained by providing it with a set of historical project data inputs and the corresponding known actual values for project schedule and/or cost. The model then iterates on its training algorithm, automatically adjusting the parameters of its estimation functions until the model estimate and the actual values are within some prespecified delta. The specification of a delta value is important. Without it, a model could theoretically become overtrained to the known historical data, adjusting its estimation algorithms until it is very good at predicting results for the training data set, but weakening the applicability of those estimation algorithms to a broader set of more general data.

Wittig [Wittig 1995] has reported accuracies of within 10 for a model of this type when used to estimate software development effort, but caution must be exercised when using these models as they are often subject to the same kinds of statistical problems with the framing data as are the standard regression techniques used to calibrate more traditional models. In particular, extremely large datasets are needed to accurately train neural networks with intermediate structures of any complexity. Also, for negotiation and sensitivity analysis, the neural networks provide little intuitive support for understanding the sensitivity relationships between cost-driver parameters and model results. They encounter similar difficulties when used in planning and control.

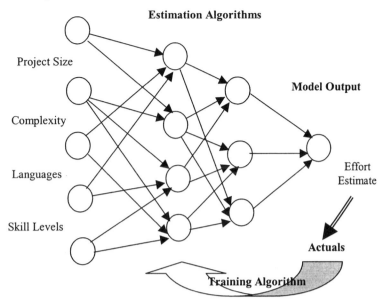

Data Inputs

Estimation Algorithms

Project Size

Complexity

Model Output

Languages

Skill Levels

Effort
Estimate

Actuals

Training Algorithm

Figure 6. A neural-network estimation model.

Dynamics-Based Techniques

Dynamics-based techniques explicitly acknowledge that software project effort or cost factors change over the duration of the system development; that is, they are dynamic rather than static over time. This is a significant departure from the other techniques highlighted in this paper, which tend to rely on static models and predictions based upon snapshots of a development situation at a particular moment in time. However, factors like deadlines, staffing levels, design requirements, training needs, and budget all fluctuate over the course of development and cause corresponding fluctuations in the productivity of project personnel. This in turn has consequences for the likelihood of a project coming in on schedule and within budget—usually negative. The most prominent dynamic techniques are based upon the system-dynamics approach to modeling originated by Jay Forrester nearly 40 years ago [Forrester 1961].

System Dynamics Approach

System dynamics is a continuous-simulation modeling methodology whereby model results and behavior are displayed as graphs of information that change over time. Models are represented as networks modified with positive and negative feedback loops. Elements within the models are expressed as dynamically changing levels or accumulations (the nodes), rates or flows between the levels (the lines connecting the nodes), and information relative to the system that changes over time and dynamically affects the flow rates between the levels (the feedback loops).

Figure 7 [Madachy 1999] shows an example of a system dynamics model demonstrating the famous Brooks' law, which states that "adding manpower to a late software project makes it later" [Brooks 1975]. Brooks' rationale is that not only does effort have to be reallocated to train the new people, but the corresponding increase in communication and coordination overhead grows exponentially as people are added.

Madachy's dynamic model as shown in the figure illustrates Brooks' concept based on the following assumptions:

1. New people need to be trained by experienced people to improve their productivity.
2. Increasing staff on a project increases the coordination and communication overhead.
3. People who have been working on a project for a while are more productive than newly added people.

As can be seen in Figure 7, the model has two flow chains representing software development and personnel. The software chain (seen at the top of the figure) begins with a level of requirements that need to be converted into an accumulation of developed software. The rate at which this happens depends on the number of trained personnel working on the project. The number of trained personnel in turn is a function of the personnel flow chain (seen at the bottom of the figure). New people are assigned to

217

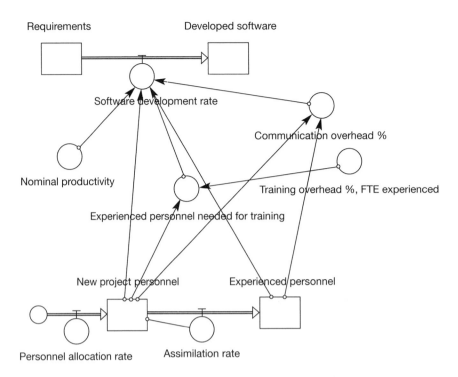

Requirements

Developed software

Software development rate

Nominal productivity

Communication overhead %

Training overhead %, FTE experienced

Experienced personnel needed for training

New project personnel

Experienced personnel

Personnel allocation rate

Assimilation rate

Figure 7. Madachy's System Dynamics Model of Brooks' law.

the project according to the personnel allocation rate, and then converted to experienced personnel according to the assimilation rate. The other items shown in the figure (nominal productivity, communication overhead, experienced personnel needed for training, and training overhead) are examples of auxiliary variables that also affect the software development rate.

Within the last ten years, this technique has been applied successfully in the context of software engineering estimation models. Abdel-Hamid has built models that will predict changes in project cost, staffing needs and schedules over time, as long as the initial proper values of project development are available to the estimator [Abdel-Hamid 1989a, 1989b, 1993; Abdel-Hamid and Madnick 1991]. He has also applied the technique in the context of software reuse, demonstrating an interesting result. He found that there is an initial beneficial relationship between the reuse of software components and project personnel productivity, since less effort is being spent developing new code. However, over time this benefit diminishes if older reuse components are retired and no replacement components have been written, thus forcing the abandonment of the reuse strategy until enough new reusable components have been created, or unless they can be acquired from an outside source [Abdel-Hamid and Madnick 1993].

More recently, Madachy used system dynamics to model an inspection-based software lifecycle process [Madachy 1994]. Dynamics-based techniques are particularly good for planning and control, but particularly difficult to calibrate.

Regression-Based Techniques

Regression-based techniques are the most popular ways of building models. These techniques are used in conjunction with model-based techniques and include "standard" regression and "robust" regression.

"Standard" Regression—Ordinary Least Squares (OLS) Method

"Standard" regression refers to the classical statistical approach of general linear regression modeling using least squares. It is based on the ordinary least squares (OLS) method discussed in many books such as [Judge et al. 1993; Weisberg 1985]. The reasons for its popularity include ease of use and simplicity. It is available as an option in several commercial statistical packages such as Minitab, SPlus, and SPSS.

The OLS method is well suited when

1. A lot of data are available. This indicates that there are many degrees of freedom available and the number of observations is many more than the number of variables to be predicted. Collecting data has been one of the biggest challenges

218

in this field due to lack of funding by higher management, coexistence of several development processes, lack of proper interpretation of the process, and so on.

2. No data items are missing. Data with missing information could be reported when there is limited time and budget for the data collection activity, or due to lack of understanding of the data being reported.

3. There are no outliers. Extreme cases are very often reported in software engineering data due to misunderstandings or lack of precision in the data collection process, or due to different "development" processes.

4. The predictor variables are not correlated. Most of the existing software estimation models have parameters that are correlated to each other. This violates the assumption of the OLS approach.

5. The predictor variables are easy to interpret when used in the model. This is very difficult to achieve because it is not easy to make valid assumptions about the form of the functional relationships between predictors and their distributions.

6. The regressors are either all continuous (e.g., database size) or all discrete variables (ISO 9000 certification or not). Several statistical techniques exist to address each of these kinds of variables but not both in the same model.

Each of the above is a challenge in modeling software engineering datasets to develop a robust, easy-to-understand, constructive cost-estimation model.

A variation of the above method was used to calibrate the 1997 version of COCOMO II. Multiple regression was used to estimate the b coefficients associated with the five scale factors and 17 effort multipliers. Some of the estimates produced by this approach gave counterintuitive results. For example, the data analysis indicated that developing software to be reused in multiple situations was cheaper than developing it to be used in a single situation, hardly a credible predictor for a practical cost-estimation model. For the 1997 version of COCOMO II, a pragmatic 10 weighted-average approach was used. COCOMO II. 1997 ended up with a 0.9 weight for the expert data and a 0.1 weight for the regression data. This gave moderately good results for an interim COCOMO II model, with no cost drivers operating in noncredible ways.

"Robust" Regression

Robust regression is an improvement over the standard OLS approach. It alleviates the common problem of outliers in observed software engineering data. Software project data usually have a lot of outliers due to disagreement on the definitions of software metrics, coexistence of several software development processes, and the availability of qualitative versus quantitative data.

There are several statistical techniques that fall in the category of "robust" regression. One of the techniques is based on least mean squares method and is very similar to the OLS method described above. The only difference is that this technique reduces the mean of all the r_i^2.

Another approach that can be classified as "robust" regression is a technique that uses the datapoints lying within two (or three) standard deviations of the mean response variable. This method automatically gets rid of outliers and can be used only when there are a sufficient number of observations, so as not to have a significant impact on the degrees of freedom of the model. Although this technique has the flaw of eliminating outliers without direct reasoning, it is still very useful for developing software estimation models with few regressor variables due to lack of complete project data.

Most existing parametric cost models (COCOMO II, SLIM, Checkpoint, etc.) use some form of regression-based techniques due to their simplicity and wide acceptance.

Composite Techniques

As discussed above, there are many pros and cons of using each of the existing techniques for cost estimation. Composite techniques incorporate a combination of two or more techniques to formulate the most appropriate functional form for estimation.

Bayesian Approach

An attractive estimating approach that has been used for the development of the COCOMO II model is Bayesian analysis [Chulani et al. 1998].

Bayesian analysis is a mode of inductive reasoning that has been used in many scientific disciplines. A distinctive feature of the Bayesian approach is that it permits the investigator to use both sample (data) and prior (expert-judgement) information in a logically consistent manner in making inferences. This is done by using Bayes' theorem to produce a "postdata" or posterior distribution for the model parameters. Using Bayes' theorem, prior (or initial) values are transformed into postdata views. This transformation can be viewed as a learning process. The posterior distribution is determined by the variances of the prior and sample information. If the variance of the prior information is smaller than the variance of the sampling information, then a higher weight is assigned to the prior information. On the other hand, if the variance of the sample information is smaller than the variance of the prior information, then a higher weight is assigned to the sample information, causing the posterior estimate to be closer to the sample information.

The Bayesian approach provides a formal process by which a-priori expert judgement can be combined with sampling information (data) to produce a robust a-posteriori model. Using Bayes' theorem, we can combine our two information sources as follows:

$$f(\beta|Y) = \frac{f(Y|\beta)f(\beta)}{f(Y)}$$

where β is the vector of parameters in which we are interested and Y is the vector of sample observations from the joint density function $f(\beta|Y)$. In the above equation, $f(\beta|Y)$ is the posterior density function for β summarizing all the information about β, $f(Y|\beta)$ is the sample information and is algebraically equivalent to the likelihood function for β, and $f(\beta)$ is the prior information summarizing the expert-judgement information about β. The above equation can be rewritten as

$$f(\beta|Y) \propto l(\beta|Y)f(\beta)$$

In words, this means

$$Posterior \propto Sample \cdot Prior$$

In the Bayesian analysis context, the "prior" probabilities are the simple "unconditional" probabilities associated with the sample information, whereas the "posterior" probabilities are the "conditional" probabilities given knowledge of sample and prior information.

The Bayesian approach makes use of prior information that is not part of the sample data by providing an optimal combination of the two sources of information. As described in many books on Bayesian analysis [Learner 1978; Box 1973], the posterior mean, b^{**}, and variance, $Var(b^{**})$, are defined as

$$b^{**} = \left[\frac{1}{s^2}X'X + H^*\right]^{-1} \times \left[\frac{1}{s^2}X'Xb + H^*b^*\right]$$

and

$$Var(b^{**}) = \left[\frac{1}{s^2}X'X + H^*\right]^{-1}$$

where X is the matrix of predictor variables, s is the variance of the residual for the sample data, and H^* and b^* are the precision (inverse of variance) and mean of the prior information, respectively.

The Bayesian approach described above has been used in the most recent calibration of COCOMO II over a database currently consisting of 161 project data points. The a-posteriori COCOMO 11.2000 calibration gives predictions that are within 30 of the actuals 75% of the time, which is a significant improvement over the COCOMO II. 1997 calibration, which gave predictions within 30 of the actuals 52% of the time, as shown in Table 3. (The 1997 calibration was not performed using

Table 3. Prediction accuracy of COCOMO II.1997 versus COCOMO II.2000

COCOMO II	Prediction accuracy	Before stratification	After stratification
1997	PRED(.20)	46%	49%
	PRED(.25)	49%	55%
	PRED(.30)	52%	64%
2000	PRED(.20)	63%	70%
	PRED(.25)	68%	76%
	PRED(.30)	75%	80%

Bayesian analysis; rather, a 10 weighted linear combination of expert prior vs. sample information was applied [dark et al. 1998].) If the model's multiplicative coefficient is calibrated to each of the major sources of project data, that is, "stratified" by data source, the resulting model produces estimates within 30% of the actuals 80% of the time. It is therefore recommended that organizations using the model calibrate it using their own data to increase model accuracy and produce a local optimum estimate for similar type projects. From Table 3 it is clear that the predictive accuracy of the COCOMO 11.2000 Bayesian model is better than the predictive accuracy of the COCOMO II. 1997 weighted linear model, illustrating the advantages of using composite techniques.

Bayesian analysis has all the advantages of "standard" regression and it includes prior knowledge of experts. It attempts to reduce the risks associated with imperfect data gathering. Software engineering data are usually scarce and incomplete, and estimators are faced with the challenge of making good decisions using this data. Classical statistical techniques described earlier derive conclusions based on the available data. But to make the best decision it is imperative that in addition to the available sample data we should incorporate nonsample or prior information that is relevant. Usually, a lot of good expert-judgment-based information on software processes and the impact of several parameters on effort, cost, schedule, quality, and so on is available. This information does not necessarily get derived from statistical investigation and, hence, classical statistical techniques such as OLS do not incorporate it into the decision making process. Bayesian techniques make best use of relevant prior information along with collected sample data in the decision-making process to develop a stronger model.

Summary of Cost Estimation Techniques

This section has presented an overview of a variety of software estimation techniques, providing an overview of several popular estimation models currently available. The important lesson in this section is that no one method or model should be preferred over all others. The cost estimating expert should deploy a variety of methods and tools to achieve a reasonable level of satisfaction with software estimation.

4. Benefits of Software Engineering Economics

The major benefit of an economic perspective on software engineering is that it provides a balanced view of candidate software engineering solutions and an evaluation framework that takes account not only of the programming aspects of a situation, but also of the human problems of providing the best possible information processing service within a resource-limited environment. Thus, for example, the software engineering economics approach does not say, "we should use these structured structures because they are mathematically elegant" or "because they run like the wind" or "because they are part of the structured revolution." Instead, it says "we should use these structured structures because they provide people with more benefits in relation to their costs than do other approaches." And besides the framework, of course, it also provides the techniques that help us to arrive at this conclusion.

Benefits of Software Cost Estimation Technology

The major benefit of a good software cost estimation model is that it provides a clear and consistent universe of discourse within which to address a good many of the software engineering issues that arise throughout the software life cycle. It can help people get together to discuss such issues as the following:

- Which and how many features should we put into the software product?
- Which features should we put in first?
- How much hardware should we acquire to support the software product's development, operation, and maintenance?
- How much money and how much calendar time should we allow for software development?
- How much of the product should we adapt from existing software?
- How much should we invest in tools and training?

Further, a well-defined software cost estimation model can help avoid the frequent misinterpretations, underestimates, overexpectations, and outright buy-ins that still plague the software field. In a good cost estimation model, there is no way of reducing the estimated software cost without changing some objectively verifiable property of the software project. This does not make it impossible to create an unachievable buy-in, but it significantly raises the threshold of credibility.

A related benefit of software cost estimation technology is that it provides a powerful set of insights into how a software organization can improve its productivity. Many of a software cost model's cost-driver attributes are management controllables: use of software tools, personnel capability and experience, and software reuse. The cost model helps us determine how to adjust these management controllables to increase productivity, and further provides an estimate of how much of a productivity increase we are likely to achieve with a given level of investment.

Finally, software cost estimation technology provides an absolutely essential foundation for software project planning and control. Unless a software project has clear definitions of its key milestones and realistic estimates of the time and money it will take to achieve them, there is no way that a project manager can tell whether his project is under control or not. A good set of cost and schedule estimates can provide realistic data for the PERT charts, work breakdown structures, manpower schedules, earned value increments, and so on that are necessary to establish management visibility and control.

Note that this opportunity to improve management visibility and control requires a complementary management commitment to define and control the reporting of data on software progress and expenditures. The resulting data are therefore worth collecting simply for their management value in comparing plans versus achievements, but they can serve another valuable function as well: they provide a continuing stream of calibration data for evolving more accurate and refined software cost estimation models.

Recent Developments in Knowledge Management across the Software Life Cycle

The focus of the software economics and measurement research work described in this paper and that of much of the software measurement community is on building models for software cost, schedule, and quality prediction. The extent of the quality prediction is in determining the defect density of the product when its fully operational in the field in terms of defects/KSLOC (thousands of lines of code) or defects/FP (function point), where a defect is viewed as problem resulting in some change of code distributed to the customer. Although this metric may represent quality adequately from the development point of view, a typical "customer" for software does not take into account the size or complexity of the product in judging the quality of the product. In addition, defect density does not really capture the overall customer satisfaction experienced by the users of the software product. For example, when a customer has difficulty with product installation, he calls in for service and this user problem is not necessarily coded as a defect as it may not require a change in the code base. Thus, even though the customer may not be satisfied, the currently available quality/cost models do not incorporate this dissatisfaction in any way.

Recently, a software engineering knowledge management pilot study was done at IBM with participants from different groups within the software organization encompassing most of the entities of the software product life-cycle, in particular, product development teams, service teams, and customer satisfaction analysts. The product development teams are the primary producers of the product, whereas the service teams work with the customers once the product is generally available and help the customer if the customer experiences any problems with the product. The customer satisfaction analysts capture and analyze several different marketing aspects of the organization and products, such as brand name satisfaction and trends in the marketplace with respect to product customer satisfaction and its relationship with competitor products' customer satisfaction. Often, these different groups are separate entities with different focus areas.

The theme of this study is to recognize and exploit the benefits of using data and information across these teams together to make better decisions that improve the quality of the entire life cycle. Example questions answered by this study include:

1. What is the relationship between kinds of customer problems (e.g., duplicate problem report, problem affecting a data record, etc.) and product attributes (i.e., performance, reliability, usability, etc.)?
2. Does the defect density or the time to resolution have a higher impact on overall customer satisfaction?
3. Does a desired decrease in time to resolution impact other parameters causing a decrease in customer satisfaction?

In-depth correlation studies establish relationships between the data and information available across development, service, and customer satisfaction teams. Several regression models are built using the customer satisfaction data as response variables and the service and development data as predictor variables. These models facilitate improvements in the development/service activities that have a positive impact on customer satisfaction. Early results of this effort were published in [Chulani et al. 2001]

Value-Based Software Engineering

The customer satisfaction analysis initiative just discussed is exemplary of an increasing trend in software engineering organizations to focus more on the benefits realized via software, and on the integration of cost and benefit considerations into a value-based approach to software engineering. If estimating software costs is difficult, it has at least the advantage of a common framework of activities and product artifacts upon which to build estimation models. In contrast, estimating the benefits realized by software development in such areas as office automation, international currency trading, and automotive electronics must relate gains in software quality and productivity to very different models of value in these different applications domains.

Still, there are a number of areas in which considerable progress is being made in benefits estimation and value-based software engineering. As summarized in [Boehm-Sullivan 2000], these include:

- The DMR Consulting Group's Benefits Realization Approach, including the Results Chain approach linking software initiatives to benefit outcomes realized [Thorp 1998].
- Software business case analysis techniques for evaluating the relative costs and benefits of alternative initiatives [Reifer 2002].
- Spiral model process extensions more explicitly linking evaluation of alternatives to objectives and constraints (MBASE) [Boehm and Port 1999] and to goals, questions, and metrics (CeBASE Method) [Boehm and Basili 2001].
- Techniques for reconciling multistakeholder value propositions such as Quality Function Deployment [Eureka and Ryan 1988] or WinWin [Boehm, Gruenbacher, and Briggs 2000], and for multicriterion decision making [Hammond, Keeney, and Raiffa 1999].
- Strategic design techniques for assessing the economic value of modularity and options creation in software architecting and design [Baldwin and Clark, 1999; Sullivan et al. 2001].
- New techniques for assessing increasing returns to scale in network-based systems [Shapiro and Varian 1999].

Software Estimation: The Receding Horizon

In the early days of the software estimation field, we thought we would be like the Tycho Brahes in the sixteenth century, compiling observational data that later Keplers and Newtons would use to develop a quantitative science of software engineering. As we went from unprecedented to precedented software applications, our productivity would increase and our error in estimating software costs would continue to decrease, as on the left side of Figure 8.

However, this view rested on the assumption that, like the stars, planets, and satellites, software projects would continue to behave in the same way as time went on. But this assumption turned out to be invalid. The software field is continually being reinvented via structured methods, abstract data types, information hiding, objects, patterns, reusable components, commercial packages, very high level languages, and rapid application development (RAD) processes.

With each reinvention, software cost estimation and other software engineering fields need to reinvent pieces of themselves just to keep up, resulting in the type of progress shown on the right side of Figure 8. And the rate of reinvention of the software

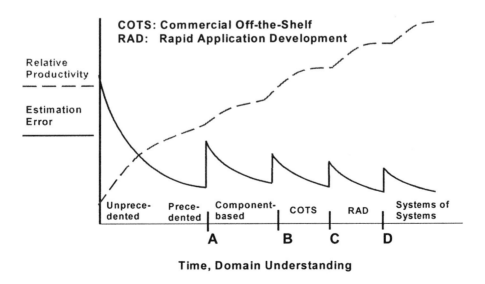

Figure 8. Software estimation—the receding horizon.

field continues to increase. The most encouraging thing in Figure 8, though, is that leading companies are able to build on this experience and continue to increase our relative productivity in delivering the huge masses of software our society increasingly depends on. Our biggest challenge for the future is to figure out how to selectively prune the parts of the software engineering experience base that become less relevant, and to conserve and build on the parts with lasting value for the future.

Software Engineering Economics Challenges

The opportunity to improve software project management decision making through improved software cost and benefit estimation, planning, data collection, and control brings us back full circle to the original objectives of software engineering economics: to provide a better quantitative understanding of how software people make decisions in resource-limited situations.

Even accepting the fact that we will be dealing with a receding software economics horizon, the more clearly we as software engineers can understand the quantitative and economic aspects of our decision situations, the more quickly we can progress from a pure seat-of-the-pants approach on software decisions to a more rational approach that puts all of the human and economic decision variables into clear perspective. Once these decision situations are more clearly illuminated, we can then study them in more detail to address the deeper challenge: achieving a more quantitative and intuitive understanding of how people work together in the software engineering process.

References

Abdel-Hamid, T. (1989a), "The Dynamics of Software Project Staffing: A System Dynamics-based Simulation Approach," *IEEE Transactions on Software Engineering,* February 1989.

Abdel-Hamid, T. (1989b), "Lessons Learned from Modeling the Dynamics of Software Development," *Communications of the ACM,* December 1989.

Abdel-Hamid, T., and Madnick, S. (1991), Software Project Dynamics, Prentice-Hall, 1991.

Abdel-Hamid, T. (1993), "Adapting, Correcting, and Perfecting Software Estimates: a Maintenance Metaphor," *IEEE Computer,* March 1993.

Abdel-Hamid, T., and Madnick, S. (1993), "Modeling the Dynamics of Software Reuse: an Integrating System Dynamics Perspective," presentation to the 6th Annual Workshop on Reuse, Owego, NY, November 1993.

Abts, C. (1997), *COTS Software Integration Modeling Study,* Report prepared for USAF Electronics System Center, Contract No. F30602-94-C-1095, University of Southern California, 1997.

Abts, C., Bailey, B., and Boehm, B (1998), "COCOTS Software Integration Cost Model: An Overview," in *Proceedings of the California Software Symposium,* 1998.

Albrecht, A. (1979), "Measuring Application Development Productivity," in *Proceedings of the Joint SHARE/GUIDE/IBM Application Development Symposium,* Oct. 1979, pp. 83–92.

Baird, B. (1989), *Managerial Decisions under Uncertainty,* Wiley, 1989.

Baldwin, C., and Clark, K. (1999), *Design Rules: The Power of Modularity,* MIT Press, 1999.

Banker, R., Kauffman, R., and Kumar, R. (1994), An Empirical Test of Object-Based Output Measurement Metrics in a Computer Aided Software Engineering (CASE) Environment," *Journal of Management Information Systems,* 1994.

Boehm, B. (1981), *Software Engineering Economics,* Prentice-Hall, 1981.

Boehm, B., Abts, C., Brown, A.W., Chulani, S., Clark, B., Horowitz, E., Madachy, R., Reifer, D., and Steece B. (2000), *Software Cost Estimation with COCOMO II,* Prentice-Hall, 2000.

Boehm, B., and Sullivan, K. (2000), "Software Economics: A Roadmap," in *The Future of Software Engineering,* IEEE/ACM, 2000.

Boehm, B., and Port, D. (1999), "Escaping the Software Tar Pit: Model Clashes and How to Avoid Them," *ACM Software Engineering Notes,* January 1999, pp. 36–48.

Boehm, B., and Basili, V. (2001), "The CeBASE Model of Strategic Software Development and Evolution," *Proceedings, EDSER 3,* June 2001.

Boehm, B., Clark, B., Horowitz, E., Westland, C., Madachy, R., and Selby, R. (1995), "Cost Models for Future Software Life-cycle Processes: COCOMO 2.0," *Annals of Software Engineering Special Volume on Software Process and Product Measurement,* J. D. Arthur and S. M. Henry (Eds.), J. C. Baltzer AG, Science Publishers, Amsterdam, The Netherlands, Vol. 1, 1995, pp. 45–60.

Boehm, B., Gruenbacher, P., and Briggs, R. (2001), "Developing Groupware for Requirements Negotiation: Lessons Learned," *IEEE Software,* May/June 2001, pp. 46–55.

Box, G., and Tiao, G. (1973), *Bayesian Inference in Statistical Analysis,* Addison-Wesley, 1973.

Bozoki, G. (2001), "An Expert Judgment Based Software Sizing Model," *Target Software,* www.targetsoft-ware.com.

Briand, L., Basili V., and Thomas, W. (1992), "A Pattern Recognition Approach for Software Engineering Data Analysis," *IEEE Transactions on Software Engineering,* Vol. 18, No. 11, November 1992.

Brooks (1975) *The Mythical Man-Month,* Addison-Wesley, 1975.

Cash, J. (1979), "Dallas Tire Case," Harvard Business School, 1979.

Chidamber, S., and Kemerer, C. (1994), *A Metrics Suite for Object Oriented Design,* CISR WP No. 249 and Sloan WP No. 3524-93, Center for Information Systems Research, Sloan School of Management, Massachusetts Institute of Technology.

Chulani, S. (1997), "Modeling Defect Introduction," in *California Software Symposium,* Nov 1997.

Chulani, S. (1998), *Incorporating Bayesian Analysis to Improve the Accuracy of COCOMO II and Its Quality Model Extension,* Ph.D. Qualifying Exam Report, University of Southern California, Feb 1998.

Chulani, S., Boehm, B., and Steece, B. (1998b), *Calibrating Software Cost Models Using Bayesian Analysis,* Technical Report, USC-CSE-98-508, June 1998.

Clark, B., Chulani, S., and Boehm, B. (1998), "Calibrating the COCOMO II Post Architecture Model," in *Proceedings International Conference on Software Engineering,* Apr. 1998.

Chulani, S., Santhanam, P., Moore, D., Leszkowicz, B., and Davidson, G. (2001), "Deriving a Software Quality View from Customer Satisfaction and Service Data," in *Proceedings ESCOM 2001,* London, UK

Eureka, W., and Ryan, N. (1988), *The Customer-Driven Company: Managerial Perspectives on QFD,* ASI Press, 1988.

Forrester, J. (1961), *Industrial Dynamics,* MIT Press, 1961.

Gray, A., and MacDonell, S. (1996), "A Comparison of Techniques for Developing Predictive Models of Software Metrics," *Information and Software Technology,* No. 39, 1997.

Hammond, J., Keeney, R., and Raiffa, H. (1999), *Smart Choices,* Harvard Business School Press, 1999.

Helmer, O. (1966), *Social Technology,* Basic Books, 1966.

Henderson-Sellers, B. (1996), *Object Oriented Metrics—Measures of Complexity,* Prentice-Hall, 1996.

Jensen R. (1983), "An Improved Macrolevel Software Development Resource Estimation Model," in *Proceedings 5th ISPA Conference,* April 1983, pp. 88–92.

Jones, C. (1997), *Applied Software Measurement,* 1997, McGraw-Hill.

Judge, G., Griffiths, W., and Hill, C. (1993), *Learning and Practicing Econometrics,* Wiley, 1993.

Kauffman, R., and Kumar, R. (1993), *Modeling Estimation Expertise in Object Based ICASE Environments,* Stem School of Business Report, New York University, January 1993.

Khoshgoftaar T., Pandya A., and Fanning, D. (1995), "Application of Neural Networks for Predicting Program Faults," *Annals of Software Engineering,* Vol. 1, 1995.

Learner, E. (1978), *Specification Searches, Ad Hoc Inference with Nonexperimental Data,* Wiley, 1978.

Madachy, R. (1994), *A Software Project Dynamics Model for Process Cost, Schedule and Risk Assessment,* Ph.D. dissertation. University of Southern California, 1994.

Madachy, R. (1999), CS577a class notes. University of Southern California, 1999.

Minkiewicz, A. (1998), *Measuring Object Oriented Software with Predictive Object Points,* PRICE Systems, 1998.

Miranda, E. (2000), "Improving Subjective Estimates Using Paired Comparisons," *IEEE Software,* January/February 2001, pp. 87–91.

Nelson, E. (1966), *Management Handbook for the Estimation of Computer Programming Costs,* Systems Development Corporation, Oct. 1966.

Park R. (1988), "The Central Equations of the PRICE Software Cost Model," in *Proceedings of 4th COCOMO Users' Group Meeting,* November 1988.

Putnam, L., and Myers, W. (1992), *Measures for Excellence,* Yourdon Press Computing Series, 1992.

Reifer, D. (2002), *Making the Software Business Case,* Addison-Wesley, 2002.

Rubin, H. (1983), *ESTIMACS,* IEEE, 1983.

Shapiro, C., and Varian, H. (1999), *Information Rules: A Strategic Guide to the Network Economy,* Harvard University Press, 1999.

Shepperd, M., and Schofield, M. (1997), "Estimating Software Project Effort Using Analogies," *IEEE Transactions on Software Engineering,* Nov. 1997, vol. 23, no. 12.

Sullivan, K., Cat, Y., Hallen, B., and Griswold, W. (2001), "The Structure and Value of Modularity in Software Design," in *Proceedings, ESEC/FSE 2001,* ACM Press, pp. 99–108.

Symons, C. (1991), *Software Sizing and Estimating—Mark II FPA,* Wiley, 1991.

Thorp, J. (1998), *The Information Paradox,* McGraw-Hill, 1998.

USC-CSE (1997), *COCOMO II Model Definition Manual,* Center for Software Engineering, Computer Science Department, University of Southern California, Los Angeles, CA. 90007, website: http://sunset.usc.edu/COCOMOII/cocomo.html, 1997.

Weisberg, S. (1985), *Applied Linear Regression,* 2nd ed., Wiley, 1985.

Wittig, G. (1995), *Estimating Software Development Effort with Connectionist Models,* Working Paper Series 33/95, Monash University, 1995.

Web Development:
Estimating Quick-to-Market Software

Donald J. Reifer, *Reifer Consultants, Inc.*

Developers can use this new sizing metric called Web Objects and an adaptation of the Cocomo II model called WebMo to more accurately estimate Web-based software development effort and duration. Based on work with over 40 projects, these estimation tools are especially useful for quick-to-market development efforts.

Over the years, I have become confident in my ability to estimate software costs and schedules. Such confidence comes naturally to someone who has developed many hundreds of estimates. To accomplish this feat in a disciplined and repeatable manner, I have, of course, inserted mature processes, metrics, and estimating models. For predictability and control, I have then invested in data collection and tuned the processes, refined the metrics, and calibrated the models.

During the past few months, I found a simple way to rid myself of my self-assurance: I tried to estimate the cost and schedule for a Web development project. Seemingly, developers use hypertext markup language, Java applets and script, and visual programming languages to generate software for the Web in the blink of an eye. But such projects defeat my processes, defy my models, and make my size metrics obsolete.

By generating thousands of Web objects and making them operational in just a few months, this quickened pace raises pressing questions. For example, as we move to the Web and embrace electronic commerce business models, how do we estimate the software project costs and schedules? How do we examine the breakeven points and jus-

tify the investments needed to bring in the e-commerce bounty? More important, how do we adapt our existing processes, size metrics, and models and make them work? In this article, I will try to answer these and other questions about getting a handle on Web software development costs.

Characterizing Web Development Projects

A banner on my Web site recently announced that electronic commerce reached US$3 billion in sales last year. That's a marvelous achievement, but in good news there is also bad. The bad news is that the headline heralds a change to the way we go about developing and deploying software. In summarizing these changes, Table 1 high-

Reprinted from IEEE Software, November/December 2000.

227

Table I

Characteristics of Traditional versus Web Development Projects

Characteristics	Traditional development	Evolving Web development
Primary objective	Build quality software products at minimum cost	Bring quality products to market as quickly as possible
Typical project size	Medium to large (hundreds of team members)	Small (3–5 team members)
Typical timeline	10–18 months	3–6 months
Development approach employed*	Classical, requirements-based, phased and/or incremental delivery, use cases, documentation-driven	Rapid application development, gluing building blocks together, prototyping, Rational Unified Process,[1] MBASE[2]
Primary engineering technologies used	Object oriented methods, generators, modern programming languages (C++), CASE tools, and so forth	Component-based methods, fourth- and fifth-generation languages (HTML, Java, and so forth), visualization (motion, animation), among others
Processes employed	Capability Maturity Model-based	Ad hoc
Products developed	Code-based systems, mostly new, some reuse, many external interfaces, often complex applications	Object-based systems, many reusable components (shopping carts, etc.), few external interfaces, relatively simple
People involved	Professional software engineers typically with 5+ years of experience in at least two application domains	Graphic designers, less experienced software engineers (2+ years), new hires right out of school
Estimating technologies used	Analogy using historical data as its basis, SLOC or function point-based models, Work Breakdown Structure (WBS) approach for small projects	Analogy based upon current experience, "design-to-fit" based on available resources, WBS approach for small projects

*Often a function of best processes used in the past by the firm or industry

lights the move to component-based software development, systematic reuse, and visual technologies. It identifies the move to quick-paced developments and quick-to-market software: Getting their software to market first is the top priority for firms doing business on the Web.

The way we develop software is changing. Rather than develop software from requirements through the waterfall, Web development firms glue together building blocks and reusable components using rapid application development methods and continuous prototyping. While exciting, management of such projects can cause nightmares. Things happen so quickly that it is hard to get a handle on their status and whether they are making suitable progress. Web developments are also hard to estimate. Especially in firms with limited resources, software developers need to better predict the time and effort required to pull off such projects successfully.

In estimation, source-lines-of-code (SLOC) and function-point (FP) estimating models such as Cocomo, Price-S, Slim, and SEER are the mainstay tools used for traditional development.[3–6] The reasons for this are simple; the software development community has

- extensively studied the phenomenology associated with development and the parameters that drive cost;
- developed, validated, and commercialized estimating models that take this phenomenology into account over a period of 20+ years;

- calibrated the models using normalized historical data to accurately predict cost and schedule; and
- developed, refined, and optimized processes that incorporate the models into the planning and control processes firms use to manage their businesses.

Addressing the Estimating Challenges

The estimating community currently has not agreed on how to develop estimates for Web-based projects. The trouble is that the characteristics of the Web-based projects that are listed in Table 1 make it difficult for estimators to adapt and put existing processes, metrics, and models to work operationally. Table 2 highlights the challenges estimators face in Web estimation. For comparison, this table also identifies the more traditional approaches projects use to develop their estimates.

Devising New Size Metrics

Many professionals would like to use the more traditional processes, metrics, and models for estimating Web projects. However, as Table 2 notes, these traditional approaches do not seem to address the challenges facing the field. The major concern estimators face is in estimating size, because size drives most of their models. In response, they need new size metrics to accurately scope the work involved in projects that currently cannot be accurately estimated using SLOC and FPs.

Table 2

Web-Based Estimating Challenges

	Traditional approach	Web-based challenges
Estimating process	Most use analogy supplemented by lessons gleaned from past experience	Job costing done ad hoc based on inputs from the developers (often too optimistic)
Size estimation	Because systems are built to requirements, SLOC or function points are used. Separate models are used for COTS and reused software (generate equivalent new lines that are merged into the estimates).	Applications are built using templates and a variety of Web-based objects (html, applets, components, building blocks). No agreement on a size measure for Web applications has yet been reached within the community.
Effort estimation	Effort is estimated via regression formulas modified by cost drivers (plot project data to develop relationships between variables)	Effort is estimated by breaking the job down into tasks and identifying what is needed to do the work. Little history is available.
Schedule estimation	Schedule is estimated using a cube root relationship with effort	Schedule is estimated based upon analogy. Models typically estmate schedules high because cube root relationship doesn't hold.
Quality estimation	Quality is measurable from internal metrics like defect rates and system properties	Quality is hard to measure. New metrics are needed to assess "quality" of multimedia.
Model calibration	Measurements from past projects are used to calibrate models to improve accuracy[7]	Measurements from past projects are used to identify folklore (too few to be used yet)
"What if" analysis	Estimating models are used to perform *quantitative* "what if" and risk analysis. They are also used to compute return-on-investment (ROI) and cost/benefits.	Most "what if" and risk analysis is *qualitative* because models do not exist. ROI and cost–benefit analysis for electronic commerce applications remain an open challenge.

The first major question is "How do I measure size?" Developers involved in most working Web projects agree that SLOC might not be suitable for early estimation because they are design-based, while FPs might be inappropriate because applications do more than just transform inputs to outputs. In response, dozens of size metrics have emerged for Web development (object points, application points, and multimedia points, for example).[8] Researchers seem to agree only that they cannot agree which of these size metrics is best.

Let's muddy the waters a bit more. Based upon my research, I believe I have developed yet another size metric that resolves the current debate over size metrics. My proposed metric, Web Objects, computes size by considering each of the many elements that comprise the Web application. The metric computes size using Halstead's equation[9] for volume (that is, a proposed measure of size that is language independent and related to the vocabulary used to describe it in terms of *operands* and *operators*) as follows:

$$V^* = N \log_2(n) = (N_1^* + N_2^*) \log_2 (n_1^* + n_2^*)$$

where

N = number of total occurrences of *operands* and *operators*

n = number of distinct *operands* and *operators*

N_1^* = total occurrences of *operand* estimator

N_2^* = total occurrences of *operator* estimators

n_1^* = number of unique *operands* estimator

n_2^* = number of unique *operators* estimators

V^* = volume of work involved represented as Web Objects

Using the predictors listed in Table 3 to compute the number of Web Objects, I have been able to predict a Web application's size repeatably and robustly. These predictors let me consider the elements that contribute to the Web application's size. I can represent each predictor by the unique number of *operands* and *operators* that they contribute to the application. Like function points, the key to developing repeatable predictor counts is a well-defined set of counting conventions. This approach lets me achieve consistency across organizations and resolve conflicts, because size estimates are formulated using such standards.

By their very nature, such counts must clearly separate *operands* from *operators* because the latter represent what we do to an object, not what the object does. Table 3 also provides examples of *operands* and *operators* to clarify what is counted as I develop our Web Object estimates. In addition, Table 4 shows a worksheet I developed to weight the predictors to reflect the actual data I collected on 46 completed projects, which

Table 3

Web Based Predictors of Size

Web Object predictors	Example operands	Example operators
Number of building blocks	Fine grained components (ActiveX, DCOM, OLE, etc.), widgets, ...	Create, apply, call, dispatch, interface, terminate, ...
Number of COTS components (includes any wrapper code)	Commercial packages, library routines, objects like shopping carts, ...	Initiate, terminate, apply, bind, customize, export, wrap, ...
Number of multimedia files	Text, video, sound, 3D objects, plug-ins, metatags (no graphics files), ...	Create, cut, paste, clear, edit, animate, broadcast, ...
Number of object or application points[3] (or others proposed)	# server data tables, # states, # client data tables, percent reuse, ...	Transform (inputs to outputs), access, generate, modify, ...
Number of xml, sgml, html and query language lines	# lines including links to data attributes	Create, call, browse, link, find, search, retrieve, optimize...
Number of Web components	Applets, agents, guards, ...	Create, schedule, dispatch, ...
Number of graphics files	Templates, pictures, images, ...	Apply, align, import, export, insert, ...
Number of scripts (visual language, audio, motion, and so forth)	Macros, containers, ...	Create, store, edit, distribute, serialize, generalize, ...
Other		

ranged in size from 20 to 100 Web Objects. I developed the worksheet weightings much as Alan Albrecht and John Gaffney used a software engineering approach to validate how well function points fit their data.[10]

To use this worksheet, you must first identify the Web elements that contribute to the job you are estimating. You would start by selecting the applicable items listed in the predictor column. For example, you would enter application or object points, but not both, depending on which of the estimates you had available. If the item you need to size your project does not appear in the column, you would use "other" to account for it. Next, you would determine how each of these elements contributes to the total size by counting the unique number of *operands* (the objects) and *operators* (actions that can done to the object) involved in the application. Then, you would classify each set of *operands* and *operators* in terms of its complexity and enter the number into the appropriate worksheet column. Next, you would apply the complexity ratings and compute the total number in each column. Finally, you would sum the columns to compute the number of Web Objects. (I initially had the number of function points in this list, but I took it out because I could not get the data I needed to estimate this predictor on any of the 46 projects I analyzed.)

Computing size this way offers important advantages:

- The metric used has a solid mathematical foundation.

- It can be easily extended to include new predictors as new elements are introduced for Web applications (video markup languages, motion, sound, and so forth).
- The approach lets us address the unique characteristics of Web-based developments.

The approach also has some disadvantages:

- Some in the metrics community would argue against the use of software science because of its statistical mathematical basis. My research shows that the literature is full of arguments for and against use of the technique. Independent of who is right, use of software science as a basis is controversial.
- The planning and data collection costs rise as you add predictors to handle new elements. Temperance is needed or it might take you longer to estimate than develop your Web applications.
- Web Object counts tend to be very sensitive to counting conventions. For example, the size and complexity of multimedia components can vary from single objects such as buttons to long video sequences.

To address these challenges, I am currently documenting counting conventions as I collect and analyze project data. Based on my current rate of progress, I am at least a year away from publishing definitive guidelines for this endeavor.

Table 4

Web Object Calculation Worksheet

Web Object predictors	Complexity-weight		
	Low	Average	High
Number of building blocks	1	2	4
Number of COTS components	2	4	6
Number of multimedia files	1	2	4
Number of object or application points	*	*	*
Number of Web components	2	4	6
Number of xml, sgml, html, and query lines	3	5	8
Number of graphics files	2	4	6
Number of scripts	1	2	3
Other	2	4	6

* We assume weights have already been applied (otherwise would result in double counting).

Formulating New Models

Having a metric for size is just the first step in developing a model that accurately estimates Web development costs and schedule. The mathematical issues associated with predicting effort and duration must be reconciled before such models launch. The major issues revolve around the form of the mathematical equations and the schedule law. Analysis of data reveals that the equations can be expressed as regressions. However, the traditional cube-root relationship between effort and duration in most estimation models does not seem to accurately predict Web development schedules. Barry Boehm at the University of Southern California is looking at using a square-root relationship to more precisely represent the relationship. Larry Putnam has published several papers arguing that such relationships can be represented by a fourth power trade-off law.[11]

My initial data analysis reveals that the square-root relationship seems to exist for projects smaller than 100 Web Objects. For larger projects, the cube-root relationship seems to produce a better fit. Such a variable schedule law relationship is expected because software science scales effort mathematically as a function of length and volume to predict duration. As I continue gathering additional project data, I will look at how the equations scale for different-sized projects.

Now that these mathematical issues are out of the way, let's take a good look at the model that I propose for estimating Web development costs. I call the new model WebMo, the Web Model, because it is an extension of the Cocomo II early design model. I developed the model using a mix of expert judgment and data from 46 projects using regression analysis. Its mathematical formulation rests upon parameters from both the Cocomo II and SoftCost-OO software cost-estimating models.[12] I have computed exponents for both equations by segmenting the estimating trends into the following three domains: Web-based electronic commerce, financial and trading applications, and information utilities. Figure 1 shows the WebMo model for estimating equations for effort (in person-months) and duration (in calendar months).

As noted, the resulting effort estimation model has nine cost drivers and fixed power laws. I deviated from the Cocomo II formulation because I observed colinearity between cost drivers as I performed a regression analysis. In the duration estimation model, I switched from a cube- to square-root relationship with effort based upon built-in scaling rules to improve the accuracy of my estimates.

Table 5 summarizes the values for all of the model's parameters except the cost drivers. Tables 6 through 9 provide a quick rating scheme for each of my cost drivers, while Table 10 provides the values for each of the settings. The cost drivers include

Figure 1. WebMo model.

$$\text{Effort} = A\prod_{i=1}^{9} cd_i(\text{Size})^{P1} \qquad \text{Duration} = B(\text{Effort})^{P2}$$

Where: A and B are constants

P1 and P2 are power laws

cd_i are cost drivers

Size is the number of Web Objects

Table 5

Web Development Model Parameter Values

	A	B	P1	P2
Web-based electronic commerce	2.3	2.0	1.05	*
Financial/trading applications	2.7	2.2	1.05	*
Business-to-business applications	2.0	1.5	1.00	*
Web-based information utilities	2.1	2.0	1.00	*

Either 0.5 or 0.33 depending on the scaling (>40 Web Objects)

- RCPX: product reliability and complexity (product attributes);
- PDIF: platform difficulty (volatility of platform and network servers);
- PERS: personnel capability (skills, knowledge and abilities of the workforce);
- PREX: personnel experience (the breadth and depth of the team's experience);
- FCIL: facilities (tools, equipment and colocated facilities);
- SCED: schedule (degree of risk taken to shorten duration);

Table 6

Rating Scale for RCPX and PDIF

Driver	VL	L	N	H	VH
CPLX	Client side	Client–server	Client–server	Client–server	Client–server
	No distribution	Limited distribution	Fully distributed	Wide distribution	Full distribution
	Invocation	Adaptation	Integration	Synchronization	Collaborative
	Simple math	Standard math	Statistics	Math intensive	Soft real-time
	Simple I/O	File management	DBMS	Distributed database	Persistent database
	Limited data	Some files	Databases	Virtual database	Virtual database
	Reliability not a factor	Easy to recover from losses	Moderate recovery goal	High financial loss due to error	Errors cause risk to life
PDIF	Rare changes to platform	Few changes to platform	Platform stable	Frequent changes to platform	Platform not stable
	Speedy net	Fast net service	Acceptable net performance	Slow network performance	Unacceptable performance
	Best possible connectivity	Rare loss of connectivity	Acceptable connectivity	Poor connectivity	Unacceptable connectivity
	No computer resource limitations	Few computer resource limitations	Must watch use of computer resources	Lack of computer resources causing problems	Timing and storage impacts

Table 7

Rating Scale for PERS and PREX

Driver	VL	L	N	H	VH
PERS	15th percentile	35th percentile	55th percentile	75th percentile	90th percentile
	Major delays due to turnover	Minor delays due turnover	Few delays due to turnover	Infrequent delays due to turnover	No delays due to turnover
PREX	≤ 2 months average tool, language, platform, and applications experience	≤ 6 months average tool, language, platform, and applications experience	≤ 1 year average tool, language, platform, and applications experience	≤ 3 years average tool, language, platform, and applications experience	≤ 6 years average tool, language, platform, and applications experience

Table 8

Rating Scale for FCIL, SCED, and RUSE

Driver	VL	L	N	H	VH
FCIL	International Phone/fax Ad hoc methods Language tools Basically no collaboration	Multisite Phone/email Phase-dependent methods Basic CASE Limited collaboration	One complex LAN Life-cycle methods Tools support methods Integrated product teams	Same building WAN Integrated methods Integrated toolset Collaborative teams	Colocated Broadband State-of-the-art method Integrated toolset that supports collaboration
SCED	Must shorten 75% nominal	Must shorten 85% nominal	Keep as is Nominal	Can relax 130% nominal	Can extend 160% nominal
RUSE	Not used	Not used	Not used	Not used	Not used

Table 9

Rating Scale for TEAM and PEFF

Driver	VL	L	N	H	VH
TEAM	No shared vision Stakeholders do not work to meet each others' goals Teamwork limited	Little shared vision Stakeholders talk and build respect for each other Some teamwork	Some shared vision Stakeholders pull together and work joint goals Basic teamwork	Considerable shared vision Stakeholders respect each others' goals and collaborate Integrated teams	Extensive shared vision Stakeholders pull together and focus on goals Seamless teams
PEFF	Totally ad hoc, confused process Reliance on heroes to get job done	Project-based processes Reliance on management leadership to meet goals	Streamlined process tailored for the job Reliance on process for guidance	Efficient process matched to job Process is how engineers do their work	Effective process that meets goals Everyone uses and believes in the proces

- RUSE: reuse (degree of reuse planned and executed);
- TEAM: teamwork (the ability to work synergistically as a team); and
- PEFF: process efficiency (streamlined for the business)

I do not convert my size estimates from Web Objects to SLOC in the equation for effort. Rather, I used my initial data set to calibrate directly the relationships that existed between size in Web Objects and effort in person months. Another open issue that I will research is whether it makes sense to develop back-firing ratios from Web Objects to and from SLOC as the function point community has done.

Several of these ratings differ greatly from the original models. For example, SCED is flat when extended past its estimated duration in Cocomo II. But, my data shows that schedule adheres to a bell-shaped curve, consistent with the similar factor in the SoftCost-OO model. In other words, it costs more to both compress and elongate the nominal estimated duration.

Table 10

Values for Cost Drivers

Driver	VL	L	N	H	VH
RCPX	0.63	0.85	1.00	1.30	1.67
PDIF*	0.75	0.87	1.00	1.21	1.41
PERS	1.55	1.35	1.00	0.75	0.58
PREX	1.35	1.19	1.00	0.87	0.71
FCIL	1.35	1.13	1.00	0.85	0.68
SCED*	1.35	1.15	1.00	1.05	1.10
TEAM	1.45	1.31	1.00	0.75	0.62
PEFF	1.35	1.20	1.00	0.85	0.65
RUSE	Not rated	Not rated	1.00	Not rated	Not rated

*Significant differences from original model observed

233

About the Author

Donald J. Reifer is a teacher, change agent, consultant, contributor to the fields of software engineering and management, and author of *Tutorial on Software Management, Fifth Edition*. He is president of Reifer Consultants, Inc., and serves as a visiting associate at the Center for Software Engineering at the University of Southern California. He is also a member of the *IEEE Software* editorial board and editor of its Manager column. Contact him at d.reifer@ieee.org.

I plan to address the numerous open issues by gathering and analyzing more data from completed Web development projects. As I've discussed, the most important of these is developing consistent counting conventions for Web Objects. I will work with clients to collect the data I need to both resolve counting issues and improve the model's estimating accuracy. Currently, I can estimate Web development projects in my database within 30%, 60% of the time by segmenting the databases by the application domains in Table 5. But the accuracy of the model must be improved for commercialization. I want to improve this accuracy incrementally using project data to refine ratings developed through expert opinion. I aim to gather data on at least another 30 projects so that I can improve the model's accuracy for both effort and schedule to within 20% of actuals at least 80% of the time. This will take me about a year to accomplish. 🐝

References

1. P. Kruchten, *The Rational Unified Process*, Addison-Wesley, Reading, Mass., 1999.
2. B.W. Boehm, "Transitioning to the CMMI via MBASE," *SoCal SPIN Meeting Presentation*, Dept. Computer Science, Univ. Southern California, Los Angeles, 2000.
3. B.W. Boehm et al., *Software Cost Estimation with Cocomo II*, Prentice-Hall, Upper Saddle River, N.J., 2000.
4. R.E. Park, "The Central Equations of the PRICE Software Cost Model," *Proc. Fourth Cocomo User's Group*, 1988.
5. L.H. Putnam and W. Myers, *Measures of Excellence*, Prentice-Hall, Upper Saddle River, N.J., 1992.
6. *Parametric Cost Estimating Handbook*, US Dept. of Defense, Washington D.C., 1995.
7. D.V. Ferens and D.S. Christensen, "Does Calibration Improve Prediction Accuracy?," *CrossTalk*, Vol. 13, No. 4, Apr. 2000, pp. 14–17.
8. A.J.C. Cowderoy, "Size and Quality Measures for Multimedia and Web-Site Production," *Proc. 14th Int'l Cocomo Forum*, 1999.
9. M.H. Halstead, *Elements of Software Science*, Elsevier North Holland, Dordrecht, The Netherlands, 1977.
10. A.J. Albrecht and J.E. Gaffney, Jr., "Software Function Points, Source Lines of Code, and Development Effort Prediction: A Software Science Validation," *IEEE Trans. Software Eng.*, Vol. SE-9, No. 6, 1983, pp. 639–47.
11. L.H. Putnam and D.T. Putnam, "A Data Verification of the Software Fourth Power Trade-off Law," *Proc. Int'l Soc. Parametric Analysts Conf.*, 1984.
12. D.J. Reifer, *SoftCost-OO Reference Manual*, Reifer Consultants, Inc., Torrance, Calif., 1993.

Software Size Estimation of Object-Oriented Systems

LUIZ A. LARANJEIRA, STUDENT MEMBER, IEEE

Abstract—Software size estimation has been the object of a lot of research in the software engineering community due to the need of reliable size estimates in the utilization of existing software project cost estimation models. This paper discusses the strengths and weaknesses of existing size estimation techniques, considers the nature of software size estimation, and presents a software size estimation model which has the potential for providing more accurate size estimates than existing methods. The proposed method takes advantage of a characteristic of object-oriented systems, the natural correspondence between specification and implementation, in order to enable users to come up with better size estimates at early stages of the software development cycle. Through a statistical approach the method also provides a confidence interval for the derived size estimates. The relation between the presented software sizing model and project cost estimation has also been considered.

Index Terms—Functional specification, object-oriented systems, software cost estimation, software size estimation.

I. INTRODUCTION

THE software crisis has focused the attention of the software engineering community on the research of disciplined techniques for software development in the attempt to reduce and control the alarming growth of software systems development and maintenance costs. In particular, the commonly noticed tendency in software systems development for gross cost overruns and undesirable project delays has caused a lot of work to be done in developing project cost and effort estimation models. Accurate cost and scheduling estimations provide highly valuable aid in a number of management decisions, budget and personnel allocations, and in supporting reliable bids for contract competition.

Cost estimation models today available for the software engineering practitioner include: the Walston–Felix model [36], the Doty model [11], the Putnam model [25], the RCA PRICE S model [8], the Bailey–Basili model [2], the COCOMO (COnstructive COst MOdel) model [3], the SOFTCOST model [34], and, recently, the Jensen model [14]. An overview of each of these models is presented in [7]. In [3], a complete description of the COCOMO model together with a very detailed approach for its utilization on the daily life of an organization can be found. The discussion we carry out here will be generally valid for any of the mentioned cost models, although we concentrate something more on COCOMO in terms of examples

Manuscript received July 25, 1988; revised October 15, 1989. Recommended by C. G. Davis.

The author is with the Department of Electrical and Computer Engineering, University of Texas at Austin, Austin, TX 78712.

IEEE Log Number 9034386.

and details due to a more complete documentation available for this model.

The reception of cost estimation models in the software community has been usually good. Managers feel more comfortable using estimation models than just relying on rules of thumb and entirely subjective judgments when planning budgetary and personnel resources for a new project. Even though estimation models have some limitations that managers need to be aware of [3], [24], [7], they may be viewed as valuable tools in the software engineering process.

A common point concerning the above mentioned models is that they base their effort and scheduling predictions on the estimated size of the software project at hand, in terms of number of lines of code (LOC), or thousands of lines of code (KLOC). Generally the effort estimation is based upon an equation similar to

$$E = A + B*(\text{KLOC})^C$$

where E stands for estimated effort (usually in man-months), A, B, and C are constants, and KLOC is the expected number of thousands of lines of code in the final system. From the above equation it is easy to see that a given percentage error in the size (KLOC) may cause an even larger percentage error in the estimated effort. For instance, in COCOMO a 50% error in the size estimate will roughly result in a 63% error in the effort estimate. In other terms, size estimation error causes cost estimation error, since cost estimates are derived based on effort prediction.

Existing software cost estimation models assume that a plans and requirement analysis phase (Fig. 1), and consequently the system specifications, has been carried out before the model is applied. Their cost and schedule estimations cover the subsequent phases of the software development cycle (product design, detailed design, coding, integration, and test). Maintenance costs are estimated in a slightly different way, since by maintenance time the system is already entirely developed and its actual size is known.

It is obvious that, concerning development cost estimation, if a model would only produce effort estimates, let us say, after the detailed design or coding phase, such an estimation would have relatively low value for the project management and control. We surely need estimates in the early stages of the software life cycle in order that these estimates may cause a real impact on the development process. As a consequence, size estimations must be provided in the early phases of the software life cycle.

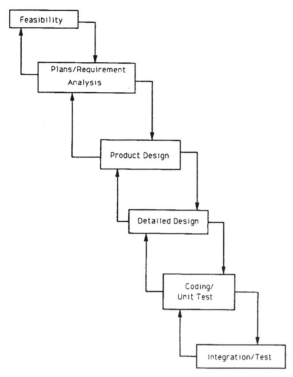

Fig. 1. Software life cycle phases.

Despite the above stated need, existing cost estimation models do not provide an integrated, detailed rationale and guidelines for producing system size estimates with required accuracy. This inconsistency has been pointed out by Bryant and Kirkham [6].

This paper attempts to focus on the problem of early size estimation. We will consider previously proposed size estimation techniques, discuss the nature of software size estimation and present a technique, based on an object-oriented specification model (for an object-oriented software implementation) and on statistical methods, that might turn out to provide more reliable software size estimates.

II. Existing Software Size Estimation Techniques

Several approaches for predicting software size have been proposed in the literature. They could be divided in two subsets: subjective techniques and objective models.

A. Subjective Techniques

The most popular sizing technique used is the PERT method where practitioners rely on expert judgment to estimate the ultimate size of a project. Such estimates are based on analogy with projects of similar characteristics, experience, or, when all else fails, on the intuition of the estimators [24].

In this approach the project is decomposed in its major functions, during the plans and requirements phase of the software life cycle (Fig. 1), and an estimation is made for each of them. The estimated size of the total system will be the sum of the estimates of the composing functions [39].

As an example, let us consider a software system to be developed for secure message communication. Project scope indicates a microprocessor based system linked in a network, providing for communication between government agencies. Evaluation of the system indicates the following major functions: user interface and control facilities, edition module, encryption/decryption modules, and communication modules. Table I shows the size estimates for each major function and for the entire system.

Putnam and Fizsimmons [26] suggested a method for adding some objectiveness to this technique. The expected number of lines of code (S_i) for each function is calculated as a weighted average of the optimistic (O_i), the most likely (M_i), and the pessimistic (P_i) size estimates. The estimated size of the total system (S_s) will again be the sum of the estimated function sizes. For example

$$S_i = \frac{O_i + 4M_i + P_i}{6} \qquad S_s = \sum S_i.$$

Considering that there is a very small probability that the actual size values do not fall in between the optimistic and pessimistic estimates, the deviation for each function estimate (D_i) and for the total system size estimate (D_s) will be

$$D_i = \frac{O_i - P_i}{6} \qquad D_s = \left(\sum D_i^2 \right)^{1/2}.$$

These equations are based on a beta distribution which means that 68% of the time the real size of the final software should be within $S_s + D_s$ and that the estimates are unbiased toward either underestimation and overestimation. Table II extends the simple expert judgment example using this PERT approach.

Despite the common utilization of subjective techniques for early software size estimation, two points can be clearly observed which expose the weaknesses of such an approach:

1) Experience has shown that expert judgment varies widely due to psychological and personal factors, and usually cannot provide estimates with required accuracy. Reference [7] quotes a study performed by Yourdon Inc., where several experienced managers estimated the size of 16 software projects on the basis of the complete specification for each project. The average expert predictions are presented in Table III together with the actual size of each software project, after completed. It may be easily seen that the discrepancy between estimated and real size values is large enough to raise questions about the applicability of the method.

2) The assumption, considered in the PERT technique, that estimates are unbiased toward underestimation or overestimation, is not confirmed by current experience. It can be noticed in Table III that 12 of the 16 projects were underestimated by experts. The reasons for this underestimation tendency include the desire to please management, incomplete recall of previous experiences, lack of familiarity with the entire software job, and lack of enough

TABLE I
SIMPLE EXPERT ESTIMATION FOR SECURE MESSAGE COMMUNICATION SYSTEM SIZE

Function Module	Estimated Size
User Interface/Control	2,500
Editor	1,500
Encription/Decription	800
Communications	1,000
Total Project	5,800

TABLE II
PERT ESTIMATION FOR SECURE MESSAGE COMMUNICATION SYSTEM SIZE

Function Module	Optimistic Size	Most Likely Size	Pessimistic Size	Expected Size	Deviation
UI/Cont	1,800	2,500	3,200	2,550	283
Editor	1,000	1,500	2,000	1,500	167
Enc/Dec	500	800	1,000	784	83
Commun	700	1,000	1,300 ·	1,000	100
Tot Proj	4,000	5,800	7,800	5,584	353

TABLE III
ACTUAL AND PREDICTED SIZE OF 16 SOFTWARE PROJECTS

Product	Actual Size	Predicted Size
1	70,919	34,705
2	128,837	32,100
3	23,015	22,000
4	34,560	9,100
5	23,000	12,000
6	25,000	7,300
7	52,080	28,500
8	7,650	8,000
9	25,860	30,600
10	16,300	2,720
11	17,410	15,300
12	33,900	105,300
13	57,194	18,500
14	21,020	35,400
15	8,642	3,650
16	17,480	2,950

knowledge of the particular project being estimated. These considerations show the need of more accurate software sizing techniques.

B. Objective Models

There have been several attempts to come up with an objective model for predicting software size. Generally the size of a system is expressed as a function of some known quantities that reflect characteristics of the system. In [18], Levitin classifies these models in two groups, according to the type of the quantities upon which the estimates are made. These groups can be called external (specification level) models or internal (implementation level) models.

Specification Level Objective Models: Specification level models express size as a function of a number of quantities which can usually be determined early in the software life cycle from system specifications. One of these methods, derived by Albrecht (see [1] and [33]), base software sizing on the so-called "function points." These are characteristics of the system such as the number of input and output files, the number of logical internal files, the number of inquiries, etc. The calculation of the "function points" is performed as a weighted sum of these quantities, adjusted by some complexity factors. The estimated size is related to the number of "function points" (FP) by an equation of the type

$$ES = (B * FP) - A$$

where ES is the estimated software size in thousands of lines of code (KLOC), and A and B are constants. Table IV shows briefly the steps for calculating the "function points" for a given application. First the total unadjusted function points (TUFP) are calculated. The calculation of TUFP is based on weighting the system components (external inputs, external outputs, etc.) and classifying them as "simple," "average," or "complex" depending on the number of data elements in the component and other factors [Table IV(a)]. Then the technical complexity factor (TCF) is calculated by estimating the degree of influence (DI) of some 14 characteristics of the component [Tables IV(b) and IV(c)]. Finally, the function points (FP) are given by multiplying the total unadjusted function points (TUFP) by the technical complexity factor (TCF) [see formula below Table IV(c)].

Another method, similar to Albrecht's one, was derived by Itakura and Takayanagi [12]. This model bases its estimations on quantities such as the number of input and output files, the number of input and output items, the number of items of transaction type reports, etc. These quantities are presented in Table V with corresponding designators (X_i's). The model equation is as follows

$$ES = A_i * X_i$$

where ES is the estimated software size in thousands of lines of code (KLOC), the X_i's are the quantities based on which the estimation is made, and the A_i's are the corresponding coefficients.

Although these models attempted to achieve a somewhat more scientific approach to software sizing, it can be generally stated that they still present a number of difficulties which point to the need of further research in the field. We could summarize these points in the following considerations:

1) These methods were derived to be used in banking and business applications. Therefore, they lack generality concerning the nature of the systems to which they might be applicable.

2) Generally, the quantities upon which the estimates are based are related to the interactions between the system and the environment (inputs and outputs). Albrecht also attempted to consider the effects of complexity factors in his sizing model. It is not difficult to understand that programs having the same type and number of interactions with the environment might have totally different sizes. It has also been noticed by Boehm, in [3], that complexity does not necessarily relate to size. In this sense we might have very complex functions which have a relatively short sized implementation, or relatively lengthy simple housekeeping functions.

TABLE IV
FUNCTION POINTS CALCULATION: (a) UNADJUSTED FUNCTION POINTS
CALCULATION, (b) TECHNICAL COMPLEXITY FACTOR CALCULATION, (c)
VALUES CORRESPONDING TO DIFFERENT DEGREES OF INFLUENCE.

| Description | Level of Information Processing Function | | | Total |
	Simple	Average	Complex	
External Input	--- *3 = ---	--- *4 = ---	--- *6 = ---	---
External Output	--- *4 = ---	--- *5 = ---	--- *7 = ---	---
Logical Internal File	--- *7 = ---	--- *10 = ---	---*15= ---	---
External Interface File	--- *5 = ---	--- *7 = ---	--- *10= ---	---
External Inquire	--- *3 = ---	--- *4 = ---	--- *6 = ---	---
	Total Unadjusted Function Points (TUFP)			---

(a)

ID	Characteristic	DI	ID	Characteristic	DI
C1	Data Communications	--	C8	On-Line Update	--
C2	Distributed Functions	--	C9	Complex Processing	--
C3	Performance	--	C10	Reusability	--
C4	Heavily Used Configuration	--	C11	Installation Ease	--
C5	Transaction Rate	--	C12	Operational Ease	--
C6	On-Line Data Entry	--	C13	Multiple Sites	--
C7	End User Efficiency	--	C14	Facilitate Change	--
	Total Degree of Influence (TDI)				--

$$TCF = 0.65 + 0.01 * TDI$$

(b)

DI Values	
No Influence = 0	Average Influence = 3
Insignificant Influence = 1	Significant Influence = 4
Moderate Influence = 2	Strong Influence = 5

$$FP = TUFP * TCF$$

(c)

TABLE V
SOFTWARE SIZING FACTORS IN ITAKURA AND TAKAYANAGI'S MODEL

X1	number of input files
X2	number of input items
X3	number of output files
X4	number of output items
X5	number of items of transactions type records
X6	number of vertical items in two-dimensional table type reports
X7	number of horizontal items in two-dimensional table type reports
X8	number of calculating processes
X9	existence of sorting
X10	sum of output items in reports (X5 + X6 + X7)
X11	sum of output items in both files and reports (X4 + X5 + X6 + X7)

3) Another difficulty arises when we think about how to extend these models to applications such as scientific programs, text processing, communications systems, and others, which emerge day to day in the computer software field. There is no easy way to find the quantities upon which we should base our estimates. A study conducted in the Navy, based on a database of avionics and sonar software data, attempted to investigate quantitative size estimating relationships in these systems. The result of this study [10] states that "no attribute factors have been found to be statistically significant for sizing adjustments, except language."

We conclude that much research needs to be done in order to have defined quantifiable system attributes upon which to base reliable size estimates. Despite the above criticism, the work of Abrecht, and Itakura and Takayanagi, represents a move from plain subjective expert estimation to more objective ways of quantifying software size early in the software development process. However, it seems clear that the goal they looked for needs to be pursued further yet.

Implementation Level Objective Models: Implementation level models attempt to express size as function of some characteristics which are more closely related to the program itself, whose values can be determined at detailed design, before actual coding begins. These quantities are, mainly, the number of operators and the number of unique variables and constants in the program. These models do not address our basic concern of early cost estimation. However they are included here for the sake of completeness of our discussions. A number of implementation level objective models for software size estimation have been proposed in the literature, such as the work of Fitsos [9] with the Software Science length equation, the work of Wang [37], and the work of Britcher and Gaffney [5]. Details of these models are provided by Levitin [16]-[18].

It is interesting to observe that, although more accurate estimates could be expected from using these models, due to more knowledge of the project which is available after the detailed design phase (Fig. 1), the results obtained by Levitin do not support this expectation. Her conclusion in [18] says that "program size cannot be estimated from the number of program variables with required accuracy. The problem is not our lack of knowledge of a right formula but rather the simple fact that programs with the same number of variables may differ considerably in their size." This conclusion is quite similar to ours in our previous considerations on specification level objective sizing models.

III. THE NATURE OF SOFTWARE SIZE ESTIMATION

From the discussion carried out in the previous section we may say that the models and techniques available today for software sizing are not yet reliable enough to be consistently used with existing cost estimation models. On the one hand, subjective estimation, as it has been used in the software industry, lacks a solid enough basis to be able to provide sufficiently accurate sizing estimates. On the other hand, the attempts which aim to relate the size of a system to the number of certain external attributes of this system seem equally unable to be successful.

The task of software size estimation has been compared by Boehm [3] to the estimation of the number of pages of a novel before the novel is actually written. Let us suppose that a certain author is planning to write a novel which has four central characters, who influence each others' lives profoundly, and twenty incidental characters. The story happens in three different locations, it has a two year time span, and includes five detailed flashbacks. Suppose now that for some reason the editor wants to know in advance how many pages this novel will have after it is written. How could one estimate this quantity based solely on the given information? It is clear that the provided information is not enough to make possible such an estimate. In order to do that one would need additional information such as the complete relation of the events to take place in the novel, the detailed interrelationships between characters, the aspects on which the author wants to focus, etc. In other words, specific knowledge about the product would be necessary. Although the software sizing problem might not have all of the aspects of the novel sizing problem, the second gives us a good appreciation of the first.

The considerations so far presented seem to point out that specific knowledge about the nature of a software system which size one wants to estimate is a must. This includes knowledge of the system functions in terms of scope, complexity and interaction. Boehm studied the uncertainty in software project cost estimates as a function of the life cycle phase of a product [3]. The graphic in Fig. 2 shows the result of this study, which was empirically validated [3, Section 21.1] for a human–machine interface component of a program. The exponential curve in the figure resembles a "learning curve" and shows clearly that the uncertainty in cost estimates is related to the amount of knowledge (or lack of it) about the system at each phase of the software life cycle. Although the referred study was done with respect to cost estimation aspects of a project, the same concept can be easily extended to size estimation aspects.

With this in mind, it is not difficult to understand that subjective techniques fail because of lack of the necessary level of system knowledge, and the major flaw with objective models is that the factors they intend to base their estimates upon are not representative of all aspects of a system which might influence its final size.

If we want to have accurate software estimates we need new software sizing models which might be able to overcome the weaknesses of the existing ones. Furthermore, new models need also to solve the following problems:

1) We need specific knowledge of a system in its early stages of development.

2) We need to be able to relate, as accurately as possible, this knowledge to the physical size of the program.

3) Given that the ultimate level of information about a system in the early stages of its development is clearly

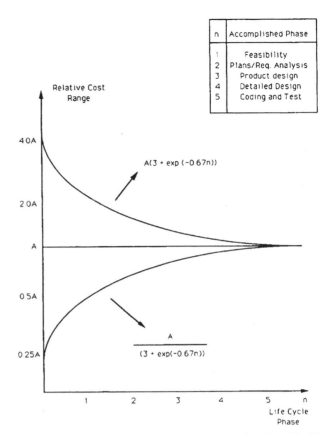

Fig. 2. Software project cost estimation accuracy as a function of the life cycle phase.

limited, we need to find a way to cope with this limitation and still have reliable sizing estimates, as well as be able to evaluate the degree of accuracy of the estimates.

The methodology we propose in this paper attempts to address these issues. In order to capture and represent knowledge about the system we use a functional requirements specification model, which enables decomposition of complexity and provides for understandability of its functionality. This model represents the system and associated environment as a number of semiautonomous objects acting asynchronously one upon another, just as the real world is. This representation points to the object-oriented approach for software development as a strong match to relate the knowledge embedded in the functional model to the final system size. This is so due to the fact that the representation of a real world problem with an object model will correspond to a great extent to the implementation of the corresponding system in an object-oriented programming environment. Finally, a statistical analysis provides for the necessary uncertainty evaluation. This analysis is based on the exponential curve of Fig. 2, adapted for the software sizing problem.

IV. THE OBJECT MODEL FOR FUNCTION REQUIREMENTS AND SOFTWARE SIZE ESTIMATION

Functional requirements are a must in any software system development in order to make it possible for developers and customers to understand the system they are both developing and proposing. The days of top-of-the-head functional specifications are already passed since the great majority of current large complex software systems demand a formal model to represent and document their functionality. Modeling the functionality of a software system is a task undertaken during the requirement analysis phase of the software life cycle.

The major role of a functional model is to provide for the understandability of the system it represents. The main problem here is how to decompose the system's complexity using a divide and conquer strategy. In [40], Yeh *et al.* point to three powerful and desirable properties of a functional model. They are as follows.

1) Abstraction: An abstraction represents several objects, suppressing details and concentrating on essential properties. It allows one to represent a system in several layers, called levels of abstraction [19], forming a natural hierarchy. Each level sees the level below as a virtual machine, with specified properties and functionality.

2) Partition: The partitioning of a system represents it as a sum of its parts, allowing one to concentrate on system components one at a time. High level components may also be partitioned, as well as its component parts. This leads to the idea of levels of partitioning. A component may also have an abstraction hierarchy. In this case a system would have both a horizontal and a vertical decomposition.

3) Projection: A projection of a system represents the entire system with respect to a set of its properties. This allows us to understand a system from different viewpoints, separating particular facets. An example of that could be the descriptive geometry description of a three-dimensional physical object which is composed of vertical and horizontal two-dimensional projections.

The object-oriented model for functional specification that we propose reflects these characteristics as we will discuss later. A number of researchers (Booch [4], Stark and Seidewitz [29]–[31]), have contributed to a general object-oriented methodology. Although they have concentrated somewhat more on design aspects of the object-oriented life cycle, the specification model we adopted here was largely influenced by their ideas.

In the proposed object model, each entity of the problem domain, or real world, is represented by an object. An object may be a person, a machine, a sensor, etc. Each object is composed by a state that characterizes it, and a set of functions, called methods, that manipulate the data corresponding to its state [32]. As a consequence, we may view an object as having two projections. One is the data structure that represents its state. The other is composed by the functions that determine its behavior. An object acts upon another by requesting the second object to perform a certain function on its data (state) and return some results to the requesting object. No object can act directly on another object's data. This concept is known as information hiding [22]. The fact that an object requests some action of another is represented in the model by an arrow directed from the object which requests the action to the object which performs the action. Therefore, an object is fully characterized by its state, its internal functions and its interactions with other objects (we will talk later about a fourth characteristic of an object—nonfunctional requirements it possibly needs to meet). We believe that a real world problem is easily represented by a set of objects that interact with one another.

At its top level a system may be represented by a single object that interacts with external objects. Beginning at this level each object of the system may be refined into component objects on a lower level of partitioning. This partitioning may continue until objects are completely decomposed into primitive objects. A primitive object would be one in which internal state (data) and corresponding methods (internal functions) are simple enough, in terms of complexity and size, to be considered an undecomposable entity of the system. The result of this process is a set of levels of partitioning that represents the system (Fig. 3). Furthermore, each partition may be viewed as a set of layers (or levels of abstraction). Each layer defines a virtual machine which provides service for senior layers. Any layer can request operations in junior layers but never in senior layers (Fig. 4). It should be noted that not all objects in a certain level of partitioning will be amenable for further partitions.

A specification effort should begin by identifying the entities in a problem domain and their interrelationships, and continue further by detailing the functions performed by and the internal state of each object. The next step would be to identify which objects could allow partitioning and the layers of abstraction in each partitioning level. A major advantage of such specification object model is that it makes possible a direct and natural correspondence with the real world, since problem domain entities are extracted directly into the model without any intermediate buffer such as traditional data flow diagrams [20]. This also makes the model quite understandable, which is an essential characteristic of a functional specification model.

The above considerations lead us to the fact that an object-oriented representation of a system is a more suitable model for accurate software size estimates than one achieved through a more traditional approach. The point here is that the implementation of the system, provided that it is also object-oriented, will match to a great extent its functional specification. This matching has been observed by Seidewitz in [31], where he reports that some projects designed and developed at Goddard Space Flight Center with an object-oriented approach, turned out to have a very smooth transition from specifications to code. We should notice that this matching does not necessarily occur with other specification methods such as common data flows, state transition diagrams, or data-oriented models. Although some of these models may also be used to specify systems in a hierarchical fashion, they lack the above mentioned correspondence between specification and implementation that favors the object-oriented model as a better choice for providing support for better software size estimates.

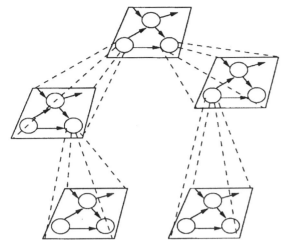

Fig. 3. Levels of decomposition (partitioning).

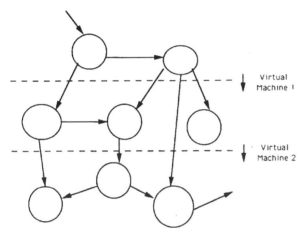

Fig. 4. Layers of abstraction.

We will not go into further detail about this object-oriented functional model, since our main goal here is to show its advantages for early software size estimation. In this scenario it is worth noting that we will be much more interested in the partitioning aspect of the objects of a system than in the aspect of layers of abstraction, although both aspects are needed when the specifications are derived. Whereas the second aspect is not needed for size estimation it will be very important concerning the development of the system.

The size estimation process of a system, whose functional model is characterized by a certain number of levels of decomposition (partitioning), may be summarized in the following steps:

1) Beginning with the lowest level of decomposition evaluate the size of each object. This evaluation should consider each function executed by the object, as well as the code corresponding to the data structures which will hold its internal state.

2) Continue to higher levels taking into account that higher level object sizes may receive contributions of component objects as well as of its own data and functions.

3) It may be necessary to include "utility objects" to account for housekeeping functions.

4) The estimated size of the whole system will be the sum of the size estimates of the objects in the top level of decomposition plus the size of possibly existing "utility objects."

It has been advocated in the literature [18] that one cannot expect to have reliable software size estimates based on specification models. Weinberg's experiment [38] is usually taken as the basis for this thesis. In that experiment, five programmer teams came up with considerably different program sizes for the same functional specifications. However, it should be said clearly that those teams were given quite different objectives during the development effort. One team was asked to minimize the amount of memory required for the program, another was to optimize program understandability, another was to minimize program length, another was to minimize the development effort, and the last one was to produce the clearest possible output. As it can be seen, although the general problem statement was the same for the five teams, they had quite different nonfunctional specifications. The conclusion we reach is that very restrictive nonfunctional specifications might influence software size. If some of them are present in a development, they should be considered in the size estimation process. This fact does not invalidate the sizing technique we present here, since our proposition is that estimates should be based on the available knowledge of the system. Whereas we consider project decomposition and functional specifications as major tools for detailing and representing system knowledge, other sources of knowledge such as nonfunctional requirements might also provide a contribution. A way to do that would be, for instance, to add to the characterization of each object a fourth element (other than data, methods or interactions) that would be called nonfunctional constraints. This would be a statement of restrictive nonfunctional requirements (if any) each object needs to fulfill. This information would also be used in the size estimation of that object.

Finally, we would like to point out that it is our belief that the most suited people for estimating software size are the future developers of the system. One reason for this is that each programmer has his own personal programming style, which often influences software size [17]. Another reason is that system developers, such as designers and programmers, are the people with the best conditions for accounting for the influence of nonfunctional specifications on system size.

V. SOFTWARE SIZING: A STATISTICAL MODEL

Fig. 2 shows a plot of the accuracy of software project estimates as a function of the software life cycle phase. This resulted from Boehm's study of projects in TRW. The meaning of this graph is that there is a very small probability that cost estimates will be out of the boundaries represented by the two converging exponential curves shown in the figure. If we put this in an analytic form we have

$$x(n) <= A * (3 + e^{-B*n}) \quad \text{(upper exponential)}$$

$$x(n) >= \frac{A}{3 + e^{-B*n}} \quad \text{(lower exponential)}.$$

Here $x(n)$ is a cost estimate, A is the actual cost of the system, and n relates to the phase in the life cycle when the estimate was done. The value of B, in that experiment found to be 0.67, determines how fast estimates converge, that is, what is the improvement in the accuracy of estimates as we go from one phase to the next in the software life cycle.

Whereas Fig. 2 was primarily sketched with cost estimation in mind, we can extend the same concept to the problem of estimating software size. This extension is based on the fact that both cost and size estimates rely on the available knowledge of the system, as discussed before.

Fig. 5 shows the learning curve concept adapted to software size estimation. This figure differs from Fig. 2 in some aspects. Rather than relating size estimates throughout life cycle phases, it reflects the variation of size estimation accuracy, as one increasingly details the functional specification of the system by means of object decomposition, during the requirements analysis phase of the software development process. A feasibility phase is considered to be completed at this time. Therefore, the crossing points between the boundary exponentials and the vertical axis will be different from Fig. 2, where the feasibility phase is still considered. The value of n is now related to the level of decomposition of system objects in the specification based on which the estimate was done. In this scenario, $n = 0$ means that no functional specification was carried out yet, $n = 1$ means that a top level specification has been accomplished, $n = 2$ means that the objects in the top level were partitioned one level below, and so forth. The value of B accounts for how fast estimates converge to the actual size A, as we pursue in decomposing system objects down to lower and lower levels.

The hypothesis we base this upon is that the proposed object specification model will provide for a sufficiently disciplined methodology for capturing system knowledge as to cause estimates to converge smoothly to the actual size of system as further levels of object decomposition are reached. This means that an estimate made at a certain level of decomposition is not unrelated to previous estimates, obtained with less detailed levels of decomposition. This is easily seen if we consider that when going a level down in the decomposition process one just carries out the decomposition of objects in the current lower level. In this scenario, the amount of knowledge corresponding to undecomposed objects (not all objects will be decomposable) will remain the same, and the new knowledge achieved by the increased detail of decomposed objects will be a refinement of some less accurate knowledge that was already available before. The conclusion we reach is

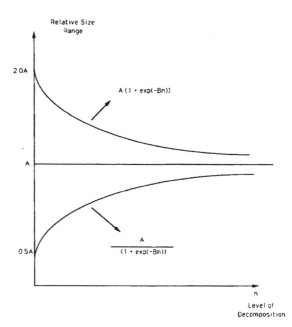

Fig. 5. Software size estimation accuracy as a function of object decomposition level in the functional model.

that, although extraneous estimates may show up here and there in the process, in general the pattern of estimates should converge monotonically to the actual size value. These considerations point to possible patterns of project size estimates as those shown in Fig. 6.

Additional important information, needed for the application of this technique, is how to obtain the value of B, which sets the rate for the exponential decay of upper and lower boundary curves of Fig. 5. After a lot of study and experimentation it is now well agreed upon among software engineering researchers and practitioners that any software metrics model needs to be tunned to the specific environment where it will be applied. In this work, the value of B is exactly the one which will incorporate with the estimating process the characteristics and previous experiences of the organization where a particular software project will take place. It should be calculated by analyzing a representative number of already accomplished projects with sizes estimated by using the proposed methodology. One would plot the values of project size estimates as a function of n, the level of decomposition of objects in the functional model, and look for the exponential boundary curves which are the "envelopes" for the entire range of estimates. This can be done by curve fitting statistical techniques.

Going further in the development of the model, we have that, for a particular estimate $x(n)$, evaluated considering n levels of objects decomposition, the following will hold

$$x(n) <= A * (1 + e^{-B*n}) \quad \text{(upper exponential)}$$

and

$$x(n) >= \frac{A}{1 + e^{-B*n}} \quad \text{(lower exponential)}.$$

242

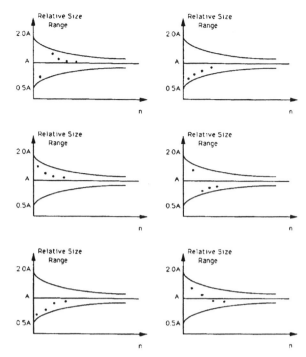

Fig. 6. Possible patterns for size estimates (assuming that subsequent estimates are not independent from one another).

These relations yield

$$A \geq \frac{x(n)}{1 + e^{-B*n}} \quad \text{and} \quad A \leq x(n) * (1 - e^{-B*n})$$

which can be rewritten as

$$A \geq L1(n) \quad \text{and} \quad A \leq L2(n)$$

where

$$L1(n) = \frac{x(n)}{1 + e^{-B*n}}$$

and

$$L2(n) = x(n) * (1 + e^{-B*n})$$

and finally,

$$L1(n) \leq A \leq L2(n).$$

Given B and n, we can also calculate a confidence interval for the estimates. This confidence interval turns out to be independent of A, the actual program size. The negative and positive deviations, $d1(n)$ and $d2(n)$, which characterize the confidence interval, can be calculated as

$$d1(n) = \frac{\frac{A}{1 + e^{-B*n}} - A}{A}$$

and

$$d2(n) = \frac{A * (1 + e^{-B*n}) - A}{A}$$

working with the above expressions we get

$$d1(n) = \frac{-e^{-B*n}}{1 + e^{-B*n}} \quad \text{and} \quad d2(n) = e^{-B*n}.$$

As $d1(n)$ and $d2(n)$ are independent of A, given a certain B we can plot their values as a function of n. Table VI shows the values of $d1(n)$ and $d2(n)$ for $B = 0.47$, with n varying from 1 to 6. We notice that the positive deviation is generally larger than the negative one, accounting for the biasing towards underestimation observed in reported software sizing experiences. The expected value for a size estimate given a certain $n = N$ will be

$$E(N) = \frac{L1_{max}(n) + L2_{min}(n)}{2}$$

where

$$L1_{max}(N) = \max \left[L1(n) \right] \quad \text{for } n \leq N$$

and

$$L2_{min}(N) = \min \left[L2(n) \right] \quad \text{for } n \leq N.$$

For $n = N$ there will be a very large probability that the actual program size A will be within the interval

$$\left[E_{min}(N), E_{max}(N) \right]$$

where

$$E_{min}(N) = E(N) * (1 + d1(n))$$

and

$$E_{max}(N) = E(N) * (1 + d2(n)).$$

It is interesting to note that, since the expected negative and positive deviations, $d1(n)$ and $d2(n)$, are independent of the actual size A, it is possible for one to know in advance the number of decomposition levels needed to achieve a desired accuracy. This fact provides the method with a criterion by which one can know whether it should or not be used in a particular project to be developed in a given organization. There will be cases when this technique will not be worth using. This will happen for small values of B, such that the convergence of the estimates with n will be so slow that, even if one gets to the lowest possible level of decomposition, the confidence interval will not satisfy the accuracy required for the particular project. The decision of using or not this technique will depend on the value of B, as well as on the required accuracy for a particular project cost estimation.

Detailing the method, we would have the following steps in the estimation process:

1) Given the value of B, plot in a table the values of $d1(n)$ and $d2(n)$ as a function of n.

2) Given the required accuracy for the estimation, check in that table what is the necessary level of object decomposition to go through in the functional specification model. Call it N.

3) Work the correspondent functional specifications

243

TABLE VI
PLOT OF NEGATIVE AND POSITIVE DEVIATIONS AS A FUNCTION OF n, FOR B = 0.47

n	$d1(n)$	$d2(n)$
1	-0.385	0.625
2	-0.281	0.391
3	-0.196	0.244
4	-0.133	0.153
5	-0.087	0.095
6	-0.056	0.060

TABLE VII
SIZE ESTIMATION CALCULATIONS FOR PROJECT I, WITH B = 0.47

n	$x(n)$	$L1(n)$	$L2(n)$	$L1(n)$ max	$L2(n)$ min	$E(n)$	$E(n)$ min	$E(n)$ max
1	7,000	4,308	11,375	4,308	11,375	7,842	-3,019	4,091
2	13,000	9,348	18,078	9,348	11,375	10,362	-2,912	4,052
3	12,200	9,806	15,174	9,806	11,375	10,590	-2,076	2,584

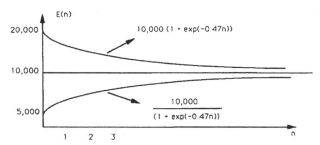

Fig. 7. Learning curve for Project I size estimates $E(n)$.

one level of decomposition down. If this is the first step, model the system with top level objects.

4) Estimate system size as suggested in Section IV, yielding $x(n)$.

5) Calculate $L1(n)$, $L2(n)$, $L1_{max}(n)$ and $L2_{min}(n)$.

6) Calculate the expected system size $E(n)$, and the maximum and minimum expected sizes, $E_{max}(n)$ and $E_{min}(n)$, for this level of decomposition n.

7) If $n = N$ stop. Consider $E_{min}(N)$, $E(N)$, and $E_{max}(N)$ as the minimum, expected, and maximum values for system size. If $n < N$ and the objects in the functional model cannot be decomposed one more level, stop and disregard results so far achieved. The method will not provide enough accuracy in this case. If objects still allow decomposition, go one step further to item (4).

As the proposed method is very sensitive to the value of B, it is important to consider that this value will not be static for a particular environment. In other words, estimators may "learn" how to come up with better estimates by getting more used to the methodology and the environment characteristics, and by relying more and more on the experiences of past projects. With this in mind, it would be wise to recalculate B when comparison between estimates and actual size values shows that the method is yielding too broad confidence intervals in face of the increased accuracy of estimates.

We can illustrate the application of the proposed technique with two examples. Project I is a relatively small business application. The actual size of the system was found to be 10,000 lines of code, after the project was accomplished. The value of B for the corresponding organization has been evaluated as 0.47, and, as the entire cost of the project is relatively low, an overall accuracy of 25% was considered acceptable. Looking at Table VI we notice that we will need up to three levels of decomposition in the functional model. Table VII shows the values of the quantities calculated in the estimating process, and Fig. 7 presents a graph of the expected size $E(n)$ provided by the model. We can see that the first estimate shows a gross discrepancy with respect to the actual achieved size, but subsequent ones converge smoothly to the value of A. By the end of the process the expected size in lines of code is 10,590, with possible deviation values of -2076 and +2584.

Project II, carried out in the same company, corresponds to the development of an operating system. This project required an accuracy of 10% due to organization budget constraints at the time. Since B is the same as in Project I, Table VI shows that functional specifications should go through 5 levels of object decomposition. Table VIII presents the values calculated in the estimating process. The expected size value was 37,505 lines of code, and deviation values -3263 and +3563. As actual program size was found to be 40,000 lines of code, we can see in Fig. 8 that model estimates $E(n)$ converge smoothly to A as n increases.

VI. RELATING SIZE TO COST

As seen in the previous section, the size estimation method proposed in this paper allows one to estimate system size with a specified confidence interval. This confidence interval depends on the value of B, the exponential decay of the size estimates exponential "envelope" curve, and on the value of n, the level of object decomposition in the functional specifications model. Since our ultimate goal in estimating program size is to be able to predict program cost as accurately as possible, it would be nice, now, to relate our size estimation results to cost. In other words, we would like to know how much to budget for a certain software project and what level of variance should be expected from this estimation. In order to do that we can use, for instance, the COCOMO model [3] to calculate the estimated development cost of Project I and Project II, the examples of the previous section.

COCOMO predicts project cost, in man-months, primarily based on the estimated number of thousands of lines of code for the system. This nominal estimation is then adjusted by a number of effort multipliers, whose overall product is called Effort Adjustment Factor (EAF). COCOMO effort multipliers are summarized in Table IX. Observation of the nature of effort multipliers shows that the necessary system knowledge for their evaluation is

TABLE VIII
SIZE ESTIMATION CALCULATIONS FOR PROJECT II, WITH $B = 0.47$

n	x(n)	L1(n)	L2(n)	L1 (n) max	L2 (n) min	E(n)	E (n) min	E (n) max
1	28,000	17,231	45,500	17,231	45,500	31,366	-12,076	19,604
2	32,500	23,011	45,901	23,011	45,901	34,456	-9,682	13,472
3	34,700	27,891	43,712	27,891	43,172	35,532	-6,964	8,670
4	35,200	30,540	40,571	30,540	40,571	37,885	-5,039	5,796
5	37,350	34,098	40,912	34,098	40,912	37,505	-3,263	3,563

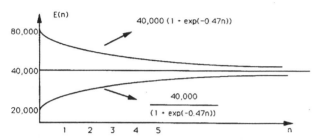

Fig. 8. Learning curve for Project II size estimates $E(n)$.

certainly available by the requirements/specifications phase of the software life cycle, i.e., at $n = 0$.

For these examples, as we use COCOMO, our assumptions will be rather simple, since our purpose here is not to detail COCOMO itself, but to relate the presented size prediction method to cost estimation. In this scenario, we can consider the top level objects in the functional model as the system components referred to in Intermediate CO-COMO. For the sake of simplicity we assume that effort multipliers are the same for all system components (top level objects) in Project I and Project II. This assumption allows us to view each of these objects, for cost estimation purposes, as having just one component. We also assume that both systems are developed from scratch. Another point is that the development team has extensive experience in working with related projects, allowing us to classify these projects as organic, in COCOMO terminology [3]. Intermediate COCOMO formulas for effort estimation of organic projects are

$$(MM)_{nom} = 3.2 * (KEDSI)^{1.05}$$

$$(MM)_{adj} = (MM)_{nom} * EAF$$

$$EAF = \prod EM_i$$

where KEDSI (thousands of expected delivered source instructions) is the estimated program size in thousands of lines of code, and the EM_i's are the effort multipliers.

Table X and Table XI show the calculated effort adjustment factor (EAF) for Project I and Project II, respectively. Table XII and Table XIII summarize the cost estimation process for Project I and Project II, respectively. The KEDSI values in these tables estimated using the proposed sizing method. In order to express project cost in dollars, the average equivalence in dollars per man-month was also considered for each project.

TABLE IX
COCOMO EFFORT MULTIPLIERS

EM	Significance	EM	Significance
RELY	Required Soft. Reliability	AEXP	Application Experience
DATA	Data Base Size	PCAP	Programmers Capability
CPLX	Product Complexity	VEXP	Virtual Machine Experience
TIME	Execution Time Constraint	LEXP	Prog. Language Experience
STOR	Main Storage Constraint	MODP	Use of Modern Prog. Practice
VIRT	Virtual Machine Volatility	TOOL	Use of Software Tools
TURN	Computer Turnaround Time	SCED	Required Development Schedule
ACAP	Analysts Capability		

TABLE X
EFFORT ADJUSTMENT FACTOR CALCULATION FOR PROJECT I

EM	Rating	Value
RELY	Nominal	1.0
DATA	Low	0.94
CPLX	Nominal	1.0
TIME	Nominal	1.0
STOR	Nominal	1.0
VIRT	Nominal	1.0
TURN	Low	0.87
ACAP	High	0.86
AEXP	Nominal	1.0
PCAP	High	0.86
VEXP	Nominal	1.0
LEXP	Nominal	1.0
MODP	Low	1.10
TOOL	Nominal	1.0
SCED	Nominal	1.0
EAF		0.67

TABLE XI
EFFORT ADJUSTMENT FACTOR CALCULATION FOR PROJECT II

EM	Rating	Value
RELY	Very High	1.40
DATA	Low	0.94
CPLX	Nominal	1.0
TIME	High	1.11
STOR	Nominal	1.0
VIRT	Nominal	1.0
TURN	Nominal	1.0
ACAP	High	0.86
AEXP	High	0.91
PCAP	Nominal	1.0
VEXP	Nominal	1.0
LEXP	Nominal	1.0
MODP	Nominal	1.0
TOOL	Nominal	1.0
SCED	Nominal	1.0
EAF		1.14

TABLE XII
COST ESTIMATION FOR PROJECT I

Component	KEDSI	EAF	MM nom	MM adj	$K/MM	Cost ($K)
Text Processing System	Minimum 8.51	0.67	30	20	5.0	Minimum 101.54
	Expected 10.59	0.67	38	26	5.0	Expected 127.74
	Maximum 13.71	0.67	48	32	5.0	Maximum 160.61

The size estimation technique proposed in this paper enables us to say that the ultimate size of Project I will be 10.59 KEDSI, with possible deviation interval of -2.08 KEDSI, $+2.58$ KEDSI. For Project II the expected final size is 37.51 KEDSI, with possible deviation interval of -3.26 KEDSI, $+3.56$ KEDSI.

As a consequence, we may also say that the cost of Project I will be \$127,740 (dollars), with possible devia-

TABLE XIII
COST ESTIMATION FOR PROJECT II

Component	KEDSI	EAF	MM nom	MM adj	$K/MM	Cost ($K)
Operating System	Minimum 34.24	1.14	131	149	5.5	Minimum 819.74
	Expected 37.51	1.14	144	164	5.5	Expected 902.14
	Maximum 41.07	1.14	158	180	5.5	Maximum 992.24

tion interval of −$26,200 (dollars), +$32,870 (dollars), and the cost of Project II will be $902,140 (dollars), with possible deviation interval of −$82,400 (dollars), +$90,100 (dollars). This type of follow-through of dollarizing fulfills the manager's needs of cost and risk assessment.

VII. CONCLUDING REMARKS

A technique for software size estimation has been proposed. The basis for estimates, when using this method, is the available knowledge of the considered system. In order to capture and represent this knowledge, an object-oriented functional model has been adopted. This functional model provides for a disciplined methodology for decomposing system complexity. This methodology is the key in the process of detailing the functionality of the system in order to enable estimators to achieve more reliable estimates. The object-oriented paradigm plays an important role in this process since it embeds a strong correspondence between specifications and implementation. This characteristic makes it easier to relate an object functions, sometimes called methods, and data to the amount of code necessary to implement it.

In order to relate previous experience with size estimation in a certain organization, the proposed sizing technique incorporates a statistical approach. This approach also enables one to have an objectively derived confidence interval for the estimates, what has been a desire among software metrics researchers.

The presented methodology is still subjective, since it ultimately depends on expert estimations. Nevertheless, this subjectiveness is controlled by disciplined capturing of system knowledge and statistical correlation with past experience. The methodology also provides a criterion that enables one to know when the amount of subjectiveness related to the estimates prevents its use. Also, certain issues like nonfunctional requirements influence and low biasing in software estimations have been considered in this sizing method.

Finally, we saw that the utilization of this sizing technique with cost estimation models enables these models to predict system cost with known accuracy, what provides for better controlled and managed software projects.

ACKNOWLEDGMENT

We are thankful to Dr. G. Cobb (with Lockheed, Austin), for various insights concerning the ideas upon which this paper is built, and to the reviewers, for their helpful suggestions.

REFERENCES

[1] A. J. Albrecht and J. E. Gaffney, "Software function, source lines of code, and development effort prediction: A software science validation," *IEEE Trans. Software Eng.*, vol. SE-9, no. 6, pp. 639-647, Nov. 1983.
[2] J. W. Bailey and V. R. Basili, "A meta-model for source development resource expenditures," in *Proc. Fifth Int. Conf. Software Engineering*, 1981, pp. 107-116.
[3] B. Boehm, *Software Engineering Economics.* Englewood Cliffs, NJ: Prentice-Hall, 1981.
[4] G. Booch, "Object-oriented development," *IEEE Trans. Software Eng.*, vol. SE-12, no. 2, pp. 211-221, Feb. 1986.
[5] R. N. Britcher and F. E. Gaffney, "Reliable size estimation for software decomposed as state machines," in *Proc. COMPSAC 1985*, pp. 104-106.
[6] A. Bryant and J. A. Kirkham, "B. A. Boehm software engineering economics: A review essay," *ACM SIGSOFT Software Eng. Notes*, vol. 8, no. 3, pp. 44-60, July 1983.
[7] S. D. Conte, H. E. Dunsmore, and V. Y. Shen, *Software Engineering Metrics and Models.* New York: Benjamin/Cummings, 1986.
[8] F. R. Freiman and R. E. Park, "Price software model version 3: An overview," in *Proc. IEEE-PINY Workshop Quantitative Software Models*, Oct. 1979, pp. 32-41.
[9] G. P. Fitsos, "Vocabulary effects in software science," in *Proc. COMPSAC 1980*, pp. 751-756.
[10] S. Gross, K. B. Tom, and E. E. Ayers, "Software sizing and cost estimation study," in *Proc. 19th Annu. Dep. Defense Cost Analysis Symp.*, Xerox Training Center, Leesburg, VA, Sept. 17-20, 1985.
[11] J. R. Herd, J. N. Postak, W. E. Russel, and K. R. Stewart, "Software cost estimation study—Study results," Doty Associates, Inc., Rockville, MD, Final Tech. Rep. RADC-TR-77-220, June 1977.
[12] M. Itakura and A. Takayanagi, "A model for estimating program size and its evaluation," in *Proc. Sixth Int. Conf. Software Engineering*, Sept. 1982, pp. 104-109.
[13] K. A. Jamsa, "Object-oriented design vs structured design—A student's perspective," *ACM SIGSOFT Software Eng. Notes*, vol. 9, no. 1, pp. 43-49, Jan. 1984.
[14] R. W. Jensen, "A comparison of the Jensen and COCOMO schedule and cost estimation models," in *Proc. Int. Soc. Parametric Analysis*, 1984, pp. 96-106.
[15] L. Ledbetter and B. Cox, "Software ICs," *Byte*, vol. 10, no. 6, pp. 307-316, June 1985.
[16] A. V. Levitin, "On predicting program size by program vocabulary," in *Proc. IEEE COMPSAC 1985*, pp. 98-103.
[17] ——, "How to measure program size and how not to," in *Proc. IEEE COMPSAC 1986*, pp. 314-318.
[18] ——, "Investigating predictability of program size," in *Proc. IEEE COMPSAC 1987*, pp. 231-235.
[19] B. Liskov and J. Guttag, *Abstraction and Specification in Program Development.* Cambridge, MA: MIT Press, 1986.
[20] T. de Marco, *Structured Analysis and System Specification.* Englewood Cliffs, NJ: Prentice-Hall, 1979.
[21] D. L. Parnas, "A technique for the specification of software modules with examples," *Commun. ACM*, vol. 15, pp. 330-336, May 1972.
[22] ——, "On the criteria to be used in decomposing systems into modules," *Commun. ACM*, vol. 15, pp. 1053-1058, Dec. 1972.
[23] G. A. Pascoe, "Elements of object-oriented programming," *Byte*, vol. 11, no. 8, pp. 139-144, Aug. 1986.
[24] R. Pressman, *Software Engineering: A Practitioner's Approach.* New York: McGraw-Hill, 1982.
[25] L. H. Putman, "A general empirical solution to the macro software sizing and estimation problem," *IEEE Trans. Software Eng.*, vol. SE-4, no. 4, pp. 345-361, July 1978.
[26] L. H. Putnam and A. Fitzsimmons, "Estimating software costs," *Datamation*, pp. 189-198, Sept. 1979; continued in *Datamation*, pp. 171-178, Oct. 1979, pp. 137-140, Nov. 1979.
[27] C. V. Ramamoorthy, A. Prakash, W. Tsai, and Y. Usuda, "Software engineering: Problems and perspectives," *Computer*, pp. 191-209, Oct. 1984.
[28] D. T. Ross and K. E. Scoman, "Structured analysis for requirements definition," *IEEE Trans. Software Eng.*, vol. SE-3, no. 1, Jan. 1977.
[29] M. Stark and E. Seidewitz, "Towards a general object-oriented de-

velopment methodology," Goddard Space Flight Center, Greenbelt, MD, Internal Rep., 1986.

[30] ——, "Towards a general object-oriented ADA life-cycle," in *Proc. Joint Ada Conf.*, Mar. 1987, pp. 213-222.

[31] E. Seidewitz, "General object-oriented software development: Background and experience," in *Proc. 21st Hawaii Int. Conf. System Science*, Jan. 1988.

[32] M. Stefik, "Object-oriented programming: Themes and variations," *AI Mag.*, pp. 40-62, Jan. 1986.

[33] C. R. Symons, "Function point analysis: Difficulties and improvements," *IEEE Trans. Software Eng.*, vol. 14, no. 1, pp. 2-11, Jan. 1988.

[34] R. C. Tausworthe, "Deep space network software cost estimation model," Jet Propulsion Lab., Pasadena, CA, Publ. 81-7, 1981.

[35] L. Tesler, "Programming experiences (with object-oriented languages)," *Byte*, vol. 11, no. 8, pp. 195-206, Aug. 1986.

[36] C. E. Walston and C. P. Felix, "A method of programming measurement and estimation," *IBM Syst. J.*, vol. 16, no. 1, pp. 54-73, 1977.

[37] A. S. Wang, "The estimation of software size and effort: An approach based on the evolution of software metrics," Ph.D. dissertation, Dep. Comput. Sci., Purdue Univ., Aug. 1984.

[38] G. W. Weinberg and E. L. Schulman, "Goals and performance in computer programming," *Human Factors*, vol. 16, no. 1, pp. 70-77, 1974.

[39] R. W. Wolverton, "Software costing," in *Software Engineering*, C. R. Vick and C. V. Ramamoorthy, Eds. New York: Van Nostrand, 1981.

[40] R. T. Yeh, P. Zave, A. P. Conn, and G. E. Cole, Jr., "Software requirements: New directions and perspectives," in *Software Engineering*, C. R. Vick and C. V. Ramamoorthy, Eds. New York: Van Nostrand, 1981.

Luiz A. Laranjeira (S'89) was born in Belo Horizonte, Brazil, in 1958. He received the B.S. degree from the University of Brasilia, Brasilia, Brazil, in 1979, and the M.Sc. degree from the Federal University of Rio de Janeiro, Rio de Janeiro, Brazil, in 1983, both in electrical engineering.

From 1984 until 1987 he was with the Research and Development Center for Communications, Brasilia, as Software Manager of the Division of Digital Projects. Since 1987 he has been a graduate student with the Department of Electrical and Computer Engineering of the University of Texas at Austin. His research interests are software engineering, parallel algorithms, and fault tolerance.

Mr. Laranjeira is a member of Tau Beta Pi.

Chapter 7

Organizing for Success

We trained hard . . . but it seemed that every time we were beginning to form into teams, we would be reorganized. I was to learn later in life that we tend to meet any new situation by reorganizing; and a wonderful method it can be for creating the illusion of progress while producing confusion, inefficiency, and demoralization.

—Petronius Arbiter, 210 BC

Overview

For most managers, the term "organization" means some formalized structure of roles or positions from which they must operate to get their jobs done. To arrive at this structure, firms define management's span of control and authority–responsibility, staff–project–line, and departmental relationships. Some of these resulting structures are flat, whereas others are hierarchical. Some are bureaucratic, whereas others are not. Some are product-oriented, whereas others are customer based. Some are functional, whereas others are grouped into projects. None stay static.

Unfortunately, most software managers have little to say about how the firm organizes. Instead, their influence is directed toward creating structures that allow them to communicate, coordinate, and work within and across operational units. Such structures include software councils, process groups, working groups, committees, and interdisciplinary teams. These structures allow managers to use all of the talent available within the firm to accomplish the task at hand. Being able to go across organizational boundaries is important because needed skills may reside in other units (the legal department has licensing skills, systems engineering may have the architectural skills, etc.).

New forms of organization are appearing as firms streamline their operations, become more global, and strive to be more service-oriented. In addition, technologies like the Internet, groupware, and distance education have made it possible for organizations whose workforces are geographically dispersed to operate in a virtual environment that appears as a single entity to team members.

The three articles that follow explain why leaner organizations continue to be so popular. The important concepts of core competency and service are explained as various organizational options are reviewed and analyzed. Although organizations frequently change, the principles upon which they are founded do not. As a reflection of this fact, I have not changed any papers in this chapter from the last edition. However, I have included papers on distribution under emerging management topics in Chapter 14.

Article Summaries

Staffing and Organization in the Engineering of Systems, by David W. Oliver. This new article provides a good introduction to the human issues associated with staffing an organization. It discusses organizational structure from a behavioral point of view by focusing on individual and group dynamics in the context of single and shared reward systems. It goes on to investigate organizing by product/service teams, function, and cooperation and competition. The paper was selected because it provides a good introduction to organizational theory.

The Core Competence of the Corporation, by C. K. Prahalad and Gary Hamel. The concept of core competency has made many companies rethink how to structure their corporations. In essence, this concept stimulates organizations to cluster products around the competencies that they have identified as the root of their competitive advantage (e.g., the key to market dominance in computers is competency in semiconductors). When viewed from a global context, such clustering permits cross-functional teams from geographically separated units to cooperate across business unit boundaries to put strategies into practice. This article provides insight into the reasons why firms have moved to new organizational structures as they downsize.

Survival Patterns in Fast-Moving Software Organizations, by Lena Holmberg and Lars Mathiassen. This article discusses how to survive in an environment in which you must respond quickly to technological options and market needs. It uses a case study to highlight the survival patterns that drive innovation, management priorities, and improvement. The article highlights the lessons learned as choices were made and as the organization in the case study struggled for survival.

Key Terms

Five terms, defined as follows, are important to understanding the topic of organization as used within this chapter:

1. **Functional organization.** An organization that groups people by skill or specialty (such as software or hardware engineering) in one department, reporting to a single manager.
2. **Line organization.** That part of the functional organization to which the authority for performing a task has been designated.
3. **Matrix organization.** A combination of function and project forms of organization in which the line is responsible for providing skilled people and the project for programmatic performance.
4. **Organizing.** Those management activities conducted to structure efforts that involve collaboration and communication so that it is effectively performed.
5. **Project organization.** The form of organization in which all of the people working on the project report to the project manager.

For Your Bookshelf

I am still looking for a good text to recommend on the topic of organization. Most of the books that are on the market treat the topic too traditionally. They do not take changes in organizational theory and technology into account. They fail to address globalization issues. They are masters of the obvious, lack vision, and do little to help you structure organizations for the modern corporation. Few of these texts assess the impact of software business functions on the organization nor do they look at software core competencies. With the exception of the book by McMahon, *Virtual Project Management,* reviewed in the Bibliography under emerging software management paradigms, even fewer of the books that I reviewed discuss distributing the work and building a collaborative work environment in which tasks are managed remotely across distances using current technology and tools. Perhaps other books will be published in the near future to correct this imbalance.

Staffing and Organization in the Engineering of Systems

David W. Oliver

Model Based Systems, Inc.

133 Ashdown Road, Ballston Lake, N.Y. 12019

dwoliver@ix.netcom.com

Abstract

The techniques of model based systems engineering are applied to the human issues of staffing, organization, and culture. This supplements IEEE standards and contributions by IEEE ECBS and INCOSE working groups on the technical process, the management process, a taxonomy for tools to automate the processes, and a mapping of the process onto tools. This paper draws on abstractions and representations from the fields of anthropology and psychology and recasts them in executable models. This results in greater rigor in expression and analysis, and the potential to automate efficient capture of data and its transformation into the notations and views wanted by other disciplines. It provides a basis for rigorous discussion of staffing, organization, and culture through review and improvement of models. The analysis connects goals, rewards and tasks to classes of cultural behavior, and to four basic organization architectures. It applies to business re-engineering.

1. Introduction

The success of systems projects depends upon the staffing and organization of the activity as well as upon the more technical issues like a technical process, a management process, automation, and documentation. The manner of staffing and organizing has a direct bearing on the effectiveness of inter-communication among the persons and groups performing the work. The importance of inter-communication to success was pointed out in a review [1] of the status and needs of the engineering of computer based systems reported by the IEEE Technical Committee on Engineering of Computer Based Systems.

This paper applies to staffing and organization issues, the process and modeling methods which have been applied previously to define the discipline of engineering systems, [2], [3], [4], [5]. The approach used here recognizes that the appropriate organization and staffing for a particular organization depends upon the culture of that organization. Accordingly this paper models and describes the basic abstractions associated with organizations and culture. From these abstractions a description of organization and staffing alternatives is derived. There is an extremely large body of ex-

isting literature which describes organizations and culture. No attempt is made here to review that literature. Instead the basic abstractions and alternatives are modeled with the executable models which have been applied to the description of systems. The notation used here to model the basic abstractions of structure is Object Modeling Technique, OMT, [6].

2. A Taxonomy for Cultural Behavior

This description of culture begins by providing a simple model for groups and a classification of several kinds of cultural behavior for people acting in a group. Real organizations may consist of groups built from other different smaller groups. Figure 1. models how groups are built. The diamond is the symbol for aggregation.

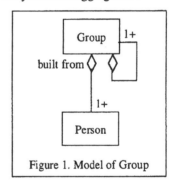

Figure 1. Model of Group

The simplest top level classification as shown in Figure 2.

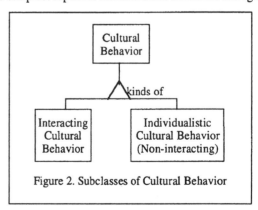

Figure 2. Subclasses of Cultural Behavior

This classification of the cultural behavior of groups or per-

Reprinted from *Proceedings of the 1997 Workshop on Engineering of Computer-Based Systems (ECBS '97).*

sons divides them into classes where the groups or persons either interact or do not interact. The triangle is the symbol for classification.

A non-interacting person or group or has defined its own goals, tasks, and rewards independent of any larger aggregation. Such a group, person, and their behavior is commonly termed individualistic. Individualistic behavior is noted as one of the important types, but is not modeled in further detail.

It is useful to refine the description of Cultural Behavior by examining its relationships to goals, rewards and tasks. Groups and persons pursue goals by executing tasks and are motivated by the rewards they receive which are a result of what is achieved. The reward is based on what was accomplished and the tasks performed. These relationships are modeled in Figure 3.

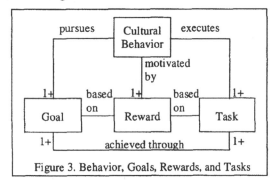

Figure 3. Behavior, Goals, Rewards, and Tasks

Three independent classifications for interacting cultural behavior shown in Figure 4. These classes are based on the

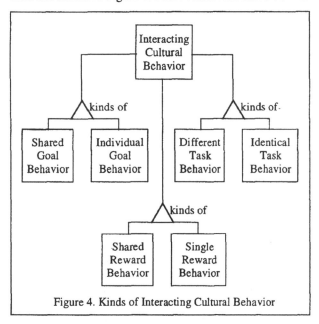

Figure 4. Kinds of Interacting Cultural Behavior

observation that the groups or persons may share or not share the same goals. They may share the reward or it may

go to one group or person. They may perform identical tasks or they may perform different tasks.

The six independent subclasses of Interacting Cultural Behavior in Figure 4. can be combined in eight ways. If one adds the subclass of Individualistic Cultural Behavior, then there are nine subclasses that have been enumerated based on the basic abstractions of interaction, goals, rewards, and tasks. It is useful to examine the characteristics of each of these nine subclasses to see how they correspond to the literature on culture and to our common words for cultural behavior. Table 1. lists the characteristics of the subclasses that have been described.

TABLE 1.

Goal	Reward	Task	Inter-act	Stable	Subclass Name
share	share	diff.	yes	yes	1. Cooperative
share	share	same	yes	yes	2. Competitive
not sh	not sh	diff	yes	yes	3. Rivalry
not sh	not sh	same	yes	yes	4. Rivalry
not sh	share	diff	yes	no	5.
not sh	share	same	yes	no	6.
share	not sh	diff	yes	no	7.
share	not sh	same	yes	no	8.
don't care	don't care	don't care	no	yes	9. Individualistic

Subclasses 5. - 8. are not stable and hence no attempt was made to name them. The lack of stability arises from their characteristics regarding goals and rewards. If the goals are shared, and the groups or persons are interacting, but reward is not shared (one gets it all), then the groups or persons over time are strongly discouraged from continuing the interaction. The subclass 7. and 8. are unstable. Note that the reward might be part of the product produced, money, respect, adulation, status, etc. If the goals are not shared and the groups or persons are interacting, and reward is shared, then the groups or persons become dissatisfied over what is being accomplished. Subclasses 5. and 6. are unstable.

In subclass 1., Cooperative Behavior, the goals and rewards are shared, but the tasks are different. This subclass is stable provided the participants view the distribution of tasks and reward to be appropriate. Rewards do not have to be identical. It is the type of behavior that is observed within

252

a team playing a sport like basketball or in the development of systems by an integrated product team. Because of the differences in tasks it is very difficult to judge the relative performance of persons or groups except by those who are directly participating and have depth of knowledge about the contributions that have been made. The reward scheme works well when team results are rewarded relative to other teams, and the team members agree with distribution of reward within the team. A frequent emotional response in well functioning cooperative behavior is a strong feeling and focus on being an accepted part of a successful group. Group identity and pride become strong. Responsibility to the group becomes strong. Individual proclivities are suppressed to enhance group performance and cohesion.

Subclass 2., Competitive Behavior differs from that of Cooperative Behavior in that the tasks are identical. Because the tasks performed are identical, the performance of groups or persons can be carefully measured and publicized. This is the subclass of behavior that enables groups or persons to improve their skills and performance. It is important that the reward be distributed among the competitors and not go exclusively to one competitor. It is important that the distribution of reward among competitors be judged by the competitors to be appropriate relative to the performances. In the world of sports, the golf and tennis tours are organized on this basis. When Reginald Jones was retiring from GE, his direct reports competed to replace him. One of them, Jack Welch, became CEO of GE. The others, however, were supported and rewarded by GE in other ways, because there was only one CEO position. Stan Gault, for example, became CEO of Rubbermaid where he produced outstanding results. His desire to become a CEO was both recognized and supported. Competiton proceeds based on a set of formal or informal rules as to what one is allowed to do and not allowed to do. The emotional responses to competition are feelings of competence, and of respect for those with both greater and lesser skills. Pride is developed in doing one's best and in the competition activity itself.

In the common use of english language, the word competition is often used in ways that overlap the meanings of rivalry or antagonism. The distinction is fuzzy. It is important to capture the difference between subclass 2. and subclass 3. In this paper the words competition and rivalry are used with very distinct and different meanings.

In subclasses 3. and 4., both named Rivalry, neither the goals nor the rewards are shared. It is characteristic that one group or person gets all the reward and others get nothing. The focus of the activity is more on eliminating other competitors than in improving one's skills. It is an extremely important subclass because it does exist and has important uses. It is critical that it exist to enforce the rules that provide security and stability to society and groups. It applies

sanctions against unwanted behavior to redirect it toward desired behavior. A criminal and the crime victim are rivals. A criminal and the justice system are rivals. A referee in sports is a rival to an angry player who refuses to accept a ruling and attacks him. This is the subclass of control, enforcing rules, warfare and vengeance. In a situation of promotion to a single position, it is the subclass of removing competitors who receive nothing or are eliminated by discrediting them or physically injuring them. The emotional response is one of victory or of having been vanquished. When the victors continue, this often occurs by engaging another competitor.

The classification of Cultural Behavior in Figure 4. can now be restructured into a useful set of four subclasses as shown in Figure 5.

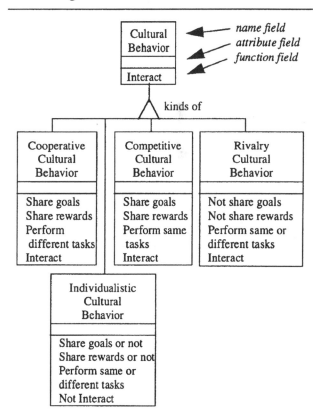

Figure 5. Reclassified Kinds of Cultural Behavior

Large and small industrial organizations are often built from a hierarchy of groups of people. A single organization often contains groups with all three kinds of behavior. A single individual may need to follow any of the three behaviors, depending upon the group in which he is participating and the role which he is playing. A person may be in competition with peers on similar tasks or for advancement. The same person may be in cooperation with another set of peers in design, production or management team projects. The same person may be a rival to a peer, subordinate, or superior in the personnel hierarchy if the established rules are violated and sanctions are to be applied. The three types of behavior frequently exist together because it is important to set and enforce rules for the organization, it is important to cooperate to meet goals, and it is important to compete to improve performance. Individualistic behavior is often counterproductive to the needs of an organization and often needs to be channeled into one of the other forms.

In the Japanese Quality Circles, teams are organized to perform their work cooperatively. A set of teams is assigned the same industrial task, and their relative performance is carefully measured and publicly rewarded, competition among teams. Information is shared about the successful work innovations. Teams are free to adopt these successful innovations or to improve upon them. Management sets the conditions and rules and applies positive rewards through a cooperative process. Management applies sanctions in the few cases where that was required, a rivalry behavior. The predominant behavior is a mixture of cooperation and competition which combines the advantages of cohesive group effort toward a common goal, with competition to improve performance through experimentation and measurement of results.

These considerations apply not only to industrial organizations, but also to cultures in general. Anthropological studies have used this same classification structure to correlate the cultures of primitive peoples, [7]. The classification has been shown to be useful through practical application. The classification has general applicability because, as shown here, it is based on the realities of basic abstractions: goals, rewards, tasks, interaction, and stability. The research results of anthropology are a bountiful source of techniques and representations for describing organizations and their culture. It is an important and useful result that the modeling techniques for describing systems can capture the abstractions and representations used in fields such as anthropology and psychology. The model based systems engineering approach can be applied to human systems.

The anthropology and psychology literatures provide much more extensive taxonomies and abstractions for describing organizations and behavior than are touched on by this paper. For example, the analysis above considers only the person or group performing the work. A more complete description of cultural behaviors would include a person or group outside the one performing the work. These additions lead to additional behaviors like altruism: vicarious but constructive and instinctually satisfying service to others. In altruism the goals and the rewards are for the benefit of others who do not perform the work. A more complete set of behaviors than described here have been discussed as personal and group coping behaviors which range from beneficial to pathological in their consequences, [8]. They are useful in a more detailed analysis and management of staffing and organization than undertaken here.

The psychology literature also provides detailed taxonomies and definitions for the structure of organizations. One of these taxonomies is useful here to distinguish the kinds of organizations being considered and those excluded in this paper, [9]. It provides a framework for the context studied in this paper. It classifies organizations according to how their membership is chosen. The subclasses are:

- Obligatory Groups, membership is required of the members. An example is prisoners in a prison.
- Accidental Groups, membership is a matter of chance rather than choice. An example is birth into a family, or a social caste.
- Voluntary Groups, membership is chosen by the members because they enjoy the fellowship and is terminated at will. An example is a group of friends who meet to play poker.
- Conditional Groups, membership is contractual and the members agree to terms of participation in return for a role and reward they are given in exchange for their participation. An example is becoming an employee for a business.

The organizations considered in this paper are limited to conditional groups.

A deeper understanding of the meaning of Individualistic Behavior, as defined here, flows from this last taxonomy. The culture of the United States is often described as being individualistic. However, individualistic persons and groups follow their own course without interacting with others. According to the definitions of this paper, the culture of the United States primarily is a combination of Competitive Behavior with Cooperative Behavior; and Rivalry Behavior is imposed for safety and security. At the time of the American revolution the European royalty-class system and the caste system of India restricted cooperation and especially competition based on the Accidental Group into which one was born. This was enforced by the sanctions of Rivalry Behavior in those societies. Courageous persons sought opportunity and freedom to both compete and cooperate freely by immigrating to the United States. The distinction between the U.S. and the class based societies or totalitarian obligatory societies is the ability to freely compete and cooperate under moderate and popularly determined laws and sanctions. The success of the American culture in penetrating other societies around the world is due to the heightened efficiency and better results obtained by combining the effectiveness of cooperative group efforts with the improvements in performance from competitive efforts.

3. Application to Conditional Organizations

Structural architectures are considered only for Conditional Organizations because these are the predominant type in business in the free world. Such an organization is built from a management organization, workers who create the product/service which is sold, infrastructure staff who provide support to management and product/service workers, and physical plant. This aggregation is shown in Figure 6., which includes typical functions performed by each of the organization components. Analysis is not provided here for the infrastructure staff or the physical plant components.

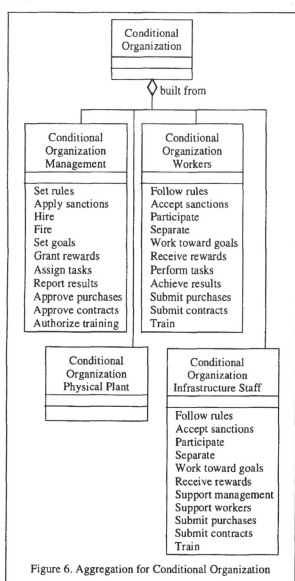

Figure 6. Aggregation for Conditional Organization

It is necessary for the workers to engage in both cooperative and competitive behavior. They must cooperate to create and sell product competitively with other organizations. They must compete to improve their own skills, to find more efficient ways to work, and to provide a basis for performance evaluation. It is necessary for the management to engage in cooperative and competitive behaviors as de-

scribed above, and also in rivalry behaviors. They must be prepared to enter rivalry behavior where issues require sanctions or even firing of subordinates.

3.1 Organization by Product/Service Teams

Current trends emphasize flattening of the management hierarchy. One person can potentially supervise between about four and twenty subordinates depending upon the intensity of supervision required. The fan out ratio in the management roles hierarchy can be increased to flatten the organization if the degree of autonomy, accountability, and responsibility is increased at lower levels. An effective way to accomplish this is to establish cooperating teams which contain the span of skills needed to develop, manufacture, and sell product. Large businesses have multiple customers and products. Teams are then organized around product/customer goals. This is a classic mode of organization based on customers and product, as shown in Figure 7.

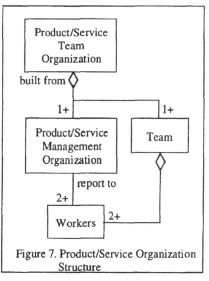

Figure 7. Product/Service Organization Structure

In the most advanced forms the team staffing includes persons from management who have familiarity with business strategy, and people from infrastructure staff who provide finance, purchasing, contractual, human resources expertise, etc. The multiple disciplines on a team need to intercommunicate. Modeling, which is rigorous and executable, facilitates the communication by removing ambiguity and providing for transformation of information as needed by disparate disciplines.

The team approach also applies to management itself, where multi discipline teams may be formed to examine and change business strategy, business organization, business culture, or business skills and resources. Communication between these teams and the product/service teams has traditionally faced barriers in precisely what is being stated. This is particularly true for important customer related information which is not in financial form, [10]. A large number of management techniques have been developed to capture this non-financial information. The basic abstractions which they contain are customer perceived quality attributes and customer perceived value attributes, [11]. These management abstractions are transformed into the effectiveness measures of systems engineering.

With the Product/Service Team Organization goals are achieved by the whole team and it is difficult to measure comparative performance for improving efficiency and providing appropriate rewards

3.2 Organization by Function

The traditional way of organizing to emphasize skills is to create an organization hierarchy based on function or discipline: finance, engineering, manufacturing, etc., as shown in Figure 8.

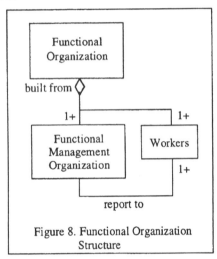

Figure 8. Functional Organization Structure

It tends to create barriers for any single project as the work transitions between one function and another. It impedes design for manufacture, assembly, and field service.

3.3 Organization for Cooperation and Competition, Matrix

The traditional way to structure the organization to account for both teams (cooperation) and skill improvement (competitive) is to use a matrix organization built from team product/service oriented managers, functional managers, and teams composed of workers. Workers are assigned from their functional organizations to teams and report to two managers, as shown in Figure 9.

For matrix organization there exists a substantial literature which includes appropriate conditions for creating such an organization and some of the pathologies that occur with this style of organization, [12]. Matrix organization requires great cooperation among managers in decision making, and an effective resolution mechanism when managers from the functional side and product side have overlapping responsi-

bility and do not agree about the resolution of an important issue. It tends to be expensive in management cost.

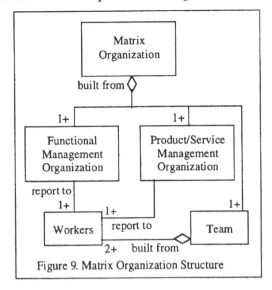

Figure 9. Matrix Organization Structure

3.4 Organization for Cooperation and Competition, Dual Team Organization

A dual team organization is shown in Figure 10, built from a management organization and teams.

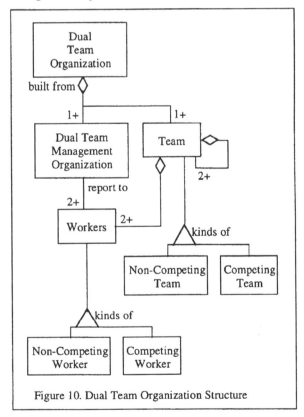

Figure 10. Dual Team Organization Structure

256

A dual team architecture can be created for an organization by using competition among teams and among sets of workers in a single team.

For large projects, the work may be organized in teams composed of teams, a hierarchy of teams, shown by the recursive aggregation on the object, Team. Competition between teams or workers can be applied whenever there is sufficient work for comparable tasks to which several groups or people can be applied. Performance is measured on the comparable tasks. This structure works best where the people or teams in competition participate in the evaluation of work and where the criteria for evaluation are clearly defined and are accepted. Some teams and workers will be competing and some will not. This organization works well where there is public knowledge throughout the organization of the competitive criteria and results, and where the tangible (money, responsibility) and intangible (respect, acknowledgment) rewards are public. This organization structure combines the advantages of cooperative and competitive cultures with a lean management structure. As workers and managers cycle through assigned roles in their careers, they experience the effects of both competition and cooperation. Quality Circles often exhibit this structure.

Appropriate leadership behavior follows from this analysis. The leader:

1. Cares for his subordinates by accepting goals with reasonable risk, assigning tasks commensurate with skills and stretch efforts, and distributing appropriate rewards.
2. Refuses unreasonable risks, tasks, or rewards for subordinates
3. Cares for the interests of his superior based on 1. and 2.
4. Cooperates and competes with peers
5. Applies rivalry when subordinates beyond limits, firing where necessary
6. Applies rivalry when superior out of limits, resigns where necessary

Typical pathologies exist: individualistic behavior looking out for own interests. An example is: submissive behavior toward superior at expense of subordinates coupled with the superior demanding unreasonable risk, tasks, or rewards for subordinates and refusing to hear their information.

4. Selection of Organization Structure

The selection of the organization structure that best fits a particular business is based on the standard best practices of the systems engineering process [13] which employ trade-off analysis based on well defined criteria called effectiveness measures, [14]. The effectiveness measures are the few top level requirements which are so essential that the system will succeed or fail based on meeting them in a near optimal manner.

A reasonable set of effectiveness measures for selecting an organization structure for a business are:
1. High customer perceived product quality
2. Low customer perceived product cost
3. Low product development cost
4. Short time to market
5. Expert and efficient engineering staff

The selection of particular subsets of these effectiveness measures leads to a trade-off that results in selection of a particular organization structure.

Organization by Function

Organization by Function emerges from trade-off when the dominant effectiveness measure is:

5. Expert and efficient engineering staff.

In this organization structure the engineering is not most strongly customer focussed.

Organization by Product/Service Teams

Organization by Product/Service Teams emerges when the dominant effectiveness measures are jointly:

1. High customer perceived product quality

2. Low customer perceived product cost

3. Low product development cost

4. Short time to market

In this structure the engineering is not most strongly focused on maintaining, improving, and rewarding engineering expertise.

Organization for Cooperation and Competition, Matrix

Organization by Matrix emerges when the dominant effectiveness measures are jointly:

1. High customer perceived product quality

2. Low customer perceived product cost

4. Short time to market

5. Expert and efficient engineering staff

In this structure the engineering is not most strongly focussed on engineering development cost and overhead.

Organization for Cooperation and Competition, Dual Team Organization

This organization structure emerges from equal weighting of all five effectiveness measures. It requires observant management, monitoring the quality of both competitive and cooperative work, and a carefully structured reward system to be able to reward both cooperation and competition. Implementation often requires management training.

5. Conclusion

The best practices and rigorous modeling techniques of model based systems engineering have been successfully applied to the human issues of staffing, organization, and culture. They are very useful in re-engineering businesses, and effectively define and link structure, behavior, culture, and reward systems.

The models utilize some of the abstractions and representations that have been developed in the fields of anthropology and psychology. The models provide a more rigorous set of definitions and descriptions than provided by that literature in text form. This results in greater rigor in expression of the abstractions, the potential to automate the descriptions and representations for efficient capture, and the potential to transform the information to the notations and views wanted by other disciplines. It provides a basis for rigorous discussion of staffing, organization, and culture through review and improvement of models.

The modeling analysis has produced a useful taxonomy of cultures based on the fundamental realities of goals, rewards, tasks, interaction, and organization stability. It shows how goals, tasks, and rewards must be treated in each of the cultures. The sanctions of rivalry culture are necessary to modify behavior toward the desired cultural norm and to limit extreme disruptive behaviors. The combination of cooperation and competition is shown to be a powerful basis for organizing businesses. Four basic organization architectures are modeled: Functional Organization, Product/Service Team Organization, Matrix Organization, and Dual Team Organization architectures. Which of these architectures are used in an organization depends upon the present status of that organization, and on the goals and effectiveness measures that are appropriate to that organization in its marketplace.

6. References

[1] Stephanie White, Mack Alford, Julian Holtzman, Stephen Kuehl, Brian McCay, David W. Oliver, David Owens, Colin Tully, and Alan Willey, "Systems Engineering of Computer Based Systems", Computer, Vol 26, pp. 54, Nov. 1993

[2] Ken Jackson and David W. Oliver, "Report of the ECBS Process and Information Model Working Group", 1994 Tutorial and Workshop on Systems Engineering of Computer-Based Systems, pp. 170, May, 1994, Stockholm

[3] Ian Pyle, Peter Hruschka, Michael Lissandre, and Ken Jackson, Real Time Systems, John Wiley, 1993

[4] David W. Oliver, "Systems Engineering & Software Engineering, Contrasts and Synergies", Fifth Annual International Symposium of the National Council on Systems Engineering, Vol. I, pp. 701, St. Louis, MO., July 1995

[5] David W. Oliver, "Creating Object Models - Design and Architecture", International IEEE Symposium and Workshop on Engineering of Computer-Based Systems, March 11-15, 1996, Friedrichshafen, Germany

[6] James Rumbaugh, Michael Blaha, William Premerlani, Frederick Eddy, and William Lorensen, Object-Oriented Modeling and Design, Prentice Hall, 1991.

[7] Margaret Mead, editor, Cooperation and Competition among Primitive Peoples, McGraw-Hill Book company, 1937

[8] George E. Valiant, Adaptation to Life, Little Brown and Company, Boston, 1977

[9] Eric Berne, The Structure and Dynamics of Organizations and Groups, page 168, J.B Lippincott Company, 1963

[10] Bradley T. Gale, Managing Customer Value: Creating Quality and Service That Customers Can See, The Free Press, New York, 1994.

[11] David W. Oliver, Timothy P. Kelliher, and James G. Keegan Jr., Engineering Complex Systems Using Models and Objects, Chapter 15, McGraw-Hill, New York, 1996

[12] Stanley M. Davis and Paul R. Lawrence, Matrix, Addison Wesley Publishing Company, Reading, Massachusetts, 1977

[13] David W. Oliver, "An Analysis of the Model Based Systems Engineering Process", Sixth Annual International Symposium of the National Council on Systems Engineering, Vol. I, pp. 369, Boston, MA., July 1996

[14] David W. Oliver, "Trade-of Analysis in Model Based Systems Engineering", Sixth Annual International Symposium of the National Council on Systems Engineering, Vol. I, pp. 307, Boston, MA., July 1996

The Core Competence of the Corporation

by C.K. Prahalad and Gary Hamel

The most powerful way to prevail in global competition is still invisible to many companies. During the 1980s, top executives were judged on their ability to restructure, declutter, and delayer their corporations. In the 1990s, they'll be judged on their ability to identify, cultivate, and exploit the core competencies that make growth possible—indeed, they'll have to rethink the concept of the corporation itself.

Consider the last ten years of GTE and NEC. In the early 1980s, GTE was well positioned to become a major player in the evolving information technology industry. It was active in telecommunications. Its operations spanned a variety of businesses including telephones, switching and transmission systems, digital PABX, semiconductors, packet switching, satellites, defense systems, and lighting products. And GTE's Entertainment Products Group, which pro-

C.K. Prahalad is professor of corporate strategy and international business at the University of Michigan. Gary Hamel is lecturer in business policy and management at the London Business School. Their most recent HBR article, "Strategic Intent" (May-June 1989), won the 1989 McKinsey Award for excellence. This article is based on research funded by the Gatsby Charitable Foundation.

duced Sylvania color TVs, had a position in related display technologies. In 1980, GTE's sales were $9.98 billion, and net cash flow was $1.73 billion. NEC, in contrast, was much smaller, at $3.8 billion in sales. It had a comparable technological base and computer businesses, but it had no experience as an operating telecommunications company.

Yet look at the positions of GTE and NEC in 1988. GTE's 1988 sales were $16.46 billion, and NEC's sales were considerably higher at $21.89 billion. GTE has, in effect, become a telephone operating company with a position in defense and lighting products. GTE's other businesses are small in global terms. GTE has divested Sylvania TV and Telenet, put switching, transmission, and digital PABX into joint ventures, and closed down semiconductors. As a result, the international position of GTE has eroded. Non-U.S. revenue as a percent of total revenue dropped from 20% to 15% between 1980 and 1988.

NEC has emerged as the world leader in semiconductors and as a first-tier player in telecommunications products and computers. It has consolidated its position in mainframe computers. It has moved beyond public switching and transmission to include such lifestyle products as mobile telephones, facsimile machines, and laptop computers – bridging the gap between telecommunications and office automation. NEC is the only company in the world to be in the top five in revenue in telecommunications, semiconductors, and mainframes. Why did these two companies, starting with comparable business portfolios, perform so differently? Largely because NEC conceived of itself in terms of "core competencies," and GTE did not.

Rethinking the Corporation

Once, the diversified corporation could simply point its business units at particular end product markets and admonish them to become world leaders. But with market boundaries changing ever more quickly, targets are elusive and capture is at best temporary. A few companies have proven themselves adept at inventing new markets, quickly entering emerging markets, and dramatically shifting patterns of customer choice in established markets. These are the ones to emulate. The critical task for management is to create an organization capable of infusing products with irresistible functionality or, better yet, creating products that customers need but have not yet even imagined.

This is a deceptively difficult task. Ultimately, it requires radical change in the management of major companies. It means, first of all, that top managements of Western companies must assume responsibility for competitive decline. Everyone knows about high interest rates, Japanese protectionism, outdated antitrust laws, obstreperous unions, and impatient investors. What is harder to see, or harder to acknowledge, is how little added momentum companies actually get from political or macroeconomic "relief." Both the theory and practice of Western management have created a drag on our forward motion. It is the principles of management that are in need of reform.

NEC versus GTE, again, is instructive and only one of many such comparative cases we analyzed to understand the changing basis for global leadership. Early in the 1970s, NEC articulated a strategic intent to exploit the convergence of computing and communications, what it called "C&C." Success, top management reckoned, would hinge on acquiring competencies, particularly in semiconductors. Management adopted an appropriate "strategic architecture," summarized by C&C, and then communicated its intent to the whole organization and the outside world during the mid-1970s.

NEC constituted a "C&C Committee" of top managers to oversee the development of core products and core competencies. NEC put in place coordination groups and committees that cut across the interests of individual businesses. Consistent with its strategic architecture, NEC shifted enormous resources to strengthen its position in components and central processors. By using collaborative arrangements to multiply internal resources, NEC was able to accumulate a broad array of core competencies.

NEC carefully identified three interrelated streams of technological and market evolution. Top management determined that computing would evolve from large mainframes to distributed processing, components from simple ICs to VLSI, and communications from mechanical cross-bar exchange to complex digital systems we now call ISDN. As things evolved further, NEC reasoned, the computing, communications, and components businesses would so overlap that it would be very hard to distinguish among them, and that there would be enormous opportunities for any company that had built the competencies needed to serve all three markets.

NEC top management determined that semiconductors would be the company's most important

> **Why did NEC enter myriad alliances between 1980 and 1988? To learn and absorb other companies' skills.**

"core product." It entered into myriad strategic alliances – over 100 as of 1987 – aimed at building competencies rapidly and at low cost. In mainframe computers, its most noted relationship was with Honeywell and Bull. Almost all the collaborative arrangements in the semiconductor-component field were oriented toward technology access. As they entered collaborative arrangements, NEC's operating managers understood the rationale for these alliances and the goal of internalizing partner skills. NEC's director of research summed up its competence acquisition during the 1970s and 1980s this way: "From an investment standpoint, it was much quicker and cheaper to use foreign technology. There wasn't a need for us to develop new ideas."

No such clarity of strategic intent and strategic architecture appeared to exist at GTE. Although senior executives discussed the implications of the evolving information technology industry, no commonly accepted view of which competencies would be re-

1. For a fuller discussion, see our article, "Strategic Intent" HBR May-June 1989, p. 63.

quired to compete in that industry were communicated widely. While significant staff work was done to identify key technologies, senior line managers continued to act as if they were managing independent business units. Decentralization made it difficult to focus on core competencies. Instead, individual businesses became increasingly dependent on outsiders for critical skills, and collaboration became a route to staged exits. Today, with a new management team in place, GTE has repositioned itself to apply its competencies to emerging markets in telecommunications services.

The Roots of Competitive Advantage

The distinction we observed in the way NEC and GTE conceived of themselves – a portfolio of competencies versus a portfolio of businesses – was repeated across many industries. From 1980 to 1988, Canon grew by 264%, Honda by 200%. Compare that with Xerox and Chrysler. And if Western managers were once anxious about the low cost and high quality of Japanese imports, they are now overwhelmed by the pace at which Japanese rivals are inventing new markets, creating new products, and enhancing them. Canon has given us personal copiers; Honda has moved from motorcycles to four-wheel off-road buggies. Sony developed the 8mm camcorder, Yamaha, the digital piano. Komatsu developed an underwater remote-controlled bulldozer, while Casio's latest gambit is a small-screen color LCD television. Who would have anticipated the evolution of these vanguard markets?

In more established markets, the Japanese challenge has been just as disquieting. Japanese companies are generating a blizzard of features and functional enhancements that bring technological sophistication to everyday products. Japanese car producers have been pioneering four-wheel steering, four-valve-per-cylinder engines, in-car navigation systems, and sophisticated electronic engine-management

systems. On the strength of its product features, Canon is now a player in facsimile transmission machines, desktop laser printers, even semiconductor manufacturing equipment.

In the short run, a company's competitiveness derives from the price/performance attributes of current products. But the survivors of the first wave of global competition, Western and Japanese alike, are all converging on similar and formidable standards for product cost and quality – minimum hurdles for continued competition, but less and less important as sources of differential advantage. In the long run, competitiveness derives from an ability to build, at lower cost and more speedily than competitors, the core competencies that spawn unanticipated products. The real sources of advantage are to be found in management's ability to consolidate corporatewide technologies and production skills into competencies that empower individual businesses to adapt quickly to changing opportunities.

Senior executives who claim that they cannot build core competencies either because they feel the autonomy of business units is sacrosanct or because

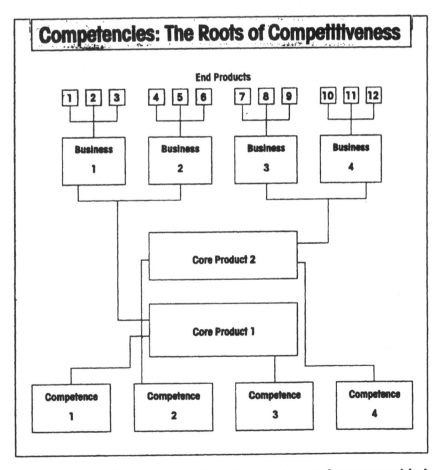

Competencies: The Roots of Competitiveness

The corporation, like a tree, grows from its roots. Core products are nourished by competencies and engender business units, whose fruit are end products.

their feet are held to the quarterly budget fire should think again. The problem in many Western companies is not that their senior executives are any less capable than those in Japan nor that Japanese companies possess greater technical capabilities. Instead, it is their adherence to a concept of the corporation that unnecessarily limits the ability of individual businesses to fully exploit the deep reservoir of technological capability that many American and European companies possess.

The diversified corporation is a large tree. The trunk and major limbs are core products, the smaller branches are business units; the leaves, flowers, and fruit are end products. The root system that provides nourishment, sustenance, and stability is the core competence. You can miss the strength of competitors by looking only at their end products, in the same way you miss the strength of a tree if you look only at its leaves. (See the chart "Competencies: The Roots of Competitiveness.")

Core competencies are the collective learning in the organization, especially how to coordinate diverse production skills and integrate multiple streams of technologies. Consider Sony's capacity to miniaturize or Philips's optical-media expertise. The theoretical knowledge to put a radio on a chip does not in itself assure a company the skill to produce a miniature radio no bigger than a business card. To bring off this feat, Casio must harmonize know-how in miniaturization, microprocessor design, material science, and ultrathin precision casing – the same skills it applies in its miniature card calculators, pocket TVs, and digital watches.

> **Unlike physical assets, competencies do not deteriorate as they are applied and shared. They grow.**

If core competence is about harmonizing streams of technology, it is also about the organization of work and the delivery of value. Among Sony's competencies is miniaturization. To bring miniaturization to its products, Sony must ensure that technologists, engineers, and marketers have a shared understanding of customer needs and of technological possibilities. The force of core competence is felt as decisively in services as in manufacturing. Citicorp was ahead of others investing in an operating system that allowed it to participate in world markets 24 hours a day. Its competence in systems has provided the company the means to differentiate itself from many financial service institutions.

Core competence is communication, involvement, and a deep commitment to working across organizational boundaries. It involves many levels of people and all functions. World-class research in, for example, lasers or ceramics can take place in corporate laboratories without having an impact on any of the businesses of the company. The skills that together constitute core competence must coalesce around individuals whose efforts are not so narrowly focused that they cannot recognize the opportunities for blending their functional expertise with those of others in new and interesting ways.

Core competence does not diminish with use. Unlike physical assets, which do deteriorate over time, competencies are enhanced as they are applied and shared. But competencies still need to be nurtured and protected; knowledge fades if it is not used. Competencies are the glue that binds existing businesses. They are also the engine for new business development. Patterns of diversification and market entry may be guided by them, not just by the attractiveness of markets.

Consider 3M's competence with sticky tape. In dreaming up businesses as diverse as "Post-it" notes, magnetic tape, photographic film, pressure-sensitive tapes, and coated abrasives, the company has brought to bear widely shared competencies in substrates, coatings, and adhesives and devised various ways to combine them. Indeed, 3M has invested consistently in them. What seems to be an extremely diversified portfolio of businesses belies a few shared core competencies.

In contrast, there are major companies that have had the potential to build core competencies but failed to do so because top management was unable to conceive of the company as anything other than a collection of discrete businesses. GE sold much of its consumer electronics business to Thomson of France, arguing that it was becoming increasingly difficult to maintain its competitiveness in this sector. That was undoubtedly so, but it is ironic that it sold several key businesses to competitors who were already competence leaders – Black & Decker in small electrical motors, and Thomson, which was eager to build its competence in microelectronics and had learned from the Japanese that a position in consumer electronics was vital to this challenge.

Management trapped in the strategic business unit (SBU) mind-set almost inevitably finds its individual businesses dependent on external sources for critical components, such as motors or compressors. But these are not just components. They are core products that contribute to the competitiveness of a wide range of end products. They are the physical embodiments of core competencies.

How Not to Think of Competence

Since companies are in a race to build the competencies that determine global leadership, successful companies have stopped imagining themselves as bundles of businesses making products. Canon, Honda, Casio, or NEC may seem to preside over portfolios of businesses unrelated in terms of customers, distribution channels, and merchandising strategy. Indeed, they have portfolios that may seem idiosyncratic at times: NEC is the only global company to be among leaders in computing, telecommunications, and semiconductors *and* to have a thriving consumer electronics business.

But looks are deceiving. In NEC, digital technology, especially VLSI and systems integration skills, is fundamental. In the core competencies underlying them, disparate businesses become coherent. It is Honda's core competence in engines and power trains that gives it a distinctive advantage in car, motorcycle, lawn mower, and generator businesses. Canon's core competencies in optics, imaging, and

> Cultivating core competence does *not* mean outspending rivals on R&D or getting businesses to become more vertically integrated.

microprocessor controls have enabled it to enter, even dominate, markets as seemingly diverse as copiers, laser printers, cameras, and image scanners. Philips worked for more than 15 years to perfect its optical-media (laser disc) competence, as did JVC in building a leading position in video recording. Other examples of core competencies might include mechantronics (the ability to marry mechanical and electronic engineering), video displays, bioengineering, and microelectronics. In the early stages of its competence building, Philips could not have imagined all the products that would be spawned by its optical-media competence, nor could JVC have anticipated miniature camcorders when it first began exploring videotape technologies.

Unlike the battle for global brand dominance, which is visible in the world's broadcast and print media and is aimed at building global "share of mind," the battle to build world-class competencies is invisible to people who aren't deliberately looking for it. Top management often tracks the cost and quality of competitors' products, yet how many managers untangle the web of alliances their Japanese competitors have constructed to acquire competencies at low cost? In how many Western boardrooms is there an explicit, shared understanding of the competencies the company must build for world leadership? Indeed, how many senior executives discuss the crucial distinction between competitive strategy at the level of a business and competitive strategy at the level of an entire company?

Let us be clear. Cultivating core competence does *not* mean outspending rivals on research and development. In 1983, when Canon surpassed Xerox in worldwide unit market share in the copier business, its R&D budget in reprographics was but a small fraction of Xerox's. Over the past 20 years, NEC has spent less on R&D as a percentage of sales than almost all of its American and European competitors.

Nor does core competence mean shared costs, as when two or more SBUs use a common facility – a plant, service facility, or sales force – or share a common component. The gains of sharing may be substantial, but the search for shared costs is typically a post hoc effort to rationalize production across existing businesses, not a premeditated effort to build the competencies out of which the businesses themselves grow.

Building core competencies is more ambitious and different than integrating vertically, moreover. Managers deciding whether to make or buy will start with end products and look upstream to the efficiencies of the supply chain and downstream toward distribution and customers. They do not take inventory of skills and look forward to applying them in nontraditional ways. (Of course, decisions about competencies *do* provide a logic for vertical integration. Canon is not particularly integrated in its copier business, except in those aspects of the vertical chain that support the competencies it regards as critical.)

Identifying Core Competencies – And Losing Them

At least three tests can be applied to identify core competencies in a company. First, a core competence provides potential access to a wide variety of markets. Competence in display systems, for example, enables a company to participate in such diverse businesses as calculators, miniature TV sets, monitors for laptop computers, and automotive dashboards—which is why Casio's entry into the handheld TV market was predictable. Second, a core competence should make a significant contribution to the perceived customer benefits of the end product. Clearly, Honda's engine expertise fills this bill.

Finally, a core competence should be difficult for competitors to imitate. And it *will* be difficult if it is a complex harmonization of individual technologies and production skills. A rival might acquire some of the technologies that comprise the core competence, but it will find it more difficult to duplicate the more or less comprehensive pattern of internal coordination and learning. JVC's decision in the early 1960s to pursue the development of a videotape competence passed the three tests outlined here. RCA's decision in the late 1970s to develop a stylus-based video turntable system did not.

Few companies are likely to build world leadership in more than five or six fundamental competencies. A company that compiles a list of 20 to 30 capabilities has probably not produced a list of core competencies. Still, it is probably a good discipline to generate a list of this sort and to see aggregate capabilities as building blocks. This tends to prompt the search for licensing deals and alliances through which the company may acquire, at low cost, the missing pieces.

Most Western companies hardly think about competitiveness in these terms at all. It is time to take a tough-minded look at the risks they are running. Companies that judge competitiveness, their own and their competitors', primarily in terms of the price/performance of end products are courting the erosion of core competencies—or making too little effort to enhance them. The embedded skills that give rise to the next generation of competitive products cannot be "rented in" by outsourcing and OEM-supply relationships. In our view, too many compa-

> Unlike Chrysler, Honda would never yield manufacturing responsibility for its engines— much less design of them.

nies have unwittingly surrendered core competencies when they cut internal investment in what they mistakenly thought were just "cost centers" in favor of outside suppliers.

Consider Chrysler. Unlike Honda, it has tended to view engines and power trains as simply one more component. Chrysler is becoming increasingly dependent on Mitsubishi and Hyundai: between 1985

and 1987, the number of outsourced engines went from 252,000 to 382,000. It is difficult to imagine Honda yielding manufacturing responsibility, much less design, of so critical a part of a car's function to an outside company—which is why Honda has made such an enormous commitment to Formula One auto racing. Honda has been able to pool its engine-related technologies; it has parlayed these into a corporatewide competency from which it develops world-beating products, despite R&D budgets smaller than those of GM and Toyota.

Of course, it is perfectly possible for a company to have a competitive product line up but be a laggard in developing core competencies—at least for a while. If a company wanted to enter the copier business today, it would find a dozen Japanese companies more than willing to supply copiers on the basis of an OEM private label. But when fundamental technologies changed or if its supplier decided to enter the market directly and become a competitor, that company's product line, along with all of its investments in marketing and distribution, could be vulnerable. Outsourcing can provide a shortcut to a more competitive product, but it typically contributes little to building the people-embodied skills that are needed to sustain product leadership.

Nor is it possible for a company to have an intelligent alliance or sourcing strategy if it has not made a choice about where it will build competence leadership. Clearly, Japanese companies have benefited from alliances. They've used them to learn from Western partners who were not fully committed to preserving core competencies of their own. As we've argued in these pages before, learning within an alliance takes a positive commitment of resources—travel, a pool of dedicated people, test-bed facilities, time to internalize and test what has been learned.[2] A company may not make this effort if it doesn't have clear goals for competence building.

Another way of losing is forgoing opportunities to establish competencies that are evolving in existing businesses. In the 1970s and 1980s, many American and European companies—like GE, Motorola, GTE, Thorn, and GEC—chose to exit the color television business, which they regarded as mature. If by "mature" they meant that they had run out of new product ideas at precisely the moment global rivals had targeted the TV business for entry, then yes, the industry was mature. But it certainly wasn't mature in the sense that all opportunities to enhance and apply video-based competencies had been exhausted.

In ridding themselves of their television businesses, these companies failed to distinguish be-

---

2. "Collaborate with Your Competitors and Win," HBR January-February 1989, p. 133, with Yves L. Doz.

tween divesting the business and destroying their video media-based competencies. They not only got out of the TV business but they also closed the door on a whole stream of future opportunities reliant on video-based competencies. The television industry, considered by many U.S. companies in the 1970s to be unattractive, is today the focus of a fierce public policy debate about the inability of U.S. corporations to benefit from the $20-billion-a-year opportunity that HDTV will represent in the mid- to late 1990s. Ironically, the U.S. government is being asked to fund a massive research project—in effect, to compensate U.S. companies for their failure to preserve critical core competencies when they had the chance.

In contrast, one can see a company like Sony reducing its emphasis on VCRs (where it has not been very successful and where Korean companies now threaten), without reducing its commitment to video-related competencies. Sony's Betamax led to a debacle. But it emerged with its videotape recording competencies intact and is currently challenging Matsushita in the 8mm camcorder market.

There are two clear lessons here. First, the costs of losing a core competence can be only partly calculated in advance. The baby may be thrown out with the bath water in divestment decisions. Second, since core competencies are built through a process of continuous improvement and enhancement that may span a decade or longer, a company that has failed to invest in core competence building will find it very difficult to enter an emerging market, unless, of course, it will be content simply to serve as a distribution channel.

American semiconductor companies like Motorola learned this painful lesson when they elected to forgo direct participation in the 256k generation of DRAM chips. Having skipped this round, Motorola, like most of its American competitors, needed a large infusion of technical help from Japanese partners to rejoin the battle in the 1-megabyte generation. When it comes to core competencies, it is difficult to get off the train, walk to the next station, and then reboard.

From Core Competencies to Core Products

The tangible link between identified core competencies and end products is what we call the core products—the physical embodiments of one or more core competencies. Honda's engines, for example, are core products, linchpins between design and development skills that ultimately lead to a proliferation

of end products. Core products are the components or subassemblies that actually contribute to the value of the end products. Thinking in terms of core products forces a company to distinguish between the brand share it achieves in end product markets (for example, 40% of the U.S. refrigerator market) and the manufacturing share it achieves in any particular core product (for example, 5% of the world share of compressor output).

Canon is reputed to have an 84% world manufacturing share in desktop laser printer "engines," even though its brand share in the laser printer business is minuscule. Similarly, Matsushita has a world manufacturing share of about 45% in key VCR components, far in excess of its brand share (Panasonic, JVC, and others) of 20%. And Matsushita has a commanding core product share in compressors worldwide, estimated at 40%, even though its brand share in both the air-conditioning and refrigerator businesses is quite small.

> Maintain world manufacturing dominance in core products, and you reserve the power to shape the evolution of end products.

It is essential to make this distinction between core competencies, core products, and end products because global competition is played out by different rules and for different stakes at each level. To build or defend leadership over the long term, a corporation will probably be a winner at each level. At the level of core competence, the goal is to build world leadership in the design and development of a particular class of product functionality—be it compact data storage and retrieval, as with Philips's optical-media competence, or compactness and ease of use, as with Sony's micromotors and microprocessor controls.

To sustain leadership in their chosen core competence areas, these companies *seek to maximize their world manufacturing share in core products.* The manufacture of core products for a wide variety of external (and internal) customers yields the revenue and market feedback that, at least partly, determines the pace at which core competencies can be enhanced and extended. This thinking was behind JVC's decision in the mid-1970s to establish VCR supply relationships with leading national consumer electronics companies in Europe and the United States. In supplying Thomson, Thorn, and Telefunken (all independent companies at that time) as well as U.S. partners, JVC was able to gain the cash and the diversity of market experience that ultimately enabled it to outpace Philips and Sony. (Philips developed videotape competencies in parallel with JVC, but it failed to build a worldwide network of OEM relationships that would have allowed it to accelerate the refinement of its videotape competence through the sale of core products.)

JVC's success has not been lost on Korean companies like Goldstar, Sam Sung, Kia, and Daewoo, who are building core product leadership in areas as diverse as displays, semiconductors, and automotive engines through their OEM-supply contracts with Western companies. Their avowed goal is to capture investment initiative away from potential competitors, often U.S. companies. In doing so, they accelerate their competence-building efforts while "hollowing out" their competitors. By focusing on competence and embedding it in core products, Asian competitors have built up advantages in component markets first and have then leveraged off their superior products to move downstream to build brand share. And they are not likely to remain the low-cost suppliers forever. As their reputation for brand leadership is consolidated, they may well gain price leadership. Honda has proven this with its Acura line, and other Japanese car makers are following suit.

Control over core products is critical for other reasons. A dominant position in core products allows a company to shape the evolution of applications and end markets. Such compact audio disc-related core products as data drives and lasers have enabled Sony and Philips to influence the evolution of the computer-peripheral business in optical-media storage. As a company multiplies the number of application arenas for its core products, it can consistently reduce the cost, time, and risk in new product development. In short, well-targeted core products can lead to economies of scale *and* scope.

The Tyranny of the SBU

The new terms of competitive engagement cannot be understood using analytical tools devised to manage the diversified corporation of 20 years ago, when competition was primarily domestic (GE versus Westinghouse, General Motors versus Ford) and all the key players were speaking the language of the same business schools and consultancies. Old prescriptions have potentially toxic side effects. The need for new principles is most obvious in companies organized exclusively according to the logic of SBUs. The implications of the two alternate concepts of the corporation are summarized in "Two Concepts of the Corporation: SBU or Core Competence."

Obviously, diversified corporations have a portfolio of products and a portfolio of businesses. But we believe in a view of the company as a portfolio of competencies as well. U.S. companies do not lack the technical resources to build competencies, but their top management often lacks the vision to build them and the administrative means for assembling resources spread across multiple businesses. A shift in commitment will inevitably influence patterns of diversification, skill deployment, resource allocation priorities, and approaches to alliances and outsourcing.

We have described the three different planes on which battles for global leadership are waged: core competence, core products, and end products. A corporation has

Two Concepts of the Corporation: SBU or Core Competence

	SBU	Core Competence
Basis for competition	Competitiveness of today's products	Interfirm competition to build competencies
Corporate structure	Portfolio of businesses related in product-market terms	Portfolio of competencies, core products, and businesses
Status of the business unit	Autonomy is sacrosanct; the SBU "owns" all resources other than cash	SBU is a potential reservoir of core competencies
Resource allocation	Discrete businesses are the unit of analysis; capital is allocated business by business	Businesses and competencies are the unit of analysis: top management allocates capital and talent
Value added of top management	Optimizing corporate returns through capital allocation trade-offs among businesses	Enunciating strategic architecture and building competencies to secure the future

to know whether it is winning or losing on each plane. By sheer weight of investment, a company might be able to beat its rivals to blue-sky technologies yet still lose the race to build core competence leadership. If a company is winning the race to build core competencies (as opposed to building leadership in a few technologies), it will almost certainly outpace rivals in new business development. If a company is winning the race to capture world manufacturing share in core products, it will probably outpace rivals in improving product features and the price/performance ratio.

Determining whether one is winning or losing end product battles is more difficult because measures of product market share do not necessarily reflect various companies' underlying competitiveness. Indeed, companies that attempt to build market share by relying on the competitiveness of others, rather than investing in core competencies and world coreproduct leadership, may be treading on quicksand. In the race for global brand dominance, companies like 3M, Black & Decker, Canon, Honda, NEC, and Citicorp have built global brand umbrellas by proliferating products out of their core competencies. This has allowed their individual businesses to build image, customer loyalty, and access to distribution channels.

When you think about this reconceptualization of the corporation, the primacy of the SBU—an organizational dogma for a generation—is now clearly an anachronism. Where the SBU is an article of faith, resistance to the seductions of decentralization can seem heretical. In many companies, the SBU prism means that only one plane of the global competitive battle, the battle to put competitive products on the shelf *today*, is visible to top management. What are the costs of this distortion?

Underinvestment in Developing Core Competencies and Core Products. When the organization is conceived of as a multiplicity of SBUs, no single business may feel responsible for maintaining a viable position in core products nor be able to justify the investment required to build world leadership in some core competence. In the absence of a more comprehensive view imposed by corporate management, SBU managers will tend to underinvest. Recently, companies such as Kodak and Philips have recognized this as a potential problem and have begun searching for new organizational forms that will allow them to develop and manufacture core products for both internal and external customers.

SBU managers have traditionally conceived of competitors in the same way they've seen themselves. On the whole, they've failed to note the emphasis Asian competitors were placing on building leadership in core products or to understand the criti-cal linkage between world manufacturing leadership and the ability to sustain development pace in core competence. They've failed to pursue OEM-supply opportunities or to look across their various product divisions in an attempt to identify opportunities for coordinated initiatives.

Imprisoned Resources. As an SBU evolves, it often develops unique competencies. Typically, the people who embody this competence are seen as the sole property of the business in which they grew up. The manager of another SBU who asks to borrow talented people is likely to get a cold rebuff. SBU managers are not only unwilling to lend their competence carriers but they may actually hide talent to prevent its redeployment in the pursuit of new opportunites. This may be compared to residents of an underdeveloped country hiding most of their cash under their mattresses. The benefits of competencies, like the benefits of the money supply, depend on the velocity of their circulation as well as on the size of the stock the company holds.

Western companies have traditionally had an advantage in the stock of skills they possess. But have they been able to reconfigure them quickly to re-

> How strange that SBU managers should be made to compete for corporate cash but never for key people.

spond to new opportunities? Canon, NEC, and Honda have had a lesser stock of the people and technologies that compose core competencies but could move them much quicker from one business unit to another. Corporate R&D spending at Canon is not fully indicative of the size of Canon's core competence stock and tells the casual observer nothing about the velocity with which Canon is able to move core competencies to exploit opportunities.

When competencies become imprisoned, the people who carry the competencies do not get assigned to the most exciting opportunities, and their skills begin to atrophy. Only by fully leveraging core competencies can small companies like Canon afford to compete with industry giants like Xerox. How strange that SBU managers, who are perfectly willing to compete for cash in the capital budgeting process, are unwilling to compete for people—the company's most precious asset. We find it ironic that top management devotes so much attention to the capital budgeting process yet typically has no comparable mechanism for allocating the human skills that embody core competencies. Top managers are sel-

Vickers Learns the Value of Strategic Architecture

The idea that top management should develop a corporate strategy for acquiring and deploying core competencies is relatively new in most U.S. companies. There are a few exceptions. An early convert was Trinova (previously Libbey Owens Ford), a Toledo-based corporation, which enjoys a worldwide position in power and motion controls and engineered plastics. One of its major divisions is Vickers, a premier supplier of hydraulics components like valves, pumps, actuators, and filtration devices to aerospace, marine, defense, automotive, earth-moving, and industrial markets.

Vickers saw the potential for a transformation of its traditional business with the application of electronics disciplines in combination with its traditional technologies. The goal was "to ensure that change in technology does not displace Vickers from its customers." This, to be sure, was initially a defensive move: Vickers recognized that unless it acquired new skills, it could not protect existing markets or capitalize on new growth opportunities. Managers at Vickers attempted to conceptualize the likely evolution of (a) technologies relevant to the power and motion control business, (b) functionalities that would satisfy emerging customer needs, and (c) new competencies needed to creatively manage the marriage of technology and customer needs.

Despite pressure for short-term earnings, top management looked to a 10- to 15-year time horizon in developing a map of emerging customer needs, changing technologies, and the core competencies that would be necessary to bridge the gap between the two. Its slogan was "Into the 21st Century." (A simplified version of the overall architecture developed is shown here.)

Vickers is currently in fluid-power components. The architecture identifies two additional competencies, electric-power components and electronic controls. A systems integration capability that would unite hardware, software, and service was also targeted for development.

The strategic architecture, as illustrated by the Vickers example, is not a forecast of specific products or specific technologies but a broad map of the evolving linkages between customer functionality requirements, potential technologies, and core competencies. It assumes that products and systems cannot be defined with certainty for the future but that preempting competitors in the development of new markets requires an early start to building core competencies. The strategic architecture developed by Vickers, while describing the future in competence terms, also provides the basis for making "here and now" decisions about product priorities, acquisitions, alliances, and recruitment.

Since 1986, Vickers has made more than ten clearly targeted acquisitions, each one focused on a specific component or technology gap identified in the overall architecture. The architecture is also the basis for internal development of new competencies. Vickers has undertaken, in parallel, a reorganization to enable the integration of electronics and electrical capabilities with mechanical-based competencies. We believe that it will take another two to three years before Vickers reaps the total benefits from developing the strategic architecture, communicating it widely to all its employees, customers, and investors, and building administrative systems consistent with the architecture.

Vickers Map of Competencies

Electronic Controls
- Valve amplifiers
- Logic
- Motion
- Complete machine and vehicle

Fluid Power
- Electrohydraulic
- Pumps
- Control valves
- Cartridge valves
- Actuators
- Package systems
- Pneumatic products
- Fuel/Fluid transfer
- Filtration

Electric Power
- AC/DC
- Servo
- Stepper

Sensors
- Valve/Pump
- Actuator
- Machine

System Engineering
- Application focus
- Power/Motion
- Control
- Electronics
- Software

Electric Products
- Actuators
- Fan packages
- Generators

Offering
- Systems
- Packages
- Components
- Service
- Training

Focus Markets
- Factory automation
- Off-highway
- Missiles/Space
- Automotive systems
- Commercial aircraft
- Defense vehicles
- Plastic process
- Military aircraft
- Marine

dom able to look four or five levels down into the organization, identify the people who embody critical competencies, and move them across organizational boundaries.

Bounded Innovation. If core competencies are not recognized, individual SBUs will pursue only those innovation opportunities that are close at hand—marginal product-line extensions or geographic expansions. Hybrid opportunities like fax machines, laptop computers, hand-held televisions, or portable music keyboards will emerge only when managers take off their SBU blinkers. Remember, Canon appeared to be in the camera business at the time it was preparing to become a world leader in copiers. Conceiving of the corporation in terms of core competencies widens the domain of innovation.

Developing Strategic Architecture

The fragmentation of core competencies becomes inevitable when a diversified company's information systems, patterns of communication, career paths, managerial rewards, and processes of strategy development do not transcend SBU lines. We believe that senior management should spend a significant amount of its time developing a corporatewide strategic architecture that establishes objectives for competence building. A strategic architecture is a road map of the future that identifies which core competencies to build and their constituent technologies.

By providing an impetus for learning from alliances and a focus for internal development efforts, a strategic architecture like NEC's C&C can dramatically reduce the investment needed to secure future market leadership. How can a company make partnerships intelligently without a clear understanding of the core competencies it is trying to build and those it is attempting to prevent from being unintentionally transferred?

Of course, all of this begs the question of what a strategic architecture should look like. The answer will be different for every company. But it is helpful to think again of that tree, of the corporation organized around core products and, ultimately, core competencies. To sink sufficiently strong roots, a company must answer some fundamental questions: How long could we preserve our competitiveness in this business if we did not control this particular core competence? How central is this core competence to perceived customer benefits? What future opportunities would be foreclosed if we were to lose this particular competence?

The architecture provides a logic for product and market diversification, moreover. An SBU manager would be asked: Does the new market opportunity add to the overall goal of becoming the best player in the world? Does it exploit or add to the core competence? At Vickers, for example, diversification options have been judged in the context of becoming the best power and motion control company in the world (see the insert "Vickers Learns the Value of Strategic Architecture").

The strategic architecture should make resource allocation priorities transparent to the entire organization. It provides a template for allocation decisions by top management. It helps lower level managers understand the logic of allocation priorities and disciplines senior management to maintain consistency. In short, it yields a definition of the company and the markets it serves. 3M, Vickers, NEC, Canon, and Honda all qualify on this score. Honda *knew* it was exploiting what it had learned from motorcycles—how to make high-revving, smooth-running, lightweight engines—when it entered the car business. The task of creating a strategic architecture forces the organization to identify and commit to the technical and production linkages across SBUs that will provide a distinct competitive advantage.

It is consistency of resource allocation and the development of an administrative infrastructure appropriate to it that breathes life into a strategic architecture and creates a managerial culture, teamwork, a capacity to change, and a willingness to share resources, to protect proprietary skills, and to think long term. That is also the reason the specific architecture cannot be copied easily or overnight by competitors. Strategic architecture is a tool for communicating with customers and other external constituents. It reveals the broad direction without giving away every step.

Redeploying to Exploit Competencies

If the company's core competencies are its critical resource and if top management must ensure that competence carriers are not held hostage by some particular business, then it follows that SBUs should bid for core competencies in the same way they bid for capital. We've made this point glancingly. It is important enough to consider more deeply.

Once top management (with the help of divisional and SBU managers) has identified overarching competencies, it must ask businesses to identify the projects and people closely connected with them. Corporate officers should direct an audit of the location, number, and quality of the people who embody competence.

This sends an important signal to middle managers: core competencies are *corporate* resources and may be reallocated by corporate management. An in-

> Send a message to your middle managers: the people critical to core competencies are *corporate* assets to be deployed by corporate management.

dividual business doesn't own anybody. SBUs are entitled to the services of individual employees so long as SBU management can demonstrate that the opportunity it is pursuing yields the highest possible pay-off on the investment in their skills. This message is further underlined if each year in the strategic planning or budgeting process, unit managers must justify their hold on the people who carry the company's core competencies.

Elements of Canon's core competence in optics are spread across businesses as diverse as cameras, copiers, and semiconductor lithographic equipment and are shown in "Core Competencies at Canon." When Canon identified an opportunity in digital laser printers, it gave SBU managers the right to raid other SBUs to pull together the required pool of talent. When Canon's reprographics products division undertook to develop microprocessor-controlled copiers, it turned to the photo products group, which had developed the world's first microprocessor-controlled camera.

Also, reward systems that focus only on product-line results and career paths that seldom cross SBU boundaries engender patterns of behavior among unit managers that are destructively competitive. At NEC, divisional managers come together to iden-tify next-generation competencies. Together they decide how much investment needs to be made to build up each future competency and the contribution in capital and staff support that each division will need to make. There is also a sense of equitable exchange. One division may make a disproportionate contribution or may benefit less from the progress made, but such short-term inequalities will balance out over the long term.

Incidentally, the positive contribution of the SBU manager should be made visible across the company. An SBU manager is unlikely to surrender key people if only the other business (or the general manager of that business who may be a competitor for promotion) is going to benefit from the redeployment. Cooperative SBU managers should be celebrated as team players. Where priorities are clear, transfers are less likely to be seen as idiosyncratic and politically motivated.

Core Competencies at Canon

	Precision Mechanics	Fine Optics	Micro-electronics
Basic camera	■	■	
Compact fashion camera	■	■	
Electronic camera	■	■	
EOS autofocus camera	■	■	■
Video still camera	■	■	■
Laser beam printer	■	■	■
Color video printer	■		■
Bubble jet printer	■		■
Basic fax	■		■
Laser fax	■		■
Calculator			■
Plain paper copier	■	■	■
Battery PPC	■	■	■
Color copier	■	■	■
Laser copier	■	■	■
Color laser copier	■	■	■
NAVI	■	■	■
Still video system	■	■	■
Laser imager	■	■	■
Cell analyzer	■	■	■
Mask aligners	■		■
Stepper aligners	■		■
Excimer laser aligners	■	■	■

Every Canon product is the result of at least one core competency.

Transfers for the sake of building core competence must be recorded and appreciated in the corporate memory. It is reasonable to expect a business that has surrendered core skills on behalf of corporate opportunities in other areas to lose, for a time, some of its competitiveness. If these losses in performance bring immediate censure, SBUs will be unlikely to assent to skills transfers next time.

> ## Top management's real responsibility is a strategic architecture that guides competence building.

Finally, there are ways to wean key employees off the idea that they belong in perpetuity to any particular business. Early in their careers, people may be exposed to a variety of businesses through a carefully planned rotation program. At Canon, critical people move regularly between the camera business and the copier business and between the copier business and the professional optical-products business. In mid-career, periodic assignments to cross-divisional project teams may be necessary, both for diffusing core competencies and for loosening the bonds that might tie an individual to one business even when brighter opportunities beckon elsewhere. Those who embody critical core competencies should know that their careers are tracked and guided by corporate human resource professionals. In the early 1980s at Canon, all engineers under 30 were invited to apply for membership on a seven-person committee that was to spend two years plotting Canon's future direction, including its strategic architecture.

Competence carriers should be regularly brought together from across the corporation to trade notes and ideas. The goal is to build a strong feeling of community among these people. To a great extent, their loyalty should be to the integrity of the core competence area they represent and not just to particular businesses. In traveling regularly, talking frequently to customers, and meeting with peers, competence carriers may be encouraged to discover new market opportunities.

Core competencies are the wellspring of new business development. They should constitute the focus for strategy at the corporate level. Managers have to win manufacturing leadership in core products and capture global share through brand-building programs aimed at exploiting economies of scope. Only if the company is conceived of as a hierarchy of core competencies, core products, and market-focused business units will it be fit to fight.

Nor can top management be just another layer of accounting consolidation, which it often is in a regime of radical decentralization. Top management must add value by enunciating the strategic architecture that guides the competence acquisition process. We believe an obsession with competence building will characterize the global winners of the 1990s. With the decade underway, the time for rethinking the concept of the corporation is already overdue. ☐

Reprint 90311

271

Survival Patterns in Fast-Moving Software Organizations

Lena Holmberg, *Sydney Systems*

Lars Mathiassen, *Aalborg University*

Software practices change. Many managers adopt software process improvement initiatives to increase their organizations' ability to develop high-quality services and institutionalize state-of-the-art disciplines.[1-3] At the same time, approaches such as open source[4,5] and Extreme Programming[6] introduce new and innovative ways to develop software and force most organizations to choose between improving present practices and supporting innovation.

Fast-moving software organizations must respond quickly to changing technological options and market needs. They must also deliver high-quality products and services at competitive prices. The authors describe how to deal effectively with such dilemmas and opportunities.

This article reports our work with improvement initiatives in a fast-moving software organization called Linq. Since the company's start in 1996, it has grown from five to 340 employees and undergone major changes in organization, technology, and strategy. Adapting improvement ideas was challenging because commitment and responsiveness to improvement fluctuated depending on the organization's preoccupation with other challenges.

The key to addressing this issue lies in the emerging cultures of such organizations. The culture is the result of the organization's attempts to deal effectively with its environment;[7] it is not explicitly created. Rather, it emerges through behavioral responses to challenges and problems. We can express such behaviors as *survival patterns.*[8] These patterns are activated in our daily work, and they help us make priorities, solve problems, and do things, but they can collide when new work practices challenge traditions. From this context, we examine how to understand and facilitate improvement in dynamic software organizations while preserving their capacity for innovation.

A fast-moving software company

Linq sprang from the idea of using collaborative software to support workflow and projects in knowledge companies.[9] Although the company changed from consulting to software product development, the basic business idea remained the same—and it profoundly affected the way the company conducted SPI.

Creation

In January 1996, Michael Mandahl and Jan Morath founded Linq. They wanted to start a company that would help its customers make their employees contribute more value to the organization by working together. The company had a simple structure,[10] with Man-

Reprinted from *IEEE Software,* November/December 2001.

This approach to improved project practices— based on the Linq business idea—was named LinQing.

dahl as CEO and the rest working on projects.

Linq grew steadily, and although most employees came fresh from universities, experienced IT consultants also joined. A customer-specific solution turned into a product, although the major part of the business still focused on consulting.

The founders soon discovered that although customer satisfaction was high, efficiency was too low. The organization changed from a simple structure into one composed of four teams headed by a team manager,[10] but employees still conducted projects in an ad hoc fashion, and learning from experience was difficult.

Professionalization

During the summer of 1997, the founders realized that they needed help to accomplish process improvement, so they hired an SPI consultant. Top management committed to SPI, forming four task forces to improve project start, requirements management, testing, and customer management and appointing an SPI manager to coordinate the groups. Although all the task forces produced results, implementation was slow.

To make the improvements more visible, management set a clear objective: Linq would perform at Software Capability Maturity Model (CMM) Level 2 by September 2000. An internal assessment in September 1998 started the initiative. The results, although devastating, encouraged new commitments. Four new task forces formed (after the initial four completed their missions): project method development, formal reviews, electronic project room, and training and diffusion. Carefully selected project members from all parts of the organization joined the groups to ensure a broad reach. This approach to improved project practices—based on the Linq business idea—was named LinQing. Linq internally developed the LinQing framework for cooperation in software projects. The purpose was to create a collaborative space for innovation and learning through joint use of simple control mechanisms. One of this article's authors, Lars Mathiassen of Aalborg University, helped develop it.

The process started with Steve McConnell's *Software Project Survival Guide*.[11] The task forces presented the resulting templates and instructions in Lotus Notes databases, and training started in spring 1999. From the start, two emphases characterized LinQing:

- collaboration and competence transfer between Linq and the customer, and
- using the customer and IT to support the project process.

Implementing LinQing was never mandatory under the SPI recommendations, but performing in accordance to CMM Level 2 was an objective. Unfortunately, the innovation-oriented founders did not always use LinQing in their own projects, which created a mixed message. In spring 1999, many employees expressed their frustration with the way projects were accomplished and demanded more structure, which resulted in further diffusion and finalizing of LinQing.

From September 1997 to June 1999, Linq grew from 30 to 100 employees. The projects involved larger and more demanding customers, and the company reached a higher level of professionalism—with formal contracts, formal project plans, and systematic tracking and oversight.

Transformation

In spring 1999, a window of opportunity opened for Linq—namely, to produce LinqPortal, a corporate portal product based on Microsoft technology. In June 1999, the company reorganized, separating product development from consulting.[10] Simultaneously, plans for a larger and faster European expansion emerged, and a search for investors began. The product, the CEO's entrepreneurship, the tight upper-management team, and the company's performance impressed investors. The investors also stressed the existence and practical use of LinQing as one of the organization's key assets. The company grew from 100 employees to 340, and new offices opened in several countries.

Although the consultants still worked with customers, the company focused more on designing and delivering a product for a perceived market need and on building a sales force. A major R&D project started in the summer: developing a mobile version of LinqPortal.

When starting the new product division, the chief technology officer decided that all projects should use LinQing. The SPI manager formed and headed a formal SPI unit in the product division. The team's five members worked part-time in product development or as consultants to ensure diffusion of the results and development of the right relevance criteria.

Because LinQing was designed for consulting, the SPI unit started working on special editions for product development. The team incorporated training into new-employee orientation, and Linq initiated a simple metrics program that emphasized the packaging of relevant LinQing features. The SPI unit produced product information sheets, put together physical folders in addition to the information presented on the intranet, and introduced a special strategy for corporate portal projects: instant deployment. The SPI initiative was thus quickly tailored to the organization's specific needs—to support product development and sales of LinqPortal.

In early spring 2000, the SPI unit was dissolved and diffused on the SPI manager's initiative into the rest of the organization. It had delivered special editions of LinQing, and the organization needed to focus on applying them. Members of the former SPI group continued diffusion work by arranging training courses and presenting information at meetings.

Epilogue

The focus then changed to developing and selling a new product. Management considered producing customer satisfaction and delivering a product that could meet market demand to be vital.

Major changes occurred in the organization. Sales separated from consulting, product management separated from product development, and the number of consultants decreased to reduce costs (which was necessary to attract new investors).[10] The business and product divisions started deciding how to best use legacy practices to improve production. At this point, Linq had the infrastructure and competence needed to perform at CMM Level 2, but actually using it would require increased commitment throughout the organization.

On 23 April 2001, Linq filed for liquidation in Sweden. Although LinqPortal received recognition as one of the best of its kind, the market had not evolved as predicted. The investors quickly decided not to go through with their long-term plans, and liquidation was the only alternative. The business was split into parts and sold to other companies. The

	Survival pattern	
Level	**Innovation**	**Improvement**
Operational (behavior)	Network	Deliver
Tactical (organization)	Flexible	Supportive
Strategic (environment)	Dynamic	Stable

Table 1. Two complementary survival patterns

founders and approximately 50 other employees now work in a new software company that focuses on LinqPortal's mobilility.

Survival patterns

Two survival patterns drove Linq's behavior and management priorities: *innovation* and *improvement* (see Table 1). Each one is characterized by the behavior of the employees, the organization's requirements, and assumptions about the nature of the environment.

Innovation

The innovation pattern is strategy-driven. A fast-moving software organization's environment is extremely dynamic: technology and market conditions change constantly, inviting or forcing the organization to adapt or change its behavior. Investing in infrastructures does not pay for the organization because they make it difficult to respond effectively to new environmental conditions. To facilitate learning, foster new ideas, and create the dynamics needed to respond quickly to new opportunities and demands, all members of the organization must interact with each other, customers, and external players with relevant knowledge and experience. In other words, to create innovations at a reasonable speed, networking is important.

Throughout Linq's rather short history, it underwent major changes as a result of responses to internal and external opportunities and challenges. The shift from Lotus Notes to Microsoft-based solutions was one such example of market-driven considerations. Similarly, moving from focusing on projects for specific customers to emphasizing internally developed products for corporate portal solutions was another major change. The company needed many major innovations to develop new management practices in response to its fast growth, gradually transform into an international rather than a national player, and successfully develop LinQing. The innovation culture emerged from the start, with the behavior of the two founders, and it flourished and continued to develop in response to a highly dynamic environment.

Table 2
The dynamics of Linq's survival patterns

Pattern	Creation	Professionalization	Transformation
Innovation	95%	30%	80%
Improvement	5%	70%	20%

Improvement

Software people want to do a good job—as professionals, they want to deliver high-quality solutions in response to customer or market needs. The organization must develop solutions that satisfy its customers and generate sufficient revenue—or it won't survive. At the operational level, a mission to deliver satisfactory solutions drives this pattern. To achieve this, the organization must offer a supportive infrastructure that makes it easy (and possible) to reuse successes from one project to the next and a management tradition that encourages (rather than hinders) professional practices. To build such a supportive infrastructure, you must make certain assumptions about the types of projects, technologies, and solutions to support. In this way, we see certain parts of the environment as being stable.

The founders imported an improvement culture in response to problems experienced with projects. It also had to change from a simple structure to one composed of teams and team managers, and an infrastructure developed to make better projects. This improvement initiative combined Linq's collaboration and networking techniques with state-of-the-art ideas on SPI. Initiated by design, the improvement pattern grew to become an integral part of Linq's culture.

Dynamics

The innovation and improvement patterns are complementary, but tensions easily arise between them. The innovation pattern generates a pull toward minimal and highly flexible infrastructures; the improvement pattern generates a contradictory pull toward supportive and more elaborate infrastructures.

The innovation culture naturally dominates in the beginning with its ad hoc structures and mutual adjustment as key coordination mechanisms.[10] As the software organization grows and matures, more elaborate structures develop and different forms of standardization occur to exploit past successes and increase management control.[10] The defining property of quickly evolving software organizations is, however, their strategic drive to respond effectively to the opportunities and challenges gen-erated through their environments. We should therefore expect a constant struggle between the innovation and improvement cultures, with changing patterns of domination but the innovation paradigm having the upper hand.

Although Linq experienced both patterns, their role and relationship changed (see Table 2). During the creation phase, innovation values nearly exclusively drove the behavior. The Linq concept was developed and implemented through intensive collaborations with customers, but little attention was paid to improvement values (beyond each individual project) and few resources were used to develop organizational infrastructures.

Driven by the company's experiences and pressure to improve, this picture changed dramatically as Linq moved into its professionalization phase. During this period, management initiated and heavily supported improvement activities, and most members of the organization took an active part in attempts to build supportive infrastructures.

In response to new business opportunities, Linq entered the transformation phase to pursue corporate portal technologies and emphasize product development. Management heavily downsized the improvement efforts, new SPI processes were not developed, and the emphasis was solely on maintaining the current position.

Lessons learned

Each software organization has its own history and needs to make strategic decisions that fit its unique environment. Linq's lessons are therefore not directly transferable to other software organizations. We have, however, learned certain lessons that might inspire other fast-moving software organizations in their ongoing struggle to cope with a dynamic environment while simultaneously trying to improve professional practices.

Appreciate the survival game

Everyone in a dynamic software organization must realize the reciprocal relationship between innovation and improvement. Both values and practices must be actively supported and cultivated to create a sustainable software business. Both need top management support in terms of resources and recognition, and the different talents and disciplines involved must constantly be developed and maintained.

About the Authors

Lena Holmberg is the managing director of Sydney Systems, a family enterprise focusing on knowledge management. After her PhD in educational research at Göteborg University, she joined Linq. Over five years, she held various positions such as Chief Knowledge Officer, HR Director, and consultant, and was responsible for the Software Process Improvement initiative. Contact her at Sydney Systems, N. Skattegård, Upplid 330 17 Rydaholm, Sweden; lena_sydney@hotmail.com.

Lars Mathiassen is a professor of computer science at Aalborg University, Denmark. His research is in software engineering and information systems, most of it based on close collaboration with industry. He has coauthored many books including *Computers in Context* (Blackwell, 1993), *Object Oriented Analysis and Design* (Marko Publishing, 2000), and *Improving Software Organizations: From Principles to Practice* (Addison-Wesley, 2001). Contact him at the Dept. of Computer Science, Aalborg Univ., Fredrik Bajers Vej 7E, 9220 Aalborg Øst, Denmark; larsm@cs.auc.dk; www.cs.auc.dk/~larsm.

Protect the improvement culture

Fast-moving software organizations are constantly on the move—not because they find this behavior particularly attractive, but simply because their raison d'être is to constantly adapt to an extremely turbulent environment. Recruiting resources to work with improvement and creating the necessary commitment toward improvement is therefore difficult. Innovation always receives more hype, and the urgency and energy involved in innovative activities easily become an excuse for giving low priority to improvements. When innovation dominates, protecting and maintaining the improvement culture is particularly important.

Create innovative improvements

To keep up with the organization's innovation, the people working with SPI must be agile and creative. They must anticipate the possible next steps in technology, software development, and customer relations and constantly evaluate the consequences these might have for the organization. SPI activities should adapt to changing requirements, and the SPI organization should be minimal and adaptive. Key practices should be based on active networking in which software developers, managers, and customers participate actively in creating and implementing new improvements.

Improve the ability to innovate

Improvements must be conceived as relevant and useful in the software organization. A conventional approach to SPI that starts by addressing the six key process areas on CMM Level 2 will have little chance of creating the necessary commitment in dynamic software organizations. Classical key process areas should be considered, but they must be complemented with other ideas that focus on the needs and practices of an innovative software culture. Otherwise there is little chance of success with SPI. This is why Linq used LinQing as the framing device for SPI. LinQing unifies the basic business idea of supporting collaboration between professionals using modern information technology with state-of-the-art disciplines in software project management.

Don't specialize

For the SPI organization, understanding the business is vital, so those involved in SPI must actively take part in the core processes. SPI people should develop double careers: one in SPI and one in software development or management. In that way, they build a good sense of what it takes to be fast moving. Management is well advised to make participation in SPI activities an important career step and to avoid having a small group of professionals specialize in SPI.

These basic lessons can help dynamic software organizations face their basic paradox. SPI is particularly important in such organizations—otherwise, they have little chance of surviving. At the same time, however, fast-moving organizations are the most difficult ones to improve in a sustainable way.

References

1. B. Fitzgerald and T. O'Kane, "A Longitudinal Study of Software Process Improvement," *IEEE Software,* vol. 16, no. 3, May/June 1999, pp. 37–45.
2. K. Wiegers, "Software Process Improvement in Web Time," *IEEE Software,* vol. 16, no. 4, July/Aug. 1999, pp. 78–86.
3. K. Kautz, "Making Sense of Measurement for Small Organizations," *IEEE Software,* vol. 16, no. 2, Mar./Apr. 1999, pp. 14–20.
4. E.S. Raymond, *The Cathedral & the Bazaar,* O'Reilly, Sebastopol, Calif., 1999.
5. J. Ljungberg, "Open Source Movements as a Model for Organizing," *European J. Information Systems,* no. 9, 2000, pp. 208–216.
6. K. Beck, *Extreme Programming Explained: Embrace Change,* Addison-Wesley, Reading, Mass., 1999.
7. E.K. Schein, *Organizational Culture and Leadership: A Dynamic View,* Jossey-Bass, San Francisco, 1985.
8. G.M. Weinberg, *Becoming a Technical Leader: An Organic Problem-Solving Approach,* Dorset House, New York, 1986.
9. T.H. Davenport and L. Prusak, *Working Knowledge: How Organizations Manage What They Know,* Harvard Business School Press, Boston, 1998.
10. H. Mintzberg, *Structure in Fives: Designing Effective Organizations,* Prentice-Hall, Upper Saddle River, N.J., 1983.
11. S. McConnell, *Software Project Survival Guide,* Microsoft Press, Redmond, Wash., 1998.

Chapter 8

Staffing Essentials

One-tenth of the participants produce at least one-third of the output, and increasing the number of participants merely reduces the average output

—Norman R. Augustine, *Augustine's Laws*

Overview

Staffing fills slots in organizations with people capable of satisfactorily performing assigned roles and responsibilities. Because a good staff is one of the keys to success, it is your responsibility to recruit, train, coach, grow, energize, appraise, and reward talent for a job well done. Sensitivity and compassion are needed, as are discipline and direction. Teamwork must be emphasized in addition to individual initiative, performance, and innovation. Needless to say, managers must develop an ability to get work done through other people. Doing everything yourself is counterproductive.

Often, good software engineers may opt to take technical rather than management promotions because they do not know how to or do not want to get involved with the many staffing issues that plague organizations. In addition, coaching skills and handling interpersonal relations often prove difficult for engineering managers who are uncomfortable with relationships. Engineers are used to dealing with logic and physical laws. Unfortunately, people sometimes defy logic and do irrational things. As a consequence, different skills are needed for managers to deal effectively with staff members. In response, such skills must be learned for managers to perform effectively.

This chapter contains five papers on staffing. The first three papers are new and address the plight of the rookie manager. I have selected these papers because they outline techniques that you can use to grow management staff. The more traditional staffing functions related to hiring, firing, reviewing, appraising, and rewarding staff tend to be adequately covered in textbooks and by organizational policies. Because of their potential impact on how the staffing function is performed, I have included the last two papers on the topics of teamwork to round out the chapter.

Article Summaries

Fear of Trying: The Plight of Rookie Project Managers, by Roger Pressman. This article argues that the success or failure of many software projects revolves around the persons leading the team and not the project management tools and techniques they use. If this is true, investments in training and mentoring are needed to arm managers with the skills, knowledge, and abilities needed for survival. In addition, the paper argues that communication, negotiation, organization, and facilitation skills need to be honed in order for managers to survive in the real world.

Coaching the Rookie Manager, by Luke Hohmann. This new article takes the previous article several steps further by discussing how to develop needed communication, negotiation, organization, and facilitation skills. It suggests that through mentoring and coaching, rookies can learn survival skills through experience. Learning using this approach can take place in an atmosphere of trust instead of one that relies on brinkmanship.

Training Developers in New Skills, by Ahmed Seffah. The major theme of this paper is that both software development and management skills can be developed systematically using a continuing-education approach that is aligned with new methods of apprenticeship capable of empowering and sustaining self-learning and collaboration. The author makes a solid case for relying on continuous education, including on-the-job training in organizations that are growing rapidly and experiencing a high rate of technological change.

Ten Lessons Learned from Implementing Integrated Product Teams, by Paul Popick and Sarah Sheard. This article summarizes the lessons learned using concurrent engineering and integrated product teams to get people from different disciplines to collaborate and build a product using consensus techniques. Evidence reported indicates that significant changes in the way work is organized, managed, and performed are required to make these techniques work in practice. Strong management commitment is needed and new skills need to be built. The paper builds on these themes as it offers advice aimed at leveraging lessons learned positively the next time through the process.

The Softer Side of Project Management, by Janice Strauss. This paper identifies the tools that project managers need to address human issues. It offers sound advice on what project managers can do to establish roles that people feel comfortable with, keep up morale, and maintain momentum by keeping the team satisfied. It emphasizes the use of humor and empowerment as tools to lighten up moments of stress. It suggests that being sensitive to the needs of your people and showing appreciation for a job well done goes a long way.

Key Terms

Nine terms, defined as follows, are important to understanding the topic of organization as used within this chapter:

1. **Collaborative development.** A development process characterized by a cooperative team effort that often crosses organizational or geographic boundaries.
2. **Motivation.** In management, the act of influencing the behavior of others through the combined use of incentives and rewards.
3. **Ownership.** In management, the degree to which a person, group, or team buys into plans that guide their performance.
4. **Performance.** In management, refers to a measure of a person's ability to achieve agreed-upon goals and realize forecasts.
5. **Role.** A unit of defined responsibility that may be assumed by one or more persons.
6. **Staff.** Those persons assigned to an organization to perform tasks.
7. **Staffing.** The management activities conducted to acquire, develop, and retain staff resources within an organization.
8. **Team.** A group of people organized to work together.
9. **Teamwork.** The cooperative effort by the members of a group, aimed at achieving common goals.

For Your Bookshelf

There are many books available on the general staffing topics of recruiting, appraising, evaluating, and retaining your human resources. Though few of them offer specific software advice, many of their recommendations and processes are applicable to the tasks performed within most technical fields. In addition, most firms have specific policies and procedures in place that guide how these activities are conducted. They have to, because there are laws in place that must be complied with.

For a more software-specific discussion of staffing issues, I would suggest that you pick up a copy of Tom DeMarco and Tim Lister's *Peopleware* (2nd edition) best-seller or Thomsett's book entitled *Radical Project Management.* If you are more interested in changing culture, I would recommend getting a copy of the Wieger's book, *Creating a Software Engineering Culture.*

The *Project Management Body of Knowledge (PMBOK™)* provides the project manager with plenty of useful information and guidance in the areas of organizational planning, staff acquisition, and team development. In the chapter on the human resource management project, the volume identifies the tools and techniques available to help project managers succeed in these difficult tasks. I particularly like its discussion of reward and recognition systems, as it is totally compatible with the paper in this chapter on personnel performance evaluation.

Roger Pressman

Fear of Trying: The Plight of Rookie Project Managers

Recently, a front-page article in *The Wall Street Journal* (4 April 1997) observed that "...many [technical] people don't want to be managers, and many people who are managers are, frankly, itching to jump off the management track—or already have." Describing a phenomenon that it called "management phobia," the article noted that sentiment against moving into management positions is the highest it's been in more than two decades. The article profiled young technologists, who in another era would have moved gladly toward project management, but today shun such positions. Most cited the "Dilbert Factor" as their primary reason for staying put.

Little more than a month later, *The Wall Street Journal* (14 May 1997) featured another front-page article—"A Software Engineer Becomes a Manager, With Many Regrets"—that addressed this topic from a different angle. A talented young software engineer working for an aggressive software company was promoted to lead a five-person project team. The team struggled to build a business-critical application under a tight deadline, only to have the product ship six months late. After the dust settled, the young man decided to give up his management position, saying, "Within three weeks, I'll just be spending all my time coding. I'll never have to do a review [personnel appraisal] again."

As a software engineering consultant, I've noticed this phenomenon among the ranks of software engineers in companies large and small. Most don't want the hassle of project management, feel (and often are) ill-prepared to take on the responsibility, and abhor the politics and frustrations endemic to the position.

And yet, few senior managers would argue with the notion that poor project management is the number one cause of project failure. We need good project managers, but it seems that the best and the brightest practitioners have a fear of trying the project management route. What to do?

Hundreds of books and training courses and dozens of management theories address software project management. Each discusses the techniques and tools that lead to a successful project and the attributes exhibited by successful project managers. After more than 20 years of consulting with software devel-

opment organizations, I've come to believe that successful projects have much more to do with the person leading the team than with project management techniques and tools.

So, how do we grow good project managers? What do we teach the rookies who have just been appointed to lead their first software project?

Regardless of the training or mentoring approach you use, I suggest focusing on four major attributes, which I describe in their order of importance.

COMMUNICATION

Here's the scene. An IS steering committee of senior executives summons a young project manager to report on the status of a troubled, critical project. He begins by looking at his shoes, unfolding a sheet of rumpled paper, fidgeting nervously, and then, without preamble, says "We've run into a roadblock in module TCP/IP.xcon. The status bit that should be set by module, uh, I forget it's name, anyway, its a real-time control module in the network management architecture, has, uh, given us a bit of a problem because, well, we thought that the requirements were consistent with...."

I suspect you've been there.

Project managers must understand how to communicate, and more important, how to tune their communication to their audience. It doesn't matter whether the communication is a presentation, a written report, or a phone call. It must be structured in a way that will get the message across clearly and concisely.

Some people have a natural instinct for communication, but most do not. Rookie managers should be trained to express the same idea appropriately to each different constituency. They must understand the needs of their audience and shape their presentations to meet them. On a given day, they may have to deliver the same message to executives, technologists, customers, and end users. The overall thrust of the communication may be the same, but the tone and structure will differ radically for each constituency.

Can this be taught? Yes. Can it be learned on the job? That depends. If rookie managers have competent mentors willing to spend time critiquing and advising on all communication to all constituencies, rookies *can* learn

Reptinted from *IEEE Software,* January/February 1998.

on the job. But if rookies are thrown into a project with little or no training or help and expected to "understand" how to communicate, problems will result immediately.

NEGOTIATION

Rob Thomsett, a well-known and widely respected consultant in the software project management area, talks about "first, second, and third wave" project management. In the 1960s and 1970s, during the first wave, software people held all the power and dictated delivery dates and costs to end users and customers. In the 1980s, during the second wave, a more balanced power relationship existed, at least in principle: business and software people worked together to derive requirements and mutually set deadlines and costs. Now, during the third wave, the balance of power has shifted to end users and customers. This means that they, not software developers, dictate the rules of the game. It also means that rookie project managers had best learn to negotiate—with their customers, with the technologists on their teams, and with the business executives who oversee their work.

There are many different ways to negotiate, but all of them can be summarized in the five steps every rookie project manager must learn.

1. *Establish a dialogue.* Because software project managers are no longer in a power position (as they were during the first wave), it is critical that they apply the communication skills I described earlier. They must probe, offer their own ideas and suggestions and build on the client's, and constructively criticize requirements that will lead to trouble. Project managers must work to make the customer understand that successful software will magnify the customer's new-found power, and that such software can only be created through a close working relationship.

2. *Plot a negotiating strategy.* Rookie project managers probably believe that quick thinking during discussions with end users and customers is the key to successful negotiation. In reality, it's most important to plan a negotiation strategy in advance, before you make any attempt to overcome obstacles and come to terms. In essence, managers must answer these questions: What will be negotiated? Who are the players? When and where will the meeting take place? Once they know these answers, they can better analyze their position, organize the information, and assess alternative solutions and positions that may arise. The vast majority of rookie managers walk into a customer meeting ill-prepared. They often get steamrolled as a result.

3. *Identify, then overcome, obstacles to success.* For example, while discussing requirements and delivery dates for a major legacy-system enhancement, a rookie project manager and an end user reach an impasse: the customer is insisting on an impossible deadline. What should the manager do? One approach is to initiate a change of pace. In this case, the manager might say something like, "I think we've

made good progress and I want to continue so that we can finalize things and begin this project. Why don't we take a break and then get back together at, say, 3:00 p.m.?" The customer may agree and be more willing to compromise after a break. Or, things may not be so simple. The customer may respond to this offer confrontationally or even irrationally. In cases like this, negotiation training is invaluable.

4. *Come to terms.* Once rookie managers neutralize obstacles, they must actually conduct the negotiation. To do so, they should open with a statement of purpose and review the pertinent information. Managers must recognize that both parties have needs and that these needs can be fulfilled in several different ways. They must work with clients to arrive at the best alternative. Finally, managers must "close" the negotiation. That is, they must summarize the agreement and identify both parties' responsibilities and the steps that follow.

The vast majority of rookie managers walk into a customer meeting ill-prepared.

5. *Make it happen.* Using organization and facilitation skills, software project managers begin the technical aspects of the project, but must never forget that, for the project to succeed, communication and negotiation must be ongoing activities.

The vast majority of rookie software project managers have never received *any* formal training in negotiation. Few have even read a book on the subject. They do not know these five steps and thus cannot apply them when they meet with end users and customers. The result? Misunderstandings, insane deadlines, unclear requirements, and the tension and frustration that lead to management phobia.

ORGANIZATION

Many people bumble their way through life, often just one wrong move from chaos. Amazingly, this approach can work, but not for rookie or even experienced project managers. Managers need organizational skills to administer technical work, coordinate the people who do it, and track and control the resulting products.

Organization is a partitioning process. Managers must know how to partition the work to be done. Both product functionality and the tasks associated with the software process must be partitioned and then related to one another.

Managers must also partition their interactions with project team members. It is difficult to assume the roles of advisor, confessor, parent, cheerleader, and even disciplinarian all at the same time. Attempting to do so invariably leads to chaos. Before entering a meeting, a review, or a one-to-one conference, managers should consider which roles are most important for the given situation.

Finally, managers must understand which work elements require immediate attention and which can proceed without direct supervision. On large projects, it is difficult and inadvisable to track and control all work tasks with equal emphasis. By partitioning work tasks and their relative importance to project goals, managers can prioritize and keep the project on schedule.

FACILITATION

In addition to being a communicator, negotiator, and organizer, a project manager should also be a facilitator. Stated simply, the manager's role should be to make things easy for the people who are doing technical work. In the role of facilitator, managers act as a buffer between the "techies" on the project team and those who fund, track, and control the project.

As team leader, a rookie manager should shield practitioners from the time-consuming burdens of everyday corporate bureaucracy. In software design jargon, managers apply "information hiding," treating the team as an encapsulated object in which data and the functions that manipulate that data are, to some extent at least, hidden from the outside world. Managers serve as an interface to the team. They filter communication with team members, not to keep them in the dark, but to screen out unnecessary and time-consuming distractions that have little or nothing to do with project success. Managers should minimize bureaucratic record-keeping duties and reporting functions to allow team members maximum time for productive work. Finally, meetings should be structured for effectiveness: Managers should set an agenda in advance, demand advance preparation when it's required, and ensure that records are kept and action items identified.

BOTTOM LINE

Rookie software project managers should be given the opportunity to succeed. Ideally, they should be trained in advance and given the necessary tools and resources to get the management job done. But this is the real world. In far too many cases, upper management throws the rookie into a project armed with little training and fewer resources. When that happens, things can be difficult—for the rookie manager, for the project team, and for the project. But even in this less-than-ideal situation, managers can survive if they remember four key concepts: communication, negotiation, organization, and facilitation. All the rest is detail.❖

Roger S. Pressman is president of R.S. Pressman & Associates, Inc., a consulting firm that specializes in software engineering training and process improvement strategies. For over 25 years, he has worked as a software engineer, manager, professor, author, and consultant. His books and video series on software engineering are widely used throughout the industry.

Luke Hohmann

Coaching the Rookie Manager

In last January's Manager column, "Fear of Trying: The Plight of the Rookie Project Manager," Roger Pressman asked a question critical to the future of our profession: "So, how do we grow a good project manager? What do we teach the rookie who has just been appointed to lead her first software project?"

Instead of answering this question directly, Pressman focused his article on four key skills that every project manager needs for success: communication, negotiation, organization, and facilitation. Although I agree with his key points, Pressman failed to explore the central question he first raised: just how do you "grow" the skills of a "rookie" project manager? This article is an attempt to answer that question.

COACHING: MODERN-DAY MENTORSHIP

Mentorship is a time-honored tradition for growing the skills associated with complex tasks. For centuries, apprenticeship was the only way you could learn to perform a complex task, from blacksmithing to carpentry. In "No Silver Bullet" (*The Mythical Man-Month*, Addison Wesley Longman, Reading, Mass., 1995), Fred Brooks points out that to be successful, companies must identify potentially great software designers and managers as early as possible in their careers, and "cultivate" their skills to allow them to realize their full potential: "I think the most important single effort we can mount is to develop ways to grow great designers." Brooks presents several ideas on how to do this, the most important being the assignment of "a career mentor to be responsible for the development of the prospect."

If you are a regular reader of *IEEE Software*, I suspect this is not new information. Mentoring is a powerful mechanism for growing skills in any complex arena. That said, I think a better term exists to describe an optimal relationship between a rookie project manager and the person devoted to improving their skills: Coach. Before elaborating on what I mean, take a brief moment to record your thoughts about the differences between mentoring and coaching (yes, write them down).

When I think of a "coach," I think of someone absolutely committed to the professional growth and development of his or her team, and virtually nothing else (even if it is a "team of one"). A coach's role at extremely high levels of sport becomes even more important, and the best athletes in the world not only accept coaching, they actively seek coaches who can improve their performance—they *want* to be coached.

Mentorship, on the other hand, differs subtly from coaching, primarily in the areas of advising and friendship. To illustrate, think about your willingness to record your thoughts on the differences between mentoring and coaching as I requested earlier. As your mentor, I'd simply recommend that you perform this task, possibly identifying how you might find it useful. Ultimately, however, it would be your choice whether to do this. If you didn't want to do it, you wouldn't (did you?). If I were your coach and you didn't want to do it, I'd have you do it anyway, possibly reminding you of your desire to be coached. I might not even explain why you should do it.

The concept of coaching fits our current cultural norms better than the concept of a mentor, and a coach has more easily referenced role models. By describing novice project managers as rookies, even Pressman falls into this cultural reference and motivates a coaching relationship.

Reprinted from *IEEE Software*, January/February 1999.

Which brings me to my first point: Establishing the proper relationship between rookie project manager and coach is essential for long-term performance improvement. If you are that rookie project manager, assess your own willingness to be coached. If you aren't willing to follow your coach's advice, it won't be of much value. This could mean, for example, doing tasks you think are unimportant, or cleaning up some mess you've made when you'd rather move on and do something else. Ultimately, it will mean doing something that for some reason or another you don't feel like doing.

If you are a senior project manager and have been given the task of mentoring a rookie, recast your relationship as his or her coach. You'll find a renewed commitment to that person's professional growth and an increased willingness to make demands that allow him or her to make real progress in their work. I find it easier to give negative feedback when I'm a coach than when I'm a manager or a mentor, and such feedback is usually better accepted.

LEARNING THROUGH EXPERIENCE

Learning can be thought of as the process of accumulating experience and wisdom through failure. Coaching (and certain aspects of management) can be thought of as the art of creating potential learning experiences that stretch the individual in key ways. Because these experiences are a stretch, some failure is inevitable. As a result, these learning experiences must be crafted so they do not permanently harm the individual or the company.

To get better at anything, you have to try, fail, reflect, regroup, and try again, until you succeed. Your first successes are likely to be sporadic and hard to repeat. Over time, and with enough practice and experience, you will improve your performance until you can perform skillfully. It doesn't matter if the skill is creating a good object model in UML, writing exception-safe C++ classes, or negotiating a delivery date for your next release.

A coach has many responsibilities in this process. The first is ensuring that "small" failures do not escalate and discourage rookie managers. Although initial preparatory training in management basics,

such as those Pressman described, can help, such training is largely ineffective unless actual work experiences match or exceed the rookie's skill level. When the rookie does fail, or realizes that he or she is failing and seeks help, the coach must be prepared

Coaching can be thought of as the art of creating potential learning experiences that stretch the individual in key ways.

to work with the rookie to attain a higher level of performance.

To illustrate, one of my "rookie" project managers was having trouble managing the inevitable evolution of requirements once the marketing requirements document was frozen. New issues were raised and debated, without the closure that the team needed to proceed.

If you're an experienced project manager, you've probably concluded that what my team needed was a more formal process for managing changes to requirements after they are frozen—something along the lines of a Change Control Board. But instead of telling my rookie to institute a CCB, I assessed the risks to the project of the current process. I felt that the risks were acceptable, and that the small failures the team was experiencing were not going to permanently harm the project manager, the team, or the company. So I waited.

When this manager eventually came to me, described the problems he was experiencing, and asked if I knew a better way, I had a perfect opportunity to coach him on the use of a CCB. He then modified a traditional CCB to fit our environment and introduced it. The improved process was immediately adopted.

Rolling this into my second point, prior introductory training in management can help the rookie project manager be successful. That said, such training is secondary to the actual "on the playing field" learning experiences the coach creates.

CAN I GO BACK?

Pressman identifies some of the fears a rookie project manager has when assuming a new position. One of the biggest was the "Dilbert Factor," which I interpret as the fear of appearing technically

To illustrate, consider the following interaction between Frank, a rookie project manager, and Henry, a developer assigned to his team (names have been changed). Frank told me that he had delegated a task to Henry. However, I was concerned by Frank's description; the task did not seem to be delegated with enough information to allow Henry to successfully complete it. So I asked Frank to describe, in detail, what he thought the task was. I asked the same of Henry, asking Henry not to go to Frank for clarification. Then I scheduled a meeting where the three of us reviewed the task together.

What we found was that Frank's detailed description of "what must be done" matched Henry's. This was a great victory—the task was, in fact, successfully communicated. However, Frank's description contained a section called "What Henry does not need to do to succeed." This section was missing from Henry's description of the same task.

Here was a major learning opportunity for both Frank and Henry. Henry learned that good "followership" includes asking what doesn't need to be done to be successful. And Frank learned that effective leadership means communicating these boundaries.

So how do you grow the skills of rookie project managers? Establish yourself as their coach. Craft specific work experiences designed to grow their skills. Work with them to improve their performance when they fail. Organize these experiences in a series of steps so that they can gradually, but steadily, move into management. Finally, remain vigilant, looking for every opportunity to coach, for it is through coaching, not general platitudes, that we grow effective managers and leaders.   ❖

Luke Hohmann is vice president of engineering for Aurigin Systems. Author of *Journey of the Software Professional: A Sociology of Software Development*, he spends as much time as possible coaching individuals and organizations to greater levels of performance. He can be reached at lhohmann@aurigin.com.

In the face of a growing software industry labor shortage and rapidly changing technology, effective continuing education can help organizations develop and retain accomplished software developers. The PRISE training program focuses on such critical skills as writing technical documentation, conducting cost–benefit studies, and working in teams.

Training Developers in Critical Skills

Ahmed Seffah, Computer Research Institute of Montreal

eleaguered by the software labor shortage, most software organizations know they must upgrade their developers' skills by investing in continuing education. Courses usually focus on technologies, using presentations to introduce and explain core principles and concepts. The best example is how the object-oriented approach is taught: its potential is outlined through simplified examples of how it is used. However, developers must not only learn concepts and skills but also adopt a mindset that facilitates effective and efficient technology transition and practice.[1] Today's work environment must enable software engineers to work efficiently, effectively, and with satisfaction, and it must support self-learning, collaborative learning, and the sharing of skills.

To achieve these two objectives, current continuing education approaches must be aligned with new methods of apprenticeship capable of empowering and sustaining self-learning and collaborative training. Furthermore, training must focus on learners' needs, skills, and interests, and on how technologies are used to complete tasks. Educators and project managers must anticipate and identify the skills required to create software developers accomplished in multiple technologies.

Reptinted from *IEEE Software,* May/June 1999.

Canada's Software Labor Shortage

Among all sectors of Canada's economy, employment in software, information technology, and engineering has grown the most—15 percent from 1990 to 1995, according to aggregate data from Canada's Federal Ministry of Industry. Two sectors are primarily responsible for this increase: the telecommunications equipment industry, with 48.1 percent growth, and the software development sector, with a phenomenal increase of 72.1 percent. Between 1994 and 1995 alone, software development employment in Canada grew 24.5 percent.

However, several indicators reveal that the shortage of qualified labor in the software development sector is both acute and large-scale, and will not be absorbed on its own in the next few years if action is not taken to counter it.[2] Although not exhaustive, a recent poll[3] conducted for the Canadian Advanced Technology Association revealed that 88 percent of member companies anticipate a short-term labor shortage, and 54 percent claim to currently offer positions they are unable to fill. According to CATA, approximately 16,000 jobs are currently open. These figures are comparable to those released by the Information Technology Association of America, which estimates that large and mid-sized US companies have 190,000 unfilled positions.

Despite this labor shortage in an environment of steady growth, the number of North American university graduates has remained stable, and the number of students registering in computer science programs has dropped dramatically over the past decade. According to the US Department of Education, between 1986 and 1995 the total number of bachelor's degrees, master's degrees, and PhDs awarded in computer science declined by 29 percent, from 50,303 to 35,614 graduates.[2] This decrease creates tremendous pressure in hiring. The situation is particularly alarming for software development, since few North American universities offer a full-fledged undergraduate program in software engineering. In the meantime, unfortunately, the academic community continues to analyze accreditation issues of software engineering curricula and what exactly should be taught.

The National Software Alliance in the US (http://www.software-alliance.org) estimates that through 2005 the demand for software professionals with computer science degrees will remain strong and new disciplines—especially software engineering—will continue to evolve. Software workers in the next century will be drawn from a variety of sources, reflecting greater diversity in the types of skills needed by industry. For instance, companies will intensify their search for workers who are both specialized and multidisciplinary. Software development organizations must be able to design applications that require in-depth telecommunications knowledge as well as high-level software engineering skills.

Other issues further complicate this already precarious situation:

- the rapid and perpetual evolution of software development methods and tools, especially with the advent of the Internet and its associated programming languages;
- the human factor in the software development process—for instance, the departure of a key team member, bringing new employees up to speed, or reluctance to consult a specialist;

> **Companies will intensify their search for workers who are both specialized and multidisciplinary.**

- the requirements of standards such as ISO-9000 and models such as the CMM that influence the maturity of the software development process, for example, by implementing a training program; and
- the correlation between improved productivity and investments in software development tools and technologies.

PRISE: An Alternative to Traditional Training

PRISE—in French, Programme de Réorientation des Ingénieurs Sans Emploi; in English, A Curriculum for Retraining Unemployed Engineers—is a skill-oriented training curriculum developed by the Computer Research Institute of Montréal (CRIM) in collaboration with the Ministry of Industry, Sciences, and Technologies, the Quebec Engineers Corporation, and several Montreal-based information technology and engineering companies. The objective of the program is to retrain more than 300 engineers in groups of 20 over the next three years. For each group, the training duration is one year, alternating intensive courses in CRIM's continuing training center with practical work in companies

Table 1
Required Skills Identified for PRISE

Prerequisite skills:

1. Mastering the basic principles, foundations, and standards of software engineering

2. Using Unix and Windows and programming under their APIs

3. Identifying the commonality and differences between procedural, logical, OO, and functional programming languages

Skills related to software processes:

4. Analyzing and specifying user and organizational needs

5. Evaluating according to needs, and installing and configuring software development technologies, environments, and tools

6. Programming and testing software components

7. Validating software components and applications with end users

8. Modifying and customizing existing software and generic applications

9. Contributing to project management and the improvement of software development processes and practices

Generic skills:

10. Writing, formatting, and publishing technical documentation

11. Conducting investigations and cost–benefit studies on software development tools and technologies

12. Communicating and working in teams and with clients

participating in the program. The first group started their courses in January 1999. We are implementing a Web site to provide program information and resources for both students and professors; a prototype (in French) is available at http://www.crim.ca/~aseffah/prise.

PRISE has three primary objectives:

♦ Reduce the shortage of qualified labor, which currently affects (or will affect by the year 2000) more than 80 percent of Canada's information technology companies, and help lower the unemployment rate in other areas of engineering.

♦ Maximize the benefits of continuing education at a time when organizations are questioning the relationship between productivity and computerization. According to several studies, training/learning is one of the major reasons for this situation.[4]

♦ Offer an alternative to traditional training approaches that is better suited to an environment where software development technologies are evolving rapidly and continuously.

The development of PRISE involved three stages, geared to understanding what developers do, what skills they need to do their work, and how continuing education can address these needs.

Identifying needed skills

In designing the PRISE curriculum, our first step was to analyze the varying contexts and companies in which software developers work. Another aim was to identify the skills developers need to perform their jobs. For this analysis, we used results from the following sources:

♦ interviews we conducted with two dozen software developers and managers;

♦ surveys of the human resource director, a team leader or project manager, a senior software developer, and a newly hired developer at each of five companies, where we measured the differences in their perceptions about training;[5,6]

♦ a skills grid developed by the Council of European Professional Informatics Society (we used only the skills related to software development);[7] and

♦ other surveys designed to identify the knowledge and skills required by accomplished software developers.[3]

Table 1 lists the skills we identified.

The experts we consulted all agreed on the importance of generic skills. Some noted that generic skills are so essential and so rare that positions offered in their companies remain unfilled despite the high number of applications received. They therefore suggested that these skills become a fundamental part of the PRISE training program. This view is also highlighted in an industry survey conducted by the Software Productivity Centre, which showed that the problem is not the lack of technical skills but a widespread lack of so-called "soft" skills (which correspond to generic skills in PRISE).

Building a skill definition grid

The second stage of PRISE development involved completing the definition grid for each identified

Table 2
A Sample Skill Definition Grid

Description of the skill
Programming and testing software components

Typical work situation
Based on technical specification and design documents
Using programming tools and environments

Widely used technologies
Programming in C++ and Java
Object-oriented modeling with UML and
    Rational Rose
Software architectures, design patterns, and
    frameworks

Constraints and standards that must be respected
Consideration of the international standards and organization-specific
    procedures that affect software programming and testing
Consideration of technological issues relative to the client's final
    environment and to quality and performance factors

Main steps of the process
[A] Establish the technical architecture of the
    component
[B] Build a detailed design model of the component
[C] Code the component using a programming
    language
[D] Write and integrate comments in the
    programmed component
[E] Debug the programmed component

Performance criteria
[A-1] Appropriate use of design patterns and frameworks

[B-1] Consideration of quality criteria: performance, reliability, and so on
[C-1] Adequate use of data structures and algorithmic techniques

[D-1] Relevance and readability of others' comments
[D-2] Use of appropriate vocabulary and terminology
[E-1] Consideration of different sets of test data
[E-2] Respect for the test procedures specified in international standards
    and/or company-specific procedures

---

skill. Each grid contains

- a description of the skill,
- the technologies most often used in software development organizations that require this skill,
- the main steps of the process in which the skill is required,
- the typical work situation(s),
- constraints and standards that must be respected, and
- performance criteria.

Table 2 presents a typical skill definition grid.

Associating training material with skills

Finally, PRISE associates a set of materials and learning activities with each skill. Online tutorials and expert advice can promote a greater understanding of the needed knowledge and provide ongoing information. However, an efficient training environment should provide learning materials that help software developers attain specific elements of each skill.

A good example of such material is pedagogical patterns, a promising way to teach object-oriented technology to software developers. A pattern essentially describes an abstract design template from which specific solutions can be generated, so that subsequent designers are not forced to start over when they encounter this same problem. Building on this definition, PRISE uses the notion of reusable pedagogical patterns[8] as follows:

- Patterns should be repeatable and easily adapted.
- Patterns should be described in a way that allows them to be easily "instantiated" for different lessons by different instructors.
- Patterns need not be novel or original but instead should communicate proven solutions to common problems.

For example, the DIRR (Design-Implement-Redesign-Reimplement) pattern attempts to explain new concepts and methods based on legacy concepts (for instance, learning OO fundamental concepts using traditional methods). The DIRR pedagogy provides a "relearning" methodology for reinforcing new concepts. Students are asked to design and implement programming solutions using their current paradigm. This is followed by a discussion of how the solution can be redesigned using concepts from the new paradigm. The students then reimplement their solution using the new paradigm's concepts. Further information about pedagogical patterns and their applications is available at http://www-lifia.info.unlp.edu.ar/ppp/.

Compared to traditional training approaches, the PRISE program provides a realistic solution for cost-effective continuing education. In observing the first group of students thus far, we see that we must develop more real-world case studies and examples, tools for evaluating the learner's evolution and performance, and a strategy that will facilitate customization of the curriculum to different contexts and software developers' profiles. A thorough evaluation of PRISE is scheduled before the end of this year.

However, we must also think about the ease of use (usability) and ease of learning (learnability) of software development tools and methods, as well as ways for integrating usability and learnability factors into our software engineering technologies. One such way is known as electronic performance support systems.[9] EPSSs are available on the spot and just-in-time, and designed to help their users learn and execute some task.

Because of the high rate of change in software engineering technologies, it is important to rely on approaches that truly support continuous learning. For example, Web programmers have quickly learned that the only way to keep in touch with the latest techniques is to rely on the Web itself to obtain the programming knowledge they require. Most other sources of learning become quickly obsolete.

But why should this approach of on-the-spot learning be confined to Web programming? Indeed, this principle of just-in-time learning ought to be much more widespread throughout the software development community. Our tools should not only provide help in using their features, but also provide support for understanding software engineering concepts, applying methods, providing pedagogical examples and templates, assessing performance, and so on.

We expect that the tools that provide better user interfaces and that nurture continuous learning of software development skills will be the most popular within the community; we also expect they will be a major factor in training the software workforce.   ❖

REFERENCES

1. K. Lato, "Learn to Learn: Training on New Technology," *J. Object-Oriented Programming*, Vol. 10, No. 1, 1997, pp.24-29.
2. Nat'l Software Alliance, "Software Workers for the New Millennium: Global Competitiveness Hangs in the Balance," Jan. 1998, http://www.software-alliance.org.
3. A. Reid, "Information Technology Skills Shortage Survey," Canadian Advanced Technology Assoc., 1997, http://www.cata.ca.
4. T.K. Landauer, *Trouble with Computers*, MIT Press, Cambridge, Mass., 1995.
5. M. Capelli et al., "A Survey on Training Practices in Software Development Organizations," *Proc. Int'l Conf. Management of*

Networked Enterprises 1998, Univ. of Quebec at Montreal Press, Montreal, pp. 754-762.
6. T. Lethbridge, "A Survey of the Relevance of Computer Science and Software Engineering Education," *Proc. 11th Conf. Software Eng. Education and Training*, IEEE Computer Soc. Press, Los Alamitos, Calif., 1998, pp. 56-66.
7. *European Informatics Skills Structure*, Council of European Professional Informatics Societies, London, 1992, http://www.cepis.org.
8. S. Lilly, "Pedagogical Design Patterns," *Object Magazine*, Jan. 1996, pp. 34-41.
9. O. Fisher and R. Horn, "Preface to the Special Issues on Electronic Performance Support System," *Comm. ACM*, 1997, Vol. 40, No. 7, July 1997, pp. 31-32; http://www.acm.org/pubs/contents/journals/cacm/1997-40/. Also, see http://www.epss.com.

• • •

About the Author

Ahmed Seffah is the research leader of the software development group at the Computer Research Institute of Montreal and an adjunct professor of computer science at the University of Quebec at Montreal. He earned his PhD in software engineering from the École Centrale de Lyon in France. His areas of interest range from software engineering and human–computer interaction to human factors, software process, and training methods in software development organizations. He is a member of the IEEE, ACM, the Association for the Advancement of Computers in Education, the International Association for Continuing Engineering Education, and the UNESCO International Centre for Engineering Education.

Readers may contact Seffah at the Computer Research Institute of Montreal, 550 Sherbrooke West, Suite 100, Montreal, Quebec, Canada, H3A 1B9; e-mail aseffah@crim.ca, http://www.crim.ca/~aseffah.

FOR FURTHER READING

R. Hsiao, "More Jobs than Workers: IT Companies Respond," SRI Consulting, 1997, http://www.sri.com.

"Software and National Competitiveness: An Overview," Software Human Resource Council of Canada, 1996, http://www.shrc.ca.

Ten Lessons Learned from Implementing Integrated Product Teams

Paul R. Popick and Sarah A. Sheard

Concurrent engineering (CE) and integrated product teams (IPTs) offer many advantages in product quality and cycle time reductions. Many companies are beginning to organize projects using IPTs, but the transition to CE and IPTs requires implementation details that are not commonly discussed in the literature. This article covers 10 of the most important lessons we have learned in our implementation of CE and IPTs.

Introduction

LORAL FEDERAL SYSTEMS began to adopt concurrent engineering and integrated product teams about five years ago. In working with the adoption of CE and IPTs, we have observed that the CE and IPT theories are warmly embraced in industry, as noted in IDA Report [5] and Miller [3]. However, we have also observed that CE and IPTs require changes to how we organize, manage, and perform our engineering activities, and these changes are not well understood or accepted. As described in *Fortune* [4], many companies have also found the transition to teams to be much more difficult than expected. Initially, the CE and IPT approach may not seem to be as efficient as the old approach, but we are beginning to see that it eventually provides superior results.

Reflecting upon the various implementations on projects we observed in detail in Loral Federal Systems, we see common issues and lessons that need to be considered when projects adopt CE and IPTs. We continue to see projects struggle with these same issues during implementation. By recording these issues and lessons, we hope to assist and simplify CE and IPT implementations.

Leadership

At the beginning of Loral Federal Systems' transition to CE and IPTs, there was a strong commitment from the management of the technology staff. Initially, this commitment was in the form of pilot projects, outside expert consultations, and workshops [11]. Later, it took the form of a policy statement that required all projects to implement CE and IPTs.

Even so, some people resisted the implementation of CE and IPTs. Before their resistance could be overcome, these people needed to understand the concepts, see the benefits to the project, and understand the changes to their role.

Originally presented at INCOSE 1996 Symposium.

There have been many instances when leaders have avoided or watered down the necessary CE and IPT changes. This is often due to work pressures to deliver products, uncertainty that the new methods will be as effective as the old methods, and fear that the new methods undermine management authority. For example, if a manager decides to review and approve all IPT decisions, the empowerment of the IPT is jeopardized.

Lesson 1 – Strong upper management commitment to drive the implementation of concurrent engineering and IPTs in the face of opposition is required [2].

When the CE and IPT approaches are first adopted, everyone is optimistic but as everyone grasps all the changes required, confusion and doubt develop. People begin to ask, "What is my role? Does the IPT have the authority to make this decision or do we need approval?" A crisis may develop as the uncertainty grows, and the IPTs become focused upon the IPT schedule and products. Some, perhaps most, people will advocate going back to the old approach.

The confusion and doubt are a typical step in the progression of learning the CE and IPT approach. The project leadership needs to continue to actively promote and personally use the CE and IPT approach whenever possible. This may involve refusing to review and approve some decisions in order to emphasize the IPT empowerment, using consensus decision making to demonstrate commitment to CE, or employing other CE methods. The project leadership needs to be the role model for the CE and IPT approach and realize that the IPTs will mirror the behavior of their leadership [8].

Lesson 2 – Three to six months after adopting CE and IPTs, there is a high level of frustration and a desire to revert to the familiar approaches. Strong leadership is required to continue to employ CE and IPT approaches.

IPT Set Up

Getting the IPTs off to the right start can prevent future problems. The following areas need to be addressed when setting up IPTs:

Product-oriented work breakdown structures. The process begins with a clear product-oriented work breakdown structure (WBS) for the project. The WBS needs to be closely related to the system being developed and the end items received by the customer. The WBS hierarchy needs to be organized along system, subsystem, subsubsystem, and component lines. Setting up the WBS this way enables IPTs to be established to develop tangible products. Functional discipline-oriented WBS structures inhibit the use of IPTs.

Clear IPT purpose. The project's IPTs need to be organized around end items of the WBS. The IPT mission and specific end items to be provided to the customer must be clearly specified. The cost, schedule, and technical requirements for the team's end items must be clearly defined. The relationship of the IPT's end items to other end items in the system must also be specified. This is often an iterative process among the teams.

Identification of the IPT customers. Identifying the customers of the IPT products enables the teams to better understand the expectations for their products. Customer here refers to end users, external customers, and internal customers. It also helps to identify points of contact or liaisons needed to complete the team's work.

Measures of Success and Incentives. Each IPT must have an understanding of what constitutes success and how that success is measured. Process, as well as product measures, need to be defined. The process and product measures should include cost, schedule, and technical measures. Process measures are such things as a specification outline completion, number of TBDs, plan vs. actual dates, and plan vs. actual costs. Product measures are such things as system failures, specification errors, and product cost.

Project progress reporting should be organized by the IPTs and their products, not by functional discipline. The IPTs need to be able to measure and track their progress. When subcontractor or discipline reporting is needed, the subcontract or discipline totals should be decomposed by IPT and product to allow consistency with IPT reporting.

Incentives need to be established that encourage teaming. This may take the form of team incentives when IPT performance exceeds a defined level. Incentives should reward achievement of measurable goals.

Resources. The IPTs need to be composed of all the engineering disciplines necessary to completely develop the IPT's products. IPTs that are missing one of the engineering disciplines are handicapped in trying to perform their mission. IPTs that include the customer and users are further enhanced. IPTs should assess their needed skill mix and attempt to obtain or grow the skills they lack.

Functionally oriented teams, such as a test team or a software team, eliminate many of the benefits of IPTs, since the products are only part of a complete deliverable.

Team Norms. Team norms are a set of operating principles for the IPT that the IPT members agree to follow. They include such things as meetings, which will always have agendas, decisions will be recorded and published, and team members will collaborate on and review work in progress.

The result of a properly set up IPT is that the team's domain of responsibility, empowerment, and resources are defined. Within this domain, the team has overall authority and need not seek approvals for its actions [1,6]. This IPT empowerment domain allows product decisions and the work to proceed rapidly.

Lesson 3 – Take the time to clearly define the IPT purpose, end products, customers, process and product measures, resources, and team incentives. Encourage the IPTs to act within their empowerment domains.

Decision Making

Consensus decision making allows all IPT members to contribute to IPT decisions, but the adoption of consensus decision making by IPTs has encountered several problems.

One problem has been with the IPTs reaching consensus. The people who make up the IPTs have had little or no experience with consensus decision making. They have experience with decision making by majority or by individual, but not with consensus. Many people do not understand that a consensus team decision will not be optimal for each individual but must be workable. As a result, an individual may believe that it is right to refuse to agree to a decision.

It is widely written that achieving consensus takes longer but pays off with better decisions. *We have found that initially, consensus decision making takes much, much longer until people learn how to use consensus decision making methods.* New skills and considerable practice are required to effectively employ consensus decision making.

The IPTs need to see consensus decision making work effectively. Unfortunately, consensus decision making is often abandoned before the IPTs have used it enough to become effective.

A second problem has been that IPT decisions have been overruled by people outside the IPT. Either this is because the team has made decisions outside their responsibility domain, or it is because others do not accept the team's empowerment. Many times when we delved into this, we found the team was not properly set up; there was no clear understanding of the team's purpose and domain. When an IPT's decision is overruled, it has a paralyzing effect on the IPT, creating a cynicism that there is just lip service to the IPT approach. Both the team and the program leadership must understand and agree upon the team's decision-making boundary.

A third problem has been that IPTs try to make every decision by consensus. Some decisions need to be made by an individual, some by small groups, and others by consensus. Decisions should be limited to the smallest group that they affect within the IPTs. We found that IPTs can usually agree on which decisions can be made quickly by the IPT leader, subteam, or members and which require consensus of the IPT members.

A fourth problem develops when important decisions are made by edict or by a small group of individuals. This sends the message that consensus is not a real decision-making mechanism. For consensus decision making to succeed, it must be embraced and used by

the leadership, otherwise it will never be generally accepted by the teams and the program.

Lesson 4 – Carefully define the consensus decision-making procedure and when it is to be used, and use it to make some important decisions at all levels of the organization.

An approach to implementing this lesson is to raise the team's expectation that initially consensus decision making is difficult, and using it takes discipline and practice. Try to involve everyone in defining and improving the decision-making procedures.

Two examples of basic decision-making procedures we are using in Loral Federal Systems are "thumb voting" and multivoting. Thumb voting allows everyone three alternatives: if you favor the decision, put your thumb up; if you can live with it, put your thumb to the side; and if you cannot live with it, put your thumb down. When there is a thumb down, the team takes time to understand the concerns and synthesize a new alternative that everyone favors or can live with. Calling for a visible thumb vote ensures an understanding of everyone's viewpoint and builds commitment to the decision.

Multivoting is used to select and prioritize from a brainstorm list. Usually, each member of the team is given a number of votes to identify the items that are most important. The items with the most votes are given top priority by the group. All items from the list are retained. Multivoting helps the team reach agreement on actions and directions.

We have found that when these simple decision-making procedures are practiced and used they build consensus and incorporate multidiscipline views.

Roles and Responsibilities

We have learned that people's roles and responsibilities change with the implementation of CE and IPTs. This change is difficult because the old roles and responsibilities are deeply ingrained. In the new environment, roles and responsibilities are often very different. Unless the new roles and responsibilities are defined and documented, each member of the IPT may have a different understanding of the roles. Contributing to this confusion is that people continue to associate the old responsibilities with titles such as team lead or manager.

As an example of this difficulty, let us consider the role of the team lead. In the past, many decisions were left to the manager. A lead came up with the ideas and recommendations, but the manager often had the final say. The lead expected the manager to bless a decision before acting upon it. In the new environment, the IPT has the final say, but many members of the IPT may still expect a manager to bless decisions.

Another pitfall is a manager may still want to approve ideas before the IPTs commit to implementation. The result is confusion, with some people still operating under the old system and some under the new system. The role of the managers, IPT leads, and customers are particularly difficult to define and understand.

When the roles and responsibilities are confused, the risk of abandoning the CE and IPT approach is greatest, and some justify doing so on the basis that CE and IPTs do not work as well as the theory.

Lesson 5 – Make sure the leadership (including all levels of management) and the IPTs define, record, and commit to the new roles and responsibilities. Periodically, the leadership and the IPTs should review and revise the roles and responsibilities.

The discussion that ensues on roles and responsibilities allows everyone to understand the different expectations for a particular role. People that want to still operate under the old system are identified. New expectations for each role are established.

Communication

In the CE and IPT environment, effective communication is very important. A common misconception the IPTs encounter is the expectation that most work is now done together. Questions and decisions that in the past were addressed by a single person are now discussed by the IPTs. The result may be long periods of discussion in which little is accomplished.

We have learned that in the CE and IPT environment, not all work is done by the team together; some work is best done by subteams and individuals. The IPTs need to be careful to decide which work is best done by the entire IPT, a subteam, or a team member.

When IPTs or subteams are doing work, everyone has to be involved in meeting the objectives, controlling digression, and seeking to understand one another's views. A great deal of personal discipline must be exercised by team members to only speak when they have something to add and to relate what they say clearly to the point of discussion.

One of our teams developed a does-it-matter team norm to remind themselves to focus their communication. Another common team norm is to limit war stories to one minute and debates to five minutes. After these limits are exceeded, the discussion is taken off line.

Lesson 6 – Effective and efficient team communication depends upon the IPT membership recognizing which work is best done as a team, as a subteam, and as individuals.

After a short period, properly set up IPTs begin to communicate effectively within their teams. However, communication difficulties between IPTs may arise. The IPTs become focused on their objectives and products, to the exclusion of the other IPTs. The overall program can suffer when inter-IPT communication is not addressed.

Ideally, one may think this is the role of the system IPT. However, practically speaking, it is not possible or desirable for the system IPT to address all of the inter-IPT issues. It is better to have the IPTs resolve as many problems as possible at the IPT level.

One of our teams created a liaison role to address inter-IPT communication. A liaison was chosen for each of the other IPTs to identify dependencies, track progress on the IPT dependencies, and lead resolution of inter-IPT issues.

Another program created a team of IPT leads to handle inter-IPT issues, communication, and plan adjustments. This team was able to resolve many IPT issues and actions and thereby reduce the number of issues that had to escalate up the organization for resolution [10].

Lesson 7 – Establish a formal mechanism for communication between IPTs, and identify IPT dependencies early.

Team Skills and Training

With the formation of IPTs, we have encountered four major skill-related difficulties. The first difficulty is lack of understanding of the other engineering disciplines. For the IPTs to be effective, all team members need to understand a little about the lifecycle steps across all disciplines in the development of the end item products. Cross discipline understanding allows IPT members to contribute to each other's work. Previously, the functional organization worked against the development of broader cross discipline skills.

A second difficulty is a lack of interpersonal team skills. Effective communication, listening, encouragement of other members, and the suppression of individual egos are examples of some of the skills needed to be an effective member or leader of an IPT. Lack of these skills often leads to ineffective decision making, ineffective meetings, and inferior IPTs. We have found that after a while, some IPTs began to identify their training needs.

A third difficulty is not using team methods enough to employ them effectively. Training should allow the IPTs to practice team methods (consensus decision making, facilitation, brainstorming, etc.) on real problems. Most people have to see and practice these methods effectively many times before adopting them.

Finally, the broader responsibilities assumed by all members of the IPTs require basic project management skills. Cross discipline cost and schedule estimating and tracking skills are needed.

Lesson 8 – Make sure the IPTs are supported with training that defines a core set of engineering discipline skills, interpersonal skills, IPT methods skills, and project management skills.

A Changing Work Sequence to Develop Engineering Products

In the past, our engineers have developed their engineering work products through a process of informal consultation and individual creation. After the initial creation, the engineering work product is subjected to a series of reviews and reworks until it is accepted by the customer. The different engineering discipline views are often reworked into the engineering work product through repeated reviews. This cycle of review and rework is both costly and time consuming. Invariably, the different engineering discipline views are only partially incorporated.

In a concurrent engineering environment, we are finding that the sequence of engineering product development changes. During creation of the engineering product, all disciplines necessary to create the product are identified and assigned. The development process now involves subteam creation with continuous review and comment.

The subteam creation employs the use of brainstorming, consensus decision making, and other creativity techniques. For example, brainstorming may be used to list the design characteristics from all the relevant disciplines as guidance to individuals creating their portions of the work products. The subteams and individuals iteratively refine and agree to the product content as it is being created. The result is a collaboration with shared ownership of the engineering product. In essence the work sequence is reversed with the review largely occurring prior to the individual creation.

A CE environment that enables everyone to have immediate access to engineering work products as they are being created is required to effectively implement concurrent engineering. Even with the CE environment, we have been most successful when we collocate the team including subcontractors, customers, and users and provide everyone network access to all the products under development through the CE environment.

We have encountered several problems when introducing concurrent development. First, some subteam sessions were not well focused and used a great deal of time with little accomplished. We found that for greatest effectiveness, subteam sessions needed to define specific objectives, use brainstorming, and use consensus decision-making procedures. These sessions should be followed by a consolidation step that publishes the session results. The subteams also had to train themselves to not constantly revisit decisions made in previous sessions.

Second, our engineers were surprised and overwhelmed with the number of comments received during the creation step. Many of the comments were extremely useful, but many others were not. Our engineers now expect more comments early in the creation step and are prepared to deal with them. Additionally, we have disciplined ourselves to think through our comments and only pass on those that matter.

Third, we did not recognize that some of the review and rework sequences should be eliminated from the start. We found that the IPTs and their customers must be given the expectation that the creation sessions at the beginning will reduce the reviews and rework at the end. Otherwise, the result is a longer creation step with the same or longer review and rework step.

Lesson 9 – Engineers and managers need to recognize and adopt a different approach to engineering work product development to realize the benefits of concurrent engineering.

A Balanced Systems Approach to CE and IPTs

We have learned that the implementation of CE and IPTs interacts with the overall system of management and personnel practices. IPTs often challenge the empowerment boundaries and the appraisal and reward system.

An IPT will question the domain of its empowerment. It is normal for the initial domain to be incompletely defined. Sometimes

an IPT will make a decision outside of its domain or someone not on the team may make a decision within the IPT domain. In either case, care must be taken to explain the basis for changing the decision to make sure that the CE and IPT approach is not undermined.

Following are some common IPT questions about the appraisal and reward system:

- How is the individual appraisal related to the success of the team; should not everyone on the team get the same appraisal?
- Don't individual appraisals and rewards encourage each member of the IPT to try to get individual credit for team activities?
- Why doesn't the IPT or the IPT lead do the appraisals? The IPT and the IPT lead are most aware of team member's contributions.

Lesson 10 – CE and IPT approaches require integration into the overall system of management, with a focus on establishing the IPT empowerment and determining how performance appraisals and rewards will be administered in the team environment.

Conclusion

Implementing CE and IPTs requires significant changes to the way we organize, manage, and perform work. Strong management commitment is needed to ensure the transition. The new skills require practice and time for the teams to use them effectively.

Initially, there is a great deal of optimism, but as reality hits, there is danger of creating frustration and cynicism. To avoid this, IPTs need to periodically assess their progress and plan improvements. Often, an outside team facilitator is needed to assist and advise the IPTs [7,9].

The lessons learned presented here are from implementing CE and IPTs on actual projects. Making use of these lessons will help new projects to more quickly achieve the benefits of CE and IPTs. ◆

References

1. Air Force Materiel Command, *Integrated Product Development Guide*, May 25, 1993.
2. Belasco, James A. and Ralph C. Stayer , *Flight of the Buffalo*, Warner Books, 1994.
3. Miller, *Concurrent Engineering Design*, SME Publishing, First Edition 1993.
4. *Fortune*, "The Trouble with Teams," Sept. 5, 1995.
5. Institute for Defense Analysis (IDA), Report R-338, December 1988.
6. Katzenbach, Jon R. and Douglas K. Smith, "The Discipline of Teams" *Harvard Business Review*, March-April 1993, Miller, Landon.
7. Popick, Paul R. and Craig L. Smith, "A Team Method to Capture Concurrent Engineering Lessons Learned," to be presented at INCOSE Symposium 1996.
8. Rothstein, Lawrence R., "The Empowerment Effort That Came Undone," *Harvard Business Review*, January/February 1995.
9. Scholtes, Peter, *The Team Handbook*, Joiner Associates, 17th printing 1992.
10. Sheard, Sarah A. and M. Elliot Margolis, "Team Structures for Systems Engineering in an IPT Environment," *NCOSE Proceedings 1995*.
11. Sheard, Sarah A., Paul R. Popick, and Thomas G. Van Scoyoc, "Team Workshops: A Systems Answer to IPT Issues," *NCOSE Proceedings 1995*.

About the Authors

Paul R. Popick is a deputy program manager at Johns Hopkins University Applied Physics Laboratory. Formerly a member of the Loral Federal Systems Group Staff, he taught proposal and program management and provided consulting assistance to projects implementing concurrent engineering. Popick  also teaches systems engineering and total quality management courses for the Whiting Graduate Engineering School of Johns Hopkins University. He received a master's degree in applied mathematics (computer science option) from New York University.

Paul R. Popick
Johns Hopkins University
Applied Physics Laboratory
Johns Hopkins Road
Laurel, MD 20723-6099
Voice: 301-953-6000
Fax: 301-953-6149
E-mail: popicpr1@JHUAPL.edu

Sarah A. Sheard has 15 years experience in systems engineering. She worked as a satellite engineer at Hughes Aircraft Space and Communications group and in systems at Loral Federal Systems, Air Traffic Control. Sheard is currently a process engineer at the Software Productivity Consortium where she consults and teaches systems engineering, process improvement, and teams. She received a master's degree in chemistry from the California Institute of Technology.

Sarah A. Sheard
Software Productivity Consortium
2214 Rock Hill Road
Herndon, VA. 20170
Voice: 703-742-7106
Fax: 703-742-7200
E-mail: sheard@software.org

The Softer Side of Project Management

Janice Strauss
National Security Agency

Many project managers limit themselves to techniques they have acquired through formal channels, which decreases their chances for success. I contend that there are many "softer" techniques available that have a great impact on a project. In this article, I share some of the techniques I use to increase the likelihood of achieving project goals.

TYPICALLY FOUND IN THE toolbox of project management are techniques for cost estimation, risk management, meeting staff requirements, and establishing work breakdown structures. These techniques represent essential project management skills usually acquired through formal courses, reading, or on-the-job training. These learning methods often overlook the "softer side" of project management. Understanding this side constitutes yet another tool just as critical to project success as more formal ones. A manager's ability to effectively maintain morale, motivate the team, and use resources determines whether team members have a sense of pride in their project and feel ownership of it.

This article highlights some techniques I have used to address the human side of project management. Some focus on ensuring everyone on the team feels comfortable with their role. Others establish and maintain good team morale. All help a project maintain momentum toward a successful conclusion.

Soft Project Management Techniques

A new project is about to commence. The team consists of senior engineers and computer scientists, all with many years of experience in the tools that will be used on the project. This team also has a history of working together and keeping one another well informed. "A dream team," you think to yourself, and with good reason. Such a team is not likely to be found in the real world. It is much more probable that a project will have a blend of junior and senior employees with varying experience levels. Furthermore, the team will probably have little history with one another and with the technologies, thus requiring much groundwork to initiate the project.

Pair Team Members

Getting junior employees comfortable, up to speed, and productive quickly is definitely a challenge. Formal training helps, but this requires time and money that may not be available. In this situation, I pair junior, inexperienced team members with those who have more expertise. Junior persons may shadow their mentors, observing and studying their behavior, or the pairs may work on a task together, with the senior person handling the more difficult aspects and serving as a mentor to the junior person.

This technique pays for itself in the long run. On one project, a new developer initially played the junior role for a few months. When another inexperienced person joined the team, the first was able to move up to the senior role and successfully served as mentor. This transition was a source of great pride to the entire team.

Ensure Expert Technical Support

Dealing with today's world of constantly changing technologies can make any reputable manager cringe. No sooner has one committed to a suite of tools than a new and better solution becomes apparent. In the case of technologies like Java, new releases occur at short intervals—a daunting prospect for developers. On one of my projects, the team chose Java for its many advantages including hardware independence and enhanced programmer productivity, yet no one on the team had previously used this language. To manage the risk involved, I took steps to ensure that expert technical support for Java was available and accessible to the team. This came in two forms: First, I hired a Java mentor who provided guidance to the rest of the team, introduced new Java tools, and reviewed all Java software. Second, team members were also encouraged to maintain a close relationship with the vendor to stay aware of the latest developments and to provide them with requirements for new features. With this strategy in place, Java increased the team's productivity rather than proving to be an obstacle.

Assign People with Care

Have you ever felt that management views developers as interchangeable game pieces they can arbitrarily move between projects? Many times, I have seen people placed in critical positions based on their job title rather than their skills. Putting team members in positions they cannot handle usually leads to negative consequences in terms of schedule, quality, and productivity. Just because a person is hired as senior computer scientist does not mean that person can take on every task successfully and with little monitoring. Admittedly, there will be times when it is necessary to assign team members to tasks for which they do not have the right expertise. I do this with caution—only with people who have proven track records and in whom I have great confidence. I do not expect those with newly acquired skills to take on critical or complex tasks.

Consider work habits when assigning tasks. Some people work faster than others, thrive on challenge, and withstand pressure well. Others proceed at a more cautious pace and prefer to work on the familiar. Take all these factors into account to prevent situations in

Reprinted from *Crosstalk*, July 1998.

which employees are frustrated with their assignments and cannot make a contribution.

Build a Project History

Every project uses a schedule to communicate its milestones and to guide development efforts. This provides a means to monitor progress. It is crucial to create a schedule that is both realistic and accurate. There are many documented techniques to scientifically do this. These include estimation techniques such as Constructive Cost Mode (COCOMO), Delphi Techniques, and Gantt Charts.

When I was faced with developing a schedule for my last project, COCOMO was suggested as a useful technique. But COCOMO requires parameters such as lines of code, which were not at my disposal. Past performance also might have been a useful predictor, but most of the project team was new—to both each other and the technologies. So I decided to build a project history, albeit a brief one. The team worked without a schedule for about three months. Throughout this period, we closely monitored and recorded progress on assigned tasks. Both the team members and I gained a sense of each person's capabilities, and we based our schedule on this knowledge. I met with team members to review their assigned tasks and to estimate how long each task would take. We compared performance to these estimates on a weekly basis. Within a few months, team members could predict their progress with precision.

There were other benefits derived from this schedule-building technique. The team became intimately aware of the schedule and regularly consulted it. Also, the schedule had buy-in from all members because the team built it. As a result, motivation to achieve milestone dates was extremely high.

Minimize Meetings

In the life of a project, it is a rare day that does not include at least a few meetings. No matter how justified their purpose, meetings tend to steal valuable time from designing and developing a product, which is the real business at hand. Most team members would rather be doing their "real" work and regard meetings with disdain. To combat this bombardment of meetings, one solution is obvious: minimize their number.

This is not a trivial feat. Gathering requirements, participating in design and code inspections, attending relevant briefings, and taking part in status reviews are essential software project activities. I handled this challenge by requiring only a small subset of the entire team at different meetings. For instance, inspections included only the people necessary to ensure coverage in the areas of databases, programming languages, logic, or quality assurance. Sometimes a desk review took the place of an inspection. A few team members had dedicated roles; I designated one to be the customer interface and he represented the team at all requirements meetings.

The exception to this policy is project status reviews. Valuable information-sharing and coordination of tasks occurs at these reviews, so attendance by all team members should be mandatory.

Keep the Team Satisfied

The magic bag of project management tricks amounts to naught without the team's dedication and enthusiasm. These people put in long, hard hours to get a product out the door. The project manager must create a stress-free, positive work environment. Techniques that foster such an atmosphere include showing appreciation, injecting humor whenever possible, and empowering team members.

Project managers should take every opportunity to show their appreciation. The power of cash awards is undeniable, yet these may be unavailable for fiscal or contractual reasons. For teams that consist primarily of contractors for whom cash awards are not available, another way must be found to inform their companies of their superior efforts. At significant milestones, I awarded individuals letters of appreciation and sent a copy to their supervisors. In all cases, the employees and their companies were delighted to receive this recognition.

A little humor goes a long way and should be dispersed in large doses. When an early prototype neared completion, software samples from each team member were analyzed by the Software TestWorks tool, which rates programming style and performs coverage analysis. Much to my delight, all code received high marks. To celebrate this achievement, I awarded the programmers a mock Certificate of Excellence for their efforts. Another light moment occurred during testing when the team was on an emotional roller coaster. To alleviate the tension, I decided to recognize the person who was responsible for the hundredth software discrepancy. Everyone eagerly anticipated this event, and when it finally occurred, I presented the team member with a token of appreciation. Although work continued uninterrupted, these light moments lifted the cloud of stress.

Empowering team members reaps many benefits. It provides them with ready access to all the information they need to do their jobs. Within well-defined boundaries, I allowed developers to directly contact customers and vendors when the situation called for it. Not only did this free me for other activities, but also fostered a trusting environment in which the team felt both unfettered and motivated.

Conclusion

In today's pressure-cooker environment, projects need all the help that can be mustered. Following a cookbook approach to project management probably is not the best recipe for success. Leaders must use every technique at their disposal to achieve their project goals. The tools presented in this article are meant to complement those usually found in courses and texts. Project managers need to select those tools with which they feel the most comfortable, while remembering that project management is as much an art as it is a science. Keeping more human concerns in mind will help projects overcome challenges and attain success. ◆

About the Author

Janice Strauss has been employed at the National Security Agency as a senior computer scientist for more than 13 years. She has worked in a variety of positions, most recently as a project manager. She is also actively involved in software improvement initiatives within her current organization. These have included leading a Requirements Management Technical Working Group as well as initiating a Software Process Information Exchange group, which provides a forum to trade development tools, techniques, and best practices.

National Security Agency
9800 Savage Road
Fort Meade, MD 20755
Voice: 301-688-0994
E-mail: gusstr@erols.com

Chapter 9

Direction Advice

To resolve to make your meaning plain, even at the cost of some trouble to yourself, is more important than any other single thing.

—Ernest Gowers

Overview

Direction is the art of dealing with people, behavior, and the many interpersonal aspects of management. It involves helping people determine what they have to do, empowering them to do it, celebrating their achievements, guiding their performance, providing them with feedback when they need it, and coaching them when they ask for your help. To provide proper direction, you must know how to "energize," "motivate," and "lead" teams of creative individuals. To direct effectively, you must understand what motivates people and be sensitive to their needs as well as those of the organization. You can then use factors like interesting work, advancement, the work environment, and prospects for growth to stimulate high levels of performance. You must strive to achieve good communications, build a consensus, and reward teamwork as well as individual performance. Without a doubt, the best software managers are team players who understand how to lead and motivate others towards achieving shared goals.

This chapter contains four papers on the topic of direction. These articles were selected to cover the following range of behavioral and psychological topics that are often grouped together under the heading of direction: change management, communications, conflict resolution, delegation, empowerment, leadership, and motivation. I have included papers taken from major management publications to show that modem change management, motivation and leadership techniques can be put to work within the software field. I have also added a paper on managing relationships and balancing them with business needs as the project unfolds. The trick is to focus on satisfying both staff and organization's goals as you plan and perform the work.

Article Summaries

The Human Side of Management, by Tom Teal. This is another of those modem classics that has greatly influenced current management theory. It points out that great management is about character, not technique. It talks about integrity in management and the importance of communicating clearly, being responsible, keeping promises, and fully understanding your capabilities. It discusses how to resolve conflicts between your organizational and moral masters. It confirms that you must pursue the courage of convictions with a tenacity that sometimes resembles heroism.

Motivating and Keeping Software Developers, by Ken Whitaker. This is an article on how to motivate and keep key people even when faced with difficult situations. The paper suggests that effective executive leadership revolves around the ability to satisfy both the organization's and the individual's goals. The paper goes on to discuss how to stimulate people to achieve these goals and channel their behavior accordingly. Finally, the paper suggests that you can greatly strengthen your ability to motivate and keep software developers by providing them with interesting work and the ability to grow professionally.

Successful Software Management: 14 Lessons Learned, by Johanna Rothman. This article provides pointers on how to effectively balance the needs of the business, employees, and the work environment. By focusing on lessons learned, the author is able to share her experiences in relationship management with the reader. The advice offered considers the human side of the enterprise, an area often ignored by technical people. Motivating people to exert their best efforts requires interpersonal skills that managers need to develop and tune.

A Tale of Three Developers, by Donald J. Reifer. The paper tells three stories about the trials and tribulations that new programmers face when taking on their initial assignments in firms having different corporate cultures. Although set in different locales, the stories have a common theme. Their message is that today's hot software marketplace offers these new hires, despite their fears, frustrations and uncertainties, unprecedented opportunities for advancement, and growth and learning on the job when properly energized, led, and motivated.

Key Terms

Seven terms, defined as follows, are important to understanding the topic of organization as used within this chapter:

1. **Authority.** In project management, the right to give direction and allocate resources (staff, schedule, etc.). This right should be commensurate with responsibility. However, the terms are different and distinct because they infer different behaviors.
2. **Delegation.** In management, to empower another with the authority to act or represent you in the performance of your responsibilities.
3. **Directing.** Those management activities conducted to energize, motivate, and guide staff to achieve organizational goals.
4. **Motivation.** m management, the act of influencing the behavior of others through the combined use of incentives and rewards.
5. **Responsibility.** In management, responsibility infers obligation, not authority to perform a task. In other words, responsibility relates to duties, both real and imaginary, that one feels obliged to perform.
6. **Team.** A group of people organized to work together.
7. **Teamwork.** The cooperative effort by the members of a group aimed at achieving common goals.

For Your Bookshelf

Recommended readings again include the Tom DeMarco and Tim Lister's *Peopleware* (2nd edition) and the Thomsett's *Radical Project Management,* books that look at how to motivate software people and direct their behavior. The *Team Handbook* (2nd edition) is another useful book on the topic of people and teams. It arms you with tools and techniques that you can use to build teams and address the conflicts that occur whenever people have to work together.

Chapter 9 of the *Project Management Book of Knowledge (PMBOK™),* published by the Project Management Institute, offers some excellent advice on team development. I particularly like the brief but pointed discussion of the reward and recognition systems that need to be put into place in order to motivate team performance.

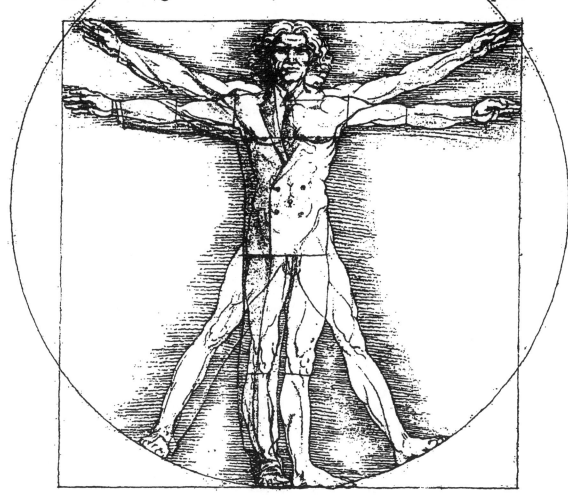

Great management is about character, not technique.

The Human Side of Management

by Thomas Teal

Look closely at any company in trouble, and you'll probably find that the problem is management. Ask employees about their jobs, and they'll complain about management. Study large corporations, and you'll discover that the biggest barrier to change, innovation, and new ideas is very often management. Make an inventory of the things that have stifled your own creativity and held back your own career; summarize the critical factors that have stood in the way of your organization's success; name the individuals chiefly responsible for the missed opportunities and bungled projects you yourself have witnessed. Managers will top every list.

There is so much inferior management in the world that some people believe we'd be better off in completely flat organizations with no managers at all. Most of us spend the better part of our working lives convinced that we could do the boss's job better than the boss. Something about management looks so easy that we watch one anemic performance after another and never doubt that we could succeed where others

Thomas Teal is a former senior editor of the Harvard Business Review. This article is adapted from his introduction to First Person: Tales of Management Courage and Tenacity, published by the Harvard Business School Press in April 1996.

repeatedly fail. Of course, a few of us *would* be terrific managers. But just as clearly, most of us would not. We know this is true because so many of us eventually get the chance to try.

As for the argument that management is unnecessary, think for a moment about what the world was like before the principles of scientific management rationalized production, democratized wealth, commercialized science, and effectively doubled life expectancy. Good management works miracles.

And still the troublesome fact is that mediocre management is the norm. This is not because some people are born without the management gene or because the wrong people get promoted or because the system can be manipulated – although all these things happen all the time. The overwhelmingly most common explanation is much simpler: capable management is so extraordinarily difficult that few people look good no matter how hard they try. Most of those lackluster managers we all complain about are doing their *best* to manage well.

In one form or another, managing has become one of the world's most common jobs, and yet we make demands on managers that are nearly impossible to meet. For starters, we ask them to acquire a long list of more or less traditional management skills in finance, cost control, resource allocation, product development, marketing, manufacturing, technology, and a dozen other areas. We also demand that they master the management arts – strategy, persuasion, negotiation, writing, speaking, listening. In addition, we ask them to assume responsibility for organizational success, make a great deal of money, and share it generously. We also require them to demonstrate the qualities that define leadership, integrity, and character – things like vision, fortitude, passion, sensitivity, commitment, insight, intelligence, ethical standards, charisma, luck, courage, tenacity, even from time to time humility. Finally, we insist that they should be our friends, mentors, or guardians, perpetually alert to our best interests. Practicing this common profes-

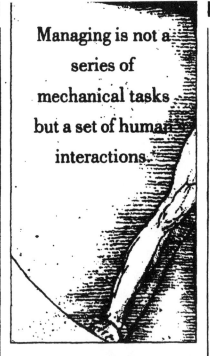

Managing is not a series of mechanical tasks but a set of human interactions.

sion *adequately*, in other words, requires people to display on an everyday basis the combined skills of St. Peter, Peter the Great, and the Great Houdini. No wonder most managers seem to underperform.

And still not *all* of them do. Easy as it is to point out mediocre managers – and you can hardly swing a cat in the average workplace without hitting several – nearly everyone gets to see a few exemplary managers in the course of a career. These people fall into two categories: first, the good or very good managers, who are exceedingly rare because they actually meet the inhuman requirements for adequacy; second, the great managers, or rather the occasional bosses we don't hesitate to call great managers in spite of the fact that they lack a dozen of the skills and virtues that we would normally insist on (and that the job description probably requires). We need to take a closer look at this second category, great managers, because although their numbers are small, they tend to loom exceptionally large in the lives of the people around them.

One reason for the scarcity of managerial greatness is that in educating and training managers, we focus too much on technical proficiency and too little on character.

The management sciences – statistics, data analysis, productivity, financial controls, service delivery – are things we can almost take for granted these days. They are subjects we know how to teach. But we're still in the Dark Ages when it comes to teaching people how to *behave* like great managers – somehow instilling in them capacities such as courage and integrity that can't be taught. Perhaps as a consequence, we've developed a tendency to downplay the importance of the human element in managing. Managers are not responsible for other people's happiness, we say. The workplace isn't a nursery school. We've got market share and growth and profits to worry about, and anyway, power is too useful and entertaining to dribble away on relationships – we've got our own nests to feather. But the only people who become great managers are the ones who understand in their guts that managing is not merely a series of mechanical tasks but a set of human interactions.

In the course of seven years at this magazine, I was lucky enough to come in contact with a surprising number of great managers. As editor of a department we called First Person, I was in a position to help several such people – many of them entrepreneurs or CEOs – tell their own stories about critical problems they had faced, analyzed, grappled with, and sometimes but not always resolved. Not all those stories ended happily, but all of them showed how extraordinarily difficult firstrate management can be. They all showed something else as well – that management is a supremely human activity, a fact that explains why, among all the preposterous demands that we make on managers, character means more to us than education. We may love and work hard for a manager who knows too little about computers or marketing but is a fine human being. We almost invariably dislike and thwart managers who are stingy or mean-spirited, however great their technical abilities. Look back three paragraphs to that long list of requirements. As it glides upward from acquirable skills to primal virtues, each item on the list grows less and less dispensable. Without courage and tenacity, for example, no manager can *hope* to achieve greatness. Consider a few of the other absolute prerequisites.

Great management requires imagination. If a company's vision and strategy are to differentiate its offerings and create competitive advantage, they must be original. Original has to mean unconventional, and it often means counterintuitive. Moreover, it takes ingenuity and wit to bring disparate people and elements together into a unified but uniquely original whole. There is even a name for this capacity. It's called esemplastic imagination, and although it's generally attributed only to poets, consider the Rosenbluth family.

When Hal Rosenbluth's great-grandfather Marcus opened a travel business in Philadelphia in 1892, he did not see himself as just another travel agent. Unlike his competitors, whose goals were limited to writing and selling tickets, he saw himself in the immigration business. For $50, he supplied poor Europeans with steamship tickets, assistance clearing the hurdles at Ellis Island, and transport to Philadelphia. And he didn't stop there. Since immigration was not usually an individual affair but involved entire families, Marcus Rosenbluth set himself up as a kind of banker for immigrants as well. When his immigrants were settled and had jobs, he collected their savings, five and ten cents at a time, until there was enough money to bring over a second member of the family and a third and a fourth, until the whole clan was safely in America. From the day it was born, Rosenbluth Travel had the competitive advantage of imagination.

Years later, when immigration slowed (and when the company was forced to give up one of its licenses – travel or banking), Rosenbluth Travel moved into the business of leisure travel. Then in the late 1970s, nearly 90 years after the whole enterprise got off the ground, Hal Rosenbluth took over the business and reinvented it once again. Deregulation had just created turmoil out of order and stability. Between any two given cities, two or three standard airfares

had suddenly mushroomed into a chaos of new airlines, schedules, and tariffs, all subject to change without notice. Customers were frustrated and angry trying to figure out what the fares really were, and travel agents, unable to cope or make sense of the confusion, were close to desperation. Hal saw it all as a grand opportunity, partly because he saw that the solution lay in another recent innovation – computers. He subscribed to every airline's electronic reservation network (in those days, the airlines charged for access), and he amalgamated all the fares on a computerized system of his own. He bought terminals for his agents and built a new spirit of teamwork using enthusiasm, incentives, and a determination to pay so much attention to his employees' interests that they would feel free to pay attention to the customers'. He guaranteed clients the lowest airfare on every route, and he set out to nail as many corporate accounts as he could find. But, as Hal put it, "I think our biggest competitive advantage was to understand that as deregulation changed the rules, we were no longer in the travel business as much as we were in the information business." The Rosenbluth imagination was

Integrity in management means being responsible, communicating clearly, keeping promises, knowing oneself.

still at work after four generations and nearly 100 years.

Another characteristic of great managers is integrity. All managers believe they behave with integrity, but in practice, many have trouble with the concept. Some think integrity is the same thing as secretiveness or blind loyalty. Others seem to believe it means consistency, even in a bad cause. Some confuse it with discretion and some with the opposite quality – bluntness – or with simply not telling lies. What integrity means in management is more ambitious and difficult than any of these. It means being responsible, of course, but it also means communicating clearly and consistently, being an honest broker, keeping promises, knowing oneself, and avoiding hidden agendas that hang other people out to dry. It comes very close to what we used to call honor, which in part means not telling lies to yourself.

Think of the way Johnson & Johnson dealt with the Tylenol poisoning crisis or how Procter & Gamble withdrew Rely Tampons, a newly launched product, because of an unproved but potentially serious health risk. Compare those cases with the way Johns-Manville handled the asbestos catastrophe. As a Manville manager for more than 30 years, Bill Sells witnessed what he calls "one of the most colossal corporate blunders of the twentieth century." This blunder was not the company's manufacture and sale of asbestos. Companies have been producing deadly chemicals and explosives for hundreds of years. According to Sells, the blunder that killed thousands of people and eliminated an industry was self-deception. Manville managers at every level were simply unwilling to acknowledge the evidence available in the 1940s, when so much of the damage was done, and their capacity for denial held steady through the following decades despite mounting evidence about old and newly identified hazards. The company developed a classic case of bunker mentality: refusing to accept facts; assuming that customers and employees were aware of the hazards and used asbestos at their own risk; denying the need for and the very possibility of change at a company that had successfully hidden its head in the sand for 100 years. Manville funded little medical research, made little effort to communicate what it already knew, and took little or no proactive responsibility for the damage asbestos might do. Captive to the notion that investments that make no product can make no contribution to success, the company pursued only haphazardly the few safety practices that were in place – with tragic consequences for workers' health and decidedly negative effects on maintenance costs, productivity, and profit. Once when he raised objec-

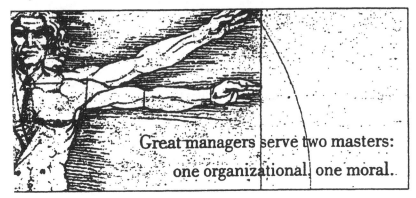

Great managers serve two masters: one organizational, one moral.

tions, Sells was told by his boss, "Bill, you're not loyal," to which he replied, "No, no, you've got it wrong. I'm the one who *is* loyal."

After eight years with the company, Sells was promoted in 1968 to manage a troubled asbestos facility in Illinois, where it was his job to juggle responsibilities that sometimes seemed to conflict – keeping the plant profitable, keeping it productive, and keeping it safe. Slowly and painfully over the next year and a half, he came to understand that labor relations, productivity, dust abatement, profitability, health, and safety were all aspects of the same issue – business integrity – and he launched a half-million-dollar program to replace or rebuild nearly all the safety equipment in the building. By the early 1970s, unfortunately, it was too late to save asbestos or its victims. But Sells did put his insight into practice in the 1980s, when he headed the company's

fiberglass division. Among other things, the division funded arm's-length studies and practiced immediate total disclosure (by phone, fax, letter, news conference, videotape, live television, and printed warnings) of everything the company learned about the potential hazards and health risks of the product and made no disingenuous effort to put a procompany spin on the results.

Of course, business integrity means accepting the business consequences of a company's acts, but for great managers, it also means taking personal responsibility. The boss who accused Sells of disloyalty didn't want to hear uncomfortable facts or opposing points of view. But when Sells took over his own division, he opened himself to criticism and argument. This is stressful work for managers, partly because it means serving two masters – one organizational, one moral – and partly because they're not likely to get support for doing it, not even for doing it well. The rewards for great managers are more subtle.

In the early 1980s, William Peace was the general manager of the Synthetic Fuels Division at Westinghouse, a relatively small unit that faced liquidation as a result of declining oil prices unless he could make it attractive enough to sell. In an effort to pare costs, he decided to eliminate a number of the division's 130 jobs because he thought potential buyers would see them as inessential, and, under the circumstances, he had no choice but to lay off the people who held those jobs in spite of their sometimes excellent performance records. He and his de-

partment heads drew up the list of 15 positions in a long, emotional meeting, and when it was over and his senior managers were about to go off and convey the bad news, Peace stopped them. He felt this was news he had to communicate himself, in part because he didn't want the entire workforce to conclude that a wave of layoffs was in the making, in part because he felt he owed the individuals involved a face-to-face explanation.

The meeting with the 15 innocent victims the next morning was funereal. People wept openly or stared dejectedly at the floor. Peace walked through his reasoning, insisted that the layoffs were based on job descriptions, not individual performance, and begged the 15 victims to understand if not forgive the need to sacrifice some employees in order to save the division and all its other jobs. They argued, pleaded, and accused him of ingratitude and heartlessness. Peace commiserated, sympathized, accepted their criticism and disapproval, and did his best to give a frank, detailed answer to every question, taking all the heat they cared to give. Gradually the anger faded and the mood shifted from despondency to resignation and even to some grudging understanding and actual interest in the prospects for a sale. Peace recalls it as the most painful meeting he ever took part in. But by the time he shook their hands and wished them luck, he hoped and believed they had come to appreciate his motives if not his choice of sacrificial lambs.

It was months later that he learned how the confrontation had played to those 15 people. A buyer had been found for the division, Peace had been kept on as general manager, and the new owner was investing money in the enterprise. Suddenly Peace was in a position to rehire many of the people he'd laid off, and when he made them the offer, everyone, without exception, came back to work for him, even when it meant giving up good jobs found elsewhere. This is a story about moral and humanitarian compunctions. Equally to the point, however, it's about a manager drawing attention to his own responsibility in adversity, a piece of courage that in this case led to the eventual recapturing of loyal, experienced employees.

Great management has to involve the kind of respect Peace showed for his subordinates, and it must also involve empowerment. The managers people name with admiration are always the ones who delegate their authority, make subordinates feel powerful and capable, and draw from them so much creativity and such a feeling of responsibility that their behavior changes forever. In 1980, when Ricardo Semler took over Semco, his family's business in São Paulo, Brazil – five factories that manufactured, among other things, marine pumps, commercial dishwashers, and mixing equipment for everything from bubble gum to rocket fuel – productivity was low, new contracts were a rarity, and financial disaster loomed. Furthermore, the company was mired in regulations, hierarchy, and distrust. There were intricate rules for travel – strict ceilings on hotel expenses, calls home limited to a set number of minutes, and all the usual red tape about turning in receipts. Factory workers underwent daily theft-prevention security checks, needed permission to use the bathroom, and were generally treated like delinquents.

Semler swept this old world out the door. He reduced the hierarchy to three levels, threw out the rule book (putting in its place what he called the rule of common sense), initiated collegial decision making, and began submitting certain company decisions – such as a factory relocation and several critical acquisitions – to companywide democratic votes. He set up a profit-sharing

plan, and, to make it work, he cut the size of the operating units to which it was tied and opened the company's books to everyone on the payroll. On the theory that he should not be sending people he didn't trust around the world to represent his company, he eliminated expense accounting and simply gave people whatever they claimed to have spent. On the theory that it was indecent to treat people like children who in private life were heads of families, civic leaders, and army reserve officers, he put hourly workers on monthly salaries, did away with time clocks and security checks, and let people on the factory floor set their own work goals, methods, and even work hours. He calculated that people whose bonuses depended on profits were neither going to waste the company's money on luxury hotels and cars nor sit around on their hands at work.

He was right. Sales doubled the first year, inventories fell, the company launched eight new products that had been lost in R&D for years, quality improved (for one product, the rejection rate dropped from more than 30% to less than 1%), costs declined, and productivity increased so dramatically that the company was able to reduce the workforce by 32% through attrition and incentives for workers to take early retirement. Semler had reversed the usual practice. Instead of choosing a few responsibilities he could delegate, he picked out a handful of responsibilities that had to remain his own – contracts, strategy, alliances, the authority to make changes in the style of company management – and gave away everything else. Perhaps, he says, some people take advantage of uncontrolled expense accounts or

unlocked storage rooms – he would certainly prosecute anyone he found stealing – but his delegation of authority has been so radical and thorough (and effective) that he has no good way of finding out and no desire to know.

In some cases, however, urging people toward shared responsibility and authority is like pulling teeth, and when it means repressing your own instinct to control, like pulling your own teeth. The truth is, people often fail to embrace the opportunities they claim to want, and managers often fail to yield the authority they aim to delegate. Ralph Stayer of Johnsonville Sausage in Wisconsin is another CEO who, in the early 1980s, tried to empower and invigorate his workforce with large helpings of profit sharing and responsibility. But Stayer was his own worst enemy. He was still so deeply in love with his own control that he held onto it in ways that he was not even conscious of. By giving advice to every subordinate who asked him for help in addressing a problem, he continued to run the company and own the problems. By continuing to collect production data, he stayed in charge of production. By continuing to check the quality of the product, he effectively prevented successful delegation of quality control. His subordinates were simply afraid to make decisions unless they knew which decisions he wanted them to make. The only real difference was that now instead of telling them what he wanted, he was making them guess. Not surprisingly, they quickly became experts at correctly interpreting his tone of voice, deciphering his body language, inferring entire policies from a single offhand remark. Once he realized what he

Motivating and Keeping Software Developers

Ken Whitaker, USDATA Corp.

The focus of the new Management column is to address the needs of those of us responsible for managing or leading computing professionals. The first column is about motivating and rewarding software developers. The author has survived the wars of managing the development of numerous shrinkwrapped software products. Over the past 24 years, he has led teams at Data General, Software Publishing Corp., and A.C. Nielsen. He wrote Managing Software Maniacs, *Wiley, 1994 and is a frequent speaker at software development conferences.*

—Mark Haas

So you're a software-development manager who must keep the "herd" motivated, yet somehow also release a product on schedule. If that's not enough, you must remind yourself, your team, and especially product management about the importance of quality.

First and foremost, you need to keep your folks motivated. This is especially difficult in a competitive job market that emphasizes high salaries and multiple opportunities for each software developer.

Two important issues you need to handle are

- making certain that developers understand their roles, and
- keeping developers happy, using either rewards or incentives.

CLEAR ROLES AND RESPONSIBILITIES

A software-development team always executes better when it uses a process—as long as everyone is accountable and everyone understands each milestone requirement. If handled properly, schedule leadership can be a motivator rather than a threat to creativity. This applies to start-ups as well as established software organizations.

Anyone can wing software development. But if everyone works under hacker rules, your folks will be doing rework throughout the project, no matter how talented they are. Hacker rules include

- Working without an agreement with marketing on the product concept.
- Working without agreed-upon schedules.
- Getting no customer feedback until the product is almost done.
- Having no agreement on a *pro forma,* the product line's profit-and-loss analysis.

Each milestone must have a certain degree of implied quality measurement. In addition, each milestone should

- be easy to understand,
- validate major achievements,
- provide value to the organization so that everyone knows their role, and
- help determine if a project is on schedule.

Milestones require a goal, a deliverable, and a definition of the most-important role for each organization that is a part of the product team. Typical product-team organizations include engineering, testing, documentation, sales, production, product management, and customer support. They should also include quality expectations, which management uses as a barometer to help determine a project's

> **It's especially difficult to keep your folks motivated in a competitive environment.**

status. As long as everyone involved is objective about evaluating the quality issues needed to attain the next milestone, the project team will keep on track toward a successful project delivery.

For example, say the goal of the beta milestone is "technical completeness." In this case, the engineer's role might be, "Hand off the code to the testing group." One quality metric, for the user interface, might be "Every menu should bring up the expected dialog box or action without any crashes."

As long as the team agrees that every organization's goal has been fulfilled and that the necessary quality metric is met, the alpha milestone has been achieved.

Whatever you do, don't fall into the trap of reducing testing time to regain a release schedule. And don't redefine a milestone goal to accommodate a product deficiency. You'll only pay for these decisions later!

REWARDS VERSUS INCENTIVES

How many times have you heard these

two lines from upper management, sales, or marketing: "Couldn't we release the software project (commonly known as "the Pig") sooner if your programmers put in more hours?" Or, "Let's dangle cash to motivate the engineers to deliver three months earlier!"

Motivating developers is a difficult skill to master. The motivational techniques you use will depend mostly on your company's culture. Now, "culture" is a word I despise. Why? Because a culture can take on a life of its own that defies reason, especially in software-development groups. Ultimately, culture becomes an excuse to justify any company, customer, or management decision.

Nevertheless, your motivational techniques should consider the effect of your company's culture and values. If you choose the right techniques, they can have dramatic impact long after the release of your current product. If your company is very aggressive (a couple come to mind) and the goal is to get products out at any cost, then by all means offer cash incentives. But be prepared to pay the consequences.

Most of us are in the software business because we like the technical challenge. This applies to writers, testers, and software engineers (*all* of whom I consider to be software developers). But we all need to make a living, and it is difficult to pass up money and other bonuses. You also expect that the more you learn and the more success you achieve, the more compensation you'll get. Unless it is for a startup opportunity, a software developer will not typically go from one company to another for *less* money. And even with startups, the opportunity to get "lots of money" down the road is the incentive to take a pay cut.

Consider what motivates other organizations in your company: Salespeople are motivated by closing the sale, attaining quotas, being recognized, and making more money. Marketing professionals have a similar motivation: If the products they are managing are successful, sales will do well and the company will grow, and so will their wallets. The folks in finance are anxious for any reduction in expenses or increase in revenues, to save face with the board of directors and stockholders.

Deciding whether to use rewards or incentives is a key management challenge that most software organizations have to face. I find that this issue comes up about once every six months, like clockwork. A reward is typically some bonus associated with some accomplishment. Usually, the recipient is not expecting a reward. An incentive is typically some bonus associated with a future goal or milestone. The recipient normally has advanced expectations of the opportunity for an incentive. Don't make the mistake of publicly presenting recognition. I'm constantly amazed at how effective a *private* award is regarded by the employee and how ineffective a *public* award can be to the individual and the team.

Developers should be rewarded after they have accomplished some goal. Although a project has many milestones, there is nothing like delivering a quality product that satisfies customer requirements on or ahead of schedule. Let's look at an example.

The wrong way

Not too long ago, a famous software company announced that each developer and a guest would be awarded a vacation in Hawaii upon product delivery. The catch? The product, which was already late to market, had to be completed by a much-publicized date. Some spouses started shopping for resortwear. Morale was high. Music was blasting down the halls and source code was flying everywhere at all hours of the night.

As weeks became months, the desired delivery date came and went. The software product was not completed on time. What was senior management to do? What would you do as the development leader?

Development and marketing management assumed that maybe the original dates were not realistic. So they drew another line in the sand and told the team that Hawaii was still on, but the new date *must* be made. No expense was spared: cots and pizza were brought in! No music was allowed; it was now viewed as distracting. The longer developers worked, the more teamwork and quality programming went out the window. In fact, team meetings became so unruly that the beta milestone was somehow achieved three times!

The second release date was not met. Executive management became furious. Stockholders had lost patience and the board of directors was convinced that the product would never be released. This time, management mandated that a third scheduled release date had to be met and that all incentives were withdrawn. The company was suffering major losses and, frankly, the developers were paid enough and were expected to deliver.

Can you guess what happened? Yep, the best developers left the company, betrayed by what they considered to be ridiculous management and unrealistic goals. The remaining team members were so burned out, they practically had to start the project over to attempt to build the product right because the developers had taken so

> **Deciding whether to use rewards or incentives is a key management challenge that most software organizations have to face.**

many shortcuts to achieve the scheduled milestones.

The product was finally released 18 months later.

The right way

Another company, also faced with an important deadline, prioritized the product features and built a product that had only the *must-have* features. Once the alpha milestone (the barely limping milestone) was achieved, the best developers (two engineers, one tester, and one writer) received private rewards and a personalized letter from the president of the company. You see, these four were the technical stars, and their excitement could encourage the rest of the team. At the beta milestone (the functionally complete milestone), several other developers received similar rewards, including one of the engineers that received an award at alpha.

An unusual by-product of the second company's approach was that the developers actually added a few features that were in the *nice-to-have* category, a pleasant surprise for marketing.

Software development includes several disciplines. Don't make the mistake of taking care of only the engineers when the testers probably went through as much hell releasing a quality product. If you depend on teamwork in your organization to deliver products, the best way to destroy teamwork is by rewarding only a portion of the team.

Last but not least, realize that timing is crucial when issuing rewards. Don't wait a couple of months after a major accomplishment before you reward someone for that accomplishment. A key technique to reduce project risk is to reward key developers early in a product cycle—even as early as the alpha milestone.

GOAL SETTING AND CAREER PLANNING

It's not enough to motivate software developers when they work on high-profile, neat projects. There are some other critical success factors that can be more important to keep a developer over the long term.

If your company has a "strategy of the day," you run the risk of training developers to see the future only in terms of the next project, not as the fulfillment of an overall strategy. Most software companies are extremely weak at strategic planning. In the disturbing movie, *Miller's Crossing*, one bad guy was asked to "terminate" another bad guy. "I can't do it without a plan," he protested. "There's *got* to be a reason."

What is your career plan? In other words, if a developer in your group is not clear on what their goals are and what it takes to get to the next step, you are vulnerable to losing that developer. Presenting a career plan can be done in three easy steps:

1. Compare the developers' current job descriptions with the next higher one.
2. List and analyze the developers' strengths and weaknesses in their current job. This is good practice for preparing their annual performance appraisal.
3. Prepare a set of actions, their intended results, and how success will be measured for each. This helps set realistic expectations so that the next job level does not appear to be unattainable and the criteria for achieving it unmea-

surable. If you are not clear in your communication, your motivational meeting could turn into a demotivational meeting.

Do you feel it's not worth the effort to deal with any form of career planning? If so, you would do well to consider who does do a tremendous job of career planning: In one five-minute phone call, a recruiter can do this job for you.

COMPENSATION

Last, but not least, you need to constantly check that you are compensating people appropriately. Do annual salary surveys, and adjust salaries accordingly. I can assure you that during the past 12 months, the market value for software developers has skyrocketed. If you fail to recognize and react to market trends, you will lose key developers. This surge in compensation is not just in key metropolitan cities—it is nationwide.

If yours is a public company, consider awarding stock. Some companies restrict the distribution of stock to reward only a chosen few. Then they try to motivate all employees by reminding them how important stockholder equity is. How do developers feel, when they look in their pocket and realize that they don't have any way to get that equity other than buying stock on the open market?

Management usually reacts to a wave of departing developers rather than proactively doing the right things to make certain that developers don't even think about leaving. Do the right thing now.

To motivate and keep developers:

- Define a product delivery process and clear roles.
- Reward—don't use incentives.
- Set goals and make career plans on a regular basis.
- Compensate to keep people. ❖

Ken Whitaker is a certified leader of software lunatics at USDATA, a leading producer of SCADA/MMI graphics in Richardson, Texas. Contact him at kwhitaker @usdata.com.

Successful Software Management:
14 Lessons Learned[©]

Johanna Rothman
Rothman Consulting Group, Inc.

Successful managers realize that they need to balance the needs of the business, the employees, and the work environment to be effective. In this article, the author summarizes her experiences in determining the work to accomplish and planning it, managing successful relationships with the group, and managing reactions to typical management mistakes.

Shortly after becoming a manager, I dragged myself home from work, flopped on the couch, and said to my husband, "This management stuff is hard. Nothing I learned in school prepared me for this people stuff. And that *management training*, that was just form-filling-out nonsense. The soft skills – dealing with people – are the hardest." My husband chuckled and commiserated.

If you are like me, and you started your professional career as a technical person, this *management stuff* is difficult to do. Not the forms, although the forms can be irritating, but the difficult part is knowing how to deal with people, and completing the work your organization expects of you. I have now had more than 15 years of management experience, and have learned a number of lessons about managing people.

Define the Manager's Role
When you become a manager, your role is to organize purposefully [1]. For me, that means creating an environment where people can perform their best work. As a software manager, that means I work to create business value by balancing the needs of the business, the employees, and the environment. There is no *one right way* to do this; every organization is different. However, the following lessons have served me well in numerous organizations.

1. Know What They Pay You to Do
I have been a manager of developers, testers, and support staff. You would think it would be easy to know what the company paid me to do. However, my mission as a test manager – to report on the state of the software – is sometimes different from what the organizations desire: to find the Big Bad Bugs before the customer does, or bless this software. Even my mission as a development manager – develop the team members as much as the software – was different from what another organization desired: create software just good enough that we can be

Reprinted from *Crosstalk,* December 2003.

bought out.

My mission does not have to be the same as yours, and you may modify your mission as your organization changes. However, delivering on your mission as a manager is what your organization pays you to do. What is important is to notice when your title, your mission, and what the company pays you to do are not synchronized.

One quality assurance (QA) manager said it this way, "My management only wants to me to manage the testing, not raise risks, look for process improvement

> ## "When you align yourself with your manager's priorities, you do the work they pay you to do."

opportunities, or even gather and report on what I think are standard metrics. My manager and I are both frustrated. Focusing on just the testing is wrong." This QA manager has at least one alternative – change his title so that he and the organization both know that he is not attempting to perform organization-wide process improvement, to clarify expectations in the organization.

Doing what the organization pays you to do, and not doing what they do not pay you to do makes a huge difference in how successfully you and your group can accomplish your mission. Make sure you clarify your mission at your organization so you can create to-do and not-to-do lists. These lists help you plan the work – for you and your group.

One development manager who temporarily took over installations from the tech support people realized that he no longer had a development team, but an installation support team. The development manager put installations on his not-to-do list and developed a plan to move

installations back to tech support.

When you align yourself with your manager's priorities, you do the work they pay you to do.

2. Plan the Work: Portfolio Management
It is easy to be reactive at work and feel buffeted by the requested changes of your group. It is harder and necessary to be proactive and plan your group's work, even if that work changes every week. For me, planning includes these activities: identifying the project portfolio (i.e., new work, ongoing work, periodic work, *ad hoc* work), developing strategies for managing the work for each project, and knowing what done means for each project. One of the questions I like to ask is, "How little can we do?" I do not want to shortchange any project, so by asking about the minimum requirements, I can accommodate more projects successfully.

Part of planning the work is assigning the people to projects. I assign people to one important project then allow them to take on little bits and pieces of less important work when they need a break or are stuck on the important project. I avoid context switching (moving from one unrelated task to another) as much as possible.

3. Accept Only One No. 1 Priority at a Time
I have worked for many managers who demanded that my staff and I work on several top-priority projects simultaneously.

Senior managers perform different work than first-line and middle managers. It is not possible for senior managers to work on more than one top-priority task at a time. However, because they tend to have more wait states in their work, these senior managers are under the illusion that they are working on several top-priority projects at the same time.

Middle and first-line managers can only work on one No. 1 priority task at a time. However, sometimes we confuse urgency and importance [2]. At one organization, I would arrive at work in the morning, check my voice mail, and respond to all message requests. That took until noon. Again after lunch, I would check my e-mail and voice mail and run around responding to those urgent requests. After a week of this, I realized I was not performing any of the important work such as planning for the group and lab, reviewing critical development plans, or planning my hiring strategy. I also realized that although people marked their e-mails and voice mails *high priority*, they did not utilize the information I had given them at the time I responded.

I stopped responding immediately to urgent requests and re-planned my days. While I still checked voice mail and e-mail, I tended to ask more questions about the deadlines for requests. Prioritizing requests helped me manage my management time. I still had the problem of too many high priority projects coming into my group, so I asked my manager these questions:

- If you could have one project first, which one would it be?
- What are the consequences if we release any of these projects late?

We talked and negotiated which projects had to be completed when and why. When I understood the trade-offs between projects, I was able to manage the work coming into my group.

4. Commit to Projects After Checking With Your Staff

Business needs change. Sometimes your manager will grab you in the hall and say, "Hey, can you do this project now, and finish it in two months?" Or, a senior management planning committee will call you into its meeting and say, "We need this project now. Can you commit to it?"

It is very tempting to say yes. However, saying yes is exactly the wrong thing to do. You can say, "Let me check to see if my previous estimate is still accurate, and I'll get back to you before 5 p.m. today."

If you say yes, you are training your senior management to ask you for answers when you do not know the answers. You have also committed your staff to a project that may not be within the scope you originally estimated.

5. Hire the Best People for the Job

Especially if you manage many projects, your greatest leverage point is in hiring appropriate staff. Too often, we hire people who have similar technical skills and personalities as the people already in our groups. Hiring people who are *just like the ones we have now* does not always gain the best people for the job.

When you hire people your staff thinks are great, you increase morale in the group, and you increase your group's capacity over time. I recommend you develop a hiring strategy that identifies the technical and soft skills you are looking for, and that you choose a variety of techniques for interviewing.

I have found auditions [3, 4, 5] to be an essential technique for interviewing technical staff. I normally create 30- to 45-minute auditions to see how a person works in a particular setting. Auditions help candidates show what they can do. If you organize a congruent audition, you do not trip people up on esoteric ideas or jargon; you create a simplified situation that

---

"Hiring people who are just like the ones we have now does not always gain the best people for the job."

---

the candidate could encounter at work. Watching the candidate, or having the candidate explain their answers/results is a powerful interview technique.

You can create auditions for any position, including project managers, developers, testers, writers, support staff, analysts, systems engineers, product managers, program managers, and people managers. Define the behaviors you require in a position, and then create an audition using your products or open source products to see the person at work. Create auditions that are 30 minutes long to start. If you are having trouble deciding between multiple candidates, define another audition that is one hour long and invite the candidates back to see how they manage that audition. Auditions show you how the person works at work — priceless information.

I also recommend behavior-description interview questions [5, 6] to understand how a candidate has performed in previous jobs. Behavior-description questions are open-ended and ask the candidate to tell you the story of previous work. For example, to understand how a project manager deals with a project team who has not yet met a schedule, ask this closed question: "Have you ever managed a project where the team had trouble meeting the schedule?" If the answer is no, you can decide if the project manager has enough experience to manage your team. If the answer is yes, ask the open-ended behavior-description question, "What did you do? What actions did you take on that project to help the project team meet the schedule?" The answers you hear will help you assess that candidate's ability to work in your organization.

6. Preserve Good Teams

Part of my hiring strategy is to hire people who fit into my already-existing team, but sometimes you inherit teams or a project has completed and a team is ready to move on. When a team is successful, I try to keep them together so they can continue working well together. I may bring more people into the team, one at a time, especially if the team has been highly productive. But I do not scatter the productive team and hope they will form more productive teams. That just reduces their productivity.

Teams can overcome bad management and bad processes, but they cannot overcome a team un-jeller. A team un-jeller is the person who walks into the lunchroom, and suddenly everyone else leaves. Or, the un-jeller creates an argument out of every conversation. If you have a team un-jeller, find another place for that person to work, preferably for your competitor.

7. Avoid Micromanaging or Inflicting Help

Many of us were software developers, testers, analysts, or some other technical role before we became managers. When we were technical contributors, we knew how to perform the technical jobs. However, once you have been a manager for a while, you probably will not know precisely how to perform the employee's job.

I once had a boss who liked to creep into my office, stare over my shoulder, and say, "On line 16, shouldn't that be a ..." By the time he reached "16," I had jumped out of my chair, become flustered, and lost my concentration. Micromanagement neither gets the job done faster, nor does inflicting advice or help.

On the other hand, you and the employee both need to know that the employee is progressing. I ask my staff to decide when they have been stuck for too long (time-box the work). Some tasks require weeks of study, but most tasks require days or hours. If the employee spends more than the agreed-upon time on the task, their job is to ask for help. As the manager, your job is to find them help, not necessarily inflict your help.

8. Treat People Individually and With Respect

Buckingham and Coffman [7] claim that each employee's relationship with his or her manager is key to that employee's success and long-term happiness in the organization. That means we need to treat people fairly, but uniquely, so that we build and maintain the best possible relationships with each employee.

Everyone has his or her own preferences, especially in their communication patterns, and how they organize their thoughts about work. Some people prefer e-mail communications; some prefer in-person discussions. Some people want to understand all the reasons behind your requests, and others will take the request at face value. Some people need to gather data to make decisions; others will develop a model about the situation and make a decision based on that model.

It does not matter if people work top-down or bottom-up, or if they want to talk in person or by e-mail. What matters is that you, within reason, accommodate everyone's uniqueness.

I once managed two very talented developers who shared a large office. Begrudgingly, they allowed me to have 20-minute one-on-ones with each of them every two weeks. In between, if I wanted to talk to either of them, I had to e-mail them first – dropping in was not allowed. I treated them differently than the other people in my group, but fairly, considering their preferences.

They frequently worked on the same software. They never spoke to each other aloud, they only communicated via e-mail even though they shared an office. Because they were so successful at their work together, and even mentored others in the organization by e-mail, their communications preferences were a bit odd but acceptable. If I had tried to change them to meet my needs and work with them the same way I worked with the other people, none of us would have been happy.

9. Meet Weekly With Each Person

Even if you have hired stars, you still need to know each person's progress on their tasks, and how the project as a whole is

progressing. I use one-on-ones weekly to meet with each person. We discuss the employee's progress on his or her tasks. Sometimes, tasks are amorphous and it is difficult to know when to stop or if the employee needs help. I ask each employee to show me visible progress on each task: drafts of plans, multiple designs, prototype test results, anything that shows me the employee is making progress and is not stuck. If the employee needs help completing the task, we discuss what kinds of help are appropriate.

I receive many benefits from these weekly meetings. I learn what everyone is doing and can track it in my notebook. It is easy to write up useful performance evaluations, including examples of successful and not so successful actions the employee has taken over the year. And, because we meet weekly, I can give feed-

---

"Buckingham and Coffman [7] claim that each employee's relationship with his or her manager is key to that employee's success and long-term happiness in the organization."

---

back then, not when we make time. I also reduce the number of staff interruptions because everyone knows they can ask me non-urgent questions during the one-on-one. I can perform weekly career development and learn if my staff has personal issues affecting their ability to do their jobs.

If I am managing more than eight people, I meet biweekly with more senior staff because they need less direct supervision.

Some of you are probably thinking you do not have time to meet with everyone once a week. However, if you do not set up specific times to meet with everyone, you tend to either not know what people are doing, or you are interrupted frequently by your staff with questions.

10. Plan Training Time Each Week

Technical work is constantly changing; most of the technical people I know enjoy

learning new things. If you have a budget for formal training, that is great. Even if you do not have a budget, plan weekly training time in the form of brown-bag lunches, presentations from other groups in your organization, an internal user-group meeting of one of your tools, or presentations from people in your group about their successes or difficulties.

I use the weekly group meeting as a time to deliver the training. When I managed development groups, I organized this internal training, including technical leads of other sub-projects to explain their architecture and application programming interface (API) to other groups, testers to explain patterns of defects they found, different techniques for peer review, or discussion of a particularly interesting article in one of the technical magazines someone had read.

11. Fire People Who Cannot Perform the Work

Even when you meet regularly with your staff and encourage them to acquire help when they need it, some people in your group may not be able to perform at the level you require. First, make sure you have been specific and have given feedback to the employee with examples of inadequate behavior. If the employee understands the lack of performance, you can choose whether to coach the person or perform a get-well plan, or in radical circumstances, escort the employee out the door.

Retaining non-productive employees has direct and indirect costs. The direct costs are easier to define: You are paying a salary and benefits and not receiving the expected work. The indirect costs are much subtler and more damaging.

When you continue employing an inadequate employee, the morale of the entire workgroup declines. If morale declines enough, your best people will leave. Not only do you have someone in your group who is not successful, that person has driven away the people who are the most successful.

In addition to low morale, you and your group accomplish less than you expected. You are not just accomplishing less because of the one employee who cannot work at the level you require; that person probably has to hand off work to others in the group, and those other people will be delayed by the inadequate work.

I once inherited a group where the previous management had *spared* an employee from layoffs because he was having personal problems. Those personal problems affected his work – he did not always come to work, he was late on every deliverable, and he was unable to perform most of his work. In my one-on-ones with the employee, I gave him examples of his work and asked if he was able to continue to work. He said yes. (If he had said no, we would have put him on short-term or long-term disability.) We chose to perform a get-well plan, which the employee stopped after a week. After the employee left, the morale in the group jumped dramatically and we were able to accomplish more work.

12. Emphasize Results, Not Time

I have worked for senior managers who rewarded individuals based on their work hours, i.e., those who started early and stayed late. Unfortunately, these managers had no ability to understand the results the long-working employees imposed on the rest of the organization: buggy code, inadequate designs, and tests that did not find obvious problems. When people work long hours, their productivity decreases, not increases [8]. In "Slack" [3], Tom DeMarco says, "Extended overtime is a productivity-reduction technique." The longer people stay at work, the less work they do. Instead, they perform the life activities they are not performing outside of work.

Make it possible for people to only work 40 hours a week. The less overtime people put in, the better their work will be.

If people tell you they are working long hours because they cannot accomplish anything in their regular work weeks, ask them where they spend their time. Look for patterns such as multi-tasking, or meetings that do not have any productive output. Use your management power to discover and remove the obstacles preventing people from working a 40-hour week.

13. Admit Your Mistakes

Sometimes, those obstacles to people completing their work successfully in 40 hours arise from your management mistakes. It is difficult, and sometimes embarrassing to have to admit you have made a mistake. In my experience, when I admitted mistakes to my staff, they have respected me more for it.

14. Recognize and Reward Good Work

Money is not an adequate reward for many technical people. If people think they are paid fairly, then more money is not reward enough. Recognition of good work and the opportunity to perform meaningful work [9] is much more important. Lack of money can be a demotivator, but only money is not sufficient when recognizing good work.

Kohn says, "[Rewards] motivate people to get rewards." If your organization has trained employees to expect money as a reward, this appreciation technique may seem small. Try it anyway.

When I use appreciation as a recognition technique I say, "I appreciate you, Jim, for your work on the blatz module and API definition. Your work made it possible for Joe to write great tests and for me to predict the project's progress." Appreciation between peers could mean even more than money from you. When you appreciate a person for good work and you explain what the work meant to you, you are motivating the person to continue performing similar work.

In addition, consider time off, group activities, movie tickets, or funny awards such as *best recursion of the week* as recognition techniques.

The most important part of a reward is to make sure it is congruent with each person's performance. Your staff knows who is performing well and who is coasting. If you recognize and reward evenly, you are not differentiating between outstanding performance and adequate performance. Make sure you reward a person's entire contribution (the entire work product, including how good the work product is, the timeliness of the deliverable, the person's ability to work with others, and whatever else is important to you), not just the size or quality of the work.

Summary

Managers exist to help people do their best work to serve the business of the organization. Technical people can make great managers as long as they understand people and want to succeed at working with them. Many successful technical managers took the time to learn about management, putting as much effort (if not more) than the effort they took to learn the necessary technical background for the technical jobs. Managers do not have to be perfect; they have to be good enough to create a working environment for their employees to deliver great work.◆

Acknowledgements

I thank Dwayne Phillips and the CROSSTALK reviewers for their input on this article.

References

1. Magretta, Joan. What Management Is: How It Works and Why It Is Everyone's Business. New York: The Free Press, 2002.
2. Covey, Stephen R. The Seven Habits of Highly Effective People. New York: Simon & Schuster, 1989.
3. DeMarco, Tom. Slack. New York: Broadway Books, 2001.
4. Weinberg, Gerald M. "Congruent Interviewing by Audition." Amplifying Your Effectiveness: Collected Essays. New York: Dorset House, 2000.
5. Rothman, Johanna. Hiring Technical People. New York: Dorset House, 2003.
6. Janz, Tom, et al. Behavior Description Interviewing. Englewood Cliffs, NJ: Prentice Hall, 1986.
7. Buckingham, Marcus, and Curt Coffman. First, Break All the Rules: What the World's Greatest Managers Do Differently. New York: Simon & Schuster, 1999.
8. DeMarco, Tom, and Tim Lister. Peopleware: Productive Projects and Teams. 2nd ed. New York: Dorset House, 1999.
9. Kohn, Alfie. Punished by Rewards. New York: Houghton-Mifflin, 1993.

About the Author

Johanna Rothman consults on managing high technology product development, which helps managers, teams, and organizations become more effective. Rothman uses pragmatic techniques for managing people, projects, and risks to create successful teams and projects. A frequent speaker and author on managing high technology product development, she has written numerous articles and is now a columnist for Software Development, Computerworld.com, and StickyMinds.com. Rothman served as the program chair for the Software Management conference and is the author of "Hiring Technical People."

Rothman Consulting Group, Inc.
38 Bonad Road
Arlington, MA 02476
Phone: (781) 641-4046
Fax: (781) 641-2764
E-mail: jr@jrothman.com

A Tale of Three Developers

Donald J. Reifer, Reifer Consultants Inc.

In many ways, today's software industry is experiencing the best of times and the worst of times. Technology advances at the breakneck pace known as Internet time, while legacy systems provide the golden ball-and-chain that keeps dragging us back from the future. Massive government and industry projects progress with measured, process-perfect strides, while Java and commercial software programmers—who must be first to market or perish—work on death march projects and code from the hip.

With so many companies hungry for new programming talent, software developers fresh out of college face a bewildering number of opportunities. As the three stories that follow show, no matter which segment of the industry you choose to work in, you will reap benefits and encounter frustrations in varying proportions. Whether your career path is lined with roses or hedged with thorns, however, it will lead you to a deeper understanding of your craft.

TRUDGING THROUGH DEATH MARCH VALLEY

John joined a Silicon Valley software house that developed e-commerce products. His mentor, a seasoned workaholic

Editor: Barry Boehm, Computer Science Department, University of Southern California, Los Angeles, CA 90089; boehm@sunset.usc.edu

Despite its frustrations and uncertainties, software development today offers unprecedented opportunities for growth.

fond of discussing the wealth his stock options were generating, taught John how to code Java applets. Surrounded by a talented and supportive team, John found himself challenged, stimulated, and acquiring knowledge rapidly. Yet the work, while interesting, nearly overwhelmed him. The firm's fast pace and lack of structure unsettled John—every day brought a new crisis.

A few weeks into their current project, the team fell behind schedule and began working 12- to 14-hour days. When this effort proved insufficient, the team held meetings on Saturdays and Sundays. Then the rework started cropping up.

Although the firm's management felt that peer reviews and process were a waste of resources, they did hire an independent test organization to evaluate products prior to beta testing. The testers began finding many bugs. When senior management reviewed the project's bug metrics, they demanded that the team report to them weekly and describe how it planned to get a stable product out the door. Work harder and smarter, they commanded.

Onboard only six weeks, John had already stumbled into a major disaster. His supervisor suggested that the team work longer hours and weekends until the product shipped, even though the team already averaged 12-hour days, six days a week.

When longer hours failed to speed development, management hired a consultant who cited Ed Yourdon's *Death March* (Prentice Hall, Upper Saddle River, N.J., 1997) and said this project exhibited all the signs of such a disaster. He then used rate-of-progress charts to forecast project completion in no less than six months. After extensive interviews with team members and management, the consultant suggested the following actions:

- Freeze the requirements and don't let marketing change them one iota.
- Replan the project based upon a cost- and schedule-to-complete exercise.
- Institute peer reviews or inspections to focus the team on defect removal.
- Hire the consultant himself to lead the effort and keep it on track.

John's boss thought these suggestions ludicrous. Team members reacted in different ways. Some felt jealous of the consultant and tried to discredit him. Others agreed with him, seeing many of their opinions reflected in his recommendations. Management approved the consultant's suggestions, accepted the current project manager's resignation, then hired a new manager who quickly turned the project around. She replanned the project and set realizable milestones, despite marketing's objections. She then steered the project and kept it focused by tightening the controls used. After orga-

Reprinted from *Computer,* November 1999.

nizing groups into teams and instituting peer reviews, she tracked progress and used metrics to assess the product's quality. Besides learning a lot about team building, leadership, and good project control from his new manager, the reforms she made actually allowed the team some much-needed downtime.

You can get real value from staying the course on a troubled project in your early years. Although not all managers are created equal, take heart that you can learn from both positive and negative examples. Don't be afraid to take a step backward when disaster looms. Most projects begin with overly optimistic schedules and budgets. Calling in a credible and competent consultant who can rapidly assess the situation when reality strikes can be a life saver.

WHERE DINOSAURS ROAM

To aid her pursuit of an MS in computer science, Susan took a government work-study job. Despite the position's low status and pay, she immediately became responsible for a large information-system procurement project. Told to manage a contractor developing multi-million-dollar software on a performance-based contract, she asked in vain for help from her overworked boss. Worse, her contractor stonewalled her attempts to monitor their progress.

Trapped in the stone age

Although she enjoyed her graduate software engineering classes, work conflicts soon arose. Her high-profile assignment lacked a job description. Before disappearing into endless meetings, her boss explained cryptically that she need only tell the contractor what to do, not how to do it. Meanwhile, the contractor disclosed that a recent government audit had identified their project's need for a software manager. Given two weeks to fix the problem, they had hired Susan to fill the gap. Determined not to let the situation bother her, Susan strove to make the most of her position.

A short course on providing technical oversight and direction gave her a disturbing insight: The contractor's software development techniques came straight from computer science's stone age. For example, the project's staff spent all their time developing, updating, and refining specifications, arguing that they couldn't build the system without requirements. Yet these thick, unreadable documents served as paperweights and little else.

She suggested instead that they work with the user representative to develop use cases and rapidly prototype the application's GUI front end. The contractor dismissed her ideas as impractical. Her boss refused to support her recommendations, admitting that he knew nothing about software even though the government had put him in charge of a software-intensive project.

> **Although not all managers are created equal, you can learn from both positive and negative examples.**

Forcing evolution

In desperation, Susan turned to a colleague for advice. Immediately sympathetic, he observed that local industry teemed with dinosaur engineers who built antiquated systems. Comfortable with the status quo and afraid of failure, they feared anything new. To overcome their resistance, she must convince them that her ideas would increase their chances of success. The trick, he said, was to make them think her good ideas were theirs.

At first, the contractor ignored her suggestions. Then she had a brainstorm and established a working group that included her savvy colleague. The right-hand rule, recommended by Susan's software-test people, proved key to the group's success in communicating with the contractor. This rule empowers the current speaker, once that person has finished talking, to pass the podium to the first person on the right. Participants honor the next person's right to talk and avoid interrupting—or pay a dollar fine for doing so. The fines fund snacks for the next meeting—and usually leave the staff stuffed with doughnuts until participants adapt to the new protocol.

Whenever multiple players collaborate, working groups and techniques that facilitate open communication offer the best hope for achieving consensus. Once you achieve consensus, implementation occurs quickly. Be patient, especially at first—facilitate, don't force. Teach people to respect others' right to speak, listen, and voice their opinions. Despite a bureaucracy blind to her problems and a contractor deaf to her suggestions, Susan learned to implement change using proven techniques that toppled the political and psychological barriers defending the status quo.

BUSTED BY THE PROCESS POLICE

Pradeep took a rotational position with a large Midwestern telephone company, receiving an excellent salary, extensive benefits, and exposure to a succession of different assignments. His manager suggested that he start in software maintenance because maintaining 20-year-old legacy software, written in C and assembly code, would prepare Pradeep to handle anything.

Detained in maintenance

He naively accepted the assignment and joined the firm's hundreds of other maintenance programmers. He soon discovered that no one older than 23 worked in maintenance. New and inexperienced, none of them could turn to senior developers for help.

On the plus side, the relaxed, structured environment let him spend his first month in training and orientation. Along with domain-knowledge courses on telephone systems and self-paced tutorials in programming languages, Pradeep also learned about the Software Engineering Institute's Capability Maturity Model (Mark C. Paulk et al., *The Capability Maturity Model: Guidelines for Improving the Software Process*, Addison-Wesley, New York, 1995). Employees took pride in the firm's integrated business and development processes, which worked so well that the company had recently earned a CMM Level 3 rating.

Training complete, Pradeep joined a small team led by a dynamic, goal-oriented individual. Even though theirs was a maintenance effort, the team held software inspections when they reached the design, code, and test gates, using metrics to assess the software's progress. For example, testing could not be completed unless the test metrics indicated that remaining error rates fell within expected limits. Pradeep felt proud to be employed by a company that used the development methods his college instructors had touted as best practices.

> ## When process managers become enforcers instead of facilitators, they must be removed.

The transition from theory to practice, however, proved problematic. Even though the team's project involved upgrading a small system, each module underwent at least five inspections. Worse, management mandated that, to track the project's progress, the team must attend at least a hundred meetings over the next six months.

Crime and punishment

Finally, if the team omitted an inspection, or submitted abnormal metrics, the "process police" intervened. Senior engineers from the firm's software process group, the process police monitored implementation of company standards.

Pradeep learned to his horror that some team members had resorted to inserting bugs into their code after tests showed fewer defects than expected. The offenders justified their actions by noting that producing code better than the norm would earn them the punishment of listening to endless lectures on the virtues of process.

Pradeep had never encountered references to the process police in his study of software development. Veteran developers referred to them as "born again" process evangelists who made everyone follow the standard process to the letter. Many process police came from the ranks of retired software managers who, during their active tenure, had cared nothing for process. Their motto now? Whether the process makes sense or not, just use it. They came down hardest on maintenance and small projects, which benefited least from the company's process model.

Yet to reach CMM Level 4 by year's end—the company's stated goal—the police had to apply the process to previously exempt small projects. The company's just-published process-tailoring guidelines assumed that maintenance simply replayed development. Those who openly disputed this approach exposed themselves to criticism and worse. Thus, Pradeep quickly learned to play along.

He also learned, however, that you must do more than adopt a one-size-fits-all process. You must tailor that process to all sorts of projects: small and large, research and development, maintenance and production. He also saw the dire consequences of toxic zeal. When process managers become enforcers instead of facilitators, they must be removed before they spread disillusionment and deception throughout the workforce.

The adversity these neophyte developers encountered will help shape them. Each will see the good, the bad, and the ugly before moving into management. Once they become software managers, they can make the lives of other developers better. I challenge them—and all succeeding generations of programmers—to do so, righting the wrongs they, and you, experience. Above all, listen to your people and your instincts, and embrace change and new ideas. ❖

Donald J. Reifer is a teacher, change agent, consultant, contributor to the fields of software engineering and management, and author of Tutorial on Software Management, *fifth edition (IEEE CS Press, Los Alamitos, Calif., 1997). Contact him at d.reifer@ieee.org.*

Chapter 10

Visibility and Control

Design engineers will fiddle and tinker forever. If you let them alone, you are guaranteed to have schedule slippages and cost problems. Nothing will come out of the end of the pipe unless you push it out.

—J. Ronald Fox, in *Arming America*

Overview

Control is the function that assesses status, tracks progress and provides you with the feedback you need to determine whether or not you are proceeding according to plan. It measures performance against goals and plans, identifies when and where deviations exist, and, by acting in a timely manner to correct these deviations, helps you make sure things get done when they are supposed to and requirements are satisfied. Planning and control are intimately related. At times, feedback from the control process may force you to either reallocate resources or develop a new plan.

There are many tools and techniques available for control. However, none of them work well if you have not developed a good plan. Your plan represents the baseline against which you control deviations, measure performance, and assess progress. Even the best control tools will not pinpoint your problems if the plan is inconsistent, incomplete, and poorly structured. The moral of the story is to devote time to planning. It pays off in the end through better visibility and control.

The primary tool that you use to structure your plan is the work breakdown structure (WBS). The WBS provides you with the means to track task progress and address problems when milestones are on the critical path throughout your schedule. It allows you to relate milestone completions to task accomplishments and calculate earned value based upon actual performance instead of expenditures.

The primary control techniques that you have available are the product baselines you use to control the work in progress, the metrics and measurements you use to assess progress, and feedback from the audits, reviews, and inspections you conduct to assess product quality. That is the primary reason we elected to discuss the topics of earned value, configuration control, and quality assurance in this chapter. Besides providing you control over your work products, the techniques discussed also provide the necessary tools to control deviations to plans, your process, and product standards.

Unfortunately, over the years, the volume of material I attempted to cover in this chapter grew to be unmanageable. To correct this problem, I stripped out various topics and created separate chapters for them when there was a sufficiently rich set of materials available. In the fourth and fifth editions, I added chapters on measurement and risk management for this reason. I updated these chapters in the sixth edition. Instead of adding even more chapters, I have tried to streamline the material in this the seventh edition in order to make its contents simpler to understand and use.

The five papers that follow were selected to give you an overview of the tools and techniques that are available for control. As in my other chapters, I have included definitions and pointers to references should you desire more information on this topic.

Article Summaries

Controlling Software Projects, by Paul Rook. This survey article on project control sets the stage for the articles that follow by discussing background, motivation, and industry trends relative to the topic. In addition to reviewing techniques that provide you with visibility into and control over your performance (relative to plans), the article introduces you to the related topics of configuration management, quality assurance, verification and validation, and metrics and measurement, and discusses how they can be used effectively. The paper provides a good explanation of the relationships between planning, estimation, measurement, and control. It also provides an excellent summary of the many tools and techniques that you can use to quantify, manage, and control your progress as your plans unfold. I have tried repeatedly to find a replacement for this article. However, it has stood the test of time and others that I have reviewed just do not compare when it comes to its depth and breadth of coverage.

Earned Value Management, by Quentin W. Fleming and Joel M. Koppelman. This paper explains the concept of earned value in layman's terms. It provides step-by-step instructions on how to calculate this metric and use the results to determine how well your project is performing. Earned value provides a system of measurement that enables you to determine whether your rate of spending is commensurate with the progress you are making as determined by milestone achievements. Using variances, earned value lets you probe to determine the root cause of the problem. It is useful because it provides early budget and/or schedule problem identification.

Software Configuration Management: A Discipline with Added Value, by Tresa Butler, Veria Standley, Elaine Sullivan, and Faith Turner. This paper provides an overview of the discipline of software configuration management and its underlying functions of planning, identifying, controlling, auditing, and reporting. The paper clearly and concisely summarizes what configuration management is trying to do, why this is important, and how its concepts can be used to improve control over changes to baselines. It also discusses tools and metrics issues and has a useful section on workforce education and training approaches.

Managing Software Quality with Defects, by David Card. This paper describes two common approaches to using defect metrics and models to provide visibility into and control over product quality as the project progresses through its life cycle. The paper shows how defect budgets can be established and used for making the difficult trade-offs between cost, schedule, and quality based on consequences. The paper also discusses how decision making relative to releases can be improved even further through the use of six sigma and other quantitative quality modeling techniques. Because of their popularity, this paper was included.

Why Bad Things Happen to Good Projects, by Karen Mackey. This article discusses two often unrelated but repeated problems that plague projects independent of size or industry: the quality–capacity syndrome and the missing-tools crisis. After digging into the problems at hand, the author offers a solution to the problems that have a potential to scale up. Lessons learned when implementing these recommendations are also shared, as are suggestions for doing things better. I included this paper because it shared various experiences about what people do to regain control once they are confronted with a problem.

Key Terms

Twelve terms, defined as follows, are important to understanding the topic of organization as used within this chapter:

1. **Audit.** An independent examination of a work product or set of work products to assess compliance with specifications, standards, contracts, or other criteria.
2. **Baseline.** A work product that has been formally reviewed and agreed upon and that can be changed only through formal change control procedures. A baseline work product may form the basis for further work activity(s).
3. **Configuration management (CM).** A discipline applying technical and administrative direction and surveillance to identify and document both the functional and physical characteristics of a configuration item, control changes to these characteristics, record and report change processing and implementation status, and verify compliance with requirements.
4. **Controlling.** Those activities conducted to determine whether or not progress is being made according to plan. Control involves measuring, monitoring, and acting on information obtained throughout the development to correct deviations, focus resources, and mitigate risk.
5. **Earned value.** In project management, a technique used to assess progress and budgetary performance using milestone completions. Actuals and projections are compared to earned value to compute trends and variances.
6. **Infrastructure.** The underlying framework used by management for making decisions and allocating resources.
7. **Inspection.** A formal evaluation technique in which software products are examined in detail by a person or group other than the author to detect errors/faults, violations of standards, and other problems.
8. **Monitoring.** In management, keeping constant surveillance over and tracking what is actually happening on a project.
9. **Quality.** The totality of features and characteristics of a product or service that bears on its ability to satisfy given needs or customer requirements.
10. **Quality assurance (QA).** A planned and systematic pattern of all actions necessary to provide adequate confidence that the item or product conforms to agreed-upon technical requirements.

11. **Review.** A process or meeting during which a work product, or set of work products, is presented to project personnel, managers, customers, users, or other interested parties for examination and comment.

12. **Tracking.** In management, the process of identifying cost and schedule variances by comparing actual expenditures to projections.

Acronyms

The following acronyms are used within the articles in this chapter:

ACWP	Actual cost of work performed
ASQC	American Society of Quality Control
BAC	Budget at completion
BCWP	Budgeted cost of work scheduled
BCWS	Budgeted cost of work scheduled
CCB	Change control board
CM	Configuration management
CMMI	Capability Maturity Model Integration
CPI	Cost performance index
CV	Cost variance
EAC	Estimate at completion
EVS	Earned Value System
IEEE	Institute of Electrical and Electronics Engineers
ISO	International Standards Organization
QA	Quality assurance
SEI	Software Engineering Institute
SV	Schedule variance
WBS	Work breakdown structure

For Your Bookshelf

For those interested further in the fundamentals of control, I suggest you read Wysocki's *Effective Project Management* (2nd edition) and play with the accompanying CD. Like a game, the built-in software mentor will provide you with feedback on how well you are doing. Devauz's book entitled *Total Project Control* provides an excellent introduction to managing multiple tasks and making project-based decisions. I have also included a new book in the Bibliography entitled *Software Endgames* that focuses on using defects as a release management tool. It is an interesting book that is full of relatively new ideas that might capture your imagination. (It captured mine.).

Two good texts on software configuration management and three on software quality management are included in the Bibliography. All of these books serve as useful references on these topics. I especially like Schulmeyer's *Handbook of Software Quality Assurance* (3rd edition) because it provides the reader with all of the material he or she needs to learn how to receive the American Society for Quality Control's (ASQC) Software Quality Engineer Certificate.

The Project Management Book of Knowledge (PMBOK$^{TM)}$ provides many project-based tools, rules, and techniques that you can use to control scope, budget, schedule, and other types of changes. Just about every chapter in the book discusses how to use the infrastructure the PMBOK^{TM} to help you improve visibility into and control over the project as it unfolds. I particularly liked the discussion in the chapter on project risk management that was focused on how to mitigate risks once they were detected using the processes advanced by the authors.

In addition, the IEEE Computer Society has published several useful standards and guides for topics discussed in this chapter. Specifically, the following six documents might be of interest to you:

1. *IEEE Standard for Software Quality Assurance Plans,* 730-1998.
2. *IEEE Guide for Software Quality Assurance Planning,* 730.1-1995.

3. *IEEE Standard for a Software Quality Metrics Methodology,* 1061-1998.

4. *IEEE Standard for Software Configuration Management Plans,* 828-1995.

5. *IEEE Guide to Software Configuration Management,* 1042-1987 (R1993).

6. *IEEE Standard for Software Reviews,* 1028-1997.

You can order these standards directly from the IEEE Service Center in New Jersey via phone at 800-678-4333 or e-mail at customer.service@ieee.org.

Controlling software projects

by Paul Rook

In recent years the software industry has seen the increasing imposition of structure and discipline on technical development activities in an attempt to improve the efficiency of software development and the reliability of the software produced. The clear emphasis in the modern approach to software engineering is to focus attention on the overall development process and the co-ordination of all aspects of software development. This paper examines the principles of managing and successfully controlling software development from a software engineering basis.

1 Introduction

The management of a large software development is a complex and intrinsically difficult task: a large software system is itself very complex and its production may involve hundreds of man-years of skilled effort with correspondingly large budgets.

Nearly every software development project is faced with numerous difficulties. When a project is successful it is not because there were no problems but because the problems were overcome. Many of the problems are technical but often the critical ones are managerial. Software development depends on documentation and communication — it is only structured if a structure is imposed and controlled. Everything that is done right in software development is done early — there is very little opportunity for catching up when things are discovered to be going wrong later in the development.

There is much discussion about comparisons between managing software development and managing hardware development. There are genuine differences between hardware and software, as follows:

- Software has no physical appearance.
- Few software quality metrics exist.
- Software has much higher complexity than hardware.
- It is deceptively easy to introduce changes into software.
- Effects of software change propagate explosively.
- Software includes data as well as logic.
- Software development makes very little use of pre-existing components.

However, in many important ways software development is like hardware development and ought to be managed and controlled using very similar techniques to those used in hardware engineering development. The genuine dissimilarities listed above are the very factors which make an engineering approach much more critical for software development.

Contributing to the difficulties of software management is the much publicised view of the programmer as the unbridled genius, whose creative process will be stifled by any of the recommended project management controls, design standards and programming standards.

Forced to contend with this view is the software manager, often a recently promoted analyst or programmer who has worked on projects managed as a collection of creative artists doing their independent thing. Management's job in these projects was to try, somehow, to steer this collection of individualists in a common direction so that their products would accomplish the project goals, be able to interface with each other, be finished within the project cost and schedule constraints, and, with a little luck, come reasonably close to accomplishing what the customer had in mind for the software. Such a software manager has been well grounded in how a project should not be managed, but has had little exposure or training in the use of effective software management techniques.

2 Structuring software development

To tackle these problems, the software industry has seen the increasing imposition of discipline on technical development activities in an attempt to improve the reliability of software development. Thus we have seen, in turn, the techniques of structured programming, structured design and structured analysis.

Structured programming provides rules for choosing the building blocks for programs. Structured design helps the designer to distinguish between good and bad designs. Structured analysis assists in the production of a specification that is correct and consistent and can be determined to be complete. The introduction in turn of each of these three techniques has thrown up problems which have been introduced through lack of discipline in the earlier stages of the development process.

In addition to this stage by stage attack on the problems of development, it is clear that all activities will have problems unless the goals of each activity are clearly stated and set within the context of the structure for the whole project.

The clear emphasis in the modern approach to software engineering is to focus attention on the overall development process. This is the aim of structured software development, which breaks down the project into a series of distinct phases, each with well defined goals, the achievement of which can be verified, ensuring a sound foundation for the succeeding phase. It also breaks down the work to be performed into a series of discrete manageable packages, and creates the basis for the appropriate organisational structure. This allows overall planning of 'how' the software is going to be developed as well as considering 'what' is going to be developed as the product.

3 Computer-based tools

An equally important development has been the introduction of computer-based tools to assist with specific tasks. The earliest tools were concerned with the production of code. These have been followed by tools which assist, for example, specification, design, estimating, planning, documentation and configuration management. In fact tools are now available to support most of the software development activities.

The right tools assist in increasing productivity and visibility of work achieved, provide a source of data for future proposal preparation, estimation and project planning, and maintain continuity between projects. They also provide automated testing and reduce iteration of work and thus aid improved quality. Tools are especially useful in detecting errors early, when they are less expensive to correct, thus leading to a more successful software project and product.

Although tools alone will not ensure success, the selection and installation of the right set of tools is seen to be necessary for an effective software development project.

4 The management of complexity

Thus the key to the management of the complex task of large software development is twofold:

• reducing complexity by imposing a structure on to the process
• using computer-based tools to make the remaining complexity more tractable.

5 Software development methodology

In planning how to develop the software, it is the responsibility of project management to ensure that a coherent system of methods and tools is chosen, integrated and supported.

However, differences in organisation structures, applications and existing approaches make it impractical to prescribe a single scheme that can be universally followed. Methods. tools. management practices or any other element of the total development environment cannot be chosen without considering each element in its relationship to the other parts of the development system.

Software engineering has introduced the term 'software development meth-

odology' to describe a systematic set of procedures followed from the original conception of a system through the specification, design, implementation. operation and evolution of the software in that system. A methodology not only includes technical methods to assist in the critical tasks of problem solving. documentation, analysis, design, coding. testing and configuration management, but also includes management procedures to control the development process and the deployment of the technical methods.

The management and technical aspects of the methodology support and gain strength from each other: the technical methods provide the basis needed for effective managerial control. while the management procedures provide the organisation and resources which enable the technical development to proceed effectively. Tools support the methodology and provide the information needed by project management.

6 Project control

The software development process is inherently subject to risks which are manifested as financial failures (time scale overrun, budget overrun) and technical failures (failure to meet requirements, over/under-engineered). The sources of risk can be placed in three main categories:

• perturbations (requirement changes, detection of problems. errors and failures)
• personnel (wrong people available. too many/too few people available)
• project environment (undefined methodology. unknown quality, errors

detected late, inadequate control, technical skill, support and visibility).

If the project is to be successful, then potential risks must be identified, and eliminated or controlled. A control system for a project is based on the usual principle of establishing suitable feedback loop(s) to ensure that the controlled system is oriented to its objective. The objective of a software development project is to produce the correct product on time and to budget.

Fig. 1 illustrates, in a simplified form, a project control system for software development. Technical development is what is controlled and project management is the controller. Estimating is a prerequisite for control, and a number of feedback loops are set up which operate via status and progress reports to compare actual progress with the plans based on the estimates.

The feedback loops operate directly from the technical development and also from the quality and configuration management systems. Fig. 1 illustrates a continuous process, as indicated by the inner product loop of feedback of intermediate development products to the activities of technical development. The quality and configuration management systems operate continuously in the development process, not only on the products finally delivered to the customer.

While the inner loop represents the work on the product, the outer feedback loops represent the basis for control. Control consists of obtaining information to make decisions and ensuring timely detection and correction of errors, thus controlling time scale and budget and minimising technical risks.

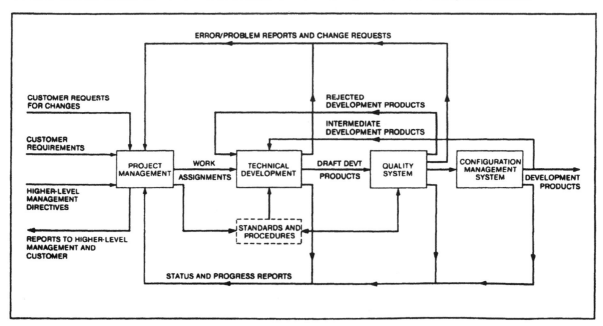

Fig. 1 Basic operation of a project control system

The upper control loops represent inevitable paths for changes, which the project manager must control through appropriate procedures, such as a change control board. The lower control loops represent the monitoring system established by the project manager to obtain information on which to make decisions and to be able to check that the consequences of those decisions are carried through and have the intended effects.

For the project to be successfully controlled the lower control loops must dominate the upper control loops. This is achieved by establishing sufficient strength in the lower loops and also by constraining the upper loops.

The operation of project control illustrated in Fig. 1 depends on an organisation with clearly defined responsibilities and disciplines related to the four functions shown — project management, technical development, quality system and configuration management system.

7 Project management

The establishment of the project environment, obtaining the personnel and dealing with perturbations (see the sources of risk listed in the previous Section) are the responsibility of the project manager. The responsibility also includes the software development methodology used on the project. In some cases a standard methodology will be available, together with the appropriate support

facilities. In other cases the project manager will have to select and establish a methodology specifically for the project. In either event, project management has the final responsibility of ensuring (or confirming) the suitability of the methodology for the project and defining precisely the details of its application.

Software development techniques such as formal specification, structured design, stepwise refinement, structured programming and correctness proofs are examples of progress in software engineering in recent years. These techniques, together with documentation standards, test methods, and configuration management and quality assurance procedures, address elements of the software development process.

The methods selected must be matched to the characteristics of the development, the imposed schedules and other operational considerations. Once selected, the methods must be implemented and controlled.

However, careful selection of software development techniques does not in itself guarantee success. Success or failure is primarily determined by the approach to project management. No matter how sophisticated the design and programming techniques, a systematic approach to project management is essential.

Project management deals with planning, defining and assigning the work to the technical development teams, monitoring status and progress, making decisions, re-planning and reporting on

the project to higher-level management and the customer.

Fig. 2 shows project management, expanded from the single box of Fig. 1, as a set of interacting processes. While the diagram is rather simplistic it does illustrate the fact that control of the project depends on the quality of information that these processes generate and the use made of it.

7.1 Decision making

The most important aspect of project management consists of making decisions (or ensuring that decisions are made), which includes making sure that timely technical decisions are made on the product as well as making the more obvious project decisions. Responsibility for decisions rests with the project manager. While he can, and must, appropriately delegate authority and decision making, he cannot avoid ultimate responsibility for customer relationship, specification, correctness of design and implementation, quality, use of allocated resources and staff, meeting time scale and budget, standards and procedures, anticipation and resolution of problems and ultimate delivery and acceptance of the product.

7.2 Planning

The planning process includes the activities of planning, scheduling, budgeting and defining milestones. This is based

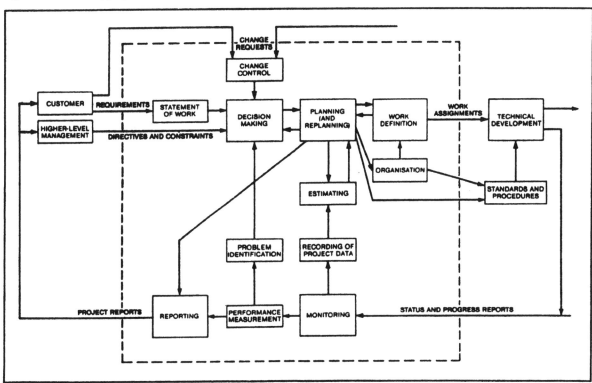

Fig. 2   The processes of project management

on the work breakdown structure (WBS) produced by the work definition process. It depends on estimating, with reference to the recorded project database derived from previous projects (and earlier stages of the current project), and, of course, is based on the input of the customer or system requirements and management constraints.

The project manager produces a project plan (to be publicly viewed and reviewed), which shows estimates, deliverable inter-relationships and timing dependencies, and the allocation of resources to produce deliverables. It is accompanied by definition of the project organisation and the standards and procedures to be used in technical development.

It is important for the project plan to be dynamic. Through the normal processes of iterative analysis, design and implementation changes, resource problems, customer or environment changes and estimation errors, the project plan will require updating and revision. Storable copies of each version of the project plan should be kept in the project history file together with the reasons for revision.

7.3 Work definition

The work definition process relies on a method of doing the work in order to be able to define the detailed work packages (the lowest level of the WBS) which are the basis for the planning process. For software development this is based on the tasks defined by the matrix of activities and phases of the life cycle model shown in Fig. 5.

These work packages define a series of products for project work and management. The WBS not only requires management and customer concurrence on the specification of the product but also requires agreement on the methodology to be used for the project.

7.4 Monitoring

The monitoring process involves measuring actual performance and handling minor schedule and resource requirements revisions that can be accommodated by the team. This process is also related to quality assurance through technical reviews and walkthroughs, and is used to maintain the project data file, which provides updated information for estimating.

Based on written reports and meetings, the monitoring process involves evaluation of expected progress in deliverables against actual progress and provides the basis for project reporting.

7.5 Reporting

The reporting process stores, analyses and filters information of project progress

fed to it by the monitoring process. It compares actual with expected performance, and yields relevant information for the project teams, management and customer.

The project manager reviews the status, progress and problems identified as a foundation for decisions, which closes the loop of internal project control.

There is also an outer loop which depends on reports to the customer and higher-level management.

The information for management should be a filtered subset of the information needed by the project manager when tracking progress within the project. The information needed by management is to answer the questions: 'Is the project on schedule?', and if not, 'Can the team handle the schedule stoppage within its own area of responsibility, or does management need to do something to help the project return to an in-control state?'

The information on measured achievement must be presented effectively to management and the customer so that project progress can be approved at critical points and the correct decisions made.

8 The life cycle model

In order to structure the software development project it is necessary to define the development process — in other words. to adopt some model of the process as an expansion of the technical development function shown in Fig. 1. A model which defines phases in the development of a software product is referred to in software engineering as a 'life cycle model'.

There are numerous life cycle models in use and described in the literature. the specific phases and names varying in detail from one model to another.

Any modern model should be easy to relate to the following phases:

- project initiation
- requirement specification
- structural design
- detailed design
- code and unit test
- integration and test
- acceptance test
- maintenance
- project termination
- product phase-out.

8.1 Baselines

Each development phase is defined in terms of its outputs, or product. The products of each phase represent the points along the development path where there is a clear change in emphasis, where one definition of the emerging product is established and is used as the basis for the

next derived definition. As such, they are the natural milestones of the development progression and offer objective visibility into that progression.

To transform this visibility into effective management control, a software development methodology based on the life cycle model uses the concept of baselines. A 'baseline' established at any stage in the development process is a set of information constituting the definition of the product at that stage.

The completion of each phase is determined by the satisfactory review of the defined products of that phase by development personnel, other project and company experts and, in many cases, customer and user personnel. These products then form the baseline for the work in the next phase. The products of the next phase are then measured and verified against previous baselines before themselves forming a new baseline. In this way confidence in project progress is progressively built on successive baselines.

The process is illustrated in the form of a V-diagram in Fig. 3. In this diagram the rectangular boxes represent the phases and the oval boxes represent the baselines. The form of the diagram shows the symmetry between the successive decomposition of the design and the building of the product by successive stages of integration and test. Each design phase is verified against the previous baseline. Each integration phase is verified against the corresponding design or specification baseline on the other side of the diagram.

8.2 Practical application of the life cycle model

The above description of the life cycle model and its representation in Fig. 3 could be interpreted as suggesting that no phase can be considered complete, and the following phases started, until all the prescribed documents have been completed to specified standards. Although the intended rigour of such an approach is commendable, it is quite unrealistic to interpret the life cycle model in such a simplistic way, particularly on large-scale software developments. For example, in a real software project:

- Exploratory work on a subsequent phase is usually required before the current phase can be completed (for example, design investigation is almost invariably required before it can be stated that a user requirement can be met).
- Problems encountered in a later phase may involve re-working the products of earlier phases — failure to recognise this leads to earlier documentation becoming inaccurate and misleading.
- The user's perceived requirement

may not remain constant during a protracted software development process, and it may be necessary to consider changed requirements and consequent design changes during later phases.

• The project plan may call for incremental development, with different increments of the product in different phases of development.

The concept of distinct phases of software development, representing the achievement of certain defined states in the development of the product, can be regarded as a device, imposed by project management to cope with complexity and improve visibility.

In practice, on a large-scale project, the precise breakpoints between the project phases are not easy to define clearly and depend to some extent on project management decision. Because completely rigid phase control is impractical, status and risk analysis at milestones is particularly important. This can only be obtained from a system of technical reviews.

However, once this reality is recognised, it does not lead to the conclusion that the life cycle model is impractical. Having escaped the simplistic interpretation, the life cycle model does represent a realistic recognition of what is actually involved in the technical work of software development.

Phases do indeed have to be imposed by project management; they will not happen of their own accord. The definitions and concepts in the life cycle model represent the best current understanding of software development methodology — gained from experience in applying software engineering to development projects.

These definitions are the worked-out basis for real control of software development, but that control has to be explicitly planned, based on an implemented methodology actually used by the development staff, and actually applied. It does not happen naturally, as is apparent from the response from some projects that the life cycle model does not correspond to reality. Project management has to *make* its version of the life cycle model realistic.

8.3 Software development life cycle phases

Listed below are the baseline outputs of each phase of the software development life cycle:

• *Project initiation phase:* A validated system architecture, founded on a design study with basic hardware-software allocations, and an approved concept of operation including basic human-machine allocations. A top-level project

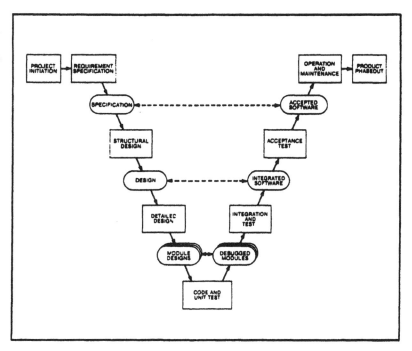

Fig. 3 The stages in software development confidence

plan, with milestones, resources, responsibilities, schedules and major activities. Defined standards and procedures.
• *Requirement specification phase:* A complete, validated specification of the required functions, interfaces and performance for the software product. A detailed project plan.
• *Structural design phase:* A complete, verified specification of the overall hardware-software architecture, control structure and data structure for the software product, along with such other necessary components as draft user's manuals and test plans.
• *Detailed design phase:* A complete, verified specification of the control structure, data structure, interface relations, sizing, key algorithms and assumptions for each program component.
• *Code and unit test phase:* A complete, verified set of program components.
• *Integration and test phase:* A properly functioning software product.
• *Software acceptance test phase:* An accepted software product handed over to the customer.
• *Maintenance phase:* A fully functioning update of the software product. This goal is repeated for each update, which follows the complete development sequence each time.
• *Project termination phase:* A completed project history document comparing estimates and plans with actual development schedule and costs as a contribution to the accumulated database of experience.
• *Product phase-out:* A clean transition of the functions performed by the product to its successors (if any).

9 Software development work

In the same way that the progress of a software development project may be partitioned into a number of discrete phases, so may the technical work involved be divided into a number of clearly identified 'activities'.

A close parallel has been deliberately adopted between the names assigned to the project phases and the technical activities, respectively. This means that, in most cases, the name of a development phase, structural design, for example, indicates the principal activity taking place within that phase. This is not to say that structural design is the only activity taking place during the structural design phase.

Conversely, not only must significant initial structural design work be performed prior to the structural design phase, but also there must be a continuing activity to deal with updates to the design during subsequent phases.

Similarly, although coding a module does not properly commence before the completion of the detailed design of that module, some programming activities must be performed during the earlier phases, such as planning coding methods and facilities, the acquisition and installation of tools and, in some cases, exploratory investigations into algorithms and operations.

Errors detected in the integration phase will require code and unit test activity even though the phase of that name has been completed.

In general, all activities continue across all phases of the project, although the emphasis shifts from activity to activity as the project proceeds from phase to phase. It follows that, in a large software development, each activity should be staffed by a distinct group of people, whose numbers might expand and contract as the emphasis of the project changes but whose existence is identifiable from project start to project end. This is illustrated in the example shown in Fig. 4.

9.1 Technical control

Since the technical activities are performed by members of a number of teams, it is vital to ensure the overall technical correctness of the product, which can be distinguished from such concerns as schedule, budget, organisation, staffing etc. which are solely the responsibility of project management. This concern with technical matters is referred to as 'technical control'.

Technical control is regarded as part of technical development (see Fig. 1) and is defined as the continuous process of making certain that what is being produced is technically correct, coherent and consistent.

It includes planning ahead for all the necessary modelling and testing. Its role is strategic in that it makes certain that the overall technical integrity of the product is not lost in the tactics of the individual technical activities. It requires an overall technical authority but does not necessarily imply managerial authority over the development staff. When sub-contractors are involved in the project, the activity of technical control becomes even more important in co-ordinating the technical aspects of all the work between the subcontractors and the integrity of the subcontract products.

Primary examples of technical control are the maintenance of the integrity of the design in the presence of changes following the completion of the structural design phase, and test planning. Test planning is a strategic activity from the very start of the project which defines and co-ordinates all the test methods, tools and techniques to be used throughout the life cycle. It also identifies critical components that need the most testing, what test data is required, and when it is to be prepared.

While it can be seen to be difficult to separate the two activities of project management and technical control and it is reasonable on very small projects for the project manager to undertake both activities, on large projects such a combination of roles is very rarely workable. Firstly, it is rare to find people who combine both the strong management talent and strong technical talent necessary for large projects. Secondly, and more

importantly, on a project of even a reasonable size, each activity is necessarily a full-time job, or more.

It is hard for the project manager to delegate the project management tasks to allow time for technical work. It is impossible for the technical controller to delegate technical control duties without compromising the conceptual integrity of the product. It is sometimes possible to run a project with the technical control exercised by the senior manager in charge of the project and almost all project management tasks delegated to a second-in-command. It is much more usual for the project manager to be in command, with the technical controller having the technical authority. In this case it is important that the technical controller does have enough authority for decisions without being in management line above all the project teams.

9.2 Quality system

In the context of product development the word 'quality' is defined as the degree of conformance of the product to its stated requirements, i.e. 'fitness for purpose'. This definition is applied to the intermediate products of the development as well as to the final product. The development process is fundamental to the ability of the project to produce products of acceptable quality. Quality is built into the product by the activities of the software development staff as a continuous process of building the product to the specified quality.

Quality is everybody's responsibility — it cannot be added by any testing or control on the products of phases. Such testing and quality control activities do, however, provide early warning of problems: changes can be made at much lower cost than in the later stages of development, provided, as always, that proper change control procedures are followed.

The quality system comprises two distinct activities: verification, validation and test (V&T), and quality assurance (QA).

9.3 Verification, validation and test

The terms are defined as follows:

• *Verification:* To establish the correspondence between a software product (documentation or code) and its specification — 'Are we building the product right?'
• *Validation:* To establish the fitness of a software product for its operational mission — 'Are we building the right product?'
• *Testing:* The actual running of code to produce test results.

V&T is checking the correctness of the products of each phase (baselines) and is performed by the software development staff. The activity should, as far as possible, be carried out by staff within the project organisation, but not by the originators of the work. For this reason it is the only development activity which may be the responsibility of a series of different teams as the project proceeds through the life cycle phases.

9.4 Quality assurance

Quality asssurance (QA) is checking the correctness of the procedures being followed, i.e. whether the development staff are following the intended procedures (in all their work, not just the V&T activities). This is carried out by QA staff either from a separate QA department or from staff assigned to QA work within the project. The checking of procedures is backed by audits (spot checks) of the quality (and conformance to standards) of the products to find out if the procedures are effective. Generally the QA staff provide an independent voice on all quality issues, especially on the setting up of standards and procedures at the beginning of the project (i.e. 'how' the project will develop the 'what' defined in the requirement specification). The responsibilities of the QA staff are:

• advising on standards and procedures
• monitoring the procedures actually employed on the project
• auditing and certifying the quality of products achieved.

9.5 Configuration management system

The successful realisation of a software product requires the strictest control over the defining, describing and supporting documentation and the software code constituting the product. It is inevitable that the definition will be subject to continuous pressure for change over the life cycle of the product, to correct errors, introduce improvements and respond to the evolving requirements of the marketplace. Configuration management provides the disciplines required to prevent the chaos of uncontrolled change.

A comprehensive approach to configuration management requires:

• clear identification of software items and documents, and their successive versions and editions
• definition of the configuration of software products, and their related configuration items
• physical control over the master files

of software code and documentation
- control of the introduction of changes to these files by a change control board and a set of change procedures
- maintenance of a system of configuration records, reflecting the definition of products in the field.

The output of each development phase should be verified and validated against the relevant preceding baselines. Configuration management disciplines ensure that all necessary corrections are introduced before this output, in turn, is baselined and that only up-to-date definitions of baselines are used by subsequent phases. The configuration management system should be able to react to the time scales needed by different phases of the project.

Once a baseline has been formally established its contents may only be changed by the operation of the formal change control process. This has the following advantages:

- No changes are made thereafter without the agreement of all interested parties.
- The higher procedural threshold for change tends to stabilise the product.
- There is always available a definitive version of the product, or of any of the controlled intermediate products (baselines).

9.6 Documentation

The output of each phase of the whole software development project consists entirely of documentation or of documentation and code. Furthermore, during the design phases, documents are the sole means by which the successive stages of the design process are recorded, and against which each phase is validated. So much of the output of a software project is in the form of documentation that it is impossible to separate the scheduling of the documentation constituting the baselines from that of the project as a whole. Therefore careful attention to the planning, structure, content, preparation, presentation and control of documentation is vital.

Documentation produced by the software development process may:

- define the software product in terms of requirement and design specifications
- describe the product to the customer or to current or future members of the development team
- support the product in the field in the form of the user's manual, operator's manual and maintenance manual.

9.7 Software development model

Having discussed all the activities of a software development project, the full list of ten activities covering all the management and technical work can be defined as follows:

- *Project management:* Project level management functions. Includes project level planning and control, contract and sub-contract management, customer interface, cost/schedule performance management, management reviews and audits, and includes acquisition of management tools.
- *Technical control:* Responsibility for the technical correctness and quality of the complete product. Responsibility for maintaining the integrity of the whole design during the detailed design, programming and testing phases. Specification, review and update of integration test and acceptance test plans and procedures. Acquisition of requirements and design verification and validation tools. Acquisition and support of test drivers, test tools and test data.
- *Requirement specification:* Determination, specification, review and update of software functional, performance, interface and verification requirements, including acquisition of requirements analysis and specification tools. Development of requirement specification level defining and describing documentation. A continuing responsibility for communication between customer requirements and the technical development.
- *Structural design:* Determination, specification, review and update of hardware-software architecture, software design and database design, including acquisition of design tools. Development of structural design level defining documentation.
- *Detailed design:* Detailed design of individual computer program components. Development of detail design level defining documentation. When a signifi-

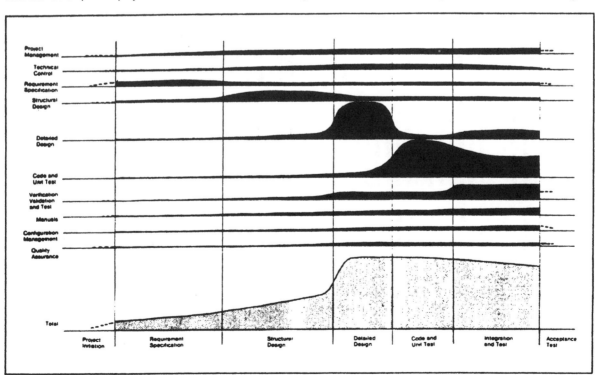

Fig. 4   Software development teams

333

Activity \ Phase	Project initiation	Reqmnt specification	Structural design	Detailed design	Code and unit test	Integration and test	Acceptance test	Maintenance
Project management	project estimating, planning, scheduling, procedures, organisation etc.	project management, project planning, contracts, liaison etc.	project management, status monitoring, contracts, liaison etc	project management, status monitoring, contracts, liaison etc.	project management, status monitoring, contracts, liaison etc.	project management, status monitoring, contracts, liaison etc.	project management, status monitoring, contracts, liaison etc.	support management, status monitoring, contracts, liaison etc.
Technical control	technical strategy, technical plans, technical standards	system models and risk analysis, acceptance test plan, acquire V and V tools for reqmnts and design, top-level test plan	design quality, models and risk analysis, draft test plans, acquire test tools	design integrity, detailed test plans, acquire test tools	design integrity, detailed test plans, install tools	design integrity, support test tools, monitor testing	design integrity, support test tools, monitor acceptance	design integrity, risk analysis, test plans
Requirement specification	analyse requirements, determine user needs	analyse existing system, determine user needs, integrate document and iterate requirements	update requirements	update requirements	update requirements	update requirements	update requirements	determine user needs and problems, update requirements
Structural design	design planning	develop basic architecture, models, prototypes	develop structural design, models, prototypes	update design	update design	update design	update design	update design
Detailed design	identify programming methods and resources	prototypes of algorithms, team planning	models, algorithms investigation, team planning	detailed design, component documentation	update detailed design	update detailed design	update detailed design	detailed design of changes and enhancements
Code and unit test	identify programming methods and resources	identify programming tools, team planning	acquire programming tools and utilities, team planning	integration planning	code and unit test	integrate software, update code	update code	code and unit test of changes and enhancements
Verification validation and test	V and V requirements	V and V specification	V and V structural design	V and V detailed design, V and V design changes	V and V top portions of code, V and V design changes	perform product test, V and V design changes	perform acceptance test, V and V design changes	V and V changes and enhancements
Manuals	define user's manual	outline portions of user's manual	draft users, operators manuals, outline maintenance manual	draft maintenance manual	full draft users and operator's manuals	final users, operators and maintenance manuals	acceptance of manuals	update manual
Configuration management	CM plans and procedures	CM plans, procedures, identify CM tools	CM of requirements, design, acquire CM tools	CM of requirements, design, detailed design, install CM tools, set up library	CM of requirements, design, code, operate library	CM of requirements, design, code, operate library	CM of requirements, design, code, operate library	CM of all documentation, operate library
Quality assurance	QA plans, project procedures and standards	standards, procedures, QA plans, identify QA tools	QA of requirements, design, project standards, acquire QA tools	QA of requirements, design, detailed design	QA of requirements, design, code	QA of requirements, design, code, testing	QA of requirements, design, code, acceptance	QA of maintenance updates

Fig. 5 Project tasks by activity and phase

334

cant number of staff are involved, this activity includes team level management functions.

● *Code and unit test:* Code, unit test and integration of individual computer program components, including tool acquisition. When a significant number of staff are involved, this activity includes team level management functions.

● *Verification, validation and testing:* Performance of independent requirements validation, design verification and validation, integration test and acceptance test, including test reports.

● *Manuals production:* Development and update of product support documentation — user's manual, operator's manual and maintenance manual.

● *Configuration management:* Product identification, operation of change control, status accounting, and operation of program support library.

● *Quality assurance:* Consultancy on the choice of project standards and procedures, monitoring of project procedures in operation, and quality audits of products.

10 The complete software development model

Fig. 5 shows a matrix of the ten activities for eight software development phases. Tasks corresponding to the specific work of an activity in a phase are shown. The tasks can be sub-divided, where relevant, to sub-systems and modules of the product.

These tasks then provide the basis for the work breakdown structure for estimating, planning and assignment of work to the development team. Thus the principles of software development methodology are unified into a single model for software development project control. In fact the matrix of tasks can be considered as a slice through a cube, as shown in Fig. 6.

Having derived the matrix of tasks and already noted that the documentation system (specification and design documents) corresponds to the work of software development, we can now briefly consider the remaining slices in the cube.

10.1 Techniques and tools

Earlier in this paper it was emphasised that one of the important elements of a modern approach to software engineering is the selection of appropriate techniques and the use of computer-based tools. The careful selection and implementation of such tools is crucial to the objective of improving control and raising productivity and product quality. Mechanisation of software development processes, where practicable, in addition to increasing efficiency, encourages consistent process quality.

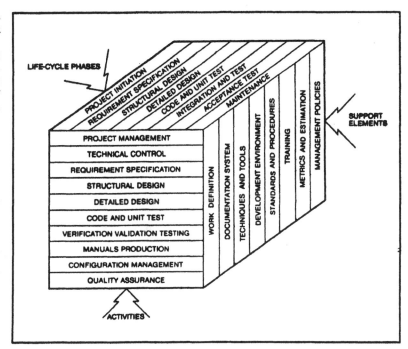

Fig. 6   The software development model

Any suggested technique or set of techniques and the supporting tools can be matched against the model to test how complete an integrated project support environment (IPSE) is provided to support all the tasks in the matrix.

This type of model provides an additional benefit: as techniques and tools are changed or improved from project to project their impact on the development process and product quality can be identified and evaluated.

10.2 Development environment

Development environment is intended to cover all aspects of the computer environment underlying the tools: namely the matters of operating system, database and file facilities, workstations, networking and mainframe computers.

10.3 Standards and procedures

A software development team can only operate effectively when each member knows the answers to the basic questions regarding the job:

● What is expected of me?
● Why is it expected?
● How do I do what is expected?
● What must I produce?
● How will my product be evaluated?
● What tools are available to me?
● What training is available to me?

A set of development procedures and standards improves communications and reduces the probability of misinterpretations among developers. Verification and

validation are much easier to implement and more effective when the product is created in accordance with standards.

The model represented by the cube gives us the basis for a set of standards and procedures that are complete and non-redundant if they cover every cubicle in the cube. This is just the same method as for identifying a complete set of tools. If any standard or procedure is missing then there is a hole in the cube. Standards and procedures should be brief and to the point — they need not be bulky and complicated. In fact the cube defines a structure which can simplify the presentation of the standards and procedures documents. If everything in the cube is covered then the software development team know how they are going to develop the product.

10.4 Training

Training is vital to the success of the programming environment. Having a defined technique is useless unless every member of the team knows how to use the technique. Training should be provided not only on the techniques and tools but on all the support elements.

10.5 Metrics and estimation

We need objective metrics on both the process and the generated products (including all intermediate products for all phases). Measurements provide the immediate benefit of refining the development plan and the long-term benefit of characterising the effectiveness of the current development methodology. Whatever the measurement, it must be defined before development begins.

Collection of data, according to the activities and phases of the model, provides the basis for estimating future projects. In turn, running the project according to the model provides the means of collecting such data and the motivation to use it to succeed in controlling successful projects. All such data collection, metrics, analysis, estimation, planning and project control are much more effective when suitable computer-based tools are used.

10.6 Management policies

Management policies define the life cycle phases and the job functions. They are descriptions of what should be performed by each job function in every life cycle phase. These descriptions may be called a methodology, a corporate policy, an instruction or a procedure. Whatever they are called they must be in place at the beginning of a software development project if the project is to be managed with a high chance of successful completion on time, within budget and with a product which operates correctly to the satisfaction of the customer organisation.

11 Conclusion

The major reason for the slow evolution of software project management over the past two decades is the persistent view that programming is an art, rather than a science. This view lingers and has contributed to delays in the development of a well defined, well structured software management methodology. The problem persists despite the great advances in computer hardware technology, the introduction of software engineering, and the definition of new development approaches, such as design decomposition, structured design, structured programming, hierarchical input-output definition and team management concepts.

These factors foster the perspective in business and project management that software management must continuously evolve and change to keep up with advances in software development technology. Yet these conclusions are seldom applied to management of the rapidly advancing electronics field. Since hardware development projects, in the midst of phenomenal technology advances, can be managed in a disciplined, systematic manner based on past decades of project management experience, why should it be assumed that software projects cannot?

Software engineering recognises both technological and managerial aspects. Improvements in the technology of software development have reached the point where the major issues have been identified and considerable progress has been made in addressing these issues. Practical working tools to support improved software production are commonly available and a firm methodology for technical software development is well defined.

Published papers over the last ten years show that software development is manageable and software productivity can be significantly improved for the benefit of the business. The common denominators in the successes reported are firstly that they are usually the better developers of software making even greater improvements, and secondly that they are backed by management commitment.

Given that making software engineering methodology really work is always difficult, it follows that success depends on more than just the wish to improve control and productivity of software development: management support and the willingness to invest is necessary in order to obtain the due return on the investment.

The technical methods, tools and disciplines are the basis for the production of reliable software, on time and within budget, but it is also necessary to have an overall management framework which allows senior management to understand, and project managers to control, large software developments. The increasing complexity of the large software systems being developed and advances in software technology and tools mean that there will be a continuing evolution in technical software development, but the primary basis for the control of software development will continue to be the principles outlined in this paper.

P. E. Rook is Software Development Manager with GEC Software Ltd., 132–135 Long Acre, London WC2E 9AH, England.

Earned Value Project Management
A Powerful Tool for Software Projects

Quentin W. Fleming and Joel M. Koppelman
Primavera Systems, Inc.

Earned value can provide any project manager with an early warning tool that sends out a signal from as early as the 15 percent completion point on a project. This signal allows the project manager to forecast the final required funds needed to finish the job within a narrow range of values. If the final forecasted results are unacceptable to management, steps can be taken early to alter the final requirements. The end benefit is that software projects can be completed that contain more final features—if the project's management monitors the true cost performance from the beginning of the project.

OVER THE LAST THREE decades, a proven but yet underutilized project management technique has emerged and taken its place alongside other valuable tools: *earned value*. In its formal application, it has been found to be an effective device to oversee and manage major new systems acquisitions by U.S. government agencies. In a more basic form, earned value can be a useful technique in the management of any project—including, and in particular, software projects.

Earned value requires that the project be fully defined at the outset and then a bottom-up plan be created. This allows measurement to take place during the entire period of performance, from 1 percent to 100 percent of the project's lifecycle. The power in this tool is that it provides accurate and reliable readings of performance from as early as 15 percent into the project. As shown in Figure 1, any project manager can use these performance readings to predict how much it will cost to complete the project within a narrow band of values. If these early warning signals convey unacceptable readings to the project manager, steps can be immediately taken to avoid the undesired results.

This technique is of particular interest to software project managers. No longer must software projects use up all their resources before there is a harsh realization that much of the work has not been completed, forcing features to be dropped to stay within the added budget authorized by management. Earned-value project management can be most helpful to any software project manager who has made a firm commitment to complete all the features within a definitive schedule and for a finite amount of funds.

Introduction to the Earned-Value Concept

Earned value has been mandated by the U.S. government for decades in an inflexible, formalized manner that has kept many organizations from attempting to use the technique. This mandated, formalized version began in 1967 when the Department of Defense (DoD) issued a directive that imposed 35 Cost/Schedule Control Systems Criteria (C/SCSC) on all private industrial firms that wished to participate in future major government systems in which some type of cost-reimbursable

or incentive contract was to be used. Thereafter, any time a new major system would be procured by the U.S. government in which the "risk" of cost growth was retained by the government, these 35 criteria had to be satisfied by the contractor.

The effect of the C/SCSC mandate was to require a formal version of the "earned-value" concept of cost and schedule management on selected major new projects. A certain minimum contract dollar value (in millions) and a minimum program duration (of 12 months or more) had to be present before the criteria were to be applied. Essentially, these earned-value criteria were intended only for major system procurements.

The C/SCSC concept has been consistently applied for over 30 years and has set the standard for major government systems acquisitions. Other government agencies in the United States and in other nations such as Australia, Canada, and Sweden have adopted similar earned-value criteria in the management of their major system acquisitions. A practical body of scientific management knowledge has been developed on the use of the earned-value concept, primarily compiled by the DoD and by the Air Force Institute of Technology (AFIT).

Although some people consider these 35 C/SCSC standards a Utopian ideal for all private firms to emulate, many within private industry have had difficulty employing these

Figure 1. *Cost risks can be managed with an "early warning" signal.*

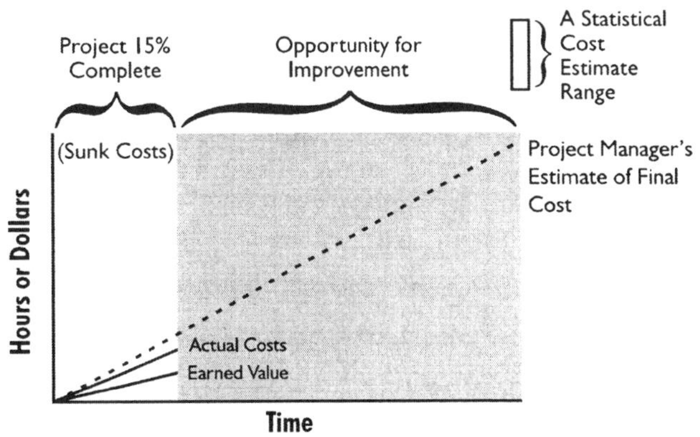

Reprinted from *Crosstalk,* July 1998.

rigid criteria on all their projects—particularly commercial projects. Their perception is that there are too many nonvalue-added requirements in the formalized C/SCSC for them to be universally employed on all their commercial projects.

Industry's acquired distaste for the C/SCSC implementation of earned value is unfortunate because earned value performance measurement provides a sound project management tool. When properly employed, it can give the project manager an early warning signal that the project is heading for a cost overrun unless immediate steps are taken to change the spending plan. The software world needs something less formal than the full C/SCSC, something that can be scaled downward and precisely tailored to fit broader project management applications. Today, it is likely that more than 99 percent of the projects in the world do *not* employ the earned-value cost management concept. Instead, to monitor costs status, they merely compare their spend plan to their actual costs, and that is unfortunate. There are opportunities to use a simplified form of earned value on any project of any size within the military or commercial sectors.

The Genesis and Evolution of Earned Value

To properly understand the earned-value concept, we must go back in time to the early part of this century and trace the origin of earned value as it came initially from the factory floor.

The Factory Floor in the Early 1900s

The earned-value concept originally came from industrial engineers in factories who for years have employed a three-dimensional approach to assess true "cost-performance" efficiencies. To assess their cost performance, they have been comparing their *earned standards* (the physical factory output) against *actual costs* incurred. Then they compare their earned standards to the original *planned standards* (the physical work they planned to accomplish) to assess the

schedule results. These efforts provided earned value in its most basic form.

Most important, the industrial engineers defined a *cost variance* as the difference between the actual costs spent and the earned standards in the factory. This definition of a cost variance is perhaps the litmus test to determine whether one uses the earned-value concept.

PERT/Cost 1962-1965

The Program Evaluation and Review Technique (PERT) was introduced by the U.S. Navy in 1957 to support the development of its Polaris missile program. PERT attempted to simulate the necessary work to develop the Polaris missile by creating a logic network of dependent sequential events. The initial focus of PERT was on the management of time and on predicting the probability of program success. But before PERT was accepted by program management in industry, the U.S. Air Force came up with an extension of PERT by adding resource estimates to the logic networks. *PERT/Cost* was thus born in 1962, and the initial PERT was thereafter known as *PERT/Time.*

The significance of PERT/Cost, however, was not the technique, but what evolved from it. The earned-value measurement concept was first introduced to the American defense contracting community when the government issued the *DoD and NASA Guide to PERT/Cost* in 1963, which provided a simple definition of earned value. Instead of relating cost plans to cost actuals, which had been the custom, PERT/Cost related the *value* of physical work performed against the cost actuals to determine the utility and benefits from the funds spent. What was *physically accomplished* for what was *spent* was a simple but fundamentally important new concept in program management.

For various reasons, the DoD gave up on the PERT/Cost technique in the mid-1960s but correctly held on to the earned-value concept. When the DoD formally issued the C/SCSC in 1967, the earned-value concept was solidly contained therein.

C/SCSC 1967 to 1996

Since the issuance of the C/SCSC by the DoD, the concept's application has been limited only to contracts in which the government has retained the risks of cost growth, i.e., on cost- or incentive-type contracts and subcontracts. Perhaps the most significant aspect of C/SCSC employment has been the body of scientific knowledge that has been accumulated in its use on major highly technical projects. The DoD has been accumulating data on the use of earned value to assess project performance and has been using the results attained to predict final cost and schedule results with amazing accuracy.

Earned Value Management Systems Criteria 1996 to Present

After years of earned value being imposed on industry by the government as a unilateral mandate, private industry asked for and was allowed to have a say in the wording of the requirements being imposed on them. In 1995, private industry, as represented by the National Security Industrial Association (NSIA), was allowed to assess the utility of the earned-value criteria.

After a year-long study, the NSIA subcommittee came up with its version of the criteria, reworded significantly to be more palatable to the project management community. The industry standard was called the Earned Value Management System (EVMS) and the number of criteria was reduced from 35 to 32. This major development was endorsed by the DoD in December 1996.

However encouraging these recent advancements may be, going from 35 to 32 criteria still leaves the earned-value concept with far too many nonvalue-added requirements. We believe the earned-value concept will never be universally accepted by project managers in its current form, embedded as a part of the 32 formal EVMS criteria. There are too many rules and terms one must master to employ this approach. Instead, what is needed is a return to the simple concept that originally came from the industrial factory floors. The industrial engineers did not use checklists and interpretations to employ their concept;

338

rather, they used common sense to determine what was needed and what did or did not work.

Listed below are 10 earned-value "musts" that, when followed, capture the critical essence of the earned-value concept and enhance the management of all projects, large and small, from any industry.

Ten Musts to Implement Earned Value on All Projects

Define Work Scope
You must define 100 percent of the project's work scope using a work breakdown structure (WBS). Perhaps the most critical and most challenging requisite to employing earned value is to define the project's total work scope. This is a difficult task for any project, and particularly so for software projects. Yet, if you do not define what constitutes 100 percent of the assumed work, how can you measure the project's performance in a definitive way? Without a 100 percent reference point, how can anyone ascertain whether you have completed 10 percent, 20 percent, or 25 percent of a job?

Realistically, no one can define a new job with absolute precision, but you must make some intelligent assumptions about a new project to quantify the work with sufficient confidence that the defined effort can be planned, scheduled, and estimated with some degree of certainty. Anything less, and management must commit to a job by authorizing a "blank check" for the project.

How does one define a job when specific details are often lacking? There are no absolute answers, but one of the most useful of all tools available to any project manager is the WBS. The WBS is to the project manager what the organization chart is to the executive—it allows the project manager to define a new endeavor by laying out all the assumed work, then decomposing each task into measurable work packages. Once the WBS is assumed to constitute a reasonable portrayal of the new project, it can be used to take the next steps in the project planning process,

including the make-or-buy analysis, risk assessment, planning, scheduling, estimating, and authorization to proceed.

Create an Integrated Bottom-Up Plan
You must combine critical processes, including defined work scope, schedule, and estimated resources, into an integrated bottom-up plan of detailed measurement cells called Control Account Plans (CAPs). Earned value project management is implemented within detailed CAPs, which therefore constitute formal bottom-up project planning. The individual CAPs represent the integration of all critical processes such as work scope, planning, scheduling, estimating, and authorization.

The performance measurement will take place within the detailed CAPs, and the total project's performance is the summation of what was reflected in the detailed CAPs. In essence, each project CAP is a subproject of the total project that is managed, measured, and controlled by a CAP manager.

Formally Schedule CAPs
Each of the defined CAPs must be planned and scheduled with a formal scheduling system. This is perhaps the single most critical tool required to implement earned value. The project's scheduling system will portray the approved work scope, which is carefully placed into a specific timeframe for performance. In earned-value vernacular, this scheduled work will constitute the project's *planned value.* As performance takes place on the project, the portion of the planned value that is physically accomplished becomes the earned value. Both the planned value and the resulting earned value must use the same metrics to measure their performance.

The project's scheduling system is, therefore, critical to the employment of earned value because it is the vehicle to represent the project's scope, planned value, and earned-value measurement. The *project master schedule* is vital to the project because it constitutes the project manager's specified planned value for everyone to follow.

Assign Each CAP to an Executive for Performance
Each of the defined CAPs must be assigned to a permanent functional executive for performance. This assignment effectively commits the executive to oversee the performance of each CAP. Projects are by their nature transient within any firm's permanent organizational structure—they are authorized, implemented, and performed, then eventually go out of existence. Many (perhaps most) of those who manage the detailed performance that takes place within the CAPs will not carry the formal title of "manager" within the firm's permanent organizational structure; rather, many or most of these CAP managers are functional employees temporarily assigned and matrixed into the project by one of the permanent functional organizations. To secure a firm commitment from the functional executives who have the authority and resources to make the plan happen, it is wise to have each of the defined project CAPs essentially adopted by a senior function person with a title such as vice president, director, or manager.

Establish a Baseline that Summarizes CAPs
A total project performance measurement baseline must be established, which represents the summation of the detailed CAPs. The next required step is to form a total baseline against which project performance may be measured. Such baselines must include all defined CAPs plus any management (contingency) reserves that may be held by the project manager. If management reserves are not given to the project manager but are instead controlled by a senior management committee, they should be excluded from the project performance baseline.

On a commercial-type contract, the baseline may include such things as indirect costs—and even profit or fee—to match the total authorized project funds. Internal projects will typically not contain indirect costs, profits, or management reserves. Most internal project baselines will be the sum of the defined CAPs.

Measure Performance Against Schedule

Periodically, you must measure the project's schedule performance against its planned master project schedule. The formally issued and controlled project master schedule constitutes the project's planned scope. Each task described on the project master schedule can be loaded with estimated resources, such as hours or dollars, which are embedded within the authorized CAPs. As performance takes place within the CAPs, you can quantify the relationship between the value of the work scheduled as compared to the value of the work accomplished. The difference between the work scheduled and work accomplished constitutes the *schedule variance* in earned value.

A negative schedule variance means that the value of the work accomplished does not match the value of the work scheduled, i.e., the project is falling behind in its scheduled work. Each behind-schedule task can be assessed regarding its criticality to the project. If the late task is on the critical path, or if the task carries a high risk to the project, efforts can be made to get the late task back on schedule. Conversely, if a task has positive variance or is not considered a high risk to the project, added resources should not be spent to accelerate its performance.

Measure Cost Efficiency Against the Costs Incurred

You must periodically measure the project's cost performance efficiency rate, which represents the relationship between the project's earned value performed and the costs incurred to achieve the earned value. The single most important benefit of employing earned value is the cost efficiency readings it provides. The difference between the value of work performed and the costs incurred to accomplish the work provides the cost-efficiency factor. If you are spending more on the project than it receives in value, this reflects an overrun condition. Absolute overruns have been

found to be nonrecoverable. Overruns expressed as a percentage value have been found to deteriorate unless the project takes aggressive actions to mitigate the condition.

Perhaps of greatest benefit, the cost efficiency rate has been found to be usably stable from the 15 percent point of a project completion and progressively more stable as it goes from the 20 percent to 30 percent to 40 percent completion point. Therefore, the cost efficiency factor is an important metric for any project manager or enterprise executive to monitor.

Forecast Final Costs Based on Performance

Periodically, you must forecast the project's final cost requirements based on its performance against the plan. One of the more beneficial aspects of the earned-value concept is its ability to independently forecast the total required funds at the end of a project, commonly called the "estimate at completion." Based on project performance against the plan, a project manager can accurately estimate the total funds required to finish the job within a finite range of values.

These statistical estimates are something like a grass-roots sanity check against estimates based more on wishful thinking because they provide a more realistic estimate of the values needed to finish the job—unless someone has a preconceived notion of what that value should be. As reflected in Figure 1, if the earned-value statistical estimates are greater than the "official" project estimates to complete the project, someone in a senior management position should reconcile these professional differences of opinion.

Manage Remaining Work

You must continuously manage the project's remaining work. The results achieved to date on a project, good or bad, are in effect "sunk costs"—gone forever. Thus, any improvements in performance must come from future work—tasks ahead of the latest status date. Earned value allows the project manager to accurately measure the cost

and schedule performance achieved to date. If the results thus far are less than desired, the project manager can exert a more aggressive posture on all future work. Earned value, because it allows the project to accurately quantify the value of its work achieved, allows the project manager to also quantify the value of the work ahead to stay within the objectives set by management.

Manage Baseline Changes

You must continuously maintain the project's baseline by managing all changes to the baseline. The project performance measurement baseline you put in place at the start of the project is only as good as your management of all proposed changes to the baseline during the duration of the project. Any performance baseline quickly becomes invalid if you fail to incorporate changes into the approved baseline either by the addition to or elimination of added work scope.

All new changes of project work must be addressed either by the approval or rejection of changes. For the initial baseline to remain valid, every change must be closely managed. Maintaining a baseline is as challenging as the initial definition of the project scope at the start of the project.

Conclusion

The earned value project management concept as a part of the more formal C/SCSC or EVMS has been demonstrated to be an effective technique in the management of major projects. Unfortunately, most of the experience with the concept has been restricted to those applications where the U.S. government has imposed the technique on major new systems acquisitions for which it retains the risk of cost growth.

However, the best opportunities for earned-value employment may well lie in the management of thousands of smaller projects that are being directed by people who may well be unaware of earned value. We believe the concept should be considered any time the risk of cost growth resides with a project manager, any time a lump sum or fixed price contract is used, and on all in-house funded developmental projects where a firm commitment is made to management. It should be considered any time a project manager could benefit from receiving an early warning cost signal in time to alter the ultimate direction of a project. Software projects can especially benefit from the employment of a simple earned-value approach. ◆

About the Authors

Quentin W. Fleming, senior staff consultant to Primavera Systems, Inc., has over 30 years industrial project management experience. He held various management assignments with the Northrop Corporation from 1968 until 1991, served on an earned-value corporate review team, and wrote the corporate policy directive on scheduling.

He is president of the Orange County Project Management Institute (PMI) chapter and developed and taught four PMI Project Management Professional tutorial courses covering scope, cost, time, and procurement management. He has a bachelor's and a master's degree in management and is the author of seven published textbooks including *Earned Value Project Management*, which he co-wrote with Joel M. Koppelman.

E-mail: QuentinF@Primavera.com

Joel M. Koppelman is president of Primavera Systems, which provides a family of project management software products. Before co-founding Primavera in 1983, he spent over 12 years planning, designing, and managing major capital projects in the transportation industry, including duties as vice president and chief financial officer for Transportation and Distribution Associates, Inc. Before that, he was affiliated with the management consulting firm of Booz Allen Hamilton, Inc.

Koppelman is a registered professional engineer with a bachelor's degree in civil engineering from Drexel University and a master's of business administration degree from the Wharton School of the University of Pennsylvania. He is a frequent speaker at universities and for international management organizations.

E-mail: JKoppel@Primavera.com

Software Configuration Management: A Discipline with Added Value

Tresa Butler, Verla Standley, Elaine Sullivan
Ogden Air Logistics Center, Technology and Industrial Support

Faith Turner
Scientech, Inc.

From the beginning of our software engineering organization to our current Capability Maturity Model® (CMM®) Level 5 quality practices, the implementation of the software configuration management (SCM) discipline combined with management and engineering practices has been critical to our weapon-system software sustainment activities. The focus of this article is to discuss how SCM adds value to our organization by establishing and maintaining continuity of the engineering workflow and provides information to help establish a strong SCM function in maturing software organizations.

The word "Kaizen" is a Japanese term used to define the discipline of continuous improvement. For example when an automotive assembly line is considered to be perfect, it is pushed past its limits until a malfunction occurs; the anomaly is found and corrected, and then the limits are tested again. When applied in the workplace, Kaizen means continuing improvement involving everyone – managers and workers alike.

Software configuration management[1] (SCM) is the one discipline where development, sustainment, support, and software Kaizen are accomplished to achieve quality products. SCM defines, implements, and manages product life cycles by planning, identifying, controlling, auditing, and improving the elements by which they are created.

During the early years of our Software Engineering Division (TIS) at Hill Air Force Base, Utah, SCM was not a term commonly used. Most engineers were aware of SCM, but would prefer to ignore it. SCM meant processes and procedures. The engineers were there to write software and did not want to be bothered with process and paperwork. Every individual or team had their own way of doing things, resulting in little work uniformity. They did, however, want to have quality software with as little rework as possible.

This desire to provide quality software forced us to look at how we did business and to search for ways to improve. Management chose to use the Software Engineering Institute's Capability Maturity Model® (CMM®), and after an initial review began building toward process improvement. This decision really

---

® *The Capability Maturity Model and CMM are registered in the U.S. Patent and Trademark Office.*

introduced SCM as a key process for better software to everyone within the division. In order to become a CMM Level 2 organization we needed to have consistent policies for managing our software projects. The standards set by the CMM for this level were requirements management, software project planning, software project tracking and oversight, software subcontract management, software quality assurance, and SCM.

During our CMM implementation, software quality assurance became tied to SCM and evolved as a major player within the structure of the organization. This was not an easy road for the SCM team. Many people within the division did not want the change and did not want the extra demands that SCM would put on them. It meant being accountable for every line of code as well as documenting every change.

Until this point, each engineer was accountable for his or her own configuration management. Now it was necessary to have a separate group of individuals with the sole purpose of providing quality assurance as well as managing the elements of each project injected into the processes.

It meant following a process that was rigid enough to keep everyone on the same track, but flexibile enough to allow each team to develop its products based on customer demands. Over time, SCM has become the discipline that assures quality software. In short, SCM has become the *glue* to an organization that produces quality products.

Developing the Glue

During the developmental stages of our weapon-system software activities, SCM plays a major role in planning and manag-

ing the schedules and milestones used during the project life cycles, as well as identifying product configuration items (CIs). Within TIS, SCM defines and records the origin and details involved in the inception of the product by establishing baselines. When SCM disciplines are used during this initial developmental stage of the product life cycle, it is comparable to the parable of the man who built his house upon the rock. A solid SCM discipline provides a firm foundation upon which software development and sustainment are achieved.

It is during the sustainment stage of weapon-system software activities that the SCM discipline provides consistency and strength. It is no longer adequate to simply create a product using a set of established ground rules and guidelines; now a structured enforcement of processes is a must. SCM provides continuity to the workflow by establishing the processes and procedures for controlling and auditing CI's throughout the product life cycle to ensure quality, integrity, and accountability levels are met and maintained.

SCM plays an integral part in scheduling, attending, and recording pertinent information during the definition portion of the project. SCM enhances the sustainment stage of the product by carefully tracking each software activity, thus blending in integrity and quality through repeatable auditing and data control. Establishing traceable metrics to track costs, identify weaknesses, and determine recovery capabilities ensures SCM as a value-added entity to the product life cycle of our organization. It assures that every requirement, problem, action item, etc., is tracked to closure, and that metrics data for each of these activities are updated.

Reprinted from *Crosstalk*, July 2001.

SCM maintains a configuration status accounting (CSA) record of requirements compliance, cost control, source lines of code, and more. This data is used in information exchanges such as program management reviews to make well thought-out, informed decisions. SCM's data management of workflow, as well as maintenance of product life cycles, provides sustainment for past, present, and future projects.

The Life Cycle Workflow

Within our organization, the SCM function defines, implements, and manages product life cycles by planning, identifying, controlling, and auditing the current workflow. Having a well-defined process has enabled us to adapt new hardware and software workloads into our organizational workflow.

One thing that has proven to be very beneficial to our organization is the ability to tailor our formal configuration management (CM) process to the needs of each individual project. This way each individual team does not have to adhere to strict procedures; instead, each team is allowed flexibility within their own programs. SCM has been very helpful to each team in setting up procedures that comply with the process, but also fit individual needs. Following is an outline of that workflow process:

Planning: Management utilizes SCM to establish and maintain CM and project plans that define project activities and deliverable work products. This includes processes and procedures for the life span of the project. SCM is used to attend and record project directives, schedules, data requirements, peer reviews, and configuration control boards (CCB). These boards define milestones, deliverable work products, and cost and schedule.

Within our organization, the CCB is held prior to initiation of any work to define requirements, schedules, and deliverables, which are incorporated into a project directive and project requirements document. These signed documents represent the agreement between our organization and our customer defining project milestones and deliverables. CM configures these documents for referral throughout the life of the project, and these documents are reviewed periodically for additions/deletions.

```
                         _P_R_O_J_E_C_T___R_E_P_O_R_T_

TV3.2  CANDIDATES
Tue Apr 10 12:11:08 2001
--------------------------------------------------------------------------------
Project: #C1-R0      Parse Configuration and BE Data
SYS DES:                                                          Status: OPEN
INT TEST:                                SYS:    0 Mhrs      ICR:    0  Mhrs

SUB     DESIGN ENGINEER      HRS  SOFTWARE ENG          HRS  SLOC  ERT ENGINEER
---     ---------------      ---  ------------          ---  ----  ------------
AFMSS                             STARRETT, BETH         13    50  F Montierth
--------------------------------------------------------------------------------
Project: #C2-R0      Time-Line Data
SYS DES:                                                          Status: OPEN
INT TEST:                                SYS:    0 Mhrs      ICR:    0  Mhrs

SUB     DESIGN ENGINEER      HRS  SOFTWARE ENG          HRS  SLOC  ERT ENGINEER
---     ---------------      ---  ------------          ---  ----  ------------
AFMSS   RICHARDSON, JIM       24  RICHARDSON, JIM        48   280  F Montierth
--------------------------------------------------------------------------------
Project: #C3-R0      Export TableView Data
SYS DES:                                                          Status: OPEN
INT TEST:                                SYS:    0 Mhrs      ICR:    0  Mhrs

SUB     DESIGN ENGINEER      HRS  SOFTWARE ENG          HRS  SLOC  ERT ENGINEER
---     ---------------      ---  ------------          ---  ----  ------------
AFMSS                             STARRETT, BETH         14   160  F Montierth
--------------------------------------------------------------------------------
Project: #C4-R0      Allow Multiple Lists in Table View Data
SYS DES:                                                          Status: OPEN
INT TEST:                                SYS:    0 Mhrs      ICR:    0  Mhrs

SUB     DESIGN ENGINEER      HRS  SOFTWARE ENG          HRS  SLOC  ERT ENGINEER
---     ---------------      ---  ------------          ---  ----  ------------
AFMSS   RAISOR, KENNETH        3  RAISOR, KENNETH        12  1300  F Montierth
--------------------------------------------------------------------------------
Project: #C5-R0      Allow For All File Extensions
SYS DES:                                                          Status: CLOSED
INT TEST:                                SYS:    0 Mhrs      ICR:    0  Mhrs
```

Figure 1: *Sample Project Report*

Identifying: Upon completion of the upper level planning, the CSA database is populated by SCM to begin the task of identifying each configuration item and to begin gathering metrics for the life-cycle updates. By obtaining metrics for proposed work products, SCM provides management and engineering with the necessary data to make judicious decisions regarding weapon-system software sustainment activities. This is the heart of the continuous process improvement of our Level 5 organization.

The SCM team works with the program managers to identify the project's CIs. SCM populates the tracking databases by creating work products and their related data management objects and ensures that all requirements approved during the planning state are incorporated into the update. This requires creation, maintenance, and closure of work products for schedules, engineering change proposals, system design change requests, subsystem design change requests, software change requests, source lines of code, etc. The database then provides pertinent information for accumulating proposed weapon-systems upgrades.

Our organization uses our CSA system to record many types of metrics as well as actual man-hours and lines of code dedicated to each change request produced. These actual metrics are later used when accessing assets and manpower for new workloads. Figure 1 is a sample project report that includes the project identifier, project name, engineer assigned to the project, man-hours, lines of code, and other information that may be required during project development. There are several other reports that can be pulled to show the status of projects, percent complete, and other valuable metrics.

Controlling: SCM enforces control of CIs by establishing processes and procedures to maintain accountability of configured software enhancements throughout the life cycle of the upgrade. Incremental configuration at each stage/milestone ensures incorporation of approved source code and maintains traceability of known anomalies. Within our organization, the CM functions to update the CSA database at intervals during the product life-cycle, providing a current snapshot of the program at any given time. This means that when addressing both current and archived projects, the historical data regarding incremental releases describes during which phase anomalies were identified, along with in which release the anomalies were corrected.

Figure 2 (see page 6) is an example of a Software Change Request (SCR) form as it is recorded within our database. Within this process several metrics are recorded for future use. Dates are tracked as each milestone is passed such as the completion of a final peer review and the approval of the CCB, as well as the man-hours spent reviewing SCRs, time spent in peer

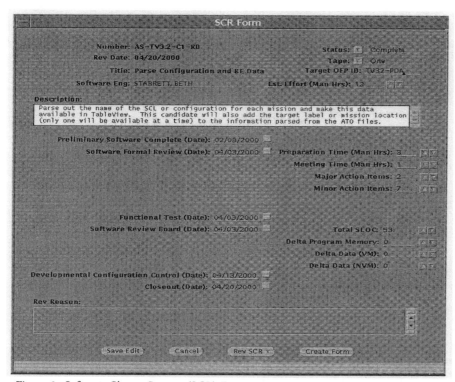

Figure 2: *Software Change Request (SCR) Form*

and did not include all CI and identifiers needed. Additional hardware modification requirements were not identified until after we began upgrading the software. Identifying, correcting, and implementing the anomaly at such a late date impacted the software release cycle. To prevent this anomaly from reoccurring, a corrective action to tailor SCM processes resulted in a preliminary review of all documentation. This has eliminated 90 percent of the problems we had previously encountered. This resulted in the CCB receiving a better product to review and more accurate estimates of program cost/schedule.

Tools and Metrics

Tools are one of the key capabilities within our software sustainment environment. Tools provide the identification and control of the software and its related components as they change during the software's life cycle. There are numerous off-the-shelf SCM tools available in today's market, some of which we use in our organization. But we have developed many organic tools to comply or adapt specifically to our processes and corporate culture. There are traditional CM tools that provide check-in/check-out control of code as well as the ability to compile or build. Within our organization we have tools that provide process management such as the ability to track anomalies and provide problem

reviews, number of action items, their priority, source lines of code, and memory changes.

Anomalies are found during various testing phases. As they are detected the engineer responsible for finding the error enters them into the database. The database assigns the anomaly a tracking number after which the anomaly becomes a configured item. SCM tracks the error until it is fixed or determined not to be an error. Figure 3 is an example of a report used to show the status of anomalies.

Auditing: SCM produces audits at incremental steps throughout the software-building process to ensure quality, integrity, and adherence to established processes and procedures. Additionally, SCM incorporates quality assurance throughout the life cycle of the product by being a separate entity and maintaining continuity and accountability of the engineering workflow. Our CM processes include audits and quality checks ensuring that specifications are being updated incrementally as software lines of code are being developed.

An example of these audits within our organization occurs after a change request has been reviewed, comments recorded, and the author has accomplished a re-edit to include peer review comments. Our peer review process requires that an audit of the document be performed to ensure

that the author incorporated all the approved changes. If the audit is not passed, the change request repeats this step of the process.

One of our lessons learned occurred when a customer provided us with documentation that required an upgrade prior to releasing new software. The customer requirements were vague and undefined

Figure 3: *Anomoly Status Report*

```
Text Editor - TV3.2_SPAR_Summary_ALL.rpt

File   Edit   Format   Options                                    Help

            _S_U_M_M_A_R_Y_  _S_P_A_R_  _R_E_P_O_R_T_
Baseline: TV3.2
Group: ALL
Wed Apr 11 10:37:24 2001
SPAR Grp    Pri Status         Class       Title

    1 AFMSS   LOW Deferred        U   AOI disabled when map is not available
    2 AFMSS   MED Fixed           U   ICDs Not Updated for C5
    3 AFMSS   LOW Cancelled       U   SDD File List Tables Outdated
    4 AFMSS   LOW Fixed           U   Table View Shape Column
    5 AFMSS   MED Cancelled       U   GUI ICD References Non-Existent Laydown
                                       Functions
    6 AFMSS   LOW Fixed           U   Can't build Editor for PFPS 3.01
    7 AFMSS   HI  Fixed           U   The Check Laydown Function does not work.
    8 AFMSS   HI  Fixed           U   ACO Set ID GEOLINE Is Not Being Parsed.
    9 AFMSS   MED Fixed           U   Installation Auto Selection fails with
                                       PFPS 3.1.1
   10 AFMSS   HI  Fixed           U   Laydown Editor Fails to Launch
   11 AFMSS   HI  Fixed           U   Can't Compile Laydown Editor
   12 AFMSS   MED Fixed           U   Laydown Editor can't open some files.
   13 AFMSS   MED Fixed           U   Can't parse all formats of EFFLEVEL
   14 AFMSS   MED Fixed           U   Confirm Build Mission Dialog needs
                                       scrolled list
   15 AFMSS   MED Fixed           U   Extra Square Box in Table View
   16 AFMSS   HI  Fixed           U   Points may not be sorted in the proper
                                       order
   17 AFMSS   HI  Fixed           U   TableView ACO List Errors
   18 AFMSS   HI  Fixed           U   Text button displays wrong info in
                                       TableView
   19 AFMSS   HI  Fixed           U   TableView Column Headers
   20 AFMSS   HI  Fixed           U   Target Columns do not show all points
   21 AFMSS   HI  Fixed           U   Customize TableView Problems
   22 AFMSS   LOW Deferred        U   FalconView Covers TaskView Window On
```

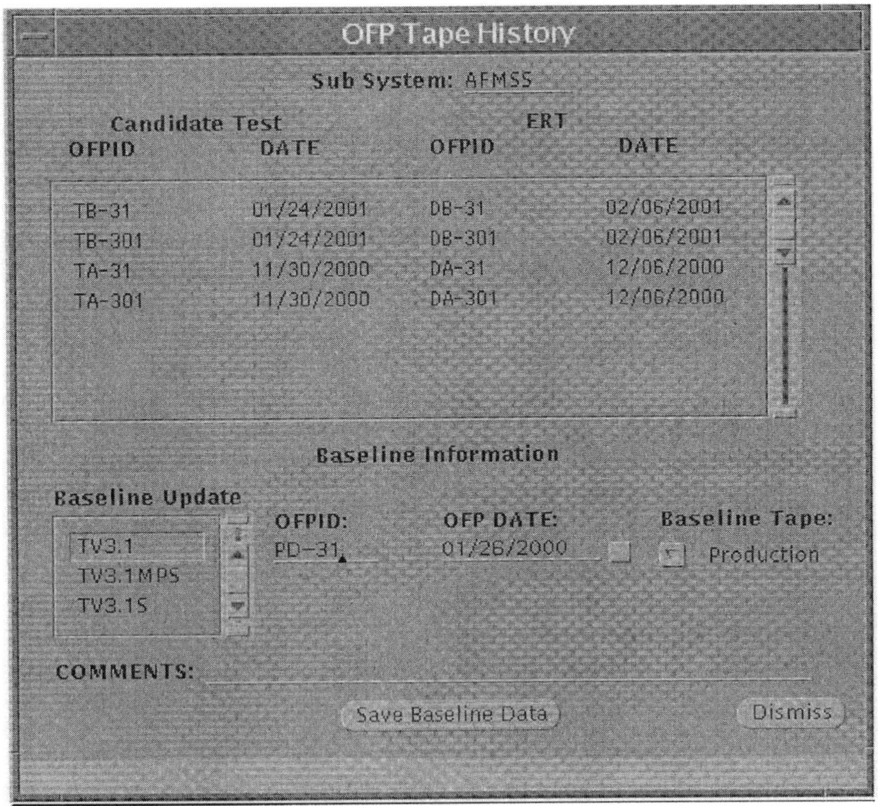

Figure 4: *Operational Flight Program Tape History*

reports. We also have commercial off-the-shelf tools that have been tailored to fit into our process and provide us with the necessary quality checks and balances.

One of the key areas within SCM is status accounting. To have true CM, tools are required to track the status of all CIs as well as problems or anomalies. We have developed tools within our organization that provide the ability to track several complex systems as well as to collect data and generate numerous reports. These tools also provide versatility in adapting to a variety of different workloads. One of the advantages of an organic tool is the ability to adapt or to change the tool as new requirements come in or as processes are updated.

An example of a new requirement added to our database recently is the Tape History dialog box shown in Figure 4. This history helps us to track the baseline used to develop the current update of the Operational Flight Program (OFP). It tracks all version releases of the software identified by the OFP Identification Number and the dates they were compiled. As a result this has helped us to track baselines for individual subsystems

and enables us to pull reports for those who need this information.

Throughout the different stages of process improvement, from being a CMM Level 1 to a CMM Level 5 organization, we have learned many valuable lessons. One of the most valuable being the importance of creating your processes and then buying or developing a tool that compliments that process. If you buy a tool without knowing where you are going and what your overall goals are, you end up having to adapt your process to fit the tool. That may not be the best for your organization.

One of the benefits of a good status accounting tool is the metrics and reports that can be obtained. This has been very beneficial to our organization and to our customers. We are able to track estimated costs, man-hours, source lines of code, anomalies, memory requirements, rework, and much more. This gives us the ability to compare estimated data to actual data. It is this historical information that gives us a solid track record and helps us greatly in bidding on future workload, as well as supplying our customers with information in creating project requirements.

Training

Training for each member of the SCM team is a must. SCM is an evolving field. Not only is it necessary to keep up with new ideas and tools, but to keep up with the industry on how SCM is being interpreted by the world or even in other parts of our own division. In order to provide customers with current processes and procedures, we must be aware of changes and improvements made within the industry. This enables assigning appropriate authorities and responsibilities to all SCM activities within our organizations.

Management, engineers, and configuration managers must understand the processes within their respective organizations. It is necessary to be knowledgeable enough to tailor SCM practices to the needs of each customer/workload. Configuration managers are involved in all stages of development; they must become an integral part of the process. Here, they are depended on for their expertise in decision making to facilitate process improvement and provide a quality assurance role. Detailed knowledge, formal training, and on-the-job experience result in the ability to recognize problems – to stop work, address issues, correct problems, and continue moving ahead. When problems are encountered, knowledgeable configuration managers are invaluable in resolving issues. Some training examples that benefit our organization follow:

- First is mentorship between trained pesonnel and new/untrained personnel.
- Second is CM training courses. These courses give a broad overview of SCM and usually benefit anyone interested in becoming knowledgeable of basic SCM fundamentals.
- Third, and most importantly, is on-the-job training, which provides the most insight to SCM processes and procedures.

Properly trained SCM personnel result in procedures that produce repeatable quality products. Members of the SCM team are not technical or engineering people. The team is comprised of individuals who are competent in the skills needed to provide insight and background to SCM policies and procedures. Within our organization, this has provided an avenue for individuals to pursue the set criteria for developing configuration management skills, which results in opportunities for advancement. Proper training creates knowledgeable configuration managers who can teach others the value of the SCM discipline. Trained configuration managers perform their duties with confidence and professionalism. These software professionals make the SCM discipline a vital function in maturing a software organization.

Conclusion

Maintaining a SCM discipline is critical to our CMM Level 5 software sustainment activities. Proper implementation of SCM enables us to plan, identify, control, and audit product life cycles. SCM along with management and engineering guide our organization to continuously improve our ability to meet expectations of high quality, low cost, and on time deliveries.

Continuous improvement, or Kaizen, can be achieved when practitioners are provided with proper tools, adequate training, and empowered with a quality process.◆

Note

1. Configuration management definition is as defined by the Configuration Management Training Foundation (CMTF), Magalia, Calif.

About the Authors

Tresa Butler is a software configuration manager at the Ogden Air Logistic Center, Software Engineering Division at Hill Air Force Base, Utah. She has worked for the Department of Defense for 13 years with the past nine years in data management and software configuration management. She participated in the software configuration team that was assessed by the Software Engineering Institute as a Capability Maturity Model Level 5. She is currently the Software Configuration Management lead for F-16 Operational Flight Programming workload. Butler attended Weber State University and plans to continue her education in the fall.

    6137 Wardleigh Road
    Hill AFB, UT 84056-5843
    Phone: (801) 777-6809
    DSN: 777-6809
    E-mail: tresa.butler@hill.af.mil

Faith Turner is a software configuration manager contracted through the F-16 (SPO) at Ogden Air Logistics Center in Utah, to provide configuration management support for software development at Hill Air Force Base (HAFB). She played an integral role on the software configuration management team during a Software Engineering Institute assessment that resulted in the first Capability Maturity Model Level 5 rating at a government organization. Turner has 16 years experience in the configuration status accounting and configuration management field. She has been a member of the F-16 software configuration management team for six and one-half years. Turner attended Texas Women's University and is continuing her education at Park College, HAFB.

    Scientech, Inc.
    6137 Wardleigh Road
    Hill AFB, UT 84056-5843
    Phone: (801) 775-3104
    DSN: 775-3104
    E-mail: faith.turner@hill.af.mil

Verla Standley is a software configuration manager for the Automatic Test Equipment (ATE) in the Software Engineering Division at Hill Air Force Base. She has worked for the government for 22 years and has been a configuration manager for 10 years. Standley was a member of the software configuration team that was assessed by the Software Engineering Institute as a Capability Maturity Model Level 5. For the past three and one-half years she has been the Software Configuration Management lead over the ATE workload. Verla attended Weber State College and has taken several configuration management classes.

    7278 4th Street
    Hill AFB, UT 84056-5205
    Phone: (801) 777-0960
    DSN: 777-0960
    E-mail: verla.standley@hill.af.mil

Elaine Sullivan is a software configuration manager in the Ogden Air Logistics Center, Software Engineering Division at Hill Air Force Base, Utah. She has been involved with configuration of F-16 software since 1988 and is currently the Software Configuration Management lead over the Avionics Intermediate Shop Workload. Sullivan developed and implemented the configuration process for her area and was instrumental in writing the configuration processes for the division and branch. She was an integral part of the software configuration team during a Software Engineering Institute assessment that resulted in the first Capability Maturity Model Level 5 rating at a government organization. She has an associate's degree from Ricks College, Rexburg, Idaho.

    6137 Wardleigh Road
    Hill AFB, UT 84056-5843
    Phone: (801) 775-2878
    DSN: 775-2878
    E-mail: elaine.sullivan@hill.af.mil

"If I had to sum up in one word what makes a good manager, I'd say decisiveness. You can use the fanciest computers to gather numbers, but in the end you have to set a timetable and act."

— Lee Iacocca

Managing Software Quality With Defects[1]

David N. Card
Software Productivity Consortium

This article describes two common approaches to measuring and modeling software quality throughout the software life cycle so that it can be made visible to management. Both approaches involve developing a life-cycle defect profile, which serves as a "quality budget." This article also provides actual examples using each approach.

Many factors contribute to an increased practical interest in managing software quality. This means treating software quality as a key dimension of project performance, equal to cost (effort) and schedule. Corporate initiatives based on the Capability Maturity Model® (CMM®) [1], CMM Integration℠ (CMMI℠) [2], and Six Sigma [3] provide some examples of forces promoting an interest in quality as a management concern.

General management activities include planning, monitoring, and directing. In order to manage quality, it must be planned; accomplishment of the plan must be tracked, and appropriate corrective action must be taken as necessary. Nearly all projects establish budgets for effort and/or cost so that these dimensions can be managed. These budgets are plans for the expenditures of labor and/or dollars during the life of the project. Budgets typically identify planned total expenditures as well as expenditures during specific intervals such as life-cycle phases or months. Managing quality also requires establishing a budget for quality.

This article presents a simple approach to measuring and modeling software quality across the project life cycle so that it can be made visible to management. Next in the article are examples of applying this measuring and modeling approach in real industry settings. Both of the examples presented come from CMM Level 4 organizations. Whether or not the CMM or CMMI explicitly requires this type of analysis is beyond the intended scope of this article. More importantly, the approach has been shown to be practical and useful to project managers.

Software Quality and the Defect Profile

There are many views of software quality. The ISO/IEC 9126 [4] defines six:
- Functionality.
- Efficiency.
- Reliability.
- Usability.
- Maintainability.
- Portability.

Some of these quality factors are difficult to measure directly. Intuitively, the occurrence of defects is negatively related to functionality and reliability. Defects also interfere, to some degree, with other dimensions of quality. Both of the approaches discussed here involve developing a life-cycle defect profile. This defect profile serves as a *quality budget*. It describes planned quality levels at each phase of development just as a budget shows planned effort (or cost) levels. Actual defect levels can be measured and compared to the plan, just as actual effort (or cost) is compared to planned effort (or cost). Investigating departures from the plan leads to corrective actions that optimize project performance.

Software development consists of a series of processes, each of which has some ability to insert and detect defects. However, only the number of detected defects in each phase can be known with any accuracy prior to project completion. The number of defects inserted in each phase cannot be known until all defects have been found. Confidence in knowing that approximate number comes only after the system has been fielded. Consequently, this approach focuses on defects detected.

The techniques presented here depend on two key assumptions:
- Size is the easily quantifiable software attribute that is most closely associated with the number of defects. The basic test of the effectiveness of complexity models and other indicators of defect-proneness is to ask, "Does this model show a significantly higher correlation with defects than just size (e.g., lines of code) alone?" [5].
- Defect insertion and detection rates tend to remain relatively constant as long as the project's software processes remain stable. While the rates are not exactly constant, they perform within a recognized range.

The first assumption appears to be inherent to the nature of software. CMM Level 4 organizations actively work to make the second assumption come true. That is, they are acting to bring their processes under control.

An Empirical Model

The simplest approach to generating a defect profile for intended projects within the organization is to collect actual data about the insertion and detection rates in each life-cycle phase. This can be accomplished in the following four steps:
- First, historical data are collected. Table 1 shows a simple spreadsheet used to tabulate defect discovery and detection data using example data. In addition, the size of the project from which the defect data is collected must be known. The size measure must be applied consistently, but this approach does not depend on using any specific measure. Lines of code, function points, number of classes, etc., may be used as appropriate. (The data in Table 1 are simulated, not real.)
- Second, an initial profile of the number of defects found in each phase is gener-

Table 1: *Example of Empirical Defect Profile (Simulated Data)*

| | Phase Inserted | | | | | |
Phase Detected	Analysis	Design	Code	Developer Test	System Test	Total
Analysis	0					0
Design	50	200				250
Code	50	100	300			450
Developer Test	25	50	150	0		225
System Test	18	38	113	0	0	169
Operation	7	12	37	0	0	56
Total	150	400	600	0	0	1,150

® Capability Maturity Model and CMM are registered in the U.S. Patent and Trademark Office.
℠ Capability Maturity Model Integration and CMMI are service marks of Carnegie Mellon University.

Reprinted from *Crosstalk,* March 2005.

ated as shown in Figure 1. The bars in that figure represent the totals in the last column of Table 1.

- Third, this initial profile is scaled to account for differences between the size of the project(s) from which the profile was developed and the size of the project to which it is applied. This is accomplished by multiplying by the ratio of the project sizes. For example, if the defect profile in Figure 1 were to be used to develop a defect profile for a project twice the size of the project providing the data that went into Figure 1, then the bars of the profile representing the new project would be twice the size of those in Figure 1.

- Fourth, the scaled defect profile is adjusted further to reflect the planned performance of the project. For example, if the project plan called for the automatic generation of code from design instead of hand coding as previously done, then the number of defects inserted in the implementation phase would be adjusted downward to reflect this change in the coding process. Also, changes in the project's process may be induced in order to reach a specified target in terms of delivered quality if previous performance did not yield the required level of quality. The target might be specified as a result of a customer requirement or an organizational goal.

Actual defect counts can then be compared with this final plan (defect profile) as the project progresses. Suggestions for this activity are provided in a later section of this article. Note that the defect profile does not address defect status (i.e., *open* vs. *closed* problems/defects). All detected defects, regardless of whether or not they ever get resolved, are included in the defect counts.

Figure 2 shows an example of a defect profile developed empirically [6] for an actual military project. This figure shows the predicted number of defects to be injected and detected in each phase, based on previous projects. However, only actual counts are shown for the number of defects detected, because the actual number injected cannot be determined with any confidence until after software delivery.

The project in Figure 2 was about two-thirds of the way through software integration at the time data were reported. Two-thirds of the predicted number of defects had been found in software integration. The project's quality performance was tracking the plan. This illustrates that the real value of the defect profile lies in its ability to make quality visible during development, not as a post-mortem analysis technique.

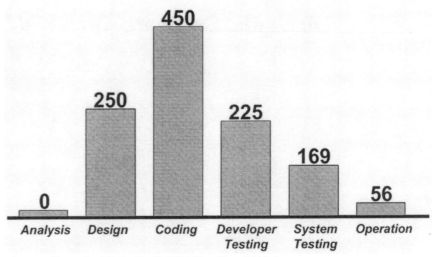

Figure 1: *Example of Defect Profile With Data From Table 1*

The project in Figure 2 actually was completed after this graph was prepared. The planned and actual defect levels never differed by more than 10 percent. The project team handed their product over to the customer with a high degree of confidence that it met the targeted level of quality.

An Analytical Model

Defect profiles may also be generated analytically. Many early studies of defect occurrence suggest that they followed a Rayleigh dispersion curve, roughly proportional to project staffing. The underlying assumption is that the more effort expended, the more mistakes that are made and found.

Gaffney [7] developed one such model:

$$Vt = E \, (1 - \exp(-\,B(t^{**}2\,)))$$

Where:
Vt = Number of defects discovered by time t.

E = Total number of defects inserted.
B = Location parameter for peak.

The time periods t can be assumed to be equal to life-cycle phase transition boundaries in order to apply the model to project phases rather than elapsed time. The location parameter B fixes the time of the maximum (or peak) distribution. For example, $B=1$ means that the peak occurs at $t=1$.

The analytical approach involves applying regression analysis to actual phase-by-phase defect data to determine the values of B and E that produce a curve most like the input data. Many Software Productivity Consortium member companies use our proprietary software, SWEEP [8] (based on the Gaffney model), to perform this analysis, but it can easily be implemented in Microsoft Excel.

The effectiveness of the analytical approach depends on the satisfaction of additional assumptions, including the following:

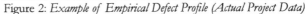

Figure 2: *Example of Empirical Defect Profile (Actual Project Data)*

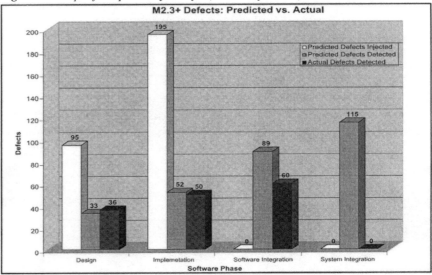

- Unimodal staffing profile.
- Life-cycle phases of similar (not exactly equal) duration (not effort).
- Reasonably complete defect reporting.
- Using only observable/operational defects.

To the extent that these assumptions are satisfied, this model gives better results. Analytical models such as this are useful when the organization lacks complete life-cycle defect data or desires to smooth existing data to provide an initial solution for new projects without prior historical data. The defect profile obtained from the actual data can be easily adjusted to fit projects with different numbers of life-cycle phases and processes by selecting appropriate values of E and B.

Figure 3 provides an example of a defect profile for another actual military project generated by SWEEP. The light bars in Figure 3 represent the expected number of defects for each phase, based on the model. For this specific project, the actual number of defects discovered is substantially lower than planned during design. Consequently, additional emphasis was placed on performing rigorous inspections during code, with the result that more defects than anticipated were captured during code, putting the project back on track to deliver a quality project as shown at post release.

A detailed discussion and analysis of applying the Gaffney model to a military project using SWEEP can be found in [9].

Interpreting Differences

During project execution, planned defect levels are compared to actual defect levels. Typically, this occurs at major phase transi-

tions (milestones). However, if a phase extends beyond six months, then consider inserting additional checkpoints during the phase (as in the example in Figure 1 where analyses were conducted at the completion of each one-third of integration testing). Since real performance never exactly matches the plan, the differences must be investigated. This involves three steps:

- Determine if the differences are significant and/or substantive. This might be accomplished by seeking visually large differences, establishing thresholds based on experience, or applying statistical tests such as the Chi-Square [10].
- Determine the underlying cause of the difference. This may require an examination of other types and sources of data such as process audit results as well as effort and schedule data. Many techniques have been developed for causal analysis (e.g., [11]), but they fall beyond the scope of this article.
- Take appropriate action. This includes corrective actions to address problems identified in the preceding step, as well as updates to the defect profile to reflect anticipated future performance.

Differences between planned and actual defect levels do not always represent quality problems. Potential explanations of departures from the plan include the following:

- Bad initial plan (assumptions not satisfied, or incomplete or inappropriate data).
- Wrong software size (more or less than the initial estimate).
- Change in process performance (better or worse than planned).

- Greater or lesser software complexity than initially assumed.
- Inspection and/or test coverage not as complete as planned.

Analyzing departures from the defect profile early in the life cycle provides feedback for our understanding of the size and complexity of the software engineering task while there is still time to react.

Summary

Relatively simple models of software quality based on defect profiles are becoming increasingly popular in the software industry as organizations mature. These models establish a *quality budget* that helps to make trade offs among cost, schedule, and quality visible and reasoned, rather than choices made by default. Defect profiles present quality performance to the project manager in a form that he or she understands. Thus, the consequences of a decision such as "reducing inspection and testing effort to accelerate progress" can be predicted. Unintended departures from planned quality activities can be detected and addressed.

Moreover, the ability to model quality across the project life cycle is a necessary prerequisite to implementing design for Six Sigma techniques [3] in software development. Achieving Six Sigma requires measuring and managing quality at each software production step, not just during the final testing stages prior to delivery.

Defect models can become very rich. The concept of orthogonal defect classification [12], for example, involves developing separate profiles for each of many different defect types. These defect classifications facilitate the causal analysis process when potential problems are identified.

This article discussed two very simple approaches to building and using defect profiles. These techniques make quality visible so that it can be managed.◆

References

1. Paulk, Mark, et al. Capability Maturity Model: Guidelines for Improving the Software Process. Boston: Addison-Wesley, June 1995.
2. Software Engineering Institute. Capability Maturity Model® Integrated SM. Pittsburgh: SEI.
3. Harry, Mikel J., and Richard Schroeder. Six Sigma: The Breakthrough Management Strategy Revolutionizing The World's Top Corporations. New York: Doubleday, Dec. 1999.
4. ISO/IEC Standard 9126. "Information Technology – Software Quality, Part 1." 1995.
5. Card, David, and William Agresti.

Figure 3: *Example of Analytical Defect Profile (Actual Project Data)*

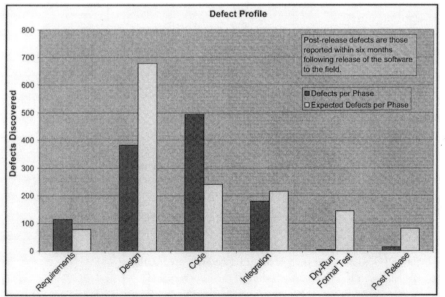

"Resolving the Software Science Anomaly." Journal of Systems and Software Vol. 7 (1990): 29-35.

6. Card, David. "Quantitatively Managing the Object-Oriented Design Process." Canadian National Research Council Conference on Quality Assurance of Object-Oriented Software. Feb. 2000.

7. Gaffney, John. "Some Models for Software Defect Analysis." Lockheed Martin Software Engineering Workshop, Gaithersburg, MD, Nov. 1996.

8. Software Productivity Consortium. SWEEP Users Guide. SPC-98030-MC, 1997.

9. Harbaugh, Sam. "Crusader Software Quality Assurance Process Improvement." Technical Report. Integrated Software, Inc., 2002.

10. Hays, William, and Robert Walker. Statistics: Probability, Inference, and Decision. Austin, TX: Holt, Rinehart, and Winston, 1970.

11. Card, David. "Learning From Our Mistakes With Defect Causal Analysis." IEEE Software Jan. 1998.

12. Chillarge, R., et al. "Orthogonal Defect Classification." IEEE Transactions on Software Engineering Nov. 1992.

Note

1. An earlier version of this article was published in the proceedings of the Institute of Electrical and Electronics Engineers' Computer Software and Applications Conference, Aug. 2002.

About the Author

David N. Card is a fellow of the Software Productivity Consortium where he provides technical leadership in software measurement and process improvement. During 15 years at Computer Sciences Corporation, Card spent six years as the director of Software Process and Measurement, one year as a resident affiliate at the Software Engineering Institute, and seven years with the research team supporting the NASA Software Engineering Laboratory. Card is editor-in-chief of the *Journal of Systems and Software*. He is the author of "Measuring Software Design Quality," co-author of "Practical Software Measurement," and co-editor of ISO/IEC standard 15939:2002 "Software Measurement Process." Card is a senior member of the American Society for Quality.

Software Productivity
Consortium
2214 Rock Hill Road
Herndon, VA 20170
Phone: (703) 742-7199
Fax: (703) 742-7200
E-mail: card@software.org

WEB SITES

Software Quality HotList

www.soft.com/Institute/HotList
The Software Research Institute maintains a list of links to selected organizations and institutions that support the software quality and software testing area. Organizations and other references are classified by type, by geographic area, and then in alphabetic order within each geographic area. The institute's aim is to bring to one location a complete list of technical, organizational, and related resources.

The Quality Assurance Institute

www.qaiusa.com
The Quality Assurance Institute (QAI) is exclusively dedicated to partnering with the enterprise-wide information quality profession. QAI is an international organization consisting of member companies in search of effective methods for detection-software quality control and prevention-software quality assurance. QAI provides consulting, education services, and assessments.

Software Technology Support Center

www.stsc.hill.af.mil
The Software Technology Support Center is an Air Force organization established to help other U.S. government organizations identify, evaluate, and adopt technologies to improve the quality of their software products, efficiency in producing them, and their ability to accurately predict the cost and schedule of their delivery.

Why Bad Things Happen to Good Projects

KAREN MACKEY, *Lotus Development Corporation*

When building a relatively complex system that involves multiple computers and multiple users, Murphy's law inevitably strikes: Something will go wrong. This article characterizes two common pitfalls, the Quality-Capacity Syndrome and the Missing-Tools Crisis, and shows how to overcome them.

At the start of a distributed software project, have you ever felt that you could finally "do it right the first time?" You have all your plans laid out, a super team, and you're primed to use the latest software technologies and development methodologies. But telling yourself you're going to "do it right" can be dangerous: You are likely to set yourself up for failure because of unforeseen complications.[1] Furthermore, if you share your optimism with your managers and they build business schedules around it, you're likely to both lose their trust and put your job or enterprise at risk.

If you're building a relatively complex system involving multiple computers and multiple users, and if the system entails significant innovation — such as new technology or expanded scale — something will inevitably go wrong. Realizing this might encourage you to use both design and user-interface prototypes[2,3] and the spiral model of development[4] so that you can look ahead and assess risks as you go. Before you start a major project, you need to understand what problems can affect it, even if you use the best available techniques and methods.

Reprinted from *IEEE Software,* May 1996.

This article characterizes two possible pitfalls: the Quality-Capacity Syndrome and the Missing-Tools Crisis. Since both have occurred with some frequency in unrelated software-development projects, they appear to be inde-

pendent of individual and management skills — factors responsible for a large variance in project success.[5] Likewise, since the affected projects followed reasonably good development practices, the appearance of these problems serves to underscore that serious problems can occur even in the best-intentioned multiuser, distributed-application development project.

To examine these two pitfalls, I pasted together a fictitious development project called GEMS, Greatest Electronic Mail Systems. GEMS is a composite of real projects that experienced the Quality-Capacity Syndrome and Missing-Tools Crisis. Managers of the various projects were so sensitive about their project's problems that the only way they would release the information was for me to create a composite project. This sensitivity underscores the difficulty within our industry of having open discussions about lessons learned, while the problems I describe under the guise of GEMS emphasize the need for such discussions.

GREATEST ELECTRONIC MAIL SYSTEM

The creators of GEMS wanted to create a uniform user interface for an electronic mail service in a heteroge-

neous environment comprised of IBM and Amdahl mainframes and DEC minicomputers. The existing mail service was an internal system developed by the company's computer services department. It provided mail service across the different systems, but on each system the mail command behaved differently. Also, because each system had unique software, it was difficult to maintain software and add features. The developers and maintainers of the existing system decided to create a replacement. They were going to do it again, and they were going to do it right.

The developers designed the new system top-down. First they found out what the users needed, and then they developed requirements. They worked from an understanding of the problem to the design of a solution, rather than conversely. The developers employed functional decomposition, carefully separating the transport facility and the mail-handling functions. They also used modularization[6] within the confines of decomposition to encapsulate related functionality. The design decomposed functions in a layered style, with complex layers built on top of more rudimentary layers, rising to a crescendo of sophisticated user capabilities at the highest layer. Furthermore, since the existing mail system was working, the team had time for a thoughtful design.

The design goal was to maximize portability between the different systems. A standard mail interface buffered the GEMS software from the idiosyncrasies of different operating systems. By using a single high-level language that had compilers on the various systems, the developers could port much of the software. The portability in turn helped improve maintainability, because a bug in the portable portion of the code had to be fixed only once.

The developers designed in many fault-recovery features: Point-to-point

protocols detected errors and initiated retransmissions; end-to-end protocols resent mail if network hardware failed during delivery; the system automatically restarted if the code failed; if the destination host was down, a queue held the mail; the mail queue was crash-resistant and audited at every restart to protect mail integrity. In summary, the developers were doing things right. In fact, they considered GEMS a really neat project.

GEMS was originally deployed on a three-node pilot system. As problems arose, the team solved them. In general, the users were quite happy. Because the system seemed to be working just fine, the developers added five more hosts to the pilot system and made near-term plans to expand GEMS to 80 to 100 more hosts. That's when both the Quality-Capacity Syndrome and Missing-Tools Crisis struck, and GEMS took a critical turn for the worse: The mail wasn't being delivered and the system was unresponsive. Users couldn't tell whether their individual systems were locked up or the mail software was just taking a long time. Users were no longer happy, and the system administrators faced a major quandary.

QUALITY-CAPACITY SYNDROME

Quality means how well a system is working. In the GEMS context, it corresponded to the inverse of the number of recovery actions per time interval. Quality problems like software bugs, hardware failures, and resource contention would trigger the fault-recovery features built into GEMS. *Capacity* refers to how much work a system can do, which in this case meant the number of messages GEMS delivered per time interval. Measures taken to increase quality directly reduced capacity.

The Quality-Capacity Syndrome has three symptoms:

- With a light load, a system performs well.
- As system load increases, system quality falls sharply.
- Even if the quality problems are solved, the capacity remains unsatisfactory.

GEMS's system quality was good at a low mail volume. As the number of messages increased, the system had lots of retransmissions and code restarts. However, the main problem was that system capacity fell rapidly as traffic increased. Message queues backed up and had to be processed at night. System capacity seemed to be limited by the implementation, not just the bugs.

Causes. Why did GEMS develop the Quality-Capacity Syndrome? Two things contributed to the problem: the design/development methodology and the pilot project.

GEMS was inherently complex, so it was essential to use a good design/development methodology. The use of modularity, clean interfaces, common functions, a high-level language, and a general-purpose operating system did result in less efficient code. However, once the designers understood where the inefficiencies were, they could improve efficiency fairly quickly. Poorly designed software would not have permitted such easy efficiency improvements.

The GEMS design methods encouraged functional partitioning and localization of concerns. Partitioning allowed the designers to break the project into development tasks that could proceed in parallel. However, because all developers were assigned a specific partition, there were no system generalists who understood thoroughly how the pieces fit together. Without this perspective, it was very difficult to debug across interfaces or boundaries. For example, when a bug surfaced between the transport mechanism and the mail-handling layer, the two teams

assigned to those layers wasted a lot of time chasing the bug back and forth across the interface. Unfortunately, a lot of demoralizing blaming and finger-pointing accompanied the chase. The project needed someone who understood the interface from both sides.

The pilot project also contributed to the Quality-Capacity Syndrome. Both prototypes and pilot projects are important to developing large, complex systems. In general, these are positive activities. In this case, however, a demonstration of functionality early on gave a false impression of progress. The GEMS pilot succeeded in getting a message to go between system A and system B, so the developers broke out the champagne and moved up the schedule. The problem was that they — and even worse, their bosses — thought the project was further along than it really was.

The focus of the pilot project was to demonstrate feasibility and usability, not test failure legs. With all the fault-recovery features in GEMS, the latter was a sizable task. The developers simply got caught up in the pilot project's success and failed to assess accurately what essential testing they still needed to do.

Treatment. How do you treat Quality-Capacity Syndrome? The GEMS crew applied the Hass Cure, named after R.J. Hass of AT&T Bell Laboratories, who first characterized, named, and treated the syndrome. This "cure" assumes that the underlying system architecture is in fact capable of handling the desired capacity. Without this guarantee, no amount of work can overcome the limitations.

The Hass Cure has four steps:
1. Stabilize the system.
2. Separate the quality and capacity concerns, which work at cross-purposes.
3. Address quality problems.
4. Address capacity problems.

To stabilize the system, you reduce

the load to the level at which the system runs well, then take baseline measurements. To improve quality, reduce and control change so you can identify the sources of problems. To improve capacity, seek out changes that will have a large effect. Neither teams nor people can focus effectively on both thrusts at the same time. Thus, you can either have a single development team that deals first with quality issues and then with capacity, or if you have sufficient staff you can form a group to address quality and one to address capacity. In either case, you'll need systems generalists to complete a timely cure.

The initial focus of the cure should be to improve quality until the system can handle an acceptable load. For GEMS, this meant reducing the number of restarts, rather than raising the throughput level. Once this was accomplished, the team could look for ways to improve capacity. The developers discovered a traffic pattern in

> The initial focus of the cure should be to improve quality until the system can handle an acceptable load.

GEMS in which 70 percent of the messages passed through one host. Blocking the text in the message transfers through this host increased the transfer rate by two to five times. This improved the overall system capacity and successfully cured the Quality-Capacity Syndrome.

MISSING-TOOLS CRISIS

When the Quality-Capacity Syndrome struck GEMS, the system administrators faced a major crisis that they were ill-equipped to handle. Although the GEMS team had plenty of development, debugging, and testing tools, their administration tools were totally inadequate. In addition to the quality-capacity crisis, administrators were faced with the crisis of missing tools.

The Missing-Tools Crisis has four characteristics:

♦ A major problem — such as bugs,

Many system designers had little or no system-administration experience.

hardware failures, or a full-fledged Quality-Capacity Syndrome — illuminates the tool deficit.

♦ The system lacks adequate monitoring and control tools.

♦ Administrators lack adequate tools to change the software in the deployed system.

♦ The existing system administrative procedures and tools do not scale up adequately.

In GEMS, the Missing-Tools Crisis emerged in the wake of the Quality-Capacity Syndrome. GEMS notified users of the success or failure of mail delivery, but offered them no window to watch their mail progress through the system. Even system administrators had no way to monitor what was going on and had no tools to take corrective action. If a problem arose, system restart was the main recourse.

One illustration of the importance of monitoring and control tools involved a clever adaptive algorithm for routing messages around failed components. When a memory overwrite confused GEMS, it responded by looping messages around the network. This looping was detected not by sys-

tem administrators — who had no tools for this sort of surveillance — but by frustrated users who never received delivery notification. To reinitialize and resynchronize the system, administrators had to bring down the entire system and restart it. Monitoring and control tools could have prevented such a drastic measure.

To overcome the Quality-Capacity Syndrome, the GEMS team needed to integrate changes into the running software quickly. Using the standard procedure, this integration was slow. At one point, a message with a bad address slipped through GEMS defenses and blocked the message queues. It brought the system to its knees for a week — despite the fact that the developers understood the problem and provided a solution within a day. They needed a more responsive way to insert changes into the system.

In place of an administrative interface designed for the new system, GEMS had different ad hoc tools on each host system. Even the logged messages generated by GEMS software were messages for debugging rather than management — but they were all that administrators had to work with. Furthermore, the administrators managed the system using one terminal per host. With the three-node pilot, this management strategy was possible. With the eight-node network, the task became cumbersome. With a projected addition of 80 to 100 nodes, it would be impossible. The makeshift administrative interface simply did not scale up.

Causes. Why did the system develop the Missing-Tools Crisis? How could developers have overlooked such critical needs? Again, the two main contributors to the problem were the design/development methodology and the pilot project. Actually, it was more the "religion" of the methodology than the methodology itself: People did not consider monitoring and control tools and the need for making cor-

rective changes because they felt the system was going to work correctly. The GEMS designers thought the system would be totally automated and self-correcting; they never foresaw the need for humans to manage the system.

Also, many system designers had little or no system-administration experience. In many companies and universities, software engineers have their own personal computers and get little exposure to distributed-systems management. They are genuinely naive — and understandably so. Few career paths lead through systems administration into development, except in small enterprises where the developer does both. Even worse, a class distinction sometimes exists between system administrators and developers, which inhibits rapport and sensitivity to the management side of distributed systems.

Another unfortunate influence on the design/development methodology came from the focus infused into the development process: The user functions justified the funding for the GEMS project. With this orientation, support functions got slighted; they were unimportant until the users grew more sophisticated and demanded better performance.

Yet another influence came from assumptions about the users. When GEMS was designed, developers envisioned small, single-page messages going between users. This was in the early days of e-mail, before its usefulness for file transfer was established, and developers didn't anticipate a user sending a 3-Mbyte message and the impact it would have on the system. Because they failed to imagine things a user could do with the system, developers provided no means to monitor and control them.

The pilot project also helped bring on the Missing-Tools Crisis by, again, giving a false sense of progress. The pilot project focused on user functions rather than administration. It did make some sense not to build elaborate management tools before the feasibility of user functions was proven. Also, since the pilot focused on small-scale feasibility, management needs were not obvious. Scaling up the project uncovered the need for administrative interface and management tools.

Treatment. Treating the Missing-Tools Crisis is straightforward:

♦ retrofit an interface for monitoring and control tools,

♦ create quick-change tools and procedures so developers can make code corrections quickly, and

♦ have the developers both use and manage the system they have built.

GEMS developers had to modify the system design to accommodate monitoring and control features, as the developers of many network systems — including DECNet, IBM SNA, and the ISO OSI model — have done before them. The advantage of incorporating tools after the system is running is that developers have a better idea of what administrative tools the system needs and how users are likely to use the system. If the software is well designed, adding this interface can be relatively easy. The work the GEMS designers put into their original design paid off here: the solid design allowed them to add the tools fairly quickly.

Many arguments show how much more expensive it is to make changes late in the development process than to get it right the first time.[7] However, even though GEMS developers were extremely careful and followed a good development methodology, they still had to make late-stage or post-deployment code changes. Large, complex systems can require several rounds of corrections, so every system should incorporate quick-change tools.

A few years ago, a former student of mine went on a job interview. At that time, the academic community *had just* fully embraced structured

coding as a useful software-engineering technique. Wanting to make sure that the company he might work for was forward-looking and used up-to-date software practices, the student asked the interviewer if they did structured coding. The interviewer said yes, they structured their code with a block of assembly code followed by a block of reserved memory called a patch area. If they needed to insert a change, they could zap out the offending code, branch down to the corrected code loaded into the reserved block, then branch back in-line.

When he related the story in class, we all had a good, self-righteous laugh at the interviewer's old-fashioned definition of structured coding. However, as I realized later, we missed the usefulness of this "antiquated" technique for quickly fixing problems in deployed systems. We still have much to learn from solutions out of our pre-structured-coding and pre-object-oriented past, even though newer software-engineering practices might alter their exact form.

Finally, having developers use what they build has gained widespread acceptance in the software-engineering community as a way of improving understanding of user needs. However, system administration often remains an unexplored perspective. Managing the system for a period of time definitely enhanced GEMS developers' awareness of the need for administrative tools.

DOING THINGS BETTER

To avoid the Quality-Capacity Syndrome, G. Scott Graham suggested the following steps in a University of Santa Cruz seminar:

♦ Build a simple analytic performance model early in the design process, even as early as during system definition, and improve it as the design progresses.

♦ Build a picture of logical resource use or resource demand. For example, determine how many disk accesses a routine might make.

♦ Tie logical resource use to physical resource use. For example, tie the disk accesses to the actual disk-access time.

♦ Use the analytic model to identify the most-used modules, then optimize those modules.

♦ Conduct a walkthrough explicitly to review the design for performance.

♦ Design into the system an interface to capture data that measures quality and capacity.

Frequently, capacity and performance goals get shelved during development. After the system is built, we push it off a cliff and see if it flies. It would be better to keep capacity goals in mind during design/development and to get performance feedback all along. Conducting an explicit performance walkthrough and designing in appropriate data-collection mechanisms are tangible activities that will elevate the design's performance aspects. To improve capacity, you can form a capacity group that follows behind the implementation group.

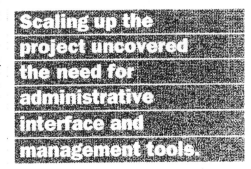

Scaling up the project uncovered the need for administrative interface and management tools.

Using the system model's numeric assumptions and analysis as the starting point, the group can measure the actual capacity and improve it.

Finally, an absolute necessity for avoiding or treating the Quality-Capacity Syndrome is to assign one or more developers the role of systems generalists. You must identify and cultivate systems generalists throughout the development process.

To avoid the Missing-Tools Crisis, try the following suggestions:

♦ Design interfaces into the system that support monitoring and control tools. You don't have to build all the envisioned monitoring and control tools at the onset of the project, but at least design a control scheme and build in the appropriate interfaces, with extra attention to manual overrides of clever adaptive algorithms.

♦ Conduct a systems-administration walkthrough, and include actual administrators. Also, bring in the people who will be using the system so they can share their perspectives.

♦ Have the developers manage the system prior to deployment. It's especially helpful to study the administration procedures in light of the scale of the final deployment.

♦ Develop the tools and procedures to support quick changes. A vital online system will undoubtedly need them.

The developers of multiuser distributed systems are particularly vulnerable to the pitfalls of Quality-Capacity Syndrome and Missing-Tools Crisis. What makes them so deadly is that they tend to occur together just as the project is nearing completion, putting the schedule in jeopardy. The Quality-Capacity Syndrome teaches us to start both performance modeling and model validation early. The Missing-Tools Crisis teaches us to consider the administration and management of the system under development.

Perhaps the best lesson learned from this experience is that we should beware of relying too heavily on our ability to "do it right." There's always a pitfall waiting to educate us. ♦

REFERENCES

1. F.P. Brooks, Jr., *The Mythical Man-Month*, Addison-Wesley, Reading, Mass., 1975.
2. L. Bernstein, "Get the Design Right!," *IEEE Software*, Sept. 1993, pp. 61-63.
3. H. Ledgard, *Software Engineering Concepts*, Addison-Wesley, Reading, Mass., 1987.
4. B.W. Boehm, "A Spiral Model of Software Development and Enhancement," *Computer*, May 1988, pp. 61-72.
5. T. DeMarco and T. Lister, *Peopleware*, Dorset House, New York, 1987.
6. D.L. Parnas, "On the Criteria to Be Used in Decomposing Systems into Modules," *Comm. ACM*, Vol. 5, No. 12, Dec. 1972, pp. 1,053-1,058.
7. B.W. Boehm, *Software Engineering Economics*, Prentice-Hall, Upper Saddle River, N.J., 1981.

Karen Mackey is a development manager at Lotus Development Corporation, a subsidiary of IBM. Previously, she was a software engineer and manager at TRW and AT&T Bell Laboratories.

Mackey received a PhD in computer science from Pennsylvania State University, University Park. She is a member of the IEEE Computer Society, ACM, and Silicon Valley SPIN.

Address questions about this article to Mackey at 1229 Susan Way, Sunnyvale, CA 94087; kmackey@best.com.

Chapter 11

Software Risk and Recovery Management

Have I not walked without an upward look?
Of caution under stars that very well
Might have missed me when they shot and fell
It was a risk I had to take—and took
—Robert Frost, *Bravado*

Overview

Risk and risk management have become topics of great interest within the software management community. This has become especially true as new opportunities in the field have opened and worldwide competition for software business has become keener. A decade ago, risk taking was frowned upon. The reason for this was that most organizations were apprehensive of software and did not know how to manage its development. Now that firms have gotten better at predicting and controlling their software costs, schedules, and technical performance, they can attempt to gain the competitive advantage by bringing high-quality products to market before their competitors.

I believe that all project management is a form of risk management. Risk in this context refers to those factors—political, technical, and managerial—that are threats to your success and/or pose major problems in getting your job done. For example, volatile requirements, feature creep, gold plating, and loss of key personnel are common risks that project managers need to guard against in most software development efforts. Risk management is the process of identifying these threats, analyzing them, quantifying their effects, and implementing plans that counteract their negative effects. For example, developing a rapid prototype early during the project to reduce potential requirements volatility, gold plating, and feature creep is considered an effective risk management technique.

This chapter contains five papers on the topics of risk and recovery management. The first two articles provide summaries of the concepts, tools, and techniques that are available for risk management. The third paper is more profound. It argues that those who gain the most are those who risk the most. The article goes on to suggest that improved risk management is therefore essential for your survival in this competitive world. The fourth article provides a discussion of risk metrics, and the fifth and final paper discusses how to get software projects back on track (recovery management). It provides some good ideas on what to do to recover from catastrophe.

Article Summaries

Understanding Risk Management, by the Software Technology Support Center Staff. This paper provides a tutorial on the topic of risk management. Its focus is process. As such, it steps you through the activities of risk assessment, mitigation, and monitoring. Similar to most risk papers, it focuses on managing mitigation actions during development to proactively address risk as it occurs. As an added benefit, it provides a cursory checklist for use in assessing whether your risk program is addressing what the authors feel are the risk management process requirements.

Software Risk Management: Principles and Practices, by Barry Boehm. This tutorial provides you with a good summary of the basics of software risk management. It begins by giving you an overview of the fundamental concepts, processes, tools, and techniques associated with the discipline. The paper then takes you step by step through the risk identification, assessment, and control processes, using realistic examples whenever possible to illustrate how to get the job done with a minimum of fuss and overhead. Throughout the article, the author discusses the merits and disadvantages of various risk management tools and techniques in a fair and revealing way.

Large-Scale Project Management Is Risk Management, by Robert Charette. This paper picks up where Boehm left off to discuss application of risk management concepts in large software developments. The article argues convincingly for establishing a risk-taking ethic in which risk is not feared but thought of as something you can profit from. The paper argues that those who risk the most gain the most. Using this entrepreneurial definition, risk should be considered as decisions are made and actions agreed upon. It suggests that risk can then be tracked, managed and controlled as you innovate and act based upon opportunities to reap potential rewards.

A Project Risk Metric, by Robert Ferguson. This article proposes a risk metric to be used across projects to provide management with visibility into project uncertainty. The metric ranks cost, schedule, and quality risk probabilistically and uses the resulting numbers to quantitatively portray the amount based on potential impacts. The article ends with a discussion of the challenges associated with implementing risk measurement.

Catastrophe Disentanglement: Getting Software Projects Back on Track, by E. M. Bennatan. This paper tackles the difficult questions associated with what you must do to straighten out a troubled project. It starts by providing you with guidance on how to determine whether your project is a catastrophe. It then suggests a ten-step approach for developing a get-well plan. It emphasizes the need for an external, unbiased evaluation. It suggests that abandoning the project may be a feasible alternative. The paper ends with a briefcase study. The paper is one of the few that I have come across that addresses this topic. It is easy to read and insightful, especially for those of you who are in trouble.

Key Terms

Six terms, defined as follows, are important to understanding the topic of organization as used within this chapter:

1. **Contingency.** In management, an amount of design margin, time, or money used as a safety factor to accommodate future growth or uncertainty.
2. **Risk.** In management, refers to those factors, both technical and managerial, that are threats to success and/or major sources of problems.
3. **Risk avoidance.** The act of changing plans to eliminate a risk or to protect the project objectives from being impacted by it.
4. **Risk management.** The process of identifying, analyzing, quantifying, and developing plans to eliminate or mitigate risk before it does harm to a project.
5. **Risk mitigation.** The act of seeking to reduce the probability and/or the impact of a risk to below an acceptable threshold level.
6. **Uncertainty.** In management, the degree of entropy associated with the information used to make a decision.

For Your Bookshelf

In recent years, several good books on the topic of software risk management have appeared. Karolak's *Software Engineering Risk Management* and McManus's *Risk Management in Software Development Projects* are the two texts that I like most on the topic. Both are abstracted in the Bibliography that appears at the rear of this tutorial.

The Project Management Book of Knowledge (PMBOK™), published by the Project Management Institute, contains a chapter on project risk management. This chapter identifies processes that can be used to plan, identify, quantify, analyze, and manage your risk mitigation activities.

In addition, there have been many excellent articles on risk management and case studies published in the professional literature. For example, the IEEE Computer Society journal has published special issues on the topic. Most of this literature emphasizes what to do about risk, not how to take advantage of it. Those interested in risk taking are referred to the many marketing texts that treat the subject from a risk-versus-return viewpoint.

Understanding Risk Management

Software Technology Support Center

The U.S. Air Force's Software Technology Support Center offers an updated and condensed version of the "Guidelines for Successful Acquisition and Management of Software-Intensive Systems" (GSAM) on its Web site <www.stsc.hill.af.mil/ resources/tech_docs>. This article is taken from Chapter 5 "Risk Management" of the GSAM (Version 4.0). We are pleased that all editions have been so well received and that many individuals and programs have worked hard to implement the principles contained therein. The latest edition provides a usable desk reference that gives a brief but effective overview of important software acquisition and development topics, provides checklists for rapid self-inspection, and provides pointers to additional information on the topics covered.

Risk is a product of the uncertainty of future events and is a part of all activity. It is a fact of life. We tend to stay away from situations that involve high risk to things we hold dear. When we cannot avoid risk, we look for ways to reduce it or its impact upon our lives. Yet even with careful planning and preparation, risks cannot be completely eliminated because they cannot all be identified beforehand. Even so, risk is essential to progress.

The opportunity to succeed also carries the opportunity to fail. It is necessary to learn to balance the possible negative consequences of risk with the potential benefits of its associated opportunity [1]. Risk may be defined as the possibility to suffer damage or loss. The possibility is characterized by three factors [1]:

1. The probability or likelihood that loss or damage will occur.
2. The expected time of occurrence.
3. The magnitude of the negative impact that can result from its occurrence.

The seriousness of a risk can be determined by multiplying the probability of the event actually occurring by the potential negative impact to the cost, schedule, or performance of the project:

Risk Severity = Probability of Occurrence x Potential Negative Impact

Thus, risks where probability of occurrence is high and potential impact is very low, or vice versa, are not considered as serious as risks where both probability of occurrence and potential impact are medium to high.

Project managers recognize and accept the fact that risk is inherent in any project. They also recognize that there are two ways of dealing with risk. One, risk management, is proactive and carefully analyzes future project events and past projects to identify potential risks. Once risks are identified, they are dealt with by taking measures to reduce their probability or to reduce their impact. The alternative to risk management is crisis management. It is a reactive and resource-intensive process, with available options constrained or restricted by events [1].

Effective risk management requires establishing and following a rigorous process. It involves the entire project team, as well as requiring help from outside experts in critical risk areas (e.g., technology, manufacturing, logistics, etc.). Because risks will be found in all areas of the project and will often be interrelated, risk management should include hardware, software, integration issues, and the human element [2].

Process Description

Various paradigms are used by different organizations to coordinate their risk management activities. A commonly used approach is shown in Figure 1. While there are variations in the different para-digms, certain characteristics are universally required for the program to be successful [2]:

- The risk management process is planned and structured.
- The risk process is integrated with the acquisition process.
- Developers, users, procurers, and all other stakeholders work together closely to implement the risk process.
- Risk management is an ongoing process with continual monitoring and reassessment.
- A set of success criteria is defined for all cost, schedule, and performance elements of the project.
- Metrics are defined and used to monitor effectiveness of risk management strategies.
- An effective test and evaluation program is planned and followed.
- All aspects of the risk management program are formally documented.
- Communication and feedback are an integral part of all risk management activities.

While your risk management approach should be tailored to your project needs, it should incorporate these fundamental characteristics. The process is iterative and should have all the components shown in Figure 2. Note that while planning appears as the first step, there is a feedback loop from the monitoring activity that allows planning and the other activities to be redone or controlled by actual results, providing continual updates to the risk management strategy. In essence, the process is a standard approach to problem solving:

1. Plan or define the problem-solving process.
2. Define the problem.
3. Work out solutions for those problems.
4. Track the progress and success of the solutions.

Figure 1: *Software Engineering Institute's Risk Management Paradigm [3]*

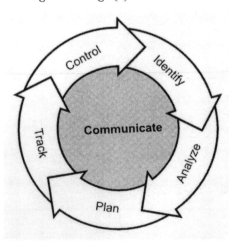

The following sections expand upon the risk management approach.

Planning

Risk planning includes developing and documenting a structured, proactive, and comprehensive strategy to deal with risk. Key to this activity is establishing methods and procedures to do the following:

1. Establish an organization to take part in the risk management process.
2. Identify and analyze risks.
3. Develop risk-handling plans.
4. Monitor or track risk areas.
5. Assign resources to deal with risks.

A generic sample risk management plan can be found in Appendix B of the "Risk Management Guide for DoD Acquisition" [4].

Assessment

Risk assessment involves two primary activities: risk identification and risk analysis. Risk identification is actually begun early in the planning phase and continues throughout the life of the project. The following methods are often used to identify possible risks [1]:

- Brainstorming.
- Evaluations or inputs from project stakeholders.
- Periodic reviews of project data.
- Questionnaires based on taxonomy, the classification of product areas and disciplines.
- Interviews based on taxonomy.
- Analysis of the Work Breakdown Structure.
- Analysis of historical data.

When identifying a risk it is essential to do so in a clear and concise statement. It should include three components [1]:

1. **Condition:** A sentence or phrase briefly describing the situation or circumstance that may have caused concern, anxiety, or uncertainty.
2. **Consequence:** A sentence describing the key negative outcomes that may result from the condition.
3. **Context:** Additional information about the risk to ensure others can understand its nature, especially after the passage of time.

Table 1 is an example of a risk statement [1].

The other half of assessment is risk analysis. This is the process of examining each risk to refine the risk description, isolate the cause, quantify the probability of occurrence, and determine the nature and impact of possible effects. The result of this process is a list of risks rated and prioritized according to their probability of occurrence, severity of impact, and relationship to other risk areas [2].

Once risks have been defined, and probability of occurrence and consequences assigned, the risk can be rated as to its severity. This facilitates prioritizing risks and deciding what level of resources to devote to each risk. Figure 3 depicts an assessment model using risk probability and consequence levels in a matrix to determine a level of risk severity. In addition to an overall method of risk rating, the model also gives good examples of probability levels and types and levels of consequences. The ratings given in the assessment guide matrix are suggested minimum ratings. It may be necessary to adjust the moderate and high thresholds to better coincide with the type of project.

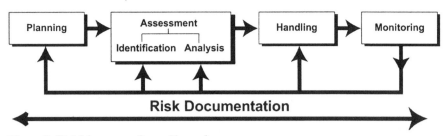

Figure 2: *Risk Management Process Example*

Condition	End users submit requirements changes even though we are in the design phase and the requirements have been baselined.
Consequence	Changes could extend system design cycle and reduce available coding time.
Probability and Impact	80%. $2 million.
Mitigation Actions	Who, what, and when?

Table 1: *Risk Statement Example*

Figure 3: *Defense Acquisition University Assessment Model [4]*

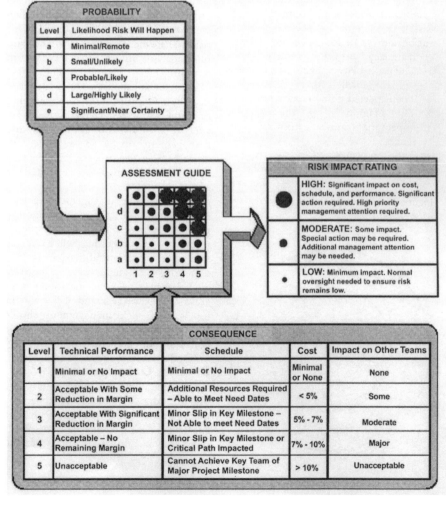

Figure 4: *Risk Handling Process*

Handling

Risk handling is the process that identifies, evaluates, selects, and implements options for mitigating risks, as shown in Figure 4. Two approaches are used in handling risk. The first is to employ options that reduce the risk itself. This usually involves a change in current conditions to lessen the probability of occurrence. The second approach, often employed where risk probability is high, is to use options that reduce the negative impact to the project if the risk condition should occur. Improving jet engine maintenance and inspection procedures to reduce the risk of in-flight engine failure is an example of the first approach. Providing a parachute for the pilot, to reduce loss if the risk condition should occur, is an example of the second approach.

Monitoring

Risk monitoring is the process of continually tracking risks and the effectiveness of risk handling options to ensure risk conditions do not get out of control. This is done by knowing the baseline risk management plans, understanding the risks and risk handling options, establishing meaningful metrics, and evaluating project performance against the established metrics, plans, and expected results throughout the acquisition process. Continual monitoring also enables new risks to be identified if they become apparent over time. Monitoring further reveals the interrelationships between various risks [2].

The monitoring process provides feedback into all other activities to improve the ongoing, iterative risk management process for the current and future projects.

Documentation

Risk documentation is absolutely essential for the current, as well as future, projects. It consists of recording, maintaining, and reporting risk management plans, assessments, and handling information. It also includes recording the results of risk management activities, providing a knowledge base for better risk management in later stages of the project and in other projects [2]. Documentation should include – as a minimum – the following information:

- Risk management plans.

- Project metrics to be used for risk management.
- Identified risks and their descriptions.
- The probability, severity of impact, and prioritization of all known risks.
- Description of risk handling options selected for implementation.
- Project performance assessment results, including deviations from the baseline plans.
- Records of all changes to the above documentation, including newly identified risks, plan changes, etc.

Risk Management Checklist

This checklist is provided to assist you in risk management. If you answer no to any of these questions, you should examine the situation carefully for the possibility of greater risks to the project. This is only a cursory checklist for such an important subject. Please see [5, 6] for more detailed checklists.

❑ Do you have a comprehensive, planned, and documented approach to risk management?

❑ Are all major areas/disciplines represented on your risk management team?

❑ Is the project manager experienced with similar projects?

❑ Do the stakeholders support disciplined development methods that incorporate adequate planning, requirements analysis, design, and testing?

❑ Is the project manager dedicated to this project, and not dividing his or her time among other efforts?

❑ Are you implementing a proven development methodology?

❑ Are requirements well defined, understandable, and stable?

❑ Do you have an effective requirements change process in place, and do you use it?

❑ Does your project plan call for tracking/tracing requirements through all phases of the project?

❑ Are you implementing proven technology?

❑ Are suppliers stable, and do you have multiple sources for hardware and equipment?

❑ Are all procurement items needed for your development effort short lead-time items (no long-lead items)?

❑ Are all external and internal interfaces for the system well defined?

❑ Are all project positions appropriately staffed with qualified, motivated personnel?

❑ Are the developers trained and experienced in their respective development disciplines (i.e., systems engineering, software engineering, language, platform, tools, etc.)?

❑ Are developers experienced or familiar with the technology and the development environment?

❑ Are key personnel stable and likely to remain in their positions throughout the project?

❑ Is project funding stable and secure?

❑ Are all costs associated with the project known?

❑ Are development tools and equipment used for the project state-of-the-art, dependable, and available in sufficient quantity, and are the developers familiar with the development tools?

❑ Are the schedule estimates free of unknowns?

❑ Is the schedule realistic to support an acceptable level of risk?

❑ Is the project free of special environmental constraints or requirements?

❑ Is your testing approach feasible and appropriate for the components and system?

❑ Have acceptance criteria been established for all requirements and agreed to by all stakeholders?

❑ Will there be sufficient equipment to do adequate integration and testing?

❑ Has sufficient time been scheduled for system integration and testing?

❑ Can software be tested without complex testing or special test equipment?

❑ Is a single group in one location developing the system?

❑ Are subcontractors reliable and proven?

❑ Is all project work being done by groups over which you have control?

❑ Are development and support teams all collocated at one site?

❑ Is the project team accustomed to working on an effort of this size (neither bigger nor smaller)?

Summary

Project managers recognize and accept the fact that risk is inherent in any project. The most successful project managers choose to deal proactively with risk. They carefully analyze future project events and past projects to identify potential risks. Once risks are identified, managers take steps to reduce their probability or reduce the impact associated with them by establishing and following a rigorous process, which involves the entire project team as well as outside experts. Risk management should include hardware, software, integration issues, and the human element. A risk management process includes planning, assessment, handling, monitoring, and documentation. Risk is a product of the uncertainty of future events and is a part of all activity. Learning to balance its possible negative consequences with its potential benefits is the key to successful risk management.◆

References

1. Software Technology Support Center. "Life Cycle Software Project Management." Project Initiation. Hill Air Force Base, UT, 9 Oct. 2001.
2. Department of Defense. "Risk Management Guide for DoD Acquisition." Washington, D.C.: DoD Feb. 2001: Chap. 2 <www.dsmc.dsm.mil/pubs/gdbks/risk_management.htm>.
3. Higuera, Ron, and Yacov Haimes. "Software Risk Management." Pittsburgh, PA: Software Engineering Institute, 28 June 1996 <www.sei.cmu.edu/publications/documents/96.reports/96.tr.012.html>.
4. Department of Defense. "Risk Management Guide for DoD Acquisition." Washington, D.C.: DoD, Feb. 2001: Appendix B <www.dsmc.dsm.mil/pubs/gdbks/risk_management.htm>.
5. Arizona State University. "Question List for Software Risk Identification in the Classroom." <www.eas.asu.edu/~riskmgmt/qlist.html>.
6. Department of Energy. Risk Assessment Questionnaire. <http://cio.doe.gov/sqse/pm_risk.htm>.

About the Author

The **Software Technology Support Center** (STSC) produced the "Guidelines for Successful Acquisition and Management of Software-Intensive Systems." Visit the STSC Web site at <www.stsc.hill.af.mil/resources/tech_docs> to access all 17 chapters of this document. The STSC is dedicated to helping the Air Force and other U.S. government organizations improve their capability to buy and build software better. The STSC provides hands-on assistance in adopting effective technologies for software-intensive systems. The STSC helps organizations identify, evaluate, and adopt technologies that improve software product quality, production efficiency, and predictability. Technology is used in its broadest sense to include processes, methods, techniques, and tools that enhance human capability. The STSC offers consulting services for software process improvement, software technology adoption, and software technology evaluation, including the Capability Maturity Model® Integration, software acquisition, project management, risk management, cost and schedule estimation, configuration management, software measurement, and more.

**Software Technology
Support Center
6022 Fir AVE BLDG 1238
Hill AFB, UT 84056-5820
Phone: (801) 586-0154
DSN: 586-0154
E-mail: stsc.consulting@hill.af.mil**

Software Risk Management: Principles and Practices

BARRY W. BOEHM,
Defense Advanced Research Projects Agency

◆ *Identifying and dealing with risks early in development lessens long-term costs and helps prevent software disasters.*

It is easy to begin managing risks in your environment.

Like many fields in their early stages, the software field has had its share of project disasters: the software equivalents of the Beauvais Cathedral, the *HMS Titanic*, and the "Galloping Gertie" Tacoma Narrows Bridge. The frequency of these software-project disasters is a serious concern: A recent survey of 600 firms indicated that 35 percent of them had at least one runaway software project.[1]

Most postmortems of these software-project disasters have indicated that their problems would have been avoided or strongly reduced if there had been an explicit early concern with identifying and resolving their high-risk elements. Frequently, these projects were swept along by a tide of optimistic enthusiasm during their early phases that caused them to miss some clear signals of high-risk issues that proved to be their downfall later.

Enthusiasm for new software capabilities is a good thing. But it must be tempered with a concern for early identification and resolution of a project's high-risk elements so people can get these resolved early and then focus their enthusiasm and energy on the positive aspects of their product.

Current approaches to the software process make it too easy for projects to make high-risk commitments that they will later regret:

♦ The sequential, document-driven waterfall process model tempts people to overpromise software capabilities in contractually binding requirements specifications before they understand their risk implications.

♦ The code-driven, evolutionary development process model tempts people to say, "Here are some neat ideas I'd like to put into this system. I'll code them up, and

Reprinted from *IEEE Software,* January 1991.

if they don't fit other people's ideas, we'll just evolve things until they work." This sort of approach usually works fine in some well-supported minidomains like spreadsheet applications but, in more complex application domains, it most often creates or neglects unsalvageable high-risk elements and leads the project down the path to disaster.

At TRW and elsewhere, I have had the good fortune to observe many project managers at work firsthand and to try to understand and apply the factors that distinguished the more successful project managers from the less successful ones. Some successfully used a waterfall approach, others successfully used an evolutionary development approach, and still others successfully orchestrated complex mixtures of these and other approaches involving prototyping, simulation, commercial software, executable specifications, tiger teams, design competitions, subcontracting, and various kinds of cost-benefit analyses.

One pattern that emerged very strongly was that the successful project managers were good *risk managers*. Although they generally didn't use such terms as "risk identification," "risk assessment," "risk-management planning," or "risk monitoring," they were using a general concept of risk exposure (potential loss times the probability of loss) to guide their priorities and actions. And their projects tended to avoid pitfalls and produce good products.

The emerging discipline of software risk management is an attempt to formalize these risk-oriented correlates of success into a readily applicable set of principles and practices. Its objectives are to identify, address, and eliminate risk items before they become either threats to successful software operation or major sources of software rework.

BASIC CONCEPTS

Webster's dictionary defines "risk" as "the possibility of loss or injury." This definition can be translated into the fundamental concept of risk management: risk exposure, sometimes also called "risk im-

pact" or "risk factor." Risk exposure is defined by the relationship

RE = P(UO) * L(UO)

where RE is the risk exposure, P(UO) is the probability of an unsatisfactory outcome and L(UO) is the loss to the parties affected if the outcome is unsatisfactory. To relate this definition to software projects, we need a definition of "unsatisfactory outcome."

Given that projects involve several classes of participants (customer, developer, user, and maintainer), each with different but highly important satisfaction criteria, it is clear that "unsatisfactory outcome" is multidimensional:

♦ For customers and developers, budget overruns and schedule slips are unsatisfactory.

♦ For users, products with the wrong functionality, user-interface shortfalls, performance shortfalls, or reliability

shortfalls are unsatisfactory.

♦ For maintainers, poor-quality software is unsatisfactory.

These components of an unsatisfactory outcome provide a top-level checklist for identifying and assessing risk items.

A fundamental risk-analysis paradigm is the decision tree. Figure 1 illustrates a potentially risky situation involving the software controlling a satellite experiment. The software has been under development by the experiment team, which understands the experiment well but is inexperienced in and somewhat casual about software development. As a result, the satellite-platform manager has obtained an estimate that there is a probability P(UO) of 0.4 that the experimenters' software will have a critical error: one that will wipe out the entire experiment and cause an associated loss L(UO) of the total $20 million investment in the experiment.

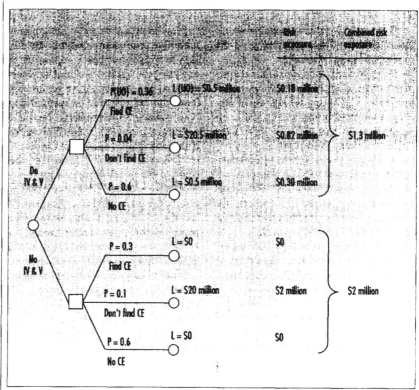

FIGURE 1. DECISION TREE FOR WHETHER TO PERFORM INDEPENDENT VALIDATION AND VERIFICATION TO ELIMINATE CRITICAL ERRORS IN A SATELLITE-EXPERIMENT PROGRAM. L(UO) IS THE LOSS ASSOCIATED WITH AN UNSATISFACTORY OUTCOME, P(UO) IS THE PROBABILITY OF THE UNSATISFACTORY OUTCOME, AND CE IS A CRITICAL ERROR.

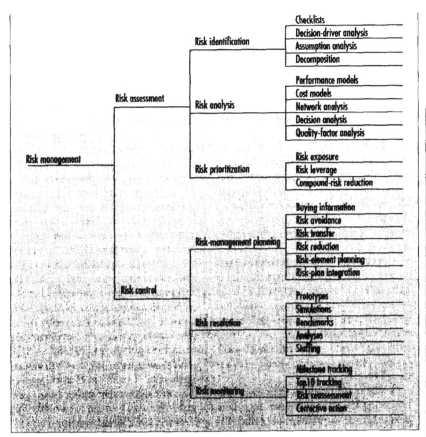

FIGURE 2. SOFTWARE RISK MANAGEMENT STEPS.

The satellite-platform manager identifies two major options for reducing the risk of losing the experiment:

♦ Convincing and helping the experiment team to apply better development methods. This incurs no additional cost and, from previous experience, the manager estimates that this will reduce the error probability P(UO) to 0.1.

♦ Hiring a contractor to independently verify and validate the software. This costs an additional $500,000; based on the results of similar IV&V efforts, the manager estimates that this will reduce the error probability P(UO) to 0.04.

The decision tree in Figure 1 then shows, for each of the two major decision options, the possible outcomes in terms of the critical error existing or being found and eliminated, their probabilities, the losses associated with each outcome, the risk exposure associated with each outcome, and the total risk exposure (or expected loss) associated with each decision option. In this case, the total risk exposure associated with the experiment-team option is only $2 million. For the IV&V option, the total risk exposure is only $1.3 million, so it represents the more attractive option.

Besides providing individual solutions for risk-management situations, the decision tree also provides a framework for analyzing the sensitivity of preferred solutions to the risk-exposure parameters. Thus, for example, the experiment-team option would be preferred if the loss due to a critical error were less than $13 million, if the experiment team could reduce its critical-error probability to less than 0.065, if the IV&V team cost more than $1.2 million, if the IV&V team could not reduce the probability of critical error to less than 0.075, or if there were various partial combinations of these possibilities.

This sort of sensitivity analysis helps deal with many situations in which probabilities and losses cannot be estimated well enough to perform a precise analysis. The risk-exposure framework also supports some even more approximate but still very useful approaches, like range estimation and scale-of-10 estimation.

RISK MANAGMENT

As Figure 2 shows, the practice of risk management involves two primary steps each with three subsidiary steps.

The first primary step, risk assessment, involves risk identification, risk analysis, and risk prioritization:

♦ Risk identification produces lists of the project-specific risk items likely to compromise a project's success. Typical risk-identification techniques include checklists, examination of decision drivers, comparison with experience (assumption analysis), and decomposition.

♦ Risk analysis assesses the loss probability and loss magnitude for each identified risk item, and it assesses compound risks in risk-item interactions. Typical techniques include performance models, cost models, network analysis, statistical decision analysis, and quality-factor (like reliability, availability, and security) analysis.

♦ Risk prioritization produces a ranked ordering of the risk items identified and analyzed. Typical techniques include risk-exposure analysis, risk-reduction leverage analysis (particularly involving cost-benefit analysis), and Delphi or group-consensus techniques.

The second primary step, risk control, involves risk-management planning, risk resolution, and risk monitoring:

♦ Risk-management planning helps prepare you to address each risk item (for example, via information buying, risk avoidance, risk transfer, or risk reduction), including the coordination of the individual risk-item plans with each other and with the overall project plan. Typical techniques include checklists of risk-resolution techniques, cost-benefit analysis, and standard risk-management plan outlines, forms, and elements.

♦ Risk resolution produces a situation in which the risk items are eliminated or otherwise resolved (for example, risk avoidance via relaxation of requirements). Typical techniques include prototypes, simulations, benchmarks, mission analyses, key-personnel agreements, design-to-cost approaches, and incremental development.

♦ Risk monitoring involves tracking the project's progress toward resolving its risk items and taking corrective action where appropriate. Typical techniques include milestone tracking and a top-10 risk-item list that is highlighted at each

weekly, monthly, or milestone project review and followed up appropriately with reassessment of the risk item or corrective action.

In addition, risk management provides an improved way to address and organize the life cycle. Risk-driven approaches, like the spiral model of the software process,[2] avoid many of the difficulties encountered with previous process models like the waterfall model and the evolutionary development model. Such risk-driven approaches also show how and where to incorporate new software technologies like rapid prototyping, fourth-generation languages, and commercial software products into the life cycle.

SIX STEPS

Figure 2 summarized the major steps and techniques involved in software risk management. This overview article covers four significant subsets of risk-management techniques: risk-identification checklists, risk prioritization, risk-management planning, and risk monitoring. Other techniques have been covered elsewhere.[3,4]

Risk-identification checklists. Table 1 shows a top-level risk-identification checklist with the top 10 primary sources of risk on software projects, based on a survey of several experienced project managers. Managers and system engineers can use the checklist on projects to help identify and resolve the most serious risk items on the project. It also provides a corresponding set of risk-management techniques that have been most successful to date in avoiding or resolving the source of risk.

If you focus on item 2 of the top-10 list in Table 1 (unrealistic schedules and budgets), you can then move on to an example of a next-level checklist: the risk-probability table in Table 2 for assessing the probability that a project will overrun its budget. Table 2 is one of several such checklists in an excellent US Air Force handbook[5] on software risk abatement.

Using the checklist, you can rate a project's status for the individual attributes associated with its requirements, personnel, reusable software, tools, and support environment (in Table 2, the environment's availability or the risk that the environment will not be available when needed). These ratings will support a probability-range estimation of whether the project has a relatively low (0.0 to 0.3), medium (0.4 to 0.6), or high (0.7 to 1.0) probability of overrunning its budget.

Most of the critical risk items in the checklist have to do with shortfalls in domain understanding and in properly scoping the job to be done — areas that are generally underemphasized in computer-science literature and education. Recent

TABLE 1.
TOP 10 SOFTWARE RISK ITEMS.

Risk item	Risk-management technique
Personnel shortfalls	Staffing with top talent, job matching, team building, key personnel agreements, cross training.
Unrealistic schedules and budgets	Detailed multisource cost and schedule estimation, design to cost, incremental development, software reuse, requirements scrubbing.
Developing the wrong functions and properties	Organization analysis, mission analysis, operations-concept formulation, user surveys and user participation, prototyping, early users' manuals, off-nominal performance analysis, quality-factor analysis.
Developing the wrong user interface	Prototyping, scenarios, task analysis, user participation.
Gold-plating	Requirements scrubbing, prototyping, cost-benefit analysis, designing to cost.
Continuing stream of requirements changes	High change threshold, information hiding, incremental development (deferring changes to later increments).
Shortfalls in externally furnished components	Benchmarking, inspections, reference checking, compatibility analysis.
Shortfalls in externally performed tasks	Reference checking, preaward audits, award-fee contracts, competitive design or prototyping, team-building.
Real-time performance shortfalls	Simulation, benchmarking, modeling, prototyping, instrumentation, tuning.
Straining computer-science capabilities	Technical analysis, cost-benefit analysis, prototyping, reference checking.

368

TABLE 2.
QUANTIFICATION OF PROBABILITY AND IMPACT FOR COST FAILURE.

Cost drivers	Probability		
	Improbable (0.0-0.3)	Probable (0.4-0.6)	Frequent (0.7-1.0)
Requirements			
Size	Small, noncomplex, or easily decomposed	Medium to moderate complexity, decomposable	Large, highly complex, or not decomposable
Resource constraints	Little or no hardware-imposed constraints	Some hardware-imposed constraints	Significant hardware-imposed constraints
Application	Nonreal-time, little system interdependency	Embedded, some system interdependencies	Real-time, embedded, strong interdependency
Technology	Mature, existent, in-house experience	Existent, some in-house experience	New or new application, little experience
Requirements stability	Little or no change to established baseline	Some change in baseline expected	Rapidly changing, or no baseline
Personnel			
Availability	In place, little turnover expected	Available, some turnover expected	Not available, high turnover expected
Mix	Good mix of software disciplines	Some disciplines inappropriately represented	Some disciplines not represented
Experience	High experience ratio	Average experience ratio	Low experience ratio
Management environment	Strong personnel management approach	Good personnel management approach	Weak personnel management approach
Reusable software			
Availability	Compatible with need dates	Delivery dates in question	Incompatible with need dates
Modifications	Little or no change	Some change	Extensive changes
Language	Compatible with system and maintenance requirements	Partial compatibility with requirements	Incompatible with system or maintenance requirements
Rights	Compatible with maintenance and competition requirements	Partial compatibility with maintenance, some competition	Incompatible with maintenance concept, noncompetitive
Certification	Verified performance, application compatible	Some application-compatible test data available	Unverified, little test data available
Tools and environment			
Facilities	Little or no modification	Some modifications, existent	Major modifications, nonexistent
Availability	In place, meets need dates	Some compatibility with need dates	Nonexistent, does not meet need dates
Rights	Compatible with maintenance and development plans	Partial compatibility with maintenance and development plans	Incompatible with maintenance and development plans
Configuration management	Fully controlled	Some controls	No controls
Impact			
	Sufficient financial resources	Some shortage of financial resources, possible overrun	Significant financial shortages, budget overrun likely

initiatives, like the Software Engineering Institute's masters curriculum in software engineering, are providing better coverage in these areas. The SEI is also initiating a major new program in software risk management.

Risk analysis and prioritization. After using all the various risk-identification checklists, plus the other risk-identification techniques in decision-driver analysis, assumption analysis, and decomposition, one very real risk is that the project will identify so many risk items that the project could spend years just investigating them. This is where risk prioritization and its associated risk-analysis activities become essential.

The most effective technique for risk prioritization involves the risk-exposure quantity described earlier. It lets you rank the risk items identified and determine which are most important to address.

One difficulty with the risk-exposure

TABLE 3.
RISK EXPOSURE FACTORS FOR SATELLITE EXPERIMENT SOFTWARE.

Unsatisfactory outcome	Probability of unsatisfactory outcome	Loss caused by unsatisfactory outcome	Risk exposure
A. Software error kills experiment	3-5	10	30-50
B. Software error loses key data	3-5	8	24-40
C. Fault-tolerant features cause unacceptable performance	4-8	7	28-56
D. Monitoring software reports unsafe condition as safe	5	9	45
E. Monitoring software reports safe condition as unsafe	5	3	15
F. Hardware delay causes schedule overrun	6	4	24
G. Data-reduction software errors cause extra work	8	1	8
H. Poor user interface causes inefficient operation	6	5	30
I. Processor memory insufficient	1	7	7
J. Database-management software loses derived data	2	2	4

quantity, as with most other decision-analysis quantities, is the problem of making accurate input estimates of the probability and loss associated with an unsatisfactory outcome. Checklists like that in Table 2 provide some help in assessing the probability of occurrence of a given risk item, but it is clear from Table 2 that its probability ranges do not support precise probability estimation.

Full risk-analysis efforts involving prototyping, benchmarking, and simulation generally provide better probability and loss estimates, but they may be more expensive and time-consuming than the situation warrants. Other techniques, like betting analogies and group-consensus techniques, can improve risk-probability estimation, but for risk prioritization you can often take a simpler course: assessing the risk probabilities and losses on a relative scale of 0 to 10.

Table 3 and Figure 3 illustrate this risk-prioritization process by using some potential risk items from the satellite-experiment project as examples. Table 3 summarizes several unsatisfactory outcomes with their corresponding ratings for P(UO), L(UO), and their resulting risk-exposure estimates. Figure 3 plots each unsatisfactory outcome with respect to a set of constant risk-exposure contours.

Three key points emerge from Table 3 and Figure 3:

♦ Projects often focus on factors having either a high P(UO) or a high L(UO), but these may not be the key factors with a high risk-exposure combination. One of the highest P(UO)s comes from item G (data-reduction errors), but the fact that these errors are recoverable and not mission-critical leads to a low loss factor and a resulting low RE of 7. Similarly, item I (insufficient memory) has a high potential loss, but its low probability leads to a low RE of 7. On the other hand, a relatively low-profile item like item H (user-interface shortfalls) becomes a relatively high-priority risk item because its combination of moderately high probability and loss factors yield a RE of 30.

♦ The RE quantities also provide a basis for prioritizing verification and vali-

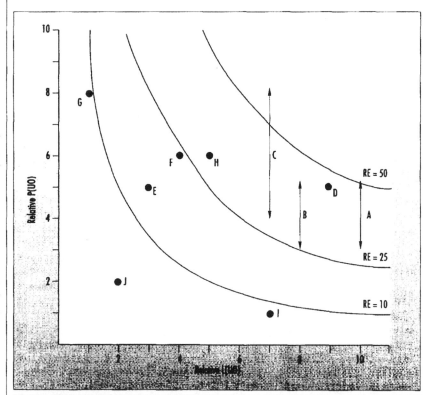

FIGURE 3. RISK-EXPOSURE FACTORS AND CONTOURS FOR THE SATELLITE-EXPERIMENT SOFTWARE. RE IS THE RISK EXPOSURE, P(UO) THE PROBABILITY OF AN UNSATISFACTORY OUTCOME, AND L(UO) THE LOSS ASSOCIATED WITH THAT UNSATISFACTORY OUTCOME. THE GRAPH POINTS MAP THE ITEMS FROM TABLE 3 WHOSE RISK EXPOSURE ARE BEING ASSESSED.

1. Objectives (the "why")
♦ Determine, reduce level of risk of the software fault-tolerance features causing unacceptable performance.
♦ Create a description of and a development plan for a set of low-risk fault-tolerance features.
2. Deliverables and milestones (the "what" and "when").
  ♦ By Week 3.
    1. Evaluation of fault-tolerance options
    2. Assessment of reusable components
    3. Draft workload characterization
    4. Evaluation plan for prototype exercise
    5. Description of prototype
  ♦ By Week 7.
    6. Operational prototype with key fault-tolerance features.
    7. Workload simulation
    8. Instrumentation and data reduction capabilities.
    9. Draft description, plan for fault-tolerance features.
  ♦ By Week 10
    10. Evaluation and iteration of prototype
    11. Revised description, plan for fault-tolerance features
3. Responsibilities (the "who" and "where")
  ♦ System engineer: G.Smith
    Tasks 1, 3, 4, 9, 11. Support of tasks 5, 10
  ♦ Lead programmer: C.Lee
    Tasks 5, 6, 7, 10. Support of tasks 1, 3
  ♦ Programmer: J.Wilson
    Tasks 2, 8. Support of tasks 5, 6, 7, 10
4. Approach (the "how")
  ♦ Design-to-schedule prototyping effort
  ♦ Driven by hypotheses about fault-tolerance-performance effects
  ♦ Use real-time operating system, add prototype fault-tolerance features
  ♦ Evaluate performance with respect to representative workload
  ♦ Refine prototype based on results observed
5. Resources (the "how much")
    $60K — full-time system engineer, lead programmer, programmer
          (10 weeks)*(3 staff)*$2k/staff-week)
    $0 — three dedicated workstations (from project pool)
    $0 — two target processors (from project pool)
    $0 — one test coprocessor (from project pool)
    $10K — contingencies
    $70K — total

FIGURE 4. RISK-MANAGEMENT PLAN FOR FAULT-TOLERANCE PROTOTYPING.

dation and related test activities by giving each error class a significance weight. Frequently, all errors are treated with equal weight, putting too much testing effort into finding relatively trivial errors.

♦ There is often a good deal of uncertainty in estimating the probability or loss associated with an unsatisfactory outcome. (The assessments are frequently subjective and are often the product of surveying several domain experts.) The amount of uncertainty is itself a major source of risk, which needs to be reduced as early as possible. The primary example in Table 3 and Figure 3 is the uncertainty in item C about whether the fault-tolerance features are going to cause an unacceptable degradation in real-time performance. If P(UO) is rated at 4, this item has only a moderate RE of 28, but if P(UO) is 8, the RE has a top-priority rating of 56.

One of the best ways to reduce this source of risk is to buy information about the actual situation. For the issue of fault tolerance versus performance, a good way to buy information is to invest in a prototype, to better understand the performance effects of the various fault-tolerance features.

Risk-management planning. Once you determine a project's major risk items and their relative priorities, you need to establish a set of risk-control functions to bring the risk items under control. The first step in this process is to develop a set of risk-management plans that lay out the activities necessary to bring the risk items under control.

One aid in doing this is the top-10 checklist in Figure 3 that identifies the most successful risk-management techniques for the most common risk items. As an example, item 9 (real-time performance shortfalls) in Table 1 covers the uncertainty in performance effect of the fault-tolerance features. The corresponding risk-management techniques include simulation, benchmarking, modeling, prototyping, instrumentation, and tuning. Assume, for example, that a prototype of representative safety features is the most cost-effective way to determine and reduce their effects on system performance.

The next step in risk-management planning is to develop risk-management plans for each risk item. Figure 4 shows the plan for prototyping the fault-tolerance features and determining their effects on performance. The plan is organized around a standard format for software plans, oriented around answering the standard questions of why, what, when, who, where, how, and how much. This plan organization lets the plans be concise (fitting on one page), action-oriented, easy to understand, and easy to monitor.

The final step in risk-management planning is to integrate the risk-management plans for each risk item with each other and with the overall project plan. Each of the other high-priority or uncertain risk items will have a risk-management plan; it may turn out, for example, that the fault-tolerance features prototyped for this risk item could also be useful as part of the strategy to reduce the uncertainty in items A and B (software errors killing the experiment and losing experiment-critical data). Also, for the overall project plan, the need for a 10-week prototype-development and -exercise period must be factored into the overall schedule, to keep the overall schedule realistic.

Risk resolution and monitoring. Once you have established a good set of risk-management plans, the risk-resolution process consists of implementing whatever prototypes, simulations, benchmarks, surveys, or other risk-reduction techniques are called for in the plans. Risk monitoring ensures that this is a closed-loop process by tracking risk-reduction progress and applying whatever corrective action is necessary to keep the risk-resolution process on track.

Risk management provides managers with a very effective technique for keeping on top of projects under their control: *Project top-10 risk-item tracking.* This technique concentrates management attention on the high-risk, high-leverage, critical success factors rather than swamping management reviews with lots of low-priority detail. As a manager, I have found that this type of risk-item-oriented review saves a lot of time, reduces management surprises, and gets you focused on the high-leverage issues where you can make a difference as a manager.

Top-10 risk-item tracking involves the following steps:

♦ Ranking the project's most significant risk items.

♦ Establishing a regular schedule for higher management reviews of the project's progress. The review should be chaired by the equivalent of the project manager's boss. For large projects (more than 20 people), the reviews should be held monthly. In the project itself, the project manager would review them more frequently.

♦ Beginning each project-review meeting with a summary of progress on the top 10 risk items. (The number could be seven or 12 without loss of intent.) The summary should include each risk item's current top-10 ranking, its rank at the previous review, how often it has been on the top-10 list, and a summary of progress in resolving the risk item since the previous review.

♦ Focusing the project-review meeting on dealing with any problems in resolving the risk items.

Table 4 shows how a top-10 list could have worked for the satellite-experiment project, as of month 3 of the project. The project's top risk item in month 3 is a critical staffing problem. Highlighting it in the monthly review meeting would stimulate a discussion by the project team and the boss of the staffing options: Make the unavailable key person available, reshuffle project personnel, or look for new people within or outside the organization. This should result in an assignment of action items to follow through on the options chosen, including possible actions by the project manager's boss.

The number 2 risk item in Table 4, target hardware delivery delays, is also one for which the project manager's boss may be able to expedite a solution — by cutting through corporate-procurement red tape, for example, or by escalating vendor-delay issues with the vendor's higher management.

As Table 4 shows, some risk items are moving down in priority or going off the list, while others are escalating or coming onto the list. The ones moving down the list — like the design-verification and -validation staffing, fault-tolerance prototyping, and user-interface prototyping — still need to be monitored but frequently do not need special management action. The ones moving up or onto the list — like the data-bus design changes and the testbed-interface definitions — are generally the ones needing higher management attention to help get them

TABLE 4.
PROJECT TOP-10 RISK ITEM LIST FOR SATELLITE EXPERIMENT SOFTWARE.

| Risk item | Monthly ranking | | | Risk-resolution progress |
	This	Last	No. of months	
Replacing sensor-control software developer	1	4	2	Top replacement candidate unavailable
Target hardware delivery delays	2	5	2	Procurement procedural delays
Sensor data formats undefined	3	3	3	Action items to software, sensor teams; due next month
Staffing of design V&V team	4	2	3	Key reviewers committed; need fault-tolerance reviewer
Software fault-tolerance may compromise performance	5	1	3	Fault-tolerance prototype successful
Accommodate changes in data bus design	6	—	1	Meeting scheduled with data-bus designers
Test-bed interface definitions	7	8	3	Some delays in action items; review meeting scheduled
User interface uncertainties	8	6	3	User interface prototype successful
TBDs in experiment operational concept	—	7	3	TBDs resolved
Uncertainties in reusable monitoring software	—	9	3	Required design changes small, successfully made

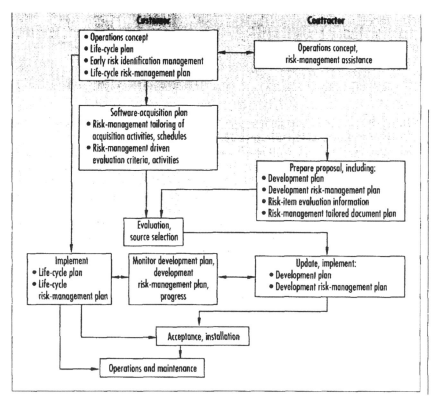

- Operations concept
- Life-cycle plan
- Early risk identification management
- Life-cycle risk-management plan

Operations concept,
risk-management assistance

Software-acquisition plan
- Risk-management tailoring of
  acquisition activities, schedules
- Risk-management driven
  evaluation criteria, activities

Prepare proposal, including:
- Development plan
- Development risk-management plan
- Risk-item evaluation information
- Risk-management tailored document plan

Evaluation,
source selection

Implement
- Life-cycle plan
- Life-cycle
  risk-management plan

Monitor development plan,
development
risk-management plan,
progress

Update, implement:
- Development plan
- Development risk-management plan

Acceptance, installation

Operations and maintenance

FIGURE 5. FRAMEWORK FOR LIFE-CYCLE RISK MANAGEMENT.

resolved quickly.

As this example shows, the top-10 risk-item list is a very effective way to focus higher management attention onto the project's critical success factors. It also uses management's time very efficiently, unlike typical monthly reviews, which spend most of their time on things the higher manager can't do anything about. Also, if the higher manager surfaces an additional concern, it is easy to add it to the top-10 risk item list to be highlighted in future reviews.

IMPLEMENTING RISK MANAGEMENT

Implementing risk management involves inserting the risk-management principles and practices into your existing life-cycle management practices. Full implementation of risk management involves the use of risk-driven software-process models like the spiral model, where risk considerations determine the overall sequence of life-cycle activities, the use of prototypes and other risk-resolution techniques, and the degree of detail of plans and specifications. However, the best implementation strategy is an incremental one, which lets an organization's culture adjust gradually to risk-oriented manage-

ment practices and risk-driven process models.

A good way to begin is to establish a top-10 risk-item tracking process. It is easy and inexpensive to implement, provides early improvements, and begins establishing a familiarity with the other risk-management principles and practices. Another good way to gain familiarity is via books like my recent tutorial on risk management,[3] which contains the Air Force risk-abatement pamphlet[5] and other useful articles, and Robert Charette's recent good book on risk management.[4]

An effective next step is to identify an appropriate initial project in which to implement a top-level life-cycle risk-management plan. Once the organization has accumulated some risk-management experience on this initial project, successive steps can deepen the sophistication of the risk-management techniques and broaden their application to wider classes of projects.

Figure 5 provides a scheme for implementing a top-level life-cycle risk-management plan. It is presented in the context of a contractual software acquisition, but you can tailor it to the needs of an internal development organization as well.

You can organize the life-cycle risk-

management plan as an elaboration of the "why, what, when, who, where, how, how much" framework of Figure 4. While this plan is primarily the customer's responsibility, it is very useful to involve the developer community in its preparation as well.

Such a plan addresses not only the development risks that have been the prime topic of this article but also operations and maintenance risks. These include such items as staffing and training of maintenance personnel, discontinuities in the switch from the old to the new system, undefined responsibilities for operations and maintenance facilities and functions, and insufficient budget for planned life-cycle improvements or for corrective, adaptive, and perfective maintenance.

Figure 5 also shows the importance of proposed developer risk-management plans in competitive source evaluation and selection. Emphasizing the realism and effectiveness of a bidder's risk-management plan increases the probability that the customer will select a bidder that clearly understands the project's critical success factors and that has established a development approach that satisfactorily addresses them. (If the developer is a noncompetitive internal organization, it is equally important for the internal customer to require and review a developer risk-management plan.)

The most important thing for a project to do is to get focused on its critical success factors.

For various reasons, including the influence of previous document-driven management guidelines, projects get focused on activities that are not critical for their success. These frequently include writing boilerplate documents, exploring intriguing but peripheral technical issues, playing politics, and trying to sell the "ultimate" system.

In the process, critical success factors get neglected, the project fails, and nobody wins.

The key contribution of software risk management is to create this focus on critical success factors — and to provide the techniques that let the project deal with them. The risk-assessment and risk-control techniques presented here provide the foundation layer of capabilities needed to implement the risk-oriented approach.

However, risk management is not a cookbook approach. To handle all the complex people-oriented and technology-driven success factors in projects, a great measure of human judgement is required.

Good people, with good skills and good judgment, are what make projects work. Risk management can provide you with some of the skills, an emphasis on getting good people, and a good conceptual framework for sharpening your judgement. I hope you can find these useful on your next project. ◆

REFERENCES

1. J. Rothfeder, "It's Late, Costly, and Incompetent — But Try Firing a Computer System," *Business Week*, Nov. 7, 1988, pp. 164-165.
2. B.W. Boehm, "A Spiral Model of Software Development and Enhancement," *Computer*, May 1988, pp. 61-72.
3. B.W. Boehm, *Software Risk Management*, CS Press, Los Alamitos, Calif., 1989.
4. R.N. Charette, *Software Engineering Risk Analysis and Management*, McGraw-Hill, New York, 1989.
5. "Software Risk Abatement," AFSC/AFLC pamphlet 800-45, US Air Force Systems Command, Andrews AFB, Md., 1988.

Barry W. Boehm is director of the Defense Advanced Research Project Agency's Information Science and Technology Office, the US government's largest computer/communications research organization. In his previous position as chief scientist for TRW's Defense Systems Group, he was involved in applying risk-management principles to large projects, including the National Aeronautics and Space Administration's space station, the Federal Aviation Administration's Advanced Automation System, and the Defense Dept.'s Strategic Defense Initiative.

Boehm received a BA in mathematics from Harvard University and an MA and PhD in mathematics from UCLA.

Address questions about this article to the author at DARPA ISTO, 1400 Wilson Blvd., Arlington, VA 22209-2308.

Large-Scale Project Management *Is* Risk Management

ROBERT N. CHARETTE, *ITABHI Corporation*

Because large-scale software projects increasingly affect the public good, the "normal science" paradigm is proving insufficient to model their complexity and potential consequences. The "postnormal science" paradigm offers a better fit, using a robust management approach predicated on a risk-taking ethic.

Two years after the start of the US Federal Aviation Administration's $4.3 billion Advanced Automation System project contract in 1990, the Government Accounting Office stated that continuing delays in the deployment of the Initial Sector Suite System, a key component of the AAS, could "have the potential for affecting FAA's ability to handle safely the predicted increases in traffic into the next century."[1] Later that year, the AAS project schedule was extended by 19 months. The FAA blamed the delay on their underestimating the development and testing time for the ISSS software, as well as on unresolved differences in the system specifications caused by changes to the requirements.

By April of 1994—following an additional 14-month schedule delay in early 1993 (blamed once again on ISSS-related software problems)—FAA management declared the AAS project "out of control." At that point, the cost for AAS completion was predicted to reach over $7 billion, with yet another schedule slip of up to 31 months possible. At this point, the FAA effectively suspended the AAS program.

Reprinted from *IEEE Software,* July 1996.

The FAA recently announced that a reduced-functionality ISSS under a restructured and curtailed AAS program called the Display System Replacement project will become operational in 1998—six years late, fourteen years after the project started, and seventeen years after it was initially defined. The current estimated cost-to-complete for the DSR project totals $5.6 billion.

Until that time, and assuming no further setbacks, the FAA and the flying public can only hope that the current air traffic control system, with its over taxed and breakdown-beset 1960's era computer systems, will not become the source of a catastrophic accident.

BEYOND NORMAL SCIENCE

Large-scale software projects like the AAS or the US Defense Department's Strategic Defense Initiative—which were estimated to require more than 2.3 and 10 million code statements respectively—are characterized by high decision stakes and high levels of system uncertainty. As such, they are poor candidates for being planned or developed under the prevalent "normal science" model of project management.

Normal science assumes that large-scale software projects are like puzzles to be solved: using reasoned trial and error, based on accepted engineering paradigms, the pieces will fall in place. However, as Frederick Brooks has pointed out, creating software systems is one of the most complex tasks ever undertaken. No matter how we might otherwise pretend, for large-scale software projects there are no edge pieces to guide us, no picture on the box we can refer to when stuck, and no assurance that we have all the pieces or even that they fit together.

Increasingly, large-scale projects most closely fit into what is called "postnormal science." They have objectives that are unprecedented in breadth and depth—such as reliability requirements of 99.99999 percent in the AAS. Ambiguity, continuous change, and complicated feedback loops dominate our project-management decision making. Because our endeavors are often unique, no one has the requisite expertise we need for planning and implementation. Project success or failure affects the public directly and indirectly, often creating unintended socio-economic impacts. As they continue to increase in size, complexity, and the potential for ill effects if they fail, more and more of our projects will fall into the "postnormal" category.

The implications for project management are two fold. First, many of the assumptions underpinning traditional project management are tenuous at best and incorrect at worst. A combination of change, complexity, discontinuities, diseconomies of scale, nonlinearities, and the consequences of failure serve to undermine them. Second, project management should—I believe, *must*—be propelled foremost by a process and philosophy of risk management; it should be the central actor in project management instead of just another member of the supporting cast.

NORMAL VERSUS POSTNORMAL SCIENCE

In 1962, scientific historian and philosopher Thomas Kuhn published a breakthrough book, *The Structure of Scientific Revolutions*. In it, Kuhn wrote that scientific paradigms, what he called "normal science," are "accepted examples of actual scientific practice—examples of which include law, theory, application, and instrumentation together—[that] provide models from which spring particular coherent traditions of scientific research."[2] Scientists and engineers operate under these accepted conceptual world views or para- digms to attack important contemporary problems and to define legitimate areas of research.

Scientific progress, Kuhn asserts, takes place by a continuous process of "puzzle-solving," that is, scientists use the accepted paradigm to solve current

Normal science assumes that large-scale software projects are like puzzles to be solved.

questions of interest as well as to resolve paradigm–nature anomalies—areas where the paradigm doesn't seem to quite fit reality.

Occasionally, an anomaly is of such significance that it directly calls into question the whole paradigm. The scientific community then shifts from unanimity into crisis, conflict, and turmoil until a new paradigm emerges to explain the anomaly. Things then run relatively smoothly until another crisis-causing anomaly is discovered and the process repeats itself once again. Thus, Kuhn contends, scientific progress is a matter of relatively peaceful periods of paradigm refinement punctuated by intense periods of dynamic change. Our move from an Aristotelian to an Einsteinian concept of physical laws, for example, required several such transformations.

Changing times. In the mid-1980s, other scientific historians and philosophers, notably Silvio Funtowicz and Jerry Ravetz, began to argue that Kuhn's view of scientific progress was too narrow.[3] Funtowicz and Ravetz contend that while Kuhn's model may have been representative of past scientific progress, it is no longer entirely applicable. They claim that "normal science" presumes an insular community of scientific interest from which the public is generally excluded; discussion of what is beneficial scientific advancement is limited to the scientists themselves. This view implies that there is a scientific answer to pressing societal

Not all hypotheses can be tested by experimental means.

problems, with scientists—because of their objectivity and expertise—ideally positioned to address them.

Funtowicz and Ravetz point out that today, however, scientists are being asked to reach solutions for complex *public* problems such as genetic re-engineering, global warming, and the like. With these types of problems

♦ the facts of the matter are uncertain,

♦ the values involved are in dispute,

♦ decision stakes are high and decisions urgently needed, and

♦ the public is deeply involved in making decisions and deeply affected by those that are reached.

Funtowicz and Ravetz maintain that the normal-science model, with its practice of using "hard" scientific inputs to make "soft" policy decisions, is not prepared to resolve these new, complex types of questions where "hard" policy decisions have to be made using "soft" scientific inputs. They go on to argue that normal science's tradition of being objective and ethically neutral does not fit many of the questions being asked of it today. An example? "Are the implications of human gene re-engineering, such as politically motivated eugenics, value free or ethically neutral?" The skills scientists require to fully address complex questions like this are usually beyond standard training. Scientists performing human-genetics research are not trained as ethicists nor are medical insurance actuaries trained as public-health policymakers. Still, each area is affected by what these scientists discover.

Funtowicz and Ravetz assert that science and its practice cannot be automatically separated from how it is used, above all when the consequences can

greatly affect the public good. They further assert that even paradigm change à la Kuhn is not sufficient, nor will it ever be sufficient, to solve the messy technology-cum-public issues now upon us.

Paradigm departure. To deal with the pressing scientific problems of today, Funtowicz and Ravetz propose a trans-science model they call "postnormal science." This new model does not imply that the scientific method is invalid, but rather that certain questions or problems now being posed do not fit the scientific process; not all hypotheses can be tested by experimental means. A major argument brought against SDI, for example, was that the system could not be "fully tested" except in actual use.[4] As a result, the confidence that it would work when needed could never be attained. The implications of deploying such a system are not difficult to imagine.

Likewise, postnormal science does not imply that the normal-science model is irrelevant, but only that it is most germane when *both* problem uncertainty and decision stakes are low. Once either factor starts to increase, the usefulness of the normal-science approach decreases rapidly; solutions will be based upon group judgment rather than objective "facts." Normal science, therefore, should be viewed as a subset of postnormal science—applicable to many (if not most) problems, but certainly not to all.

PROJECT MANAGEMENT AND NORMAL SCIENCE

Contemporary project management has been heavily influenced by normal science over the course of its theoretical and practical development. Beginning at the turn of the century, in a period of intense scientific achievement, several management theorists and practitioners believed work could be improved by the application of scientific methods.[5]

Notable among them was Frederick W. Taylor, who codified this belief into four principles of management, published in *Principles of Scientific Management*. According to Taylor, management should

(1) replace individual workers' rule-of-thumb methods with specialized, scientifically developed approaches;

(2) select, train, and develop workers using scientific methods, so each worker performs the right job;

(3) bring together scientifically selected workers and scientifically developed work to gain the optimal results; and

(4) ensure an equal division of work and responsibility between management and workers, and foster close cooperation between the two.

Project-based structure. Many people later refined Taylor's principles, including organizational theorist Luther Gulick. In 1937, Gulick presented the idea that a project-type organizational structure—one responsible for achieving a specific organizational purpose—could be more effective than the more traditional functional forms advocated by Taylor and others. Gulick's idea seemed to be supported by the numerous successful scientific and engineering efforts of World War II—particularly that of the Manhattan Project.

The success of difficult or "impossibly large" projects during the war years helped spawn further refinements of the project concept, culminating in the archetypes of modern project-management theory and practice: the 1950's era US Navy's Polaris Missile Special Projects Office and, for software particularly, the SAGE air defense system.[6]

With so many years of success in applying Gulick's concept behind us, we tend to passively take for granted the premises underlying project management. However, even a cursory glance at those premises highlights the influence of normal science.

♦ A project is defined as a clear-cut

investment activity with an explicit purpose and a distinct beginning, duration, and end.

♦ A project represents the lowest opportunity cost: It is the most beneficial option for expending scarce resources.

♦ At least one solution exists given the project's purpose, meaning that the project is *feasible* (it can be technically accomplished), *suitable* (it can be managerially accomplished), and *acceptable* (the project's purpose can be achieved).

♦ The time and resources required can be accurately predicted.

♦ The environmental context is well-understood and fixed, and "success" can be defined and measured.

♦ The risks involved, including their worst-case consequences, can be contained.

♦ Failure to meet the project's objective is caused by a lack of proper skills or their employment, rather than because the project is infeasible, unsuitable, or unacceptable.

This description is admittedly ideal. On even the most well-formed project, you would be hard pressed to completely meet any of the characteristics, let alone all of them. The description also contains a presupposition: That you have not only sufficient information to define a project, but that the information is accurate enough to let you predict future events. However, even in small software projects, information can be in short supply and of suspect accuracy, and thus prediction becomes difficult. Insufficient and inaccurate information forms small cracks in the premises of your project's foundation. Usually, the cracks do not undermine its structural integrity and you can successfully field the project, although often slightly late or over-budget from your original predictions.

When your project is large and complex and the amount of information and its accuracy decline rapidly, prediction becomes more akin to fortune telling.

Structural anomalies or fissures start to appear in each premise. Like water seeping through an earthquake-weakened dam, the cracks reveal themselves through project consequences: missed schedules, exceeded budgets, and delivered systems that don't operate correctly or at all. For large-scale software projects—50 to 65 percent of which are ultimately canceled—the flow through the cracks has become a torrent.[7]

PATCHING THE PARADIGM

According to Kuhn, when cracks appear in a paradigm steps are taken to patch them up, first through a series of refinements. Over the years, various refinements in software engineering's basic paradigm, the waterfall life-cycle model (which is itself a codification of earlier stagewise development models), have been suggested. Requirements traceability, design inspections, code reviews, configuration management, quality assurance, process improvement, abstraction, iteration, rapid development, and so on have all been added to what is now considered good if not essential software engineering practice, especially for large-scale software projects.

Efforts taken to shore up project management or the control aspect of software engineering's paradigm continue to receive the most attention, as it is almost universally perceived as the major fissure eroding project success. Over the last decade, risk management has increasingly been seen as a useful patching material to fill the project management fissure and strengthen its surrounding walls.

Risk first. Barry Boehm's spiral model was the first major endeavor to make risk management a formal software engineering activity, especially in large DoD software projects.[8] The spiral model sought to consolidate previously

proposed process-model refinements—such as the evolutionary development and transform model—into a single, unifying meta-process model, as well as to make risk management a much more visible and important part of project management.

The spiral model uses a basic four-stage, cyclic, risk-driven decision process as a metaproject management control mechanism.

1. Determine project objectives, constraints, and so on.
2. Identify risks, evaluate alternative courses of action, and resolve risks in the course chosen.
3. Implement the selected course and verify its completion.
4. Determine whether the risks are at an acceptable level to proceed to the next decision stage.

The decision process overlays the individual phases of the meta-process model. Before a life-cycle phase is initiated, management must decide whether the project situation is currently acceptable, feasible, and suitable. The spiral model uses the level of risk exposure as a key decision metric for determining this. If you perceive project risks as being too great at any phase, you must reduce them before proceeding. For example, you might have to develop prototypes to reduce feasibility risk or select a special case of the meta-process

> **When your project is large, prediction becomes more akin to fortune telling.**

model to lower suitability risk. Thus, in the spiral approach, how well you manage risk is the overriding factor in developing and managing software.

Risk experience. The spiral model has been used by many companies, particularly in the aerospace industry, with varying degrees of success. It was refined by The Software Productivity Consortium to strengthen its risk management and implementation aspects.[9]

At the start of a large project, accurate cost or schedule predictions are unlikely.

Still, few organizations have the requisite risk management expertise to apply the spiral model properly.[10] Generally, software project managers are not conversant with formal risk management, its relationship to decision making, nor how to integrate risk management into existing project management activities. The spiral model has increased the visibility of risk as an issue to be seriously considered in software project management, albeit not to the degree that might be wished.

To overcome the lack of risk management expertise in the software engineering community, several efforts have taken place since the spiral model first appeared.

♦ The Software Engineering Institute has an established software risk management program.

♦ The UK Government's Centre for Information Systems has created guidebooks on risk management for enterprise-, program-, and project-level managers in computing and telecommunications.

♦ The DoD, under its Software Acquisition Best Practices Initiative, developed a guide to acquiring best practices, designating formal risk management as a paramount practice.

Also, as the references at the end of this article show, numerous books and articles on the subject have also appeared in recent years.

SHATTERING THE PARADIGM

Despite efforts to improve its practice, risk management is still primarily regarded as an additional support activity of project management and not as project management's central tenet. More often than not, risk management is not considered at all because to do so "contradicts" a core premise underlying a software project. By definition, a project should be doable, not "risky"; except under exceptional circumstances, a project's chance for success should be significantly greater than the likelihood of failure. A project should also be well-defined, represent the lowest opportunity cost, and so on. After all, if it weren't, it wouldn't have been approved, right?

The risk stigma. Until they are completed or canceled, all projects have risk. However, for project managers to admit to "riskiness" can be seen as admitting to "not fully understanding the problem" or being "overly pessimist," or worse, "not a team player," among other things. This association of risk with something being wrong leads to cognitive dissonance: A belief is held in spite of evidence to the contrary. Many large-scale, extremely complex, and unprecedented DoD software projects, for example, are universally seen as risky yet are declared by fiat to be "low-risk" so as not to imperil future funding. Similar things happen in industry, and not only on large-scale software projects. Given this mindset, it is difficult to make a case for performing risk management.

At best, risk management is viewed as one of those "self-evident" activities: software projects obviously involve risks that need to be managed. However, few project managers see any compelling reason or need to make risk management a separate, formal activity, let alone the quintessence of project management. This is unfortunate. In my experience, project suc-

cess—particularly for large-scale software projects—is severely limited by this perspective.

As software projects become large-scale, the effects of complexity, ambiguity, change, and uncertainty dominate, acting like a confluence of storm-swollen rivers that rapidly undermine the premises that "normal" project management is built upon. That a project is feasible, suitable, and acceptable cannot automatically be presumed for large-scale software projects.

Cracking premises. Consider acceptability, for example. What does it mean in an AAS-like project? How can you clearly define investment objectives when the project spans multiple communities of interest with conflicting expectations and definitions of success? For a project of this sort, the primary community of interest includes not only the FAA customer, but the airlines, the companies that depend upon the airlines for routine business, and millions of passengers, not to mention Congress. Each of these groups is affected to varying degrees by the project's success or failure, and the consequences of the latter are much greater than merely the project's cost. Unintended consequences and attendant risks are also almost universally overlooked.

The acceptability premise is further weakened by the fact that large-scale projects are long-lived, and thus their objectives will assuredly change as economic conditions shift, technology improves, experience clarifies needs from desires, and so on. Each change in turn affects technical feasibility and managerial suitability as well. Accurately predicting cost or schedule at the start of such a project is highly unlikely, not only because of insufficient data, but because the premise of a fixed environmental context is violated as well.

Other assumptions are also eroding. In normal software projects, a definite end to the project is presumed. However, for large-scale software projects, with their long development and operational lives, their deep connection to a vast community of interests, and their tight coupling into huge programs made up of similar projects, this premise is severely eroded if not completely washed away. For example, the current DSR project is only one part of a much larger FAA modernization program that totals over $30 billion. Whatever happens with DSR has ripple effects well after it is officially delivered. Even DSR success will bring about changes in ways that are unanticipated. To paraphrase John Donne, no large-scale software project is an island, entire of itself.

Normal projects are assumed both to be beneficial and to represent the lowest opportunity cost option. For large-scale projects, neither assumption may hold. The realizable benefits of the FAA's air traffic control modernization program have been in dispute since its inception.[11] Furthermore, it is sometimes the case that not doing a large-scale project is better than trying and failing because of the way public perceptions are permanently shaped. As originally defined, SDI, and to a degree AAS, are cases in point.

LIVING IN A POSTNORMAL WORLD

With such strained or shattered "normal" project premises confronting us, we have two choices. We can continue to try to repair the normal-science paradigm of projects and project management and hope failure rates decline. Or we can decide on an alternative view.

Large-scale projects such as AAS or SDI fit the postnormal perspectives much better than the normal-science view because

♦ the "facts" of the situation are highly uncertain,

♦ project values and expectations are in constant dispute,

♦ decision stakes are very high,

♦ decisions are needed urgently, and

♦ whatever happens, a broad community of interest will be deeply affected.

Not all large-scale software projects meet these criteria, of course, as not all have a public face per se. It could be argued that most don't, at least not at the present time. However, this situation is likely to change. As software becomes ever more ubiquitous, increasing numbers of large-scale software projects are directly affecting our lives. Indirect impacts are also growing.

New criteria. The assumption that large-scale software projects are just like small ones, only bigger, must be abandoned. To effectively deal with postnormal-type software projects, project managers must adopt a different operating premise: Large-scale software projects belong to the postnormal world until proved otherwise.

However, scaling back to the "normal" project domain should not be seriously considered unless the following criteria are met:

♦ The project's risks (and rewards) are fully and completely understood by all parties potentially affected.

♦ The risks are thoroughly, continuously, and visibly assessed and managed.

♦ Project management provides the leadership to actively control the risks.

To ensure that the project's risks are fully and completely understood by the parties potentially affected, managers must openly define and share risk (and success). When they do, not only will all parties better understand the project's purpose and benefits, but when inevitable difficulties arise they are likely to respond with rational action rather than gut reaction. Each manager must also articulate the point of unacceptable risk, where the project is no longer beneficial,[12] the risks outweigh the rewards, or a project turns out not to be doable in its present form. To continue stubbornly past these points believing that something can be salvaged is not only

folly, but invariably creates problems when you attempt the idea again in the future with a different approach.

New ethic. We must develop an extra sensitivity to risk or, more appropriately, a *risk-taking ethic*[13] which holds that

♦ success entails taking on risks, sometimes very great risks, but doing so intelligently;

♦ risk is not something to be feared or avoided, but something we can profit from;

♦ change is not feared, but embraced; and

♦ by mastering the details, the risks can be mastered as well.

A postnormal project is filled with dilemmas to manage as opposed to problems to solve, and every decision has a potential for negative consequences. The high uncertainty and high decision stakes dictate that *every* decision, whether it be made by the project sponsor, project manager, the software team leader, or the individual programmer must be at a level of acceptable risk to the greatest possible degree. In other words, each decision must be assessed for risk.

Decision making. It is essential to implement a quality decision-making process that has risk as the overriding

> # Large-scale software projects are postnormal until proved otherwise.

concern and that actively searches for risk in every decision, assesses risk to see if it is too great, and if it is, takes positive action to reduce it.[14] A primary characteristic of such a decision process is that it must be visible, repeatable, and measurable. This ensures that a base level of consistency is achieved, helps others to understand why and how a decision was made as well as how to improve future decisions, and if needed, how a decision can be reversed with minimal damage.

Estimating the current situation is a powerful way to organize your thoughts and propose action.

To be most effective, the decision process must pragmatically support how project members make decisions involving risk on a daily basis. This implies that process cannot be bolted on as an afterthought, be ad hoc in nature, nor performed once a quarter or life-cycle phase. It must be embedded into everyday work practices. The process must also support different decision makers' perspectives and work contexts. It should help program managers, project managers, or programmers answer specific questions about financial, technical, legal, political, or any other risk or combination of risks involved in the decision making relevant to *their* work environment. Just as a rancher sees a cow differently than a microbiologist, a project manager sees a risk differently than a programmer.

It is imperative that you assess risks at a fine level of granularity so informed decisions can be made, but also at a level coarse enough that actions taken to manage them are efficiently implemented. Take, for example, two statements: "There is a timing risk in the system design" and "There is a 30-percent chance of the message buffer overflowing resulting in a 10-milliseconds delay." The former is useful to the project manager, the latter to a software team leader.

Information concerning risks and implications of risk management actions must also flow freely across the project, as well as include multidisciplinary concerns of the stakeholders. Otherwise, incomplete or suboptimal decisions are the likely result.

In a postnormal environment, the most effective decision process accounts for risks from the initial project definition time until the project is retired. It does little good for a project plan to be developed and then checked for risk afterwards; risk must be the first input to any initial project definition and be continually reassessed throughout the project's development and operation.

Because decisions are so interlocked in large-scale projects, the consequences of a few or even one risky decision can be quickly multiplied a hundredfold to disastrous effect. Because our knowledge of a decision's effect is limited, even good knowledge of the separate risks involved can't prevent mistakes in an individual's intuitive judgment of the effects of managing those risks today. A postnormal project can only succeed when a project team has a risk-taking ethic and sees itself as operating in an enterprise situation on an undertaking of scope, complication, and most of all, risk.

Leadership. Even if the risks are fully and completely understood by all parties potentially affected, and the risks are thoroughly, continuously, and visibly assessed and managed, you still need a project management team that can provide leadership and actively control the risks. Without leadership, "risk-taking ethic" is just a meaningless phrase. Management must be proactive, or as Stephen Covey puts it, more than "merely taking the initiative," management must create a culture where risk is not synonymous with disaster.[15]

Being proactive means taking responsibility for the choices made on the project. It means spending the time necessary to understand how decisions are made and how they can

be improved. It means looking at decisions as correct or incorrect, rather than right or wrong, and being able to reverse decisions that are incorrect. And it means management directs its energies at achieving success, not laying blame. Proactive, risk-taking project management stresses cooperation, collaboration, integration, and balance of action.

Paradigms are important to the way we see the world. They create a framework of thought for understanding and explaining reality. They also define the rules that we act under and what we consider acceptable behavior. If the paradigm is wrong, however, we will end up taking actions that we think are fitting, but are in reality detrimental.

The concept of postnormal science is meant to challenge how science is used today in attacking complex, societal questions, how society values, relates to, and uses science, and what the proper role is of scientists and practitioners of science. such as engineers. in addressing these questions. Although the postnormal concept may not be a perfect analogy or substitute for large-scale software project management, it is clear that the current reliance on a normal-science paradigm is severely wanting. At the very least. by taking a postnormal view of large-scale software projects based upon a risk-taking ethic, risk, uncertainty, and the potential impact of failure can at last be acknowledged and dealt with forthrightly, not ignored or hidden like some dark family secret.

Clearly, projects striving for goals like those of the AAS are needed, and sometimes the "performance envelope" needs to be pushed. Only through experimentation can true learning, and hence progress, take place. However, it should be remembered that one definition of insanity is when a person, failing at a task, tries the same thing over and over again, expecting a different result. Given the success rate of large-scale software projects, you decide. ◆

REFERENCES

1. T. Perry, "Special Report: Air Traffic Control — Improving the World's Largest, Most Advanced System," *IEEE Spectrum*, Feb. 1992, pp. 22-36.

2. T. Kuhn, *The Structure of Scientific Revolutions*, University of Chicago Press, Chicago, 1962.

3. S. Funtowicz and J. Ravetz, "PostNormal Science: A New Science for New Times," *Scientific European*, Mar. 1992, pp. 95-97.

4. D. Parnas, "Parnas: SDI 'Red Herrings' Miss the Boat," (Letter to the Editor) *Computer*, Feb. 1987, pp. 6-7.

5. T. S. Bateman and C. P. Zeithaml, *Management: Function and Strategy*, Irwin, Boston, 1990.

6. H. Sapolsky, *The Polaris System Development*, Harvard Univ. Press, Cambridge, Mass., 1972.

7. C. Jones, *Patterns of Software Systems Failure and Success*, International Tomson Computer Press, Boston, 1996.

8. B. Boehm, "A Spiral Model of Software Development and Enhancement," *Computer*, May 1988, pp. 61-72.

9. *Encyclopedia of Software Engineering*, vol. 1, J. Marciniak, ed., John Wiley & Sons, New York, 1994.

10. R. Charette, *Applications Strategies for Risk Analysis*, McGraw-Hill, New York, 1990.

11. "Federal Aviation Administration's Advanced Automation System Investment," Government Accounting Office, GAO/T-IMTEC-88-2, March 31, 1988.

12. R. Charette, *Software Engineering Risk Analysis and Management*, McGraw-Hill, New York, 1989.

13. R. Charette, "On Becoming a Risk Entrepreneur," *American Programmer*, Mar. 1995, pp. 10-15.

14. S. Funtowicz and J. Ravetz, "Risk Management as a Postnormal Science," *Risk Analysis*, Mar. 1992, pp. 95-97.

15. S. Covey, *The 7 Habits of Highly Effective People: Restoring the Character Ethic*, Simon & Schuster, New York, 1989.

Robert N. Charette is president of the ITABHI Corporation of Fairfax, Virginia. His interests are in entrepreneurism, unified approaches to proactive risk management, systems engineering, and very large-scale systems definition and management.

Charette is the chair of the SEI risk-management program advisory board, the author of the lead guidebook on risk management for the UK Government's Centre for Information Systems, and has written numerous papers, articles, and books on the management of risk. He can be reached at PO Box 1929, Springfield, VA 22151; 7500.1726@compuserve.com.

A Project Risk Metric

Robert W. Ferguson
Software Engineering Institute

A risk metric is proposed that is normalized across projects. The purpose of the metric is to provide management visibility into project uncertainty. This works best in an organization that manages multiple projects. The proposed metric can be applied early and throughout the project. It has been useful for identifying or canceling projects in trouble. It has also been useful for identifying projects that do not yet have a satisfactory risk plan.

The Standish Group published its original "Chaos Report" [1] in 1994 declaring that American companies spent $81 billion on cancelled projects. Additional Standish Group data in Figure 1 shows that the situation has not improved as much as one would hope.

Even projects that are not cancelled may deliver such reduced functionality that most people would not count them as successful projects. Often there has been early evidence that the project was headed for disaster. The project manager may even have issued warnings to senior management or sponsors about the problems. There simply seemed to be no way to *pull the plug* until the project was already over budget, late, and at the point where the customer was ready to give up or worse.

The problem may be a failure to examine the risks of the project from a systemic view. When risks are faced one problem at a time, the management team may convince themselves that every problem can be addressed, or that each problem has a low probability of occurrence. However, the collected problems may still be too much to manage. By its very nature, risk is statistical. It is possible to examine the collection of risks and make some projections about the project's likely success or failure. The result can even suggest that certain projects should be cancelled very early. Such projects can be rescoped and rebudgeted in a way that improves the focus and likelihood of success.

Figure 1: *Standish Group Project Results*

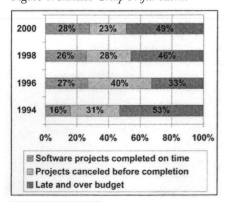

Risk Management Process

The Project Management Body of Knowledge (PMBOK) [2] includes a chapter on risk management. It describes the process steps as follows:
1. Risk Planning.
2. Risk Identification.
3. Qualitative Risk Analysis.
4. Quantitative Risk Analysis.
5. Risk Response Planning.
6. Risk Monitoring and Control.

> *"A standard definition of risk is an uncertain event that would cause an uncertain impact on project schedule, cost, or quality."*

The metric proposed in this article fits the Qualitative Risk Analysis stage so it can be used as early as possible throughout the project duration. Rough estimates are available at this step, and are sufficient for an assessment of the overall project risk. However, the rough estimates will not suffice for risk items requiring real risk-response strategies such as mitigation and avoidance plans where more detailed work is needed.

In this metric, the distinction between steps three and four of the process model is important. The metric supports the viewpoint of senior management who wants to determine which of several projects has significant uncertainty. The project itself must deal with specific risks and quantitative analysis. As such, a risk manager on a large project will not find this metric as useful. He or she must have much more specific information.

History and Metric Definition

Risk is both old and new. The written history of risk begins in 1491 with the "Pacioli Puzzle," which arises from gambling when the game is stopped before completion [3]. The problem was solved by Pascal and Fermat in 1654 and so began the use of risk in forecasting. Today, risk is the core concept in insurance and has become a major focus in project management.

A standard definition of risk is an uncertain event that would cause an uncertain impact on project schedule, cost, or quality. Both the event and the impact have the element of uncertainty. The definition from probability theory is a bit more restrictive but it provides us with the metric:

$$R = P \times V$$

The metric value of risk (R) is the product of the probability (P) of the event with the most likely value (V) of the outcome. If the risks are independent, we can add these estimates together for a combined estimate. So overall project risk is the sum of the separate risks.

$$\text{Total Risk} = \text{Sum of all } (P \times V)$$

The Total Risk value and trends of Total Risk provide a picture of the project, making it easy for people to see some good and bad project patterns without delving into the statistical theory. The assumption about independence is necessary for the theory. However, in practice, risk management experts are aware that risks are not always independent. The metric is based on the theory derived from gambling where the assumption holds true.

Getting the Probability

There have been a few sociological studies showing the range of errors people demonstrate in estimating risk. Choosing an appropriate range helps when no historical data is available. Table 1 and its heuristics have been useful in avoiding the problems of underestimating and overestimating risk. Remember, most project managers see only three to five projects in their career at any one company so they work from a very restricted sample. They need heuristics for estimates.

Five levels of probability seem to work well. Colleagues have not had a problem assigning an event to one of the recommended levels, so the suggested ranges provide good separation.

Analyzing the Impact

The impact of a project risk-event needs to be similarly divided into a few classifications and assigned a numeric value to manage risk. Making the numbers match conceptually when one risk affects schedule, another cost, and another quality or scope can be a bit of a stretch so a method is required to normalize the numbers.

A quick simplifying assumption works for the qualitative analysis stage: assign a single impact type. Choose from one of the following three image types: schedule, cost, or customers (sales). It is true that a risk event may affect more than one of these, however, coming up with a value for all the possible effects is challenging and probably not a worthwhile exercise until quantitative analysis. Narrowing the discussion of a risk event to a single type impact also focuses attention on the most useful response plans. This approach helps to avoid the problem of overthinking the impact of a risk. Here is an example of the kind of thinking to avoid at this early stage.

> Some employees are due for sabbatical leaves of two months. One may take that sabbatical during the project. You propose that turnover is a risk for the team. If this risk event occurs, it may cost some additional schedule time and additional resource cost to hire and train staff. If you lose schedule time, you may also lose some sales. What is the appropriate impact for this event – schedule, cost, or sales?

Experienced risk managers will understand that additional impacts will have to be considered when developing the risk-response plans.

Normalizing Risk Impact

The next challenge is normalizing the various impacts to arrive at a single numeric value for schedule, cost, and sales. Capers Jones reported that in 1996 "the typical project is 100 percent over budget when it is cancelled" [4]. This suggests that a useful normalizing factor is to set maximum risk impact at project cancellation. That impact value should be cost or schedule

Label	Description	Value
Very Low	In your career, you have never seen this happen, but it could.	5% Range 1-9%
Low	It has happened on occasion.	25% Range 10-29%
Moderate	Sometimes it happens and sometimes not.	50% Range 30-69%
High	Most of the time this event will occur.	75% Range 70-89%
Very High	It has happened on every project, and you think it always will, but there is a chance of escape.	95% Range 90-99%

Table 1: *Risk Event Probability Estimates*

overrun of 100 percent, or when there is no customer or no potential first-year sale.

Of course, no project will be allowed to overrun to such an extent without senior management intervention, but that is precisely the point. Senior management should intervene when the uncertainty suggests the project is in trouble. Since the metric is applied at qualitative analysis, there is time to recover.

A Second Aside

Why would we develop a product without customers? No one plans a project for a non-existent market, but the market can disappear or be misjudged. It happens all the time. Some well-known examples are the Newton tablet computer, the Iridium satellite telephone, and New Coke. Everyone also has an example of the *pet project* that was developed but was never used. Many organizations are surprised to learn that it is possible to cancel a project when sales or number of customers are factored into the risk management effort.

Using the possibility of cancellation as the highest risk impact, assign a value of five to cancellation. Five levels of risk should be enough. Creating the other levels again requires a bit of psychology. The PMBOK states an order of magnitude estimate is plus or minus ($\pm$) 35 percent of the base estimate. Using a range of 1 ± 0.35 is a range of 0.65 to 1.35. The ratio of these two numbers is $1.35/0.65 = 2.08$, approximately a factor of two.

Thus to have a range that clearly separates the estimates, we must use a larger value. Using ± 50 percent yields a ratio of 1.5/0.5, which equals a factor of three.

Experience suggests the psychology works, and people are comfortable with the results. Therefore, assign five to cancellation and divide the cancellation level by three successively to arrive at the other values. The following example points the way.

Consider a project that is scheduled for

18 months with a projected cost of $30 million and projected first-year sales of $27 million. This would be a project of about 100 people with about $5 million in external expenses. A risk event with an impact level of five would cause the following:

- Overrun by 18 months.
- Overspend by $30 million.
- Achieve no first-year revenue.

A risk event with an impact level of four (divide by three) would cause the following:

- Overrun by six months.
- Overspend by $10 million.
- Lose $9 million in sales (achieves $18 million).

A risk event with an impact level of three would cause the following:

- Overrun by two months.
- Overspend by $3.3 million.
- Lose $3 million in sales.

A risk event with an impact level of two would cause the following:

- Overrun by three weeks.
- Overspend by $1.1 million.
- Lose $1 million in sales (one customer).

A risk event with an impact level of one would cause the following:

- Overrun by one week.
- Overspend by $300,000.
- Lose $300,000 in sales (customer delays six months).

A useful interpretation is to say that the project manager can manage one or two risk events of impact level one within the project contingency and without unusual reporting. It would be necessary to generate a special report for any occurrence of impact level two. Any risk event at impact levels three or higher will require senior management's involvement to determine the response.

There is one more step in calculating the final impact. The numbers one through five were calculated by successive division by three. The final value has to put that back into a geometric scale.

Impact = 3^(level-1)

Impact Level	Impact Value
5	81
4	27
3	9
2	3
1	1

Table 2: *Impact Value Adjustment*

So a risk event with an impact level of five has an impact value of 3x3x3x3=81, as shown in Table 2.

The factor *three* is not arbitrary but is derived from the observation that order-of-magnitude estimates use a factor of two for the error range.

There is a temptation to turn the numbers back into dollars. This is a lot of work as revenue dollars are not the same as cost dollars or schedule days. The extra work makes sense for the top risks but not in general. Using the impact number instead of a dollar value also normalizes the risk metric across projects.

Risk Calculation

The final risk calculation follows the original equation:

Risk = Probability x Impact Value

The highest risk is 95% x 81 = 76.95
The lowest is 5% x 1 = 0.05

Normal usage is the sum of the highest 20 project risks. It seems that 20 risks at a time is a sufficient number to track for all but some mega-projects (over three years and more than 500 people). Barry Boehm, TRW professor of software engineering at the University of Southern California and author of the COCOMO estimating model, has suggested that projects manage the top 10 risks. There are two reasons this metric recommends watching the top 20.

The first is that 20 risks x 5% = 100%. That is the recommended cancellation level so it makes for a convenient metric. The second reason is to make certain the project team investigates more than the first 10 risks to be certain that it manages the top 10.

Project Risk Score =
Sum (highest 20 project risks)

Implications

The Project Risk Score should be charted so senior management can see scale and trends. Since there is a threshold (threatened cancellation) implicit in a risk with impact level five, that threshold should also appear on the chart. An impact level equal to five translates into an impact value of 81. Figure 2 is a sample chart from an actual project.

There are many implications in the chart and its use. The threshold is a powerful concept. Senior management will focus a lot of attention on a project that is above the threshold. The fact is, projects with risk higher than the threshold simply will be late, over cost, or fail to meet project quality goals. Some projects have risk levels that are astronomically high. It is theoretically possible to see a value of 1,539 with 20 risks that are very likely to occur and have an impact rating of five. Of course, such a project should be cancelled and restarted. I have actually seen only one project risk value over 400. That project had to make major changes to deliver even a subset of the desired functionality. If the threshold concept had been introduced at the start of that project, it would never have gotten into so many problems.

A somewhat opposite situation also can occur when a project shows particularly low risk. The project manager or senior man-

agement may have a sense that a project is at significant risk, but the metric does not show it. Use that low number as a signal that a risk collection effort is needed. The project manager must gather a wider audience and run a facilitated session to identify those other risks. Make sure to include stakeholders from other locations and groups outside the development team. Develop the organization taxonomy for risks like the one in the "Continuous Risk Management Guidebook" [5] from the Software Engineering Institute to make the data collection more complete and rigorous.

A normal response when the project risk is high is to manage that risk down. This can happen several ways:
* The time for the risk event may pass without incurring the problem.
* The team may adopt an avoidance plan so that the event cannot occur.
* The team may adopt a mitigation plan to reduce the impact.
* The team may transfer the risk to another organization.
* The event may occur and the project eats the contingency.

The last four responses cause the project to incur a specific cost that should appear in the project planning and reporting. Each of the responses requires the project manager to make some update to the risk database.

Finally, product managers (not project managers) should be hesitant to select a project of very low risk. If the risk is so low, why not address a more aggressive product plan? Risk avoidance is not generally a winning strategy in the marketplace. The point is to manage risk to appropriate levels for the organization, product, and project. Risk management is a systemic study and not a technological one.

Implementation

There are several challenges in adopting the project risk metric. The following is a list of the top challenges:
* **A database for collecting and managing risks.** There are a number of products that will do the job. Implementing one will require the addition of project and sub-project identification and organizational process support. This work cannot be institutionalized without an automated system.
* **A process model.** The basic framework is available in the PMBOK, the Continuous Risk Management Guidebook, or the Institute of Electrical and Electronic Engineers standard for risk management [6]. The process model has to be extended to cover a risk taxonomy that is appropriate to

Figure 2: *Sample Project Risk Score*

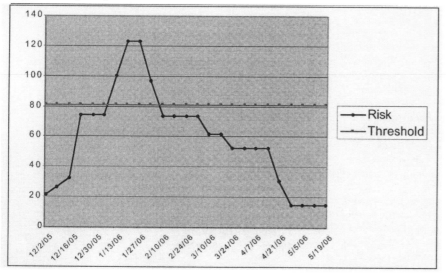

the organization.

- **Automated reporting.** Chances of success are better if the project risk chart is automated and is required as a part of the regular project management review. The risk metric should be checked at least monthly.
- **Training.** Training is a big effort. Training project managers to do risk management takes days, not hours. Writing good risk scenarios requires at least eight hours of training and much practice. Learning the organization taxonomy of risk takes time. Evaluating impacts probably takes three hours of training. Directors and senior managers also need at least three hours of training. Do not attempt to implement a project risk metric without decent training on risk management.

Summary

Many seasoned project managers say that advanced project management is mostly risk management. This metric makes that statement visible and concrete to a much larger audience. It provides fast visibility and has a high emotional impact on managers.

The project risk metric, however, has been tested in only one location and on only a dozen projects. The simplifying assumptions made in order to develop and use the metric make it suspect for use by risk practitioners who must perform detailed quantitative analyses and develop risk mitigation and avoidance plans.

It does provide a comparison between projects that is useful to senior management. If senior management is presented with one risk at a time, they are likely to develop a confidence that they can deal with each risk as it comes. Dealing with each risk separately and successfully may convince them that the project cannot really be in trouble. Management may then come to believe that the project team is whining about problems instead of dealing with problems, and real risks may not be addressed in a timely fashion. Presenting senior management with a picture of the total project risk will encourage them to take appropriate systemic actions when these are necessary. Product managers on projects with high risk will need additional justification and resources to add scope. The development team may have an easier time getting training or adding consultants when needed.

The key is presenting senior management with better visibility into the project so that project change-management becomes faster and easier, and finally, so that product delivery becomes predictable.◆

References

1. The Standish Group International, Inc. CHAOS Chronicles Ver. III. West Yarmouth, MA: The Standish Group, 2003 <www.standishgroup.com/chaos/toc.php>.
2. Project Management Institute. A Guide to the Project Management Body of Knowledge (PMBOK Guide). Newton Square, PA: Project Management Institute, 1996 <www.pmibookstore.org/productdetail.asp?productid= 4106>.
3. Bernstein, Peter L. Against the Gods: The Remarkable Story of Risk. Hoboken, NJ: John Wiley and Sons, 31 Aug. 1998 <www.wiley.com/Wiley CDA/WileyTitle/productCd-0471295639.html>.
4. Jones, Capers. Patterns of Software Failure and Success. Boston, MA: International Thompson Computer Press, 1996.
5. Durofee, Audrey J., et al. Continuous Risk Management Guidebook. Pittsburgh, PA: Software Engineering Institute, 1996 <www.sei.cmu.edu/publications/books/other-books/crm guidebk.html>.
6. Institute of Electrical and Electronic Engineers. "Software Engineering: Software Life-Cycle Processes, Risk Management." Proposed Standard. New York: IEEE, 2004 <http://standards.ieee.org/announcements/pr_p1540. html>.

About the Author

Robert W. Ferguson is a member of the Technical Staff at the Software Engineering Institute. He has more than 30 years of software development and management experience in several industries. Ferguson is a member of the Computer Society of the Institute of Electrical and Electronic Engineers and the Project Management Institute. He has been active in the software process improvement community for several years and is past chairman of the Chicago Software Process Improvement Network.

Software Engineering Institute
Carnegie Mellon University
4500 Fifth AVE
Pittsburgh, PA 15213
Phone: (412) 268-9750

Catastrophe Disentanglement: Getting Software Projects Back on Track©

E.M. Bennatan

Advanced Project Solutions, Inc.

If you are responsible for a late and over-budget software project, you are not alone — software project overruns are all too common. But if serious problems have existed for quite a while and the situation is getting worse, not better, you may have a project catastrophe on your hands. At this point, there is no established rescue process to follow. Dealing effectively with an out-of-control project is as much an emotional challenge as it is a managerial and technical one. This article describes a 10-step process to disentangle a software project catastrophe and get it back on track.

In Spencer Johnson's "Who Moved My Cheese?" [1], the *little people* keep coming back to where the cheese used to be even though it is not there anymore. It is a natural tendency to continue doing what we have always done even when, to an outside observer, it no longer makes sense. This behavior is quite common when projects get into trouble. We keep plodding away at the project hoping that the problems will go away and the *cheese* will miraculously reappear. In all too many cases, it does not.

Just as the smart thing to do when a ball of twine seems hopelessly entangled is to stop whatever we are doing with it (otherwise the tangle gets worse), so it often is with a disastrous project: The longer we keep at it, the worse it gets. At some point, we need to halt all activity and reassess what we are doing.

Disastrous software projects, or *catastrophes*, are projects that are completely out of control in one or more of the following aspects: schedule, budget, or quality. They are by no means rare – 44 percent of surveyed development organizations report that they have had software projects cancelled or abandoned due to significant overruns, and 15 percent say that it has happened to more than 10 percent of their projects (see Figure 1).

But, obviously, not every overrun or quality problem means a project is out of control, so at which point should we define a software project as a catastrophe? What are the criteria for taking the drastic step of halting all activities, and how do we go about reassessing the project? Most importantly, how do we get the project moving again? The answers to these questions are the essence of the concept of *catastrophe disentanglement*.

When Is a Project a Catastrophe?

Organizations and projects vary to such an extent that there can be no universal criteria for branding a software project a catastrophe. The expectations from mission-critical, life support, or banking software are significantly different than from most consumer- or Internet-based software applications. But experience shows that in virtually all cases, projects are in deep trouble if serious problems have existed for quite a while and the situation is getting worse, not better. How is this reflected in terms of schedule, budget, and quality?

Schedule

Software projects rarely or never strictly follow their schedule; delays often grow and shrink like an accordion. It is a sad reality that software project delays are an excessively common occurrence (see Figure 2[1]). But we are not looking at just any delay; the issue here is to identify those projects where the delay is growing uncontrollably.

To determine if the delay is out of control, divide the total development schedule into 12 phases, and look at each of the last three. Has the delay steadily grown in each phase? Is the total delay now greater than three phases (i.e., 25 percent of the total project schedule)?

On a one-year schedule, for example, look at the last three months and ask the following questions:

1. Was the delay significant two months ago?
2. Was the delay even greater one month ago?
3. This month, has the delay grown again?
4. Has the delay growth been steady (that is, not two small delays and one major delay caused by an identifiable event)?
5. Is the total delay now greater than three months?

If the answer to these questions is yes, it is probably a good idea to halt the project and reassess it.

Budget

A project is a budget catastrophe if its remaining projected cost far exceeds what the development organization is willing to pay for it. In software projects, major budget overruns are often the result of schedule overruns or of attempts to reduce schedule overruns (e.g., by adding staff). The following are points to consider:

1. Does the project schedule appear to be a catastrophe? If so, project cost projections have little value at this time.
2. If the project schedule appears to be under control, then extrapolate budget overruns for the past three phases up to the end of the most current project schedule (assume that every future phase will continue to exceed the budget at a similar rate). Is this a cost your organization can bear?
3. Do you have current feedback from the project's customers and users? Do you have updated market research data? Is the original cost/value analysis for this project still valid?

Quality

A software project is a quality catastrophe if (a) the list of serious quality problems has been substantial for three periods and is not decreasing, or if (b) customers/users who have evaluated the software that is being developed are exceptionally critical of it.

The project problem list is a good indicator of how serious the problems are. The list is commonly divided into (a) critical, (b) serious, and (c) minor problems. The following are points to consider:

1. Is the critical problem list growing? Are problems being resolved? How fast are new problems being added?
2. The second level of serious quality problems can also indicate the gravity of the situation if the list is particularly long and not getting any shorter.
3. Another indicator to monitor is how well the quality problem lists are being maintained. Are problems being categorized correctly? Are problems being removed prematurely from the list? Are new problems being withheld from the list?

Reprinted from *CrossTalk*, October 2004.

Severe quality problems (those that are either critical or most serious) are often difficult, if not impossible, to see in the early stages of a project. In fact, many severe quality problems emerge only toward the end of a project (and sometimes only after its release). Even the *last-three-phases* technique can be ineffective during the first half of a project because too often problem lists have not yet been compiled or well maintained.

But project quality issues can be monitored from the outset if there is someone whose job it is to do so. This means assigning an independent software quality assurance (SQA) professional to every project team as soon as the project is launched. For small development teams, one SQA professional can be responsible for two or three projects, though large projects should have their own indigenous SQA team.

Customer and user feedback is the best source for evaluating project quality. Unfortunately, it is sometimes difficult to get feedback until a project is close to release. For large projects, it is often worth investing in prototypes and pre-releases, thus getting preliminary versions of the software into the users' hands for early evaluation and feedback. This investment is like an insurance policy: It reduces the risk of major product quality issues – but at a cost.

The Project Is a Catastrophe – Now What?

The following 10 steps describe the process for disentangling a failing software project and getting it back on track. Because these steps intrude on the responsibilities of the team members – most especially the project manager – the process should be confined to getting the project back on track and nothing more. Ultimately, the new project plan must gain the unreserved support of the development team members, and the details should be left up to them.

1. Stop

Once you have determined that a software project is unlikely to be completed with any reasonable degree of success, the next step is painful but clear: Stop all activities immediately. This is a difficult decision because it will always be open to harsh criticism from some circles. It is also a tough decision because, as we have seen, there is really no airtight algorithm for determining that a project is a catastrophe. Ultimately, the decision is a combination of data analysis and management experience.

Stopping a project should never leave a team idle. There is much to do in preparing the project for assessment, including the following:
- Collecting and updating project documentation and data.
- Preparing status reports for each team member and each team.
- Bringing the project software to the nearest point (backward, not forward) for demonstration. This means that except for minor exceptions, no new code should be written and no new features should be added or integrated (otherwise there is a risk that the demonstration will take too long to prepare).
- Assisting the project evaluator.

In addition, other activities should be prepared and held in reserve such as training and assistance to other projects.

2. Assign An Evaluator

Virtually all software projects in trouble have strong emotional and political hallmarks that often produce passionate advocates and opponents. Therefore, the importance of using an *external* project evaluator cannot be overstated. This will increase the likelihood of getting an unbi-

Ten Steps to Disentangle a Software Project Catastrophe

1. Stop.
2. Assign an external, unbiased evaluator.
3. Evaluate true project status (what has been achieved and what has not).
4. Evaluate team capabilities.
5. Define new minimal goals and requirements with senior (executive) management and customers.
6. Determine if minimum goals can be achieved (if not, then abandon, find alternative to the project).
7. Rebuild the project team.
8. Perform high-level risk analysis.
9. Develop reasonable estimates.
10. Install an early warning system.

ased and unemotional evaluation.

Whom should you choose? Ideally, you should assign a reliable, pragmatic, experienced, and successful project evaluator who (a) understands the project technology, (b) has good social skills, and (c) can reprioritize other responsibilities to allow sufficient time for the evaluation.

For very large projects, use an evaluation team of two or more evaluators but

Figure 1: *Percentage of Abandoned or Cancelled Software Projects Due to Significant Cost or Time Overruns in the Past Three Years [2]*

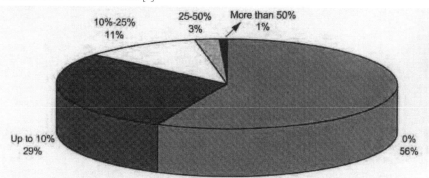

Figure 2: *Percentage of Software Projects Completed Within 10 Percent of Original Estimated Time in the Past Three Years [2]*

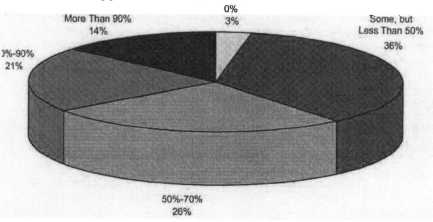

with a clearly designated chief evaluator.

3. Evaluate Project Status
The first challenge in evaluating a project is to determine its true status. Most failed software projects will have produced many status reports – some may even be quite positive – but they will not necessarily be objective or dispassionate. In establishing an unbiased view of the project status, do the following:
- Reduce tension by involving the project team in your evaluation and by being completely open (no secrecy or mysterious behind-closed-doors discussions).
- Consider only observable facts (e.g., not, "This feature used to work well but something has gone wrong.").
- Consider accomplishments, not effort.
- For almost completed tasks, apply the 90-50 rule. *(It takes 50 percent of the time to do 90 percent of the work and another 50 percent to do the remaining 10 percent.)*
- Present your evaluation to the team before finalizing it and consider their responses (look for details and facts that you overlooked or misunderstood, while resisting undue pressure to amend your findings).

4. Evaluate the Team
Evaluating a team is a sensitive activity that should be handled both resolutely and tactfully. This step is purely part of the evaluation process and does not, at this point, result in any restructuring of the team. The following are questions to be considered:
- Does the project team have the necessary skill set and experience to successfully deliver the project?
- Do the team leaders have the leadership, technical skills, and the personality necessary to lead their team?
- Does the project manager have the required leadership, technical skills, and personality necessary to lead the project team, and does he or she command the respect of the team members?
- Are there any internal team conflicts or tensions that could disrupt the project?
- What is the level of team spirit and morale? If low, then why? (Are there reasons beyond the failing of the project?)

5. Define Minimum Goals
The emphasis here is on the word minimum; the project should be reduced to the smallest size that achieves only the most essential goals. This resetting of goals and objectives can only be performed with the active involvement of senior (executive) management and the customer[2]. Divide all project requirements into three sets:
- **Set One:** Essential requirements without which the project has no value.
- **Set Two:** Important requirements that greatly improve the project but are not essential.
- **Set Three:** Nice-to-have requirements that add to the project, but are not especially important.

Now, start by retaining the requirements from set one, and initially eliminating sets two, and three. This will often create tremendous opposition, but remember – we are dealing with a project that was totally out of control and may otherwise be cancelled. Occasionally, some elements from set two can be added, but this should be rare. All remaining requirements (from sets two and three) should be targeted for subsequent releases of the software.

Here is a word of caution: Be prepared to forestall the ploy by some stakeholders to second-guess the whole evaluation process by their insistence on listing all (or most) requirements in set one.

6. Can Minimum Goals Be Achieved?
The main challenge here is to determine whether the requirements in set one can reasonably be achieved. The questions to be addressed are the following:
- Is set one a genuine and significant reduction of the project scope?
- Is there a single requirement in set one that adds an order of magnitude to the complexity of the project? If so, are members of management aware of this and will they reconsider its inclusion[3]?
- Are the new project goals now achievable? Is there now a reasonable chance that the team will be able to deliver the requirements in an acceptable time-frame, within a reasonable budget, and with an acceptable quality level?
- How genuinely confident are the team members (and especially the project manager) in their ability to achieve the new set of goals?

If the minimum goals appear unachievable (and they are truly minimal), a recommendation to cancel the project may be the only remaining realistic course of action.

7. Rebuild the Team
Based on the evaluation of the team (see step four) it may be necessary to restructure and even partly re-staff the team to handle the new set of goals.

A halted software project can mean a team that is demotivated and demoralized. But in all probability, if the project was in deep trouble before it was halted, then the low morale did not start with the decision to halt the project. However, the issue of team morale should be a major consideration in rebuilding the project team (this will be further discussed later).

In rebuilding the team, consider the following points:
- **Team Structure.** Is the project team structured optimally for the success of the project?
- **Team Functions.** Are the necessary team functions staffed?
- **Team Members.** Are there team members who should be replaced?
- **Team Leaders.** Are there team leaders who should be replaced?
- **Project Manager.** Is the project manager the right person to lead this project?

8. Risk Analysis
In all phases of a software development project, risk analysis is virtually an indispensable tool – this is particularly true of a failing project trying to get back on track. The process identifies risk events, mitigation steps and contingency plans, and assigns tracking responsibilities[4].

High-level risk analysis (i.e., anticipating the most serious potential problems) should be performed as part of the project evaluation process. The analysis will not only help evaluate the chances of success in restarting the project, it will also help restore a level of confidence within the project team.

9. New Estimates and Schedule
Based on the minimal goals and the rebuilt team, new reasonable high-level estimates and a new schedule need to be prepared and the cost-effectiveness of the renewed project plan should be established. If the schedule is firm, ensure that budget, staffing level, and feature set are not also all fixed (or another catastrophe will ensue).

In many cases, it may be prudent to focus primarily on the schedule and feature set (the other parameters, such as budget and staffing levels, can initially be sidelined). This means that if the minimal feature set is firm, then calculate the project delivery date and vice versa. Remember that even a generous budget and an unrestricted staffing level may not be enough to resolve the problem of a fixed feature set with an uncompromising delivery date.

Here is a note on cost effectiveness: In analyzing the cost of completing a software project, only future costs (not costs already expended) should be considered. The cost of project completion should then be compared to the value of the completed project.

10. Establish Clear Project Review Milestones

Put in place an early warning system to ensure that the project does not slip back into catastrophe mode. Such a system should include the following:

- The introduction of an efficient and reliable project data collection and analysis system.
- Clear project evaluation criteria for management.
- A schedule of frequent project reviews with well-defined measurable milestones.

After successful completion of these project evaluation steps, and after determining that the renewed project plan is achievable and cost effective, the project can be restarted.

Case Study

A failing project is often like a hand in a cookie jar: to get some cookies out, you first have to let some go. Such was the case at Motorola with the software for a wireless telephony[5] control and maintenance center (CMC) that we delivered several years ago as part of a 200,000-subscriber project to one of the emerging Eastern European countries (see [5]). The specially tailored CMC was a last minute add-on to the wireless telephony contract and was consequently not well defined.

The CMC was developed with a subcontractor team, based on an existing control system. The first phase of the project was devoted to producing a voluminous set of requirements, none of which could be omitted (according to the customer). The schedule was dictated – 16 months, which was set as close as possible to the date the subscriber telephony system was to become operational. Needless to say, every month was critical.

Five months into the project, key dates were already being missed. Seven months into the project, doubts began arising among senior management about whether the project would be ready on time. Nine months into the project, senior management was trying to calculate how much the late delivery penalties would cost, and a frantic marketing team was looking for alternatives. At all junctures, the development team was adamant that they would deliver the project on time.

At the end of nine months, amid significant resistance from the development and marketing teams, we brought the project almost to a complete halt (some tasks did continue). Two activities were then launched: (a) a total external review of the project, and, in parallel, (b) customer negotiations were reopened on the CMC requirements.

- The project status was evaluated and it was confirmed that the then-current rate of progress would lead to a major project overrun. The team was moving forward at a steady pace but there was no way that they could meet the delivery date, or any date close to it.
- Because the CMC was critical for the operation of the whole system, the customer was cooperative in reevaluating the project's software features. Thus, a new set of minimal requirements was prepared.
- The project was rescheduled with two release dates: the first with the minimal feature set and the second with the remaining features.
- On the development team side, instead of using a single team for development, installation, and support, a cooperative effort was launched together with a local support team.
- Frequent project progress reviews were initiated by management with key development team members together with the customer.

As a result, a working CMC system was delivered on time and the full telephony system became operational as planned. The additional CMC features were provided as part of a later second release.

The Customer Perspective

Some software organizations' attitude toward customers is reminiscent of the librarian who disliked readers removing books from the library shelves because they disrupted the tidy placement of the books on the shelves. The librarian had confused means (the library) with goals (reading books). In software development, we also sometimes tend to confuse means (the project) with goals (customer satisfaction[6]).

There is justification for a project only as long as there are willing customers for its product. Hence, it is wise for both management and the project team to keep an ever-watchful eye on the customers: their needs, their expectations, and their opinion of the software being developed. After all, the continued development of a product that no longer has a willing customer (or user) is the ultimate project catastrophe.

Post-Project Reviews

Getting a failed software project back on track is an admirable accomplishment, but an even greater one is not having it go off track in the first place. Therefore, part of the catastrophe disentanglement procedure is preventing future recurrences of similar catastrophes. This is achieved

---

Warning Signs to Watch for in a Project:
- It is late and getting later.
- It is over budget and getting more so.
- Performance is poor and getting poorer.
- Criticism from customers/users is severe.

Choosing a Project Evaluator
- External (this might be the time to use a good consultant).
- Reliable, pragmatic, and experienced.
- Understands the project technology.
- Has good social skills.
- Can devote sufficient time.

The Post-Project Review
- What happened? (25%)
- Why did it happen? (25%)
- How to do better in the future? (50%)
- Who/what is to blame? (0%)

---

through a special review process held after the project has ended (successfully or otherwise).

The post-project review is a process intended to facilitate an understanding of why a project evolved the way it did. What was done right? What was done wrong? What can be done better next time[7]? The review is a structured process that is not intended to find the guilty or to lay any blame, and is best done with a trained facilitator.

The output of the review includes a list of operational, procedural, and organizational changes and actions to ensure that mistakes are not repeated and successes are. In fact, the U.S. Army recommends that 50 percent of the review be devoted to discussions on how to do better in the future; the remaining time is devoted to what happened (25 percent), and why (25 percent) [7].

The Human Factor

The process of disentangling catastrophes is traumatic not just for the project team, but for the organization itself. Clearly, halting a project does not add to the motivation of a project team. Similarly, declaring a project to be a catastrophe does not add to the prestige of a development organization – though the courage to make such a decision often deserves praise.

While a highly motivated team is certainly one of the primary factors for project success, the fear of demotivating a team or tarnishing an organization's image should never be a reason to allow a team to continue in the wrong direction. Catastrophe disentanglement should be viewed like corrective surgery: just as the body undergoes trauma in order to heal, so does the development organization.

One of the problems with the rather drastic measures of catastrophe disentanglement is that the knowledge that an organization will take such measures can inhibit the flow of accurate information (particularly bad news) to senior management. But successful corrective action, just like successful surgery, depends on the flow of truthful and accurate information even, in fact especially, when the news is bad.

The ability to bring bad tidings and make unpopular decisions is a desirable, if not entirely common, part of an organization's culture. Former Intel Chief Executive Officer Andy Grove said:

… If you are a middle manager you [may] face … the fear that when you bring bad tidings you will be punished, the fear that management will not want to hear the bad news from the periphery. Fear that might keep you from voicing your real thoughts is poison. Almost nothing could be more detrimental to the well-being of the company. [8]

Grove's point is that effective corrective action requires accurate information – a reality not unfamiliar to those of us who drive a car: We cannot effectively steer a vehicle on the road if we cannot get accurate data. Thus, an organization that wants to be able to effectively evaluate its activities with processes such as the one described here, needs to promote the flow of accurate information by ensuring the following:

* The process is open and fair (not secretive).
* The staff is briefed about the process and the reason it is being adopted.
* The organization promotes a mistake-tolerant culture[8]. Blame and punishment need to be eliminated from the evaluation process (mistakes should be addressed in normal performance reviews alongside successes and achievements).

Conclusion

Most software catastrophes were troubled projects that went on for too long. Part of the trauma of dealing with them is the realization that "this shouldn't have happened," or "we should have seen it coming." Realizing this, the call to action is: "Something has to change around here."

Returning to Johnson's "Who Moved My Cheese?" the tale continues:

The littlepeople were outraged, shocked, scared, and befuddled when the cheese disappeared. In their comfort, they didn't notice the cheese supply had been dwindling, nor that it had become old and smelly. They had become complacent. [1]

How better to describe the failing of a software project?◆

References

1. Johnson, Spencer, and Kenneth H. Blanchard. Who Moved My Cheese? An Amazing Way to Deal With Change in Your Work and in Your Life. Putnam Pub Group, 1998.
2. Bennatan, E.M. "The State of Software Estimation: Has the Dragon Been Slain?" Part 1. Executive Update 3.10. The Cutter Consortium, July 2002.
3. Brooks, Fredrick P. "The Mythical Man Month After 20 Years." The 17th International Conference on Software Engineering, Seattle, WA, Apr. 23-30, 1995.
4. Bennatan, E.M. On Time Within Budget: Software Project Management Practices and Techniques. 3rd ed. John Wiley & Sons, 2000.
5. Bennatan, E.M. "Wireless Local Loop in Hungary – A Case Study." New Telecom Quarterly 2nd Quarter, 1997 <www.tfi.com/pubs/ntq/auth -BennatanElli.html>.
6. Sullivan, Gordon R., and Michael V. Harper. Hope Is Not a Method. Times Business, Random House, 1996.
7. Meliza, Larry L. A Guide to Standardizing After Action Review (AAR) Aids. Report No. A348953. Orlando, FL: U.S. Army Research Institute, Field Unit, 1998 <www.stormingmedia.us/ 34/3489/A348953.html>.
8. Grove, Andrew S. Only the Paranoid Survive. HarperCollins Business, 1996.
9. Farson, Richard E., and Ralph Keyes. "The Failure-Tolerant Leader." The Harvard Business Review 1 Aug. 2002.

Notes

1. To be statistically accurate, the results may have included some projects that were finished early, but we risked the speculation that such cases (if any) would only represent a small fraction of the results.
2. The term *customer* here refers to the entity that requested the project or that will use its product, or more generally, for whom the project is being developed.
3. Fred Brooks [3] tells the story of a senior naval officer's last minute requirement after many months of negotiating features, schedule, and cost for a new navy helicopter. "It must be able to fly across the Atlantic," he stated. Only after laboriously explaining to him the enormous complexity that it added to the project was the officer willing to drop the requirement.
4. For an overview of basic software project risk analysis, see [4].
5. *Telephony* here refers to the provision of telephone-related services.
6. Yes, profitability is usually a good goal, too.
7. A useful overview of a generic, after-action review process, which can be easily adapted for software projects, is given in [6].
8. For an interesting discussion of a mistake-tolerant business culture, see [9].

About the Author

E.M. Bennatan is president of Advanced Project Solutions, Inc., where he assists development companies in software project catastrophe disentanglement, introduction of orderly process into ad-hoc organizations, organizational structure, simplification of existing processes, and management of multinational development. Bennatan spent many years as senior director at Motorola leading multinational design centers and developing wireless access systems. He was also responsible for program management of Motorola's High Availability Systems corporate-wide initiative. Before Motorola, Bennatan spent several years developing defense and aerospace systems in the U.S. and overseas. Bennatan has authored several articles and books, including "On Time Within Budget: Software Project Management Practices and Techniques," and is a senior member of the Institute of Electrical and Electronics Engineers and a member of the Association for Computing Machinery.

Advanced Project Solutions, Inc.
One Northfield Plaza
Northfield, IL 60093
Phone: (847) 441-3229
E-mail: bennatan@advancedps.com

Chapter 12

Metrics and Measurement

Exact scientific knowledge and methods are everywhere, sooner or later to replace rules-of-thumb.
—Frederick Taylor

Overview

As the software field has matured, considerable progress has been made in the field of software metrics and measurement. By collecting, analyzing, and using measurement data, software engineers and managers can better evaluate their status, track progress, analyze trends, and ensure success. They can get feedback on how well they are doing and, more importantly, forecast important trends and have sufficient lead times to do something about them.

Software metrics refer to a standard way of measuring some useful attribute of the software development effort. For example, rework rate, task size, cost and difficulty, and productivity are attributes that provide you insights into the nature of the work you have pursued. I like grouping things into separable baskets so I can understand their nature and impact they have on one another more fully. Breaking metrics considerations down by process, product, and people makes a lot of sense because it allows me to better comprehend the relationships that exist between these variables.

Process metrics are used to quantify useful attributes of the software development process and its environment. They provide you feedback as to whether or not the process is functioning optimally as they report on attributes like cycle time and rework rate. The goal is to do the correct job right the first time through the process. Metrics provide the feedback you need to achieve this goal.

Product metrics are used to quantify useful attributes of the products you are generating, including those delivered internally as well as externally. They provide feedback about the product you are generating and assess if it is acceptable as they report on attributes like usability, reliability, maintainability, and portability. The goal in any product development is to build the products your customers want and make sure they have the features and functionality that will satisfy the user. Metrics help you determine whether the product meets specifications, is ready to ship, and is fit for use.

People metrics are used to quantify useful attributes of the people who are generating the products using the processes, methods, and tools (the infrastructure) at their disposal. They provide you feedback as to whether the people are being productive and whether you are experiencing personnel problems as they report on attributes like turnover rates, productivity, and absenteeism. The goal with people is to keep them happy, motivated, and focused on the task at hand. Metrics provide you with the feedback you need to determine whether or not these goals are being realized.

The five papers that follow provide you insights into what metrics are and how to use them with measurement concepts to accomplish the goals set out above for the process, products, and people. They were selected to demonstrate what can be done when a metrics philosophy was adopted.

Article Summaries

Metrics and Management: A Primer, by Donald Reifer. This updated opening piece sets the stage for the papers that follow. After reviewing the metrics state of the technology, the paper looks at current trends to determine whether or not innovations being made in the field of measurement and modeling can help you better gauge your project's and organization's actual performance. The paper then discusses where metrics can help and hinder in getting the job done. Suggestions are offered along the way on how to overcome common problems so that you can use identified metrics and measurement concepts more effectively. The paper provides examples of how you can use metrics and measurement techniques to answer tough questions raised by customers, executives, and peer managers during software development.

Back to the Basics: Measurement and Metrics, by Tim Perkins, Roald Peterson, and Larry Smith. This article discusses what it takes to put a successful metrics and measurement program in place. It is tutorial in nature and highlights the use of proven tools and techniques like the GQM (Goal–Question–Metrics) paradigm to achieve business objectives. The article does not identify specific metrics. Instead, it provides you with a process for defining those that are meaningful for your firm. Valuable checklists are provided at the end of the paper to help you start up, implement, and evaluate a metrics initiative once you have put it into place within your organization.

Implementing Effective Software Metrics Programs, by Tracy Hall and Norman Fenton. This paper presents a more corporate view of the challenges associated with implementing a measurement program. The paper summarizes the results of a case study that looked at how two organizations, one dealing with embedded products and the other with information systems, addressed the challenges. Both organizations provide the reader insight into what works and what does not under different operational conditions. The most important result is the list of an emerging set of assessment criteria for a metrics program that appears in the finale of the paper.

Software Defect Reduction Top 10 List, by Barry W. Boehm and Victor R. Basili. This paper presents a list of ten defect truths or principles that were products of the experience factory established by the National Science Foundation (NSF) as part of their attempt to put software engineering on a more scientific basis. Each of the ten principles shared provides an insightful look at what you can do to improve the quality of your products through defect reduction. For example, you might adopt perspective-based reviews because the empirical data indicate that they catch 3.5 more defects than more open-ended, nondirected reviews.

Metrics for Small Projects: Experiences at the SED, by Ross Grable, Jacquelyn Jerigan, Casey Pogue, and Dale Divis. This paper summarizes the U.S. Army Missile System Command's experience in establishing a comprehensive metrics program for their programs. The metrics program was created to set in place a foundation for improvements being made in area project management and process improvement. The paper discusses how the Software Engineering Directorate (SED) approached implementing metrics, what metrics they selected, and what they did with them. Its aim is provide some guidance for those of you that are working on small development and maintenance projects.

Key Terms

Six terms, defined as follows, are important to understanding the topic of organization as used within this chapter:

1. **Error.** (1) The difference between the computed, observed, or measured value or condition and the true, theoretically correct, or specified value or condition; (2) An incorrect step, process, or data definition; (3) An incorrect result; and (4) a human action that produces an incorrect result.

2. **Indicators.** In management, a device that identifies a prescribed state of affairs relative to managerial or financial performance.

3. **Measurement.** In management, the process of collecting, analyzing, and reporting metrics data useful in assessing status, progress, and trends.

4. **Metric.** A quantitative measure of the degree to which a system, process or component possesses a given attribute. For example, error density is an indicator of software reliability.

5. **Productivity.** In economics, productivity is defined as the ratio of output to input. It allows you to determine how efficiently input resources (people, equipment, facilities, etc.) are used to produce outputs that you and your customers consider valuable.

6. **Quality.** The totality of features and characteristics of a product or service that bears on its ability to satisfy given needs or customer requirements. Reliability, which infers freedom from error, is one of these characteristics.

Acronyms

The following acronyms are used within the articles in this chapter:

CeBASE	Center for Empirically Based Software Engineering
DoD	Department of Defense
GQM	Goal–Question–Metric paradigm
NASA	National Aeronautics and Space Administration
NSF	National Science Foundation
PSM	Practical systems and software measurement

SED	Software Engineering Directorate (of the U.S. Army Missile Command)
SEI	Software Engineering Institute
SLOC/SM	Source lines of code/staff month (measure of productivity)
SSCI	Systems and Software Consortium Inc.

For Your Bookshelf

There are some excellent texts on the topic of metrics and measurement on the market today. My favorites are abstracted for you in the annotated Bibliography at the rear of this volume. McGarry et al.'s *Practical Software Measurement* highlights the contributions made in the field of measurement by the initiative of the same name. The books by Ebert et al. and Florac and Carleton present useful ideas on how to use metrics and measurements concepts to improve performance on projects and process improvement efforts. Grady and Caswell's *Software Metrics: Establishing a Company-Wide Program* continues to be one of my favorites on the topic. This classic provides you with a step-by-step process for setting up a metrics program within your firm.

The IEEE Computer Society has also published the following useful standards on metrics-and-measurement-related topics:

1. *IEEE Standard Dictionary of Measures to Produce Reliable Software*, 982.1 -1988.
2. *IEEE Guide for the Use of IEEE Standard Dictionary of Measures to Produce Reliable Software*, 982.2-1988.
3. *IEEE Standard Classification for Software Anomalies*, 1044-1993.
4. *IEEE Guide for Classification for Software Anomalies*, 1044.1-1995.
5. *IEEE Standard for Software Productivity Metrics*, 1045-1992.

Metrics and Management: A Primer

Donald J. Reifer

Introduction

We have made a lot of progress in the fields of metrics and measurement during the past decade. Many of us adopted metrics-based management methods as we tried to improve our processes, standardize our products, and professionalize our workforces. Such methods capture "hard" measurement data during our software development efforts that provide us with quantitative indicators of progress against plans and relative to customer expectations. They also provide us with indicators of trouble so we can prioritize issues and work them proactively as they occur.

When I think of metrics and measurement, I think of the statement, "You can't control what you can't measure."[1] I also think of the many papers and excellent books I have read on the topic of software measurement.[2,3,4] However, being the pragmatist that I am, I also think of the many experiences I have had relative to helping firms use this valuable technology operationally. Needless to say, there is a wide divergence between the theory of measurement and the current state of the practice.

Metrics and Measurement: Theory Meets Practice

Let us quickly review the state of the art in software metrics and measurement. During the past two decades, software project managers have defined many useful metrics to provide them with visibility into and control over their software development progress. They use progress-oriented metrics to investigate how well they are performing relative to their plans and to determine if they will realize their cost, schedule, and technical performance targets based upon trend analysis. They evaluate the quality of their products by looking at complexity and defect densities. They collect data naturally as a by-product of their processes and use these measurements to answer questions throughout the software life cycle. Examples of the questions they ask and the metrics and the data they use to answer them are provided in Table 1. As shown, managers at different levels of the enterprise ask different questions as the information goes up and down the organization structure.

Software project managers want to determine whether or not they are making suitable progress. They want to determine where they are relative to their budget, schedule, and technical performance. They use budgets and schedules as control devices. They want to pinpoint problems so that they can take action and fix them while there still is time to get things right. Their primary goal is to deliver an acceptable, high-quality product to their customers on schedule and within budget.

In contrast, managers of software organizations are concerned with organizational efficiency and team productivity. They have implemented metrics-based management methods to determine whether or not the processes they use and the products they generate are any good. The metrics they have adopted tend to look at the quantity of the work their staff has performed and the quality of the products generated by them. Examples of such organizational metrics and the data used to quantify them are again provided for your review in Table 1.

Managers of software-intensive enterprises (software firms, computer manufacturers, etc.) are primarily concerned with their profitability. They use standard business-oriented metrics to determine whether they are making money and being profitable. They look at things like how costs are allocated between budget centers (engineering, marketing, research, and development, etc.) to determine whether or not they are within the norms. They often benchmark their competitiveness and overall performance using metrics like price/earnings ratios to get a handle on enterprise-wide performance. Examples of such enterprise-oriented metrics are also provided in Table 1.

As you might expect, the metrics and measurement practices each of these levels of management employ in most enterprises is well behind that of the state of the art. Some of the many reasons for this phenomenon include:

Table 1. Examples of software metrics different people use

Category	Examples	How defined?	Questions answered
Project performance the budget?	Budget performance	Actuals versus targets	Is our rate of expenditure in line with
	Schedule performance	Rate of progress of milestone achievements	Is our rate of progress as planned?
	Earned value performance	Value earned for milestones achieved versus budget set for work to be performed and actual expenditures	Is the progress we are making commensurate with our rate of expenditure and our budget?
	Technical performance	Indicators like: • Requirements growth • Size growth	Are we making suitable progress relative to the indicators? For example, have our requirements stabilized or are they volatile? Is growth under control?
Process performance	Rework rate	Number of times it takes you to get it right	Is the process working the first time through?
	Defect rates	Number of defects discovered and removed as a function of time	Are defects being detected versus fixed at anticipated rates?
Product quality	Product complexity	Cyclomatic number or some similar metric	Is the product overly complex?
	Defect density	Number of defects as a function of size	Is the defect density as expected?
Personnel performance	Personal productivity	Individual output as function of inputs used to generate them	Are staff members generating products at anticipated rates?
Organizational performance	Process maturity	SEI rating using either the discrete or continuous models of the CMMI	Are projects using organizational processes?
	Product quality	Complaint rate	Are customers happy with the product?
	Productivity	Group output as function of inputs used to generate them	Are teams producing at anticipated rates?
Enterprise performance	Profitability	Price/earnings ratio	Is the enterprise profitable?
	Return on equity	Earnings as a function of capital used to generate it	Are investments generating acceptable earnings?
	Cost of sales	Dollars spent on sales as a function of revenue earned	Is the cost of sales acceptable?
	Competitiveness	Productivity versus benchmarks or competitive figures	Are we as productive as our competition?

- There is no standardization in the industry relative to what metrics to collect and what software measurements to capture. Definitions for key terms vary (e.g., what is a line of code?), as do the techniques different managers use to gain visibility into and control over their progress.

- It is often difficult, time-consuming and expensive to collect the data needed to quantify these metrics. If data collection is done manually, the task can impede the software development team's progress because it forces them to perform a lot of extra work that is viewed as not contributing directly to product development.

- It takes considerable time to insert a metrics-based management philosophy operationally. Because metrics requires that good management practices be in place first, many enterprises need to worry about putting basic project management practices (e.g., planning, tracking, configuration management) into place before metrics. That is why the SEI suggests that organizations wait until they are mature before inserting metrics practices.

- The state of software technology is rapidly progressing. As discussed in this volume, new paradigms and more agile methods are being used as firms focus on speeding products to market. As a result, metrics that we used in the past to determine the progress of large projects are not always applicable in this new environment. In addition, new size metrics like object points and Web objects[5] are gaining popularity. New metrics may be needed for these reasons. Such metrics may force you to reeducate your workforce. Such reeducation adds to the burden because it takes time and effort to successfully perform.

Current Trends

Sprinkled throughout this tutorial are examples of metrics and best measurement practices used by project and functional software managers. These can be classified simply using the "3 Ps of software management" organized under the headings of process, product, and people. When you look more closely at Table 1, you will see that that is what I tried to accomplish. Use of such metrics and measurement concepts is commonplace in mature organizations. Most of the firms that I have worked with that are CMM Level 3 and above on the SEI rating scale tend to have excellent metrics programs in place. However, standardization of the metrics used to assess progress and pinpoint problems across organizations has not been achieved. The Practical Systems and Software Measurement6 program can help you do this. As indicated in the article in this section, this initiative provides those seeking to put measurement programs in place with a structure for deciding on metrics and an action framework for accomplishing this important task.

I am glad to report that good progress is being made in the field of metrics and measurement. As shown in the Bibliography, books, articles, and experience reports are readily available for those of you who want to venture forth in this area. In addition, a wide range of metrics have been defined that have been used operationally by firms for improved visibility and control purposes. In addition, many organizations are willing to share their experience, good or bad, as part of a fact-finding or competitive-benchmarking exercise.[6] The major issues you face in metrics and measurement tend to be more management-based in scope than technical. They revolve around psychological issues associated with the misuse of numbers and the costs associated with data collection and reporting.

Metrics Make Good Managers Better

I believe metrics and measurement can provide managers who are ready to adopt them with valuable insights. The trick is to know what you are ready for and what you can adopt with minimum effort. All too often, organizations rush to put a metrics program in place before they figure out what they want to measure and why. Adopting such an approach has and will continue to lead to disaster. Instead, managers need to focus their metrics programs on answering questions that they are concerned about. The six key lessons we have learned about using metrics and measurement to improve one's ability to manage are summarized as follows:

1. *Make measurement part of the system.* Weave metrics and measurement into the infrastructure you use to manage your projects. Make use of numbers a natural part of the way you run your project. For example, have each of your work groups report rate of progress information weekly up the management chain. For example, if a group's rate of progress is 10% behind expectations, have the group leader report why to his or her boss.
2. *Capture metrics and measurement data at their source.* Make collection and reporting of metrics and measurement data easy by collecting the data at its source as part of your software trouble reporting, change management, and progress measurement systems. Collect the core measures associated with your metrics using industry standards to guide your definitions.
3. *Understand what the numbers mean.* Precisely define what the numbers mean before you use them. Get down to details. Make sure that your numbers relate to your past performance by correlating your experience and using it as a benchmark. Remember that senior managers will never forget a number. Therefore, be careful that you use numbers carefully and wisely.
4. *Set meaningful thresholds.* Delegate management authority by using the numbers to establish thresholds for action. For example, let group leaders decide how to recoup from a problem when budget and schedule performance for a subprogram are 10% out of line. Elevate the action to the next level of management when performance at the program level is 10% off.
5. *Once validated, believe the numbers.* After you validate the numbers, believe them and use them effectively. You will find that software engineers can come up with the most inventive reasons for running late. "Trust me," they will say, "we will get there." Be skeptical of such statements when the cost and schedule-to-complete forecasts show that there is no way that they will be able to correct their performance. Instead, update your plans and allocate your reserves.
6. *Use the numbers to make decisions.* Once you believe the numbers, you are ready to use them to provide insight into problems and help make decisions. Realize that numbers are not infallible. They can portray the symptoms, not the root cause of the problems. For example, you may be behind schedule and under budget because you are having difficulties staffing the project up.

Are You Ready for Metrics and Measurement

After reading this, you are probably asking, "Am I ready for metrics and measurement?" Let us look at the following criteria for you to use to determine whether or not using the numbers to help manage will help or hinder you in getting the job done:

- *Level of process maturity.* Metrics and measurement will typically help those firms rated at the higher levels of process maturity implement the statistical process and quality controls needed to raise their SEI rating to Level 4 organizationally. Firms rated lower than Level 3 often have more basic problems at the project level to be worried about than metrics and measurement.

- *Availability of methods and tools.* Organizations who plan to use proven methods and production quality tools to define and implement their metrics and measurement program will have a higher probability of success. No matter how hard you try, you will have difficulties if you have to capture a lot of measurement data manually.

- *Degree of standardization.* Organizations that have spent time defining standardized metrics and measurements (i.e., those that are precisely defined) are not likely to get into trouble with counting conventions. They can also benchmark their performance against others in their industry relatively easily because comparisons to norms are simple to make.

- *Ease of understanding.* A simple and understandable set of core metrics that look at the things that matter to management and provide insight into problems and progress works for most people. Those who overwhelm management with too much data fail to get their support because they fail to communicate the root causes of the problems.

- *Ease of use.* Just generating numbers is not what the practice of measurement is all about. Metrics captured should be presented in such a way that they answer the key questions your managers are asking about project progress, product quality, organizational productivity, and/or enterprise profitability.

Sometimes, premature adoption of a metrics and measurement program can lead to more pain than benefits. For example, I recently watched a major firm try to adopt function points as their preferred sizing measure. They published a policy stating that function points were to be used across divisions. Unfortunately, they neither prepared their workforce for the switch over to function point usage nor examined the issues associated with capturing and counting before making the transition. They failed to get commitment as a result and nobody paid any attention to the numbers they published. They could have avoided the problems by carefully introducing the technology after they had readied their staff to accept it.

Using Metrics and Measurement Effectively

If you are interested in establishing a metrics capability, I would recommend that you employ the ten-step approach that follows. I also suggest that you look the paper that I have included in this tutorial[7] to help guide your development of a workable framework. This approach advanced in these papers is consistent with the recommendations in Grady and Caswell's book,[8] which describes Hewlett-Packard's experience in metrics insertion:

1. Define your measurement objectives and strategy.
2. Assign responsibility for metrics. Establish a procedure and get the stakeholders involved in defining what is needed and how to put recommendations into practice.
3. Define the initial metrics to collect and precisely define what your terms mean.
4. Establish an education and training program for metrics and measurement.
5. Baseline your organizational norms for this metrics set using whatever data you have at your disposal.
6. Sell the metrics program by educating management about what the numbers mean.
7. Acquire tools for automated data collection and analysis and make them part of your software engineering environment.
8. Publicize your successes and encourage an exchange of ideas and data across organizations.
9. Create a metrics database. Use the database to develop benchmarks and calibrate your estimating models.
10. Be flexible and establish ways to change the program based upon experience.

These steps allow you to systematically insert a metrics program into your firm. However, let me warn you about the psychological factors associated with a metrics program. It is important to not use metrics data as a rating tool. Your people may respond to any inappropriate use of metrics by sabotaging the numbers and manipulating data to make themselves look good.

Take the time to educate and train your staff so that they understand what you are trying to do and will support you. Use the metrics to fix the processes that cause the problem. Provide feedback to those generating the numbers so that they see the fruits of their efforts and can take advantage of them.

Summary, Conclusions, and Recommendations

Metrics and measurement is a very important topic. The numbers supply you with the hard data that you need to manage your projects. You can also use these data to satisfy your management's hunger for measures of progress, organizational productivity, and enterprise profitability. As stated in this and the rest of the papers that follow in this chapter, metrics use can have a profound impact on your ability to effectively manage your software efforts. From a positive point of view, they can be used to confirm that you are making suitable progress and will deliver an acceptable product on schedule and within budget. They can also provide you with insight into negative trends so you can take action and head off potential problems before they occur. From a negative viewpoint, measurement can be a costly and time-consuming activity that can generate numbers that are easily misunderstood and often misused. Fear of this misuse can cause your staff to take actions to sabotage or manipulate the numbers in their own best interest.

In conclusion, I would like to offer the following three recommendations when it comes to metrics and measurement:

- If you are an immature organization per the SEI Software CMM rating scale (e.g., Level 1 or 2), focus your organizational improvement efforts on getting your processes and building codes in order before taking on the issues associated with metrics and measurement. As I have repeatedly stated in this paper, you have more fundamental issues to worry about than metrics. However, even at these low levels of maturity, project managers can still use metrics and measurement techniques effectively to gain insight, improve visibility, reduce risk, and improve control.
- If you decide to start up a metrics initiative, do so systematically and carefully. Start by defining your goals. Then establish the infrastructure you need to get organizational buy-in for your recommendations. Then try using the metrics before making them your standard.
- Get your management to sponsor you and spend the time needed to define metrics that make sense and measurements that are easy to capture and understand. Make the business case for metrics.[9] Use the savings that will accrue as control is improved to justify your cause.
- Finally, build from the basics to more advanced metrics iteratively by relating what you measure to the work your people perform. In other words, make your metrics and measurements a natural way you conduct your business.

I hope you enjoy reading the articles that follow in this tutorial. They were selected to whet your appetite. They address a number of issues pertinent to metrics programs, like metrics for small projects. As already noted, many interesting articles and books on the topic are now available (see the annotated Bibliography that I have included at the end of this volume for some pointers to recommended readings). I encourage you to check some of them out.

References

1. DeMarco, Tom, *Controlling Software Projects,* Yourdon Press, 1982, p. 3.
2. Lawrence H. Putnam and Ware Myers, *Executive Briefing: Controlling Software Development,* IEEE Computer Society, 1996.
3. Department of Defense, *The Program Manager's Guide to Software Acquisition Best Practices,* Software Acquisition Best Practices Initiative, 1995.
4. Capers Jones, *Applied Software Measurement,* McGraw-Hill, 1991.
5. Donald J. Reifer, "Web Development: Estimating Quick-to-Market Software," *IEEE Software,* December 2000, pp. 57–64 (included in Chapter 6 of this tutorial).
6. Robert C. Camp, *Benchmarking,* ASQC Quality Press, 1989.
7. Tracy Hall and Norman Fenton, "Implementing Effective Software Metrics Programs," *IEEE Software,* March/April 1997.
8. Robert B. Grady and Deborah L. Caswell, *Software Metrics: Establishing a Company-Wide Program,* Prentice-Hall, 1987.
9. Donald J. Reifer, *Making the Software Business Case: Improvement by the Numbers,* Addison-Wesley, 2001.

Back to the Basics: Measurement and Metrics

Tim Perkins and Roald Peterson
Software Technology Support Center/SAIC

Larry Smith
Software Technology Support Cente

Measurements and metrics are key tools to understanding the behaviors, successes, and failures of our programs and projects. This article highlights the basic principles of measures and metrics and encourages the reader to improve his or her use of these tools. The article is adapted from [1].

According to Tom DeMarco, "You cannot control what you cannot measure" [2]. Imagine going on a road trip of over a thousand miles. This is easy because most of us really have done this several times. Now imagine that your car has no speedometer, no odometer, no fuel gauge, and no temperature indicator. Imagine also that someone has removed the mile markers and road signs from all the roads between you and your destination. Just to complete the experiment, remove your watch.

What was once a simple journey becomes an endless series of guesses, fraught with risks. How do you know where you are, how far you have gone, or how far you have to go? When do you gas the car? Should you stop here or try to make the next town before nightfall? You could break down, run out of gas, be stranded, take the wrong road, bypass your destination, or waste time trying to find your location and how to reach your destination. Clearly, some method of measuring certain indicators of progress is essential for achieving a goal.

Imagine again going on a road trip. This time the cockpit of the car is filled with instruments. In addition to what you have been accustomed to in the past, there are now the following gauges:

- Speed in feet and yards per second, and as a percentage of c (light speed).
- Oil pressure in millibars.
- Estimated time to deplete or recharge the battery.
- Fuel burn rate and fuel weight.
- Oil viscosity and transparency indicators.
- Antifreeze temperature and pressure.
- Engine efficiency.
- Air conditioning system parameters (pressures, temperatures, efficiency).
- Elevation, rate of climb, heading, accelerometers for all directions.
- Indicators for distance and time to destination and from origin.
- Inside air temperatures for eight different locations in the car.

Also, there are instruments to count how many cars pass, vibration levels, and sound pressure levels within and outside the car. There are weather indicators for outside temperature, humidity, visibility, cloud ceiling, ambient light level, true and relative wind speeds and directions, warning indicators for approaching storms and seismic activity, etc. Along the roads will be markers for every hundredth mile and signs announcing exits every quarter mile for five miles before an exit is reached. Signs in five-mile-per-hour increments will announce speed changes.

> *"Metrics are measurements of different aspects of an endeavor that help us determine whether we are progressing toward the goal of that endeavor."*

To some, this may seem like a dream come true, at least the cockpit part. However, careful consideration will soon reveal that the driver will be inundated and quickly overwhelmed with unnecessary, confusing data. Measurement, in itself, is no prescription for achieving a goal. It can even make the goal unattainable.

Introduction

Metrics are measurements of different aspects of an endeavor that help us determine whether we are progressing toward the goal of that endeavor. They are used extensively as management tools to provide some calculated, observable basis for making decisions. Some common metrics for projects include schedule deviation, remaining budget and expenditure rate, presence or absence of specific types of problems, and milestones achieved. Without some way to accurately track

budget, time, and work progress, a project manager can only make decisions in the dark. Without a way to track errors and development progress, software development managers cannot make meaningful improvements in their processes. The more inadequate our metrics program, the closer we are to herding black cats in a dark room. The right metrics, used in the right way, are absolutely essential for project success.

Too many metrics are used simply because they have been used for years and people believe they might be useful [3]. Each metric should have a purpose providing support to a specific decision-making process. Leadership too often dictates metrics. A team under the direction of leadership should develop them. Metrics should be used not only by leadership but also by all the various parts of an organization or development team. Obviously, not all metrics that are useful to managers are useful to the accounting people or to developers. Metrics must be tailored to the users. The use of metrics should be defined by a program describing what metrics are needed, by whom and how they are to be measured and calculated. The level of success or failure of your project will depend in large part on your use or misuse of metrics – on how you plan, implement, and evaluate an overall metrics program.

While this article introduces and describes key metrics ideas and processes and can point you in the right direction, it is recommended that you gain more insight, depth, and specific examples by downloading and reading the material listed in "Additional Reading" in the online version of this article at <www.stsc.hill.af.mil/crosstalk>. Of particular value to Department of Defense users is [4] better known as the "Practical Software and System Measurement Guidebook," where a more specific and detailed terminology and methodology can be found.

Process Description

Metrics are not defined and used solely

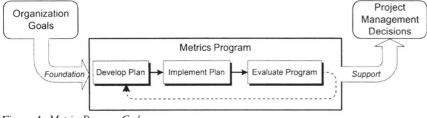

Figure 1: *Metrics Program Cycle*

Figure 2: *Basili's Goal, Question, Metric Paradigm*

but are part of an overall metrics program. This program should be based on the organization's goals and should be carefully planned, implemented, and regularly evaluated for effectiveness. The metrics program is used as a decision support tool.

In relation to project management metrics, if the information provided through a particular metric is not needed for determining status or direction of the project, it is probably not needed at all. Process-related metrics, however, should not necessarily be dismissed so harshly since they indicate data useful in improving performance across repeated applications. The role of the metrics program in the organization and its three major activities are shown in Figure 1.

Developing a Metrics Program Plan

The first activity in developing a metrics program is planning. Metrics planning is usually based on the goal-question-metric (GQM) paradigm developed by Victor Basili (see Figure 2). The GQM paradigm is based on the following key concepts [3]:

1. Processes, including software development, program management, etc., have associated goals.
2. Each goal leads to one or more questions regarding the accomplishment of the goal.
3. Each question leads to one or more metrics needed to answer the question.

4. Each metric requires two or more measurements to produce the metric (e.g., miles per hour, budget spent vs. budget planned, temperature vs. operating limits, actual vs. predicted execution time, etc.).
5. Measurements are selected to provide data that will accurately produce the metric.

The planning process is comprised of the three sub-activities implementing the GQM paradigm and one that defines the data collection process. Each of these is discussed in the following sections.

Table 1 shows two examples of goals and their related questions and metrics. Note that there could be one or more metrics associated with each question. As the initial list of questions and metrics is written and discussed, the goal is usually refined, which then causes a further refinement in the accompanying questions and metrics.

Define Goals

Planning begins with well defined, validated goals. Goals should be chosen and worded in such a way that they are verifiable; that is, their accomplishment can be measured or observed in some way. Goals such as meeting a specific delivery schedule are easily observable. Requirements stating "software shall be of high quality" are highly subjective and need further definition before they can be used

as valid goals.

You may have to refine or even derive your own goals from loosely written project objectives. The selection or acceptance of project goals will determine how you manage your project, and where you put your emphasis. Goals should meet the following criteria:

- They should support the successful accomplishment of the project's overall or system-level goals.
- They should be verifiable, or measurable in some way.
- They should be defined in enough detail to be unambiguous.

Derive Questions

Each goal should evoke questions about how its accomplishment can be measured. For example, completing a project within a certain budget may evoke questions such as these: What is my total budget? How much of my budget is left? What is my current spending rate? Am I within the limits of my spending plan?

Goals related to software time, size, quality, or reliability constraints would evoke different questions. It should be remembered that different levels and groups within the organization might require different information to measure the progress in which they are interested. Questions should be carefully selected and refined to support the previously defined project goals. Questions should exhibit the following traits:

- Questions only elicit information that indicates progress toward or completion of a specific goal.
- Questions can be answered by providing specific information. (They are unambiguous.)
- Questions ask all the information needed to determine progress or completion of the goal.

Once questions have been derived that elicit only the complete set of information needed to determine progress, metrics must be developed that will provide that information.

Develop Metrics

Metrics are the information needed to answer the derived questions. Each question can be answered by one or more metrics. These metrics are defined and associated with their appropriate questions and goals. Each metric requires two or more measurements. Measurements are those data that must be collected and analyzed to produce the metric.

Measurements are selected that will provide the necessary information with the least impact to the project workflow.

Table 1: *Goals and Their Related Questions and Metrics*

	Common Example	Product Example
Goal	*Run competitively in a 10 kilometer (10K) race.*	*Improve customer satisfaction with the current release of the product.*
Questions and Metrics	*What is a competitive time for an individual of my age and rank?* • Age and ranking figures for run times.	*Are customers buying our product?* • Sales rate (up or down) as compared with competing products, product return rate, etc.
	Am I capable of running at a competitive time? • Time to complete 10K, post-run recovery time, etc., repeated over each practice run.	*What are the key attributes of customer satisfaction?* • Metrics related to reliability, safety, functionality, performance, etc.
	What current injuries are impacting my ability to race? • Injury prognosis and recovery time.	*How satisfied are our customers (in relation to the above attributes)?* • Customer survey data, defects reported, etc.
	Am I sustaining my health and weight by eating and sleeping properly? • Hours of sleep per night, weight, dietary intake, etc.	*How are we resolving problems that affect customer satisfaction?* • Defect resolution rate, post-release defect density, etc.

Figure 3 summarizes the process of turning measurements into goal status.

Choosing measures is a critical and nontrivial step. Measurements that require too much effort or time can be counterproductive and should be avoided. Remember, just because something can be measured does not mean it should be. An in-depth introduction to measurements, "Goal-Driven Software Measurement – A Guidebook," has been published by the Software Engineering Institute and is available as a free download [5].

In addition to choosing what type of data to collect or measure, the methods of processing or analysis must also be defined in this step. How do you turn the measurements into a meaningful metric? How does the metric then answer the question? The analysis method should be carefully documented. Do not assume that it is obvious.

This activity is complete when you know exactly what type of data you are going to collect (what you are going to measure and in what units), how you are going to turn that data into metrics (analysis methods), and in what form (units, charts, colors, etc.) the metrics will be delivered.

Define the Collection Process

The final step of the metrics planning process is to determine how the metrics will be collected. At a minimum, this part of the plan should include the following:

- What data is to be collected?
- What will be the source of the data?
- How is it to be measured?
- Who will perform the measurement?
- How frequently should the data be collected?
- Who will the derived metrics be delivered to, and in what format?

Implementing a Metrics Program

A good rule of thumb to follow when starting a measurement program is to keep the number of measurements between five and 10. If the metrics program is well planned, implementing the program should be reduced to simply following the plan. There are four activities in the metrics implementation cycle, shown in Figure 4 [6].

Data is collected at specific intervals according to the plan. Data is then validated by examining it to ensure it is the result of accurate measurements, and that the data collection is consistent among members of the group if more than one individual is collecting it. In other words, is it being measured in the

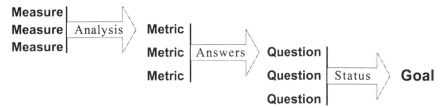

Figure 3: *Goal, Question, Metrics Examples*

same way, at the same time, etc.? Once the data is determined to be valid, the metrics are derived by analyzing the data as documented in the metrics program plan. Metrics are then delivered to appropriate individuals and groups for evaluation and decision-making activities. This process is repeated until the project is complete.

Evaluating a Metrics Program

It is likely that a metrics program will not be perfect in its first iteration. Soon after its initial implementation and at regular

---

"Too many metrics are used simply because they have been used for years, and people believe they might be useful."

---

intervals after that, the metrics program should be evaluated to determine if it is meeting the needs of the metrics users, and if its implementation is flowing smoothly. If metrics prove to be insufficient or superfluous, the program plan should be modified to provide the necessary information and remove any unneeded activity. The objective of a metrics program is to provide sufficient information to support project success while keeping the metrics program as simple and unobtrusive as possible. The following are areas that should be considered when reviewing a metrics program:

- Adequacy of current metrics.
- Superfluity of any metrics or measures.
- Interference of measurements with project work.
- Accuracy of analysis results.
- Data collection intervals.

- Simplification of the metrics program.
- Changes in project or organization goals.

Metrics Repository

A final consideration is establishing a metrics repository where metrics history is kept for future projects. The availability of past metrics data can be a gold mine of information for calibration, planning estimates, benchmarking, process improvement, calculating return on investment, etc. At a minimum, the repository should store the following:

- Description of projects and their objectives.
- Metrics used.
- Reasons for using the various metrics.
- Actual metrics collected over the life of each project.
- Data indicating the effectiveness of the metrics used.

Measurement and Metrics Checklist

This checklist is provided to assist you in developing a metrics program, and in defining and using metrics. If you cannot answer a question affirmatively, you should carefully examine the situation and take appropriate action. The checklist items are divided into three areas: developing, implementing, and reviewing a metrics program.

Developing a Metrics Program

☐ Is your use of metrics based on a documented metrics program plan?

☐ Are you using the GQM paradigm in developing your metrics?

☐ Are your metrics based on measurable or verifiable project goals?

☐ Do your goals support the overall system-level goals?

☐ Are your goals well defined and unambiguous?

☐ Does each question elicit only information that indicates progress toward or completion of a specific goal?

Figure 4: *Metrics Implementation Cycle*

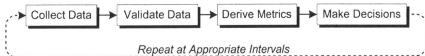

- ☐ Can questions be answered by providing specific information? (Is it unambiguous?)
- ☐ Do the questions ask for all the information needed to determine progress or completion of the goal?
- ☐ Is each metric required for specific decision-making activities?
- ☐ Is each metric derived from two or more measurements (e.g., remaining budget vs. schedule)?
- ☐ Have you documented the analysis methods used to calculate the metrics?
- ☐ Have you defined those measures needed to provide the metrics?
- ☐ Have you defined the collection process (i.e., what, how, who, when, how often, etc.)?

Metrics Program Implementation

- ☐ Does your implementation follow the metrics program plan?
- ☐ Is data collected the same way each time it is collected?
- ☐ Are documented analysis methods followed when calculating metrics?
- ☐ Are metrics delivered in a timely manner to those who need them?
- ☐ Are metrics being used in the decision-making process?

Metrics Program Evaluation

- ☐ Are the metrics sufficient?
- ☐ Are all metrics or measures required, that is, non-superfluous?
- ☐ Are measurements allowing project work to continue without interference?
- ☐ Does the analysis produce accurate results?
- ☐ Is the data collection interval appropriate?
- ☐ Is the metrics program as simple as it can be while remaining adequate?
- ☐ Has the metrics program been modified to adequately accommodate any project or organizational goal changes?◆

References

1. Software Technology Support Center. Condensed Version (4.0) of Guidelines for Successful Acquisition and Management of Software-Intensive Systems. Hill Air Force Base, Utah: Software Technology Support Center, Feb. 2003.
2. DeMarco, Tom. Controlling Software Projects. New York: Yourden Press, 1982.
3. Perkins, Timothy K. "The Nine-Step Metrics Program." CROSSTALK, Feb. 2001 <www.stsc.hill.af.mil/crosstalk/2001/feb/perkins.asp>.
4. Bailey, Elizabeth, et al. Practical Software Measurement: A Foundation for Objective Project Management Ver. 4.0b1. Severna Park, MD: Practical Software and Systems Measurement, Mar. 2003 <www.psmsc.com/PSMGuide.asp> under "Products."
5. Park, Robert E., et al. Goal-Driven Software Measurement – A Guidebook. Pittsburgh, PA: Software Engineering Institute, Aug. 1996 <www.sei.cmu.edu/publications/documents/96.reports/96.hb.002html>.
6. Augustine, Thomas, et al. "An Effective Metrics Process Model." CROSSTALK June 1999 <www.stsc.hill.af.mil/crosstalk/1999/jun/augustine.asp>.

About the Authors

Tim Perkins has been involved in software process improvement for the past 11 years, including leading the effort to initiate software process improvement at the then five Air Force Air Logistics Centers. As the Software Engineering Process Group leader at the Software Engineering Division at Hill Air Force Base, Utah, he led the division in reaching Capability Maturity Model® (CMM®) Level 3. The division has gone on to achieve CMM Level 5. Perkins is Acquisition Professional Development Program Level 3 certified in Project Management and System Planning, Research, Development, and Engineering.

Software Technology Support Center
OO-ALC/MASE
6022 Fir Ave.
Bldg. 1238
Hill AFB, UT 84056
Phone: (801) 775-5736
Fax: (801) 777-8069
E-mail: tim.perkins@hill.af.mil

Roald E. Peterson is a senior systems engineer with Science Applications International Corporation. He has 22 years of electronic systems development experience, specializing in communications, architecture, and software development. Peterson was an editor and contributor for the "Guidelines for the Successful Acquisition and Management (GSAM) of Software Intensive Systems" and is the author of the "Condensed GSAM Handbook." He has a bachelor's degree in physics and master's degrees in computer resources management and electrical engineering.

Science Applications
International Corporation
920 W. Heritage Park Blvd.
Suite 210
Layton, UT 84041
Phone: (801) 774-4705
Fax: (801) 728-0300
E-mail: roald.e.peterson@saic.com

Larry Smith is a senior software engineer and project manager for the Air Force's Software Technology Support Center at Hill Air Force Base, Utah. He provides software engineering, software process improvement, and project management consulting for the U. S. Air Force and other Department of Defense organizations as well as commercial and nonprofit organizations. Smith is a faculty member at the University of Phoenix. He is also certified by the Project Management Institute as a Project Management Professional. Smith has a bachelor's degree in electrical engineering and a master's degree in computer science.

Software Technology Support Center
OO-ALC/MASE
6022 Fir Ave.
Bldg. 1238
Hill AFB, UT 84056
Phone: (801) 777-9712
Fax: (801) 777-8069
E-mail: larry.smith4@hill.af.mil

Implementing Effective Software Metrics Programs

TRACY HALL, *University of Westminster*
NORMAN FENTON, *City University*

Increasingly, organizations are foregoing an ad hoc approach to metrics in favor of complete metrics programs. The authors identify consensus requirements for metric program success and examine how programs in two organizations measured up.

Until relatively recently, software measurement in the Western world has been a rather *ad hoc* affair focused on measuring individual, product-based software attributes. This rather one-dimensional approach to software measurement is now changing. Increasingly, organizations are integrating complete software metrics programs into their software development processes. That is, they are habitually using a balanced range of product and process measures in their micro and macro decision making systems.

There are several reasons that partially explain the recent move toward complete metrics programs. Not only has the process improvement bandwagon raised a general awareness of metrics, but to reach higher Capability Maturity Model levels, organizations must incorporate metrics into their development process. Moreover, there now appears to be consensus about the need for

Reprinted from *IEEE Software,* March/April 1997.

Characteristic	Embedded Systems	Information Systems
General profile	Engineering company	Large public-sector organization (in the process of transferring into the private sector)
Applications	Defense-related Embedded control software 90% of applications are safety-critical	Online data processing systems
Development environment	Variety of advanced approaches, including formal methods and code, analyzing tools	State-of-art in using new methods Keen on using project management methods and tools
Quality framework	Strong (on the surface), but suboptimal use of reviews and inspections AQAP certified (defense quality certificate)	Well-used framework Consistent use of basic quality controls In the process of seeking software quality certification
Management framework	Very complex staff structure Steep hierarchy Low morale score Two-year pay freeze High staff attrition rate	Simple staff structure Flattish hierarchy Average morale score Stable staff group

metrics programs within improvement initiatives.[1] However, perhaps the most important positive push for metrics programs was the publication of Robert Grady and Deborah Caswell's 1987 book, *Software Metrics: Establishing a Company Wide Program.*[2] The book—and its 1992 revision[3]—describes the Hewlett-Packard software metrics program. Grady and Caswell identify many important, and usually neglected, organizational issues surrounding software measurement. In particular, they proposed, along with other commentators,[3-5] various criteria for achieving a successful metrics program. After studying this and other research, we identified a consensus on requirements for metric program success.

♦ *Incremental implementation.* Implementing a metrics program over time holds significantly less risk than a "big bang" approach.

♦ *Transparency.* The metrics program must be obvious to practitioners. Practitioners must understand what data is being collected, why it is being collected, and how it is being used.

♦ *Usefulness.* The usefulness of metrics data should be obvious to all practitioners. If usefulness is not transparent (or, worse, if the data is not actually useful), practitioners will collect data without enthusiasm and the data will probably lack validity.

♦ *Developer participation.* Developers should participate in designing the metrics program. With high levels of developer participation, buy-in is more likely, as is the implementation of a more incisive metrics program.

♦ *Metrics integrity.* Practitioners should have confidence in the collected data. They should believe it is sensible to collect, accurately collected, and not being "fiddled."

♦ *Feedback.* When practitioners get feedback on the data they collect, it gives them a clear indication that the data is being used rather than going into a black hole. This makes practitioners more likely to view the program positively. Commentators suggest several feedback mechanisms including newsletters, newsgroups, and graphical posters.

♦ *Automated data collection.* This should be done wherever possible. Minimizing extra work for developers also minimizes developer resistance to metrics. It also means that the data collected is more likely to be valid.

♦ *Practitioner training.* Case studies show that a metrics program that has a base of trained practitioners is more likely to be successful. Appropriate training must be targeted at all levels in a company and should range from awareness raising to training in statistical analysis techniques.

♦ *Gurus and champions.* Organizations can increase practitioners' initial enthusiasm by bringing in an external metrics guru (Hewlett-Packard, for example, brought in Barry Boehm; Contel brought in Dieter Rombach). Organizations should also appoint internal metrics champions to help with the difficult and arduous task of sustaining a metrics program.[6]

♦ *Dedicated metrics team.* Responsibility for the metrics program should be assigned to specific individuals.

♦ *Goal-oriented approach.* It is very important that companies collect data for a specific purpose. Usually the data will be for monitoring the attainment of an improvement goal. Unsuccessful or ineffective programs collect data for no specific reason and find they have no use for the data they have collected. The Goal-Question-Metric model[7] has been highly popular among companies implementing a goal-oriented approach to measurement.

On the last two factors, the broader software engineering community does not entirely agree. Although there is consensus on the need for some kind of dedicated metrics team, there is no clear agreement on how

TABLE 2
RELEVANT STAFF AND RESPONSE RATE

Organization	Staff Directly Affected by Metrics Program	Number Responding to Questionnaire			Response Rate (%)
		Total	Manager	Developer	
Embedded systems	24	20	10	10	83
Information systems	125	103	48	55	82

centralized it should be, nor whether metrics should be the team's sole activity. Questions have also been raised about the GQM approach.[8] For example, Hetzel highlights the fact that GQM encourages organizations to use data that is likely to be difficult to collect.[9] This directly contradicts other advice on metrics programs, which encourages organizations to use available or easily collected data.

Notwithstanding these minor doubts, the factors above appear to be commonsense advice on implementing a metrics program. However, these factors are apparently proposed on the basis of either anecdotal evidence or single program experiences.

We spent six months conducting an independent study of these factors at work in two organizations. Here, we present quantitative data that describes practitioner experiences of metrication. This data generally supports—but occasionally contradicts—existing anecdotal evidence about metrics programs.

Although both of our case study programs were structurally similar, one was judged to be successful (by the organization and by us), and the other was judged as not yet successful (by the organization's metrics group and by us). Despite the fact that anecdotal evidence suggests that most metrics programs are unsuccessful, with a few notable exceptions (such as a 1993 study by Ross Jeffery and Mike Berry[10]), only successful programs are typically reported.

Our ultimate aim in this article,

which follows on our earlier work,[11] is to present the critical success and failure factors associated with the two metrics programs. In particular, we report on each organization's metrics implementation strategy, quantify the extent to which they implemented various metrics, and detail the ongoing management of the metrics programs.

THE STUDY

Our case study involved two organizations which, for reasons of commercial confidentiality, we refer to as Embedded Systems (ES) and Information Systems (IS). Both organizations

♦ have more than 10,000 employees, are more than 20 years old, and have complex internal bureaucracies;

♦ have a large software development function, with more than 400 software staff;

♦ are fully dependent on in-house software systems to support or enhance their main (nonsoftware) products;

♦ have a progressive approach toward new development methods and tools;

♦ have mature quality programs and usually consider the software they produce to be high quality; and

♦ have had a metrics program for between two and three years.

Some metricating success or failure factors may result from organization-specific issues; Table 1 gives the organizational context of each metrics program.

Phase one: fact finding. At each organi-

zation, we started with a few fact-finding interviews with middle managers who had a high level of corporate responsibility for the metrics program. We designed this fact-finding phase to identify the context, framework, and content of the "officially" implemented metrics program. Managers commonly have an inaccurate picture of what is really happening "on the ground." Thus, we designed this phase to establish what state the organization believed its metrics program to be in. In particular, we found out about the organization (such as number of employees in various activities), applications developed, development environment, metrics collected and how they were used, and implementation and management of metrics. We used the results of phase one as a baseline for phase two.

Phase two: data collection. In phase two we wanted to find out what was really happening in the metrics program. We managed to get serious input from nearly all the relevant staff by distributing detailed questionnaires to all managers and developers affected by metrics.

The aims of the questionnaire were to

♦ identify which metrics were really being collected (as opposed to the ones managers believed were being collected),

♦ find out how the metrics program was initially implemented and subsequently managed,

♦ establish the contributions that individuals and groups made to metrics, and

TABLE 3
IMPLEMENTATION FACTORS

Implementation Factors	ES	IS
Consensus recommendations		
Incremental implementation	✓	✗
Well-planned metrics framework	✓	✗
Use of existing metrics materials	✓	✗
Involvement of developers during implementation	✓	✗
Measurement process transparent to developers	✓	✗
Usefulness of metrics data	✓	✗
Feedback to developers	✓	✗
Ensure that the data is seen to have integrity	✓	✗
Measurement data is used and seen to be used	✓	✗
Commitment from project managers secured	✓	✗
Use automated data collection tools	✓	✗
Constantly improving the measurement program	✓	✗
Internal metrics champions used to manage the program	✓	✗
Use of external metrics gurus	✗	✗
Provision of training for practitioner	✗	✗
Other Recommendations		
Implement at a level local to the developers	✓	✗
Implement a central metrics function	✗	✓
Metrics responsibility devolved to the development teams	✓	✗
Incremental determination of the metrics set	✓	✗
Collecting data that is easy to collect	✗	✗

Key: ✓ shows that the recommendation is followed; ✗ shows that it is not

♦ solicit views and experiences of the success and value of metrics.

As Table 2 shows, we had an overall response rate of 83 percent. Thus, almost everyone affected by the metrics programs at both organizations contributed to this study: 24 practitioners at ES and 125 at IS. (ES implemented metrics in only one critical department whereas IS implemented metrics throughout software development.)

Our high response rate can likely be attributed to several factors.

♦ *Topicality.* Although both metrics programs were maturing, neither was long established. Thus, metrics was still a hot issue in both organizations, and practitioners had a lot they wanted to say about it.

♦ *Desire for evaluation and improvement:* In both organizations, metrics program managers fully and publicly supported our study. Because they had not formally evaluated the metrics programs themselves, they were keen to find out their practitioners' views. Developers also seemed keen to contribute, perhaps thinking their contribution might improve the metrics program.

♦ *Independence of the study:* Practitioners were confident that their views could not be used against them by management, and, thus, we suspect, were more open and honest in their contributions.

Because of our high response rate, we're confident that our results are an accurate representation of each organization's metrics program. However, this was not a controlled experiment and does not assess each factor's impact on metrics program success. Moreover, although it would be wrong to generalize results from a case study to the industry as a whole,[12] we believe our results offer many interesting insights that are relevant and applicable to other metricating organizations.

STUDY RESULTS

At both organizations, metric program managers agreed that good metrics implementation was important. Still, as Table 3 shows, they ignored experts' key recommendations discussed above, although ES adhered to more of the proposed success factors than IS did. And, indeed, ES's metrics program was the successful one. Now the details.

Introducing metrics. No comprehensive international survey has quantified the industrial penetration of metrics since the Drummond-Tyler study.[13] Indeed, influential software commentators disagree about the extent to which metrics have penetrated the software industry. For example, Capers Jones claims an encouraging industry-wide use of measures such as function points,[14] while Bill Hetzel is much less optimistic.[9]

Measurement was initially introduced at ES only because they were given external funding to field test the Application of Metrics in Industry (ami) approach to metrication.[1] Ami combines CMM with the Goal-Question-Metric method. With it, you use the SEI CMM questionnaire to establish process maturity, then use GQM to identify metrics that are appropriate for your organization's maturity level.

Although not particularly motivated at the start, ES quickly discovered the value of metrics and implemented the program reasonably well. Metrics were implemented initially only in one development team, which meant that the metrics program was very close to the developers and could be tightly controlled by the managers.

Metrics implementation at IS was weak. The initial motivation for implementing metrics was that senior managers wanted to monitor productivity. Other studies have shown that weak motivations like this are commonplace, although the relationship between weak motivations and program failure is not clear.

IS set up a centralized metrics group to introduce metrics across the whole development function. There was no discernible use of metrication aids, nor was metrics use piloted. The implementation strategy seemed to consist solely of the metrics group instructing the development departments to start collecting specified metrics.

Developer involvement. Although managers were very involved in metrics design in both organizations, IS had little developer input into the design process. Interestingly, managers at both organizations thought developers were more involved in metrics design than developers said they were: 60 percent of managers—compared to 20 percent of developers—thought metrics design at ES was a joint effort, while 27 percent of managers and 4 percent of developers at IS thought the same.

Goal clarity. We asked practitioners to rank five software development goals according to their organization's priorities and their own. A score of 1 was awarded for the most important goal and 5 for the least important goal. Table 4 shows practitioner perception of the organization's goals. Clearly, neither ES nor IS was good at communicating development goals to their employees.

These poor results are surprising considering that ES was actively using GQM (though the model does not address the method of identifying and disseminating goals). There was, however, much less disagreement when practitioners were asked to rank their own personal goals (and not everyone ranked low costs as their least important goal).

Usefulness. As Table 5 shows, practitioners were generally positive about the usefulness of metrics, although the practitioners at ES were more positive than those at IS (90 percent of ES practitioners and 59 percent of IS prac-

TABLE 4
RANKING SOFTWARE GOALS

Embedded Systems				Information Systems			
Perceived Organizational Goals	Mean Scores			Perceived Organizational Goals	Mean Scores		
	Overall	Managers	Developers		Overall	Managers	Developers
Low costs	2.5	2.2	2.8	User satisfaction	2.6	2.6	2.6
Conformance	2.9	2.6	3.2	Speed	2.9	2.9	2.8
Speed	3.0	3.0	3.0	Reliability	3.0	3.0	3.0
Reliability	3.1	3.6	2.6	Conformance	3.1	3.2	3.1
User satisfaction	3.5	3.6	3.4	Low costs	3.4	3.3	3.5

TABLE 5
USEFULNESS OF METRICS

Metrics Usefulness	Embedded Systems			Information Systems		
	Overall	Managers	Developers	Overall	Managers	Developers
Very useful	30	40	20	15	22	9
Quite useful	60	60	60	44	50	41
Not very useful	10	0	20	25	18	30
Not useful at all	0	0	0	10	9	11
Don't know	0	0	0	7	1	10

TABLE 6
METRICS EFFICACY AND INTEGRITY

	Embedded Systems			Information Systems		
	Overall (%)	Managers (%)	Developers (%)	Overall (%)	Managers (%)	Developers (%)
1. Is the data collected accurately?						
Accurate	40	60	20	18	31	8
Not accurate	10	10	10	41	39	43
Don't know	50	30	70	41	29	50
2. Metrics feedback?						
Feedback is provided	30	50	10	18	25	11
Feedback is not provided	15	20	10	53	56	50
Don't know	55	30	80	29	19	39
3. Is the right data collected?						
Yes	40	60	20	11	13	10
No	10	0	20	46	48	44
Don't know	50	40	60	43	39	44
4. Is the data manipulated?						
Often	20	20	20	27	29	26
Occasionally	40	30	50	50	58	41
Never	5	10	0	1	0	2
Don't know	35	40	30	22	13	31
5. Who manipulates the data?						
Developers	5	0	10	15	21	9
Managers	35	40	30	40	42	39
Neither	5	10	0	2	2	2
Both	20	20	20	22	24	20
Don't know	35	30	40	20	10	30

titioners thought metrics were very useful or quite useful).

Table 6 shows practitioner confidence in each organization's metrics program. Once again, the metrics program at ES was received much more positively than the metrics program at IS. However, as the table also shows, most practitioners at both organizations were convinced that the metrics data was manipulated. Follow-up research suggests the practitioners were convinced that data was "massaged" (usually by managers) to make a situation look better than it actually was.

We also found a clear difference in metrics feedback between ES and IS. At ES, 30 percent of practitioners said feedback was provided, compared with only 18 percent at IS. Still, uncertainty reigned: 55 percent of ES practitioners and 29 percent of those at IS said they didn't know if their organization provided feedback or not.

Overall results. The approach adopted by each organization gives us a particu-

lar insight into GQM, which forces an incremental approach to identifying a metrics set. GQM thus complimented ES's incremental implementation strategy and helped it avoid problems, such as lack of transparency and developer buy-in.

IS used neither GQM nor data that was easily available. They had many problems with their metrics program. IS's approach to identifying a metrics set lacked a clear strategy. Whether GQM is being used or not, an organization must provide its practitioners a clear use for the data they collect. IS did not do this. Further, there must be a clear link between the metrics and improvement goals. If this relationship is not obvious, practitioners lack motivation to put effort into metrics collection. The validity of the data collected is thus compromised.

Our results also gave us interesting insight into the nature of metrics feedback. Practitioners at ES were reasonably satisfied with metrics feedback whereas practitioners at IS were not at

all satisfied. At ES, only 15 percent said they did not get feedback, as opposed to 53 percent of IS respondents. This surprised program managers at both organizations.

Before our study, IS managers felt confident that formal feedback mechanisms were in place (although they had not properly evaluated the effectiveness of these mechanisms). Since the study, managers at IS have taken steps to improve metrics feedback.

Managers at ES were surprised at how relatively satisfied practitioners seemed to be with feedback, as they had few formal feedback mechanisms. They did, however, use metrics on a day-to-day basis and regularly discussed results informally. ES also operated an open-house policy for metrics data. Thus, although metrics results were not formally distributed or displayed, practitioners did have access to the data. On the other hand, the program may have been an even greater success if ES had provided more formal feedback.

Finally, many practitioners marked

"Don't Know" when asked about aspects of metrication. Even at ES, where the metrics program was well established and apparently successful, many practitioners did not know, for example, whether metrics data was accurate or if the right data was collected. Practitioner ignorance was a weak spot in both programs. However, practitioners had strong views on some aspects of metrication, indicating better communication and higher practitioner interest. On metric usefulness, for example, few practitioners responded with "don't know."

EMERGING CRITERIA

In addition to the expert recommendations discussed so far, there are other, broader ways to assess a metrics program. Among the most important we identified were metrics collection effort, metrics selection, practitioner awareness, and practitioner attitude.

Choosing metrics. Table 7 quantifies the extent to which each organization collected various metrics data. The table lists a subset of the measures contained in the official metrics programs. IS's metrics list included several other measures and was considerably longer than the ES list.

We determined the most frequently used metrics in each organization based upon the activity levels in Table 7. For ES, the core metrics were
- resource estimates,
- lines of code,
- design review data, and
- code complexity data.

For IS, the core metrics were
- resource estimates,

TABLE 7
METRICS PENETRATION LEVELS

| | Total | | | | Manager | | | | Developer | | | |
| | Question One | | Question Two | | Question One | | Question Two | | Question One | | Question Two | |
	ES	IS	ES	IS	ES	IS	ES	IS	ES	IS	ES	IS
Function points[†]	-	86	-	15	-	87	-	19	-	85	-	11
Metrics for size estimates*	85	50	40	11	90	57	60	13	80	44	20	9
Metrics for cost estimates*	90	80	30	26	90	85	50	56	90	76	10	7
Metrics for effort estimates*	70	65	35	27	90	77	60	42	50	54	10	13
Analysis inspection data	40	35	10	8	50	41	20	13	30	30	0	4
Design review data	75	39	25	8	80	44	50	10	70	34	0	6
Design effort data	40	31	20	9	50	40	30	11	30	23	10	7
Code interface data	65	16	20	5	60	13	30	4	70	19	10	6
Code complexity data	70	7	20	0	90	8	30	0	50	6	10	0
Lines of code data	80	43	25	12	100	52	40	19	60	35	10	7
Coding effort data	45	20	10	12	70	49	20	19	20	26	0	6
Code inspection data	30	29	15	7	40	38	20	10	20	22	10	4
Fault rates	25	14	10	2	20	15	10	4	30	13	10	0
Defect densities	20	15	10	3	30	23	20	4	10	9	0	2
Change data	60	28	20	5	70	32	30	6	50	24	10	4
Testing effort data	40	31	10	7	60	49	20	13	20	15	0	2
Test review data	65	25	20	6	70	34	30	11	60	17	10	2

Key: Each entry represents the percentage of respondents answering "yes" to the following questions:
Question One: *Does your organization collect the following metrics data?*
Question Two: *Do you know, from personal involvement, that the following metrics data is collected?*

[†] = IS practitioners were very keen on function points, so we asked them separately about function point penetration.

* = We asked only about fairly general metrics in order to avoid fragmenting the results.

413

- function points, and
- lines of code.

Although ES was generally more active in its metrics activity, both orga-

> ## Data cannot be used to motivate productivity if people do not know it is being collected.

nizations favored a typical set of core metrics, dominated by size and effort metrics—primarily used for resource estimation and productivity measurement—rather than quality metrics. This result supports other research and runs contrary to the advice of all commentators. Overemphasis on cost-oriented data is probably another common fault of many metrics programs.

Collection effort. There is little explicit discussion in the literature about what constitutes a reasonable overhead for a metrics program, although 7 percent overall has been suggested as an average effort overhead.[15] In our study, neither program appeared to have a large effort overhead. At ES, 90 percent of practitioners said they spent less than 3 percent of their time on metrics-related activity, with the remaining 10 percent spending between 3 and 14 percent. At IS, 79 percent spent less than 3 percent, 16 percent spent between 3 and 14 percent, and 4 percent spent between 14 and 29 percent of their time on metrics activities. The fact that practitioners at ES spent less time collecting metrics data than practitioners at IS was probably because ES used automated tools.

Ironically, IS was not as effective at metricating as ES, and yet spent more effort on its metrics program. Part of this was because IS was collecting more metrics data. It is also likely that some of the IS metrics were not needed or used.

As Table 7 shows, managers at both organizations were more personally involved in metrics collection than developers, although ES had a higher overall participation level than IS. Also, while ES had a successful metrics program, there was minimal developer involvement in data collection. This is because the ES program was deliberately driven by managers and used automated data collection. The metrics program at IS seemed generally inactive, with few managers or developers directly participating in metrics collection. Indeed only 19 percent of IS managers and 7 percent of its developers said they knew from personal involvement that LOC data was collected. (IS's program did not use any special-purpose automated metrics collection tools and was largely paper-based.)

These results suggest that it is important for practitioners to know what is going on in the metrics program, but that personal involvement in collection is not very important. This finding supports other experiential reports[4,16] in which using automated tools and keeping practitioners informed seem like necessary prerequisites to metrics success.

Table 7 also shows that although ES had the most active metrics program, it lacked clarity and goal orientation in two areas.

- *Poor transparency.* Although 70 percent of ES managers said that coding effort data was collected, only 20 percent of developers knew this and no developers claimed to be involved in collecting this data. It is difficult to understand how accurate data can be collected over the life cycle without developer participation (although they may not have realized that time sheets are used for collecting coding effort data). It is also difficult to understand the purpose of collecting such data if developers do not know that it is required. It cannot be used to motivate productivity if people do not know it is being collected.

- *Poor goal-metric coupling.* Although 90 percent of managers said code complexity data was collected, only 50 percent of developers realized this and very few managers or developers were involved in collecting it. The main purpose of collecting complexity data is to control complexity. If developers do not know that complexity data is being collected, they are unlikely to take reducing complexity seriously. It also makes collecting complexity data ineffective.

Practitioner awareness. We analyzed metrics activity in terms of what practitioners knew about the measurement and how involved they were in collecting the data. Our rationale was that, although there may be an *official* metrics program in place, unless practitioners are aware of that program and see themselves as involved in it, the organization has not created the necessary measurement culture and the program is likely to be ineffective. Indeed, many of the metrics cited by both organizations as part of their "official" metrics program were so little known about and used that it is difficult to accept that they were an actual part of the metrics programs.

As Table 7 shows, ES had consistently more metrics activity than IS among both managers and developers. Although the official metrics program at IS contained many measures, awareness of these measures was generally low. Although there was a higher general level of awareness at ES, the awareness gap between managers and developers was lower at IS (an average 13-percent difference between managers' and developers' metrics awareness levels at IS and a 20 percent difference at ES). LOC metrics are a good illustration of this awareness gap: 100 percent of managers and 60 percent of developers at ES knew that lines of code data was collected (an awareness gap of 40 percentage points) compared with 52 percent of managers and 35 percent of developers at IS (an awareness gap of

17 percentage points).

Generally, practitioners at both organizations exhibited poor awareness of what was happening to review and inspection data. Both organizations used reviews and inspections regularly; the review process can be a rich source of metrics data. As Table 7 shows, the use of this data was not obvious to managers or developers at either organization, thus suggesting that the data was being used suboptimally. This is probably a common metrication weakness and is another example of organizations not heeding the published experiential advice.

Practitioner attitude. One of the most important factors in metrics program success is practitioner attitude: If you fail to generate positive feelings toward the program, you seriously undermine your likelihood of success. As Table 5 shows, in general, ES practitioners were more positive about metrics use than those at IS.

A significant influence on attitude towards metrics was job seniority. In both organizations, managers were much more positive than developers about metrics use, introduction, and management. Furthermore, the more senior managers were, the more enthusiastic they were about using metrics. At IS, for example, 87 percent of senior managers were positive about metrics compared to 72 percent of middle managers and 45 percent of junior analysts and programmers.

However, we also found that developers were more positive about metrics than conventional wisdom has led us to believe (Tom DeMarco suspected this was this case.[5]) It is generally thought, especially by managers, that developers are unenthusiastic about quality mechanisms like metrics and cannot see their value. Our results actually show that 80 percent of ES developers and 50 percent of IS developers were positive about metrics use.

It has been said that when developers are asked their opinion about software quality mechanisms, they say such things are useful, but when they're asked to participate they find many reasons why their work must be exempt. This could explain the positive attitudes toward metrics that we found in this study. If this is the case—and developers are only positive about metrics in the abstract—then organizations need to work toward realizing this positive potential. In any case, the relationship between positive perceptions and negative action warrants more research.

Table 5 supports our view that practitioners' perceptions of metrics are strongly influenced by the reality of their metrics program rather than vice versa. If this were not the case, we would expect a stronger alignment between developer and manager views between the organizations. In fact, the table shows that practitioner perceptions varied significantly, even though within each organization the perception patterns of managers and developers were very similar. This has important implications for managers: it means that what practitioners think about metrics and how they respond to them is within managers' control. Too frequently, managers assume that developers will be negative about metrics *per se*. Our results suggest that developer attitudes are built upon experience.

The integrity of metrics data also seems to have a powerful influence on practitioner attitudes, as Table 6 shows. Managers at both organizations were significantly more convinced than developers that

♦ the data collected was accurate,

♦ enough metrics feedback was provided, and

♦ the right metrics data was collected.

Such a manager/developer perception gap is troublesome. For an effective metrics program, it is important that the metrics data not only has integrity, but that developers believe that it has. Our study has not yet examined the integrity of the ES and IS metrics data, so we do not know whether the data has integrity or not. We do know, however, that many practitioners affected by metrics do not believe that the data has integrity. This perception will probably do more damage than if the data has no integrity but practitioners believe that it does. As Tables 5 and 6 show, ES developers were less negative overall about the integrity of metrics data and more positive about using metrics.

There are two probable explanations for the manager/developer perception gap that we observed. First, managers probably have more access to metrics information and data. So, for example, they probably have more feedback and are probably in a better position to judge data accuracy. Second, managers in both organizations were more actively involved in setting up and managing the metrics programs. Consequently, they are less likely to criticize something they were instrumental in setting up. This gap may be compounded by the fact that no metrics evaluations had taken place at either organization and so managers may have been unaware of the problems our study uncovered.

What practitioners think about metrics and how they respond to them is within the managers' control.

EPILOGUE

These case studies form part of a continuing longitudinal study into the quality and measurement programs in several major UK organizations. As

415

such, we continue to monitor the ES and IS metrics programs.

Our results were taken very seriously by the metrics managers at IS. Since we conducted the study two years ago, IS has either rectified, or is in the process of rectifying, many of the weaknesses we identified in its metrics programs. The program has radically improved, both because of our findings and because IS has since been taken over by a company with a more established quality and measurement regime. In particular, the IS program has been improved in the following ways:

♦ Metrics responsibility has been devolved to individual development teams and is thus much more local to developers.

♦ The centralized metrics group now acts in a more advisory rather than managerial role.

♦ Managers have made a big effort to improve transparency and feedback within the program.

♦ The actual metrics set has also been revised and is now smaller and more goal-focused, addressing the basic areas of effort, size, change, defects, and duration.

The metrics program at ES continues to be carefully managed and improved in an incremental way. The metrics set has been refined and some metrics are no longer collected. The program is viewed by ES senior managers as so successful that it is now in the process of being rolled out to all other software teams in the organization.

Neither organization has divulged to us metrics data about software quality. Thus, even at this stage, it is impossible for us to report on how the quality of software produced by ES compares to that produced by IS.

Our study confirmed that the success of a metrics program depends upon a carefully planned implementation strategy. We also found that the consensus "success" factors in the literature are generally correct, but that the advice is not always heeded. Success seems particularly linked to an organization's willingness to

♦ do background research on other metrics programs and use advice given in the published experiential reports,

♦ involve developers in metrics program design and inform them on the program's development and progress,

♦ use an incremental approach to implementation and run a pilot of the metrics program, and

♦ acknowledge developer concerns about metrics data use.

Also, in our study both metrics programs could have benefited from earlier and regular evaluations.

In contemplating the two programs, we suspect that one of the most important but intangible success factors is the approach and attitude of metrics program managers. The successful program was managed with a tenacious commitment to see metrics work. In contrast, the unsuccessful program seemed half-hearted, despite the fact that it was ambitious and expensive to implement. Indeed, at the outset, the odds were probably stacked against the successful organization: it had a weaker quality framework and lower staff morale. This suggests that organizations implementing metrics not only need to make use of the good practices, but must manage those programs with a certain amount of gusto. ♦

REFERENCES

1. *Metric Users Handbook*, ami Consortium, South Bank Univ., London, 1992.
2. R.B. Grady and D.L. Caswell, *Software Metrics: Establishing a Company-Wide Program*, Prentice Hall, Englewood Cliffs, N.J., 1987.
3. R.B. Grady, *Practical Software Metrics for Project Management and Process Improvement*, Prentice Hall, Englewood Cliffs, N.J., 1992.
4. S.L. Pfleeger, "Lessons Learned in Building a Corporate Metrics Program," *IEEE Software*, May 1993, pp. 67-74.
5. T. DeMarco, *Controlling Software Projects*, Prentice Hall, Englewood Cliffs, N.J., 1982.
6. G. Cox, "Sustaining a Metrics Program in Industry," *Software Reliability and Metrics*, N.E. Fenton and B. Littlewood, eds., Elsevier, New York, 1991, pp. 1-15.
7. V.R. Basili and H.D. Rombach, "The TAME Project: Towards Improvement-Oriented Software Environments," *IEEE Trans. Software Eng.*, Vol. 14, No. 6, 1988, pp. 758-773.
8. R. Bache and M. Neil, "Introducing Metrics into Industry: A Perspective on GQM," *Software Quality, Assurance and Measurement: A Worldwide Perspective*, N.E. Fenton et al., eds., Int'l Thompson Computer Press, London, 1995.
9. W.C. Hetzel, *Making Software Measurement Work: Building an Effective Software Measurement Programme*," QED, Wellesley, Mass., 1993.
10. R. Jefferey and M. Berry, "A Framework for Evaluation and Prediction of Metrics Program Success," *1st Int'l Software Metrics Symp.*, IEEE Computer Soc. Press, Los Alamitos, Calif., 1993, pp. 28-39.
11. T. Hall and N.E. Fenton, "Implementing Software Metrics—The Critical Success Factors," *Software Quality J.*, Jan. 1994, pp. 195-208.
12. B. Kitchenham, L. Pickard, and S.L. Pfleeger, "Case Studies for Method and Tool Evaluation," *IEEE Software*, July 1995, pp. 52-63.
13. E. Drummond-Tyler, *Software Metrics: An International Survey of Industrial Practice*, Esprit 2 Project Metkit Sema Group, South Bank Univ., London, 1989.
14. C. Jones, *Applied Software Measurement*, McGraw-Hill, New York, 1991.
15. D.H. Rombach, V.R. Basili, and R.W. Selby, *Experimental Software Engineering Issues*, Springer Verlag, Berlin, 1993.
16. M.K. Daskalantonakis, "A Practical View of Software Management and Implementation Experiences within Motorola," *IEEE Trans. Software Eng.*, Vol. 18, No. 11, 1992, pp. 998-1009.

Tracy Hall is a senior lecturer in software engineering at the University of Westminster, UK. Her research interests center around quality and measurement in software engineering.

Hall received a BA and MSc from Teesside University and is studying for a doctorate at City University, London.

Norman Fenton is a chartered engineer and a professor of computing science at the Centre for Software Reliability, City University, London. His research interests are in software metrics, safety-critical systems, and formal development methods.

Software Defect Reduction Top 10 List

Barry Boehm, University of Southern California
Victor R. Basili, University of Maryland

R ecently, a National Science Foundation grant enabled us to establish the Center for Empirically Based Software Engineering. CeBASE seeks to transform software engineering as much as possible from a fad-based practice to an engineering-based practice through derivation, organization, and dissemination of empirical data on software development and evolution phenomenology. The phrase "as much as possible" reflects the fact that software development must remain a people-intensive and continually changing field. We have found, however, that researchers have established objective and quantitative data, relationships, and predictive models that help software developers avoid predictable pitfalls and improve their ability to predict and control efficient software projects.

Here we describe developments in this area that have taken place since the publication of "Industrial Metrics Top 10 List" in 1987 (B. Boehm, *IEEE Software*, Sept. 1987, pp. 84-85). Given that CeBASE places a high priority on software defect reduction, we think it is fitting to update that earlier article by providing the following Software Defect Reduction Top 10 List.

ONE

Finding and fixing a software problem after delivery is often 100 times more expensive than finding and fixing it during the requirements and design phase.

As Boehm observed in 1987, "This insight has been a major driver in focusing industrial software practice on thorough requirements analysis and design, on early verification and validation, and on up-front prototyping and simulation to avoid costly downstream fixes."

Software's complexity and accelerated development schedules make avoiding defects difficult. These 10 techniques can help reduce the flaws in your code.

For this updated list, we have added the word "often" to reflect additional insights about this observation. One insight shows the cost-escalation factor for small, noncritical software systems to be more like 5:1 than 100:1. This ratio reveals that we can develop such systems more efficiently in a less formal, continuous prototype mode that still emphasizes getting things right early rather than late.

Another insight reveals that good architectural practices can significantly reduce the cost-escalation factor even for large critical systems. Such practices reduce the cost of most fixes by confining them to small, well-encapsulated modules. A good example is the million-line CCPDS-R system described in Walker Royce's book, *Software Project Management* (Addison-Wesley, 1998).

TWO

Current software projects spend about 40 to 50 percent of their effort on avoidable rework.

Such rework consists of effort spent fixing software difficulties that could have been discovered earlier and fixed less expensively or avoided altogether. By implication, then, some effort must consist of "unavoidable rework," an observation that has gained increasing credibility with the growing realization that better user-interactive systems result from *emergent* processes. In such processes, the requirements emerge from prototyping and other multistakeholder-shared learning activities, a departure from traditional *reductionist* processes that stipulate requirements in advance, then reduce them to practice via design and coding. Emergent processes indicate that changes to a system's definition that make it more cost-effective should not be discouraged by classifying them as avoidable defects.

Reducing avoidable rework can provide significant improvements in software productivity. In our behavioral analysis of how software cost drivers affected effort for the Cocomo II model (B. Boehm et al., *Software Cost Estimation with Cocomo II*, Prentice Hall, 2000), we found that most of the effort savings generated by improving software process maturity, software architectures, and software risk management came from reductions in avoidable rework.

THREE

About 80 percent of avoidable rework comes from 20 percent of the defects.

That 80 percent value may be lower for smaller systems and higher for very large ones. Two major sources of avoidable rework involve hastily specified

Reprinted from *Computer*, January 2001.

requirements and nominal-case design and development, in which late accommodation of off-nominal requirements causes major architecture, design, and code breakage. A tracking system for software-problem reports that records the effort to fix each defect lets you analyze the data fairly easily to determine and address additional major sources of rework.

FOUR

About 80 percent of the defects come from 20 percent of the modules, and about half the modules are defect free.

Studies from different environments over many years have shown, with amazing consistency, that between 60 and 90 percent of the defects arise from 20 percent of the modules, with a median of about 80 percent. With equal consistency, nearly all defects cluster in about half the modules produced.

Obviously, then, identifying the characteristics of error-prone modules in a particular environment can prove worthwhile. A variety of context-dependent factors contribute to error-proneness. Some factors usually contribute to error-proneness regardless of context, however, including the level of data coupling and cohesion, size, complexity, and the amount of change to reused code.

FIVE

About 90 percent of the downtime comes from, at most, 10 percent of the defects.

Some defects disproportionately affect a system's downtime and reliability. For example, an analysis of the software failure history of nine large IBM software products revealed that about 0.3 percent of the defects accounted for about 90 percent of the downtime. Thus, risk-based testing—including understanding a system's operational profiles and emphasizing testing of high-risk scenarios—is clearly cost-effective.

SIX

Peer reviews catch 60 percent of the defects.

Given that finding and fixing most defects earlier in the project development cycle is more cost-effective than finding

them later, we seek techniques that find defects as early as possible. Numerous studies confirm that peer review provides an effective technique that catches from 31 to 93 percent of the defects, with a median of around 60 percent. Thus, the 60 percent value cited in the 1987 column remains a reasonable estimate.

> **Peer reviews, analysis tools, and testing catch different classes of defects at different points in the development cycle.**

Factors affecting the percentage of defects caught include the number and type of peer reviews performed, the size and complexity of the system, and the frequency of defects better caught by execution, such as concurrency and algorithm defects. Our studies have provided evidence that peer reviews, analysis tools, and testing catch different classes of defects at different points in the development cycle. We need further empirical research to help choose the best mixed strategy for defect-reduction investments.

SEVEN

Perspective-based reviews catch 35 percent more defects than nondirected reviews.

A scenario-based reading technique (V.R. Basili, "Evolving and Packaging Reading Technologies," *J. Systems and Software*, vol. 38, no. 1, 1997, pp. 3-12) offers a set of formal procedures for defect detection based on varying perspectives. The union of several perspectives into a single inspection offers broad yet focused coverage of the document being reviewed. This approach seeks to generate focused techniques aimed at specific defect-detection goals by taking advantage of an organization's existing defect history.

Scenario-based reading techniques have been applied in requirements, object-oriented design, and user interface inspec-

tions. Improvements in fault detection rates vary from 15 to 50 percent. Further, focused reading techniques facilitate training of inexperienced personnel, improve communication about the process, and foster continuous improvement.

EIGHT

Disciplined personal practices can reduce defect introduction rates by up to 75 percent.

Several disciplined personal processes have been introduced into practice. These include Harlan Mills's Cleanroom software development process and Watts Humphrey's Personal Software Process (PSP).

Data from the use of Cleanroom at NASA have shown 25 to 75 percent reductions in failure rates during testing. Use of Cleanroom also showed a reduction in rework effort so that only 5 percent of the fixes took more than an hour, whereas the standard process caused more than 60 percent of the fixes to take that long.

PSP's strong focus on root-cause analysis of an individual's software defects and overruns, and on developing personal checklists and practices to avoid future recurrence, has significantly reduced personal defect rates. Developers frequently enjoy defect reductions of 10:1 between exercises 1 and 10 in the PSP training course.

Effects at the project level are more scattered. They depend on factors such as the organization's existing software maturity level and the staff's and organization's willingness to operate within a highly structured software culture. When you couple PSP with the strongly compatible Team Software Process (TSP), defect reduction rates can soar to factors of 10 or higher for an organization that operates at a modest maturity level. Results tend to be less spectacular if the organization already employs highly mature processes.

The June 2000 special issue of *CrossTalk*, "Keeping Time with PSP and TSP," offers a good set of relevant discussions, including experience showing that adding PSP and TSP to a CMM Level 5 organization reduced acceptance test defects by about 50 percent overall, and reduced high-priority defects by about 75 percent.

NINE

All other things being equal, it costs 50 percent more per source instruction to develop high-dependability software products than to develop low-dependability software products. However, the investment is more than worth it if the project involves significant operations and maintenance costs.

The analysis of 161 project data points for the Cocomo II model resulted in an added cost of 53 percent for its "required reliability" factor, while normalizing for the effects of 22 other factors. Does this mean that Philip Crosby's landmark book, *Quality Is Free* (Mentor, 1980), had it all wrong? Maybe for some low-criticality, short-lifetime software, but not for the most important cases.

First, in the Cocomo II maintenance model, low-dependability software costs about 50 percent per instruction more to maintain than to develop, whereas high-dependability software costs about 15 percent less to maintain than to develop. For a typical life-cycle cost distribution of 30 percent development and 70 percent maintenance, low-dependability software becomes about the same in cost per instruction as high-dependability software—again, assuming all other factors are equal.

Second, in the Cocomo II-related quality model, high-dependability software removes about four times as many defects as average-dependability software, which in turn removes about four times as many defects as low-dependability software. For example, consider an average-dependability system such as a commercial billing system, in which the operational cost of software defects—due to lost worker time, lost sales, added customer service costs, litigation costs, loss of repeat business, and so on—roughly equals life-cycle software development and maintenance costs. For such a system, the increased defect rate of using low-dependability software would make its ownership costs roughly three times higher than the ownership costs of high-dependability software.

TEN

About 40 to 50 percent of user programs contain nontrivial defects.

A 1987 study in this area (P.S. Brown and J.D. Gould, "An Experimental Study of People Creating Spreadsheets," *ACM Trans. Office Info. Sys.*, July 1987, pp. 258-272) found that 44 percent of 27 spreadsheet programs produced by experienced spreadsheet developers contained nontrivial defects—mostly errors in spreadsheet formulas. Yet the developers felt confident that they had produced accurate spreadsheets.

> **The creators of Web-programming facilities face the challenge of providing their tools with the equivalent of seat belts and air bags, along with safe-driving aids and rules of the road.**

Subsequent laboratory experiments have reported defective spreadsheet rates between 35 and 90 percent. The analysis of operational spreadsheets reveals defect rates between 21 and 26 percent; the lower rates probably stem from corrections already made during operation.

Now, and increasingly in the future, user programs will escalate from spreadsheets to Web-scripting languages capable of sending agents into cyberspace to make deals for you. The ranks of "sorcerer's apprentice" user-programmers will also swell rapidly, giving many who have little training or expertise in how to avoid or detect high-risk defects tremendous power to create high-risk defects. One study for the Cocomo II book estimated that the US will have 55 million user-programmers by 2005. If we classify active Web-page developers as user-programmers, this prediction appears to be on track.

Thus, the creators of Web-programming facilities face the challenge of providing their tools with the equivalent of seat belts and air bags, along with safe-driving aids and rules of the road. This software engineering research challenge is one of several identified by a National Science Foundation study, "Gaining Intellectual Control of Software Development," which we recently summarized in *Computer* (May 2000, pp. 27-33).

Surely, our list can benefit from refinement and further empirical research on defect reduction. Much of the data we have reported, for example, fails to account for the interaction between many of the variables that, if known, could provide answers to questions like:

- If I invest in peer reviewing, Cleanroom, and PSP, am I paying for the same defects to be removed three times?
- How much testing would this investment enable me to avoid?

We hope to involve the software community in expanding the Software Defect Reduction Top 10 List and other currently available data into a continually evolving, open source, Web-accessible handbook of empirical results on software-defect reduction strategies. We also plan to initiate counterpart handbooks for commercial off-the-shelf systems and other emerging software areas. We welcome your participation in this effort and urge you to visit the CeBASE Web site at http://www.cebase.org for further information. You can also find an expanded version of this column at http://www.cebase.org/defectreduction/ top10.

Barry Boehm is director of the University of Southern California Center for Software Engineering. Contact him at boehm@sunset.usc.edu.

Victor R. Basili is a professor in the Institute for Advanced Computer Studies and the Computer Science Department at the University of Maryland. Contact him at basili@cs.umd.edu.

Metrics for Small Projects: Experiences at the SED

Ross Grable, US Army Missile Command
Jacquelyn Jernigan, Casey Pogue, and Dale Divis, Tennessee Applied Physical Sciences, Inc.

T he Software Engineering Directorate of the Research, Development, and Engineering Center at the US Army Missile Command designs, builds, and maintains small embedded applications. These projects consist of 10,000 to 50,000 lines of source code. Some SED projects also address larger systems in their sustainment phase, which often require modifications or enhancements to only a small percentage of the overall code per build.

Organizations such as the SED that produce and maintain many small embedded application software packages can benefit from a well-organized metrics program. Since the SED's emergence in 1984, software metrics have played an increasing role in the organization's development process. Before undertaking a concerted effort to coordinate its software metrics process, the SED had inaccurate, inconsistent data reported with no validation of usefulness or relevance. There was little respect or insight into the value of the metrics or measuring process, and virtually no return on the investment of time spent in data collection.

Although earlier attempts were unsuccessful, the SED has established an organization-wide metrics program that has been functioning successfully for over a year.

Reprinted from *IEEE Software*, March/April 1999.

Most IEEE Software *submissions are experience stories from academia or from fairly large companies. Articles from small companies are very rare, especially when it comes to experience reports on process improvement. This article is one of the few that describes attempts to introduce some process improvements in small companies.*

Although the results are based on limited sample sets, they demonstrate that even in the smallest of development organizations a sensible approach to metrics can yield useful results. In this case, the results were helpful because the experiments were highly goal-oriented. The goals had a practical purpose and allowed the companies to learn something they could use for future improvements.

Provided metrics are collected with clear goals in mind, whether in large companies with sophisticated processes or in small ad hoc development environments, the results can give valuable insight into the success of improvement work. One lesson I learned from this article is that the mere existence of measurements leads to communication and discussion of results, which in turn enables teams to become more aware of key success factors in their work. Even if this was the only outcome, I believe it shows it is worth it to start taking some measurements.

—*Wolfgang Strigel, From the Trenches editor*

METRICS AT THE SED

In the SED's earlier days, development teams periodically performed panic collections of each day's code output for approximately 50 ongoing projects. The data collected was inconsistent, unreliable, and incomplete. After these early efforts, tactical missile projects began using standardized metrics for management briefings.[1] These metrics consisted of the number of people on the project, progress of the development phase, use of the target computer resources, analysis of schedule risk, resolution of trouble reports, number of delivered software projects, and supportability of software maintenance. Cooperation, completeness, and accuracy problems plagued the collection effort even though project leads presented some useful information in the quarterly progress review meetings. Scattered experiments performed on special pilot projects measured the complexity of, and effort devoted to, software developed in-house. However, the SED still lacked a coordinated effort to collect and analyze metrics data throughout the organization. Only with concerted effort and upper-management involvement did a useful software metrics program emerge.

These early attempts at metric collection, although they fostered no great revelations, taught the organization important lessons:

♦ Most project engineers routinely collected some kind of tracking data, yet resisted the imposition of centralized data collection.

♦ Project personnel expressed concern that the data collected would be used to assess individuals negatively.

♦ Project leaders expressed concern about the time taken from software development activities to collect metrics.

♦ Project leaders expressed concern about how the collected data would reflect poorly on their projects when compared to the data from other projects.

♦ Management and policy makers appreciated and used simple presentations of analysis results, such as pie charts or red-amber-green traffic-signal graphics.

♦ Measurement of an activity, initially at least, caused improvement in the activity, as predicted by the Hawthorne Effect.

♦ Variations in metric definitions made it difficult to get consistent measurements.

♦ Software cost models produced good estimates for experienced engineers, even when there were no grounds for validation.

Software Engineering Evaluation System

In 1990, the SED developed a method of gathering metrics for validation and verification, called the Software Engineering Evaluation System. The SEES metric set consists of the number of people on the project, hours worked on the project, product items, planning, preparation, and defects. SEES records these metrics for software requirements, requirements traceability, software design and code, test plans, test descriptions, test witnessing, and functional- and physical-configuration audits. The SED provided training in SEES data collection and the reporting process for project leads involved with verification and validation of software, and developed a database for maintaining these metrics. The SED completed formal documentation of the SEES process in 1994.[2] Since then, a software group of the US National Aeronautics and Space Administration has also adopted this procedure for maintaining verification and validation metrics.

Metrics Working Group

The SED published an organization metrics policy in 1994 that established a Metrics Working Group

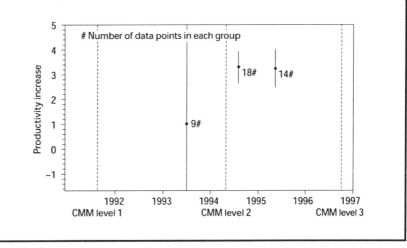

Figure 1. Annual productivity at the Software Engineering Directorate. The SED's productivity increased by a factor of approximately three between 1993 and 1994.

and laid the guidelines for collection and analysis of organization-wide metrics. This policy, still in use today, provides process audits and support funding. It requires that the information gathered be excluded from individual performance evaluations. This stipulation opened the door for integration of the metrics processes and procedures into the operational structure of the whole organization. The SED rewrote the standard operating procedures to include periodic collection and reporting of software metrics.

Overseeing the metrics initiative for the organization was the Metrics Working Group, which acts as a software metrics information center. Today the working group participates in professional metrics standards groups and leads research in metrics effectiveness. It maintains the metrics definitions for the organization, collects data from projects, and provides data analysis to management and project leads. Training provides SED personnel with an understanding of metrics policies and explains metrics definitions. The working group is also responsible for acquiring and maintaining the organization's metrics database.

The Metrics Working Group evaluated the SED's software-producing efficiency and calibrated a cost model for use in estimating future project costs.[3,4] This task began with the bulk collection of a standard dataset for internal software development projects. The set included lines of code, engineering hours, calendar months, and the number of defects discovered in peer reviews and testing.

The collection process consisted of project leads completing a metrics form that contains the needed information. Scheduled interviews with each project leader answered questions about the data. The data collected demonstrated the diversity of the organization's projects: they varied significantly in size, effort, duration, and languages used. This data formed a baseline for the organization, one that helps indicate trends and areas of process improvement.

The analysis in the following sections lists projects anonymously and shows data for the organization as a whole, not by individual projects. The projects are listed anonymously to promote the honesty of reporting the data. Managers must get data on specific projects through the project leader, not

from the Metrics Working Group. Giving the project leads authority over their own data alleviated some of their concerns about project comparisons.

Along with these tasks, there have been various experimental data-collection projects. Typical data in these acquisitions include software science metrics, function points, feature points, state entropy, cyclomatic complexity, coupling and cohesion metrics, and cleanroom metrics.

ANALYSIS

The SED actively applies the SEI's Capability Maturity Model,[5] which claims to increase the efficiency and productivity of an organization. The following analysis indicates that this claim is valid.

Efficiency analysis

The main goal of our efficiency analysis is to show productivity increases at the SED since the start of its software improvement efforts. Data collection began in January 1990, but data generated prior to 1993 is so sparse and unreliable that it was inadequate for establishing a baseline. Therefore, the efficiency analysis uses 1993 data to normalize each year's productivity mean. Figure 1 shows the productivity ratio, which is defined as each year's average productivity divided by 1993's average productivity. The data indicates that the SED's productivity increased by a factor of approximately three between 1993 and 1994. The productivity of SED projects completed in 1995 showed no significant change from the 1994 results. The large increase in productivity between 1993 and 1994 was primarily the result of appreciable software training during that interval. However, that very large productivity

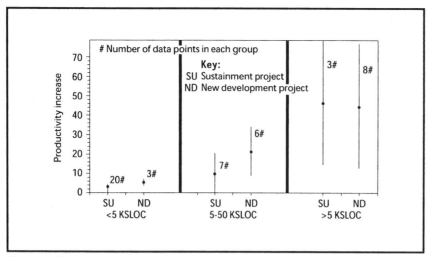

Figure 2. Average productivity for each project size category at the SED.

increase would not be expected year after year.

The productivity analysis partitioned the metrics data by size to investigate what effect project size would have on productivity. The analysis also divided the data between sustainment builds and new-development builds. Figure 2 shows the average productivity computed for each size category. The data indicates that the new-development builds are more efficient than the sustainment builds for the "very small" (less than 5,000 lines of code) and "small" (5,000 to 50,000 lines of code) size categories. The data also suggests that, for the SED, productivity increases for larger projects. This finding contradicts some experiments that show that productivity decreases for larger projects,[6] and provides an example for why organizations should gather and analyze their own data. Not all organizations should follow the standard assumptions made by most software professionals. They should measure, analyze, and develop calibration models from their own software projects.

The statistical analysis included the use of small sampling theory since, in most datasets, the number of data points in a group numbered less than 30. The small sample numbers clearly contributed to the relatively large one-standard-deviation error shown in all the figures provided. In addition, the large differences in the characteristics of these small projects also contribute strongly to the large statistical deviations. In future work, we hope that sufficient numbers of projects in each year will allow the splitting of projects into subgroups that share similar characteristics. This may allow observation of statistical differences in productivity for different project categories.

Other factors that contributed significantly to errors in the calculations include the following:

♦ Project leaders obtained much of the data from recordings made by people and not by unbiased machines. When people record data measurements on work they themselves performed, they often provide numbers in their favor or inaccurate values.

♦ Developers used several different languages to generate project code. Even though methods were used to normalize use of the various languages, large uncertainties persist.

♦ No one evaluated the education and experience levels of the contributors, even though there is general agreement that experience and education can exert a marked positive influence on productivity.

♦ Although project members recorded software error information, they did not use it to calculate the productivity values shown. This is important because a project may have relatively high lines of source code per effort value but also have a relatively high error rate. Thus, the effective productivity may not be high and certainly could be reduced.

Because of the diverse software being developed at the SED, the small number of builds with available data, and other limitations, determining conclusive results from this organizational analysis is difficult. However, we have identified several trends. Primarily, the analysis shows the importance of collecting accurate data and investigating trends in that data.

Cost model analysis

The cost model analysis investigated relationships between the metrics used in the cost models. This analysis computed linear and rank correlation coefficients and used nonlinear curve fits. The only metric pair with a "high" correlation coefficient was size (lines of code) and effort (0.80). However, this correlation does not appear in every project. Moreover, this relationship is not as strong in the sustainment builds (0.61) as in the new-development builds (0.84). This is because sustainment has much greater variability in requirements than new development.

A study of one project that measured individual code modules showed no correlation between effort and lines of code. This was, in large part, due to variations in module complexity. The project consisted of complex, tight hydraulic control loops and simple user interfaces. Nevertheless, a cost model based on estimated lines of code accurately

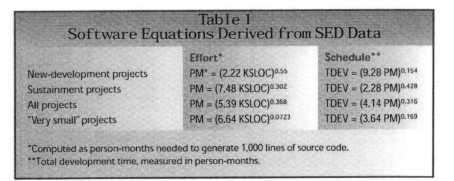

Table 1
Software Equations Derived from SED Data

	Effort*	Schedule**
New-development projects	PM* = (2.22 KSLOC)$^{0.55}$	TDEV = (9.28 PM)$^{0.154}$
Sustainment projects	PM = (7.48 KSLOC)$^{0.302}$	TDEV = (2.28 PM)$^{0.428}$
All projects	PM = (5.39 KSLOC)$^{0.368}$	TDEV = (4.14 PM)$^{0.316}$
"Very small" projects	PM = (6.64 KSLOC)$^{0.0723}$	TDEV = (3.64 PM)$^{0.169}$

*Computed as person-months needed to generate 1,000 lines of source code.
**Total development time, measured in person-months.

predicted project effort and schedule to within 10 percent. The number of actual lines of code was also within 10 percent of the estimated number.

Was the estimate a self-fulfilling prophecy? We think not, but will never know for sure. Verification of the reason behind the results requires more data than was available.

Barry Boehm's Constructive Cost Model[7] (Cocomo) is one of the most popular software development cost-estimation models. However, the coefficients given in the Cocomo textbook are not valid for all organizations. Using the collected data, we calibrated the SED cost model analogous to the Cocomo basic model. The top graph in Figure 3 shows the effort versus the size of all SED projects. We measured effort in person-months, with each PM defined as 152 person-hours. The graph also shows the best nonlinear fit computed from the data, and the results obtained from the Cocomo basic organic model.

Table 1 lists the equations computed from several different data groups. The effort equation shows the relationship between the thousands of lines of codes (KSLOC) and the project person-months to generate the value of the KSLOC. The schedule or time-of-development equation (TDEV) shows the relationship between the total person-months and the total duration to complete the project. Significantly, the effort equations in the basic Cocomo model contain an exponent greater than one. When the exponential coefficient is greater than one, the model assumes that larger projects cost more per line of code than do smaller ones. Yet the effort equations from the SED data produced exponents less than one. The Cocomo model's "diseconomy of scale" did not appear in our calibrated coefficients. With an exponent less than one (as for the SED projects), the model predicts that larger projects cost less per line of code than do small projects.

Figure 3 shows how data clusters near the origin, then spreads out as the project's size grows. Therefore, the analysis also calibrated the Cocomo

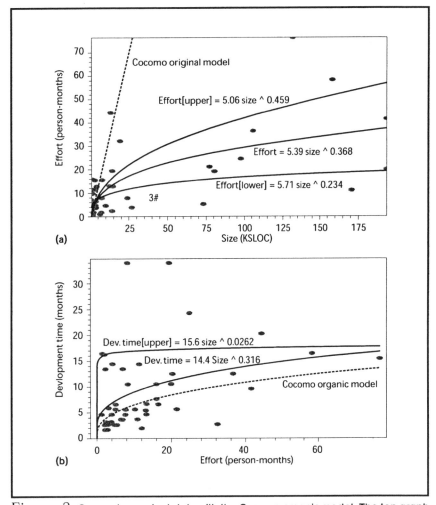

Figure 3. Comparing project data with the Cocomo organic model. The top graph (a) shows the effort in person-months vs. size for all SED projects; the bottom graph (b) shows the data related between development time and effort for all SED projects.

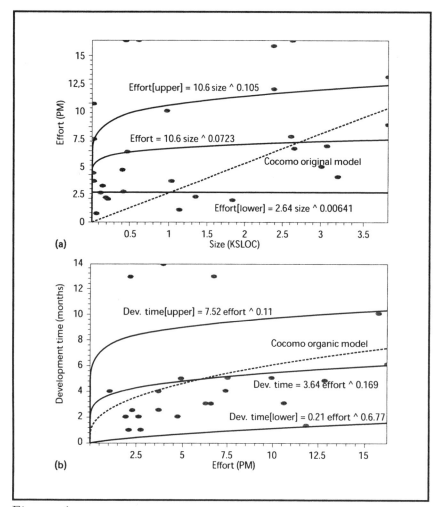

$$\text{Effort[upper]} = 10.6\ \text{size} \char`^\ 0.105$$

$$\text{Effort} = 10.6\ \text{size} \char`^\ 0.0723$$

Cocomo original model

$$\text{Effort[lower]} = 2.64\ \text{size} \char`^\ 0.00641$$

(a)

$$\text{Dev. time[upper]} = 7.52\ \text{effort} \char`^\ 0.11$$

Cocomo organic model

$$\text{Dev. time} = 3.64\ \text{effort} \char`^\ 0.169$$

$$\text{Dev. time[lower]} = 0.21\ \text{effort} \char`^\ 0.6.77$$

(b)

Figure 4. Comparing the very small project data with the Cocomo organic model. The top graph (a) shows the effort in person-months vs. size for all **SED** projects; the bottom graph (b) shows the correlation between development time and effort for all **SED** projects.

basic model for the "very small" projects (less than 5,000 lines of source code). Figure 4 shows the curves for the very small data.

The cost model analysis also computed upper- and lower-bound values for the calibrated cost model coefficients. In theory, these upper- and lower-bound coefficients should provide one standard deviation about the calibrated cost model. The upper- and lower-bound curves for the small projects contained approximately 53 percent of the SED builds. These curves also have exponents less than one.

The Cocomo basic schedule model estimated the SED builds much closer than did the effort model. The exponent for these curves was very close to the Cocomo model. The bottom graphs in Figures 3 and 4 show the SED duration in months as a function of effort hours. The upper and lower bounds of the small projects for the schedule data

contain approximately 87 percent of the SED builds.

The cost estimation analysis shows the importance of calibrating cost models. Using coefficients calibrated with data from other organizations can lead to large errors in software estimation. Textbook cost models give software practitioners a place to start; however, once data is available, analysts should compute new coefficients for their projects or organization. Metrics analysts should also update the cost model coefficients periodically to incorporate the most recent data collected.

CURRENT COLLECTION PROCEDURES

In February 1996, the SED implemented a standard procedure for the periodic collection and analysis of current-build metrics. The main goal of the SED Metrics Working Group in establishing this procedure was to make it minimally intrusive to project personnel while it gathered the needed data with more accuracy and consistency than previous attempts. Before initiating the organization-wide collection procedures, the Metrics Working Group held detailed discussions on several topics, including

♦ metrics to collect,
♦ definitions of metrics,
♦ design of the metrics collection form,
♦ metric collection time period,
♦ person responsible for data collection, and
♦ analysis procedures.

The working group decided to begin with four basic metrics: effort, schedule, defects, and size, as recommended by the Software Engineering Institute.[8] Substantial discussion and planning went into the design of the metrics collection form, incorporating suggestions from project personnel that would work for all SED projects. At first, the forms were confusing and complicated: they consisted of several sheets, with separate sheets for each metric and a different sheet for each project classification. Based on suggestions from project leaders, the final collection form consisted of one page, with all four metrics and their definitions listed on the form's back.

The effort metric consists of hours directly charged to the project for 15 activities. Of these activities, 10 deal directly with the software development process, including requirement definition, design, code, and test. Four categories address project support activities, but are not directly involved with software development or sustainment; these include management and software quality assurance. An "other" category includes activities performed on the project that may not fit any of the previous categories.

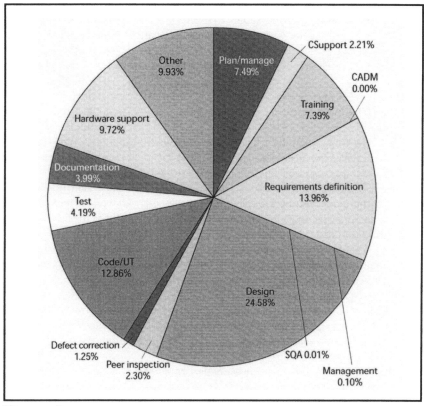

Figure 5. Sample monthly metrics report for an SED project.

The schedule metric consists of the planned date and actual date for 10 milestones, chosen to represent the main events in the software development process. A project's staff can tailor its process to have fewer milestones, in accordance with the SED procedures.

The defect metric represents the number of new and closed defects. The metric divides defects into three classes depending on the severity of the defect. Several projects use peer inspection reports for recording defects. Project leads can attach the peer inspection reports to the metrics collection sheet, which helps reduce their paperwork.

The size metric consists of the language, number of lines of source code developed or modified, and number of document pages generated. The sustainment builds also record the total lines of code in the system.

We decided to collect metrics biweekly for two reasons: government employees report their hours biweekly, and it is less intrusive than weekly collection but frequent enough to ensure the data's consistency and correctness. Project leaders collect and submit the forms to the working group, ensuring collection of all project data and helping to guarantee the data's accuracy.

The SED consists of approximately 300 government and contract personnel. Approximately 130 of these are software personnel who work on the 22 projects currently participating in the metrics collection program. Thus, within a two-week period, project leaders typically record 5,700 personnel hours on the metrics collection sheets. The number of hours collected varies, since project personnel are always changing and new projects begin as others end.

The Metrics Working Group generates monthly metrics reports for each project and sends them to the project leads. The reports consist of comparisons between actual and estimated values, percentages of effort hours spent in each category, and the number of defects open. Figure 5 contains a sample pie chart that shows the percentages of effort hours expended in each category. The pie chart summarizes the distribution of effort by activity in concise and easy-to-read form.

Other simple charts of size, defects, and schedule metrics also aid project leaders in managing their projects. These simple charts may also alert the leaders to potential problems early in the software development process and provide time for corrective action. The monthly metrics reports are still evolving; they change as project leads realize the management benefits this data provides.

Taking advantage of SED-funded training for several of its members, the Metrics Working Group began using a sophisticated database tool to manage the data. However, even though the database had some powerful features, it proved difficult to learn and use. The working group discovered that simple, inexpensive database tools and spreadsheets could adequately produce the needed results.

FUTURE PLANS

The working group is developing a network-based collection system, and plans to phase it in in small steps. Several different implementation methods are being investigated.

The group also periodically updates the cost model analysis, and it is working on a spreadsheet that incorporates the calibrated coefficients into an estimation model for project leader use. This spreadsheet will incorporate the percentage data for each effort category from completed projects to help project leads estimate hours in each effort category. Calibrating the cost models for the organization, providing training, and providing metrics tools will help increase the accuracy of software project estimation.

The Metrics Working Group continues to research new metrics and models, investigating different ways of measuring complexity. Several other areas are also being investigated as the SED begins plans for reaching CMM level 4.

Upper management's involvement and the publication of an organizational metrics policy contributed to the success of the present metrics collection program at the SED. The organization learned many lessons in the process of establishing measured feedback for its processes, including the following:

♦ A successful metrics program must have support from the highest management.

♦ Training is essential for the correct collection and analysis of data, and for management to be able to appropriately apply metrics. All managers and engineers need training in the collection and use of the data.

♦ Although metrics use does lead to better organizational performance, it requires an up-front investment of 3 to 8 percent of the project's overall cost, which must be paid at the beginning of the metrics program. This cost drops to less than 1 percent after project personnel become familiar with the program.

♦ Experiments to validate and analyze the metrics are an essential process component. Analysis of the data can validate assumptions or show that typical software process assumptions do not apply to a particular organization or project.

♦ Periodic calibration of cost models helps ensure accurate cost estimation.

♦ The metrics analysis techniques used should be statistically sound to ensure the accuracy of conclusions drawn from data analysis.

♦ A metrics collection program should be initiated with a small set of metrics that will show the benefits of collecting data. The metrics collection form should have a simple and easily understood design; a complicated form will only discourage software personnel from collecting data.

♦ Establish a metrics feedback procedure for engineers and managers to learn how to use the metrics and to help them understand the use and benefits of the measurement system.

♦ Inexpensive commercial database and spreadsheet tools are all that an organization needs to track metric data and provide meaningful reports.

The SED continues to learn important lessons from the metrics process. Our organization monitors its process improvement program's progress using the baseline established from collected data. The metrics program continues to expand as SED personnel experience the benefits of collecting and analyzing software metric data. ❖

REFERENCES

1. "Methodology for the Management of Software Acquisition," Software Engineering Directorate, Research, Development, and Engineering Center of the US Army Missile Command, Redstone Arsenal, Ala., 1991.

2. "Software Engineering Evaluation System (SEES), Volume I, SEES Executive Summary," Software Engineering Directorate, Research, Development, and Engineering Center of the US Army Missile Command, SED-SES-IES-001, Redstone Arsenal, Ala., 1994.

3. J.G. Jernigan and D.H. Divis, "Metric Analysis of Historical Data for the Software Engineering Directorate," Tennessee Applied Physical Sciences, TAPS-22-1995, Sept. 1995.

4. J.G. Jernigan, C.R. Pogue, and D.H. Divis, "Software Metric Analysis for the Software Engineering Directorate 1996," Tennessee Applied Physical Sciences, TAPS-24-1996, Sept. 1996.

5. M.C. Paulk et al., "Capability Maturity Model for Software, Version 1.1," Software Eng. Inst., Carnegie Mellon Univ., CMU/SEI-93-TR-24 or ESC-TR-93-177, Pittsburgh, 1993.

6. L.H. Putnam and W. Myers, Measures for Excellence: Reliable Software on Time, Within Budget, Yourdon Press, Englewood Cliffs, N.J., 1992.

7. B.W. Boehm, Software Engineering Economics, Prentice-Hall, Upper Saddle River, N.J., 1981.

8. A.D. Carleton et al., "Software Measurement for DoD Systems: Recommendations for Initial Core Measures," Software Eng. Inst., Carnegie Mellon Univ., CMU/SEI-92-TR-19 or ESC-TR-92-019, Pittsburgh, 1992.

About the Authors

D. Ross Grable is on the computer science faculty at the Clinch Valley College of the University of Virginia. His research interests are software and system metrics, software project management, and information system measurement techniques. He has worked with the Army Aviation and Missile Command as a senior scientist and consultant, and has also worked as a programmer, analyst, and project manager on many aerospace and military software-intensive real-time systems projects.

Ross received a BS in mathematics and physics, and an MS and a PhD in computer science from the University of Alabama Huntsville. He is a member of IEEE and the IEEE Computer Society.

Jacquelyn G. Jernigan is a weapon system analyst at Lockheed Martin Missile and Space in Huntsville, Alabama. Previously she was a senior software engineer at Tennessee Applied Physical Sciences. She has performed systems and radar analysis and developed analysis tools and radar simulations for government agencies for seven years. Her recent work includes metric analysis for the Software Engineering Directorate of the US Army Missile Command. Her current research interests include software metrics, process improvement, and system performance.

Jernigan received a BS in electrical engineering from the University of Alabama, Huntsville. She is a member of the IEEE Computer Society.

Casey R. Pogue is a computer scientist at Tennessee Applied Physical Sciences. He has developed accounting tools for small businesses and worked in computer services support. His current work includes metric analysis, Ada Compiler evaluation, and code analysis for the Software Engineering Directorate of the US Army Missile Command. His current research interests include software metrics and compiler optimization.

Pogue received a BS in computer science from Middle Tennessee State University.

Dale H. Divis is president of Tennessee Applied Physical Sciences. He has performed physics and mathematical modeling research for government agencies, and has evaluated data from physical experiments with unique statistical methods. Currently, he is involved with the statistical evaluation of software metrics data.

Divis received a BA in physics with minors in mathematics and chemistry from Rutgers and a MS in physics from Texas Christian University. He is a member of the American Physical Society.

Readers may contact Divis at Tennessee Applied Physical Sciences, Inc., P.O. Box 994, Fayetteville, TN 37334-0994, e-mail mld@vallnet.com.

Chapter 13

Acquisition Management

The only thing more costly than stretching the schedule of an established development program is accelerating it, which is itself the most costly action known to man.

—Norman R. Augustine, *Augustine's Laws*

Overview

As firms have downsized, they have moved more and more to using commercial off-the-shelf (COTS) packages and third-party suppliers to generate their software. Managing contractors generating software under contract to your specifications requires you to develop skills, knowledge, and abilities in acquisition management. You need to understand how to manage to a contract and motivate your suppliers to achieve often difficult goals by controlling work progress instead of people, using a variety of financial and nonmonetary incentives. Often, good software managers make terrible software acquisition managers because they tell their contractors how to perform the job instead of providing them with clarifications of what the job really entails.

All three papers contained in this volume were written specifically for the previous edition and are tutorial in nature. They address the fundamental concerns, processes and practices of software acquisition management and give some feedback on what does and does not work based upon experience. They focus on identifying practices that can help you to improve how you manage your suppliers using both agreements and contracts as your basis for action. As in the other chapters, I have defined key terms and provided some suggested readings along with these opening remarks.

Article Summaries

Software Acquisition Management, by John Marciniak. This paper introduces you to the topic of software acquisition management and the management and engineering environment in which it takes place. The environment is described in terms of the strategies, processes, and types of contract vehicles employed to manage those developing software for you under contract to your specification. Planning and assessment functions that are needed to acquire a capable source are discussed along with background information on contracting. Finally, the key assessment practices employed to provide visibility and control over the acquisition as it unfolds are described along with metrics that provide you with indications of progress.

Managing Subcontracts, by Kenneth E. Nidiffer, Claire L. Brown, and R. A. Neale. This paper focuses on software suppliers (subcontractors, cocontractors, vendors, etc.) and the subcontracting practices that can be used to improve how you effectively manage them. The paper emphasizes the keys to getting suppliers to perform critical tasks satisfactorily under contract, namely teamwork, trust, and a proper management infrastructure. However, the infrastructure is built by its underlying nature and differs from that used by development groups because the effort is essentially work done for hire. Therefore, management of relationships is stressed along with techniques to manage them within this paper.

Software Licensing: A Missed Opportunity, by Donald J. Reifer. This final paper examines the topic of licensing and discusses how organizations can improve the practices they utilize to purchase the rights to use software. The paper emphasizes the development of processes that revolve around enterprise-wide software licenses. It suggests that implementing such practices within most firms can save millions of dollars annually. It goes on to relate what should be included in such licenses and how firms can lever their purchasing power to get concessions from their suppliers, leading to better service and lower prices.

Key Terms

Eight terms, defined as follows, are important to understanding the topic of organization as used within this chapter:

1. **Acceptance criteria.** The criteria a system or component must satisfy in order to be accepted by a user, customer, or other party.

2. **Acquisition management.** The process of managing third parties that generate software products and/or perform related services using a contract as the legal basis for action/arbitration of disputes. In such situations, managers provide technical direction to the teams developing software per the contract's terms and conditions.

3. **Commercial off-the-shelf (COTS) software.** Software that is supplied by a third party who retains responsibility for continued development and life cycle support of the package. COTS software is used as-is (the version is not changed to address the unique needs of the user).

4. **Customer.** The individual or organization that specifies and accepts the project deliverables. The customer may be internal or external to the parent organization and may or may not be the end user of the software. A financial transaction between the customer and developer is not implied by this definition.

5. **Integrated product team.** An organization structure for a product development project that includes representatives of all functional disciplines involved with the effort from both the developer's and customer's organizations that are collectively responsible for delivering the product.

6. **Subcontractor management plan.** An acquirer's plan for managing the efforts of a subcontractor. Identifies items such as project objectives, stakeholders, work breakdown structure, roles and responsibilities, schedule, budget, risks, performance measures, resources, work products, change process, and other supporting plans.

7. **Supplier.** Any third-party organization that supplies software products and/or performs services using a written agreement or contract as the basis for action or settling of disputes (subcontractor, COTS supplier, etc.).

8. **Supplier management.** The process of managing third parties that supply software products and/or perform related services. To satisfy the intent of such agreements, stakeholders must make investments of their own assets.

Acronyms

The following acronyms are used within the articles in this chapter:

BOA	Basic ordering agreement
CM	Configuration management
CMM	Capability Maturity Model
CMMI	Capability Maturity Model Integration
COTS	Commercial off-the-shelf
CPFF	Cost plus fixed fee (contract)
CPIF	Cost plus incentive fee (contract)
FFP	Firm fixed price (contract)
IEEE	Institute of Electrical and Electronics Engineers
IPT	Integrated product team
PMBOK™	Project Management Body of Knowledge
QA	Quality assurance
RFP	Request for proposal
SAM	Supplier Agreement Management
SA-CMM	Software Acquisition Capability Maturity Model
SEI	Software Engineering Institute
SMP	Subcontract management plan
SOW	Statement of work
SSCI	Systems and Software Consortium Inc.

For Your Bookshelf

The classic reference for software managers on acquisition management is Marciniak and Reifer's *Software Acquisition Management.* Much of the material in the paper that opens this chapter was taken from this reference, which is abstracted in the Bibliography.

Two useful references on subcontract management are the excellent 1993 textbook by Fleming and Fleming entitled *Sub-*

contract Planning and Organization, and the Software Productivity Consortium (SPC) 2001 guidebook on the topic entitled *Subcontracting Products or Services for Software-Intensive Systems.* Please note that the SPC has been renamed the Systems and Software Consortium, Inc. (SSCI). Also please note that some of their publications are restricted to member firms and may not be available to the public.

The Software Engineering Institute (SEI) has recently recognized the importance of supplier management by making Supplier Agreement Management (SAM) one of the six project management process areas in the Capability Maturity Model Integration (CMMI). A good summary of the SAM process area in both its staged and continuous forms is provided in the bibliography of both CMMI references. The SAM requires that firms manage the acquisition of products and services from suppliers external to the project for which there exists a formal agreement and that:

- Agreements with the suppliers must be established and maintained.

- Both the project and the supplier must satisfy agreements with the suppliers.

- The process is institutionalized as a managed process.

The SEI has also been working to improve the ability of government program offices that manage firms that build software under contract for the Department of Defense. They have published an update to the Software Acquisition Capability Maturity Model (SA-CMM) that may be of interest to you because it presents an overview of key acquisition processes and practices:

- Jack Cooper, Matthew Fisher, and S. Wayne Sherer, *Software Acquisition Capability Maturity Model (SA-CMM), Version 1.02,* Software Engineering institute, April 1999.

The SEI has also merged the SA-CMM and the CMMI and provided guidance for using the combined model on its Web site (www.sei.cmu.edu).

The Project Management Book of Knowledge (PMBOK™) devotes a chapter to the topic of project procurement management. The emphasis of this chapter is on procurement planning and awards. The chapter also highlights best practices for managing contracts once they are awarded.

For those interested, the IEEE has published a *Recommended Practice for Software Acquisition,* IEEE Std 1062-1998. This document provides useful guidelines that can easily be adapted for use by most firms I have worked with.

Software Acquisition Management*

John J. Marciniak

Introduction

Acquisition management is a fairly new term. As near as one can tell, it arose as a discipline during the late 1980s. Several articles and at least one book on the topic [1] have been published on the subject. The term arose due to a perceived lack of management discipline for the acquisition of software systems, or systems with extensive software content (and development), sometimes called software-intensive systems.

One could reasonably ask "Why all the fuss when we have been acquiring systems for some time?" or "Why is software acquisition different or special?" The answer to these questions is rooted in the same difficulties we have had managing the development of software systems. These cases are well known and have been discussed freely in the media and within software circles. In the 1980s we began to understand that the acquisition of software systems is an area that also deserves special attention because it focuses attention on managing those who build software under contract, not under your direct supervision.

So what is *acquisition* anyway? Before we get into what it is we should understand what it is not. It is not the discipline of software development rooted in software engineering practice. And it is not the management of this process, something that we term software project management, although it is certainly related to this discipline. Whenever we buy something we are involved in an acquisition of sorts. The thing that makes software acquisition different is two conditions: First, it deals with acquiring, through an agreement, a software-intensive system, and, second, it is an acquisition that is not routine, that is, complexity and, therefore, risk are involved. Let's take a look at each of these circumstances so we have a better or clearer understanding of what this subject is about.

The first case is rather simple. It implies that we are acquiring a software system through an agreement; that is, from another party. The agreement may be formal such as a contract to develop and deliver a product, a so-called work for hire, or it may be informal such as an agreement between two parties (e.g., memoranda). The reason for the formality is principally based on the circumstances of the organizations involved. Government organizations, when they acquire systems, are bound by regulations that require a contract when they acquire from the private sector. Organizations that are not governed by formal regulations may choose an informal agreement, for example, when one part of the organization acquires a system from another part of the same organization. In this case it makes sense to have an internal, "informal" agreement.

The second case is strictly based on the complexity of the acquisition. On one extreme are the large systems acquired by government organizations such as the Federal Aviation Administration's acquisition of a new air tower control system or the traffic control systems undertaken by local governments. It is clear that these involve risk by the very nature of their being software intensive. Large-scale software development is complex and risky. In addition, the risk exposure can be quite great because large-scale systems can run into the hundreds of millions of dollars to acquire. On the other hand is the simple acquisition of an off-the-shelf

*Portions of this article have been used with permission from Donald J. Reifer and John J. Marciniak, "Acquistion Management," *Encyclopedia of Software Engineering,* 2nd ed., John Wiley & Sons.

piece of software such as a database management system (DBMS), which can be rather straightforward and not involve the risk exposure of a larger system. It is still an acquisition, but may not deserve the type of management attention that larger systems require. The agreement to buy it, in some cases, may be as simple as a purchase order. Between these two extremes lie a multitude of differing cases. Their treatment, from an acquisition management perspective, has to be gauged by the scope and complexity of the specific acquisition project.

Now that we understand what software acquisition is, let's see if we understand who is involved in it. For this, we use the implied model that we discussed above. It involves two parties: the acquirer or customer, and the supplier or developer. The acquirer wants to acquire a software system based on internal requirements and wishes to employ a development organization for the acquisition. The acquirer has decided that they will not develop the system themselves.

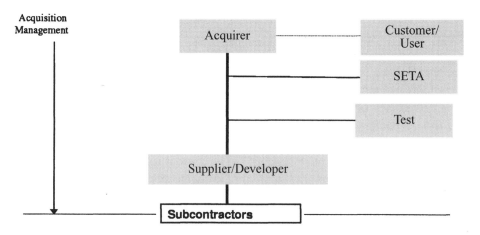

Figure 1: Acquisition Environment

Thus, we have the acquirer and developer in a relationship depicted by Figure 1. This figure draws attention to the various organizations that are involved in acquisition as well as the nature of the relationship between the acquirer and developer.

The acquirer collects requirements through a requirements elicitation process, then using a set of requirements that have been baselined, arranges for a suitable (qualified) supplier to develop the system. Typically a formal contract is used to consummate this agreement. The selection of the supplier may have been accomplished on a sole source basis or through a competitive procurement process. The acquirer is involved in an acquisition project—their role is termed *acquisition management*. The supplier is involved in a typical development situation—their role is to develop and manage the development of the software-intensive system and its delivery (project management) to the potential user or operator.

In managing the acquisition, a number of other organizations may be involved. For example, the acquirer may wish to have help in its management role and contract with a systems engineering and technical assistance (SETA) company to aid in their acquisition management capability role. Also, they may seek an independent organization to conduct system usability testing. On the other hand, the supplier may contract with other organizations for services such as the acquisition of commercial off-the-shelf (COTS) products that will be integrated into the system.

In the acquisition role a number of persons are involved aside from the traditional managers: contracting specialists, lawyers, testers, administrators, budget personnel, and so forth. Each of these persons has an "acquisition" role, some to more and some to a lesser extent. But, they are involved in acquisition management because skills other than software management are required.

Software Acquisition Capability Maturity Model® (SA-CMM®)

In 1996 the DoD put into place a process model for acquisition, the Software Acquisition Capability Maturity Model® (SA-CMM®) [2]. Industry had proved successful in improving software development processes with the use of the Capability Maturity Model® for Software (SW-CMM®) [3], but the acquirers or buyers of software-intensive systems continued to be a problem in software acquisition projects. Because of the interaction between acquirer and supplier and the perceived immaturity of acquisition organizations, a group of government and industry managers encouraged the Software Engineering Institute (SEI) to lead development of a CMM for the buyer—the Software Acquisition Capability Maturity Model® (SA-CMM®). The first version of the SA-CMM was published in 1996 and V1.02, incorporating public change requests, was published in 1999. The SA-CMM describes the acquirers' or buyers' role in software-intensive system acquisition. Its purpose is to provide a framework for benchmarking and improving an organization's software acquisition process.

Level	Focus	Key Process Areas	
5 Optimizing	Continuous process improvement	Acquisition Innovation Management Continuous Process Improvement	Quality
4 Quantitative	Quantitative management	Quantitative Acquisition Management Quantitative Process Management	
3 Defined	Process Standardization	Training Program Acquisition Risk Management Contract Performance Management Project Performance Management Process Definition and Maintenance	
2 Repeatable	Basic Project Management	Transition to Support Evaluation Contract Tracking and Oversight Project Management Requirements Development and Mgt. Solicitation Software Acquisition Planning	
1 Initial	Competent people and heroics		Risk Rework

Figure 2: The Software Acquisition Capability Maturity Model

The key process areas (KPAs) of the SA-CMM are shown in Figure 2. In line with maturity level (ML) definitions, ML 2 KPAs describe basic software acquisition project management, while ML 3 contains both organization process and proactive acquisition management KPAs. ML 4 focuses on quantitative techniques applied to the acquisition process and the products being acquired and ML 5 uses these quantitative measures as a basis for continuous improvement [3].

The SA-CMM provides a model for acquisition practice[1]. Its use, in the remainder of this article, serves as a basis for describing acquisition practices in an orderly and comprehensive manner. To do this the following subjects will be discussed (also shown is the cross-reference to SA-CMM KPAs where there is a difference of wording):

1. Software acquisition planning,

2. Requirements development and management,

3. Acquisition agreement (solicitation),

---

[1]In addition to the SA-CMM [4], other models exist that include acquisition management, notably the FAA-iCMM [5] and to a lessor extent the CMMI [6,7]. The FAA-CMM integrates the SA-CMM as well as the SW-CMM and SE-CMM into process areas and provides a mapping matrix. The CMMI merely treats supplier agreement management at ML 2, which is not a robust treatment of acquisition management. There are plans to incorporate acquisition management in a forthcoming revision to the CMMI.

4. Contract management (contract tracking/oversight, and contract performance management),

5. Project management (project management and project performance management),

6. Evaluation,

7. Acquisition risk management, and

8. Transition to support.

Each of these eight topics is briefly discussed in the following paragraphs.

Software Acquisition Planning

Planning is an activity that all managers must perform. Some may be under the impression that planning is a documentation exercise, that is, one prepares a plan for some activity. Plans are the *result* of the planning activity and serve to provide a description of the plan. Plans provide managers with benchmarks against which performance can be compared. The description, or plan, is usually an evolving document—it changes as the plan is executed and events occur or lessons are learned that dictate a change in course from the plan.

Planning is the first event that is initiated in the acquisition management life cycle of the system. Plans lay out how the system will be acquired, the management mechanisms that will be employed for managing the acquisition project, and the specific plans for areas such as testing and support of the system once it becomes operational. Planning encompasses development of all of the plans for the acquisition as well as plans to ensure support of the software-intensive system. Plans can be broken into the following three areas:

1. **Strategic plans.** These plans deal with key decisions that have to be made for the acquisition. The principal plan is the acquisition strategy, which lays out how the acquisition will be handled. It considers topics such as how the system will be acquired, for example, who will develop it, and if by a supplier the type of contracting process that will be used. For example, is the system going to be acquired from a specific supplier (i.e., sole source procurement) or is a competition warranted? It also considers issues such as whether the system can be acquired based on the technical facets of the effort, in other words, the risk of acquiring the system. In many cases, a full system acquisition (or development) may be postponed or deferred because technology will not support the acquisition within an acceptable level of risk. In these cases, a risk reduction effort may be put into place as a precursor to full-scale development.

2. **Management or tactical plans.** These documents typically are project management plans, or plans for the management of the acquisition project. Many plans need to be considered for an acquisition project. Some of these are "management" plans, test plans, solicitation plans, and evaluation plans.

3. **Support plans.** Support is an area that is often overlooked at the beginning of a project, however, early decisions can have an effect on supportability. Support plans need to outline issues such as the maintenance concept (who will provide support for the system, what facilities will be used, and what resources will be required). Supportability requirements (training, etc.) need to be collected and included in the statement of work (SOW), and life cycle cost estimates prepared (What is the life cycle cost of system support?).

Planning is documented in various ways. Usually, formal, stand-alone written plans are prepared for the acquisition strategy and management of the acquisition project. The form of the document is not important;

control and management of the plan are. Typically, the management plan is a stand-alone document. It may include other areas such as contract management, depending on the size of the acquisition project. Reifer and Marciniak recommend consideration of three formal documents as a minimum set: "There are three key planning documents in any software acquisition: the acquisition strategy document, the program management plan (PMP) and the software development plan (SDP) [8]."

Requirements Development and Management

Technical and nontechnical software contractual requirements are developed and managed throughout the acquisition cycle. The major features of requirements development and management process include:

1. Requirements elicitation,

2. Requirements baselining, and

3. Requirements management.

Requirements management actually includes the first two functions outlined above, however, it was important to stress these two areas. According to Al Davis [9], "Requirements management is the discipline of elicitation, triage, and specification of the initial and evolving requirements (q.v.) for a system." Triage is the process the acquisition team engages in to ascertain that they have the right set of requirements. Analyses can be conducted, and sometimes simulations are used, to get a better handle on requirements. For example, it has been found that static screens are useful for evaluating "display" requirements. As another example, simulation has been found useful in determining how best to satisfy performance requirements.

In requirements elicitation, requirements are gathered in a disciplined and methodological manner. This could occur in a variety of ways. In some cases, the system may be a replacement for an existing system. In that case, existing requirements need to be reviewed and additional requirements may be added. In a new system, the process is different. In this case the acquirer may wish to adopt a method for the collection of requirements. This might even include the use of a semiformal or formal method automated in a tool.

The critical part of requirements elicitation is deciding what is a real requirement and what is not, or perhaps not affordable. An initial set is collected through the selection of qualified persons who will contribute the requirements. One simply cannot go out and collect requirements from random users. Once an initial set is collected it should be subjected to some form of review. Initially this can be a peer review, but eventually the requirements must be tested against budgets, risk, and so forth, to determine the feasibility of the acquisition in terms of funding and schedule needs. The culmination of this process is a requirements statement or specification.

Once the specification is prepared and passes initial reviews, it must be placed under configuration control, a process normally called *baselining*. Creating a baseline implies that the documented set of requirements cannot be changed except by managed action (e.g., via controlled change). The reason for creating and managing a baseline is that subsequent actions are normally based on the baseline, such as procurement (selection of a supplier). If requirements are allowed to change during this period of time, it is impossible for the supplier to provide a realistic proposal for development of the system, and the integrity of the acquisition will be in serious jeopardy.

Acquisition Agreement (Solicitation)

Acquisition agreement is the process of obtaining a supplier (developer) and putting into place an agreement that describes the arrangement to which the two parties have agreed. Typically, this is accomplished through the use of a contract. If it is accomplished through some other form of arrangement, such as a teaming or strategic partnering agreement, the acquirer still has to ensure that appropriate provisions are in place so that it is clear what is to be accomplished, what is to be delivered, and what management practices are to be employed.

"A great deal of work must be done before a source can be selected. An acquisition strategy must be formulated, procurement plans prepared, management approaches developed, visibility and control provisions crystallized, documentation defined, schedule and cost estimates developed, and a draft contract readied. In addition, high-level requirements must be developed along with key performance parameters and specifications. A key part of the package is the Statement of Work (SOW) because it details the tasks that must be performed, their products, and documentation to be delivered as part of the contract [8]."

The major considerations associated with preparing a solicitation or acquisition agreement include the following:

1. Planning considers how the supplier will be acquired (sole source or some type of competition), the type of contractor that will be employed, how the supplier will be evaluated, and evaluation criteria.

2. Implementing the acquisition is a matter of following the solicitation plan. In a formal procurement, the request for proposal is issued, and the evaluation team is organized and instructed on their duties.

3. Solicitation prepares a solicitation package and selects a contractor best capable of satisfying the contract requirements.

An important part of solicitation is deciding what type of contract should be used. There are basically two different types [8]:

1. **Fixed-price contracts.** A firm fixed-price contract is the most typical fixed-price contract. It is a contract in which the acquirer agrees to pay a specified price when the goods or services are delivered and accepted. Other forms of fixed-price contacts are fixed-price with economic price adjustment (FPEPA), fixed-price incentive (FPI), and fixed-price redetermination (FPR).

2. **Cost-reimbursable contracts.** The cost plus incentive fee (CPIF) is the most commonly used cost-reimbursable contract type. It is similar to a fixed-price incentive contract; it uses fees to motivate the provider to control costs. Other forms are cost and cost sharing, cost plus award fee (CPAF), and cost plus fixed fee (CPFF).

These are the basic steps in the agreement (or solicitation) process:

1. **Preparing the solicitation.** The solicitation includes the SOW, evaluation criteria to be used in the selection process, and proposal preparation guidelines.

2. **Issuing the RFP.** The formal process of issuing the RFP to a broad and open set of prospective suppliers or to a limited set who have qualified to bid on the procurement.

3. **Proposal preparation.** The actions taken by prospective suppliers to provide a proposal based on the requirements contained in the RFP.

4. **Proposal evaluation.** The proposals are evaluated against evaluation criteria that have been prepared in advance as a part of the acquisition plan.

5. **Negotiations.** Negotiations are sometimes held with suppliers that have technically qualified to continue in the solicitation process. Usually these concentrate on cost or profit, however, they may include requirements, not from an attempt to question or change them, but to better understand them before they may be asked to present a best and final offer.

6. **Contract award.** The last step in the solicitation process, the selected supplier(s) is awarded the contract.

While these steps are often compressed or combined, they are not eliminated. The reason for this is simple. Each of these steps fills a specific purpose.

Contract Management

Contract management is the activity to manage a specific contract. It is closely related to project management; however, project management focuses on all of the aspects of the acquisition project, while contract management is principally concerned with how the supplier lives up to the agreement in place, and whether what is delivered meets the intended needs of the ultimate user of the system. This may seem like a dubious distinction to many. On large programs, several contracts (and subcontracts) may be in place. Each has to be "managed" to ensure that the supplier is meeting the terms of the agreement and what is being acquired meets the needs of the program and user. On a small effort, there may be only one supplier and, thus, one contract. In this case the activities of contract management and project management overlap in a number of areas and the contract management plan is probably integrated into the PMP or SDP. This is not important to worry about, but you should understand the basic management mechanisms that are important to use in a contract management situation.

The key management elements of contract management are as follows:

1. **Technical reviews.** Reviews start with the plans that the supplier will use to implement the program. These include a number of plans typically spelled out in the SOW. If they are not spelled out in the SOW, the acquirer should at least consider requiring review of contractor-generated plans to determine if they are adequate for the program. Plans include the software development plan (SDP), configuration management plan (CMP), test plan, and quality assurance (QA) plan. Note that the supplier also has a SDP. There are a number of plans that make sense for the acquirer and the supplier such as a project management plan, SDP, and risk management plan. At the acquirer level, these plans typically deal with the whole program to include all elements that may be involved with acquiring the system. The supplier plans, of course, deal with their specific part of the puzzle.

   Reviews of progress are also a key part of this process. The acquirer needs to specify what type of reviews will take place and their expectations for the review and ensure that a procedure is in place to carry out reviews. That procedure, typically a three-part process, calls for pre-review, during, and post-review activities. The premeeting process schedules the meeting, provides an agenda, and notifies personnel who need to attend of where and when the meeting will be held. During the meeting action items are collected, and after the meeting minutes are prepared and actions items are placed into a corrective action system so they can be managed to closure.

   The acquirer should also be concerned with the supplier's process. In concert with modern development, programs such as the SEI's SW-CMM have demonstrated that the process of development is key to reduced risk and higher productivity; in other words, key to a better chance of success. Appraisals of the supplier's process may be warranted, especially at the onset to determine if the capability to develop the system is realistic (that is, within acceptable risk). The ISO 9001 audit process is another example of the management attention that has been given to process management. Measurements from appraisals may be used to evaluate the supplier's performance and trends analyzed to ascertain schedule progress.

2. **Required contractor software planning.** If plans are expected by the acquirer, they need to be specified in the SOW so it is clear that they will be developed. Perhaps the acquirer does not want to make these a deliverable; however, they should at least require review of contractor-developed plans. Normally, if a contractor knows that the plan will be reviewed as part of the source selection activity or contract they will be motivated to not only produce one, but to be concerned with its viability and quality. If a plan needs to be delivered, and these are usually plans that bear on other contractual aspects such as support plans that the acquirer needs to use to develop and implement a proper support environment for the system, these need to be specified in the SOW and made a part of the contract.

3. **Progress Tracking.** Progress is normally tracked through formal and informal means. Informal means are through activities such as technical interchange and/or working group meetings. Formal means are through periodic progress reports that the acquirer receives and uses to assess progress. Typically, the most obvious reports are schedule and cost tracking. Schedule is tracked though key milestone achievements; cost typically is tracked through cost reporting mechanisms such as earned value management systems (see Figure 3). In the figure, the "value" of the budgeted cost of the work scheduled (BCWS) "earned" for doing the work is called *earned value* [11]. It should be obvious that supplier accounting procedures need to accommodate cost reporting procedures [10]. There are also a myriad of other techniques to track progress. Most of these are rooted in metrics that may be applied to track progress. Figure 4 shows one example of such an indicator used for tracking testing progress.

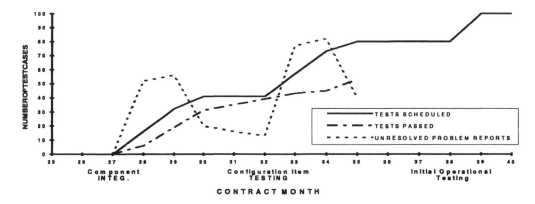

Figure 3: Earned Value

The key to tracking progress is to decide what is of special interest. All projects want to track cost and schedule—they are the standard items that people are familiar with and of high interest to senior managers. But technical items such as computer performance have to be tracked also, especially those that are of critical importance to the acquisition. There may be high-risk areas that also need tracking.

A couple of mechanisms are useful in this area that are used for the selection of metrics: Practical Software Measurement (PSM) [12,13] and the Goal-Question-Metric (G-Q-M) paradigm [14]. These measurement methodologies provide a way for determining what is important, and in the case of the PSM methodology, also suggesting the metrics that may be applied to get insight into contractor performance and assessing related development progress.

444

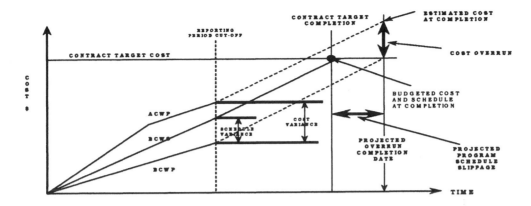

Figure 4: Test Progress

One of the key areas that needs to be tracked as a special attention item is the preparation for support of the system. In cases where the supplier is developing or providing the support environment, that should be an item that requires special attention and warrants measurement. The support environment could include a software engineering environment that those supporting and/or maintaining the system will need in order to provide keep the system operational.

4. **Change management.** The acquirer has to be able to manage changes to the system. Changes arise when the user decides that there is a need for a new or change to a requirement, or can be precipitated by other causes such as changes in technology capability. In these cases the team needs to analyze changes to see what their impact is on the performance, cost, and schedule of the acquisition project. The change should be coordinated with all affected groups and individuals, such as the contracting official, contractor, and end user. Once the change is accepted, it has to be controlled, that is, integrated into the system in a way that its identification is accounted for so that a history of the change is kept. The configuration management system supports this process.

5. **Issue/corrective action.** Every meaningful project needs to have a corrective action system in place. A corrective action system is an orderly way of keeping track of issues that arise from review meetings and interchanges. It not only lists the issues or problems, it keeps track of them from their identification to their closure. In this way issues and actions are managed to closure, ensuring the integrity of the review and management process.

Project Management

Project management is an all-encompassing activity. It is the capstone management activity of any software acquisition project. Management must be concerned with how well the suppliers are executing their tasks as well as how well the acquisition team is performing. Project management encompasses all of the basic management processes and practices for the acquisition project.

The top-level management plan is the project management plan (PMP). It contains all of the details that determine how the project will be managed, or directs the user to other documents that may provide additional detail (such as a test plan). Its key elements include these:

- *Organization.* Project team structure, roles, and responsibilities;

- Schedule;

- Resource requirements;

- Acquisition strategy;

- Project performance, cost, and schedule baselines;

- Engineering approach;

- Support requirements;

- Corrective action reporting procedures;

- End user involvement;

- Risk management;

- Training needs; and

- Interface management.

Project management is largely putting into place a sound plan, the PMP, and implementing the plan. In this implementation it is worth pointing out the following key practices:

- **Reviews.** The project team performs periodic reviews to ensure that the project is executing within its planned boundaries and that the projected needs of the end user will be satisfied. In the same manner as in contract management, reviews are held at the project level. Internal project reviews provide for communication between project members and a vehicle to communicate with users and supporting organizations (procurement) that are involved in the project. This provides for communication regarding critical issues. Reviews are also held with senior management. These reviews provide an oversight function. They typically are more concerned with cost and schedule, and the risks that would affect those two factors, however, they can look at other factors such as technical performance as well.

- **Risk management practices.** The project team must use a risk management system to examine issues, prioritize risks, implement mitigation actions, and manage the risk. These are normally accomplished as a part of the review process. A review of this area can be as simple as monitoring a top 10 risk list, or as extensive as reviewing mitigation plans and discussing mitigation actions. The project team identifies and analyzes risks and identifies specific risk mitigation actions for those risks.

- **Corrective action system.** The project team needs to organize and implement a corrective action system. Many projects leave this to the supplier;' however, this obviates the management responsibility of the acquirer and is a poor choice of alternatives except in small, one-supplier acquisition environments. The corrective actions system, as mentioned in contract management, is a disciplined way of tracking, controlling, and bringing to closure issues and actions from reviews, technical interchanges, audits, and other activities.

- **Tracking and measurement.** The project team needs to track the status of the project through factors such as funding, schedule, performance, and expenditures. A key part of this process is the collection of useful metrics. As mentioned previously cost (earned value) and schedule (e.g., Gantt charts) are commonly used. These provide a useful way of tracking, however, they need to be supplemented with measurements that get at technical issues such as processing response, Internet access, and memory availability. Also, the process of development may need to be tracked in situations where process appraisals are employed to ascertain the capability of a supplier to perform. Examples of process metrics are the effectiveness of quality assurance audits.

This tutorial volume contains numerous papers on project management topics or those interested in the subject. In addition, the bibliography at the end of the volume contains many references that should be examined for those who wish to build needed skills, knowledge, and abilities in the practice.

Evaluation

This function provides objective evidence that evolving software products and services satisfy contractual requirements. Evaluation is intended to ensure that all appropriate actions, considering the size and complexity of the system being acquired, are taken to check that the implementation meets the needs of the ultimate user.

The typical reaction to evaluation is to rely on the testing program. But, the testing program is only one of the techniques that the manager has available to support evaluation. All of the methods need to be considered and wrapped into the evaluation plan. Some of these are quality assurance, configuration management including audits such as the functional configuration audit (FCA) and the physical configuration audit (PCA), product audits that may be conducted outside the QA program, review of supplier documentation by the project team and other resources (in-plant inspectors), as well as testing of all kinds (e.g., system, acceptance, facility).

The evaluation plan, whether a stand-alone plan or part of the PMP or SDP, lays out the overall approach. It is then up to individual plans, for test, quality assurance, configuration management, and so on, to flush out the specific details of how these efforts will be conducted. Incidentally, these plans are normally supplier plans with the exception of, on large government programs, the overall test plan called the test and evaluation master plan. Although the government title includes "evaluation" the plan typically addresses only development and operational testing.

To recap what goes on here:

- The acquirer prepares an evaluation plan, which lays out the total program to evaluate the product and details other plans that flush out details.

- The supplier responds to the evaluation plan, as appropriate, with individual plans and effort in areas such as quality assurance and configuration management.

- The acquirer reviews these plans and monitors the efforts of the supplier in carrying them out.

- The evaluation results are examined, analyzed, and used as the basis for acceptance of the system/product.

Acquisition Risk Management

Risks are identified and addressed in both the acquisition planning and execution phases of the acquisition life cycle. The first considers the overall risk of undertaking the project; the second deals with risks during implementation.

A risk management program is part of an integrated and robust project management program. Risk management is an area that is often done poorly or does not consider all the risks associated with an acquisition, for example, the risks associated with the project management team being able to adequately perform its job.

The risks associated with the acquisition itself may be technical or programmatic in nature. Technical risks determine things like the acquisition approach. For example, if a part of the system has high development risk, that part may be prototyped or developed on a stand-alone basis before the major development is undertaken. This helps to keep resource expenditures low while the risk of the overall program is lowered to an acceptable level.

The second area, risk management during execution, is actually more complicated than most suspects. Many program offices rely on the supplier to manage risk. In a small program that might be acceptable, however, in programs of considerable size and complexity that is not a sound approach. Both the acquirer and the supplier need to have their own risk management programs in place. The acquirer's program manages the entire program, to include risks associated with the acquisition management team and across all of the suppliers that may be involved in the acquisition project. The supplier's program examines the risks associated with the development effort, prioritizes them based on impact, implements plans to reduce them, then follows through by closely managing risk mitigation actions throughout the life of the project.

Transition to Support

This activity is conducted to ensure the orderly transition of the software products being acquired to the eventual support organization. Support is the issue here. Any system has to be maintained once it is put into operational use. Supportability has to be planned for, in other words, it needs to be a part of initial acquisition planning. These issues need to be considered:

Who will support? On most projects, the initial effort is on getting on with the development process. People are not motivated or conditioned to think about support—it is too far off. With this mind-set, support typically gets shortchanged. After all, the objective is to provide something that people can use—not simply to develop a product. So the question about who will support is key in planning for support. In some cases the support organization is not known. But, considering the question forces a confrontation that eventually will produce an answer.

What does the developer need to do to provide for support? The developer may need to provide the capability for support—the facilities perhaps, but usually the environment—the tools, documents, and training needed to afford support. The acquirer needs to ensure that these requirements are stated in the SOW.

What facilities will be required? This is another key question that sets the planning for support into action. Quite often this is ignored until too late. It must be considered early so that the acquirer can make plans for its availability.

The key document for support is the transition to support plan. Sometimes this may have other names, such as *life-cycle support plan*. This plan can also be part of other planning documents, most notably, the PMP. In a large and complex project, however, the plan should be a stand-alone document.

A transition to support plan covers the following items [2]:

- The objectives and scope of the transition to support activities,

- Identification and involvement of the software support organization,

- Support resource requirements,

- A definition of transition activities,

- A schedule of transition activities,

- Allocation of transition responsibilities,

- Installation of products that are to be delivered, and

- Warranty and data rights provisions.

The project management team manages the implementation of the plan. A key part of this management process is the actual transition itself. During this period, there is a discontinuity when the system is placed into operation and support is handed over to a new organization. Before the system transitions it may be necessary to demonstrate that the new organization has the capability to provide support. A *capability demonstration* might be used for this purpose. Everybody involved must be clear about what is being handed over. When you buy a new car you are given an inventory of what the car contains. In like fashion, the list of deliverables needs to audited so it is clear that the supporter has all that is needed and has been promised according to the contract and transition plan. Configuration control of the product transfers to the supporter, and that transfer has to be made in a way that the integrity of the system remains intact—that is, identification of all components and supporting materials is maintained.

You are doing the right things in transition to support if you

- Plan for transition,

- Monitor the implementation of the plan, and

- Ensure that resources are available to cover transition.

Summary

Acquisition management is a serious and complex undertaking, as all software development and management activities tend to be. The techniques that have been described should provide the basis for understanding and guidance for an acquirer. They are not sophisticated or complex, but represent an initial approach to providing management mechanisms in this area. In CMM process parlance, these are basically ML 2 practices.

References

[1] John J. Marciniak and Donald J. Reifer, *Software Acquisition Management*, John Wiley & Sons, New York, 1990.

[2] J. Cooper, M. Fisher, and S. W. Sherer, *Software Acquisition Capability Maturity Model® (SA-CMM®) Version 1.02*, Technical Report CMU/SEI-99-TR-002, Software Engineering Institute, April 1999.

[3] M. Paulk. C. V. Weber, B. Curtis, and M. B. Chrises, *The Capability Maturity Model: Guidelines for Improving the Software Process*, Addison-Wesley, Reading, MA, 1995.

[4] John R. Ferguson, "Software Acquisition Capability Maturity Model," in *Encyclopedia of Software Engineering*, 2nd ed., John Wiley & Sons, New York, in preparation.

[5] Federal Aviation Administration, "Federal Aviation Administration Integrated Capability Maturity Model (FAA-iCMM)," http://www.faa.gov/aio/.

[6]   Winifred Menezes, "Capability Maturity Model Integrated," in *Encyclopedia of Software Engineering*, 2nd ed., John Wiley & Sons, New York, in preparation.

[7]   Software Engineering Institute, "Capability Maturity Model Integrated," http://www.sei.cmu.edu/cmmi/.

[8]   Donald J. Reifer and John J. Marciniak, "Acquisition Management," in *Encyclopedia of Software Engineering*, 2nd ed., John Wiley & Sons, New York, in preparation.

[9]   Alan Davis, "Requirements Management," in *Encyclopedia of Software Engineering*, 2nd ed., John Wiley & Sons, New York, in preparation.

[10] Donald J. Reifer, *Making the Software Business Case: Improvement by the Numbers*, Addison-Wesley, Reading, MA, 2002.

[11] M. Servello, "Earned Value," in *Encyclopedia of Software Engineering*, 2nd ed., John Wiley & Sons, New York, in preparation.

[12] Don S. Lucero, "Practical Software Measurement Insight: The Army-DoD Tool to Implement Issue-Driven Software Measurement," *CrossTalk*, June 1999.

[13] "Practical Software and Systems Measurement," http://www.psmsc.com.

[14] R. van Solingen, "Goal Question Metric Paradigm," in *Encyclopedia of Software Engineering*, 2nd ed., John Wiley & Sons, New York, in preparation.

Managing Subcontracts

Claire L. Brown, David "R. A." Neale, and Dr. Kenneth E. Nidiffer

Software Productivity Consortium

Recent literature in the field of software system development indicates that deteriorating subcontract relationships, late deliveries, higher than expected costs, operational disruption, and overall poor performance have led to lost business opportunities and project failures. To realize the full value from a software subcontractor, experience indicates the acquirer needs to expend significant effort to maximize supplier performance and build enduring business relationships that support the organization's goals.

This article describes the key criteria for a successful subcontract relationship and the activities to effectively manage such a relationship. These critical aspects of subcontracting are based on our consulting experience with many organizations involved in the development of software-intensive systems, as well as the best practices defined in the Software Acquisition Capability Maturity Model (SA-CMM®), the Integrated Capability Maturity Model (CMMI), and the *Project Management Book of Knowledge (PMBOK)*. Although we use the term *subcontract* throughout this article to refer to the supplier relationship, the actual form of the agreement between the acquirer and supplier may be less formal than a contract, such as a memorandum of understanding with another division within the same company.

Four key criteria are identified as being essential for successful subcontract management:

1. Mutually compatible objectives through joint development of a subcontract management plan;

2. Shared risks, resources, and responsibility through an integrated management structure;

3. Mutual trust and cooperation through acquirer's management skills; and

4. Common understanding through timely communications.

Managing the relationship encompasses the people, processes, methods, tools, and systems—within both the acquirer's and supplier's organizations—that are needed to achieve the goals and objectives of the project. The five primary activities of subcontract management include the following:

1. Monitor supplier processes.

2. Monitor performance factors.

3. Conduct reviews.

4. Manage risks.

5. Control change.

Joint Development of Subcontract Management Plan

Developing, following, and updating a subcontract management plan (SMP) are critical tasks if we are to effectively manage a supplier, particularly on large or complex projects. Involvement of the supplier early in the generation of this plan, while the subcontract is being negotiated, promotes positive cooperation in reaching project objectives and provides an understanding of the expected products and services in the context of the project's planned activities. Because of the contractual overhead involved in changing the subcontract agreement, items such as schedules and risks, which are likely to change during the period of performance, should be incorporated in the SMP and not in the subcontract agreement.

The supplier's own project plan may be incorporated or referenced in the acquirer's SMP to show their compatibility and interfaces. The acquirer and supplier must agree on how the effort will be managed, who will be responsible for what products and activities, and what mechanisms will be put in place to deal with issues as they arise. If both parties work jointly on developing the SMP, they are more likely to follow the plan, support the effort cooperatively, and work together to resolve future disagreements.

A complete SMP includes the following items:

Description of the subcontracting effort.   Describe the work to be done as well as objectives, constraints, assumptions, and the supplier's organization, personnel, location, and facilities.

Identification of the stakeholders.   Identify subcontract manager, senior management, technical personnel, support personnel, users, and customers, as applicable.

Work Breakdown Structure (WBS).   The acquirer's WBS incorporates all activities to be performed by the acquirer's staff in managing and supporting the subcontract. The supplier's WBS includes all the activities for the conduct of the effort as well as the supplier's management and support tasks.

Schedule of activities.   Plan and schedule activities for all WBS elements, including when meetings and reviews will be held and who is required to be in attendance.

Roles and responsibilities.   Identify who is responsible for planning, performing, reviewing, and approving the activities identified in the WBS.

Budget.   Allocate budget to each of the defined activities.

Risk management plan.   Identify and quantify the risks, mitigation plans, responsibilities, timeframes for action, and what to do if the mitigation actions fail.

Performance measurement plan.   Include data to be collected, when and by whom, determine who analyzes and reports the measurement analysis, and to whom and when reports are sent.

Work products.   Identify deliverables and project data that both the acquirer and the supplier will provide, when these items are due, and who is responsible for their development, review, and approval.

Resources, required skills, and knowledge.   Identify personnel qualifications. If training is needed, specify a training plan covering both acquirer and supplier staff.

Requirements change process. Describe how changes will be received, analyzed, documented, negotiated, and approved.

Quality assurance plan. This plan covers audits of the supplier's adherence to his defined process and satisfaction of contractual requirements in work products and services. It also identifies when and how reviews and audits will be conducted and to whom quality reports will be sent.

Configuration management plan. Define a plan for baselining work products and deliverables, auditing and reporting the configuration, and handling requests to change baselined products.

Communications plan. Identify what, when, how, and to whom information will be disseminated.

Tools, equipment, and facilities. Identify items that the acquirer must provide to the supplier for the effort and when these items are needed. Include software licenses, where applicable. Identify items that are to be returned at the end of the contract period.

Management Structure

A typical subcontract has a subcontract manager supported by committed technical or functional specialists, such as system engineers, configuration managers, quality assurance (QA) personnel, and contract administration, from both the acquirer and supplier organizations.

All of the staff involved with the subcontract need to have a common understanding of the project goals, performance criteria, working environment, culture, organizational values, and the roles and authority of each person on the team.

Although multiple approaches to subcontract management organizations have been designed, the integrated product team (IPT) has been shown to be an effective management structure for getting the two organizations to work cooperatively. Under the IPT approach, all functional disciplines required to acquire, define, develop, train, and support the new system are represented on a single team that meets regularly and works together to resolve issues. The system users should also be represented on the IPT, so that they are kept informed of the progress and issues and can interpret requirements appropriately. The IPT approach has been shown to reduce rework and retest, save costs, and increase teamwork and accountability [Fleming & Fleming 1993].

The IPT approach avoids the problems that inevitably occur when the acquirer and supplier work independently. The supplier delivers the product "over the transom," and the acquirer discovers that what was built is not what was needed. Requirements interpretation is almost always an issue, because the requirements statements are seldom precise enough or sufficiently detailed to represent the need clearly to all parties. So the supplier's interpretation ends up being different from the acquirer's. However, when members of the IPT discuss the ongoing activities, review each other's interim work products, and are available to answer questions and resolve issues, the misinterpretations are cleared up long before the final product is delivered.

In the case of a service supplier, an integrated services team, consisting of representatives of all the stakeholders, meets periodically in an informal manner to discuss service-related issues, identify opportunities for improvement, and clarify evolving roles and responsibilities over time. Working together to understand the needs of each of the stakeholders and the satisfaction of those needs by the service supplier avoids surprises and disagreements when the supplier's service-level performance is formally evaluated.

Another approach that has worked well for some organizations is colocation of the acquirer and supplier teams so that they are close enough to observe what's happening, to partake in informal conversations, and to understand the priorities of the other team. When the organizations are geographically separated and cannot colocate the entire team, one or more representatives of the supplier team can work at the acquirer's facility and serve as a liaison between the two teams, keeping both parties informed of ongoing activities.

If neither IPT or colocation approaches are used, the acquirer must rely on frequent status reviews, technical interchanges, and progress and performance evaluations to ensure that the supplier is meeting the contractual requirements, building the correct product, and following the development plan. Open and honest communication at these meetings is essential in this approach.

Acquirer Management Skills

The subcontract manager, who may also be the project manager, serves as a facilitator and an integrator of resources in managing the supplier relationship. He or she must understand the benefits of subcontracting, be supportive of the supplier, and be committed to flexibility because most subcontracts invariably require changes at some point. To manage the supplier relationship effectively, the subcontract manager must be skilled in negotiation, communication, strategic planning, and financial skills. Developing these skills takes years of experience and may require specific training to fill in any knowledge and skill gaps, particularly if this role is new to the subcontract manager.

Successful management of supplier relationships is built on trust and commitment to success by both parties [Greaver 1999]. For the integrated team or colocation approaches to be successful, the manager must focus on building trust among all members of both parties to effectively bring the participants together as one team. Techniques for team development include the following:

Team-building activities.   These activities can range from involving nonmanagement team members in the planning process to off-site professionally facilitated sessions designed to improve interpersonal relationships. Holding social events, at which the team members can get to know each other more personally, helps to coalesce the team.

Reward and recognition systems.   Reward systems include such things as awards, gifts, certificates, letters of appreciation, promotions, and bonuses linked to performance. Predefined supplier rewards may be built into the subcontract in the form of incentive fees, award fees, or profit sharing. But providing small, unexpected rewards to those whose actions and performance you wish to promote goes a long way toward to making the supplier feel like a welcome and appreciated part of the team.

Training.   Necessary skills training or orientation sessions may be formal, such as classroom or computer-based courses, or informal, such as on-the-job mentoring or feedback from other team members. When a supplier will be working at the acquirer's site, the subcontract manager needs to ensure that the supplier's personnel are oriented to the working environment, cultural norms, and project goals. The training plan in the SMP should identify the required training, but day-to-day mentoring supplements the more formal education mechanisms.

Timely Communication

Lack of timeliness on the part of the acquirer in responding to subcontract issues can result in supplier delays, impacts on supplier performance, and inaccurate supplier assumptions. Successful subcontract management depends on monitoring and evaluating performance factors, timely review of supplier plans, status, and procedures, providing technical comments back to the supplier on their deliverables as scheduled, mitigating and tracking risks, and addressing and resolving issues as they occur.

The contractual agreement and the SMP form the basis for managing the relationship and they define the formal channels of communication. But in an effective cooperative relationship, many informal lines of communication will be developed. As unforeseen problems arise during the subcontract period, these informal channels serve to promote faster communication and resolution of the issues.

Developing a cooperative and understanding relationship with the supplier through timely communications between members of both teams helps to facilitate requests for changes and resolution of disputes at the lowest possible levels. For instance, if the supplier's software engineers are having a technical interface problem, they can discuss and resolve the problem with the acquirer's system engineers without involving their managers. Of course, any changes to requirements necessitate going through the appropriate chain of command, the configuration control board, and the contracting officer. Ideally, the subcontract manager and the supplier's project manager should be able to resolve any programmatic issue between them without involving senior management or contracting officers, unless a change in the contract is required. When either feels that they cannot trust the other, all disputes tend to get raised to a higher-level of management and can cause contention throughout the subcontract.

When contract deliverables are provided to the acquirer, it is important that the materials be reviewed quickly and comments provided back to the supplier before further development has progressed very far. Delays in providing feedback inevitably cause extra rework and lead to frustration on the part of the supplier. If no feedback is provided, the supplier will believe that the acquirer is not even paying attention to what they are doing and will likely put much less emphasis on doing a good job.

Many different communications techniques, such as briefings, reports, status meetings, technical reviews, videoconferencing, advanced teleconferencing, collaborative online tools, e-mail, and Web pages, should be used to enhance communications between the people in both organizations. An adequate communication plan defining the communication technology and periodic face-to-face meetings should be developed as part of the SMP. This is especially important if geographic factors, such as different time zones or cultures, need to be considered.

Geographically distributed teams present a significant challenge to managers in team building and in communications development. The subcontract manager must plan on frequent trips to the supplier's facility to observe the progress and activities. Likewise, the supplier must plan on frequent interactions with the acquirer to keep the lines of communication open. In these situations, active use of collaborative online tools, e-mail, and the telephone is essential to replace the informal interactions that occur when teams are colocated. Daily updates of information during critical phases of a project may be required.

Subcontract Management Activities

Managing the subcontract relationship entails monitoring and evaluating supplier processes, deliverables, and performance factors as specified in the supplier agreement. The tasks of this process are performed in accordance with the SMP, and include periodic tracking of cost, schedule, risks, changes, and technical performance, as well as conducting informal and formal reviews of both deliverables and status.

Monitor Supplier Processes and Deliverables

The acquirer's QA and configuration management (CM) personnel need to review and evaluate the supplier's QA and CM plans and periodically the execution of these plans. These plans should be reviewed at the same time as the management review of the supplier's project plan. Review of their QA plan focuses on whether it is adequate to monitor their own process performance and work product quality. Review of their CM plan ensures its adequacy for identifying, controlling, and auditing their product configuration. Discrepancies or insufficiencies that are found must be reported to the supplier and the revised plan must be reviewed again to ensure that it has adequately addressed the issues.

Periodic review of the supplier's QA and CM process during the subcontract period ensures that they are following their plans, procedures, and standards, appropriately documenting the results, and taking corrective action as needed. The periodicity of reviews and the extent of sampling of their process depend on the supplier's overall experience and capability and the acquirer's confidence in their ability to perform QA and CM functions. If the acquirer believes that the supplier is not adequately focused on quality issues, the subcontract manager must plan a significant amount of oversight of their processes. Any issues and deviations found in these reviews must be documented and reported to both supplier and acquirer management teams.

The subcontract manager is responsible for reviewing the supplier's project plan at the beginning of the contract and checking periodically that it has been appropriately revised as a result of changes in the project. The acquirer should perform periodic audits of the performance of the supplier against their project plan to determine if they are following the current plan. For long-term subcontracts where the supplier's performance could have a significant impact on project success, the acquirer may choose to conduct a process appraisal of the supplier against an industry capability model such as the CMMI. The results of such an appraisal will indicate not only which process areas the supplier is not performing well in, but also what practices they need to institute to improve performance.

Every deliverable that the supplier provides must be reviewed for conformance to the contractual requirements, consistency with other project documentation, and technical adequacy. All deviations from the expected content, format, or performance must be reported to the supplier and tracked as action items to closure. However, this does not give the acquirer the opportunity to impose new standards, requirements, or expectations that were not identified in the supplier agreement.

Monitor Performance Factors

Monitoring objective performance factors requires consistent oversight regarding the collection and analysis of performance measures that indicate achievement of project objectives and anticipated benefits. Use the results of the performance measures to help the supplier improve performance and to nurture a long-term relationship.

The performance measurement plan in the SMP establishes the basis for performance and management reviews, provides the rationale for making changes in service levels and expectations, and helps the acquirer decide the future of the relationship at subcontract renewal time.

Performance measurements should be compatible with the supplier's processes so they do not impose an undue burden; they should be consistent with the type of contract, for example, a fixed-price contract would not expect monthly cost data but might expect monthly schedule data; and they should be supportive of the project objectives and the risks associated with the supplier so that management stays focused on tracking the important issues.

When the supplier is providing services, the users of the service should provide data on their satisfaction with the service provider. When measures such as cost, schedule, and quality data are obtained directly from the supplier, the acquirer should request the raw data and perform an independent analysis of it, rather than getting only summary data from the supplier. The specific performance measures defined in the SMP depend on the type of services or products being provided, the project objectives and issues, and the level of service that was negotiated. For more detailed information about a structured measurement approach and the types of measurements that address particular issues, see Department of Defense and U.S. Army [U.S. Army 2000].

Conduct Reviews

The open and honest communication required to effectively manage the supplier relationship can be nurtured with frequent regular reviews involving the responsible managers and staff from both organizations. These meetings must not be contentious confrontations between the parties, but rather cooperative sharing of information and joint discussions of how best to resolve any issues. Agendas must be prepared prior to the meetings to keep the discussion meaningful and on track. Action items with due dates need to be assigned during the meetings and then tracked to closure at subsequent meetings.

Typical types of reviews include the following:

Regular status.   Held weekly or monthly, these are status meetings with the supplier to review progress, performance, and current issues. Typical items to be discussed include deviations from planned schedule, effort, cost, and technical performance.

Formal reviews.   A common practice is to schedule and hold complete project reviews with the supplier, project manager, and senior-level management from both organizations at key milestones. Typical items to be reviewed include risks, dependencies, schedule, cost, technical performance, requirements or design change activity, action items, and changes in objectives, constraints, or assumptions.

Performance evaluation.   This is a periodic overall appraisal of the supplier's performance against previously negotiated goals or thresholds. The appraisal is an objective evaluation of supplier results, as shown by quantitative data, against the defined performance criteria.

Technical interchanges.   Technical personnel from both organizations meet to freely exchange knowledge and expertise on design, development, and interface issues. All affected stakeholders should be involved in these discussions.

QA reviews and audits.   QA review and audit plans are defined in the SMP, for the purpose of:

- Assessing process compliance with the subcontract and any applicable project-specific processes and procedures,

- Evaluating the satisfaction of subcontract requirements in deliverable work products and services , and

- Documenting and reporting any deviations or noncompliance issues found.

Control Risks

A continuous disciplined process of identifying, analyzing, and mitigating risks is an essential part of any project. The output of an initial risk analysis is a risk management plan documented in the SMP, which is then continuously updated throughout the project. Requiring the supplier to generate a risk management plan is one way to get them involved in the risk management process. However, the subcontract manager needs to involve and get the perspective of all stakeholders to have a true picture of the project risks. Risks that have a high probability of impacting the project must be tracked and monitored at set review times and when events occur that affect those risks.

The goals and objectives of the subcontract serve as a guide to risk determination. If a potential problem does not impact the goals or objectives, it should not be considered a project risk. Categorizing risks into areas such as cost, schedule, and technical performance helps in developing and implementing mitigation strategies that reduce related risks. The magnitude of the risk, in terms of its probability of occurrence and its impact on the project objectives, determines how much effort should be placed on trying to avoid or mitigate it.

Once mitigation strategies have been identified for the largest risks, the subcontract manager must assign actions to ensure that the mitigation is performed and regularly review the status of those actions and the effect they are having on the risks. Regular risk reviews are used to identify and analyze new risks, as well as evaluate mitigation actions for existing risks. Risks will change over time, the risks will become better understood, and the environment will change. By conducting these risk reviews, the subcontract manager can determine if the total subcontract risk is increasing or decreasing.

Manage Changes

Another key element of managing subcontracts is a well-defined and mutually agreed-upon change process. The supplier agreement should identify who can propose changes, when and to whom changes can be proposed, what approvals are necessary, and when change requires renegotiation of some aspect of the subcontract. A plan should be included in the SMP for handling changes in key personnel, project objectives, requirements of products and services, customer's needs, and technology and marketplace conditions.

Documentation of requirements changes should include a description of the change, reason for change, type of change (for example, interface, requirements, usability), amount of effort required to implement, functional impact, and implementation schedule. Summary information about such things as number of changes, total effort expended for changes, trends of change requests, and rework costs should be documented and maintained. This information can give the subcontract manager insight into whether or not the project will complete on time and within budget. The change control board made up of staff and management from both organizations reviews change requests and approves them prior to implementation.

It may be necessary to revise the contractual agreement, SMP, affected project plans, and schedules to remain consistent with approved changes in the project. If these plans are not kept up to date, no one will continue to follow them.

Regardless of how confident the acquirer is of the supplier's ability to perform, the subcontract manager should always be prepared to handle problems if and when they occur. Two mechanisms that address this issue should be part of the supplier agreement: a problem escalation process and financial incentives or penalties.

Escalation of Problems

It is preferable for subcontract problems to be resolved at the lowest possible organizational level. The subcontract management team and the supplier can resolve less significant day-to-day problems without senior management involvement. If problems cannot be resolved at this level, they must be brought to the attention of senior-level management or an oversight committee for resolution. If senior management or the committee cannot resolve the issue, then mediation or arbitration by third-party experts may be invoked as a resolution mechanism. The last resort is to proceed through the judicial system.

An important principle in managing the relationship is to define in advance the escalation process to be used for the resolution of contractual issues. The appropriate time limits for resolution at each stage of the escalation must be specified. The escalation process should be tied to an objective scoring system, for example, if projections indicate a milestone being missed by 5 to 10 percent, then appropriate corrective action is planned and agreed to by the project team; or if delivery will be missed by more than 10 percent, then escalation to senior management is required to resolve the issue.

Incentives and Penalties

Many contractual agreements have financial incentives and penalties tied to achieving selected or overall objectives. The goal of incentives and penalties is to elicit supplier behavior to fix problems and provide for continuous improvement, innovation, and proactive efforts that advance the achievement of the project goals and objectives. The key principle is to fairly and consistently apply these incentives and penalties.

The following types of incentives may be considered:

Gain-sharing.   The supplier receives a portion of any additional savings it can generate for the project through its efforts. Savings might come from driving down the costs of services or implementing new technologies.

Achievement bonuses.   Typically, one-time payments provided for reaching certain objectives, which may be tied to earlier-than-expected completion dates, higher-than-committed service levels, or better-than-expected throughput.

Performance-based pricing.   When performance in a given time period exceeds some specified criteria, additional payments apply; when it falls short, penalties are imposed [Klepper & Jones 1998].

Different types of penalties that may be imposed include the following:

Cash penalties.   Reduction in payments to the supplier due to failure to meet a contractual obligation, such as a critical schedule deadline (this could be a specific amount per day).

Credits against future payments.   To compensate for work that is not up to par but has already been paid for, future payments are reduced.

Delayed payment.   Payment for current work is delayed until a problem is resolved. Such penalties should be used only to protect the most critical items to the business. Penalties must be tightly tied to measurable performance items so that failure to meet the performance requirement is unambiguous.

Conclusion

It is possible to engage a supplier who delivers high-quality products on time and within budget, supports the overall project objectives, and improves the system's operational capability. However, the subcontract manager's actions in managing the supplier relationship have a very strong impact on the supplier's desire to do so. The type of relationship developed from the start sets the tone for interactions throughout the contract period.

A particularly effective relationship is a strategic alliance or partnership, where the supplier and acquirer together develop a strategic plan for the product or service. For instance, the acquirer may fund the development of a new product for their current system, but assign the rights to the supplier to market the product 6 months after delivery to the acquirer. Such an alliance motivates the supplier to develop the best possible product and the acquirer is ensured a head start on beating the competition to market.

Good supplier relationships are founded on the principles of sound project management and supported by an atmosphere of mutual trust and cooperation. If the subcontract manager can create situations where both sides always win their key objectives, no one loses.

References

[Fleming & Fleming 1993] Fleming, Quentin W., and Quentin J. Fleming, *Subcontract Planning and Organization*, Probus Professional Publishing, Chicago, 1993. An excellent subcontract management text that addresses the complexities of government as well as commercial contracting and follows the guidance provided in the PMBOK. It covers the decisions to make or buy, to team or not to team, and to select the most appropriate type of subcontract, and provides detailed contents of a subcontract management plan.

[Greaver 1999] Greaver II, Maurice, F., *Strategic Outsourcing, A Structured Approach to Outsourcing Decisions and Initiatives*, AMACOM, an imprint of AMA Publications, New York, 1999. This text provides a methodology with seven steps to successful outsourcing: planning initiatives, exploring strategic implications, analyzing costs and performances, selecting providers, negotiating terms, transitioning resources, and managing relationships.

[Klepper & Jones 1998] Klepper, Robert, and Wendell O. Jones, *Outsourcing Information Technology, Systems and Services*, Prentice-Hall, Upper Saddle River, NJ, 1998. This book explains the world of outsourcing relationships clearly and comprehensively. It provides extensive coverage of risks and rewards of outsourcing, the proposal and contract negotiations processes, transitioning, and managing the relationship.

[U.S. Army 2000] Department of Defense and U.S. Army, "Practical Software and Systems Measurement; A Foundation for Objective Project Management," version 4.0b, http://www.psmsc.com, 2000. The Practical Software Measurement Support Center produces a guidebook, tool, and training courses that support a measurement methodology based on defining and using measures that address the important issues and objectives of a project and organization. This well-structured methodology is practical and easy to use by novices as well as experienced measurement analysts and project managers.

Other Useful Readings

Ang, S., and C. Beath, "Hierarchical Elements in Software Contracts," *Journal of Organizational Computing*, 3(3), 329–361, 1993.

Carmel, Erran, *Global Software Teams*, Prentice-Hall PTR, Upper Saddle River, NJ, 1999.

Charette, Robert N., *Software Engineering Risk Analysis and Management*, Intertext Publications, New York, 1989.

CMMI Product Development Team, "CMMISM—SE/SW, Version 1.0," Software Engineering Institute, Pittsburgh, PA, 2001.

Cooper, Jack, Mathew Fisher, and S. Wayne Sherer, "Software Acquisition Capability Maturity Model® (SA-CMM) Version 1.02," Software Engineering Institute, Pittsburgh, PA, 1999.

Corbett, Michael F., "Disciplines of Outsourcing, Best Practices in Managing the Outsourcing Relationship," http://www.FIRMBUILDER.com, 2001.

Fox, Geraldine, "From Commodity Vendor to Strategic Partner: Moving Outsourcing Relationships Up the Value Chain," Compass America, Reston, VA, http://209.238.236.162/pubs/outvalue.htm, 1999.

Project Management Institute, *A Guide to the Project Management Body of Knowledge (PMBOK)*, Project Management Institute, Upper Darby, PA, 2000.

Marciniak, John J., and Donald J. Reifer, *Software Acquisition Management*, John Wiley & Sons, New York, 1991.

Quinn, James Brian, and Frederick G. Hilmer, "Strategic Outsourcing," *Sloan Management Review*, Summer 1994, pp. 43–55.

Rizzo, Jr., Michael A., "The U-Shaped Customer Satisfaction Effect," *PM Network*, May 2001, pp. 53–55.

Software Productivity Consortium, "Evolutionary Spiral Process Model Guidebook," SPC-91076-MC, version 03.00.05, Software Productivity Consortium, Herndon, VA, 1993.

Software Productivity Consortium, "Managing Risks Course," SPC-97083-MC, version 01.01.00, Software Productivity Consortium, Herndon, VA, 1998.

Software Productivity Consortium, "Techniques for Enterprise Measurement," SPC-98016-MC, version 01.00.03, Software Productivity Consortium, Herndon, VA, 1999.

Software Productivity Consortium, "Distributed Development Technical Report," SPC-2001014-MC, version 01.00.00, Software Productivity Consortium, Herndon, VA, 2001.

Software Productivity Consortium, "Principles of Project Management," SPC2001008-MC, version 01.00.00, Software Productivity Consortium, Herndon, VA, 2001.

Software Licensing: A Missed Opportunity

Donald J. Reifer
Reifer Consultants, Inc.

Introduction

For the past 3 years, we have been working with clients to identify best software acquisition practices. This effort has been in response to our clients who are using suppliers (contractors, subcontractors, vendors, partners, etc.) to fill their software needs. As these clients made the transition to the use of suppliers, they quickly realized that their supplier management practices were out of date. For example, while their software managers were skilled in managing software development projects, few of them knew how to motivate and manage a third party hired to do the same job under a contractual relationship. As another example, while many of these clients had what most in the business would consider mature processes [e.g., rated at least as a level 3 using the Software Engineering Institute's Capability Maturity Model (CMM) for software [1]], few of their practices adequately addressed supplier management issues such as enterprise-wide licensing, outsourcing, and contracting.

During our investigations, we conducted seven "quick-look appraisals" to determine where improvements were needed in acquisition management practices [2]. The three most promising targets of opportunity identified by our four commercial appraisals were improved software licensing, better commercial off-the-shelf (COTS) management, and more effective strategic partnering and outsourcing. In contrast, the three appraisals of government organizations that we conducted identified acquisition planning, solicitation, and evaluation practices as primary targets for process improvement. Based on these findings, we developed best practices for all six targets. However, this paper focuses on just one of these targets, software licensing, because we believe that improvement in this area is the opportunity missed most often in most of the firms with which we deal.

Current Licensing Practices

Software licenses present a challenge to most software managers. That's because licensing costs are increasingly becoming a larger part of their software budgets as more and more packaged software is being incorporated into their products. Many organizations have gotten in trouble because they didn't pay attention to the license's terms and conditions (what happens when the package doesn't perform as advertised, e.g., what recourse is available) and did not adequately manage the license once awarded (let licenses lapse, did not transfer excess licenses, etc.).

Licenses are legal contracts that are enforceable in courts of law whereby one person, the licenser, grants to another, the licensee, certain rights in specified property belonging to the licenser. Typically, software licenses are written to define the applicable law, protect intellectual property rights, and limit the liability of the licenser. For example, licenses for operating system packages like Windows limit the licenser's liability to replacement of the software. Software licenses can be expensive because they oblige the licenser to pay a fee based on their usage of the software (i.e., so much a seat or sublicense). Because licenses are legal documents, many of their terms and conditions are often unintelligible to lay personnel like programmers.

Licensing has a life cycle that parallels that used for software development. As software requirements are formulated, a make/buy analysis is performed to determine whether use of COTS software packages could be used to cut costs, speed development, and/or improve quality. Market research is conducted to identify candidate packages that satisfy these requirements and assess package and vendor capabilities including financials. Suitable candidates are then selected and purchased. The package is then delivered, accepted, and either put into operation or integrated into a product. Once operational, the package is refreshed (i.e., new versions replace old ones) and renewed (i.e., annual licenses are renewed). When the license for the package expires, the agreement is terminated.

In addition to being involved in the selection and acquisition of the package, software managers must keep track of their active licenses so they can maximize their utilization after they are acquired. To manage existing licenses, new processes and tools may need to be developed. For example, a metering tool may be needed to keep track of package utilization if there are limits on the number of concurrent users for the software. In addition, focal points for licenses must be designated, because model license agreements are developed to serve as the basis for negotiation with suppliers who are selected based on "best value" concepts.

Licensing practices used in the organizations that we appraised were for the most part ad hoc and chaotic. Most software packages were licensed on a project-by-project basis. Few of the projects that we interviewed took exceptions to the standard license terms and conditions offered by the software package vendors. Some of the organizations we interviewed did not know how many licenses they held for the software or when they expired. Transfers of licenses for unused seats between projects and leveraged procurements to take advantage of volume discounts were new ideas when we introduced them in our discussions. So was the concept of a basic ordering agreement (i.e., BOA is a prenegotiated contract that provides favorable terms and volume discounts that any project can use to order COTS packages from a vendor).

Based on our analysis, introduction of better licensing practices could save most of the organizations we appraised millions of dollars annually. By just leveraging their purchasing power with their vendors across projects, these organizations could increase their quantity discounts from 10 to 40 percent. It was therefore not surprising that they selected software licensing as a primary target for improvement once our appraisal findings were made public.

An Improved Software Licensing Approach

To improve the licensing process for our clients, we devised the recommended process pictured in Figure 1. Table 1 was developed to summarize the salient characteristics of this process. As the figure and table illustrate, the process is very comprehensive. The objective of the process is to allow organizations to lever their corporate buying power to purchase software licenses typically acquired at the project level at a reasonable cost. To accomplish this goal, many activities need to be performed and a new review held, the licensing review, prior to signing a software license with a vendor. The roles of buyer, supplier, and customer are spelled out in Table 1 along with the four primary activities, their inputs and outputs, the entry and exit criteria, the validation points, and the measures of success. The process doesn't end with acquisition. The last activity focuses attention on managing licenses once they're operational.

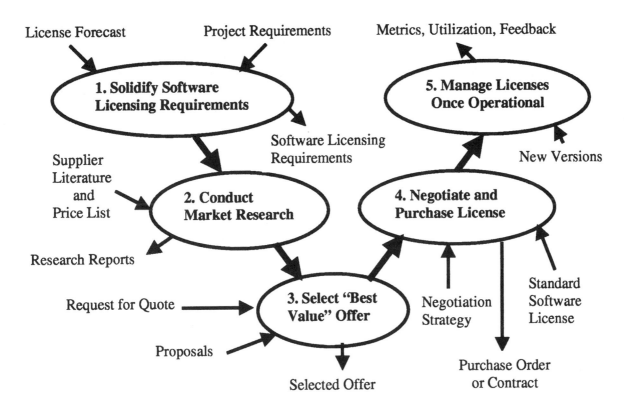

Figure 1: Licensing process flow diagram

Guiding Principles

Using Figure 1 for context, we have developed five guiding principles for use in implementing our process and its attendant best practices. Principles are strategic, while practices are tactical. We recommend that you use these principles as you put your practices into motion:

- **Know Your Licensing Requirements.** Poll your users across the organization to get a full and accurate forecast of your licensing requirements. Make sure that you include both general-purpose and project-specific needs in the tally.

- **Have a Standard License Handy.** Recognize that supplier licenses are written to protect them, not you. Insist on using your license terms instead of theirs because they were developed with your needs in mind.

- **Negotiate Licenses from a Position of Strength.** Research suppliers to understand how to gain the advantage before entering into an agreement with them. Formulate a strategy and have your numbers (past sales, order quantities, etc.) readily available.

- **Focus on Getting "Best Value" for Your Money.** Use competitive market forces whenever possible to get the most for your money. Use weighted "best value" criteria to make your selection. Avoid single sources when there are several vendors who could possibly meet your needs.

- **Pay Attention to the Details.** When it comes to licensing, the devil is in the details. Allocate the time and resources necessary to determine exactly what the license says. Then, bring in the experts to work any outstanding issues with the vendor before recommending and going ahead with the purchase.

Table 1 is a template designed to help develop a licensing process by amplifying the details of the process shown in Figure 1. In addition to summarizing activities and their inputs/outputs, it provides entry/exit criteria, measures of success, and role statements. It also calls for using a license review to validate needs and consolidate requirements. This review should be held annually just prior to solidifying the capital budget. The reason for this is simple. If the projects can't fund the licenses fully, the organization may be called on to provide financial support.

Related Best Practices

The following four "best practices" provide you with the structure for implementing the recommended process that we illustrated in Figure 1. The principles explained earlier provide a foundation for putting these practices into action.

- **Enterprise-Wide Requirements Forecasting.** Use an annual license forecast to determine licensing requirements for the organization. Tally the number of licenses each project anticipates buying into a composite list. Such a forecast allows you to lever your buying power to negotiate favorable terms with your vendors. Conduct a license review to go over your forecasts and develop acquisition strategies.

- **Market Research/Capital Planning.** Determine whether competitive products exist and whether suppliers are qualified and capable of delivering on their promises. In other words, research both the product and the supplier to determine whether they can satisfy your requirements without any difficulties. If licenses are capitalized, makes sure budgets are established in the capital plan in anticipation of their purchase.

- **Evaluation and Procurement.** Thoroughly examine the options, which provide the "best value." Emphasize past performance, relationships, and experience when selecting a vendor. Try the package before you buy it if you can to determine what it can do for you and to you. Negotiate fair and equitable terms with the vendor. Build an alliance and team with the vendor if you need to influence the direction they will take with their products in the future.

- **License Agreements and Management.** Track license utilization (batch purchasing power across projects to get deeper discounts, return unused licenses before their renewal dates, etc.) and maintain a database of pertinent licensing information. Refresh and renew licenses when necessary. Because of their cost, manage licenses as major organizational assets.

This licensing process makes use of an annual forecast to identify opportunities for cost savings and establishes win-win conditions through its "best value" criteria for both buyer and supplier. License reviews are held during the process to determine the following:

- Whether purchases are warranted (project needs have been authenticated, market research has been conducted, past performance has been examined, etc.) and

- Whether the vendor is providing "best value" (license terms and conditions are not overly restrictive, discounts are attractive, service preference for bug fixes is guaranteed, and so on).

The process assumes that a framework for evaluating packages and the vendors that supply them is in place. The framework would be used to rate criteria pertinent to making your selection decision. Several such frameworks have been advanced for screening COTS packages [3].

ENTRY CRITERIA	ACTIVITIES	EXIT CRITERIA
• Annual software license forecast • Funds appropriated for the license purchase • Legal and contracts specialists on-board	• Solidify software licensing requirements • Conduct market research • Select "best value" offer • Negotiate and acquire license • Manage licenses once operational (renew and refresh licenses)	• Acceptable license terms and conditions negotiated • Price points negotiated as a function of quantity • License executed by the proper authority • Usage of licenses tracked • Renewal and refresh of licenses justified
INPUTS	**VALIDATION**	**OUTPUTS**
• License forecast • Project requirements • Supplier literature and price lists • Request for quote • Proposals • Negotiation strategy • Standard license • New versions	• License review	• Software licensing requirements (including annual updates) • Market research reports • Selected offer • Purchase order or contract with license attached to it • Metrics, utilization, feedback (about license)
ROLES	**PURPOSE**	**MEASURES OF SUCCESS**
• *Buyer* – negotiates terms and conditions of the license agreement based upon "best value" • *Supplier* – preserves overall pricing integrity by negotiating equitable license terms • *Customer* – establishes the software license order requirements based on an accurate assessment of user needs	• Leverage corporate buying power to purchase at a reasonable cost software licenses for enough seats for the users to get their work done efficiently	• Projected number of seats to be licensed is large enough to provide negotiating leverage • Supplier and buyer remain fair and flexible during negotiations • Licensing options can be pursued (shared royalties, variable discounts, etc.) • Both buyer and supplier provide protection for their investments

Table 1: Licensing Process Summary

The process also advocates setting up a corporate software license database that can be used to facilitate management of licenses once they are placed with the vendors. This database provides those managing the licenses, the relationship managers, with information about the vendor, who is authorized to use the product, renewal dates, license terms, discounts, and how terms will be enforced. Often, such information is made available to prospective users, along with past performance data and a copy of the license agreement, so that they understand license terms more fully. In addition, many firms use specialized tools to meter the use of their licensed software and to advise users when the license is due for renewal.

Trial Use Experience

The license process was given to two commercial organizations for trial use for 2 years at the beginning of 1998 and ending in 2000 [4]. Both organizations identified software licensing as a target area of process improvement after our appraisal was completed. Both had process groups that took responsibility for process sponsorship. Both involved many stakeholders and both approached improved licensing using a philosophy of partnering with the vendors and building alliances, not maintaining an antagonistic relationship.

The first organization initiated their improvement efforts by placing a call for a license forecast. This call asked project personnel to supply specific information about products, why they were selected, in what order quantity, when they were needed, and how many dollars were committed to be spent. In parallel, the organization developed a standard license that its purchasing personnel used as a tool during vendor negotiations. This license contained nonstandard terms and conditions that would have to be agreed to prior to entering into an agreement (e.g., transfer of seat licenses between projects, maintenance upgrades, receiving priority in service calls). Based on the forecast, this organization found that they could commit to an increased number of licenses, allowing them to receive a 24 percent discount instead of a nominal 10 percent savings. Negotiations were held with three vendors. All agreed to the revised license terms and conditions. The firm realized a net savings of about $500,000 after all was said and done.

The second organization's implementation of the process resulted in even more dramatic savings. In the past, they had purchased 127 individually negotiated operating system licenses from a single vendor for use across 30 projects within one division. Needless to say, very little leverage was achieved when one project tried to negotiate licenses with the vendor because at most they were buying four to eight developer license seats. In addition, the operating system had a run-time license associated with it as well. As a result, the organization had to pay a royalty for every product they sold that contained the executable operating system. Although these costs were acceptable at the project level, the licensing costs for this software across the division were exceeding $1.0 million annually. Negotiating discounts after the fact was not something the vendor was motivated to do. However, they were much more flexible with their run-time and maintenance license costs when they were approached with a package deal that extended over several years. If successful, the firm offered to pay the vendor a premium for 24/7 support. In response, they would provide the firm priority on needed fixes and upgrades. In addition, the vendor agreed to cut the run-time license cost by 20 percent after it was brought to their attention that the firm was responsible for 12 percent of their annual revenue (neither party knew this prior to the initiation of process improvement).

Conclusions and Recommendations

Based on our experience, we believe software licensing represents a missed opportunity for many organizations. By focusing on improvements in this area, we believe that organizations can reap significant savings with minimal effort in a short period of time (i.e., 3 to 6 months). The two examples provide insight into the magnitude of the savings. Improved licensing processes provide positive return for little effort [5]. Based on the results of our client's trial usage of our licensing process and its four attendant best practices, we encourage firms to target improvements in this area in the near term.

References

[1] Paulk, M. C., Weber, C. V., Curtis, B. and Chrissis, M. B., *The Capability Maturity Model: Guidelines for Improving the Software Process*, Addison-Wesley, Reading, MA, 1995.

[2] Ragan, Tara, and Reifer, Donald J., "Adding Product Lines, Architectures and Software Reuse to the Software Acquisition Capability Maturity Model," *CrossTalk*, Vol. 11, No. 5, May 1998, pp. 14–18.

[3] Meyers, B. Craig, and Oberndorf, Patricia, *Managing Software Acquisition: Open Systems and COTS Products*, Addison-Wesley, Reading, MA, 2001.

[4] Reifer, Donald J., Kalb, George E., and Ragan, Tara, "Licensing a Target for Process Improvement," *Proceedings of the Acquisition Management Conference*, Defense Systems Management College, 1998.

[5] Reifer, Donald J., *Making the Software Business Case: Improvement by the Numbers*, Addison-Wesley, Reading, MA, 2001.

Chapter 14

Emerging Management Paradigms

The imperatives of technology and organization, not the images of ideology, are what determines the shape of economic society.

—J. Kenneth Galbraith, *The New Industrial State*

Overview

This chapter discusses emerging issues in software engineering project management. It focuses on managing the leap from early adopter to broad-scale user of a new technology. The differences in emphasis are less subtle. When you manage technology transfer, you focus your attention on the technology and the risks it presents to your organization. In contrast, managing the leap to widespread use requires you to pay more attention to the infrastructure issues because readying the organization to support the changeover is your primary concern.

Often, managers use new technology as an excuse for a culture change. They bring in new processes, tools, and management concepts and institute long-overdue organizational changes as part of the changeover. They piggyback the changes on top of some large new project so that they can use it as a pilot for determining what works and what does not as new operational concepts are implemented. As they work with the pilot, they fail to address the issues associated with transitioning the technology into broad-scale use throughout the firm. They also pursue popular technology rather than that which is needed to address the issues that are troubling the firm.

I have selected seven papers for this chapter. Two of these are new and focus on managing the transition of technology. All examine emerging issues that management is trying to cope with. The last paper addresses the need to change the way you manage the introduction of new technology. Its focus is process, not new tool and technique, adoption.

Article Summaries

Distributed Development: Insights, Challenges, and Solutions, by Paul McMahon. This article examines the challenges and experiences associated with distributed development. To cope with the communication issues that abound when staffs are geographically separated, the article presents an eight-step plan focused on minimizing conflicts. The plan attempts to build a common infrastructure and culture that act as enablers to those who must bridge time zones and space to get their jobs done. The paper argues that building trust and effective communications in such organizations requires leaders who are willing to listen and take risks.

The Evolution of Distributed Project Management, by Kenneth Nidiffer and Dana Dolan. This paper amplifies points discussed in the opening paper as it discusses how to leverage distributed work. It identifies tools, techniques, and processes that work as enablers and discusses the challenges inherent in making a cultural change. It argues that the current momentum behind distributed work and work environments is natural and that firms need to mount concentrated efforts to mature the infrastructures they develop to facilitate the transition.

Managing Product Lines, Architectures and Reuse, by Donald Reifer. This updated original article summaries my state-of-the-art approach to software reuse with an emphasis on product-line management concepts. It introduces you to opportunistic and systematic product-line strategies and comments on early adopter successes with both approaches. The paper looks at industry trends relative to component-based software engineering and product lines as it builds the case for use of this emerging technology. The paper concludes with several recommendations aimed at helping you put this promising technology to work in your organization.

Improving the Security of Networked Systems, by Julia Allen, Christopher Alberts, Sandi Behrens, Barbara Laswell, and William Wilson. This paper summarizes the security problems organizations face as they try to take advantage of networking technology to distribute work and collaborate across geographic boundaries. It is an informative paper that highlights the need to strengthen security practices and to view distribution as a risk that needs to be better managed. One of the central themes of the paper is that everyone in the organization needs to be educated and trained in the practices adopted for security engineering.

Managing at Light Speed, by Lynn Carrier. Management flexibility is a must in this era of constant technological change. This paper suggests ways to maintain this flexibility as you compete in fast-changing markets. By accelerating responsiveness and nurturing creativity, organizations can put the analytical and decision-making processes needed to survive constant change in place without disturbing existing operations.

Strategic Information Technology Management: Managing Organizational, Political, and Technological Forces, by Keith Schildt, Suzann Beaumaster, and Marcie Edwards. This survey reports how California municipalities attempt to manage change within the context of their information technology organizations. Using a strategic management model as its basis, it explores issues of concern within organizational, political, and technological spheres of influence. The paper concludes by identifying nine techniques that can be used to manage change successfully.

Information Resources Management: New Era, New Rules, by John D. Hwang. This article emphasizes that organizations must evolve beyond a focus on technology and implementation to manage the risks associated with juggling business and technical objectives. It introduces the reader to the role of the Chief Information Officer (CIO). It then discusses how people juggle priorities to fulfill these roles. Finally, it provides valuable insight into the issues that organizations face as they try to put their strategic plans into action organizationally via the CIO.

Key Terms

Sixteen terms, defined as follows, are important to understanding the topic of organization as used within this chapter:

1. **Architecture.** The structure of components, their interrelationships, and the principles and guidelines governing their design and evolution over time.
2. **Asset.** Any product of the software life cycle that can be potentially reused. This includes. architectures, requirements, designs, code, lessons learned, and so on.
3. **Asset management.** The processes/practices firms use to manage their reusable software assets and make them readily available in quality form to their potential users.
4. **Commercial off-the-shelf (COTS) software.** Software that is supplied by a third party who retains responsibility for continued development and life cycle support of the package. COTS software is used as is (the version is not changed to address the unique needs of the user).
5. **Component-based software engineering.** The process of building software systems by combining and integrating pretested and preengineered, fine-grained software objects taken from some framework or class library.
6. **Domain.** A distinct functional area that can be supported by a class of systems with similar requirements and capabilities (avionics, banking, etc.).
7. **Domain analysis.** The process of identifying, collecting, organizing, analyzing, and representing the relevant information in a domain based on the study of existing systems and their development histories, knowledge captured from domain experts, underlying theory, and emerging technology within a domain.
8. **Domain engineering.** The reuse-based processes/practices firms use to define the scope, specify the structure, and build the assets for a class of systems, subsystems, or applications.
9. **Framework.** A collection of classes that provides a set of services for a particular domain. A framework thus exports a number of classes and mechanisms that clients can use or adapt, depending on their needs.
10. **Infrastructure.** The underlying framework used by management for making decisions and allocating resources.
11. **Paradigm.** A modeling method for the software development process.
12. **Product line.** A family of similar products developed to service the market needs of a particular business area or line of business.
13. **Product-line management.** The business function that manages the definition, development, evaluation, use, and evolution of product-line assets over time.
14. **Reuse engineering.** The engineering activities performed to systematically develop, test, field, and maintain reusable software assets.
15. **Reuse library.** A software library specifically developed and built to house reusable assets. Contains a controlled collection of assets together with the procedures and support functions required to satisfy its users' needs.
16. **Technology transfer.** The process used to prove, transfer, and put technology into widespread use (within an organization).

Acronyms

The following acronyms are used within the articles in this chapter:

ACM	Association for Computing Machinery
AOL	America On-Line
CIO	Chief Information Officer
CMMI	Capability Maturity Model Integration
CPU	Central processing unit
HTML	Hyper Text Markup Language
IEEE	Institute of Electrical and Electronics Engineers
IT	Information technology
OCTAV	Operationally critical threat, asset, and vulnerability evaluation
PMSC	Policy Management System's Corporation
RAM	Random access memory
SEI	Software Engineering Institute
TQM	Total quality management
TRL	Technology readiness level
TT	Technology transfer

For Your Bookshelf

I have abstracted six books in the Bibliography under two headings. The first four discuss emerging software management paradigms like extreme programming and project retrospectives. Beck discusses some of the practices associated with agile methods in *Extreme Programming Explained,* whereas Boehm discusses how to use agile and plan-driven methods together effectively in *Balancing Agility and Discipline.* Leach puts the theory of constraints to work in *Critical Chain Management,* whereas Kerth provides guidelines for gathering lessons learned via a project postmortem in *Project Retrospective.* The final two selections in the Bibliography are McMahon's *Virtual Project Management,* on managing distributed developments, and Moore's *Crossing the Chasm,* on the challenges associated with moving new technology from early adopters into widespread use. It is a widely quoted book whose applicability is much broader than just software.

The Software Engineering Institute's (SEI) Capability Maturity Model Integration (CMMI) has replaced its Technology Management Key Practice Area (KPA) at Level 5 with Organizational Innovation and Deployment. This process area requires practices that address the following:

- Process and technology improvements that contribute to meeting quality and process performance objectives are selected.
- Measurable improvements to the organization's processes and technologies are continually and statistically employed.

The SEI also conducts seminars on the topic of change management and has an active program looking at modeling and improving the process of making institutional changes.

Tools represent one effective way to put technology to work operationally. The IEEE has published two tool standards that might be of interest to you. Their *Recommended Practice for the Adoption of CASE Tools,* IEEE Std 1348-1995, provides useful guidelines for those looking for tools to bring in new software paradigms.

Distributed Development: Insights, Challenges, and Solutions

Paul E. McMahon
PEM Systems

Today, many organizations are facing difficulties competing for new work due to a critical shortage of engineering skills. Employing the power of distributed development can increase an organization's opportunities to win new work by opening up a broader skill and product knowledge base, coupled with a deeper pool of personnel to potentially employ. By distributed development, we mean development efforts that span multiple organizations and/or multiple physical locations. This article provides an overview of key issues and challenges managers and project engineers are facing today on distributed development efforts. Insights into root causes of difficulties and recommended solutions are provided. Within this article the terms distributed and virtual are used synonymously. Information presented in this article has been excerpted and condensed with permission from the newly published Virtual Project Management: Software Solutions for Today and the Future [1].

Other authors using the terms *virtual collaboration*, *virtual development*, and *distributed development* have addressed the subject of this article. Regardless of the name used, this subject is about the issues involved when multiple organizations and/or multiple physical locations join forces on an advanced technology software-intensive effort.

It is important to note that I am not referring to traditional subcontract relationships. Rather, this article focuses on the use of *virtual teams* operating more as a single *integrated* team employing some degree (to be discussed) of common processes, support services, and technical strategies driven through a streamlined management chain.

While just a few short years ago such a project would have seemed inconceivable, modern technologies like e-mail, the World Wide Web, NetMeeting, teleconferencing and videoconferencing are today providing new possibilities for distributed teams to work in a more integrated and productive manner.

Why Care About Distributed Development?

To understand the critical importance of succeeding in a virtual collaborative environment, one only needs to examine the changes taking place inside today's workforce. According to a recent study conducted by the U.S. Bureau of Labor Statistics, approximately 25 percent of all workers age 16 or over have been with their current employer 12 months or less. This same study indicates that the average worker is now expected to change jobs every five years [2].

These statistics paint a picture of an increasingly mobile work force. The 20-year employee holding a wealth of corporate knowledge inside his head may well be a corporate asset of the past. At the same time, corporations are experiencing an increasing demand for software-intensive solutions produced from a combination of existing products and new developments. This, in turn, is driving a greater demand for personnel with increasingly specialized software skills; that is, skills geared toward specific software products. Compounding this demand for key people is the seemingly never-ending shortening of cycle times to enter and succeed in new markets.

> ## "Within this demanding environment, even the largest mega-corporations are finding they can no longer maintain inside their own corporate walls all the critical skills necessary to compete in many new markets."

Within this demanding environment, even the largest mega-corporations are finding they can no longer maintain inside their own corporate walls all the critical skills necessary to compete in many new markets. As a result, more and more companies today are reaching out in a cooperating manner to organizations previously viewed only as competitors. While the rationale for embracing virtual operations is evident, many corporations today are struggling with implementation-related challenges.

Distributed Development Challenge

Research conducted by Booz-Allen [3] has identified four characteristics common to many of today's collaborative failures:
- Cultural incompatibility.
- Leadership struggles.
- Lack of trust.
- Inbred notions of competition.

Recently, a three-year collaborative development study was documented in *Virtual Project Management: Software Solutions for Today and the Future* [1]. The results indicate that beneath these symptoms lie a number of key relationships that include both technical and non-technical factors. On the positive side, this study also indicates that, once these key relationships are understood, practical and affordable actions can be taken to aid organizations in achieving successful virtual operations. The referenced study is based on experiences derived from real distributed projects that occurred between 1994 and 2000.

The Eight-Step Plan

In this article we employ an eight-step plan (see Figure 1) as a framework to assist our investigation of distributed project challenges. This framework can be used as an aid in setting up a new distributed project, or in instituting improvements to an ongoing one.

While the eight steps identified may appear traditional and relevant to any project, our focus in this article is on specific issues related to distributed operations. It should be noted that the use of the term *steps* is not intended to imply that virtual project success can be achieved through a *cookbook* approach. Nor do we mean to imply that these steps are easily achieved. Many of the challenges faced on

Reprinted from *CrossTalk*, November 2001.

virtual projects are closely coupled to communication. Evidence of this fact can be seen throughout the eight steps starting with Step 1.

Step 1: Selecting Team Leaders

It should not be a surprise to anyone who has worked on a collaborative endeavor that one of the most important decisions to project success is the choice of team leaders. While strong conflict management skills, and a willingness to consider alternative approaches are desirable traits for leaders on any project, these leadership characteristics are particularly critical to distributed project success.

Unlike most traditional collocated projects, virtual projects face the added challenge of teammates with differing backgrounds, experiences, and technical expectations. This situation can give rise to frequent and often intense conflict. While most project conflicts faced are not insolvable, all too often timely and effective resolution falls short due to a breakdown in communication.

Conflict and Communication

Conflict is not unique to distributed projects, but it is not uncommon for traditional, collocated approaches to conflict resolution to fail in a distributed environment. To understand why, we must look closer at communication in the organization.

In the early 1980's, Alan Cox conducted a survey in which he found that more than 66 percent of middle managers believed that more than half of the communication in their organizations occurred informally [4]. Experience on distributed projects indicates this is not only true, but some of the most critical communication with respect to conflict resolution occurs in this manner. Unfortunately distance, differing experiences, and internal team competition often hinder informal communication on distributed efforts.

It should be noted that the term *informal* in this article means unplanned and undocumented.

A Partial Solution to Virtual Project Conflict

While distributed development provides the potential power of rapidly accessible personnel with key skills and key product knowledge, it often does so at a cost of interpersonal team bonds built over time through shared experiences. Although there does not exist a simple cure-all for the loss of shared experiences and tradi-

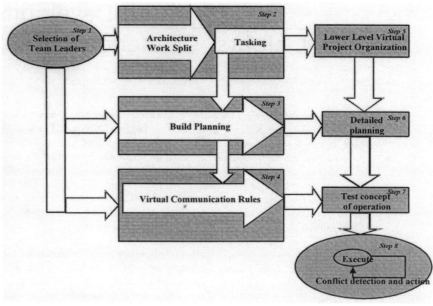

Figure 1: *Eight-Step Plan*

tional informal communication on distributed projects, a number of partial solutions do exist.

For example, experience indicates that collocating a small team of senior systems designers during the critical creative design stage of a distributed project can be effective. Studies have shown that when team members must interact frequently and for short durations, collocation offers the best opportunity for success [5]. This does not mean that full-time collocation is required for the life of the program. Cases where repeating cycles of intense collocated work followed by periods apart have worked well, especially during the early critical creative design stage.

It is also important to note that early collocation is multi-purpose. This activity supports the shared development of a project's common technical vision, but equally important it also starts the process of building interpersonal bonds among key teammates across project organizations/ sites. Other recommendations in support of a shared leadership vision are discussed in Step 7.

Step 2: Architecture, Work Split, and Tasking

While collocation of key personnel early can go a long way to getting a distributed effort off on the right foot, a significant number of managers remain skeptical about the viability of distributed development. When surveyed on this subject, many managers have expressed fear in not knowing if a remote team member is "doing the right thing [6]."

When one considers how much a new

engineer traditionally has learned about task expectations through informal means, this fear is understandable. Managers who have known only collocated operations often take informal communication for granted, but they intuitively know how much they rely upon it every day.

Even in organizations where task assignments are formally written, there is usually a significant reliance on informal communication to clarify and guide the new engineer. With respect to designing or coding a solution, this informal guidance often takes the form of an experienced engineer relaying examples of solutions patterns that he/she knows will fit that particular organization's accepted technical architecture. Although the process described is commonplace, the relationship being described among architecture, work split, and tasking has not always been well understood.

Definitions

When the term *architecture* is used, it means the "components" of a system and the rules defining how the components are connected, along with any constraints. When used, the term work split means the allocation of responsibilities across physically separated sites or organizations. Work split can also be thought of as *site-level tasking*.

Architecture as a Management Tool

Traditionally, many think of architecture as a technical issue, and work split as a separate and distinct management issue. But in practice, work split decisions can fracture a sound architecture. Furthermore, a sound technical architecture can actually provide one of the best task communication and coordination techniques.

For example, think about how a senior technical mentor guides a new engineer. The most effective mentors guide by listening first and then providing feedback that ensures the approaches chosen fit within the range of an organization's acceptable solutions. This is another way of saying that effective mentors guide through the vision of a technical architecture.

When used appropriately, a sound technical architecture can go a long way to addressing a manager's concerns about whether a remote team member is in fact "doing the right thing." Often it is through informal architecture-centric discussions that teammates gain the real insight needed to accurately meet task expectations within a specific organization. But for architecture to be effective as a task communication aid, the work split definition across physically remote sites must follow the architecture definition, not the reverse.

Architecture First

Too often we see work split decisions made without due consideration to the technical architecture. When work split decisions are forced prior to architecture definition, we often find distributed projects suffering from fuzzy task responsibilities and technical leadership struggles. Without a well defined architecture, remote groups often find themselves heading down inconsistent paths leading to project conflict and control struggles.

For example, the choice of computer hardware platform has been a topic of intense inter-site battles on many distributed efforts. By documenting agreed to platform constraints early, unnecessary project conflict during a critical project stage can often be avoided.

There are many sources available that can provide more in depth information on the key role of architecture to project success [1, 7, 8, and 9].

Do Not Delay the Work Split

There is another side to this coin that must also be adequately considered. Delaying the definition of work split too long can have equally devastating effects on a distributed project. The right answer to the problem of fuzzy task responsibilities is not always simply delaying the work split definition until the architecture is defined. When work split decisions are delayed too long, internal teams' mistrust quickly builds. Be aware that the conse-

quences of defining a work split that leaves tasking grey in certain areas has proven to be a poor solution to this challenging area. While your architecture needs to be in place when you define your work split, you should also know that architecture is an evolutionary product. Never wait for the architecture to be 100 percent complete, or you'll never get your work split defined.

"Studies have shown that when team members must interact frequently and for short durations that collocation offers the best opportunity for success."

Step 3: Planning the Builds and Site-Specific Infrastructure

While a sound architecture can aid work split definition and task management, it does not convey when product functionality is available. This is the purpose of a build plan.

Today, many companies are moving toward incremental build approaches especially on distributed projects because a build approach reduces integration risk. You can think of a build as a set of hardware and software that meets a subset of the functionality of the final deliverable product. *Planning and coordinating the builds across distributed sites may be the single greatest challenge faced on virtual projects.*

One of the keys to effective build coordination on distributed projects is found in the technical infrastructure (hardware computer platforms and software tools). The criticality of the technical infrastructure to effective build planning can best be conveyed through two competing technical infrastructure visions often found on distributed efforts. These two visions are referred to as the *maximize use of company-owned assets* vision and the *seamless* vision.

Maximize Use of Company-Owned Assets

Maximized use of company-owned assets means the use of existing company-owned organizational assets (computer hardware and software tools) to the maximum extent possible to meet project needs. Those who demand that the project's direct infrastructure costs be kept to a

minimum drive this vision. While driving hard toward this vision does reduce the up-front project expenditures, it can also increase the project's integration risk and the overall project cost since not all existing hardware and software will be the same.

Seamless Vision

On the other hand, those driving the seamless vision believe that an engineer should be able to log in and do 100 percent of his engineering work using identical tools and processes from any workstation at any remote project location. While the advantages of the seamless vision are evident, the cost of common hardware, common software tools, and software licenses can quickly become prohibitive for a single project. It is also important to keep in mind that the choice you make with respect to infrastructure (hardware, software tools) cannot be made independent from your project's process decision unless you keep your process definition high. But keep in mind that if the process definition is too high, it is more likely to lead to miscommunication. In the following section we discuss a common distributed project process pitfall.

Do Not Drive Process Commonality Too Deep

One of the most common pitfalls witnessed on distributed projects is referred to as the "let's use the most mature process available" pitfall. This pitfall usually starts with the project leadership's decision to mandate that all project sites use a common process. While at the appropriate level a common process makes sense, the pitfall is tied to what often happens next. Rather than define the common process at the appropriate level and allow individual sites the appropriate freedom to leverage site-specific procedures, oftentimes a mandate is sent across the distributed sites to drive procedure commonality (different from process commonality) as well. The common set of procedures chosen is usually supplied by the highest software maturity-rated organization on the project.

It is natural to look to your teammate with the highest process maturity for software guidance. However, procedures represent only a small part of the complete process maturity picture. They are often too site-specific to make sense for application across multiple organizations (each with their own culture and history) in conducting development activities.

When attempts are made to drive commonality too deep into a virtual organization the lack of an enabling organization, supporting infrastructure, and supporting culture at each of the remote sites is almost certain to lead this initiative to failure.

Solution to the Common Process Initiative

A process freedom line is defined to be the point in the process where a site/organization is free to make process-related decisions. For example, a project level procedure may call for a design document to be produced with specific design artifacts, but may not require a specific document format. I recommend that virtual projects define process freedom lines at the point where products and people must come together across divergent sites/organizations. It is not recommended that the project attempt to dictate how specific sites/organizations accomplish their tasks internally.

The freedom line definition essentially tells each site where they are free to leverage site-specific procedures (that can include site-specific support organizations and company-owned assets) in implementing solutions. This strategy has proven effective at balancing the management of the project's integration risk, while at the same time leveraging the strengths of individual sites/organizations.

Step 4: Virtual Communication Rules

Architecture definition and planning are critical on all projects, collocated or virtual. Virtual communication, on the other hand, presents distributed projects with new challenges not previously faced in traditional collocated environments.

Today, virtual communication is in its infancy. We are just now starting to comprehend the implications of first generation lessons on using the World Wide Web, teleconferencing and videoconferencing, NetMeeting, and e-mail. We recommend that virtual project communication lessons drive written virtual project rules (guidelines) to aid engineers in the effective application of new tools.

For example, in the early stages of a large virtual project it is not uncommon for engineering personnel to receive 50-60 e-mails per day! Think about it. If you take just four minutes to process each e-mail, at this rate you could spend half of your day just handling e-mail correspondence. E-mail flooding is the result of personnel being given a new tool and insufficient training in its use. E-mail, voice mail, teleconferencing, videoconferencing and NetMeeting all require training in more than just the mechanics of their use.

I recommend that each project create its own guidelines as it moves forward. And don't ignore rules and lessons that may seem obvious. I challenge those who

---

> ## "On virtual projects the building of trust requires a more proactive management stance."

---

have been involved in distributed efforts with the following questions:

- Does your distributed project have rules for the use of e-mail and teleconferencing?
- Have your people been trained and are they following the guidance provided?

It has been our experience that while few disagree with the concept of guidelines, most distributed projects in operation today are not doing the best job of deploying effectively virtual communication technologies, and the unfortunate part is that it could be costing you plenty in human resources. Furthermore, this recommendation is simply not that expensive to deploy!

For more examples of first-generation virtual communication lessons, see [1].

Step 5: Lower Level Virtual Project Organization

The recommendation for the lower level structure of a distributed project organization may not be a popular one. At the top end of the organization where a breath of issues must be addressed, the Integrated Product Team (IPT) structure tends to function well, and I recommend it. This is the level where *heads-up* activities exist. By heads-up activities I mean work that must look across the multiple sites and organizations of the project. But I have also observed – and many clients concur – that a strict IPT structure is weak when it comes to producing products that include detailed design, code, and test cases.

Where the *real* engineering, or what we refer to as heads-down work, occurs, I have found that on distributed efforts a *hybrid* of IPTs and functional groups is often more effective. When I use the term heads-down work I mean the engineering work associated with building and testing actual executable code.

An example of why we recommend this structure can be seen in the need for an infrastructure implementation group that provides common services that multiple product development teams may need across remote sites. Too often, when virtual projects try to drive a strict IPT structure deep into the organization, responsibility for critical common services is lost. This is because when a strict IPT structure is employed at lower levels of the organization, you often find that each of those lower level IPTs focus almost exclusively on their own specific product. As a result, each solves their own specific problem in their own specific way.

On the other hand, when organizations recognize the need for an infrastructure implementation group that is not focused on any single specific product, commonality across multiple sub-products can be more effectively achieved.

Step 6: Detailed Planning

Detailed planning is important on any project, but on a virtual project its critical relationship to work split is often misunderstood.

Often on virtual projects work split decisions get delayed. This can occur for a multitude of reasons – most are not technical. But, all too often, great pressure continues to be brought on the engineering team to complete the detailed project plan despite the uncertainties of where work will actually get done. What is too often misunderstood in these situations is the extent to which detailed planning directly depends on work location.

While some project planning can be done independent of location, think about the real issues an engineering manager faces when it comes to developing a really detailed plan that is actually executable. Here are just a few of the critical questions to be asked:

- Is the development hardware available?
- Have the software tools and licenses been procured and installed?
- Have we identified the engineering personnel that will do this job?
- Have the identified personnel been trained on the chosen platform, language, tools?

To develop a detailed plan that is executable, managers must make assumptions with regard to each of these issues. These are the real issues that truly impact project performance.

Now think about how the answers to these questions are affected when work is moved to a different location. Based on my experience, if you are doing detailed

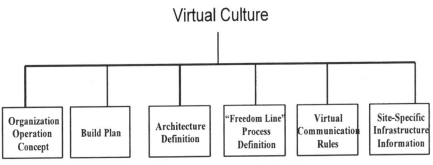

Figure 2: *Sample Virtual Culture*

planning, and the work location is still fuzzy, you can start planning right now on doing your detailed plan all over again!

Step 7: Test the Operation Concept of the Virtual Organization

It is unreasonable to expect new virtual project organizations to instantly operate as effectively as strongly cultured time-tested collocated operations. Effective organizations – collocated or virtual – do not just happen.

We recommend that newly established virtual project organizations set aside the time for project leaders to walk through key organizational scenarios that are most likely to cause leadership friction. When leaders take the time to discuss openly their visions of the virtual organization, potential problem areas can often be uncovered and resolved quickly.

Often, at the start of a new project, leaders are uncertain where the most likely trouble spots might be in the operation of the distributed organization. For example, experience has shown that when multiple organizations are involved, task management of remote personnel is a critical area. It is recommended that you walk through your task management model and your risk management model, and be sure to do it in a face-to-face setting with all your project leaders present. For more information on recommended organizational scenarios, see the referenced book [1].

Step 8: Execute

As discussed in Step 1, increased conflict is to be expected in a distributed development environment due to the lack of shared experiences and interpersonal bonds. Recognizing this fact, a key to effective process deployment on virtual projects is ensuring that leaders are aware of the warning signs of unhealthy team conflict. An example of an unhealthy

conflict warning sign is what we refer to as the repeating issue warning sign. This is the case where:

- A valid issue is raised by a virtual team member.
- The issue is worked through by the team.
- A consensus is reached and the issue is put to bed.
- One week, or one month later, the same issue returns.

Does this sound familiar? Have you ever sat in a meeting and thought you were sitting through a rerun of an old movie? If you detect the repeating issue warning sign on your distributed project be sure to deal with it rapidly before it does permanent harm to your team. See reference for more examples of unhealthy team conflict warning signs, and recommended actions [1].

Deploy A Virtual Culture

In this article I have emphasized challenges being faced today on many distributed projects. I have stressed the impact of the loss of traditional informal communication in distributed environments, and have provided related recommendations. I also recommend the deployment of what is referred to as a virtual culture.

A virtual culture [1] is a simple, yet powerful concept that brings an information-age perspective to the notion of culture. Think of a virtual culture as a physical framework that supports effective communication across distributed project sites.

The virtual culture – unlike traditional collocated engineering cultures – is product oriented. It is not intended to replace past traditional collocated cultures. In fact, I don't think you should try to replace strong local cultures. Rather, my recommendations are based on leveraging the strengths of your teammates within their proven environments.

The virtual culture complements the existing site-specific cultures providing

the critical information needed to coordinate and communicate key tasking information across distributed sites. This approach reduces the risk of rework when remotely developed products are integrated together. A sample structure of a virtual culture is provided in Figure 2. Virtual cultures can be implemented through a Web site or through a shared directory system.

It is worth noting that a key difference between a virtual culture and a traditional culture is found in its formality. Experience indicates that an effective virtual culture cannot be informal. In other words, it must be written down. We recognize that in today's world this emphasis on the written word may not be popular.

However, recommendations with respect to a more formal virtual culture should not be interpreted as a step backwards to the days of voluminous documentation. The virtual culture is not intended to include historical milestone-type documentation, but rather it focuses on those critical pieces of information that must be coordinated and communicated across distributed sites. Experience indicates that when you go virtual and utilize remote operations that more things do need to be written down in support of effective remote communication.

Conclusion

The potential gains of virtual operations are great. Nevertheless, implementation issues cut deep inside present-day engineering organizations. Inside traditional engineering environments, common cultures, common site infrastructures, and common experiences provide key ingredients supporting team trust.

In collocated environments, trust appears to just happen through little more than the passage of time. In reality, in these traditional environments there have always been numerous informal factors hard at work building trust on a daily basis. In the past these informal activities may not have received the attention they deserve. This is because in strongly cultured collocated environments the benefits of informality came to us essentially for free. In the virtual world this is no longer the case.

On virtual projects, the building of trust requires a more proactive management stance. It requires leaders who are willing to listen to alternative approaches put forth by team members who may have very different backgrounds and experiences from their own. But listening is only the first step.

When alternative ideas are accepted they must also be effectively communicated to the full team. And on virtual projects, we now know we cannot rely on traditional collocated informal mechanisms to achieve this communication. Therefore, in the virtual world, the written word takes on new and increased importance.

Think about the information that is today conveyed through unplanned meetings in hallways, at lunch, casually in cubicles and over the tops of cubicles. While experience has shown that e-mail, teleconferencing, videoconferencing and NetMeeting are all powerful distributed development communication tools, they cannot replace what collocated organizations have taken years to mature. Consider deploying the virtual culture concept on your distributed project to aid communication to all your team members. It is not that expensive to implement, but the potential cost of not implementing one is.◆

References

1. McMahon, Paul E. <u>Virtual Project Management: Software Solutions for Today and the Future</u>. Boca Raton: St. Lucie Press, An Imprint of CRC Press LLC, 2001.
2. Gannett News Service, "Job Hopping by Young Workers Increasingly Common," 29 Aug. 1999.
3. Norton, Bob, and Cathy Smith, eds. <u>Understanding the Virtual Organization</u>. Hauppauge, NY: Barron's Educational Series, 1997. 68.
4. Cox, Alan. <u>The Cox Report on the American Corporation</u>. New York: Delacorte Press, 1982. 112-114.
5. Gindele, Mark E., and Richard Rumpf, eds. "Effects of Collocating Integrated Product Teams," <u>Program Manager</u>, July-Aug. 1998: 38.
6. Haywood, Martha. <u>Managing Virtual Teams</u>. Boston: Artech House, 1998.
7. Software Engineering Institute, <www.sei.cmu.edu/architecture/definitions.html>.
8. Shaw, Mary, and David Garlan, eds. <u>Software Architecture: Perspectives on an Emerging Discipline</u>. Englewood Cliffs, NJ: Prentice Hall, 1996.
9. Bass, Len, and Paul Clements, eds. <u>Software Architecture in Practice</u>. Reading, MA: Addison-Wesley, 1998.

Additional Reading

1. Karolak, Dale Walter. Global Software Development. Los Alamitos, CA: IEEE Computer Society, 1998: 35-46.
2. Mayer, Margery. <u>The Virtual Edge</u>. Newtown Square, PA: Project Management Institute Headquarters, 1998.
3. Lipnack, Jessica, and Jeffrey Stamps, eds. <u>Virtual Teams: Reaching Across Space, Time and Organizations with Technology</u>. New York: John Wiley & Sons, Inc., 1997.
4. Reifer, Don. <u>Practical Software Reuse</u>. New York: John Wiley & Sons, 1997.
5. Royce, Walker. <u>Software Project Management</u>. Reading, MA: Addison-Wesley, 1998.
6. Highsmith, James A. <u>Adaptive Software Development: A Collaborative Approach To Managing Complex Systems</u>, New York: Dorsett House Publishing, 1999.
7. Deeprose, Donna. <u>The Team Coach</u>. New York: American Management Assoc., 1995.

About the Author

Paul E. McMahon is an independent contractor providing technical and management leadership services to large and small engineering organizations. McMahon began his career in the early 1970's as a flight simulation programmer. Before initiating independent work at PEM Systems in 1997, he held senior technical and management positions at Hughes and Lockheed Martin. Today McMahon employs his 27 years of experience in helping organizations deploy high quality software processes integrated with systems engineering and project management. He has taught software engineering as an adjunct at Binghamton University, N.Y., and published more than a dozen articles and a book on virtual project management.

118 Matthews Street
Binghamton, NY 13905
Phone: (607) 798-7740
E-mail: pemcmahon@acm.org

The Evolution of Distributed Project Management

Kenneth E. Nidiffer and Dana Dolan

Abstract

The ever-increasing growth and complexity of software-intensive systems over the last 20 years, and the ensuing rise in geographically distributed projects are trends that are here to stay. Players in the government defense-contracting industry are leading the way through this jungle, blazing a path for other industries to follow. The Systems and Software Consortium, with a membership comprised of most of the largest defense contractors, has a unique view into evolving initiatives both within and between its member companies. Solving the distributed-project-management problem is without doubt a top priority, one that relies not simply on the intelligent application of technology, but also on coordinated, complimentary efforts focused on people and processes. This paper describes an array of drivers, constraints, and enablers that are leading organizations to invest in real-time project-management information systems. The authors describe how these systems must evolve to support increased decision velocity and cohesiveness in today 's increasingly distributed world.

Keywords

Project management, complex programs, geographically distributed projects, virtual teams, collaboration, virtual collaboration, virtual development, geographically distributed development, collaborative tools, decision velocity, virtual presence, integrated digital environments.

Project Management Past—How We Got Where We Are Today

Advances in technology, the growing need for larger and more complex software-intensive systems, the customer's desire to place more risk with the developer, and the need for companies to be more competitive in the marketplace are the principal forces driving project development teams to become increasingly dispersed. Project management is a discipline that surely has existed from the beginning of our civilization. Slowly through the millennia, and more rapidly within the last century, an immense body of management knowledge has arisen. A glimpse at the history of project management shows that although these practices have served us well in the past, incremental improvements are not enough to respond to today's challenges.

In the 1970s and early 1980s, achieving effective software project management was a significant issue. Projects were often delivered late and over budget, and did not meet requirements and expectations. Thought leaders like Winston Royce, Frederick Brooks, Arthur Pyster, Richard Thayer, Richard Fairley, and Barry Boehm helped chart new directions in software project management. In those days, there were only a few complex systems, and project management teams were much more centralized than today.

As we approached the 1980s, the number of complex systems began to increase dramatically, and the problems associated with ineffective project management became more acute. Senior managers coined the phrase "software crisis" to focus attention on providing solutions to this problem; numerous government and industry initiatives were developed in response (see Sidebar 1). Collectively, these initiatives embodied a four-pronged technical and management attack: (a) standardize the process, (b) standardize the product, (c) standardize the support environment, and (d) professionalize the workforce [9].

In the mid-1980s, the SEI Software Capability Maturity Model® [1]} began to take shape. This framework has enabled many organizations to adopt the processes, methods, and tools of effective project management. Product-line management techniques, increased graduate-level education in software and systems engineering management, and the development of standards such as the Guide to the Project Management Body of Knowledge (PMBOK® [2]) also emerged in response to the recognized software crisis.

Project Management Present—Are We Where We Need to Be?

Managing a large software-intensive system is a complex and intrinsically difficult task. The system is itself complex and may involve hundreds of staff years of skilled effort, large budgets, and potentially thousands of activities. Sidebar 2 presents a number of perspectives that attest to the facts that (a) the delivery of complex systems on time, within cost, and meeting customer requirements is a significant problem; and (b) the number of complex systems is increasing. This situation does not bode well for our ability to improve the effectiveness of project management.

The discipline of project management is certainly better off today than it was 20 years ago. However, while companies were responding internally, customer behavior, industry structure, and the competitive environment were changing externally at an accelerating rate. The net effect, as evidenced by the data presented above, has stretched the limits by which projects can be effectively managed in today's environment. Coupled with the increasing rate of technological change, it is clear that the current initiatives are not enough. Project managers must adapt to a new set of *drivers,* changes in the acquisition environment and changes in the acquisition risk–award model for industry, and a new set of *enablers* for geographically distributed projects.

Our research focuses on the changes in the defense industry. This industry leads the charge into large, complex, dispersed systems because they have (1) the critical need, with the war on terror only increasing this need; (2) the ability to make long-term investments based on the public interest; and (3) a culture adapted to embrace distributed work—by its very nature, war fighting has always been a distributed project. Other industries can benefit from analyzing how the defense industry is changing to effectively meet the challenges of new drivers and enablers of complex, distributed project management; the need for increasingly complex, software-intensive systems is germane to almost any market domain.

Drivers, Part I: The Impact of Recent Federal Legislation

Major DoD/federal legislation has had significant influences on today's acquisition environment (see Sidebar 3). Look closely at the language of the legislation. Words such as *results, streamlining, reform, reduction, improvement,* and *elimination* indicate the changing culture and future direction of the acquisition community.

This legislation has influenced government agencies to approach acquisition and procurement of complex systems in a fundamentally different way. It has enabled them to say, "I am not going to tell you my requirements. I'm going to tell you the ob-

---

[1]CMM® is registered in the U.S. Patent and Trademark Office.
[2]PMBOK® is registered to the Project Management Institute, Inc.

Winning with Software, An Executive Strategy describes increasing complexity in terms of the growth of software in military aircraft [5]:

Year	Aircraft	Percent of pilot's functions supported by software
1960	F-4	8%
1982	F-16	45%
2000	F-22	80%

CHAOS report quantifies our poor ability to keep pace with complexity [12]:

- Success rates are improving, but are still dismal at 34%.
- 15% of projects are outright failures.
- A staggering 51% are significantly "challenged" (late, over budget, or lacking in anticipated capabilities).
- The level of complexity of IT projects is rising faster than our ability to effectively manage it [12].

"Defense Acquisitions: Stronger Management Practices are Needed to Improve DoD's Software-Intensive Weapon Acquisitions" [14] determined that:

- Software-intensive weapons acquisitions are increasingly critical.
- Current project management practices are insufficient to meet the challenge.

jective capabilities I want. I am willing to do business with you in different sorts of ways and if you want to do business with me, you need to play by these new rules." The government customer has taken on a new industrial awareness and commitment to achieve a business advantage that is beyond a traditional process improvement mindset. There is an expanded emphasis on improvements across the total life cycle, particularly in earlier phases, and a broader perspective on assessing the return on investment from an enterprise performance perspective. The emphasis has shifted from simply *building IT systems* to the more encompassing goal of *providing business value.*

Drivers, Part II: The Changing Acquisition/Market Environment

Changes in the acquisition/market environment, in particular the growing need for larger teams with a wide range of specialized expertise, are rapidly driving industry to a distributed project-management environment with new rules of engage-

- 1990—Chief Financial Officers Act
- 1993—Government Performance and Results Act
- 1994—Federal Acquisition Streamlining Act
- 1994—Government Management Reform Act
- 1995—Paperwork Reduction Act
- 1996—Federal Acquisition Reform Act
- 1996—Clinger/Cohen Information Technology Management Reform Act
- 1996—Federal Financial Management Improvement Act
- 1998—Government Paperwork Elimination Act
- 1998—Federal Activities Inventory Reform Act
- 2002—Homeland Security Act
- 2002—E-Government Act (includes Federal Information Security Management Act)

ment. Table 1, adapted from Kane [6], frames the business and operational environment we can expect over the next several years.

To top off all of this increased complexity, the shift in the acquisition environment is not simply in one direction (as in the shift from *requirements* to *capabilities*); industry must respond to both sides of the driver equations, and do it at a much faster pace in order to remain competitive.

Drivers, Part III: Changes in the Risk–Reward Model

These changes in legislation and in the marketplace have changed the risk–reward model for industry (see Figure 1). Historically, industry and government contracting organizations accepted certain risk–reward tradeoffs as represented toward the left side of the graph. In general, industry accepts a higher risk–reward position (as represented by point "a") than government (as represented by point "b"). For example, industry typically prefers the guaranteed profit of "cost plus fixed fee" contracts, whereas the government prefers "cost plus award fee," where some part of the contract payment is dependent on satisfactory performance. Usually, the two sides negotiate their differences to the satisfaction of both parties.

Industry today must consider much riskier acquisitions, but with the potential for greater reward (point "c"). Yet not enough risk has shifted out or reward shifted in (to approach point "d") for industry to satisfactorily negotiate the gap. Industry must find some way to either secure a greater reward (point "e") through innovation, or minimize the risk (point "f") through systematic process improvement. It is in this "green space" that industry must apply process improvements, better software engineering, better systems engineering, in short, better project management, either to yield greater predictability, greater certainty, and therefore reduce risks, or to secure productivity gains that enable them to capture the reward differential they seek.

The green triangle space a new opportunity area for project management, dependent on effective communications and information brokerage. These are the keys to overcoming the challenges of an increasingly distributed environment, and to leveraging its promise as well.

The Promise, Problems, and Challenge of Leveraging Distributed Work

Geographically distributed projects enable managers to compress schedules by employing larger workforces than could fit in a single location (i.e., collaboration on any shore), using time zone differences to increase the number of productive work hours in a day (i.e., "around-the-clock" or "24×7" operations), and securing scarce resources such as knowledge specialists and other specialized resources no matter where they reside (i.e., zero-geography staffing).

However, these benefits come with increased risks because of lack of face-to-face communication, in particular, the potential loss of trust, collaboration, and communication richness. Carmel [1] argues that teams of software engineers need at least a minimum amount of face-to-face meetings to be effective. The agile and extreme programming movements suggest ways to increase communication such as "pair programming," in which programmers share desks so that they can see each other to understand the subtleties of design and debugging. Other research, on managers engaging in complex information processing requiring rich information and frequent feedback, indicates that the more complex the organizational phenomena, the richer the information must be in order for the manager to process it effectively. The established trend toward customers placing more risk with the developer means failures at this level will inevitably impact the developer's bottom line and eventually its long-term survivability.

To successfully manage complex projects, project management practices must evolve to work in a distributed world, focusing simultaneously on people, processes, and technology. According to the CHAOS report:

> Most project management techniques were designed for co-located teams. Those techniques may prove ineffective in global, multi-site organizations. . . . CIOs understand that managing a virtual project workforce is not technology dependent. From email to cell phones and pagers, communications abound. Again, people and processes are at the heart of project management, not tools and technology. . . . Building virtual teams with a minimum of face time, clearly defining work, measuring cybernetic worker productivity and managing employee communications across time zones are major management priorities." [13]

Managing a virtual project workforce is not technology *independent,* either. Malone [8] describes how historically the high cost of communication prompted the evolution of organizations from small, decentralized firms to large, centralized hierarchies in order to gain efficiencies. The rapidly shrinking cost of communication brought about by the rise of the Internet is causing the pendulum to swing away from centralization, resulting in the rise of decentralized, networked organizations. As a

Table 1. Complexity Drivers in the Acquisition/Market Environment

Complexity Driver	Explanation	Examples	Implication
Increasing Problem Complexity. The customer acquisition model is shifting its focus from *requirements* to *objective capability* statements.	In the 1980s, customers typically framed acquisitions in terms of requirements. Now, customers often state their needs in terms of capabilities, placing the problem of figuring out the requirements on industry.	The **Missile Defense Agency** initiative has specified a set of deliverable capabilities due at designated points in the project life cycle.	Project managers must secure the required expertise to address the full scope of issues, which often translates into larger teams, frequently augmented through strategic partnerships.
Increasing Solution Complexity. Customer emphasis is shifting from the *platform* to the *enterprise*.	Software-intensive systems acquisition was much easier when customers acquired platforms, such as a specific aircraft, to be added to their existing portfolio. Today, customers frame their requirements in terms of the enterprise.	The enterprise is often codified in terms of its enterprise architecture, a systematic description of not only the pieces of the enterprise "portfolio" of systems, but also the complex interrelationships between them. Examples include **Office of Management and Budget's** *Federal Enterprise Architecture* (TEA) and *DoD Architecture Framework* (DoDAF).	With increased emphasis on providing fully integrated systems, project managers must understand their customer's business in much greater depth to address "systems of systems" interface considerations. This increases the need for larger teams with more specialized solution expertise.
Increasing Technical Complexity. Interoperability and interconnectedness integration challenges have shifted from integrating *boxes* to integration across the *layers and stacks* of the communications/network architecture.	In the 1980s, the project manager was concerned about what was needed to integrate his box with other boxes. In the new world of network centricity, a supplier still needs to integrate the boxes, but at multiple infrastructure, transport and application levels.	**Defense Advanced Research Projects Agency's** request for proposal for *Innovative Information Exploitation Technology and Systems.* Even as DoD builds a massive information grid, a new generation of software and sensors is needed to fulfill the promise of net-centricity. This will require competing firms to integrate their systems into the global information grid.	Increasingly, the project team must be extremely knowledgeable about the complexities of how their software-intensive products fit into the current and future architectures.
Increasing Compliance Complexity. The application of standards is shifting from *proprietary* to *open standards*.	In the past, industries have leveraged proprietary standards to gain competitive advantage. In today's world of strategic teaming and integration, there is much greater emphasis on interoperability.	For example, **Rockwell Collins** supplies communication products to both commercial and government clients. As part of their project-management strategy to reduce costs, they try to minimize the differences in products that satisfy different clients though increased reliance on open standards.	Through compliance with open standards, forward thinking organizations have developed a new competitive advantage. One difficulty these organizations must face is determining which standards to support.
Increasing Team Complexity. Project execution is shifting from the *dominant prime* contractor to *strategic teaming* and *mergers and acquisitions (M&A)*.	Increasingly, organizations are turning to strategic partnerships and M&A to meet these shifting customer demands. Competing organizations want to ensure that the best technologies are being brought to bear across the acquisition life cycle even if the source of that technology rests outside the current company.	In the **Army's** *Future Combat Systems,* the Department of Defense has elevated its requirement for sensors to help fend off rocket-propelled grenades and improvised explosive devices. The technologies to deal with these opportunities will come from a diverse set of sources.	The project manager will be faced with more supplier management and M&A issues than ever before. Techniques for managing these diverse relationships must be matched to the organization's differentiating features, such as its size, resources, and process maturity.

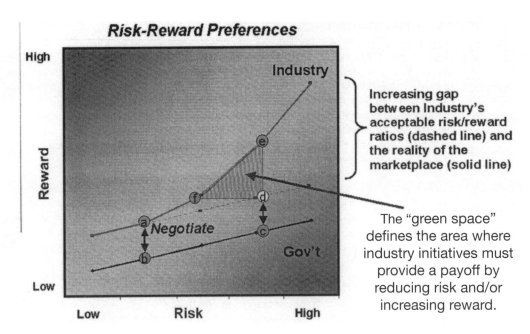

Figure 1. Navigating the "green space." Acquisition changes based on previous legislation have introduced new levels of risk. (© 2003 Systems and Software Consortium, Inc.)

result, project managers seek communication systems that combinatorially support data, voice, video, and virtual presence, and those tools are available today.

But technology by itself is not a *solution,* it is simply an *enabler*. Technological advances in communication are enabling profound changes in organizations and management, changes that simply were not possible before.

As we move forward, a number of additional issues need to be resolved before we can take full advantage of the promise of distributed work. Resolved issues have the capacity to become enablers, whereas unresolved issues act as constraints. The next section describes the Consortium's efforts to identify the top issues in implementing distributed work, with the goal of transforming these into additional enablers.

Insights From Consortium Research

The Systems and Software Consortium's not-for-profit membership model enables a unique perspective on complex systems through its ongoing research and consulting across a variety of organizations. Consortium members include the top contractors to the federal government and the top technology implementers that are transforming the way business is done. Working in partnership with these members, the Consortium recognizes the increasing use of distributed teams and their unique needs in specialty areas such as process improvement, engineering, measurement, verification and validation, and project management.

The Consortium's research in distributed work began in 2000 and continued in 2002 and 2003 with a focus on tools, processes, and measurement. In early 2003, a structured survey of Consortium members identified six issues of primary concern in the area of distributed development (see the first column of Table 2). The Consortium's ongoing work with its members is aimed at resolving these concerns, as indicated in the second and third columns.

Also in 2002, the Consortium formed a subsidiary organization, the Telework Consortium, funded with federal grants and supported by numerous high-profile and innovative technology partners. Its mission is to demonstrate how advanced tools and technologies for communications can be used as a substitute for transportation. Ongoing executive briefings and an extensive list of pilot projects continue to provide the Consortium with a unique view into the requirements and realities of working in a distributed manner. Lessons learned through Telework Consortium efforts are also incorporated into Table 2.

Toward Distributed Project Management

It is through the lens of this research that we can begin to build a vision for the next evolution of project management. The evolution toward distributed project management drives the need for improved processes, methods, and tools to input and

Table 2. Top issues in distributed development*

Issue	Potential Enablers	Current Constraints
Strategic: Difficulty leveraging available resources	Understanding common issues on distributed projects so that risks can be anticipated and managed	Best practices are often deemed proprietary.
	Knowledge management systems, especially expertise management systems	Time-consuming to implement and maintain
Project and process management: Difficulty synchronizing work between distributed sites	Integrated quality frameworks help define synchronization points between work teams.	Complex projects often involve organizations at various maturity levels, making it difficult to implement a standard process across the project. Even organizations at the same maturity level may implement processes in incompatible ways. Different organizations may subscribe to different quality frameworks altogether.
	Shared workspaces for storing files in centralized, accessible locations paired with workflow capabilities can increase efficiency for distributed teams.	Wide range of choices, each with different user interfaces that may require familiarity training. Can be costly and time-consuming to set up and maintain.
	Engineering tool vendors are beginning to release distributed versions.	Still need to integrate these into a real-time project management reporting system.
Communication: Lacking effective communication mechanisms	Asynchronous collaboration tools (e-mail, electronic bulletin boards, voicemail, search agents, change alerts, etc.)	Loss of communication richness increases the risk of miscommunication.
	Real-time collaboration tools, including virtual presence	Lack of bandwidth, robust security, and inexpensive appliances (these issues are becoming less of a challenge)
	Standardized, simplified display of information to combat "information overload"	Agreement required between partnering organizations and with customer—each have their respective informational requirements
Cultural: Conflicting behaviors, processes, and technologies	Targeted training for managers and employees on distributed projects	Hard to quantitatively justify investments in soft skills
	Advances in process, methods, and tools	Adaptation is difficult. Managers may not mind change, but they mind being changed. Very conservative, risk adverse environment.
Technical: Incompatible data formats and exchanges	XML Web Services for data exchange	Lack of industry-wide standard schema for software-intensive development projects
	Standards for real-time collaboration are converging	Leading standards are still being defined
Security: Ensuring confidentiality and privacy of electronic transmissions	Emerging standards for secure messaging, including role-based security and encryption technologies	Numerous competing standards are evolving simultaneously. Current offerings can be expensive to administer, inconvenient to use, and incompatible. No solution is fail-safe, leading to difficulty establishing appropriate limits for sharing of intellectual property across organizational boundaries

*These issues were identified through guided interviews with lead engineering managers of approximately 75% of SPC member companies from January through March, 2003. Combined annual revenue of these organizations is well over $100 billion.

share common data (e.g., technical, financial, project, and communication). The need applies across the project life cycle (e.g., research and development, concept exploration, demonstration, engineering, production, support, and disposal) and among all or selected elements of the team (primes, subcontractors, vendors, customers, oversight agencies, etc.). In our global economy, there is increasing need to decrease the time it takes to make an informed decision, to improve the "decision velocity" of the team. There also is a need for the participants to be highly visible to each other (i.e., the concept of virtual presence), despite being geographically separated, in order to increase trust for discussion, deliberation, and negotiation. These needs, in turn, require a renewed focus on the *enablers* of successful project management in a distributed world.

Enablers, Part I: Tools and Technologies

The rise of the Internet as a ubiquitous connection between distributed locations and the quickly maturing marketplace of collaborative tools are essential ingredients for complex project success.

Software vendors already have released Web-enabled versions of many familiar project management tools, enabling specialized tasks like tracking requirements, schedules, and budgets to be distributed to multiple sites and scaled for multiple users. Software engineering tool suites are beginning to follow suit as well. Similarly, organizations are increasingly employing Web-based repositories (project Web sites, portals, workspaces, etc.) for intelligently sharing and storing files both within and across corporate firewalls.

Structured collaboration tools such as these, often enhanced with workflow functionality, are instrumental in enabling project management hard skills on complex projects, but they fall short in enabling the increasingly critical soft skills like defining the business value, clarifying the vision, determining requirements, providing direction, building teams, resolving issues, and mitigating risk. Research on virtual teams treats this lack of support as a preexisting constraint, recommending face-to-face meetings as often as possible and at critical points in the project to augment communications via e-mail and telephone [1, 7].

Organizations are now beginning to leverage real-time collaboration tools to bridge the soft-skills gap for distributed teams. Tools like instant messaging, Web conferencing, whiteboards, and desktop videoconferencing provide substantially different communication possibilities than the familiar telephone, e-mail, and face-to-face options. Tools for unstructured collaboration can enhance communication by enabling more frequent collaboration between distant coworkers. In contrast to early incarnations of unstructured tools (for example, expensive room-based videoconferencing systems), these inexpensive desktop tools are designed for frequent, ad hoc use. Telework Consortium pilots indicate that these characteristics can lead to increased communications and trust, thereby facilitating quick decisions and enhanced team cohesiveness.

Looking across the IT industry, integrated digital environments for secure sharing of files and databases are being rolled out in organizations with multiple locations and trading partners, leveraging technologies from electronic data interchange (EDI) to Web services. Workflow functionality is enabling great leaps forward in productivity by minimizing lag time between tasks. Communication and collaboration tools are maturing rapidly, and despite the lack of interoperability, single-vendor applications are functional and stable enough to support distributed work in standardized environments. The emerging move toward contextual collaboration promises to bring these communication tools to our fingertips by linking them within the familiar applications we "live in." Security concerns and limited network capacity still limit the use of advanced tools such as desktop videoconferencing in some work environments, but progress is accelerating on these fronts as well.

Based on ongoing research at the Consortium, it has become clear that the technology is available to support distributed project management needs, despite the fact that incompatible data formats and exchanges remain a challenge. An array of technologies is available now, and more are coming into the marketplace at a rapid rate. A remaining issue for the project manager is how to make effective trade-offs among the different alternatives.

The recent history of knowledge management projects demonstrated that relying on the "if-you-build-it-they-will-come" principle merely led to the creation of hugely expensive and disappointingly empty repositories. The next two sections discuss the complimentary enablers of reevaluating processes and procedures, and the people issues or cultural change needed to implement an effective solution.

Enablers, Part II: Reevaluating Processes and Procedures

Existing processes must be reassessed for use in a distributed work environment. Some will be found to be inappropriate, controlling, or confining, whereas others will require more formalization to be effective for distributed work. Telework Consortium pilot projects with small distributed teams [3] show that each organization must approach the shift to distributed work with an open mind for identifying process improvements customized to their business environment. For example, when a four-person magazine staff began teleworking, they quickly recognized the inefficiency of reviewing articles by passing hand-edited paper copies to each of the three editors in turn, and then to the art director for incorporation. The electronic editing software and related processes they implemented shortened the review process by allowing the three editors to accomplish their tasks to be done in parallel, shrinking the time required for this step by a factor of three and increasing quality at the same time. The new solution was so successful that they are now considering it for use across their parent organization. This solution had always been available to them, but was never considered before the move to a distributed environment. The Consortium believes that the strategic advantage from distributed work will stem from the implementation of streamlined processes and procedures such as this.

Process improvement models such as CMMI were developed for use in a single organization. The model enumerates needs in a number of capability areas, and each organization interprets these requirements for its own environment, mapping the process activities to its own business goals. The model mandates that one process be established organization-wide, and although each project has the ability to tailor the standard procedures for its unique needs, there are certain aspects that are mandated across all projects. These mandates allow the organization to create a baseline for reporting and analysis, and ultimately for measuring the success of new initiatives. Adherence to a single framework also enables the business to implement common, shared processes across all of its business units, allowing personnel to work across different business units with minimal need for training.

But compliance to a single standard *within* the organization is not enough in our increasingly distributed world; suppliers and business partners must be a part of the process as well. For example, on DD(X), the U.S. Navy's 21st century surface combatant ship, the Consortium is working with Raytheon to ensure that suppliers achieve a minimum CMMI Level 3 rating, enabling them to leverage advanced, integrated processes across the various organizations involved.

Whether within a single organization or across them, project and process management issues associated with defining integration and synchronization points are still an issue for many distributed teams. Furthermore, there are security issues associated with ensuring confidentiality and privacy of electronic transmissions that are in part addressed by processes and procedures, and partly through the application of technologies as part of an integrated solution.

Enablers, Part III: People and Cultural Change

The rate-limiting variable for success in distributed project management is probably the human element of the project team. This variable is difficult to address because it deals with cultural changes in the areas of conflicting behaviors, processes, and technologies.

For example, distributed project management requires new human interaction skills that shift the emphasis from project *management* to project *leadership*. The manager must give up the role of benevolent dictator in a top-down hierarchical structure and develop new skills as an orchestrator of interconnected relationships. Negotiation is a core competency for the new project managemer, who needs to balance the needs of an increasingly large and diverse set of stakeholders. Herzog recommends that project managers employee 15 specific activities to increase communication and build trust within a team [4]. Management by walking around/flying around must give way to management by results. Humphrey [5] recommends several leadership activities in his Team Software Process (TSP[SM 3]), including ways to build trust, increase teamwork, and motivate teams. Looking across the range of management activities that rely heavily on soft skills, it is easy to understand why cultural change is needed to manage distributed work adequately.

Work needs to be done to move the current project management culture to a new way of thinking. Initiatives are ongoing at the Consortium, the Defense Systems Management College (Defense Acquisition University) [2], and other organizations to support this transition.

Maturing the New Culture

The availability of enabling tools, reevaluation of processes and procedures, and individual adoption of new skills for distributed work are essential, but taken individually are not sufficient to change the habits of a workforce. Senior management support for coordinated, complimentary change initiatives across all three aspects of the organization is essential to fully embrace the competitive advantages of distributed work.

One way to begin addressing the challenge is to develop a prototype and demonstration center [11] in which key practitioners and project managers can evaluate different hardware and software alternatives, assess current approaches, and make suggestions on how to tailor a selective alternative for their environment. Consortium support includes a collaboration tool data-

---

[3]TSP[SM] is a service mark of Carnegie Mellon University.

base, which contains evaluation data to support tool selection, and displays of hardware and software collaboration solutions connected to different communication mechanisms.

Another effective way to assist the project manager is by organizing a pilot that provides a set of capabilities tailored to the specific needs of the project. The Telework Consortium's pilots with distributed teams have achieved promising results by leveraging advanced virtual-presence tools. The goal of these experiments is to approximate colocated interactions as closely as possible through the use of integrated data, voice, and video communication, available frequently and spontaneously. To date, pilot results support the hypothesis that electronically enabled face-to-face communication can help minimize the impact of cultural changes and overcome the need for heavy application of processes when transitioning to a distributed work environment.

Closing Comments

Today's market environment is changing in several significant ways. The key drivers causing these changes are apt to stay relevant for some time to come, driving organizations to leverage distributed work. m response, the project manager, in order to manage and grow projects effectively, must look for mechanisms that provide integrated communications and information-sharing systems. Effective systems will incorporate not only technological advances, but also the complementary efforts required to evolve processes and culture for success in a distributed environment. By taking this action, project managers will enhance enterprise performance by reducing risks and increasing the velocity by which effective decisions can be made.

As the processes, tools, and technologies to support distributed work mature, more organizations are applying them to support their increasingly complex systems and software development projects [10]. A growing body of academic research and case studies describe the issues and considerations of successful distributed projects and show how the risks are being managed. Major initiatives at the Consortium related to distributed work are ongoing, both within the realm of systems and software engineering, and as it relates to society at large via its sponsorship of the Telework Consortium. By coupling existing research with the lessons from complex programs in the defense industry, the Systems and Software Consortium intends to place its member companies "ahead of the curve and shaping the game" in the area of distributed project management.

References

1. Carmel, Erran, *Global Software Teams, Collaborating Across Borders and Time Zones,* Upper Saddle River, New Jersey: Prentice-Hall PTR, 1999.

2. Cromar, Commander Patrick F., USN; Wiley, Lieutenant Colonel Anthony G., USA; Tremaine, Lieutenant Colonel Robert L., USAF, "Navigating The Digital Environment: A Program Manager's Perspective." Fort Belvoir, Virginia: Defense Systems Management College Press. December 1996. Available online at http://www.dau.mil/pubs/mfrpts/pdf/navdigl.pdf (accessed 09/29/04).

3. Dolan, Dana, and Arling, Priscilla, *Loudoun County Remote Work Pilots—Interim Findings Report.* Oct. 2004. Available online at http://www.teleworkconsortium.org.

4. Herzog, Valerie Lynne, "Trust Building on Corporate Collaborative Project Teams," *Project Management Journal* (March 2001), pp. 28–37.

5. Humphrey, Watts S., *Winning with Software, An Executive Strategy.* Reading, MA: Addison-Wesley, 2002.

6. Kane, James A., Presentation to the Software Productivity Consortium Executive Round Table, September 2004.

7. Lipnack, Jessica, and Stamps, Jeffery, *Virtual Teams: People Working Across Boundaries with Technology.* New York: Wiley, 2000.

8. Malone, Thomas W., *The Future of Work: How the New Order of Business Will Shape Your Organization, Your Management Style, and Your Life.* Boston, MA: Harvard Business School Press, 2004.

9. Nidiffer, Kenneth E., *Selection of Investigation Strategies which are Optimal for the Implementation of Software Environments with Particular Attention to DoD.* Dissertation, George Washington University, 1988.

10. Schmitt, John K. (BG, USA, Ret.), "Integrating the Battlespace," Presentation to the Software Productivity Consortium Executive Round Table on the Future Combat System (FCS), September 2004.

11. Schrage, Michael, Serious Play: *How the World's Best Companies Simulate to Innovate.* Boston MA: Harvard Business School Press 2000.

12. Standish Group, 2003 CHAOS Chronicles Report. The Standish Group International, Inc., 2003. Available online at http://www.standishgroup.com/press/article.php?id=2 (accessed 9/27/2004).

13. Standish Group. CHAOS: A Recipe for Success. The Standish Group International, Inc., 1999. available online at http://www.standishgroup.com/sample research/PDFpages/chaosl999.pdf (accessed 9/27/2004)

14. U.S. General Accounting Office Report to the Committee on Armed Services, U.S. Senate. "Defense Acquisitions: Stronger Management Practices Are Needed to Improve DOD's Software-Intensive Weapon Acquisitions," March 2004.

About the Authors

Dr. Kenneth Nidiffer is a Fellow at the Systems and Software Consortium (www.systemsandsoftware.org), which includes companies and affiliates from commercial industry, the information technology sector, government, and academia. His expertise in aligning an organization's technology and quality objectives to its business needs results from more than 35 years' experience as an engineering executive directing the research, development, test, maintenance, and acquisition of software-intensive systems across a wide range of business domains. A Professor Emeritus of the Defense Systems Management College and Adjunct Engineering Professor at George Mason university, Dr. Nidiffer has been widely published in the systems and software engineering community. He received his B.S. degree in Chemical Engineering in 1962 from Purdue University, Indiana, M.S. degree in Astronautical Engineering in 1969 from the Air Force Institute of Technology, Ohio, MBA degree from Auburn University, Alabama in 1975, and his D.Sc. degree from George Washington University, Washington D.C. in 1988. Dr. Nidiffer is a member of the Association of Computing Machinery (ACM), the Institute of Electrical and Electronics Engineers (IEEE), National Defense Industrial Association (NDIA), and the Air Force Society.

Dana Dolan is Director of Research at the Telework Consortium (www.teleworkconsortium.org) and senior member of the technical staff at the Systems and Software Consortium (www.systemsandsoftware.org), where she helps establish the strategic direction of their combined efforts in distributed work. Ms. Dolan has extensive experience in software architecture and development, specializing in Web-based management information systems and the collaborative development environments used to create and support them. Her current research focuses on collaborative tools for distributed work. Ms. Dolan holds a Masters of Information Systems from George Mason University and a Bachelor of Science degree in Math/Business, with a Computer Science Minor, from Wake Forest University. Ms. Dolan has extensive experience as a remote worker in a variety of situations, from running a software development business from her home beginning in 1986, to remote site and part-time telework arrangements with the Consortium, Lockheed Martin, Computer Associates, and others.

Managing Product Lines, Architectures, and Reuse

Donald J. Reifer

Introduction

Product-line management is one of the "hot" topics in software engineering today [1, 2]. As firms have moved to use open software architectures, they have started to adopt new product-line management paradigms that facilitate software reuse within and across their projects. The economic benefits of this movement have been profound. By harnessing the technology, the following significant benefits have been reported [3]:

- GTE Corp. saved $14 million in costs of software development with reuse levels of 14%.
- Hewlett-Packard cited quality improvements on two projects of 76% and 24% defect reduction, 50% and 40% increases in productivity, and 43% reduction in time to market with reuse levels of 70%.
- Nippon Electric Co. achieved 6.7 times higher productivity and 2.8 times better quality through 17% reuse. They improved quality 5–10 times over a 7 year period through the use of unmodified reuse components in two domains.
- Toshiba saw 20–30% reduction in defects per line of code with reuse levels of 60%.

The terms product line, architecture, and reuse have taken on different meanings from a decade ago. The following definitions [4] are offered to clarify their current meanings:

- **Product line.** A family of similar software products that are developed to service the market needs of a particular business area.
- **Architecture.** The structure of components, their interrelationships, and the principles and guidelines governing their design and evolution over time.
- **Software assets.** Any product of the software life cycle that can be potentially reused. This includes: architectures, requirements, designs, code, lessons learned, and so on.
- **Reuse.** To use again. The process of implementing or updating software using existing software assets.

Product Lines: The State of the Technology

Significant improvements have been made in the state of the technology in product lines. As the literature illustrates, the lessons learned as part of software reuse initiatives mounted during the last decade have been used to develop today's workable strategies for moving to product lines. These strategies can be classified as either an opportunistic or systematic approach [5]. Opportunistic reuse revolves primarily around project managers banding together to take advantage of opportunities as they arise for sharing across projects. For example, one project uses class libraries that a second project produces. Although some infrastructure changes may be needed to facilitate sharing, major organizational and cultural revisions do not have to be made. For example, the firm may establish an engineering council to coordinate sharing and handle change-control issues. It may designate owners for assets and may establish a corporate library to handle version control and distribution issues across the firm. The message is that alterations are minimal and it is business as usual.

The other major approach organizations are pursuing to take advantage of product lines is more systematic. This approach employs reference architectures as frameworks for facilitating sharing of software assets across product lines. While some line of business organization may own the architecture, a group separate from the software engineering organization may be designated the owner and assigned the task of developing assets to populate it. As an alternative, several firms have created software factories and tasked them to develop the reusable assets because they did not want to adversely impact the ability of their projects to fulfill their existing commitments. Corporate libraries are again used to store and make the assets shared across the product line readily available to the software workforce. The library is made part of the engineering environment and the associated processes are incorporated as part of the management infrastructure that the organization uses to conduct its business. The message here is that major changes must be made to the way the organization currently does business to pull this approach off in most businesses.

The component-based strategies that are popular in the literature [6] are a variant of the systematic approach. They try to make reuse integral to the business of software development by arming the people who do the work with the processes, methods, tools, and decision framework they need to incorporate reusable software assets into their deliverables. These components are typically fine-grained (i.e., small building blocks like active objects taken from a framework library). This approach builds applications using frameworks by combining and integrating pretested and preengineered fine-grained components with the help of automated tools. To put these changes to work, advocates of the methodology have taken and used many of the innovations developed by the reuse community for facilitating sharing of assets across project and project organizations.

The relative strengths and weaknesses of these two primary approaches to inserting product lines into your organization are compared above in Table 1. The six primary factors that govern selection of the strategy that is right for you are:

1. **Process maturity.** As Table 1 illustrates, organizations with low SEI process maturity ratings have more important things than product lines to worry about. They should be more concerned with defining and putting project management practices in place for processes like configuration management, project planning and tracking, and intergroup communications.

2. **Organizational focus.** The business the organization is in also impacts the selection. Software vendors have an easier time adopting product lines than service providers do. System developers and integrators may have a difficult time because they might not yet view software as an asset capable of being built and shared across projects.

3. **Organizational readiness.** Another important factor is how ready the organization is to adopt product lines. They require firms to embrace architectures as frameworks. They require new skills, knowledge, and abilities to be built. They revolve around sharing of assets. Those organizations that recognize that change is needed and have readied their staff for it will fare better than those who do not.

4. **Culture compatibility.** When making a change of this magnitude, you want to avoid culture clashes. Product lines fit well within organizations that already embrace a line of business culture. Cultures that fund projects one at a time have a more difficult time adopting a more opportunistic strategy because they are structured around projects.

5. **Degree of risk taking.** Because product lines typically force major organizational and management infrastructure changes, risk taking must be part of the culture. Making large gains requires taking large risks. Even the most mature organization might not be ready to accept the degree of organizational change and the related disruptions associated with inserting a product-line management approach operationally.

Table 1. Assessment of opportunistic versus systematic strategies

Strategy	Strengths	Weaknesses
Opportunistic	• Simple and easy to implement • Costs are reasonable • Can make near-term impact • Provides results that users are willing to pay for	• Often bureaucratic because access to assets is restricted • Taxes used to pay for services • Assets tend to be a hodgepodge of whatever is available
Systematic	• Product-line oriented • Investments based on what is needed to populate architecture • Reuse of COTS emphasized • Economies of scale possible • Product-line management becomes the way you do business • Easy to achieve	• Investments needed are large • Major culture change is needed • New management infrastructure (processes, etc.) is needed • Change takes energy and time • Existing project and products may be adversely impacted • Difficult to achieve

6. **Degree of investment.** The opportunistic approach requires less time and money to pull off. It also does not make radical changes to the way the organization currently does business. Therefore, it appeals to those looking to make near-term impacts quickly. In contrast, the product-line approach requires considerable time and investment. Because its benefits are much larger, it may appeal to those in a position with a longer-term vision.

Guidelines for Adoption Success

Software product lines are an emerging technology. Current efforts in industry are mostly aimed at bridging the chasm [7] that exists between early adopter pilot project successes and widespread adoption. The roadmap to success that I have developed is built on the following 11 principles of change management [5]:

1. **Change only if it makes good business sense.** Do not make investments in product lines unless you can reasonably expect to show some positive returns on investment within a reasonable time period. Senior managers get restless easily, especially when they see lots of money being spent with little return. You need to properly set their expectations in order to counter this negative view that occurs when initiatives do not yield immediate results.

2. **Do not become enamored with the technology.** Do not believe the technologists when they promise you miracles. Instead of generating results, use of immature technology can often force you to expend effort to refine methods and tools. This causes you to focus attention on the technology instead of using it to promulgate your product lines. Focus instead on getting the product out. Results are what counts in reality.

3. **Get your people involved at all levels.** The best way to get your people energized is to get them involved. Listen, act, and factor their opinions into your plans. Address their concerns and let them know that their opinions count. When you do this, your plan will become their plan. They will become your allies instead of your saboteurs.

4. **Focus change on product-specific improvements.** Focus your process-related changes on making your products better. Make improvements visible where they count, where the customer can see them, and where you can earn points over the competition. This approach will enable you to create bastions of support for your initiative that will help you dampen criticism by the skeptics and those who fear change.

5. **Look to the future, not the past.** Do not worry about your past mistakes. Instead, learn form them and factor them into your plans for the future. Set realistic expectations and then claim success in everything you do. Focus on being perceived as being successful. Perception is reality in the minds of most bosses and others that count in most organizations.

6. **Do not reinvent the wheel.** Build on the successes (and failures) of others. Take advantage of what others have experienced and learned relative to the strategy you have selected to build the support you will need to sustain your initiative.

7. **Remember, Rome was not built in a day.** Be patient. Make incremental impact. Build momentum slowly, but steadily. Move ahead smartly, gaining speed on every straightaway. Take detours as necessary, but continue along your planned path. Establish credibility along the way by making your results visible to all through a public relations campaign.

8. **Do the easy things first.** Make an immediate impact by doing the obvious things right away. This maneuver will buy you the time you need to figure out how to attack the harder things. It will also create the impression that you are being successful. Because success breeds success, such perceptions can go a long way toward keeping you out of trouble.

9. **Identify and manage risks.** Figure out the five to ten important things that can cause your effort to go astray and then do something about each of them. "Important" means things that can negatively impact your ability to deliver as promised on time and within budget. Worry about these issues because they represent your report card as a program manager. Realize that situations change. In response, always be on the lookout for new risks.

10. **Keep focused.** Most of the failed product-line initiatives that I have studied failed because they expanded and took on added responsibilities prematurely. They did not have a chance to succeed. Because they were trying to do so many things all at once, they lost focus and could not seem to do anything right. Fight the urge to couple other needed changes with your initiative. There will be time for them later. Instead, focus on delivering what you promise, when you promised it. When you fight for budget, you will be glad you did.

11. **Judge the initiative on the results.** As you examine the results, believe the numbers and facts that you have assembled. Everything else is usually noise. Separate hard numbers from soft data. Then use the number to develop tangible and intangible benefits. Publish results in a form management relates to. For example, publish an annual report containing a balance sheet and detailing the return on investment.

I have used these principles again and again to guide my actions as I have led initiatives and pursued changes within organizations of the magnitude described herein.

Implementation Tactics

To put my 11 change-management principles into action, I offer the following tactics:

- Define a vision and strategy. Write a vision and strategy document for upper management that clearly states what you are trying to accomplish and why it is important to the business enterprise that you are part of. Identify how product lines fit into current corporate plans and how it complements the firm's vision for the future.
- Document your operational concepts. Document your proposed technical, managerial, and technology fan-out concepts of operations. Provide senior management with some insight into the organizational and cultural changes needed to use these concepts effectively.
- Assign responsibility to a dedicated leader. You cannot institute change without dedicated leadership. Using part-timers, even when they are competent, has not worked in the past. Someone must take charge of the initiative, motivate the troops, sell management, focus energy, generate products, and publicize the results.
- Establish a plan of attack. Supplement your vision and strategy with a management plan. Show everyone concerned how you will manage the realization of your vision. Define activities, set schedules, establish budgets, describe controls, and define your measures of success. Use the organizational process whenever possible to be compatible with the way your firm does business.
- Let people know what you are trying to do and get them involved. Let people know what is going on, why it is important to them and the organization, and how they can contribute. Otherwise, they will feel left out. Listen to their suggestions, act on them whenever possible, and keep everyone informed about their contributions and your progress. Be viewed as their champion and a winner.
- Baseline your organizational norms. Get the historical cost, productivity, and quality data that you will need to show that you have made a positive impact [8]. Numbers can be your allies, especially when they can be used to show that you have made a positive impact. Articulate these numbers and carefully explain what they mean. Do not give others a chance to misinterpret them and use them against you. Realize that executives are like elephants when it comes to numbers. Utter one and they never will forget it.
- Make a positive impact as quickly as possible. Avoid "ivory towerism." Prove your worth under controlled conditions on a pilot or pathfinder project. Conduct a demonstration. Show people results; do not just tell them about your achievements. You will be surprised at how well you will be perceived when you can prove your value.
- Publicize successes and encourage the exchange of ideas. Make what you are doing and your achievements visible. Publish a monthly newsletter, articles, and press releases. Set up a Web site. Have your people make briefings and present your experience. Encourage the exchange of information and ideas. Deal from a sense of power, not weakness, as you convey the impression that you are achieving results.
- Expand as you learn. Start out small and expand slowly. Use your metrics data to decide on your next course of action. Beware of becoming a threat to those in power. Provide them with support and help other organizations that can help you protect your money and win the battle of the budget. Make others your allies by helping them solve their problems. Later, when you need their help, they will reciprocate and you will be glad that you helped them.
- Establish ways of altering course. Continuously monitor feedback on how well you are doing relative to your goals. Take suggestions, listen and act to make changes when they are warranted. Keep in touch with your sponsors, customers, and supporters. Make sure that you hold hands and keep these stakeholders happy.

Summary, Conclusions, and Recommendations

I believe that product lines can have a profound impact on the way we do our software business in the near term. People are excited about the possibilities of reuse and are trying to put the technology to work. This paper was written and the articles within this chapter were selected to emphasize this point. For those interested in getting further information, the body of literature on product lines, architectures, and component-based software engineering [9–12] is expanding and a number of good public seminars on the topic are available.

References

1. Paul Clements and Linda M. Northrop, *Product Lines: Practices and Patterns,* Addison-Wesley, 2001.
2. David M. Weiss and Chi Tau Robert Lai, *Software Product Line Engineering,* Addison-Wesley, 1999.
3. Jeffrey S. Poulin, *Measuring Software Reuse,* Addison-Wesley, 1997, pages 6–7.
4. Donald J. Reifer, *Practical Software Reuse,* Wiley, 1997.
5. Ibid, Chapter 3.
6. George T. Heineman and William T. Councill, *Component-Based Software Engineering,* Addison-Wesley, 2001.
7. Geoffrey A. Moore, *Crossing the Chasm,* HarperBusiness, 1991.
8. Donald J. Reifer, *Making the Software Business Case: Improvement by the Numbers,* Addison-Wesley, 2001.
9. Paul Alien and Stuart Frost, *Component-Based Development for Enterprise Systems,* Cambridge University Press, 1998.
10. Len Bass, Paul Clements, and Rick Kazman, *Software Architecture in Practice,* Addison-Wesley, 1998.
11. Peter Herzum and Oliver Sims, *Business Component Factory,* OMG Press, 1999.
12. Clemens Szyperski, *Component Software: Beyond Object-Oriented Programming,* Addison-Wesley, 1999.

Improving the Security of Networked Systems

By Julia Allen, Christopher Alberts, Sandi Behrens, Barbara Laswell, and William Wilson
Networked Systems Survivability Program, Software Engineering Institute, Carnegie Mellon University

As the Internet and other national information infrastructures become larger, more complex, and more interdependent, the frequency and severity of unauthorized intrusions is increasing. Therefore, to the extent possible and practical, it is critical to secure the networked systems of an organization that are connected to public networks. This article describes an emerging approach and set of activities for establishing and maintaining the security of networked systems.

Targeting the Problem

Networks have become indispensable for conducting business in government, industry, and academic organizations. Networked systems allow access to needed information rapidly, improve communications while reducing costs, enable collaboration with partners, provide better customer services, and conduct electronic commerce [1].

Organizations have moved to distributed, client-server architectures where servers and workstations communicate through networks. In addition, they are connecting their networks to the Internet to sustain a visible business presence with customers, partners, and suppliers. While computer networks revolutionize the way business is done, the risks they introduce can be fatal. Attacks on networks can lead to lost money, time, products, reputation, sensitive information, and even lives.

The *2000 Computer Security Institute/FBI Computer Crime and Security Survey* [2] indicates that computer crime and other information security breaches are still on the rise, and the cost is increasing. For example, 70 percent of the 585 respondents reported computer security breaches within the last twelve months, up from 62 percent in 1999. Furthermore, the financial losses for the 273 organizations that could quantify them totaled $265,586,240, a 100 percent increase over the $123,779,000 reported in 1999.

Engineering for ease of use is not being matched by engineering for ease of secure administration. Today's software products, workstations, and personal computers bring the power of the computer to increasing numbers of people to perform their work more effectively. Products are so easy to use that people with little technical knowledge or skill can install and operate them on their desktop computers. Unfortunately, it is difficult to configure

and operate many of these products securely. This gap between the knowledge needed to operate a system and that needed to keep it secure leads to increasing numbers of vulnerable systems [3].

Technology evolves so rapidly that vendors concentrate on time-to-market, often minimizing that time by placing a low priority on security features. Until customers demand products that are more secure, the situation is unlikely to change.

Users count on their systems being there when they need them, assuming that their information technology (IT) departments are operating all systems securely. This may not be the case. System and network administrators typically have insufficient time, knowledge, and skill to address the wide range of demands to keep today's complex systems and networks up and running. Additionally, evolving attack methods and software vulnerabilities continually introduce new threats to an organization's installed technology and systems. Thus, even vigilant, security-conscious organizations discover that security starts to degrade almost immediately after fixes, workarounds, and newly installed

technology are put in place.

Inadequate security in the IT infrastructures can negatively affect the integrity, confidentiality, and availability of systems and data.

Who has this problem? The answer is just about everyone—anyone that uses information technology infrastructures that are networked, distributed, and heterogeneous needs to care about improving the security of networked systems.

Why Improve Security?

Why should you care about this problem? Whether you acknowledge it or not, your organization's networks and systems are vulnerable to attack by both insiders and outsiders. Organizations cannot conduct business and build products without a robust IT infrastructure. In addition, users have an organizational and ethical responsibility to protect competitive and sensitive information. They must also preserve the reputation and image of their organizations and business partners. All of these can be severely compromised by successful intrusions.

In the 1980s intruders were the sys-

Figure 1. *Attack Sophistication vs. Intruder Technical Knowledge*

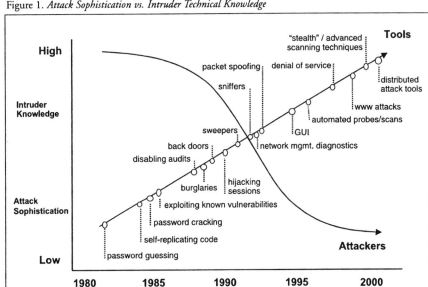

tem experts, as depicted in Figure 1. They had a high level of expertise and personally constructed methods for breaking into systems. Automated tools and exploit scripts were the exception rather than the rule. Today, absolutely anyone can attack a network due to the widespread and easy availability of intrusion tools and exploit scripts that can easily duplicate known methods of attack. While experienced intruders are getting smarter—as demonstrated by the increased sophistication in the types of attacks—the knowledge required on the part of novice intruders to copy and launch known methods of attack is decreasing. Meanwhile, as evidenced by distributed denial-of-service attacks and variants of the Love Letter Worm, the severity and scope of attack methods is increasing.

In the early to mid-1980s, intruders manually entering commands on their personal computers could access tens to hundreds of systems; today, intruders use automated tools to access thousands to tens of thousands of systems. In the 1980s, it was relatively straightforward to determine if an intruder had penetrated your systems, and discover what they did. Today, intruders are able to totally hide their presence, for example, by disabling commonly used services and reinstalling their own versions, then erasing their tracks in audit and log files. In the 1980s and early 1990s, denial-of-service attacks were infrequent and not considered serious. Today, for organizations such as Internet service providers that conduct business electronically, a successful denial-of-service attack can put them out of business. Unfortunately, these types of attacks occur more frequently each year.

Due to exploding Internet use the demand for individuals with necessary technical education far exceeds the supply required to meet the need (see Figures 2 and 3). This is true for both those in formal degree programs and those who have acquired on-the-job knowledge and skills. As a result, people who are not properly qualified are being hired or promoted from within to do the job. This trend is exacerbated by the fact that some skilled, experienced system administrators change jobs frequently to increase their salaries or leave the job market because of burnout.

Today's audit and evaluation products typically focus on the underlying system and network technologies without considering the organizational concerns (e.g., policies, procedures) and human aspects (e.g., management, culture, knowledge and skills, incentives) that can dramatically affect the security posture of IT infrastructures. As a result, incomplete or point solutions are implemented with the expectation that they will completely solve the problem.

Figure 2. *Internet Growth by Number of Hosts*

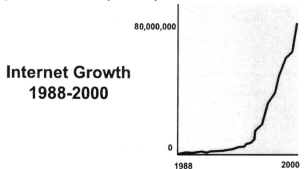

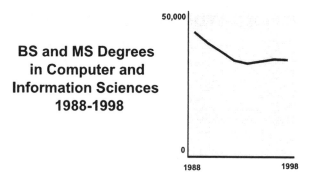

Figure 3. *Degrees in Computer and Information Sciences from 1988 to 1998*

The Meaning of Improved Security

Improving security is hard work, even if you have had a significant attack that has gotten everyone's attention. Sustaining a desired level of security can be even harder. First, you need to identify the risks to your business if the security (confidentiality, availability, and integrity) of critical data, systems, and/or networks (assets) is compromised. By compromised, we mean that the asset has been destroyed, damaged, or altered in a way that hurts your operations, or has been revealed to your competitors.

You cannot protect everything equally, so it is important to carefully choose the data you want to protect and then plan how to do so based on its value to your organization [4].

Once you know the risks to your networked system, you need to decide which ones are most likely to occur and which would cause the largest potential impact. The impact could be measured in money, time, lost productivity, or loss of market share, customers, or reputation. After deciding on a prioritized list of risks and an effective plan to mitigate them, there is still work to be done.

Suppose that a day after you create your plan, you find out that your main competitor has just launched a new e-commerce site and is ready to do business on the Internet—and you are still six months away from launching yours. Or suppose a recently fired employee has successfully penetrated your strategic planning database and posted your plans for the next 18 months on an Internet newsgroup. In other words, change and surprises introduce new risks that must be added to the ones you are already managing.

Since the technology and business environment is highly dynamic, an organization needs mechanisms for identifying critical information assets as conditions change. You need to have a way of adjusting where you invest time and energy for improving security based on this very dynamic environment.

Information Security Risk Assessment

Information protection decisions are often incomplete or ineffective because they are based on the organization's prior experience with vulnerabilities and current threats. While managing information security risks helps ensure that information protection strategies are appropriate, most risk assessments are incomplete, or are conducted by external consultants who have little knowledge of the organization's unique requirements. In order to address the widening gap between current risk management practice and the need for flexible, effective information protection, the Networked Systems Survivability (NSS) Program at the Software Engineering Institute (SEI) is developing a comprehensive, repeatable technique for identifying vulnerabilities in networked systems through organizational self-assessment.

This self-assessment, Operationally Critical Threat, Asset, and Vulnerability Evaluation (OCTAVE[SM])[1] [5], enables organizations to develop appropriate protection strategies by considering policy, management, administration, and other organizational issues, as well as technologies, to form a comprehensive view of the information security state of that organization. This method is a key component of an overarching security and information protection framework that allows an organization to identify and pursue an appropriate security posture.

An effective risk management strategy requires more than an assessment of the existing information infrastructure. An organization needs to understand:

- Value of the assets that must be protected.
- Consequences of loss of confidentiality or operational capability.
- Vulnerabilities that could be exploited to bring about the losses.
- Existing threats that could exploit the vulnerabilities.
- Likelihood that a threat might occur.
- Availability and appropriateness of options and resources to address risks and concerns.

The OCTAVE method is composed of three phases that provide a systematic, context-driven approach to managing information security risks, and enables an organization to assemble a comprehensive picture of their information security needs. Phase 1 identifies information assets and their values, as well as threats to those assets and the security requirements to protect them. This is accomplished using staff knowledge from multiple levels within the organization along with standard catalogs of information. This information can then be used to achieve the Phase 1 goal, which is to establish the security requirements of the enterprise.

Phase 2 examines the information assets of the organization in relation to the information infrastructure components to identify those components that are high priority. Then, staff evaluates the vulnerabilities within the infrastructure. At the conclusion of Phase 2, the organization has identified the high-priority information infrastructure components, missing policies and practices, and vulnerabilities.

Phase 3 builds on the information captured during Phases 1 and 2. Risks are identified by analyzing the assets, threats, and vulnerabilities. Estimates of impact and probability of the risks are made, and the risks are then prioritized, ultimately resulting in the development of a protection strategy and a comprehensive, enterprise-wide plan for managing information security risks.

OCTAVE has many unique features that extend its impact far beyond a comprehensive risk assessment. First, OCTAVE provides an organizing framework as well as a method that capitalizes on the abilities, practices, and mission of the organization performing the self-assessment. Thus, it helps organizations understand what current strategies and practices are working effectively. It also reveals needed improvements and gaps existing in strategy, technology, staff knowledge, and in the organization's ability to protect key information assets in a constantly changing environment.

Second, OCTAVE requires effective communication among all levels of staff and management. This is one of the long-lasting benefits.

Third, OCTAVE helps provide a clear picture of gaps in internal capabilities, thus enabling a strategy to be built that can include appropriate use of specialized, external experts. Ultimately the goal of OCTAVE is to improve how well information assets are protected, thus putting organizations in a better position to achieve their missions.

Inherent in the OCTAVE method is the assumption that an organization is already working to meet its mission objectives by using many good protection strategies. There are many practices that are commonplace; some are effective and some are not. The NSS Program continues to define technology and management practices that provide practical guidance, which will help organizations address important problems in network security.

Recommended Security Practices

One of the most important parts of adopting recommended security practices is selecting those that will allow you to mitigate your most critical technical risks. When considering who could most benefit from pragmatic, concise, how-to guidance about security (practices), it became obvious that the audiences with the greatest need were network and system administrators and their managers. They face the most daunting challenges as a result of the growth and complexity of their IT infrastructures, which they must keep in operation around the clock, seven days a week. They are constantly being asked to add new IT systems, networks, applications, and data to keep pace with changing business and technology demands.

Based on the actions successful organizations were taking to deal with these demands, the NSS program has developed step-by-step guidance that does not rely on a particular operating system or platform. The intent was to make the information as useful as possible. In addition, the NSS program developed UNIX- and Windows NT-specific implementations for many of the practices. All of this information can be found at the CERT® Coordination Center[2] (CERT/CC) Web site on the security improvement page.[3]
Each practice contains:

- A brief description that expands the title of the practice.
- An explanation of why the practice is important (what casualties can occur if you do not implement the practice).
- A step-by-step description of how to perform the practice.
- A collection of related policy topics that support deploying the practice successfully.

As data becomes available from organizations implementing recommended security practices, the practices will also provide:

- The cost/benefit analysis information for selecting among alternative approaches, and
- The means to measure implementation success (did it solve the problem it purported to solve, and were the benefits of the investment worth the cost?).

Some of the more frequently referenced sets of practices (each set is called a module) include Preparing to Detect Signs of Intrusion, Detecting Signs of Intrusion, Responding to

Intrusions, Securing Desktop Workstations, Securing Network Servers, Securing Public Web Servers, and Deploying Firewalls. The modules contain practices such as:

- Establishing requirements, policies, and procedures.
- Establishing secure architectures and configurations.
- Identifying and installing tools.
- Setting up logging options, examining what they produce.
- Setting up user authentication and file access control mechanisms.
- Determining how to deny network traffic that you do not want coming into your system.

Many of the practices are starting to appear in training materials and are being referenced by other web sites.

Curriculum and Certification Standards

Information systems security training at the SEI uses a variety of source material and experience in developing courses, including recommended practices and implementations. Relevant data from CERT/CC incident response and vulnerability analysis operations are used to provide current information on trends and emerging threats. CERT/CC experience in helping to foster the creation of other incident response teams around the world provides the core content for the suite of incident handling courses [7]. Research in the areas of security risk management and information survivability similarly provide core content for course development.

Comprehensive solutions for the survivability of information systems require that senior executives and managers, as well as technical staff, develop strong and diverse skills. Senior management must establish a clear sense of priority levels and appropriate policies, as well as risk-mitigation strategies, for securing various information assets. They share this guidance with technical staff responsible for the secure administration of networked systems. The first-line managers of technical staff must be able to articulate the technical implications of these decisions so cost-benefit tradeoffs can be performed.

The NSS program is in the process of developing security curricula for managers and system administrators. As a result of course development in the areas of Internet security, e.g. incident handling, secure system administration, and risk management activities, current offerings[4] include two sets of courses. One set is built around computer security response teams and incident handling. This set includes Managing Computer Security Incident Response Teams and Computer Security Incident Handling for Technical Staff [Introductory and Advanced].

The second set is built around fundamental concepts and selected practices for Internet security. This set includes Concepts and Trends in Information Security, Information Security for System Administrators, Managing Risks to Information Assets, and The Executive Role in Information Security: Risk and Survivability. Selected, tailored training courses have also been developed to accompany security improvement modules and practices for implementation at customer organizations.

Arguably, current training for system and network administrators, their managers, and users does not sufficiently address requisite knowledge, skills, and abilities for securing networked systems unless an organization has clearly identified its critical information assets and defined a set of protection strategies that guide the appropriate training. Since the technology changes rapidly, people need to update their skills frequently. Consequently, course content needs to be dynamic as well. Thus, any systematic effort to train and certify system and network administrators must account for changing technical requirements and course content.

There is a growing demand to establish a minimum set of core competencies or certification standards for system and network administrators. Several efforts are underway to address this problem. For example, the *Information Technology Security Training Requirements: A Role- and Performance-Based Model* [6] outlines an information technology security body of knowledge, topics, and concepts. Integrated Space Command and Control[5] offers the designation of Certified Information Systems Security Professional. System Administration Networks and Security[6] offers Levels 1 and 2 certification. USENIX System Administrator's Guild[7] is currently examining certification approaches and conducting job analyses to establish standards [8].

Summary

This article described the growing problem of protecting networked systems connected to public networks such as the Internet. We presented an emerging structure for improving the security of networked systems that includes conducting an information security risk assessment, which produces a recommended set of risks to be managed and protection strategies intended to mitigate those risks. Implementing protection strategies includes adopting recommended security practices. Both assessment and practice deployment require appropriate training, which, in the future, will hopefully build upon a set of security certification standards.

We welcome your feedback and look forward to hearing about your experiences as you improve the security of your organization's networked systems and work to sustain them. ◆

References

1. Allen, Julia. *Securing Networked Systems: A Technology Improvement Process.* 1999 Software Engineering Process Group Conference, Carnegie Mellon University, Software Engineering Institute, March, 1999. Available at www.cert.org/sepg99/index.htm
2. Computer Security Institute, 2000 CSI/FBI Computer Crime and Security Survey, *Computer Security Issues and Trends,* Vol. VI, No. 1, (Spring 2000).
3. Pethia, Richard. *Internet Security Issues: Testimony Before the U.S. Senate Judiciary Committee.* Carnegie Mellon University, Software Engineering Institute, May 25, 2000. Available at www.cert.org/congressional_testimony/Pethia_testimony25May00.html
4. West-Brown, Moira and Allen, Julia. SEI Interactive. Pittsburgh, Pa.: Carnegie Mellon University, Software Engineering Institute, September 1999. Available at http://interactive.sei.cmu.edu/Columns/Security_Matters/1999/September/Security.sep99.pdf
5. Alberts, Christopher; Behrens, Sandra G.; Pethia, Richard D.; and Wilson, William R. *Operationally Critical Threat, Asset, and Vulnerability Evaluation (OCTAVE^{SM}) Framework, Version 1.0.* (CMU/SEI-00-TR-017). Pittsburgh, Pa.: Carnegie Mellon University, Software Engineering Institute, June 1999. Available at www.sei.cmu.edu/publications/documents/99.reports/99tr017/

99tr017abstract.html

6. Wilson, William, ed. *Information Technology Security Training Requirements: A Role- and Performance-Based Model* (Publication 800-16). National Institute of Standards and Technology, U.S. Department of Commerce, 1998.

7. West-Brown, Moira J.; Stikvoort, Don; and Kossakowski, Klaus-Peter. *Handbook for Computer Security Incident Response Teams* (CMU/SEI-98-HB-001). Pittsburgh, Pa.: Carnegie Mellon University, Software Engineering Institute, 1998. Available at www.sei.cmu.edu/publications/documents/98.reports/98hb001/98hb001abstract.html

8   Laswell, Barbara; Simmel, Derek; and Behrens, Sandra G. *Information Assurance Curriculum and Certification: State of the Practice* (CMU/SEI-99-TR-021). Pittsburgh, Pa.: Carnegie Mellon University, Software Engineering Institute, July 1999. Available at www.sei.cmu.edu/publications/documents/99.reports/99tr021/99tr021abstract.html

Notes

1. Operationally Critical Threat, Asset, and Vulnerability Evaluation and OCTAVE are service marks of Carnegie Mellon University.
2. CERT and CERT Coordination Center are registered in the U.S. Patent and Trademark Office.
3. See www.cert.org/security-improvement
4. The current description of public offerings is available at www.sei.cmu.edu/products/courses/courses.html
    The current schedule of public offerings is available at www.sei.cmu.edu/products/calendars/calendar.html
5. See www.isc2.org
6. See www.sans.org
7. See www.usenix.org

About the Authors

Julia Allen is a senior member of the technical staff working in security improvement. She has an master's degree in electrical engineering from the University of Southern California.

Christopher Alberts is a member of the technical staff working in information security risk management. He has an master's degree in engineering from Carnegie Mellon University.

Sandi Behrens is a senior member of the technical staff working in information security risk management. She has a doctorate degree from the University of Pittsburgh with an emphasis on instructional technology and cognitive science.

Barbara Laswell is the technical manager of practices development and training. She has a doctorate degree from Stanford University in the design and evaluation of educational systems.

William Wilson is currently managing the survivable network management team. He has a master's degree in computer systems management from the University of Maryland.

Carnegie Mellon University, Software Engineering Institute
4500 Fifth Ave.
Pittsburgh, Pa. 15213
Voice: 412-268-6942
Fax: 412-268-6989
Email: Julia Allen: jha@sei.cmu.edu
          Christopher Alberts: cja@sei.cmu.edu
          Sandi Behrens: sgb@sei.cmu.edu
          Barbara Laswell: blaswell@sei.cmu.edu
          William Wilson: wrw@sei.cmu.edu
Internet: http://www.sei.cmu.edu, http://www.cert.org

Managing at Light Speed

Lynn Carrier, Policy Management Systems

Faced with the relentless pace of technological progress, businesses today need a blueprint for strategically implementing and exploiting new technologies. In *The Innovator's Dilemma* (Harvard Business School Press, 1997) Clayton M. Christensen sketches the broad outlines of this blueprint when he categorizes technology as either disruptive or sustaining. A disruptive technology is one that changes or replaces the accepted way of doing things. A sustaining technology, on the other hand, enhances an existing product or service by refining it or making its creation and delivery more efficient.

Unfortunately, the larger and more successful a company grows, the more inimical its culture becomes to the flexibility and inventiveness that innovation requires. To achieve long-term success in today's business environment, managers must learn how to accommodate the very different requirements of disruptive and sustaining technologies.

FROM SUCCESS TO STAGNATION

After excelling for years, why do great companies like Sears and IBM, who implement the best-accepted practices of good management, lose their dominant positions by failing to innovate with disruptive technology?

Christensen describes how a success-

Editor: Barry Boehm, Computer Science Department, University of Southern California, Los Angeles, CA 90089; boehm@ sunset.usc.edu

In an environment of constant technological innovation, success may be the surest path to failure.

ful company with established products gets pushed aside by newer, cheaper products that will, over time, improve and become a serious business threat. He notes that even the best-managed companies, despite their attention to customers and continual investment in new technology, remain susceptible to failure no matter what the industry—be it hard drives or consumer retailing. Christensen observes that "great companies can fail precisely because they do everything right." For example, although closely monitoring customers' needs is key to a firm's current success, doing so will not lead it to discover the innovations that customers do not know they want.

Maturity's upside: stability

Some management challenges faced today are sustaining in character. They require managerial techniques, capabili-

ties, organization structures, and decision-making processes valid only in certain conditions. A project to implement sustaining technology can benefit from the Capability Maturity Model's software process. In *Key Practices of the Capability Maturity Model, Version 1.1* (Software Engineering Institute, 1993), Mark C. Paulk and colleagues describe the chaos of the software process life cycle. They describe organizations that have not implemented CMM process-management controls as "... unpredictable because the software process is constantly changed or modified as the work progresses ...." Managers of sustaining organizations require oversight, control, and continuous process improvement to lift their organizations through CMM's five levels.

To achieve this goal, CMM's nonspontaneous model pushes organizations to strive for discipline and mature processes. Similar stable processes helped build Sears from a small catalog operation into a nationwide chain and propelled IBM into the world's leading provider of business machines with their mainframes, dumb terminals, and typewriters. Sears enjoyed 40 years of national retail sales dominance before another retail chain emerged to challenge it.

Maturity's downside: rigidity

Unfortunately, Sears's managerial discipline and mature processes let Wal-Mart replace it as market leader; Microsoft did the same thing to IBM. The old market leaders rigidly focused on what their customers said they wanted and needed, then simply provided more of the same.

CMM's effects on technology-driven strategies are unpredictable. Sometimes CMM's continuous-improvement focus enforces a rigid attention to process that can blind contractors and developers to important technology changes. Maybe *discontinuous* improvement would be better. Christensen points out that only twice during the disk-drive industry's history has that market's leading company developed the next-generation model; in six other generations, new companies used disruptive technology to replace the established leaders.

Reprinted from *Computer,* July 1999.

Customers who cannot immediately use breakthrough innovations tend to reject these disruptive technologies at first. This reaction can lead firms with a strong customer focus to let their most important advances languish. By failing to create new markets and seek new customers, such firms unwittingly bypass opportunities, opening the door for more nimble, entrepreneurial rivals.

RUNNING TO STAY IN PLACE

According to Michael A. Cusumano and David B. Yoffie (*Competing on Internet Time*, Free Press, 1998), the Honda Supercub, Intel's 8088 processor, and hydraulic excavators all show how disruptive technologies helped redefine the competitive landscape of their respective markets. By marketing first for new uses, these products cut into the marketplace's low end, then evolved to displace high-end competitors. Significantly, these products did not come from already-successful companies in established markets. Entrenched firms tend to ignore disruptive technologies because they are unproven and offer lower profit margins than existing technologies.

Netscape's entry into the corporate intranet provides another example of high-speed innovation. According to Cusumano and Yoffie, in 1995 Netscape refocused its main product "... from consumer-oriented Internet to intranets, or corporate TCP/IP-based networks" in response to customer feedback. When Netscape saw the new potential, it changed its focus almost overnight. Given how swiftly information spreads across the Internet and thus how quickly innovations can proliferate, companies that want to stay competitive must emulate Netscape's quick-response model. Making a large organization capable of such flexibility, without destabilizing it, will likely prove the greatest challenge.

STRATEGIES FOR CHANGE

Today's competitive environment requires a different managerial formula to deal with constant change. A strong vision will help companies develop the entrepreneurial agility needed to catch the next great wave of industry growth.

Accelerating responsiveness

Cusumano and Yoffie offer entrenched companies three techniques for competing in fast-changing markets:

- move rapidly toward new products and markets,
- be flexible in strategy and implementation, and
- exploit all leverage points.

Quickly responding to unforeseen opportunities and competitive threats requires organizational agility. For example, as competition between Microsoft and Netscape spread to new markets, Netscape nimbly changed from a company that produced browser software to one that produced intranet solutions, then extranet solutions, then morphed itself into a portal for e-commerce, and has just lately been split and absorbed into Sun and AOL.

Avoid repetitive thinking if you want innovative strategic planning. Shona L. Brown and Kathleen M. Eisenhardt's *Competing at the Edge: Strategy as Structured Chaos* (Harvard Business School Press, 1998) offers 10 strategies for becoming a leading-edge competitor:

- Advantage is temporary
- Strategy is diverse, emergent, and complicated
- Reinvention is the goal
- Live in the present
- Stretch out the past
- Reach into the future
- Time pace change
- Grow the strategy
- Drive strategy from the business level
- Repatch businesses to markets and articulate the whole

In the authors' view, you must thrive on ambiguity and spontaneous reactions if you hope to succeed in a market that is a moving target. By developing and maintaining a broad vision, you can exploit all leverage points and accelerate your response to market changes. Companies go blind when their strategic and operational plans derive from an external assessment of the future that's rooted in the past. To avoid this, keep

Sources and Resources

Several books give valuable insight into the challenge of balancing disruptive and sustaining technologies.

Clayton M. Christensen's *The Innovator's Dilemma: When New Technologies Cause Great Firms to Fail: Managing Disruptive Technological Change* (Harvard Business School Press, Boston, 1997) gives a detailed discussion of how well-managed companies fail to react successfully to innovator challenges powered by disruptive technology. Christensen offers a solution in the form of a new strategy for change.

Michael A. Cusumano and David B. Yoffie's *Competing on Internet Time,* (Free Press, New York, 1998) combines Cusumano's expertise in technology management with Yoffie's leading thought on competitive strategy to produce an in-depth analysis of Netscape that extends through the summer of 1998. Describing how Netscape and Microsoft battled over Internet turf, they draw lessons from direct interviews with company executives to show that corporate strategy must have a vision that allows change.

Shona L. Brown and Kathleen M. Eisenhardt's *Competing at the Edge: Strategy as Structured Chaos* (Harvard Business School Press, Boston, 1998) details the importance of valuing change. Their 10 rules provide guidelines for managing chaos, implementing strategies based on severe change, and maintaining focus in a world of unstable markets and fierce competition.

Mark C. Paulk and colleagues' *Key Practices of the Capability Maturity Model, Version 1.1* (Software Engineering Institute, Carnegie Mellon University, Pittsburgh, 1993) provides practical guidelines for implementing work processes.

your vision open enough so that you don't lock your organization into a specific path to the future. For example, the Prudential Property & Casualty insurance company developed one of the first Web-based e-commerce solutions for issuing personal-automobile policies. Prudential injected the technology of the 1990s into an industry commonly thought of as staid and slow to change.

Nurturing creativity

Keep the creative process alive by avoiding linear, cause-and-effect approaches to decision making. An approach that thrives on ambiguity and unpredictability can actually be implemented with good discipline. Consider Brown and Eisenhardt's application of complexity theory to help evolve the complex organization with their "key signals." They recommend a coherent business vision, a variety of low-cost probes into new markets, and constant but "thin" attention to future market shifts. Thin attention requires that you limit yourself to frequent peeks at what the future may bring, rather than attempting a constant scrutiny of ever-changing markets.

If your organization is a market leader, you must remember to look beyond current customer needs. Keeping close tabs on customers' expressed needs may maximize profits, but it won't foster innovation. Because no one knows how the innovations will be used, you need to observe customers. For example, Netscape saw new potential when it discovered a customer using its browser not for Internet access but for navigating the customer's own intranet.

The analytical and decision-making processes learned in best-management practices require precise quantitative information, but none exists for innovative technology. According to Christensen, your organization must, instead of planning for results, plan for learning and plan to fail. The knowledge you gain from these failures gives you an advantage when creating new markets. Your experiences also let you resolve uncertainties before investing heavily in unproven technology, products, or processes.

Leading change through strategy and harnessing disruptive technology require the active participation of developers, investors, and management. The developer sees the possibilities and problems in finding new markets for innovative technologies, then identifies and develops the organization's capability for capitalizing on them. The venture capitalist who sponsors the new technology benefits from understanding how the disruptive technologies should be managed and marketed. Finally, the disruptive-technology implementer must continually sell the customer on the new technology's advantages so that it doesn't simply replace old technology but instead achieves its full potential. ❖

Lynn Carrier is a senior business consultant who implements enterprise software system solutions and project management services at Policy Management Systems Corp. Contact him at PMSC, PO Box Ten, Columbia, SC 29202; lynncarrier@ pmsc.com.

Strategic Information Technology Management: Managing Organizational, Political, and Technological Forces

Keith Schildt,
University of La Verne
schildtk@ulv.edu

Suzann Beaumaster,
University of La Verne
beaumast@ulv.edu

Marcie Edwards
University of La Verne
medwards@anaheim.net

Abstract

This paper explores the role of Information Technology (IT) in the management of municipally-owned and operated public utilities. Through semi-structured interviews of senior management in the largest municipal electric and water systems, the paper examines the confluence of contextual factors fostering changes in an IT management strategy, which tend to be aimed at increasing efficiency and effectiveness of service delivery as well as improving customer/citizen satisfaction. The paper proposes a model of the IT strategic planning process occurring in municipal environments illustrating interplay between technological, political, and bureaucratic decision-making. The study finds that the complex nature of technology with its rapid and seemingly chaotic rate of change poses political risks for the organization attempting to manage the IT infrastructure. Successful strategic management of IT must take into account the differing value sets among its organizational and political members and how these differing motivations impact the management of the IT infrastructure.

1. Introduction

Typically, public organizations are viewed as increasingly resource scarce, and this line of thought is captured in the "doing more with less" phrase. Oddly, public organizations have an overabundance of information resources, which show no sign of diminishing in the foreseeable future and if not properly managed public administrators may end up "doing less, with more". This burgeoning resource has concomitantly occurred with a complex set of technologies offered by the marketplace to manage it. While it's one thing to have a resource and the potential power it brings, it is an entirely different matter to make effective use of that resource through management, control, and foresight. How organizations control, process, and disseminate information and how they manage the associated technologies is critical to organizational success.

Strategic management of information technologies is an involved and complicated endeavor and becomes more so with each new innovation. It is no longer enough to simply automate clerical tasks or transfer reams of data into a computer. Today's technologically savvy organization must make use of integrated information systems, which will not only allow them to process data and perform clerical tasks, but also provide services in a more effective and user-friendly way. Integrated municipal information systems can offer better ways to provide for government administration and service deliveries, but getting there is no easy matter.

Reprinted from *Proceedings of the 38th Hawaii International Conference on System Sciences—2005.*

Information Technology (IT) is no longer merely the gathering and processing of data. One the one hand, IT has become an integral managerial process that can be used to foster strategic organizational change. However, on the other hand, organizations can get caught up in chasing the advances in IT and lose sight of core organizational goals and objectives. The purpose of strategically managing information technology is to avoid goal displacement and its resulting depletion of organizational resources.

This paper sets out to explore how various California municipalities attempt to strategically manage information technology. Specifically, the paper examines the management of IT in municipally operated public utility departments (i.e., organizations that deliver water and electricity to its citizens and customers). Public utility departments were chosen for this exploratory research for two interrelated reasons: (1) the basis and history of these operations are technologically driven and (2) the juxtaposition between the old core technologies of utility systems with its very stable and relatively predictable rates of change and obsolescence and the newer information technologies with their rapid and relatively unpredictable rates of change and obsolescence. Also, municipally operated public utility systems (MOPUS) are different than the typical municipal service being delivered to citizens. MOPUS are really businesses within government and are accounted for as enterprise funds, not financed as part of the general fund. Identical to the private sector, revenues derived from sales and not from property and sales taxes finance the operation.

This research is based primarily on a series of lengthy iterative semi-structured interviews with senior management representatives of the California municipalities that operate utility systems (a total of six municipalities), as well as archival data and secondary data analyses. The aim of this exploratory study was to expand on a model of IT strategic management that incorporates the differing rates and patterns of change in technology compared to those typically found in organizational and political processes

2. ITM Strategic Management Model

The context of public administration is open and influenced by factors external to the organization but critical in its operation and act as agents of organizational change. The typical rate and pattern of change for organizations can be characterized as bureaucratic in nature. Change is a steady and incremental process. Juxtaposed with this fairly predictable process is technological change. Technological change can be characterized as rapid and relatively chaotic in comparison. The analogous difference is between a very large ocean liner and a speedboat. The latter is capable of quick shifts in direction while the former is less amiable to such sudden change.

The public administrator also exists in an environment affected by other external factors. Some of these other factors can be termed political in nature as they influence "who gets what, when, and how". Whereas technological change is rapid and chaotic and organizational change is steadier and incremental, political change is more cyclical in nature. The cycles of elections of and budgetary approval by city councils are one such example of the seasonality of the political process. Similarly, economic conditions with cycles of inflation and recession impact organizational decision making and organizational change.

Based on previous, preliminary research, the authors concluded that the management of IT occurs at the convergence of three interrelated sphere of values and activities (See Model 1). One sphere contains political processes. These are factors that are predominately envisioned as external to the organization, which tend to be control oriented and generally distributive in nature. This political sphere includes elected officials, citizens and especially more formally organized citizen groups, consultants hired by the organization, and businesses as well as state and federal regulatory agencies and their rules. The second sphere contains organizational or bureaucratic processes, which tend to be stability oriented and generally procedural in nature. This organizational sphere includes the employees of the municipality and the administrative processes. The third sphere contains technological processes, which tend to be change oriented and catalytic in nature. All these spheres are interrelated and act to establish the parameters of strategic information technology management (SITM). The interaction between what is politically viable, organizationally feasible, and technologically possible provides for a dynamic SITM situation.

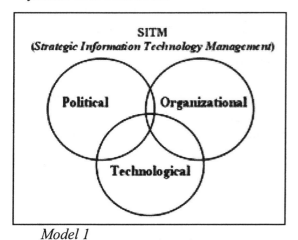

Model 1

3. Findings and Elaboration of the Basic Model

The interviews with senior management representatives of the major municipally operated public utility systems in California confirmed the basic model's assumptions about differing rates and patterns of change among the organizational, political, and technological spheres. Importantly, the interviews also identified other aspects about the interaction of the three spheres as they relate to attempts to strategically manage IT.

As previously assumed, organizational processes produce rates and patterns of change that can be best characterized as steady and incremental. When queried about the reasons for this type of change, respondents all mentioned the following as the possible reasons:

- Reward Systems. The rewards systems in government, including compensation, foster incremental decision-making. Bureaucracies tend to be risk-adverse and those managing them do not want to make what one respondent termed a "career-limiting move". A small incremental step, even if taken in the wrong direction, can be easily corrected without too much damage to the organization, its resources, or the administrator. Taken in the context as stewards of public resources, this is quite acceptable behavior. However it may act to limit innovation and precludes swift organizational change.

- Predictability. One respondent summed this up by stating, "Bureaucracies need predictability". The diverse array of services provided by municipal organizations, their complexity, and the numerous types of professions involved in the operation of the organization require an articulating mechanism; the ability to foretell what others will do allows for the organization to move forward and function.

- Time Necessary for Analysis. Respondents all agreed that it takes time to produce the type of analysis necessary for city councils to approve IT projects. All respondents spoke of creating an "authorizing environment" where administrative integrity can be fostered and a "political platform" be developed that mitigates council member concerns about the zero sum nature of expenditures; money spent for one project precluding other possible projects. This point also underscores the nature of IT projects in general. They are not easily visible by the electorate and may not create as much political capital as other more apparent expenditures afford (e.g., a new fire station).

- The Product of Public Utilities. The product being delivered by public utilities has changed very little or as one respondent stated, "water is water".

Technological change was identified as rapid and chaotic. The respondents felt that technological change was very market-driven and, implicitly, as market-manipulated. Technology by its very nature is in constant flux. Change and constant design improvements drive technology and the timeline is very short forcing obsolescence. Importantly, not only were the rapid innovations mentioned as chaotic processes but also the impact of mergers and acquisitions, which make IT management difficult. Mergers of IT providers pose problems for administrators because support services may no longer be available or may be more costly. This exacerbates the relatively quick obsolescence of IT and may force obsolescence.

Political processes and change were seen as steady as were organizational ones. However, instead of an incremental pattern in the political sphere change was seen as cyclical. The management of the organization in relation to its political sphere is the crux strategically managing IT. To strategically manage IT an administrator must manage at the "gaps". Gap management refers to the difference between the organizational realities and the technological changes the organization wishes to or is forced to undertake. Gap management requires an understanding of the political realities and harnessing those to achieve the desired outcome.

For obvious reasons, elected officials are the most proximal influence within the political sphere and were mentioned repeatedly by respondents. Importantly, all respondents also mentioned business and citizens (especially citizen groups) as important factors to be considered when managing IT. The use of outside consultants was frequently mentioned as a way to satisfy the political sphere's needs for external validation of organization requests for improved IT. Consultants are used by organizations for this external validation purpose as well as means to overcome organizational capacity issues associated with downsizing and the highly technical nature of IT. Consultants act as a bridge between the spheres occupying an important niche in government decision-making.

4. Catalysts of Change

A number of factors were identified that foster change. These change catalysts operate at the conflux of the spheres and pose special problems for strategic management of IT in public utility systems. Of primary influence to public sector utility systems is the competition from the private sector and, importantly, the perceived superiority of private sector administration.

A number of the respondents spoke of having to deal with city council discussions of selling the system to the private sector. On the one hand, this can certainly be seen as a stressful situation. However, it can also be used internally to motivate improved production and efficient service delivery among employees and externally to get champions to support the city's own publicly owned system. Other catalysts for change identified were:

- Regulatory Agencies. Regulatory agencies at the state and federal level using their rulemaking powers to force changes plays a huge role in fostering change; albeit, many times this may be seen as unfunded mandates limiting local decision making.

- Technological Change. The change in technology through innovation forces obsolescence of existing technology. Technical innovation also offers the potential for greater efficiencies with each change.

- Market Changes. The mergers and acquisitions of IT service providing companies, previously mentioned in the paper, also perforce change.

- Employee Knowledge of IT. Organizational staffing issues will impact change. The knowledge, skills, and abilities of the staff plays a role in degree to which IT will be integrated in the organization. This could act to foster IT advances in the organization, as one respondent stated, "I have a young staff, they understand technology, and I give them some leeway so they can be innovative". Conversely, one of the biggest roadblocks in this area can be that information technologies often represent completely new processes for the organization and its employees. Human beings typically reach a certain comfort level with regard to their abilities and work processes. For most people new

technologies represent a daunting learning curve and possible downsizing of their jobs. This perception introduces fear into the process and creates significant resistance to technology.

- Service Provision. All of the respondents stated the importance of customer information systems and billing operations as agents of change. The range of technologies available from automated customer service attendants to remote meter reading posed important strategic questions for the administrators. For example, all mentioned how automated customer service may reduce labor costs but they do so at the expense, as one respondent put it, "maintaining the human face of the organization" because many customers grow quickly frustrated of having to drill down through a series of prompts just to get a simple question answered.

5. Dynamics of the Spheres

One of the more notable outcomes of this research is the dynamic nature of the spheres themselves. The original model based on initial research, suggests spheres of equal proportions, with each of the areas dominating its own particular environment. Given the current research findings, the reality is much more dynamic, fluid, and contextually based than previously assumed. It is the fluid nature of organizational, political, and technological changes that determine the extent to which a given sphere dominates SITM.

All of the respondents in this study described scenarios where one sphere was more dominant than the others. Even a highly charged, politically driven municipality will defer to technological change if the current context warrants it.

This dynamic creates a scenario where the spheres expand or contract depending on the given context. There are a multitude of factors that impact the expansion or contraction of a sphere. To illustrate this point—One of the more significant issues affecting public institutions today relates to security issues. More than one municipality has found themselves the victims of computer hackers: individuals who have hacked into the customer information database creating a serious security breach. In most instances, while the insurgence was contained relatively quickly, the situation had a significant impact on all three spheres for the municipality. As the hacking was discovered, the technological sphere expanded as the immediate situation was dealt with. Once the security breach was contained, the political sphere expanded to its original level of influence. Finally the technological sphere contracted as the organizational sphere expanded to accommodate the changes necessary to prevent future, similar events from occurring. Eventually, the political sphere also contracted, as technological change became part of the organizational approach to security. In describing the interaction of all three spheres in this scenario, one of the respondents described the situation in this way, " No one owned that loophole, it was just there. The reality was that the organization was unable to manage the process in the old way because the technological situation pushed a particular issue to the forefront." This sort of technologically based situation has ramifications for the municipality, especially in terms of risk management and privacy issues

The security scenario illustrates the way in which the spheres expand and contract in a given context. Each sphere appears to respond in different ways as changes occur in the environment. As the respondents described their experiences from organizational, political, and technological contexts some patterns emerged.

The technological sphere is associated with rapid change. In most instances, technology, as it impacts the municipalities in question, is tied directly to the market. Every respondent mentioned the difficulties in dealing with the perceptions of the constant flux of technology, "we need this now" rationalizations, individual fear of technological change, and the ever-increasing rate of obsolescence. One of the key factors in this area is the historical stability of the industry in question. Utilities have historically been on a 30-50 year change plan; new technology has significantly impacted that timeframe. What was once a very stable sphere has now given way to an extremely dynamic one.

In essence, the technology sphere expands when the manager can quantify the outcomes. One of the difficulties appears to be, associating the specific technological advances, processes, and acquisitions with planning outcomes. The respondents expressed the need to quantify technological outcomes by attaching them to proposed variables whether or not the specific technologies were the true catalysts for the outcomes or not

The technology sphere also expands in the face of a perceived "uncontrolled onset of technology" and, for the respondents, this represents the point where technological expansion has gone too far. This scenario represents the random acceptance of global change and tends to be "distracting" to planned technological implementation. A respondent provided one such example in the form of the rising popularity of the Blackberry. Certain individuals in the organization saw the global purchase and use of this new technology as imperative. The push was to integrate Blackberry use in numerous aspects of the municipality. This would have necessitated a large expenditure, training, and reworking a number of organizational processes. In the end the decision was made not to make use of the technology in question, as it was not deemed a necessary change for the municipality. The respondents all argued that technology needs in-depth scenarios for decision-making. All necessary tools must be justified based on needed and desired outcomes.

The technological sphere expands when the technology need is global and inevitable, i.e. Email. But the changes must be resisted when they accommodate the needs of only a few, i.e. Blackberry. Catastrophic expansion occurs in this sphere when the change is too cutting edge and the organization cannot adapt—or when change is forced via "planned obsolescence". Respondents cited the tendency to get on board and purchase new technology too early. In the case of GIS systems, one respondent found his municipality in technological trouble when they pursued the cutting edge of the GIS push. In buying in too early the organization found themselves with proprietary software and systems that were not upgradeable and far too expensive to keep up. All respondents echoed similar experiences in this area. Another common culprit is the CIS (customer information systems). These systems were extremely complex and expensive to implement, with an initial implementation failure rate of over 60%. Utility managers have learned to wait until after the learning curve has passed on new technologies. More than one of the respondents summed this up as not wanting to be " on the bleeding edge" of technology.

The technological sphere most commonly contracts when the benefits are not quantified through their attachment to specific variables or outcomes. Contraction also occurs when the technology experiences planned obsolescence. This most commonly occurs in the form of software and hardware changes; for example, when a particular software company is bought out by a larger entity. In these cases the technology in question is often no longer supported, resulting in "stranded platforms". Municipalities are left to support themselves, "buy in" to expensive upgrades and support initiatives, or completely change the system in question, all very expensive and time intensive options. In the end, the ability to expand—and the need to contract within the technological sphere is dependent on personal track records and the credibility of both the organization as a whole and the political players.

The political sphere appears more stable than the technological sphere when it comes to its expansion or contraction. The changes in this arena are much less volatile for the most part. The political sphere tends to expand or contract in response to environmental factors brought on by external situations and the occurrences with regard to the other spheres. For example, the 9/11 tragedies and its new security implications or the hacking instance described previously.

There are some other influences that affect this sphere, the primary force being the election cycle. The desire to maintain status quo during the election process greatly affects the organizational and technological spheres. In some instances, the political sphere expands when there is a "sword to fall on". This typically occurs as a politician retires and is looking for the last big initiative. Or when political term limits expire, as occurs in some municipalities. As one respondent put it, "A politician at the end of their term can really throw a wrench in the system".

Typically it is the place of the political sphere to maintain the status quo. There is a tendency in the political realm to hesitate on the approval of new contracts for technology initiatives. Most political players do not have technology buy-in, nor do they typically understand what it is they are buying into unless there is a well-documented environmental force pushing the change or acquisition, (i.e. Y2K). For the most part the political sphere "vapor locks" until forced, as politicians are frustrated by the lack of predictability on projects and technological related outcomes. Utility managers find it necessary to provide a platform for political figures to sponsor technologically change, which gives them a platform of quantifiable and proven outcomes to stand on. In the political sphere, expansion is dependent on proven outcomes.

Much like the political sphere, the organizational sphere is dependent on outcomes. At the same time it must also be cognizant and focused on the objectives of both the municipality as a whole and the utility in particular. For the most part, the organizational sphere uses technology as a tool with the ultimate goal of "staying out of the elections". By maintaining the planning process, the organizational sphere can pursue its technological objective at the same time without it becoming a "political question".

In some cases the organizational sphere expands when a dynamic change agent is thrown into the system. That change agent may come in the form of an individual with the specific agenda to "shake things up," provide a catalyst for change, and then move on. The key in this instance is to remove the change agent before damage occurs. The organizational sphere may also expand incrementally as necessary changes are made to accommodate technological needs.

One respondent described an expansion scenario where an IT department specific to the utilities had to be created to deal with the planned technological changes because the municipalities IT staff was incapable of dealing with the needs. The existing staff did not have the capacity, training, or resources to implement the technology. The existing IT director's hands were tied due to political pressures, process regulations, and bureaucratic rules. The new IT staff was hired based on specific skills, expertise, and professionalism. The job was completed and the organizational sphere permanently expanded, as the new staff became part of the municipal IT department. This scenario was made possible due to the nature of the municipal utility departments and their ability to fund the new organizational additions.

6. Techniques for Successful IT Management

Garnered from the interviews, is a set of techniques that were thought to be associated with successful IT management by the respondents. These management strategies are derived from discussions with the respondents about successful and failed IT projects they have managed. In the aggregate they represent an attempt to first create an "authorizing environment" where the administrators create a consensus about the desirability of the IT project and gain a favorable approval from the city council, and secondly to successfully implement the project. They are not meant to be sequential or ranked in importance. Instead, they can be thought of as additional ingredients added to the management mix used individually or in combination.

Sell planned obsolescence – be sure the council understands that information technology has a shortened life span compared to more traditional technologies. Make the council aware of the rapid innovations in technology, the maintenance issues of not keeping up with technology, and the unpredictability of the technological marketplace.

Identify "hard savings", discount "soft" – Use monetary and other easily quantifiable hard savings as the primary rationale for the IT project in lieu of soft savings (e.g., increases in employee morale). Quantify IT success so political sponsors have a substantive, objective hook to hang their hat on.

Avoid stranded capital by using pilot programs and incremental rollouts - IT projects carry some inherent risks. In lieu of selling planned obsolescence, a manager could use pilot programs. An element related to technological risk is the concept of "*stranded capital*". The nature of technology with its rapid change and therefore obsolescence poses a problem because there is a lack of guarantee that the technology will be useful in the near future. The roll-out of an IT project may be implemented over a number of years and questions arise not only whether the technology will still be useful at the end of the roll-out, but additionally whether the organization can find a vendor to maintain the technology after full implementation. It is organizationally costly and politically hazardous to venture down a technological path only to find out half way through the implementation that less costly technological advances have been created, or that vendors are no longer servicing that particular program or piece of hardware and that the organization spent scarce fiscal resources on an ineffective, inefficient project. The use of pilot programs or incremental rollouts allows for small test projects to be initiated and evaluated. This technique is useful because it acts to slow the rate of technological change in the organization, which allows for staff learning curves to ramp up and buys time until the "second wave" of technology is in the market.

Ride the second waves, not the first – By being patient and not chasing after new technology, a manager can wait out the initial introduction of a new technology, which is typically costly and prone to maintenance problems. By awaiting the second-generation products the manager can also learn from others who have implemented the technology and gain from their successes (and miscues). Similarly, try to avoid "vendor pressure." Those who are marketing technology may overstate the capability of new technology, which may not always live up to the salesperson's hyperbolism.

Recognize approval shifts – The process of IT planning occurs over a relatively long time frame. During this time frame, events can occur that may make approval of IT projects more or less probable. Obviously, changes in city council membership can preclude certain projects and make others more favorable for approval. Similarly, changes in demographics as well as business needs will influence IT projects. The testing of ideas about possible projects at various points of time can help a manager recognize the ripeness of the project.

Gain political buy-in by getting a champion – Cultivate relations in the external environment to create a network of potential advocates who can champion a project through it s approval process.

Build credibility and demonstrate patience – remember that nothing works like success. If possible, start with small, do-able IT projects and use these successes to build momentum and credibility. Be perceived as not chasing after the newest technology.

Build and sell by blocs – As much as possible, provide the appearance of a unified front among all staff (and across departments where applicable) when requesting approval from city council for IT projects.

Use externalization to validate organizational desires – The use of outside consultants cultivates an aura of legitimacy around staff's IT proposals.

7. Conclusions

Successful strategies for managing IT must recognize not only the usual concepts associated with strategic planning but must also do so with a keen understanding of how organizational, political, and technological forces each originate from a different core set of values, foci, and activities.

A successful manager must be aware that technological change occurs at not only a extremely quick pace but changes chaotically as well. Whereas, organizational change tends to be slow and incremental, and change in the political realm is also slow but occurs more cyclically or episodically due to budgetary approval cycles, elections, and redevelopment activities.

8. References

Boar, B. H. (1993). *The Art of Strategic Planning for Information Technology: Crafting Strategy for the 90's.* New York, NY: John Wiley & Sons, Inc.

Braithwaite, T. (1996). *The Power of IT: Maximizing Your Technology Investments.* Milwaukee, WI: ASQC Quality Press.

Bryson, J. (1995). *Strategic Planning for Public and Nonprofit Organizations.* San Francisco, CA: Jossey-Bass.

Byrd, T.A., Sambamurthy, V, and Zmud, R.W. (1995). An Examination of IT Planning in a Large Diversified Public Organization. *Decision Sciences* 26:1, 49-73.

Goodstein, L., Nolan, T., and Pfeiffer, J. W. (1991). *Applied Strategic Planning: A Comprehensive Guide.* New York: McGraw-Hill.

Gordon, G. L. (1993). *Strategic Planning for Local Government.* Washington, D.C.: ICMA.

Harmon, R. et. al. (1998). Energy deregulation. *American Water Works Association*, 90, 26-30.

Tat-Kei Ho, A. (2002). Reinventing local governments and the E-government initiative. *Public Administration Review*, 62.

Landers, J. (2002). SafeguardingWater Utilities. *Civil Engineering*, 72, 48-56.

Newcomer, K. E. and Caudle, S. L. (1991). Evaluating Public Sector Information Systems: More Than Meets The Eye. *Public Administration Review*, 51.

Nutt, P. and Backoff, R. (1992). *Strategic Management of Public and Third Sector Organizations.* San Francisco, CA: Jossey-Bass.

Ward, J. (1995). *Principals of Information Systems Management.* New York, NY: Routledge.

Winklhofer, H. (2002). Information systems project management during organizational change. *Engineering Management Journal*, 14.

Information Resources Management
New Era, New Rules

John D. Hwang

About 20 years ago, no one had heard of a CIO and only a handful of organizations were using the phrase "information technology." There was only the information resources manager, whose primary job was to decide what platform or system the organization could afford and what it would take to implement it. The lines between business objectives and technical infrastructure were relatively distinct, so the manager's job—information resources management—was comfortably predictable. IRM was a service and support activity. Tasks consisted of planning, organizing, acquiring, maintaining, securing, and controlling information resources across the organization. The worst days were when the system went down or the vendors didn't deliver.

> *IRM must evolve beyond a focus on technology and implementation to manage the risks of juggling business and technical objectives.*

The proliferation of PCs in the 1980s and the resulting decentralized information systems architecture began to transform this neatly ordered world, and managers struggled to find meaning in established IRM tenets. About that time, CEOs began to realize that they couldn't isolate business requirements from the technology, so they altered their expectations of the already burdened information resources manager to include understanding business requirements. As technology gained more respect and acceptance, the manager's position was elevated to director of information systems, and ultimately to CIO with all the pulls of any other corporate executive.

Enter the Internet, e-commerce, and the digital era, and the CIO's job description balloons. Now CIOs must think strategically and formulate business strategies, build business relationships, and deeply understand the organization's culture—all on Internet time.

With this broader job description and accelerated schedule has come a large set of risks, some of which have little to do with the technology. Ironically, the structured world of traditional IRM can help mitigate these risks, but the old rules need some updating. The new IRM requires a proactive CIO; an information systems infrastructure that emphasizes planning, security, and risk control; and IT governance that encourages due diligence.

THE CIO

The "Agendas Then and Now" sidebar might be an exaggeration, but it correctly characterizes the CIO of the 2000s as a little of everything. Fifteen years ago, CIOs clamored to be at the executive decision-makers' table, but many are now finding that the price of admission is high. CEOs and executive managers make it their business to keep current on IT issues, and they have high expectations for the CIO. In addition to adapting value and supply chain concepts to streamline business processes, planning, and operation, CIOs must

Inside

Agendas Then and Now

Strategies for Successful IT Audits

Reprinted from *IT Pro,* November/December 2002.

and partnerships with suppliers, customers, and manufacturers; effect organizational and cultural change; and adopt the right technology at the right point in its life cycle.

Communication ability and assertiveness are particularly important. In 2002, New York executive search firm John J. Davis & Davis surveyed 200 CIOs and found that "nearly three-quarters believe they're not the first place CEOs turn to for information about new technology."

Many CEOs want CIOs to provide timely business information. US military departments as well as major telecommunications companies, for example, have real-time, information displays in their situation rooms to exhibit their resources, operational status, and preparedness.

Another critical characteristic is flexibility. CIOs must be chameleons: The characteristics the CEO finds important one day might not be as desirable in four weeks when the organization picks up a different partner or develops a new product line. Also, as Table 1 (p. 12) illustrates, different organizations have different views of a CIO and thus different ideas of what constitutes a core skill set.

A big risk for both organizations and CIOs is a mismatch of skills and assumed responsibilities. To minimize this risk, both the business and CIO should assess at the outset and at regular intervals different aspects of the business and its relation to IT. Risk decreases as the CIO's role, the agenda, and long-term expectations become clear. When a company hires a CIO, the CEO sees only a snapshot of capabilities, and the CIO has only a vague idea of expectations. An organization typically hires a CIO to solve some problem. Is it real or a product of hidden agendas and technical misinformation? For example, the CEO of a transportation company brought in an expert technologist because he was "sure" that the chaos among his European offices was due to poorly integrated technology. Five months later, he scrapped the integration project after he and the CIO discovered that the difficulties stemmed from management and cultural diversity. The technology was the least of it.

New CIOs can avoid this trap by following a few commonsense rules. Insist from day one that management list its top three priorities and explain them in depth. Recognize that priorities will shift and institute a regular reevaluation time using the first 100 days as a baseline for measuring change. An IT audit is valuable both to establish your presence and further define the baseline. Above all, be proactive in consistently

Agendas Then and Now

The late 1970s and early 1980s saw the birth of a new position: the information resources manager. Two decades later,

IRM director

6 to 8 am Take the dog for a run around the neighborhood.
Have breakfast.
Read the entire *LA Times*.
Drive to the office.

8 to 10 am Catch up on mail and review bids for a system upgrade.
Conduct staff meeting, which is over in 30 minutes.

10 am to noon Review telecommunications network design and cost charge-back with departmental principals.
Play racketball at the gym.

Noon to 2 pm Attend VIP business luncheon at the locally hosted database conference.

2 to 4 pm Browse booths for information on two or three promising new packages.
Read *Computer* magazine.

4 to 6 pm Prepare article for presentation.
Review documents and prepare for tomorrow's meetings.

6 to 8 pm Drive home.
Watch news.
Eat dinner.

8 to 10 pm Watch TV and finish painting the bookcase.
Tidy the garage.
Walk the dog.

10 pm Go to bed.

that position has vanished and in its place is the modern CIO. Admittedly these agendas are caricatures, but they accu- rately reflect the CIO's increased responsibilities and they underline the need for IRM's controls and structure.

CIO

Walk the dog to the nearest bush. Grab coffee and read the first sentences of six paragraphs in the *LA Times*, *Wall Street Journal*, and *New York Times*. Note scores for three baseball teams that the CFO follows. Plan to talk about baseball after presenting the business case for upgrading the payroll system. Review keynote speech for VIP conference at 6:30 pm.
Attend CIO Forum. Today's topic is audits. Hear horror stories about resentful staff and irate CEOs. Share story about the 65 angry e-mails after your last audit.

Review IT status and daily schedule with assistants. Note that George, who was supposed to provide an update on payroll procedures for the business case, is out sick. Call CFO to reschedule presentation.
Attend CEO's weekly executive management meeting. Topic is budget review planning. Note that the budget for the new payroll initiative is $10,000 smaller than it was at the last meeting and that the schedule is two months shorter.

Appear in city council to present brief testimony on the city's cable renewal process and Internet open access. Plan to partner with major Internet service providers and recommend that the city follow forthcoming federal guidance from the US Federal Communications Commission. Meet city CIO and principals to discuss second-generation e-government initiative.

Review material with staff while driving to a local educational TV channel for an interview about e-learning and the digital divide.
Join VIP luncheon that started at noon. Greet Japanese delegation tasked with fact finding for emergency-preparedness software and disaster communications.

Host IT staff meeting. Receive plaque from department head for department's success in implementing a customer relationship management system. Silently bless the extra hours of user training that everyone initially cursed.
Attend corporate steering committee meeting on procurement and B2B business reengineering initiative.

Review speech material with staff. Prepare to meet three corporate principals for a potential joint venture at the VIP conference. Instead, receive frantic alert that a hacker might have damaged the company's public Web site. Bring in SWAT team to conduct diagnosis and assess damage, catch evening shift to implement contingency plan by bringing up backup server and maintaining vigilance. Feel extreme gratitude that the staff managed to complete the risk management plan, formalize the SWAT team, and conduct a contingency exercise last week.

Notify CEO of progress.
Notify VIP conference that the keynote will be a half hour late.
Deliver keynote on "Role of IT in Support of Seaport Security and Supply Chain Management."

Politely decline overcooked chicken entrée at the conference dinner. Wolf down a bag of stale chips on the drive back to the office. Monitor Web site recovery, find system is OK, authorize everyone to return to normal operation, and notify CEO. Review e-mail and staff documents for early morning journal interview.

Arrive home, trip over the dog in the dark hallway, crash in a chair, watch five minutes of news, and fall asleep holding the mail.

Table 1. Three views of CIO roles and skills.

Area	Business management*	Executive ability**	Familiarity with government needs***
Business and organization	• Need a CEO who can communicate the vision • Know the business life cycle to determine needs and actions • Know the stage of growth the company is in	• Have international and global experience in other cultures and markets • Have knowledge of and experience in specific industries like banking, retailing, and insurance • Have business savvy in both the employer's business and business in general	• Demonstrate business acumen; thoroughly understand agency nuances • Adapt to cultural change; understand how technology breeds change
Information technology	• Understand Internet and e-commerce issues, such as scalability and privacy • Use technology to add value and reduce costs through enterprise resource planning, for example.	• Have expertise in aligning and leveraging technology	• Be aware of best practices in the private sector
Relationships	• Obtain employee buy in for technology • Cultivate an open work environment • Choose partners and strategic alliances that are both IT-based and promote integrated IT systems • Communicate with customers	• Have communication skills and the ability to articulate a strategy • Possess people skills to manage a variety of relationships	• Be a teacher and educator; communicate effectively • Coordinate outside help across organizational boundaries
Leadership and management	• Develop management skills in executives, using IT for training • Outsource but manage potential loss of control • Manage cash flow by reinvesting in rapid growth • Find the right employees to fill knowledge gaps when key staffers leave	• Be able to hire, develop, and retain high-quality IT professionals • Create and manage change, especially when the CIO position is new • Be experienced in project management and keep projects within schedule and budget • Be a business leader	• Derive power from leaders • Have a vision; be a strategic forward thinker, seer • Understand capital spending; make a business case and link it to the agency's budgetary process • Understand security issues such as cybersecurity and information sharing

* Chad Sanders and Yolanda Chan, "12 Challenges for Rapid Growth Firms Impacting IT," *Ivey Business J.*, Jan./Feb. 2002.
** Mark Polansky, "Ten Prerequisites in Conducting an Executive Search," *CIO*, 15 Sep. 2001.
*** Joshua Dean, "Top Dog," *Government Executive*, Apr. 2002.

managing expectations. By the time you get your report card, it's too late to address the negatives.

IT INFRASTRUCTURE RISKS

A properly run IT infrastructure—the hardware, software, databases, networks, and people that enable business operations—is a strategic advantage. It offers organizations the power to innovate, lower costs, and gain competitive advantage through mass customization and reduced time to market. It lets companies react and change business lines quickly and transition from a regional and functional orientation to an integrated, globally managed structure.

The risks come because everyone expects the IT infrastructure to run smoothly and effortlessly, and it doesn't. The

CIO's best chance is to apply IRM principles such as strategic planning, information systems life-cycle management, resource allocation, and information security. Still, some risks are inevitable and require careful consideration.

CIOs should be proactive in consistently managing expectations. By the time you get your report card, it's too late to address the negatives.

Return on IT investment

One risk is that the organization will have unrealistic expectations about what IT can do. IT's contribution has always been difficult to measure definitively or quantitatively. CIOs typically pitch IT initiatives by presenting a business case, usually to the chief financial officer, who is concerned with budget and finance, technology, and cost-benefit analyses. It is hard to persuade CFOs of any causal relationship between IT investment and performance improvements. Indeed, given the myriad intermediate variables, such as business processes, personnel, and market, it might be impossible to derive one. Three decades of research haven't produced any clear, consistent way to show technology's return.

Despite these findings, many organizations persist in their unrealistic expectations of the CIO and look to IT as the cure-all. When results aren't immediate and obvious, the CIO is "ineffective."

CEOs who understand this problem seek customer endorsement and try to establish a group of early users, rather than directly measure an investment's return. These activities tend to weed out marginal projects. If no one wants or likes the idea, it just dies, and it wastes only a few resources. Michael Dell, CEO of Dell Computers, suggests having key personnel who stand to benefit from the investment lead the project to implement the technology. These personnel are in the best position to measure progress before, during, and after development and implementation because they know exactly what contribution IT does (or doesn't) make to reduce cost and increase productivity.

Project development and implementation

IT projects are inherently full of risks because they depend on leadership, changes to business processes, personnel acceptance, adequate training, implementation variables, transition periods, and the supporting infrastructure. IT projects compete with other projects for resources and often bump up against limited funds and personnel support. Some IT project managers end up making promises that they simply can't deliver, and the project dies somewhere in the systems development life cycle. Indeed, successful implementation—on time, on budget, and with user acceptance—seems to be the exception.

One reason is that major risks are inherent in pursuing business process reengineering (BPR), and organizations are quick to blame any BPR failure on the introduction of new technologies or the implementation of new applications. In one case, a company spent $23 million to adopt a new payroll software system, decided to abandon the system, and blamed the failure to roll it out on the systems technology and database synchronization. IT didn't do a good enough job of mapping the data from the legacy system to the new databases, the company complained.

In reality, the failure stemmed from management's unwillingness to change a rigid organizational structure, existing payroll processes, and its numerous irregular payroll agreements that involved overtime and complex labor contracts. This meant that the IT department had to tailor the standard software far beyond the accepted 10 or 20 percent. Costs skyrocketed, and the organization was unable to exploit many of the features that gave the standard software its power—the reason for selecting it in the first place.

To reduce project development and implementation risk, a CIO must fully understand the organization's culture, operation, and technical maturity. A good business case is essential because it helps avoid solutions that are looking for a problem.

Enterprise resource planning

Enterprise resource planning projects have so many inherent risks that they belong in their own category. Successful ERP implementation is far more than installing software and systems. It requires a certain amount of business process change and a great deal of work to get an organization-wide commitment to that change. Six years later, after expending more than $200 million on an ERP system, the CIO of Nestle USA acknowledged that the company completely underestimated the amount of work and the complexity of change management, and will finally complete its implementation in 2003.

All the managers in the organization must review and realign their management approaches to take full advantage of ERP features. The review and approval authorities for business transactions might be different, for example. Maintaining the status quo without adopting the naturally prescribed ERP processes might call for extraordinary reprogramming to customize the application software, thus defeating one of the main advantages of adopting ERP in the first place.

Organizations must recognize that ERP projects don't succeed only because of the technologists (and sometimes they succeed in spite of them). One project manager used his knowledge of governance principles like change management and infrastructure control to oversee a major ERP project. A city government wanted a new procurement system that would provide seamless integration from requisition to check processing. It also wanted accurate and timely cost accounting, electronic fund transfers, e-commerce, and Web-based applications.

The project manager was not an IT expert and had limited top-executive support, but he managed to meet and even exceed requirements. Over the past three years, the system has reduced inventory from $37 million to $15 million, led to the closure of 14 warehouses, deleted 4,000 line items, and eliminated 40 warehousing positions. The city reaped $10 million in savings through contract consolidation. Furthermore, all department warehouses were consolidated into one department, as with accounts payable units and inventory and purchasing functions. The system has reduced organizational levels and created new staff positions with the redefinition of civil service classes, and established new standards for payment practices to vendors.

How did a non-IT expert accomplish all this?

- He understood that the ERP system implementation was change management. As such, it had to follow disciplined project management practices. He ensured that he had the suitable authority as the project manager and looked hard at the amount of change required from the project's outset. Early on, for example, he conducted a fit analysis, comparing the ERP package with the organization's functions. Attention to ERP selection and a thorough fit analysis are paramount to controlling cost and schedule.
- He aligned IT and business objectives. He articulated the change vision in creating a new procurement system, gained support at a time when the public wanted to see government reform, and capitalized on the IT organization. The CIO dedicated expert staff to conduct the initial fit analysis, support the IT infrastructure design, assist in managing the systems integrator, and generally make internal collaboration easier.
- He knew governance principles and applied them. He ensured that general management, IT specialists, and users were communicating. He set up extensive communications plans for internal and external customers; a joint labor-management committee to deal with worker issues; and advisory committees to address system, inventory, payment, purchasing, quality, and process issues.
- He provided comprehensive training on the new processes, procedures, roles, and responsibilities. He properly sequenced and repeated training, as necessary, pacing change introduction to match employees' confidence about using the new system.
- He walked the talk. He created an open environment, was straightforward, and involved everyone. To gain buy-in and trust, he proved the value of the system again and again, showing each employee what was in it for them.

Enterprise resource planning projects have so many inherent risks that they belong in their own category.

Knowledge management

A perennial problem with data and information in a business is that most IT systems still fall short of delivering timely information to decision makers. Now, knowledge management—a means to capture, retain, and distribute personnel expertise, corporate processes, and business experiences—aims to provide a business entity with a competitive advantage. Unfortunately, many CEOs view knowledge management as a technology issue and assign the CIO to develop it. In reality, the key ingredients for successful knowledge management are the people and process. The Naval War College in Newport, Rhode Island, planned its 2001 and 2002 war games to demonstrate the benefits of knowledge management through an elaborate suite of software tools, databases, and conference servers. Senior military and civilian players took so long to figure out the tools and resources that they found themselves behind in the war games and ended up canceling them for 2002.

Security

Information security has always been a priority. In the aftermath of Y2K and the events of 11 September 2001, however, the scope of information security has broadened to include business security. Compromised security can have grave consequences to business operation. To minimize security risk, CIOs must instill the philosophy that IT security is everyone's business. Contingency planning must involve the full participation of any who would be affected by unknown or unmanaged risks.

Many organizations correctly recognize that implementing overall business risk management programs might be a stretch for the CIO, and they are seeking more security directors. The new directors, CIOs, operations directors, and emergency managers will collaborate to create these programs. Still, the CIO must again be proactive in gaining resources for prevention. Organizations typically plan to spend much more to recover business continuity than to prevent its loss. With a heightened awareness of threats and of how much is at stake, this is changing. Wal-Mart, a retain chain that built its reputation on an efficient supply chain, is reversing its traditional 20-80 funding (20 percent risk prevention and 80 percent risk recovery). Other companies are likely to follow suit.

IT GOVERNANCE

Governance is generally the determination of roles and responsibilities that responsible parties exercise through the processes and procedures an organization uses to manage and carry out its functions. IT governance, then, consists of the roles and responsibilities in applying information systems and associated resources to support the organization.

"Support" in this sense also includes enhancing the organization's ability to pursue new strategies and business, which means that governance extends beyond information systems and services to organizational changes and business management. If IT enables the organization to transform its business processes to offer e-commerce, for example, the organization is not only introducing new technology but also instituting corporate-wide change.

Three domains

As Table 2 shows, the responsibility for IT governance falls across three domains—the IT department, users, and general management. It is important to manage the tensions among these domains by establishing clear policies that specify areas of responsibility. As a strategic and business leader, the CIO facilitates IT governance.

The *IT department* adds value to the business. It can create new channels for marketing and sales through e-commerce. It can create new products by transforming brick-and-mortar businesses to e-business. It can institute online banking and bill payment. All these strategies enhance business operations. The IT department also builds relationships with internal users by reaching beyond itself into the business enterprise, to suppliers and other logistical support organizations. The *users* monitor IT systems, services, and operation, making sure that they participate in and provide constructive input to all IT plans, projects, operations, and service. *General management* ensures that IT functions fit corporate-wide objectives and

that they have the proper balance between IT and user interests.

IT governance is not the same as IT management. IT management is multifaceted, sometimes centralized under a CIO, but often distributed among line organizations. IT governance attempts to be more cohesive. At the core of IRM is a carefully formulated structure, and governance is the glue that keeps the pieces together. Without it, the organization dissolves into chaos, users become confused and often hostile, the CIO accomplishes about a tenth of the agenda, and the IT department cannot exploit technology's potential to enhance the business.

Efforts to conquer the Y2K bug are a good example of this cohesiveness. Y2K was far larger than an IT problem; it affected business operations deeply. The solution wasn't about changing the date in a computer. It was about how to enlist everyone's help in maintaining business and resource continuity.

General management clarified the relationship between IT infrastructure and business objectives, and made the schedule to address issues a priority. Users became aware that organizational issues would affect usability and they took appropriate steps, such as obtaining patches. IT departments had sufficient guidance to follow the requirements, priorities, and schedule. In short, everyone who was affected collaborated.

Companies can foster similar collaboration, and it

Table 2. Three important domains in IT governance.*

Responsibility categories	IT department	Users	General management
Business and organization	• Develop IT strategic plans in concert with business change and/or networked organizational design.	• Actively participate in developing IT evolutionary plans.	• Oversee IT strategy in concert with business. • Ensure the enforcement of IT standards.
Information technology	• Introduce new technologies and applications. • Maintain IT infrastructure.	• Assist in defining IT scope consistent with the organization's IT maturity.	• Ensure technology transfer to the organization. • Encourage experiments.
Relationships	• Collaborate with users.	• Maintain IT-user interfaces.	• Maintain IT-user balance.
Leadership and management	• Maintain acquisition, central control, quick implementation, and high performance. • Manage vendors and inventory. • Retool IT staff skills.	• Plan for user investment in supporting all initiatives. • Ensure user inputs throughout the decision-making process. • Ensure that the company conducts IT audits.	• Ensure IT inventory management. • Ensure the implementation of IT planning and control processes.

* From *Corporate Information Systems Management: Text and Cases* (Lynda Applegate, F. Warren McFarlan, and James L. McKenney, McGraw-Hill/Irwin, 1999).

needn't always lead to the building of a system. The overriding goal of any IT initiative is to use IT to satisfy information needs. Thus, having the accounting staff collaborate with IT specialists to streamline the accounts-payable process results in more information to both parties. IT learns more about the procedures, and the accounting staff sees how they can process checks more quickly. Without this type of exchange, it is hard to improve work processes in a way that exploits technology.

Collaboration is not the same as participation, as one development team learned. A major city government decided to direct its resources to support businesses that could enhance service delivery to the public or create new services. The mayor and council authorized the CIO to conduct a citywide IT strategic planning effort. To ensure collaboration across the entire organization, they approved a project charter to create an executive steering committee, designate a project manager, and form a project team comprised of members from individual department project teams and outside consultants.

The project had an extremely large scope, and the team collected IT initiatives from different departments and other city stakeholders on key service areas. When the executive steering committee convened to review and select the candidate set of initiatives for elaboration and analysis, key city officials began to dictate the outcome of the planning effort, usurp the prerogative of the steering committee, and even threaten to politically torpedo the entire effort. The plan was never released because, although everyone had participated, not everyone had collaborated.

IT audits

Most companies conduct financial reporting or compliance audits, which are narrowly focused and occur with some regularity, or management audits, which evaluate management practices company-wide. IT audits are far less common. Part of the reason is that many CIOs wait for someone else to initiate them. When that happens, the initiator's agenda becomes the objective for the audit. Often CFOs will request an IT audit as part of the financial audit because they recognize that their data and database transactions are very much IT related. This unwittingly sets up an adversarial relationship because when the CFO initiates the audit, the CIO is on the defensive to prove that the technology and technical processes are not contributing to any losses.

CIOs need to become comfortable with audits and do them proactively, either internally via traditional control structures, or externally, using some third party.

The advantage of a CIO-initiated audit is that the CIO is in control of the objectives and tone. A positive audit lets the organization claim credit for progress and balances areas for improvement with accomplishments. A negative audit comes across as a witch-hunt and can turn ugly. Staff becomes defensive, and the CIO will find it harder to implement needed change.

An external audit has the advantage of unbiased benchmarking. However, it can come across as negative because the auditors are anxious to do their job, which is to find something. As the "Strategies for Successful IT Audits" sidebar describes, the CIO can ensure that the audit remains positive by discussing objectives with the auditors

Strategies for Successful IT Audits

➤ *Be proactive.* **Don't wait for someone else to initiate it. The initiator controls the objectives and sets the tone.**

➤ *Get management support and sensitize general management on issues.* **Make sure that the audit is in line with management's agenda for IT. After the audit, discuss results in a formal meeting.**

➤ *Have clear objectives and make sure everyone understands them.* **Talk with the IT staff about any concerns. A sample objective is "Enable real-time accounts payable and supplier satisfaction through the evolution of ERP systems and efficient and effective financial services."**

➤ *Schedule audits regularly, at least once a year.* **Without this regularity, audits come across more as an impromptu inspection to find faults than as a mechanism to encourage continuous improvement.**

➤ *Maintain healthy dynamics throughout the audit.* **Don't let it disintegrate into finger pointing. Rather, keep the focus on identifying problems and defining solutions. Encourage staff to provide constructive suggestions to resolve issues.**

➤ *Present a balanced appraisal when it's over—one that acknowledges accomplishments and makes constructive recommendations.* **No one will believe the audit if you find nothing to improve. On the other hand, staff will become discouraged if you find nothing right. Seek benchmark, comparable metrics, and show rationale for future improvements.**

➤ *Recognize the effects of other factors.* **The business environment and organizational culture can influence the success of audited projects. Politics and other intangibles might be the reasons for certain conditions, such as addressing labor concerns, phasing out dead-end jobs, and providing additional training to shift affected individuals to new positions.**

in depth and well before the audit.

IT audits should be comprehensive. Charles Austin and colleagues ("Managing Information Resources: A Study of Ten Healthcare Organizations/Practitioner Application," *J. Healthcare Management*, Jul./Aug. 2000) suggest including these categories (I've added the clarifying questions):

- *Strategic information systems planning.* Are strategies, plans, and budgets consistent with business goals? Are IT operational environments adequately staffed?
- *User focus in system development.* Are users actively involved in defining requirements and initial system design? Are they committed to ensuring successful system development and implementation?
- *Personnel.* Are IT services adequately staffed with skilled and experienced personnel? Are personnel receiving appropriate training with an opportunity to advance?
- *Information systems integration.* Are applications, databases, and networks evolving toward an enterprise-wide system?
- *Protection of information security and confidentiality.* Are logical security tools and physical access restrictions in place? Are information resources protected against hazards and related damages? Are business processes and information systems recoverable?
- *Project management in system development.* Are the new applications, databases, and networks (developed or acquired) consistent with management's intentions? Are system modifications consistent with management's intentions?
- *Post-implementation evaluation of information systems.* Are systems maintainable and supportable? Is system productivity consistent with business goals?

Organizations need not conduct a full audit every time. Even a partial review, addressing two or three of these areas, will give useful insights. How much and how often is largely up to the CIO and the organization.

DUE DILIGENCE

Now, more than ever, risk awareness is high. Terrorism is causing all nations to focus more intently on security, including information security. Financial and accounting scandals are causing businesses to examine their executive accountability, ethical behavior, and internal controls and auditing. IRM is timely because it forces CIOs and IT departments to do what doesn't come naturally: practice due diligence. Auditors look for documentation, rationale, and numbers—things that don't come naturally for many IT folks. IRM puts mechanisms in place like strategic planning and risk management, which help meet these requirements. Successful CIOs must build a strong IRM foundation and use it to sustain business operation and growth if they are to gain credibility as leaders in today's business world. ▪

John D. Hwang is a professor of information systems at California State University, Long Beach. In the early 1980s, he was appointed a director of information resources management at the US Federal Emergency Management Agency. More recently, he was the general manager of the Information Technology Agency for the City of Los Angeles, where his agenda was not unlike that of the CIO in "Agendas Then and Now." Contact him at jdhwang@csulb.edu.

Annotated Bibliography

This annotated list of general references provides you with what I believe are the most readable and practical texts on the topic of software management currently on the market. These are the books that I would recommend every software manager should have in his/her library.

General Management Readings

F. P. Brooks, Jr., *The Mythical Man-Month* (Anniversary Edition), Addison-Wesley, 1995. This well-written historic monograph discusses the problems and pitfalls that beset the author as he managed the development of the IBM 360 operating system. Although somewhat dated, this recently updated classic is interesting reading and full of sound advice. It continues to hold the distinction of being the best-selling software text on the market today.

S. McConnell, *Software Project Survival Guide,* Mircosoft Press, 1998. Software projects fail for two general reasons: the project team fails to comprehend what it takes to be successful or lets down their guard, once started, as distractions and dangers occur. This book arms those embarking on a project with a survival guide and checks for addressing these problems. Witty and informative, the book provides a great deal of practical advice on how to succeed.

R. S. Pressman, *A Manager's Guide to Software Engineering* (5th Edition), McGraw-Hill, 2001. A new edition of this popular book clearly explains how managers can use software engineering technology to help improve how they manage their software projects, people, and processes. Organized in four parts, the book provides a framework for putting the pieces of the software engineering puzzle together in a way that is both predictable and controllable.

D. J. Reifer, *Making the Software Business Case: Improvement by the Numbers,* Addison-Wesley, 2001. This book explains how to develop a software business case. It emphasizes how to develop, package, and use numbers to get improvement initiatives of all kinds approved and funded. It uses four case studies to illustrate the use of numbers and how to package them so that you can set realizable expectations, win the battle of the budget, and deliver what you promise.

K. E. Wiegers, *Creating a Software Engineering Culture,* Dorset House, 1996. The tactical changes needed to support process and quality improvements in modem software development shops are clearly explained in this text. It provides a variety of approaches to dealing with the day-to-day problems that confront managers as they try to create a team culture. The book provides practical guidance on how to structure and institute a culture change.

Acquisition Management

J. J. Marciniak and D. J. Reifer, *Software Acquisition Management,* Wiley, 1990. This book describes management practices used by organizations that acquire software contractually for their users. Using a buyer-versus-seller model, it covers the entire acquisition life cycle from competitive award until system retirement. It explains the contractual and legal aspects of the cycle and provides readers with tips on how to maintain visibility and control over third parties.

Software Productivity Consortium, *Subcontracting Products or Services for Software-Intensive Systems,* 2001. This guidebook describes how to implement a process for subcontracting, beginning with the decision to make or buy a product or service. The guidebook covers all aspects of subcontracting, beginning with soliciting and negotiating with a supplier and concluding with accepting and transitioning a product or service into the organization. Because the guidebook is written for those engineers who have the responsibility for managing a subcontract, it is full of practical advice.

Configuration Management

A. M. Jonassen Hass, *Software Configuration Principles and Practice,* Addison-Wesley, 2002. This comprehensive guide introduces the reader to the discipline of configuration management. It describes both how to establish a sound CM strategy and to put the strategy into action. In addition to discussing the issues, the book provides implementation guidance and examples based upon experience. The text is current in that it discusses CM for agile and safety-critical projects. It also provides insight into establishing CM for multisite developments.

D. D. Lyon, *Practical CM: Best Software Configuration Management Practices,* Butterworth, 2000. This brief but information-packed text provides a step-by-step strategy for planning, implementing, and integrating modem configuration and data management practices into businesses of all size. The book covers all aspects of configuration and data management, including the often forgotten topics of release and distribution management, and the transition to production.

Emerging Software Management Paradigms

K. Beck, *Extreme Programming Explained,* Addison-Wesley, 1999. This text explains extreme programming and highlights its agile, just-in-time concepts in simple and understandable terms. It talks about an incremental development approach and stresses the reliance on good communications, teamwork, and automation to put a lightweight, efficient, low- risk and fun way to develop software into place in your firm. I selected the book because its goal is to help you make the decision as to when you should use extreme programming and when not.

B. Boehm and R. Turner, *Balancing Agility and Discipline,* Addison-Wesley, 2004. This book provides the reader with insights on how to use agile methods within a plan-driven environment. It argues for balancing objectives so discipline is not sacrificed as developers build products quickly and without the overhead inherent in more formal methodologies. Its appendices are especially useful because they point the reader to information on methods and tools that they can use to put the book's recommendations into action.

R. Galen, *Software Endgames,* Dorset House, 2005. This book discusses how to use software defects as a management tool to determine when to release software being developed incrementally. It discusses the setup and use of a defect-tracking system to provide the metrics needed for endgame defect tracking. It is a practical volume full of lots of sage advice for those trying to determine when they have tested enough.

N. L. Kerth, *Project Retrospectives: A Handbook for Team Reviews,* Dorset House, 2001. The author describes processes that he has developed and successfully used to conduct successful project retrospectives (e.g., end-of-project reviews). Using imaginative illustrations and practical scenarios, the author shows you how to gather meaningful lessons learned from project successes and failures in an atmosphere of mutual trust among project participants.

L. P. Leach, *Critical Chain Project Management,* Artech House, 2000. This book discusses Golratt's theory of constraints and the technique of critical chain scheduling. This is required reading for those looking for a new and better way to manage their projects. This theory revolves around how budget and schedule reserves are developed, allocated, and controlled. The book weaves these thoughts into a total quality framework that managers can use productively.

P. E. McMahon, *Virtual Project Management,* St. Lucie Press, 2000. The title of this text is misleading because the focus of its coverage is on managing distributed developments, not virtual technologies. It discusses practical and affordable ways to create collaborative environments in which work is done at different locales by distributed teams. It is insightful and prescriptive relative to what the critical factors are and how you should deal with them. There are a multitude of practical examples and useful hints to help those embarking on this journey to becoming successful.

Estimation

B. W. Boehm, *Software Engineering Economics,* Prentice-Hall, 1981. This classic textbook discusses the issues, experiences, and methods used in the field of software estimation and life cycle management. It reviews common tools and techniques that engineers can use to perform economic analysis. It then goes on to describe the original version of the Constructive Cost Model (COCOMO) software cost estimation model and the assumptions, factors, constraints, and mathematical formulas upon which it is based. It explains how the model can be used to estimate the resources (duration, effort, etc.) you will need for your project.

B. W. Boehm, C. Abts, A. W. Brown, S. Chulani, B. K. Clark, E. Horowitz, R. Madachy, D. Reifer, and B. Steece, *Software Cost Estimation with COCOMO II,* Prentice-Hall, 2000. This book thoroughly reworks Dr. Boehm's original textbook to address economics when using modern software development techniques. The book introduces the reader to the COCOMO II extensions for cost and schedule estimation and to the approaches being developed to address issues surrounding estimating COTS, incremental paradigms and, rapid application development methodologies. The book was written to supplement rather than replace Dr. Boehm's 1981 classic textbook entitled *Software Engineering Economics.*

R. D. Stutzke, *Estimating Software-Intensive Systems,* Addison-Wesley, 2005. This comprehensive, fact-filled volume fills a void in many a bookshelf. Unlike other texts on the topic of estimating, this one presents factual and unbiased information about the full range of options open to those seeking to improve their skills, knowledge, and abilities in a variety of topics. It combines over 900 pages of extremely current and useful information organized for those who want pointers on how to get the job done. I especially liked the chapters on earned-value measurement, determining product quality, and measuring and estimating process performance. The CD, with its Excel spreadsheets, is an added bonus, as are the appendices explaining measurement theory and estimation accuracy.

Life Cycles

I. Jacobson, G. Booch and J. Rumbaugh, *The Unified Software Development Process,* Addison-Wesley, 1999. The authors describe the Rational Unified Process for developing software. This process serves as a model of what the characteristics that a modern software life cycle process should possess. As part of their discussions, the authors point to the four underlying principles that most modern life cycle processes support: the process is architecture-centric, iterative by nature, develops products incrementally, and employs use cases to get the users involved.

Metrics and Measurement

J. McGarry, D. Card, C. Jones, B. Layman, E. dark, J. Dean, and F. Hall, *Practical Software Measurement: Objective Information for Decision Makers,* Addison-Wesley, 2001. This book takes the reader through the process of establishing a metrics program. The book builds on the experience the authors had in implementing the concepts advocated as part of the Practical Software Measurement initiative. It provides insight into what metrics to use and why. The case studies in the appendices are illustrative of how to put its recommendations into action.

C. Ebert, Reiner Dumke, M. Bundschuh, A. Schmietendorf, and Rainer Dumke, *Best Practices in Software Measurement,* Springer-Verlag, 2004. This text offers practical guidance in software measurement based on experience. Besides explaining current measurement standards, the authors provide implementation guidance in their use by employing case studies taken from such firms as Alcatel, Deutsche Telekom, and Siemens. Besides many practical hints and checklists, readers will appreciate the pointers given to the many metrics resources they can tap into in order to improve their metrics programs.

W. A. Florae and A. D. Carleton, *Measuring the Software Process,* Addison-Wesley, 1999. The authors put into place a framework that they developed to measure software products and processes so that performance can be analyzed using statistical process control techniques like control charts. The book emphasizes how statistical process control can be used to help managers to analytically predict, control, and improve the performance of their software development process. Besides introducing you to the tools and techniques, the book also provides you with a solid set of measurement principles that can serve as a foundation for a metrics program.

R. B. Grady and D. L. Caswell, *Software Metrics: Establishing a Company-Wide Program,* Prentice-Hall, 1987. This is still the most readable book I have encountered on the topic of introducing metrics and measurement into use in an enterprise. It describes how the authors developed, sold, implemented, and continued to improve a metrics program within Hewlett-Packard (HP). It is insightful and extremely pragmatic in its views. It provides many aids, including previously used briefing charts, metrics definitions, and checklists. This book serves its readers well by discussing what it takes to set a measurement program into motion in practice.

People and Teams

T. DeMarco and T. Lister, *Peopleware* (2nd Edition), Dorset House, 1999. This classic challenges the myth that technology is the cornerstone of productivity. The book focuses on people and how to direct human behavior to achieve project goals. It makes you think about the things that you need to do to empower and enable your people to work together more effectively. The updated presentation remains witty and entertaining. There are also lots of revealing examples used to illustrate key points. The advice provided is sound and timeless. In my opinion, the book is well worth reading multiple times.

P. Scholtes, P. L. Joiner, and B. J. Streibel, *The Team Handbook* (2nd Edition), Oriel, 2000. The first edition of this handbook focused primarily on establishing cross-functional teams for improvement projects. It was updated to add approaches for building and channeling the behavior of new product development, management, and a variety of other types of teams in the 1990s. It discusses strategies and tools for getting team members to work together and to address the conflicts that arise between people, management, and management style. It is instructive and provides many examples and work-related aids aimed at helping you form teams operationally.

R. Thomsett, *Radical Project Management,* Prentice-Hall, 2002. This book is a well-written, nicely illustrated, thought-provoking treatise on how to succeed in software development. Its emphasis focuses on what matters most: people, relationships, and value propositions. In addition to providing rules for project managers to live by, Thomsett explains his XPM methodology and offers good advice along with concrete examples on how to use it.

Process and Product Improvement

D. M. Ahern, R. Turner, and A. Clouse, *CMMI Distilled: A Practical Introduction to Integrated Process Improvement* (2nd Edition), Addison-Wesley, 2003. For those of you interested in the new Capability Maturity Model for Integration (CMMI), I highly recommend this book. The authors have done an admirable job of describing the large and somewhat unwieldy new combined software and systems engineering process maturity model in a language that just about anyone can understand. It summarizes both the staged and continuous representations of the CMMI and gives practical guidelines for their use. The update provides the latest information about the framework and its associated assessment methods.

M. B. Chrissis, M. Konrad, and S. Shrum, *CMMI,* Addison-Wesley, 2003. This book defines the Software Engineering Institute's Capability Maturity Model Integration (CMMI) in more depth in terms of what are called process areas in both the continuous and staged representations of the model. The book describes each of the process areas in depth as it introduces the model. It next guides the reader in how to interpret and use the CMMI for process and product improvement. To facilitate learning, the book provides a detailed case study. This is especially useful to those who are using the updated framework for the first time because it helps pull guidance together in a way that can be implemented in practice.

W. S. Humphrey, *Managing the Software Process,* Addison-Wesley, 1989. This classic text by one of the leaders in the field of software management provides practical guidelines for assessing and improving processes used for software development. It describes the five level maturity model popularized by the Software Engineering Institute (SEI) as its framework. Key technical and managerial practices associated with each level of the model are identified along with the criteria used to make process assessments. Methods and actions needed to establish control over improvement activities are also provided, along with examples and guidelines. This is a most sought after reference by those embracing the process discipline.

N. S. Potter and M. E. Sakry, *Making Process Improvement Work: A Concise Action Guide for Software Managers and Practitioners,* Addison-Wesley, 2002. This well-written and concise guide makes it clear what process improvement is all about. It emphasizes the need to tie improvement activities to business goals. It provides real-world examples and a step-by-step approach for initiating an initiative. Besides being short, it provides practical insight into what works and what does not, based on actual experience, not hearsay or theory. The numerous case studies, graphs, and templates provide the reader with the tools to put the book's recommendations into practice in one's own organization.

Project Management

T. DeMarco, *Slack: Getting Past Burnout, Busy Work and the Myth of Total Efficiency,* Broadway, 2002. This book's message is that project managers must build slack into their schedules. Otherwise, they will burn out before the situation gets dicey.

Though short in length, the book is full of wisdom when discussing burnout work efficiency. The text at times reads like a novel. Most managers will relate to its message and the stories used to convey it. The book is insightful and deserves a prominent place on most bookshelves. Perhaps then it will remind most managers that you can run out of gas quickly if you continuously race around at 90 miles an hour.

S. A. Devauz, *Total Project Control: A Manager's Guide to Integrated Project Planning, Measuring and Tracking,* Wiley, 1999. This text takes a total systems view of management and provides you with insight into building an integrated decision-support system for use when making difficult project-related decisions. I especially like how it handles multitask projects, resource distribution, and delivery of multiple products and services in parallel. Its chapter on managing the project's entire portfolio is profound and thought provoking. The book also points out what to do when faced with adversarial situations.

H. Kerzner, *A Systems Approach to Planning, Scheduling and Controlling,* Wiley, 2003. Using a hands-on approach to management, the author answers typical questions managers pose about the systems, practices, tools, and techniques used to implement the common principles advanced for project management. The author explains all facets of project management, including approaches that can be used to assess performance and develop practitioner skills, knowledge, and abilities. The chapters on concurrent engineering, contracting, and risk management are especially timely. This is a very readable book and highly recommended for managers at all levels of an organization, from project manager to executive.

W. Royce, *Software Project Management: A Unified Framework,* Addison-Wesley, 1998. The author offers ten principles of software project management after he reviews traditional approaches and dogma associated with software development. These principles guide his discussions on how to have a successful project using state-of-the-art tools and techniques. The author then recommends changes needed to gain control over today's iterative and incremental processes. I like that he gets into the details and provides like of examples to make improving the way you manage achievable in the context of modern software developments.

R. K. Wysocki and R. McGary, *Effective Project Management: Traditional, Adaptive, Extreme* (3rd Edition), Wiley, 2003. The new edition of this tutorial provides novices with a good introduction to the topic of project management. It begins by describing proven project management tools and techniques. It then interacts with you via a savvy software mentor to help you develop skills using a simulated real-world project (using the included CD). It shows you how to break down the work into components, allocate staff, develop schedules, and use milestones to control the work in progress. New topics in this edition include extreme management methods, team selection, and risk analysis.

Quality Management

J. W. Horch, *Practical Guide to Software Quality Management* (2nd Edition), Artech House, 2003. This book provides a comprehensive guide to the topic of software quality management. It provides you with an understanding of what characterizes a quality organization and what functions it should perform. The book focuses on defect analysis and suggests a variety of techniques and tools that you could use to minimize their occurrence. The book then provides you with useful guidelines for structuring an organization and implementing a responsive set of quality practices. The new edition includes chapters on software safety and risk analysis.

S. H. Kan, *Metrics and Models in Software Quality Engineering* (2nd Edition), Addison-Wesley, 2002. This text discusses techniques for measuring and improving software quality throughout the software development life cycle. It focuses on the use of software metrics, reliability models, and program complexity analysis techniques. It goes on to discuss defect removal models and customer satisfaction measurement schemes. The case studies from several computer firms and the NASA Software Engineering Laboratory are especially enlightening.

G. G. Shulmeyer and J. I. McManus, *Handbook of Software Quality Assurance* (3rd Edition), Prentice-Hall, 1999. This handbook covers all the material you need to understand how to receive the American Society for Quality (ASQ) Software Quality Engineer Certificate. Its 21 chapters contain essays written by experts in the field on topics ranging from planning to implementation. Its coverage of metrics and statistical quality control is especially enlightening, as is its discussion of where software quality fits within an organization and why it should report independently outside of engineering. I recommend it to anyone interested in the topic.

Risk Management

D. W. Karolak, *Software Engineering Risk Management,* IEEE Computer Society Press, 1996. This book investigates just-in-time (JIT) software and risk management techniques from both technology and business perspectives. It suggests identifying risk based upon the relationships between risky situations and behavior. Approaches for risk mitigation and avoidance are reviewed along with risk metrics as the book recommends processes developed to address risk in a JIT manner. The book is straightforward, readable, and worthwhile for anyone interested in the topic.

J. McManus, *Risk Management in Software Development Projects,* Butterworth-Heinemann, 2003. This text focuses on what the practitioner needs to know about risk in order to deliver superior products on time and within budget. It describes the key components of a successful risk management process and best practices. It is especially useful for those unfamiliar with the basics. It provides checklists and examples that reinforce the use of recommended tools and techniques.

Teamwork

W. S. Humphrey, *Managing Technical People: Innovation, Teamwork and the Software Process,* Addison-Wesley, 1996. Written for project leaders and managers, this book provides practical advice on managing technical and professional workforces. The book provides tips on recruiting, motivating, organizing, directing and recognizing talented people. Most of the points the author makes are bolstered through the use of delightful anecdotes, examples, and illustrations. This book is good reading that is full of very sound advice provided by one of the masters of the trade.

E. Sullivan, *Under Pressure and On Time,* Microsoft Press, 2001. This book shares hard-won practices for developing award-winning software within a commercial start-up environment. In addition to good project management, it places an emphasis on people and teamwork as discriminators. It goes on to describe a model for creating, directing, and growing a successful software development team that can excel under pressure. It is full of good advice and provides many practical examples relative to empowering teams.

Technology Transfer

G. A. Moore, *Crossing the Chasm,* HarperBusiness, 1991. This book discusses the issues, challenges, and experiences associated with moving technology from early-adopter projects into widespread use. It is pragmatic in its orientation and full of examples. Its hypothesis states that the chasm is deep and that your technology transfer strategy needs to be adjusted using a new model before you can cross it. This is a very thought-provoking text that has become one of the classics in the field of technology transfer.

Project Management Body of Knowledge (PMBOK™)

A book that every software project manager should own is the *PMBOK™* published by the Project Management Institute (www.pmi.org) in Newtown Square, Pennsylvania. This book organizes the knowledge that experienced project managers have learned according to the following taxonomy:

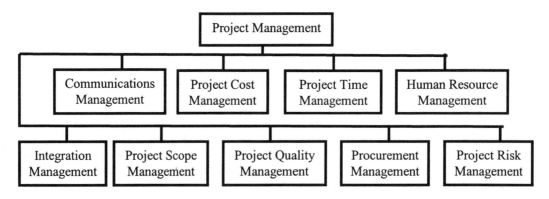

PMI Organizational Taxonomy for Project Management Knowledge

534

The *PMBOK*™ is well written, nicely illustrated, and current. It provides software managers with a single source of information about most aspects of project management. However, it does not provide insight into what works and what does not in practice. You will get this information from the many articles that I have reprinted in this volume. The third edition of the *PMBOK*™ is available at the referenced PMI Web site along with an offering of related publications.

IEEE Software Engineering Standards

The IEEE publishes 40 standards bound together in its four-volume collection along with an overview document. J. W. Moore, *The Roadmap to Software Engineering: A Standards-Based Guide,* IEEE Computer Society, 2005. This book describes the scope, roles, uses, and development trends associated with the most widely used of the IEEE's software engineering standards collection. Because there are so many standards and guides, the book serves a particularly useful purpose by establishing a context for the use of each standard and helping you filter through the material to find what is important.

The standards that comprise this collection are as follows:

Volume 1—Customer and Terminology Standards
1. *IEEE Standard Glossary of Software Engineering Terminology,* 610.12-1990.
2. *IEEE Recommended Practice for Software Acquisition,* 1062, 1998 Edition.
3. *IEEE Standard for the Application and Management of the Systems Engineering Process,* 1220-1998.
4. *IEEE Standard for Software Safety Plans,* 1228-1994.
5. *IEEE Guide for Developing System Requirements Specifications,* 1233, 1998 Edition.
6. *IEEE Guide for Information Technology—System Definition—Concept of Operations Document,* 1362-1998.
7. *Software Life Cycle Processes,* IEEE/EIA Std. 12207.9-1996.
8. *Software Life Cycle Processes—Life Cycle Data,* IEEE/EIA Std. 12207.1-1997.
9. *Software Life Cycle Processes—Implementation Considerations,* IEEE/EIA Std. 12207.2-1997.

Volume 2—Process Standards
10. *IEEE Standard for Software Quality Assurance Plans,* 730-1998.
11. *IEEE Guide for Software Quality Assurance Planning,* 730.1-1995
12. *IEEE Standard for Software Configuration Management Plans,* 828-1998.
13. *IEEE Standard for Software Unit Testing,* 1008-1987(R1993).
14. *IEEE Standard for Software Reviews,* 1028-1997.
15. *IEEE Standard for Software Verification and Validation Plans,* 10012-1998.
16. *Supplement to IEEE Standard for Software Verification and Validation: Context Map to IEEE/EIA 12207.1-1997.*
17. *IEEE Guide to Software Configuration Management,* 1042-1987 (R1993).
18. *IEEE Standard for Software Productivity Metrics,* 1045-1992
19. *IEEE Standard for Software Project Management Plans,* 1058-1998.
20. *IEEE Guide to Software Verification and Validation Plans,* 1059-1993.
21. *IEEE Standard for Developing Software Life Cycle Processes,* 1074-1997.
22. *IEEE Standard for Software Maintenance,* 1219-1998.
23. *IEEE Guide—Adoption of PMI Standard—A Guide to the Project Management Body of Knowledge,* 1490-1998.

Volume 3—Product Standards
24. *IEEE Standard Dictionary of Measures to Produce Reliable Software,* 982.1-1988.
25. *IEEE Guide for the Use of Standard Dictionary of Measures to Produce Reliable Software,* 982.2-1988.
26. *IEEE Standard for a Software Quality Metrics Methodology,* 1061-1998.
27. *IEEE Standard for Software User Documentation,* 1063-1987 (R1993).
28. *IEEE Standard Adoption of International Standard ISO/IEC 12119:1994(E)—Information Technology—Software Packages—Quality Requirements and Testing.*

Volume 4—Resource and Technique Standards
29. *IEEE Standard for Software Test Documentation,* 829-1998.
30. *IEEE Recommended Practice for Software Requirements Specifications,* 830-1998.

31. *IEEE Recommended Practice for Software Design Descriptions,* 1016-1998.

32. *IEEE Standard Classification for Software Anomalies,* 1044-1993.

33. *IEEE Guide to Classification for Software Anomalies,* 1044.1-1995.

34. *IEEE Standard for Functional Modeling Language—Syntax and Semantics for IDEFO,* 1320.1-1998.

35. *IEEE Standard for Conceptual Modeling Language—Syntax and Semantics for IDEFlX$_{97}$(IDEF$_{object}$),* 1320.2-1998.

36. *IEEE Recommended Practice for the Adoption of Computer-Aided Software Engineering (CASE) Tools,* 1348-1995.

37. *IEEE Standard for Information Technology—Software Reuse—Data Model for Reuse Library Interoperability: Basic Interoperability Data Model (BIDM),* 1420.1-1995.

38. *Supplement to IEEE Standard for Information Technology—Software Reuse—Data Model for Reuse Library Interoperability: Asset Certification Framework,* 1420. la-1996.

39. *IEEE Guide for Information Technology—Software Reuse—Concept of Operations for Inter operating Reuse Libraries,* 1430-1996.

40. *IEEE Standard Adoption of ISO/IEC 14102:199 5-Information Technology-Guidelines for the Evaluation and Selection of CASE Tools,* 1462-1998.

Project Management Resources on the Web

The Web has many resources that will help the software project manager. Some useful sites include:

- Project Management Institute's site, www.4pm.com
- Project Management Resource Center, Columbia University, www.columbia.edu/~jm2217/#Metrics
- Stanford's Advanced Project Management Site, www.projectconnections.com
- My Web site, www.reifer.com

Glossary of Software Management Terms

This glossary defines key terms used in this tutorial. By design, it is neither complete nor comprehensive. That would be impossible to accomplish because of the breadth of the field. Instead, it was developed over the years to explain terms that may be new or foreign to our more technical readers. In this edition, I have added about 20 new terms to explain the advances made in the field of software project management. These definitions support several new articles that I have included in this volume.

The over 200 entries in the glossary are arranged alphabetically. An entry may consist of a single word, such as "budget," or a phrase, such as "matrix organization." Phrases are given in their natural order (project management) instead of being reversed (management, project). Terms are spelled out prior to placing their acronyms or abbreviations in parentheses. If a term has more than one commonly accepted definition, several explanations may be listed. Ordering for these listings is random and does not convey any preference. Where necessary, examples and explanatory notes have been included to provide the clearest definition for the term possible.

The source for most of the standard definitions used comes from the following two IEEE documents, the referenced *Guide* and previous editions of this tutorial:

1. *IEEE Standard Glossary of Software Engineering Terminology,* IEEE, 1983.
2. *Glossary of Software Engineering Terminology,* ANSI/IEEE Std. 610.12-1990, IEEE Computer Society, 1990.
3. *Guide to the Project Management Body of Knowledge (PMBOK™ Guide),* Project Management Institute, 2000 Edition.

In those cases in which a definition is taken from a different source, the reference is cited in brackets following the entry. In those rare cases in which there was no acceptable definition available, I developed my own. A list of references is included at the end of the glossary.

A

Acceptance. In acquisition management, the official act by which the customer accepts transfer, title, and delivery of any item specified as part of the contract.

Acceptance criteria. The criteria a system or component must satisfy in order to be accepted by a user, customer, or other party.

Acquisition. The process of obtaining products and services through a contract.

Acquisition management. The process of managing third parties that generate software products and/or perform related services using a contract as the legal basis for action/arbitration of disputes. In such situations, managers provide technical direction to the teams developing software per the contract's terms and conditions.

Activity. A major unit of work to be completed in achieving the goals of a software project. An activity has precise starting and ending dates, has a set of tasks that need to be done, consumes resources, and results in work products. An activity may contain other activities arranged in a hierarchical order.

Agile method. A software development process that evolves a product in a series of rapid iterations, most of which are scheduled to last weeks, not months.

Allocation. In management, the process of allotting resources to performing organizations.

Allocated baseline. In configuration management, the initial approved specifications governing the development of configuration items that are part of a higher configuration.

Application. A system that provides a set of services that solve some type of user problem.

Application engineering. The processes/practices used to guide the disciplined development, test, and life cycle support of applications software.

Architecture. The structure of components, their interrelationships, and the principles and guidelines governing their design and evolution over time.

Asset. Any product of the software life cycle that can be potentially reused, including architectures, requirements, designs, code, lessons learned, and so on.

Asset management. The processes/practices firms use to manage their reusable software assets and make them readily available in quality form to their potential users.

Attrition. A gradual, natural reduction in the workforce caused by various means like retirement.

Audit. An independent examination of a work product or set of work products used to assess compliance with specifications, standards, contracts, or other criteria.

Authority. In project management, the right to give direction and allocate resources (staff, schedule, etc.). This right should be commensurate with responsibility.

B

Bar chart. A chart used to graphically portray schedule-related information.

Baseline. A work product that has been formally reviewed and agreed upon and that can be changed only through formal change-control procedures. A baseline work product may form the basis for further work activity(s).

Benchmark. In management, an industry-wide or organizational standard against which performance is measured or improvements are compared. Best practice. An engineering or management activity that directly addresses the purpose of a particular process and contributes to the creation of its output [1].

Breakage. The amount of previously delivered software that must be modified when adding more functionality to a software product.

Budget. In management, a statement of expected results expressed in numerical terms.

Budgeting. In management, allocating money to the performers of approved tasks.

Buffer. In planning, the extra time or reserve in your schedule that you can allocate to handle contingencies that arise as the project unfolds.

Build. An operational version of a software product that includes a specified subset of the capabilities provided by the final product.

Business area. A coherent market created by consumers who have similar needs. Business areas may be organized by customer, geography, product, or some other characteristic.

Business area manager. The person or organization responsible for managing the definition, using an evolution of products within a business area.

Business case. The materials prepared for decision makers to show them that the business idea under consideration is a good one and that the numbers associated with it make financial as well as technical sense for the organization [1].

C

Capability Maturity Model (Software). A description of the stages through which organizations evolve as they define, implement, measure, control, and improve their software processes. This model provides a guide for selecting a process improvement strategy [2].

Capability Maturity Model Integration (CMMI). A model that describes an organization's potential for producing quality systems, considering their institutionalized practices for performing systems engineering, software engineering, integrated product development, and supplier management.

Case study. An example employed to communicate lessons learned from trial use of a concept or idea[l].

Charter of accounts. A listing of the charge accounts for a project.

Class. A group of objects with similar properties, common behavior, common relationships to other objects, and common semantics.

Collaborative development. A development process characterized as a cooperative team effort that often crosses organizational or geographic boundaries.

Commitment. An obligation to expend resources at some future time, such as a purchase order or travel authorization, which is charged against a budget although it has not yet been paid. It also refers to an obligation to perform a set of tasks for or deliver a product to another member of a project team at a specified point in time.

Competency. The skills, knowledge, and personal attributes that enable effective work performance [3].

Computer-aided software engineering (CASE). The use of computers to aid in the software engineering process. May include the application of tools to software design, requirements tracing, code production, testing, document generation, and other software engineering activities. Commonly refers to the integrated collections of tools and a repository.

Commercial off-the-shelf (COTS) software. Refers to software that is supplied by a third party who retains responsibility for continued development and life cycle support of the package. COTS software products are used as is (the version is not changed to address the unique needs of the user).

Component-based software engineering. The process of building software systems by combining and integrating pretested and preengineered, fine-grained software objects taken from some framework or class library.

Computer software configuration item (CSCI). An aggregation of software that is designated for configuration management.

Configuration management. A discipline applying technical and administrative direction and surveillance to identify and document both the functional and physical characteristics of a configuration item, control changes to these characteristics, record and report change processing and implementation status, and verify compliance with requirements.

Contingency. In management, an amount of design margin, time, or money used as a safety factor to accommodate future growth or uncertainty.

Contracting. Refers to the process of obtaining supplies and services from third parties using the competitive contracting process.

Control charts. Graphical displays of results portrayed over time and for which control limits have been established for the process involved.

Controlling. Those management activities conducted to determine whether or not progress is being made according to plan. Control involves measuring, monitoring, and acting on information obtained throughout the development to correct deviations, focus resources, and mitigate risk.

Core competency. Those capabilities of the firm deemed essential for its continued survival.

Costing. In management, the process of developing a cost estimate for an item, task, or activity. Costing and pricing are separate but related activities typically done by different people.

Cost–benefit analysis. Management trade-offs normally conducted to determine whether or not the benefits that accrue to alternatives are worth the costs involved.

Cost center. An organization to which control over resources has been assigned and to which budgets and profit goals have been made.

Cost performance index (CPI). A cost efficiency ratio computed as the ratio of earned value to actual costs.

Critical path. In a network diagram that shows how tasks in your work plan are related, the longest path from start to finish or the path that does not have any slack, thus the path corresponding to the shortest time in which the project can be completed.

Critical chain. Refers to the chain of critical tasks in a project. The end date is forecast based upon task completions rather than scheduling hard due dates from the end date forward.

Critical path method (CPM). In project management, a technique used to determine the critical path through a cost or schedule network diagram.

Critical success factors. Those characteristics, conditions, or variables that have a direct influence on your customers' satisfaction with the products and services that you offer.

Customer. The individual or organization that specifies and accepts the project deliverables. The customer may be internal or external to the parent organization and may or may not be the end user of the software. A financial transaction between the customer and developer is not implied by this definition.

D

Decision tree. A tree representation used typically to describe the costs, risks, and rewards associated with alternatives being considered in making a management decision.

Defect. A detected fault or an observation of incorrect behavior during operation.

Defect density. The number of defects per unit of product size (i.e., the number of validated defects per thousand source lines of code).

Delegation. In management, to empower another with the authority to act or represent you in the performance of your responsibilities.

Deliverable. The end product or service that is specified by and delivered to a customer or user.

Delivery. Release of a system or component to a customer or user.

Design review. A process or meeting during which the system, hardware, or software design is presented to project personnel, the manager, customers, users, or other interested parties for review or approval.

Directing. Refers to those management activities conducted to energize, motivate, and guide staff to achieve organizational goals.

Domain. A distinct functional area that can be supported by a class of systems with similar requirements and capabilities (avionics, banking, etc.).

Domain analysis. The process of identifying, collecting, organizing, analyzing, and representing the relevant information in a domain based on the study of existing systems and their development histories, knowledge captured from domain experts, underlying theory, and emerging technology within a domain.

Domain engineering. The reuse-based processes/practices firms use to define the scope (domain definition), specify the structure (domain model), and build the assets for a class of systems, subsystems, or applications.

Dummy activity. An activity of zero duration used to show a logical relationship in a schedule network or PERT chart.

Duration. The number of time periods, excluding holidays and other scheduled periods of nonactivity, required to satisfactorily complete either a work task or activity.

E

Earned value. In project management, a technique used to assess progress and budgetary performance using milestone completions. Actuals and projections are compared to earned value to compute trends and variances.

Education. The communication of knowledge to interested parties. Quite different from training, in which the aim is developing those skills and abilities needed to perform a job.

Effort. The number of labor units required to satisfactorily complete either a work task or activity.

Error. (1) The difference between the computed, observed, or measured value or condition and the true, theoretically correct, or specified value or condition. (2) An incorrect step, process, or data definition. (3) An incorrect result and/or (4) a human action that produces an incorrect result.

Estimate. A calculated prediction, typically of the resources required to complete a project.

Evolutionary. Refers to an iterative process used to specify requirements when knowledge about them is unknown when the project starts.

Expected value. The weighted average using probabilities as weights [1].

F

Feedback. In management, the acquisition of that information needed to ascertain status or progress.

Forecasting. In management, refers to the prediction of future events. Forecasts differ from estimates in terms of the means used to derive them and their accuracy. For example, an estimate of the area of a curve is quite different from a market forecast.

Framework. A collection of classes that provides a set of services for a particular domain. A framework thus exports a number of classes and mechanisms that clients can use or adapt, depending on their needs.

Funding. In management, refers to the authorizing or appropriating of money to cover the costs of a project.

Functional organization. An organization that groups people by skill or specialty (such as software or hardware engineering) in one department, reporting to a single manager.

G

Gantt chart. A representation of a milestone schedule in which activities are pictured as horizontal lines and start and stop milestones by triangles.

H

HyperText Markup Language (HTML). The coding method used to format documents on the World Wide Web. Browsers display text, graphics, and links on Web pages by translating HTML tags that appear in the file.

I

Increment. Refers to a working version of the software that provides a specified set of functions or capabilities.

Incremental development. Refers to a process used to develop software products via capability builds that are typically organized along functional lines.

Independent verification and validation (IV&V). Verification and validation of a software product by some organization that is technically, managerially, and financially independent of the organization developing the application. See the definitions for verification and validation.

Indicator. In management, a device that identifies a prescribed state of affairs relative to managerial or financial performance.

Infrastructure. The underlying framework used by management for making decisions and allocating resources.

Inspection. A close and strict examination of a software artifact by a group of peers following a defined process and a common standard of excellence.

Integrated product team (IPT). An organizational structure for a product development project that includes representatives of all functional disciplines involved with the effort from both the developer's and customer's organizations that are collectively responsible for the product.

Institutionalization. The building of infrastructure and culture to support making whatever is changed a part of the ongoing way a firm does business.

Intellectual property. The intangible output of a rational thought process that has some intellectual or informational value.

K

Key process area. A cluster of related activities that, when performed collectively, achieve a set of goals considered to be important for establishing process capability.

Know-how engineering. The ability to transfer the know-how associated with a new technology in a manner that builds the skills, knowledge, and ability to do the job in a logical order.

Knowledge base. The codification of the organization's past engineering experience in building and sustaining similar systems.

L

Leadership. In management, the ability to influence the behavior of others and focus it toward achievement of accepted goals.

Legacy. Reusable software assets developed on one project that have the potential for use on another project. For example, an algorithm developed on one project could be used on another if it were designed to be reused.

Lessons learned. The knowledge or experience gained by actually completing a project.

Life cycle. The period of time that starts when a software product is conceived and ends when that product is retired from use.

Line manager. The manager of a functional organization that generates a product (software development, etc.) or provides a service (configuration management, etc.).

Line of business manager. The person put in charge of deciding how to fulfill customer needs within a business area with some product or product line.

Line organization. That part of the functional organization to which the authority for performing a task has been designated.

M

Management. Getting things done through the work of other people.

Management reserve. In project management, resources set aside for contingency purposes.

Manager. The person charged with the job of planning, organizing, staffing, directing, and controlling the activities of others.

Master milestone schedule. A summary-level schedule that identifies major activities, significant events, and key milestones.

Matrix organization. A combination of function and project forms of organization in which the line is responsible for providing skilled people and the project for programmatic performance.

Measurement. In management, the process of collecting, analyzing, and reporting metrics data useful in assessing status, progress, and trends.

Method. The steps, notation, rules, and examples used to structure the approach used by a person or team for problem solving.

Metric. A quantitative measure of the degree to which a system, process, or component possesses a given attribute. For example, error density is used to characterize software reliability.

Middleware. A layer of software that sits between the operating system and application and that provides distributed computing services through a simple programming interface.

Milestone. A schedule event for which some person is held accountable and that is used to demonstrate progress.

Milestone schedule. A significant event in the project, usually resulting in completion of a major task or delivery of a major deliverable.

Monitoring. In management, refers to keeping constant surveillance over and track of what is actually happening on a project.

Motivation. In management, the act of influencing the behavior of others through the combined use of incentives and rewards.

N

Network. In management, a diagrammatic display showing the logical relationships that exist between scheduled activities and their previous relationships. Not to be confused with the more technical definition referring to a communications network.

O

Object. An element of the software work breakdown structure (WBS) derived using the criteria of information hiding and abstraction. An object typically maintains complete internal knowledge of its own state and reveals hidden information through a set of services or methods. A primitive object consists of some data, a group of operations on that data, and a mechanism for selecting an operation given a command.

Opportunity cost. Net benefits forgone when pursuing alternate uses of resources [1].

Organizing. Refers to those management activities conducted to structure efforts that involve collaboration and communication so that it is effectively performed.

Organizational breakdown structure (OBS). A family tree that organizes, defines, and graphically illustrates the organizational structure used on a project.

Ownership. In management, the degree to which a person, group, or team buys into plans established and against which they are performing.

P

Parametric estimating. An estimating technique that uses statistical relationships between historical data that are a function of significant variables to develop an estimate of the resources needed to complete a software job.

Peer review. A review of a software work product, following defined procedures, by peers of the authors of the product, for the purpose of identifying defects and improvements.

Performance. In management, refers to a measure of a person's ability to achieve agreed-upon goals and realize forecasts.

Planning. Refers to management activities that establish future courses of action at all levels of the organization. At the top, plans tend to be strategic. At lower levels, plans tend to be more tactical. At all levels, plans establish the baselines against which progress is measured.

Policy. General statement or understanding developed at a corporate level to channel thinking and decision making.

Position. In management, the specific role an individual plays within an organization.

Power. In management, the perceived ability of one person to influence the action of others.

Practice. In management, a preferred course of action for getting the job done.

Pricing. In management, the process of determining how much to charge a customer or user for products or services. Costing and pricing are separate activities. Organizations can price services for less than their cost and still make a profit based upon economies of scale.

Procedure. In management, guides to action that provide a person or team with a preferred structure for the activity to be accomplished.

Process. In management, the sequence of steps, actions, or activities taken to bring about a desired result or achieve a goal.

Process improvement. Refers to a program of activities designed to improve the performance and maturity of the processes that an organization uses to perform work.

Process maturity. The extent to which a specific process is explicitly defined, managed, measured, controlled, and effective [2].

Product. A system and all of its associated work products.

Product baseline. In configuration management, the approved technical documentation (including, for software, the source code) defining a configuration item during the production, operation, maintenance, and logistics support phases of its life cycle.

Product breakdown structure (PBS). Refers to a family tree used to organize, define, and graphically illustrate the structure of the product (i.e., its bill of materials).

Product family. The realization of a product line in which products are organized according to their similarities and differences.

Productivity. In economics, productivity is defined as the ratio of output to input so that the efficiency and effectiveness with which resources (people, equipment, facilities, etc.) are used to produce output of value can be calculated.

Product line. A family of similar products developed to service the market needs of a particular business area or line of business.

Product-line management. The business function that manages the definition, development, evaluation, use, and evolution of product-line assets over time.

Program evaluation and review technique (PERT). A form of the critical-path method that uses probabilistic estimates to compute the quickest way through a network.

Program manager. A person who manages several aligned projects within a line of business.

Project. An organized undertaking that uses human and physical resources, done once, to accomplish a specific goal.

Project management. The system of management established to focus resources on achieving project goals. Project management has been defined as the art of creating the illusion that any outcome is the result of a series of predetermined, deliberate acts when, in fact, it is not.

Project manager. A person who is held responsible for planning, controlling, and directing project activities. Many times, these responsibilities involve coordinating and integrating activities and products across functional units or organizations.

Project organization. The form of organization in which all of the people working on the project report to the project manager.

Prototype. Software developed specifically to assess feasibility or risks. Prototypes typically do not contain full functionality. Once used, they should be thrown away.

Q

Quality. The totality of features and characteristics of a product or service that bears on its ability to satisfy given needs or customer requirements.

Quality assurance (QA). A planned and systematic pattern of all actions necessary to provide adequate confidence that the item or product conforms to established technical requirements.

Quality control (QC). The process of monitoring specific project results to determine if they comply with appropriate quality limits. If they do not, the function determines the cause of variability and recommends how to eliminate them and achieve satisfactory performance.

Quantitative control. Any quantitative or statistically based technique appropriate to analyze a software process, identify special causes of variations in the performance of the software process, and bring the performance of the software process within well-defined limits [2].

R

Rapid prototyping. A type of prototyping in which emphasis is placed on developing prototypes early in the life cycle to provide feedback and support further development of requirements.

Reengineer. The process of examining, altering, and reimplementing an existing software system to reconstitute it in a form acceptable to the user.

Refactoring. Refers to a method of revising software to improve its structure without changing its functionality or behavior.

Reference architecture. Refers to a software architecture defined to serve as a point of departure for a product line or family of similar systems.

Release. Refers to a working version of the software that has been delivered to the user for test or use in the field.

Reliability. Refers to the capability of a system or component to perform its required functions under specified conditions, including time [4].

Requirement. A condition or capability needed by a user to solve a problem or achieve an objective.

Reserve. Budget or schedule held in reserve to mitigate cost and/or schedule risk and growth at some future point in time in the project.

Resources. In management, the time, staff, capital, and money made available to a project to perform a service or build a product.

Resource leveling. Refers to adjusting schedules to smooth out the projected staffing curves so that staff can be allocated to schedules in a systematic manner.

Resource management. In management, the identification, estimation, allocation, and monitoring of the resources used to develop a product or perform a service.

Responsibility. In management, responsibility infers obligation, not authority to perform a task. In other words, responsibility relates to duties, both real and imaginary, that one feels obliged to perform.

Return on investment. The amount of savings gained (via increased productivity, cost savings, etc.) divided by the investments made to obtain them.

Reusable. The ability or extent to which a software component can be reused across multiple applications. To be meaningful, the software properties must be reusable and measurable.

Reusable software. Software designed and implemented for the specific purpose of being reused within a product line.

Reuse. Refers to using again (e.g., the process of implementing or updating software using existing assets).

Reuse advocate. The person charged with identifying and exploiting reuse opportunities.

Reuse engineering. The engineering activities performed to systematically develop, test, field, and maintain reusable software assets.

Reuse library. A software library specifically developed and built to house reusable assets. Contains a controlled collection of assets together with the procedures and support functions required to satisfy its user's needs.

Review. A process or meeting during which a work product, or set of work products, is presented to project personnel, managers, customers, users, or other interested parties for comment.

Rework. Actions taken to correct defective or nonconforming items in compliance with requirements.

Risk. In management, refers to those factors, both technical and managerial, that are potential threats to success and/or major sources of problems.

Risk management. Refers to the process of identifying, analyzing, quantifying, and developing plans to eliminate or mitigate risk before it does harm on to project.

Role. A unit of defined responsibility that may be assumed by one or more persons.

S

Scenario. A usage-oriented, execution-ordered sequence of activities conducted to elicit some expected system behavior.

Schedule. The actual calendar time budgeted for accomplishing the goals established for activities or the tasks at hand.

Scheduling. In management, the process of allocating and interrelating tasks to the schedule. This activity is like figuring out a jigsaw puzzle, especially when many of the tasks need to be done in parallel. Some form of network, like a PERT chart, usually is extremely helpful in the conduct of this process.

Shared asset. Refers to a reusable asset that is shared across business units and/or product lines.

Should-cost estimate. Refers to resource estimates that are used to assess the reasonableness of a contractor's cost proposal.

Slack. In networks, the term used to refer to marginal time available to complete a task or activity.

Software. Computer programs, procedures, rules, and possibly associated documentation and data pertaining to the operation of a computer system.

Software development library (SDL). A software library that contains computer-readable and human-readable information relevant to a software development effort.

Software development methodology. The overall approach selected to develop software. Hopefully, an integrated set of methods supported by mature standards, practices, and tools will be used as part of the methodology.

Software engineering environment (SEE). The supporting hardware, software, and firmware used in the production of software. Typical elements of the SEE include computer equipment, compilers, assemblers, debuggers, libraries, documentation tools, and database managers.

Software process. A set of activities, methods, practices, and transformations people employ to develop and maintain software and associated products.

Software repository. A permanent, archival storage place for software and related products.

Solicitation. A document used to solicit competitive bids or quotations from competent sources.

Spiral development. A software development process whose function is risk reduction and in which activities are performed iteratively until the software is completed and delivered.

Staff. Those persons assigned to an organization to perform tasks.

Staff loading. Refers to the process of adjusting task schedules to level out the number of staff assigned to perform the individual jobs.

Staffing. The management activities conducted to acquire, develop, and retain staff resources within an organization.

Stakeholder. Any person or organization with a vested stake in working on the project.

Standard. Mandatory requirements employed and enforced to force a disciplined and uniform approach to software development; that is, mandatory conventions and practices are viewed as standards.

Statement of work (SOW). A description of the products or services to be supplied via a contract.

Subcontract management plan (SMP). An acquirer's plan for managing the efforts of a subcontractor. The plan is used to identify items such as project objectives, stakeholders, work structure, roles and responsibilities, schedule, budget, risks, performance measures, resources, work products, change process, and other supporting plans.

Subproject. A portion of a larger project that typically delivers something of value to the customer and is used to reduce risk.

Sunk cost. An expense that has occurred before an investment decision is made [1].

Supplier. Any third-party organization that supplies software products and/or performs services using a written agreement or contract as the basis for action or settling of disputes (subcontractor, COTS supplier, etc.).

Supplier management. The process of managing third parties that supply software products and/or perform related services. To satisfy the intent of such agreements, stakeholders must make investments of their own assets.

System. Refers to a collection of interrelated components that operate together to achieve some desired function, and support organizational mission or business objectives.

T

Task. In management, the smallest unit of work subject to management accountability. A task contains a well-defined work assignment for one or more members of the project team. The specification of work needed to complete a task is documented in a work package. Related tasks are usually grouped to form activities.

Team. A group of people organized to work together.

Teamwork. The cooperative effort by the members of a group aimed at achieving common goals.

Technical performance measurement. The act of comparing technical accomplishments during execution to the project's planned schedule for technical achievements.

Technology transfer. The process used to prove, transfer, and put technology into widespread use.

Total Quality Management (TQM). A modem philosophy of management in which quality becomes the primary concern and goal in system development.

Tracking. In management, the process of identifying cost and schedule variances by comparing actual expenditures to projections.

Trade secret. Any formula, process, design, or tangible intellectual property that is protected by secrecy.

Training. The planned development of skills and abilities needed by personnel to perform their jobs.

U

Uncertainty. In management, the degree of entropy associated with the information used to make a decision.

Use case. A set of possible scenarios between users (actors) and systems in a particular environment aimed at achieving a specific goal.

V

Validation. The process of evaluating a software system or component at the end of the development process to determine whether or not it satisfies specified requirements.

Verification. The process of evaluating a software system or component to determine whether or not the products of a given development phase satisfy the conditions imposed at the start of that phase.

W

Work breakdown structure (WBS). A family tree used to organize, define, and graphically illustrate the products, services, or tasks necessary to achieve project objectives.

Work instructions. The step-by-step procedures devised to be followed as a task is performed. They are much more detailed than normal procedures, which provide structure but not detail.

Work package. A specification of the work to be accomplished in completing a function, activity, or task. A work package defines the work product(s), the staffing needs, the expected duration, the resources to be used, the acceptance criteria for the work products, the name of the responsible individual, and any special considerations for the work.

References

1. Donald J. Reifer, *Making the Software Business Case: Improvement by the Numbers,* Addison-Wesley.2001.
2. Mark C. Paulk, Charles V. Weber, Bill Curtis, and Mary Beth Crises, *The Capability Maturity Model.* Guidelines for Improving the Software Process, Addison-Wesley, 1995.
3. K. El Emam, J. N. Drouin, and W. Melo, *SPICE,* IEEE Computer Society, 1997.
4. Richard D. Stutzke, *Estimating Software-Intensive Systems,* Addison-Wesley, 2005.

About the Authors

Barry Boehm, TRW Professor of Software Engineering Computer Science Department Director, USC Center for Software Engineering. Dr. Barry Boehm is one of the leading figures in the field of software engineering. He served within the U.S. Department of Defense (DoD) as Director of the DARPA Information Science and Technology Office and as Director of the DDR&E Software and Computer Technology Office. He worked at TRW, culminating as chief scientist of the Defense Systems Group, and at the Rand Corporation, culminating as head of the Information Sciences Department. Dr. Boehm's current research interests include software process modeling, software requirements engineering, software architectures, software metrics and cost models, software engineering environments, and knowledge-based software engineering. His contributions to the field include the Constructive Cost Model (COCOMO), the Spiral Model of the software process, and the Theory W (win-win) approach to software management.

Claire Brown, Internal Process Manager Software Productivity Consortium, 2214 Rock Hill Road, Hemdon, VA 20170-4227. She has over 20 years of experience in the software engineering field as a process improvement specialist, project manager, systems engineer, and software development manager. She is experienced in MIL-STD software development and documentation, CASE tools, SEI CMM key practices and project management techniques. She is also an instructor and co-author of the Consortium's guidebook on subcontract management.

Sunita Chulani, Ph.D., Research Staff Member IBM T. J. Watson Research Center, 650 Harry Road, San Jose, CA 95120. She works as a Researcher at the Center for Software Engineering at IBM's T.J Watson Research Center. Her main research interests include software metrics and economics and knowledge management across the software product life cycle. During her graduate studies at USC, she deployed the Bayesian calibration approach on COCOMO II and developed COQUALMO, a framework for quality-based decision support systems that determines the defect density for software development projects.

John J. Marciniak, Software Process & Management, 5104 Tall Oak Court, Camp Springs, Maryland 20748. He has over 35 years of experience in computer systems, particularly software engineering management and process improvement. Ran major Satellite and Command & Control programs while a Colonel in the U.S. Air Force. For the last 12 years has been involved in process improvement, leading and participating in assessments based on the SW-CMM, SA-CMM and FAA-integrated CMM. He is the Editor in Chief of the John Wiley & Sons "Software Engineering Encyclopedia."

David "R.A." Neale, Senior Process Improvement Engineer Software Productivity Consortium, 2214 Rock Hill Road, Hemdon, VA 20170-4227. He has over 10 years of experience as a specialist in software engineering process improvement with Fortune 100 companies. He is experienced in business process re-engineering, specializing in areas of product development, globalization and knowledge management. He is also a co-author of the Consortium's guidebook on subcontract management.

Kenneth E. Nidiffer, Ph.D., Vice President Software Productivity Consortium, 2214 Rock Hill Road, Hemdon, VA 20170-4227 An experienced engineering executive possessing a comprehensive knowledge in the research, development, test, maintenance, education and acquisition of software-intensive systems across a wide range of business domains. He has specific background in cultivating high performance teams, executing critical projects, streamlining the software development process, and aligning a firm's technology and quality objectives with the needs of the business.

Donald J. Reifer, President Reifer Consultants, P. 0. Box 4046, Torrance, CA 90510-4046. He has over 35 years of progressive software management experience in government and industry in a number of responsible positions. Consultant, author and entrepreneur who built a highly successful consulting firm, led major projects, participated in project recovery teams and developed improvement strategies for a number of Fortune 500 clients.

Walker Royce, Vice President and General Manager of Professional Services Rational Software Corporation, 18920 Forge Drive, Cupertino, California. He has over 25 years of field experience as a programmer, architect, product manager, project manager, and services manager. His areas of expertise include software project management and software economics. He has

Software Management, 7th ed. Edited by Donald J. Reifer.

547

participated and contributed 1st hand to numerous successful software projects and initiatives across a broad spectrum of software businesses. He has authored a best selling book on software management and is frequently asked to speak on the topic by international groups.

Richard D. Stutzke, Ph.D., Vice President Science Applications International Corp. (SAIC), 6725 Odyssey Drive, Huntsville, AL 35806. He has more than 40 years of experience with software development and project management in military and industry, including scientific, embedded real-time, and commercial systems. He is the author of over two dozen papers and articles and teaches on the topics of software development, management and estimation. He established SAIC's Corporate Software Process Group in 1989. He recently helped an Army organization achieve a SEI SW-CMM Level 4 maturity rating.

117122